Y0-CQU-095

Transforming Learning with New Technologies

Fourth Edition

Robert W. Maloy
University of Massachusetts Amherst

Ruth-Ellen Verock
University of Massachusetts Amherst

Sharon A. Edwards
University of Massachusetts Amherst

Torrey Trust
University of Massachusetts Amherst

Director of Product Management: Linea Rowe
Product Manager: Drew Bennett
Product Management Analyst: Brooke Warner
Content Manager: Jenifer Niles
Senior Content Analyst: Rebecca Fox-Gieg
Senior Development Editor: Jeffery Johnston
Senior Content Producer: Yagnesh Jani
Managing Producer: Autumn Benson
Manufacturing Buyer: Deidra Headlee, LSC
Text Designer: Integra Software Services Pvt. Ltd.
Full-Service Project Management: Patricia H. Walcott, Integra Software Services Pvt. Ltd.
Cover Design: SPi Global, Inc.
Cover Art: Hero Images/Getty Images; Klaus Vedfelt/Digital Vision/Getty Images;
  Freer/Shutterstock; Rido/Shutterstock
Text Credits (throughout): Acknowledgments of third-party content appear on the page with the
  material, which constitutes an extension of this copyright page.

Copyright © 2021, 2017, 2014 by Pearson Education, Inc. or its affiliates. All Rights Reserved. This
digital publication is protected by copyright, and permission should be obtained from the publisher
prior to any prohibited reproduction, storage in a retrieval system, or transmission in any form or
by any means, electronic, mechanical, photocopying, recording, or otherwise except as authorized
for use under the product subscription through which this digital application is accessed. For
information regarding permissions, request forms and the appropriate contacts within the
Pearson Education Global Rights & Permissions Department, please visit www.pearsoned.com/
permissions/.

Many of the designations by manufacturers and sellers to distinguish their products are claimed
as trademarks. Where those designations appear in this book and the publisher was aware of a
trademark claim, the designations have been printed in initial caps or all caps.

Between the time website information is gathered and then published, it is not unusual for
some sites to have closed. Also, the transcription of URLs can result in typographical errors. The
publisher would appreciate notification where these errors occur so that they may be corrected in
subsequent editions.

Library of Congress Cataloging-in-Publication Data:

Names: Maloy, Robert W., author. | Verock-O'Loughlin, Ruth-Ellen, author. | Edwards, Sharon A.,
  author. | Trust, Torrey, author. | Pearson (Firm)
Title: Transforming learning with new technologies / Robert W. Maloy, University of Massachusetts
  Amherst, Ruth-Ellen Verock, University of Massachusetts Amherst, Sharon A. Edwards,
  University of Massachusetts Amherst, Torrey Trust, University of Massachusetts Amherst.
Description: Fourth Edition. | Hoboken, New Jersey : Pearson, [2019] | Third edition published
  in 2017. | Includes bibliographical references and index.
Identifiers: LCCN 2019026254 (print) | ISBN 9780134054889 (Loose-leaf) | ISBN 9780134020631
  (Paperback) | ISBN 9780133960556 (eBook) | ISBN 9780134044125 (PDF) | ISBN 9780134044057
  (ePUB)
Subjects: LCSH: Internet in education.
Classification: LCC LB1044.87 .T73 2019 (print) | LCC LB1044.87 (ebook) | DDC 378.1/7344678—dc23
LC record available at https://lccn.loc.gov/2019026254
LC ebook record available at https://lccn.loc.gov/2019026255

1 2019

Access Code Card
ISBN-10: 0-13-577302-4
ISBN-13: 978-0-13-577302-4

Rental
ISBN-10: 0-13-577316-4
ISBN-13: 978-0-13-577316-1

Instructor's Review Copy
ISBN-10: 0-13-577324-5
ISBN-13: 978-0-13-577324-6

*To the students we are learning from and
the students they are learning from,
the teachers of today and tomorrow.*

About the Authors

Robert W. Maloy is a senior lecturer in the Department of Teacher Education and Curriculum Studies in the College of Education at the University of Massachusetts Amherst, where he coordinates the history and political science teacher education programs. He also co-directs the TEAMS Tutoring Project, a community engagement/service learning initiative in which university students provide academic tutoring to culturally and linguistically diverse students in public schools throughout the Connecticut River Valley region of western Massachusetts. His research focuses on technology and educational change, teacher education, democratic teaching, and student learning. He is coauthor of eight other books: *Kids Have All the Write Stuff: Revised and Updated for a Digital Age; Wiki Works: Teaching Web Research and Digital Literacy in History and Humanities Classrooms; We, the Students and Teachers: Teaching Democratically in the History and Social Studies Classroom; Ways of Writing with Young Kids: Teaching Creativity and Conventions Unconventionally; Kids Have All the Write Stuff: Inspiring Your Child to Put Pencil to Paper; The Essential Career Guide to Becoming a Middle and High School Teacher; Schools for an Information Age;* and *Partnerships for Improving Schools.* Robert has received a University of Massachusetts Amherst Distinguished Teaching Award (2010), the University of Massachusetts President's Award for Public Service (2010), a School of Education Outstanding Teacher Award (2004), a University Distinguished Academic Outreach Award (2004), and the Chancellor's Certificate of Appreciation for Outstanding Community Service (1998 and 1993).

Ruth-Ellen Verock is a senior lecturer in the Department of Teacher Education and Curriculum Studies in the College of Education at the University of Massachusetts Amherst. She coordinates *Bridges to the Future*, a one-year intensive master's degree and secondary teacher license program serving school systems in western Massachusetts. Prior to joining the university, Ruth was an elementary school classroom and reading teacher in Virginia and Massachusetts. Her academic research focuses on new teacher education, technology in teaching, and community service learning in K–12 schools. She is coauthor with Robert W. Maloy and Sharon A. Edwards of *Ways of Writing with Young Kids: Teaching Creativity and Conventions Unconventionally.* She received the School of Education's Outstanding Teacher Award in 2007. She served as coordinator of the 2003 University of Massachusetts/WGBY National Teacher Training Institute (NTTI) and was an educational researcher for the 1999–2000 Harvard University Evidence Project.

Sharon A. Edwards is a clinical faculty member in the Department of Teacher Education and Curriculum Studies in the College of Education at the University of Massachusetts Amherst. Retired from public school teaching, she taught primary grades for 32 years at the Mark's Meadow Demonstration Laboratory School, a public laboratory school in Amherst, Massachusetts. As a clinical faculty member, she mentors undergraduate students and graduate student interns in the early childhood teacher education, constructivist teacher education, and secondary teacher education programs. Her college teaching and workshop presentations focus on children's writing, reading, and math learning; curriculum development; instructional methods; and diversity and equity in education. She also co-directs the university's TEAMS Tutoring Project. In 1989, Sharon was the inaugural recipient of the national Good Neighbor Award for Innovation and Excellence in Education given by the State Farm Insurance Companies and the National Council of Teachers of English for her work with young children's writing. She received her Doctor of Education degree from the University of Massachusetts Amherst in 1996. She is coauthor with Robert W. Maloy of two other books: *Ways of Writing with Young Kids* and *Kids Have All the Write Stuff*.

Torrey Trust, Ph.D., is an associate professor of Learning Technology in the Department of Teacher Education and Curriculum Studies in the College of Education at the University of Massachusetts Amherst, where she is the co-coordinator of the Learning, Media and Technology master's degree program. Her research and teaching focus on how technology can support teachers in designing contexts that enhance student learning. Dr. Trust is the past president of the Teacher Education Network for the International Society for Technology in Education (ISTE) (2016–2018). Her research, teaching, and service to the field of educational technology have received noticeable recognition, including the 2016 ISTE Online Learning Network Award, 2017 Outstanding Research Paper Award for the *Journal of Digital Learning in Teacher Education*, 2017 American Educational Research Association (AERA) Instructional Technology Special Interest Group Best Paper Award, 2017 ISTE Emerging Leader Award, 2017 Association for Educational Communication & Technology Division of Distance Learning Crystal Award (second place), 2018 Making IT Happen (ISTE) Award, and 2019 AERA Technology as an Agent of Change for Teaching & Learning (Special Interest Group) Early Career Scholar Award.

Brief Contents

Contents

7 Engaging in Virtual Learning with Online Resources 161

8 Solving Problems and Designing Solutions Through Coding, Makerspaces, and Serious Gaming 186

9 Communicating and Collaborating with Social Technologies 209

Preface

Welcome to the fourth edition of *Transforming Learning with New Technologies*. We have written this book to demonstrate the limitless ways teachers and students can use desktops, laptops, smartphones, tablets, apps, interactive websites, coding, makerspaces, 3-D modeling and printing, serious learning games, assistive technologies, performance assessments, and many more new and emerging technologies to create highly interactive, inquiry-based teaching and learning experiences in K–12 schools.

Our goal is to help you transform classrooms into technology-infused places of learning where teachers and students are active educational partners, working together to use and understand technology. Focusing on day-to-day realities of elementary and secondary schools, each chapter addresses the needs of future educators. We provide thoughtful perspectives, instructional examples, descriptions of technology tools and apps, and technology-integrated lesson plans from across the curriculum and for all grade levels as starting points for new teachers to use in developing technology-based learning for students.

As technology transforms every aspect of our lives and our society—from science, medicine, and business to family, entertainment, and education—this fourth edition seeks to support future teachers as they re-envision the roles of technology in schools. Our highly technological, knowledge-based society demands that teachers and students possess new knowledge and expanded talents to be successful in careers and life—what the Partnership for 21st Century Skills calls the "3 Rs and the 4 Cs" of our digital age.

The 3 Rs refer to the academic curriculum content that is taught across the grade levels where teachers add problem solving and inquiry learning to the time-honored skills of reading, writing, and number operations in the subject fields of reading/language arts, mathematics, the sciences, world languages, the arts, economics, geography, history, and government/civics. The 4 Cs are the skills and talents of critical thinking, communication, collaboration, and creativity that every teacher and student must have to understand and succeed in the world of today and tomorrow.

Teaching and learning with the 3 Rs and the 4 Cs mean teachers prepare, deliver, and assess lessons differently while students participate by thinking critically and creatively about all learning they do and what technologies they use, transforming themselves from passive consumers of information *from* technology to active creators of knowledge and understanding *with* technology.

Each of us—young and old, novice or experienced technology user—is living through social, economic, and technological revolutions that are remaking every aspect of our lives, including education. Learning about technology is the essential step in using it successfully both as a teacher and as a learner. Digital technologies directed by the creative ideas that you bring to the art and craft of teaching will continue changing K–12 schools throughout your career. You are only just beginning. In that spirit, we invite you to join us in exploring how *new technologies* create *new opportunities* to *transform teaching and learning* in schools.

New to This Edition

This edition has been substantially revised and updated to incorporate the latest developments in educational technology and digital learning. In it, you will find:

- **Chapters aligned to the newest International Society for Technology in Education (ISTE) Standards**—the first five chapters are aligned to the 2017 ISTE Standards for Educators; the final seven chapters are aligned to the 2016 ISTE Standards for Students. The ISTE Standards for Educators and Students (formerly called NETS for Teachers and NETS for Students) describe and illustrate ways for teachers and students to use technology to achieve learning goals and outcomes. Each chapter supports ISTE's broad vision of technology-infused learning by providing examples, models, and strategies for using interactive technologies to create new patterns of teaching and learning at every grade level.

- **Material on the latest highly interactive technologies and strategies for teaching and learning**—tablets and apps, flipped classrooms, computational thinking, learning to code, 3-D printing, microblogging, online learning, virtual schools, open educational resources, digital citizenship, performance assessments, and using technology with culturally and linguistically diverse learners. An emphasis on highly interactive tools and strategies reflects the changing nature of educational technology from singular devices used by individuals to collaborative tools used by groups and communities.

- **Online Application Exercises in each chapter** focus on having readers utilize digital technologies and apply them directly to their development as educators. Readers are invited to explore technology tools in more depth to experience how they might use these tools in their future classrooms.

- **Technology Transformation Plans** at the end of chapters have been renamed and refocused as "Technology Transformation Learning Plans" to emphasize the educational outcomes for students that result from the ways teachers integrate technology into classroom lessons and learning activities.

- **Designing Instruction with Technology**—the focus of Chapter 4 has been re-envisioned and re-organized to more directly address instructional design with technology. The chapter includes material on different types of educational websites and apps, as well as a step-by-step presentation of the instructional design process in action using two science lessons—one for elementary age learners, the other for middle and high school students.

- **Teachers as Technology Leaders**—a chapter on teacher leadership has added material on the SAMR Model of Technology Integration, one-to-one computing and BYOD/T programs, and the role of teachers in addressing digital inequalities facing low-income and culturally and linguistically diverse youngsters. There are also strategies for how new teachers can most effectively manage their online presence and digital reputation on social media.

- **Digital Literacies**—Expanded coverage of digital literacy includes new material on open educational resources (OERs) and public domain materials, as well as strategies for teaching students how to do online research, evaluate the quality of web materials, and recognize and reject fake and false news.

- **Problem Solving and Inquiry Learning**—An entirely revised chapter focuses on using coding, robotics, makerspaces, and 3-D printing with students in schools. The chapter features new material on serious educational games and game-based learning along with a new Technology Transformation Learning Plan: *Recreating Pre-Contact Native American Houses with a Makerspace and 3-D Printing*.

- **Technology for Diverse Learners**—A substantially reorganized chapter emphasizes using technology to support learning for culturally and linguistically diverse students as well as youngsters with special educational needs. There is material on culturally responsive teaching, teaching students who are learning English as a new language, creating digitally accessible assignments for students, and using technology to support a writing process fit for young writers.

- **MyLab Education**
One of the most visible changes in the fourth edition, also one of the most significant, is the expansion of the digital learning and assessment resources embedded in the eText and the inclusion of MyLab Education in the text. MyLab Education is an online homework and assessment program designed to work with the text to engage learners and to improve learning. Within its structured environment, learners see key concepts demonstrated through real classroom video footage, practice what they learn, test their understanding, and receive feedback to guide their learning and to ensure their mastery of key learning outcomes. Designed to bring learners more directly into the world of K–12 classrooms and to help them see the real and powerful impact of educational technology concepts covered in this book, the online resources in MyLab Education with the Enhanced eText include:

  - **Video Examples.** Embedded videos provide illustrations of educational technology principles or concepts in action. These video examples most often show students and teachers working in classrooms. Sometimes they show students or teachers describing their thinking or experiences.

- **Self-Checks.** In each chapter, self-check quizzes help assess how well learners have mastered the content. The self-checks are made up of self-grading multiple-choice items that not only provide feedback on whether questions are answered correctly or incorrectly, but also provide rationales for both correct and incorrect answers.

- **Application Exercises.** Every chapter in the fourth edition includes three interactive Application Exercises called "Application Exercises offer hands-on, technology-based opportunities to explore tools and resources that technology-using educators will want to know about and be able to use with K-12 students. Tech Tool exercises are ways to "test-drive" digital tools, experiencing first-hand how they can function instructionally in school settings. Building Your PLN exercises feature digital technologies that future teachers can add to their professional resume of skills and understandings. Growing and Leading with Technology exercises invite readers to develop their own "what would you do" responses to actual classroom scenarios. Application Exercises have thought questions to answer, after which readers can view our author feedback for each question.

1. Becoming a 21st Century Teacher
   - Application Exercise 1.1: Tech Tool: *Transforming Technology Tools for Tablets, Smartphones and Laptops*
   - Application Exercise 1.2: Building Your PLN: *Selecting Professional Pull and Push Resources*
   - Application Exercise 1.3: Growing and Leading with Technology: *Marco's "PLN Building" Activity*
2. Understanding Educational Technology Issues and Trends
   - Application Exercise 2.1: Building Your PLN: *Examining Apps for Safety and Privacy*
   - Application Exercise 2.2: Tech Tool: *Writing a Review of an Educational App*
   - Application Exercise 2.3: Growing and Leading with Technology—*Cherelle's "Using Technology in the Classroom" Activity*
3. Transforming Learning with Unique, Powerful Technologies
   - Application Exercise 3.1: Building Your PLN: *Web Resources and Apps for Critical Thinking and Problem Solving*
   - Application Exercise 3.2: Building Your PLN: *Web Resources and Apps for Digital Literacy Learning*
   - Application Exercise 3.3: Building Your PLN: *Web Resources and Apps for Digital Communication and Collaboration*
   - Application Exercise 3.4: Building Your PLN: *Web Resources and Apps for Creativity*
   - Application Exercise 3.5: Building Your PLN: *Web Resources and Apps for Digital Citizenship*

Author-Created Companion Site

To provide ongoing updates and resources for the 4th edition, we have developed a companion Google site, also called transforming learning with new technologies. It replaces transformingtech, our companion wiki for the 3rd edition. At the new site you will find material related to key topics in each chapter. As new research, materials, and resources become available, our plan is to post them on the site so everyone can find up-to-date news and information about technology, schools, and learning. THE SITE IS FREE ONLINE AT https://sites.google.com/view/transformlearningwithtech

Chapter Organization and Updates

Each chapter is organized around specific learning goals designed to provide teachers and students with information to create successful, technology-infused learning environments in K–12 schools and classrooms.

- Chapter 1 introduces the changing context of education in an increasingly multicultural, multilingual society, along with what it means to be a 21st century teacher who uses technology for teaching and learning. There is material updating Bloom's taxonomy with technology, an introduction to the newest ISTE Standards for Educators and Students, and ideas for how to use this book to begin building a PLN (professional learning network) as a new teacher.
- Chapter 2 identifies the latest issues, developments, and trends in the field of educational technology. There is material on using technology to engage students as well as the impacts of digital inequalities on student achievement gaps. Overcoming differences between student-initiated and teacher-chosen technology use is

a key to addressing a persistent digital disconnect that many students feel at school.

- Chapter 3 discusses how technology can generate unique, powerful, and transforming learning (UPT) as defined by the ISTE Standards for Students and 21st Century Student Outcomes. There are technology-based learning activities, web resources and apps for critical thinking and problem solving, digital literacy, communication and collaboration, creativity, and digital citizenship.

- Chapter 4 reviews learning theories and design processes for incorporating technology into lesson planning, classroom teaching, and student assessment, including constructivist and student-centered approaches to the essential elements of instructional design. Two science lessons, one each for elementary school and high school students, provide a step-by-step overview of the instructional design process in action.

- Chapter 5 discusses the dynamics of integrating technology into teaching while creating educational change in schools. There is a focus on using technology to address digital inequalities and student participation gaps in school classrooms, including one-to-one computing, flipped learning, and interactive educational materials. There are also strategies for college students to utilize to become technology-leading educators.

- Chapter 6 examines the multiple dimensions of information literacy and digital citizenship. Beginning with the importance of digital literacy for teachers and students, there is material on identifying fake and false news, using search engines effectively, critically assessing online materials, and utilizing open educational resources (OERs) and public domain materials. There are also strategies for teaching students how to act responsibly as digital citizens.

- Chapter 7 focuses on using online digital content for teaching and learning while also examining the growth and development of blended learning and virtual schools. Technologies and strategies for curating information include an overview of Google's collection of tools for teachers. There is also material on the strengths and drawbacks of online learning and the importance of using exploratory learning websites and apps to engage students in academic learning.

- Chapter 8 shows ways to develop students' inquiry-learning and problem-solving skills using technology. Teaching coding and robotics engages students in problem-based learning. Serious learning games, online simulations, and virtual reality applications offer students open-ended ways to practice problem solving by thinking critically. Makerspaces and 3-D modeling and printing place students in the roles of inventors, creators, and engineers of creative learning experiences.

- Chapter 9 explains how teachers and students can use digital communication technologies to enhance collaboration, share information, and promote new learning. There are strategies for utilizing e-mail, text messaging,

Twitter, and online discussions as a teacher. Blogs, wikis, and Google sites are discussed as technologies for engaging students and implementing collaborative project-based learning activities.

- Chapter 10 explores multimedia technologies and their roles in promoting multimodal learning and student creativity. There are strategies for utilizing e-books and e-readers, educational podcasts, and next-generation presentation tools. There are also ideas and tools for incorporating video in the classroom and supporting students as they engage in photo taking, digital story-telling, and movie-making.

- Chapter 11 explains how technology supports differentiated instruction and universal design for learning by emphasizing educational success for all students. There are tools and strategies for engaging culturally and linguistically diverse learners; an overview of assistive technologies that support students with special educational challenges; and tools for teaching writing within a writing process fit for young writers.

- Chapter 12 demonstrates how teachers and students can become active participants in evaluating and assessing their own growth as learners using technology. The role of assessment in K–12 education is explored along with different types of technology-based, student-centered assessments, including student performance rubrics, democratic classrooms, student feedback surveys, and student participation tools. Digital portfolios for students and teachers are also highlighted as ways for individuals to self-assess personal learning.

In-Chapter Features

CHAPTER-OPENING PEDAGOGY Each chapter begins with learning outcomes connected to each major heading in the chapter. This establishes the framework for what students should know and be able to do when they complete the chapter. Following the learning outcomes is a graphic organizer outlining the chapter's learning goals; ISTE standards connections; and apps and tools that appear in the chapter. Learning goals offer a guide for students' reading and brief vignettes of real-life situations in schools that introduce the chapter's main theme.

END-OF-CHAPTER ACTIVITIES The following materials provide a thorough review of the chapter and extend student thinking beyond the chapter focus:

- **Chapter Summaries** of the major ideas correspond to the learning outcomes found at the beginning of the chapter.

- **Key Terms** list the important terminology found in the chapter. Terms are found in bold within the chapter text and are defined in the glossary at the end of the book.

- **For Reflection and Discussion** offers end-of-the-chapter questions and exercises for the purpose of individual reflection, group dialogue, and personal writing to reinforce chapter content and its learning goals.

- **Chapter Learning Outcomes** have been consolidated to reflect the evolving emphasis on social media, apps, online digital content, and new interactive tools for teaching and learning. Each learning outcome corresponds to a section within the chapter, arranged from the conceptual to the practical so readers receive an introduction to concepts and learning goals and are then shown ways to implement them in school classrooms.

- **In Practice** is a boxed feature in every chapter that offers classroom-based examples of teachers and students using new technologies for classroom learning. Every In Practice showcases one of the key ideas or technologies being discussed in the chapter by focusing on its practical applications in K–12 schools.

TECH TOOLS   Tech Tools in each chapter profile high-quality, easy-to-use, and easy-to-obtain digital tools, apps, and web-based resources that can enhance your work as a teacher, both instructionally and professionally. We describe each tool, how it can be used educationally, and why it is important for teaching and learning. In the eText edition, each Tech Tool includes an interactive, learner-centered Application Exercise designed to help readers of the book explore tools and apps in greater depth. All Tech Tool resources have been class-tested by the authors and students.

Tech Tool 1.1

Tablets, Smartphones, and Laptops

As a college student, you may own a smartphone as well as a laptop, desktop, or tablet computer. By 2018, 95% of all Americans owned a cell phone; 75% had smartphones; three in four owned a desktop or laptop computer; half had a tablet; one in five had an e-reading device (Pew Research Center, 2018). Mobile and digital technologies provide anywhere, anytime online access to ideas, information, and learning resources—essential features of educational life for teachers and students. The three basic mobile devices include:

Tablets

Tablets are small, powerful machines that use touch-screen controls and Internet access to promote interactive learning among teachers and students who can collaborate on projects, share information, access multimedia resources, compute and calculate numbers, and perform many other learning activities. The Apple iPad (multiple models), Microsoft Surface Pro, Samsung Galaxy Tab S4, and Asus ZenPad are all highly rated tablets. The definition of what is or what is not a tablet is evolving, giving rise to a new term, *phablet*, meaning a device that combines features of a tablet and a mobile phone. Its larger size screen hosts full high definition with superior resolution for online browsing, music listening, photo taking, movie and video viewing, and e-reading.

Smartphones

Smartphones are mobile telephones that perform a range of information communication functions, including Internet access, voice communication, text messaging, and video viewing. As historian Paul Ceruzzi (2012) noted, smartphones blend the functions of technologies from the past—telephone, radio, television, phonograph, camera, and teletype—to create a multifunctional handheld device. Apple's iPhone propelled the development of smartphone technology, and now there are numerous competing models from multiple companies.

The smartphone's popularity opens up many possibilities as a learning technology. First, smartphones support anywhere,

anytime learning. Teachers and students can access a wealth of audio and video educational resources whenever they choose. Second, the portability of a smartphone lets students take course content wherever they go. Third, teachers and students can record their own podcasts and then listen to them on their phones. Although not yet total substitutes for desktops and laptops, smartphones offer on-the-go teacher options such as rapid note taking, quick texting and e-mail communicating, and easy information searching. Like tablets, smartphones run many apps for educational learning.

Laptops

Laptops (also called *notebooks*, *netbooks*, or *ultrabooks*) weigh between 2 and 8 pounds. Although their lightness is a significant bonus, the computing power of these machines makes them vitally useful for teachers. High-quality laptops offer long battery life, an easy-to-read screen display in all kinds of light, sufficient memory to run multiple applications, and enough processing speed to handle downloading information and processing files. They have enough storage to be filing cabinets and virtual libraries. Ask yourself, "What kind of laptop user am I?" If you are a frequent note taker, you may want to consider battery life. If you do lots of traveling, weight may be your number-one concern. If you store lots of data, memory may be your purchasing focus.

Tablets, smartphones, and laptops run apps, support software, and access interactive websites that can be used for thousands of instructional purposes:

- Supporting learning in every subject area—interactive world maps in social studies, online dictionaries and poetry collections in language arts, calculators and problem-solving activities in math
- Asking students to research existing apps that specifically address the needs of people in local communities
- Inviting students to envision new smartphone apps to explore pressing social or environmental problems.

DIGITAL DIALOG   A boxed feature in each chapter invites readers to use social media and in-class conversations to explore issues raised throughout the book. Brief questions focus attention on current thinking and future plans. From their own and other students' written reflections, readers learn ways to use new technologies for teaching and learning.

Digital Dialog 1.1

Looking at the Harris Poll survey findings in Table 1.1, college students who are planning to become teachers may find their experiences with technology are closer to the older generation of Millennials than the generation of students you will be teaching when you enter the classroom. Consider whether you align more closely with Gen Z or Millennials in the categories of the survey, then connect and comment online about the following questions:

- Based on what you now know about Gen Z and Gen Alpha, what digital tools might you consider using for teaching to engage your students? Explain why.
- Students use technology in so many parts of their lives outside of school. Should they be constantly connected to technology in the classroom? Why or why not?

TECHNOLOGY TRANSFORMATION LEARNING PLANS   Found at the end of Chapters 6–12, Technology Transformation Learning Plans show teachers how to infuse technology in a substantive and meaningful way using a standard lesson plan template with objectives, methods, assessment strategies, national subject area curriculum standards, and the ISTE Standards for Students. Relating directly to the learning goals and new technologies featured in the chapter, each lesson plan offers "before-and-after" insights via a table that includes one column, "Minimal Technology" (the "before" mode), describing how teachers might conduct a lesson without a significant role for technology, and a second column, "Infusion of Technology" (the "after" mode), illustrating how technologies can fundamentally enhance and transform learning for students and teachers. The Technology Transformation Learning Plans are correlated to the ISTE Standards for Students.

Technology Transformation Learning Plan

Weather Station WebQuest

Investigating Science Using Interactive Web Resources

Grade(s)	Elementary and middle school
Subject(s)	Science/social studies
Key Goal/Enduring Understanding	Weather is a naturally occurring phenomenon that may appear unpredictable but is actually a group of interconnected elements that can be studied, understood, and predicted.
Essential Question	What types of patterns do we see in weather, and how can we use those patterns to make our own weather predictions?
Academic Discipline Learning Standards	**National Science Teachers Association:** *Next Generation Science Standards* Earth and Space Sciences Earth and Human Activity **National Council for the Social Studies:** *Curriculum and Content Area Standards* **Theme III:** People, Places, and Environment **Theme VIII:** Science, Technology, and Society
Learning Objectives	Students will know how and be able to: - Recognize patterns in weather - Use tools that simulate weather patterns - Disseminate weather-related information using web-based tools - Make predictions about future weather based on weather pattern data

PROFESSIONAL LEARNING NETWORK (PLN) An expanded inside-the-chapter Application Exercise provides readers with technology exploration activities to complete as they read the book. These hands-on activities are designed to help readers develop a portfolio of knowledge and skills to use when entering the teaching job market and throughout their career. PLNs are a popular concept for new teachers, for as technology educator Torrey Trust (2012, p. 133) noted: "PLNs connect teachers to other individuals worldwide who can offer support, advice, feedback, and collaboration opportunities." PLNs also allow teachers to collect information from various websites so they can stay up-to-date on the latest teaching techniques, pedagogies, and changes in the field of education.

Support Materials for Instructors

The following resources are available for instructors to download on **www.pearsonhighered.com/educators**. Instructors enter the author or title of this book, select this particular edition of the book, and then click on the "Resources" tab to log in and download textbook supplements.

Instructor's Resource Manual and Test Bank

The Instructor's Resource Manual and Test Bank includes suggestions for learning activities, additional Experiencing Firsthand exercises, supplementary lectures, case study analyses, discussion topics, group activities, and a robust collection of test items. Some items (lower-level questions) simply ask students to identify or explain concepts and principles they have learned. But many others (higher-level questions) ask students to apply those same concepts and principles to specific classroom situations—that is, to actual student behaviors and teaching strategies.

PowerPoint Slides

The PowerPoint slides include key concept summarizations, diagrams, and other graphic aids to enhance learning. They are designed to help students understand, organize, and remember core concepts and theories.

TestGen

TestGen is a powerful test generator that instructors install on a computer and use in conjunction with the TestGen testbank file for the text. You install TestGen on your personal computer (Windows or Macintosh) and create your own tests for classroom testing and for other specialized delivery options, such as over a local area network or on the web. A test bank, which is also called a Test Item File (TIF), typically contains a large set of test items, organized by chapter and ready for use in creating a test based on the associated textbook material. Assessments may be created for both print and online testing.

The tests can be downloaded in the following formats:

TestGen Testbank file: PC
TestGen Testbank file: MAC
TestGen Testbank: Blackboard 9 TIF
TestGen Testbank: Blackboard CE/Vista (WebCT) TIF
Angel Test Bank (zip)
D2L Test Bank (zip)
Moodle Test Bank
Sakai Test Bank (zip)

Acknowledgments

We were inspired to write *Transforming Learning with New Technologies* by collaborating and learning with hundreds of teachers and students during the past four decades of teaching at the University of Massachusetts Amherst. Their drive to inspire, support, and engage students motivates us to envision technology-infused schools in which every learner can realize her or his fullest potentials.

We would like to thank the following individuals whose ideas and insights contributed to the fourth edition of this book: Trevor Takayama, Heather Dahl-Hansen, Jerry & Beverly Trust, Irene LaRoche, Dave Hale, Stacey Chapley, Brianna Ball, Erich Leaper, Emily Chandran, Marissa Best, Sinead Meaney, Stephany Pallazolla, Shannon Hirsch, Joel Flores, Brook Hansel, Colin Conkey, Allison Malinowski, Leah Mermelstein, Fred Zinn, Daryl Essensa, Jeromie Whalen, Chris Gaudreau, Lauren Goodman, Mario Valdebenito Rodas, and Maria Fabozzi.

As in any project, realizing this point would not have been possible without the assistance of numerous individuals who helped sharpen the focus and improve the content of this edition. We would like to thank the reviewers of previous editions: Stephen Cebik, who wrote the PowerPoint supplements; Agnes Helen Bellel, Alabama State University; David Bullock, Portland State University; Craig Cunningham, National-Louis University; Carrie Dale, Eastern Illinois University; Jane Eberle, Emporia State University; Loretta Enlow, Indiana Wesleyan University; Sonja Heeter, Clarion University of Pennsylvania; Barbara Jones, Golden West College; Bernadette Kelley, Florida A&M University; Valerie Larsen, University of Virginia; Ashley Navarro, Seminole Community College; Robert Perkins, College of Charleston; Andrew B. Polly, University of North Carolina-Charlotte; Ken Rushlow, Middle Tennessee State University; Diana Santiago, Central New Mexico Community College; Shannon Scanlon, Henry Ford Community College; Patricia Weaver, Fayetteville Technical Community College; Pavlo D. Antonenko, Oklahoma State University; Tracey L. Sheetz Bartos, Seton Hill University; Richard L. Holden, Mississippi University for Women; Carol L. Martin, Harrisburg Area Community College; Inge Schmidt, Ursuline College; Rebecca Fredrickson, Texas Woman's University; Dr. Elisa Beth McNeill, Texas A&M University; Steven Smith, Ed.D., Clayton State University; and Jeffrey S. Trotter, Anderson University.

Finally, we thank our editors: Product Manager Drew Bennett, Senior Development Editor Jeff Johnson, and other editors, design, and production staff. Their guidance and suggestions have crafted this edition into print and digital formats that convey our vision for technology and change.

Chapter 1

Becoming a 21st Century Teacher

SOURCE: Hquality/Shutterstock

Chapter Overview

Chapter 1 introduces skills, talents, and technologies 21st century teachers will be using to create interactive, engaging learning experiences for themselves and students. We open with an overview of technology's centrality in the lives of students and families and its integration in the work of teachers. The current International Society for Technology in Education (ISTE) Standards for Students and Educators as well as Bloom's taxonomy of educational objectives, the technological pedagogical content knowledge (TPACK), and 21st century skills are introduced to frame how new teachers think about technology's role in teaching and learning. In a final section, we introduce a professional learning network (PLN) as a framework for how new teachers can continually expand and document what they know and can do as technology-leading and learning educators. The chapter addresses the "Leader" domain of the ISTE Standard for Educators, which urges teachers to continually look for and learn about new ways for technology to improve successful learning for students.

∨ Learning Outcomes

After reading this chapter, you will be able to:

1.1 Summarize the changing diversity of American education and the roles of technology in the lives of students and families.

1.2 Discuss ways teachers utilize digital technologies in their work as educators.

1.3 Analyze how 21st century technologies can be used to create highly interactive, inquiry-based learning environments.

1.4 Organize a professional learning network (PLN) as a technology-using educator.

Chapter Learning Goal

Understand students, schools, and technologies as a 21st century technology-using teacher.

Featured Technologies

Computers

Laptops

Tablets

Smartphones

Apps

Social media

Professional learning network (PLN)

Web 2.0/3.0

Two New Teachers and Their Technologies

Hilary remembers always wanting to be a teacher. From grade school on, she imagined herself in a classroom teaching her favorite subjects. She is from a family of teachers—her father taught and coached at a local high school, and her older sister is a speech therapist in a nearby elementary school. Going to college was always in her plans, and when she arrived at her four-year school, she majored in history and teacher education.

Becoming a teacher was the furthest thing from Anthony's mind when he graduated from high school and enrolled in a local community college as a part-time student. As he gradually earned the credits to transfer to a four-year school and major in biology, the idea of teaching science to younger students began to appeal to him as a career choice.

As diverse as these two appear to be, Hilary and Anthony are constant technology users. Neither goes anywhere without a smartphone. Both enjoy watching YouTube videos and downloading music on their handheld devices. While each has an e-mail account, texting, Instagram, and Snapchat are their preferred modes of communicating with friends. Playing video games, shopping online, watching television, doing mobile banking, and streaming movies are daily parts of their media lives.

Seeing technology influencing their own learning, Hilary and Anthony sought ways to use digital tools for teaching students. Hilary helped build and expand a wiki of multimodal web resources to assist history teachers in developing technology-infused learning plans. Anthony began bookmarking online simulations and games for students to play while making science-in-the-real-world videos on his smartphone and editing them as part of inquiry-based lessons. For both Hilary and Anthony, technology for teaching became a central part of becoming an educator.

Although they took different routes to teaching, Hilary and Anthony consistently learned about technology through their use of it in their own lives. When they were in high school and college, technology meant texting, **social media**, and entertainment through **apps**, games, streaming videos, digital music, and online blogs and news sites. As teachers entering classrooms for the first time, however, they were not experienced with how to use the power of technology to transform learning. They had to learn new digital tools and discover unforeseen possibilities of technology-based learning to become 21st century teachers.

Our goal for you is to become a confident, thoughtful user of educational technologies in courses, classrooms, and professional settings while you develop your knowledge, skills, and talents as a technology-leading and learning teacher. In this opening chapter, we focus attention on four questions central to your growth and development as a teacher in the digital age:

1. What are the characteristics of today's rapidly changing, increasingly diverse schools?
2. What technologies are integral to your work as a 21st century teacher?
3. How might the ISTE Standards for Students and Educators, technological pedagogical content knowledge (TPACK), and 21st century skills shape your teaching practice?
4. How can you begin developing a professional learning network (PLN) as a teacher?

Teaching and Students Today

1.1 **Summarize the changing diversity of American education and the roles of technology in the lives of students and families.**

Students of all ages use technology for learning and socializing.

SOURCE: Rob/Fotolia (top);
SOURCE: Pressmaster/Fotolia (bottom)

Teaching is a career that matters to everyone—students, families, employers, and society. Filled with endless complexities, questions, and rewards, the profession is clearly committed to continuous professional development and academic learning. As a teacher, you are expected to:

- Convey essential academic material to students in ways they will understand, remember, and apply
- Educate, inspire, engage, and create success for every student, each of whom has a unique background of culture, social class, family income, gender, language, and individual exceptionalities
- Manage inside-the-classroom dynamics of interpersonal interactions, behavior, and community and daily routines to sustain academic learning in the lives of students, families, and communities.

As Philip Jackson (1968) chronicled five decades ago, a teacher handles some 200 separate interpersonal interactions every hour, 6 hours a day, for 180 school days each year—a huge endeavor. Faced with these multiple and often competing goals, beginning educators draw on years of personal experience as students to balance it all. They tend to teach as they have been taught, utilizing whole-group instruction with desks arranged in rows while students take notes, complete worksheets, write papers, and receive grades based on multiple-choice test scores. As a result of these established instructional routines, many classrooms feature large amounts of teacher talk while students passively listen to what teachers say.

Traditional practices, from before and throughout the 20th century, fail to engage large numbers of students, including students who are too far behind or ahead academically; students who prefer to learn by moving, drawing, or singing; and learners who are deeply connected with technology outside of school, but have to power down their devices in school. Todd Rose, in his TED talk "The Myth of Average" (2013), pointed out that "Even though we have one of the most diverse countries in the history of the world, and even though it's the 21st century, we still design our learning environments, like textbooks, for the average student." As a result, Rose concludes, "We've created learning environments that, because they are designed on average, cannot possibly do what we expected them to do, which is to nurture individual potential . . . Because every single student has a jagged learning profile, it means that the average hurts everyone, even our best and brightest."

Creating interactive and inspiring learning experiences for students is today's greatest educational challenge, made all the more complex in classrooms with students from many backgrounds, cultures, and languages who possess different levels of interest in the curriculum and have divergent learning preferences. To teach effectively, educators at every grade level must know how to utilize multiple technologies to promote and sustain student learning. Technology enables new ways to engage students by:

- Differentiating instruction to offer students diverse learning experiences
- Energizing learning with interactive tools
- Creating collaborative learning situations
- Enabling access to academic information from multiple sources
- Visiting places and observing processes that cannot be seen otherwise.

A Rapidly Changing and Diversifying Society

As you prepare to teach, you do so within the context of a rapidly changing and diversifying society in which:

- *The K–12 school population is becoming more culturally and linguistically diverse.*   Demographer William H. Frey (2018a, 2018b) refers to these changes as a "**diversity explosion.**" Hispanic, African American, Asian/Pacific Islander, and Native American students now make up more than 50% of the nation's K–12 student population, and the National Center for Education Statistics (2019) is forecasting that the percentage of non-White students in the schools will continue to increase through at least the year 2027 (see Figure 1.1).

  Cultural diversity is accompanied by linguistic diversity—the U.S. Census Bureau (2015) has reported that there are now more than 350 different languages spoken in U.S. homes. Spanish is the second-most spoken language besides English, with more than 40 million speakers, but Chinese (including Mandarin and Cantonese), Tagalog (including Filipino), Vietnamese, Arabic, French, and Korean have at least 1 million speakers as well. Nevada, Florida, California, New York, and Texas are the most diverse states. In California, half of the state's students are Hispanic, and nearly half speak a language other than English at home (Ed100.org, 2018). Diversity is also reflected in the learning needs of students. Thirteen percent of the nation's K–12 students receive special education services; more than half of those students have learning disabilities or speech and language impairments (National Center for Education Statistics, 2018a). Diverse classrooms mean that you can expect to teach in schools that will have many languages, family backgrounds, cultural traditions, and forms of gender expression in student populations.

- *Multiple achievement gaps persist among students in schools.*   **Achievement gaps** are differences in educational outcomes among groups of students. Black, Hispanic, and Native American students, despite some improvements and gains, continue

Figure 1.1 Percentage Distribution of Students Enrolled in Public Elementary and Secondary Schools, by Race/Ethnicity

SOURCE: U.S. Department of Education/National Center for Education Statistics (February 2019).

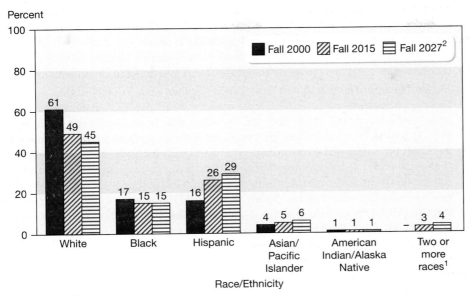

— Not available.
[1] In 2000, data on students of Two or more races were not collected.
[2] Projected.

to perform below White and Asian students in reading and math as measured by the National Assessment of Educational Progress (NAEP), the nation's report card (Hansen, et al., 2018). These youngsters lag behind White and Asian peers in graduating from high school, attending college, and graduating from college. In addition, significant numbers of English language learners, students in special education, and LBGTQ youth remain behind their peers in reading, writing, and math test scores; rates of high school graduation; and choice of math-, science-, and engineering-related careers. There are wide achievement gaps between youngsters from wealthy and poor families (defined as 90th vs. 10th percentiles of income). There are gender-based gaps as well. For instance, girls outperform boys on reading and writing in almost all school districts, while boys from affluent, predominantly White districts outperform girls in math (Reardon, et al., 2018). And even though more girls are taking the AP Computer Science test, girls are less likely than boys to pursue careers in science, technology, engineering, and math (STEM) after high school.

- *Connectivity gaps remain a pervasive educational issue.* **Connectivity gaps** are a type of **digital inequality** in which children in low-income, Black, Hispanic, and American Indian/Alaskan Native households are technologically "underconnected" from the digital resources needed for successful life and learning (National Center for Education Statistics, 2018b; Moore, Vitale, & Stawinoga, 2018). Underconnected households either lack Internet access entirely or have broadband speeds too slow to run the latest software programs, and many face the threat of having Internet service cut off at any time for unpaid bills. Connectivity gaps are everywhere. A large majority of youngsters living in rural areas—about one out of every five elementary or secondary school students in the country—report either "terrible," "unpredictable," or just "OK" access to the Internet at home and at school (Croft & Moore, 2019).

- *Connectivity gaps lead to homework gaps and reduced educational outcomes for students.* **Homework gaps** happen in many low-income households when students and adults must share a single, often outdated computer (Katz, Gonzalez, & Clark, 2017). Since 80% of eighth-graders use a computer at home for schoolwork, lack of up-to-date technology can result in severe educational disadvantages (National Center for Education Statistics, 2018b). One report documented that 13% of students have difficulty completing homework due to lack of Internet access (Evans, 2018). Another national survey found that fewer than 10% of all school districts report that every student has access to a non-shared computing device at home. Students without their own device may have difficulty completing their homework (Mayalahn, 2017). By contrast, students from higher-income families are much more likely to have high-speed Internet, use multiple digital devices, and get news and conduct business online. Phone technology also imposes limitations on students' educational experience. While most less affluent youngsters have mobile phones for accessing social media and listening to music, it is not easy to write papers, analyze materials, record data, or view simulations and interactive websites on phones as compared to using the most up-to-date desktop or tablet computers.

- *Digital inequalities persist in how technology is used in schools as well.* In theory, youngsters with reduced access to new technologies at home can overcome any educational disadvantages by being able to use and learn with digital tools at school. However, there are persistent technology-based **participation gaps** in classrooms. The same technologies get used differently in different schools, so that even when schools provide access to learning technologies for all students, schools in wealthier communities have students using those technologies in more creative and expansive ways (Reich & Ito, 2017). Students in low-income community schools tend to use technology mainly for basic skills instruction, while students in more affluent districts use technology for more creative, hands-on, exploratory learning such as coding, making games and animations with digital media, and utilizing peer collaboration tools like blogs and wikis.

- *The role of the teacher is evolving from expert in front of a classroom to facilitator of small learning groups and project-based activities.* Traditional educational practices (teachers present information while students listen and learn) fail to engage at least half and often most of the students in any given classroom. In surveys and studies, students tell researchers that they want learning in schools to resemble the active, technology-driven learning environments they routinely experience in most other parts of their lives. Multiple educational policy organizations urge teachers to create more interactive, inspiring learning environments that will connect to learners who possess different levels of interest and divergent learning preferences.

MyLab Education
Video Example 1.1
In this video, a teacher discusses the diversity of students in her school. How does the student population of this school compare with the schools you attended as a student?

- *Schools are changing in structure and format from traditional brick-and-mortar buildings to many different combinations of in-person and online learning environments.* Everywhere in the country, you will find widely varying types of schools, including public, private, independent, religious, homeschool, charter, single gender, vocational, agricultural, virtual/online, magnet, language immersion, extended day, year-round, GED preparation, school to college, Montessori, and Reggio Emilia. As a teacher, you are not just getting ready to teach in one type of school for the duration of your career, but preparing to succeed in many different schools with different approaches to teaching and learning.

- *Beyond the schoolhouse, the nature of jobs and work now places great emphasis on mental rather than physical labor.* Students today are entering the world of work, where the skills needed are constantly changing, as are the jobs themselves. Employers want employees who have learned how to learn and embrace the idea of "thinking for a living," in Ray Marshall and Marc Tucker's memorable phrase (1993). In every sector of the economy, technology-based professional, managerial, technical, and entrepreneurial careers are emerging all the time, including many that no one could have imagined even a decade ago (e.g., drone operator, 3-D printing specialist, nanotechnology designer, robot operator for surgery). One report on human-machine partnerships forecast that 85% of the jobs for workers in 2030 have not even been invented yet (Institute for the Future for Dell Technologies, 2017). You will be teaching students not only to enter the world of today, but to be prepared for discovering the exciting new opportunities of the future.

A Generation of Technology Users

The students in your future classroom will be unlike any generation of students before them. Psychologists Howard Gardner and Katie Davis (2014) have labeled them the "app generation" because they have grown up using computers, the Internet, smartphones, social media, and interactive digital technologies. The oldest of these students (those born between the mid-1990s and 2010) are members of **Generation Z** (Gen Z); they are also called "post-millennials," "screeners," or the "iGeneration" (Serafino, 2018; Caumont, 2014). The children of Gen Z are a new population cohort known as **Generation Alpha** (Gen Alpha) and includes youngsters born between 2010 and 2025. Knowing about these generations is vitally important for you as a teacher, because the more informed you are about students and technology, the better you will understand their interests, motivations, and goals, as well as the types of educational methodologies needed to successfully teach them in K–12 schools.

From the earliest ages, children from Gen Z and Gen Alpha live media-saturated lives, constantly receiving images and information from televisions, computers, video and picture sharing websites, video games, and smartphones as participants in what sociologists have called a **digital childhood** (Vandewater, et al., 2007). Growing up digital includes the following:

- Almost all infants, toddlers, and preschoolers watch television (nearly every U.S. home has one) while making increasing use of digital tablets, smartphones, and social networks (Donahue, 2015; Guernsey, 2014).

- On average, children ages 2 to 10 years spend more than 2 hours a day with screen media, about half that time viewing materials that parents consider "educational." As they get older, children's screen time increases, but the amount of educational viewing decreases (Common Sense Media, 2017).

- By 2013, nearly three of four children had access to mobile devices at home on which they spent time playing games, using apps, watching videos, and reading books (Common Sense Media, 2013).

- In their teenage years, nearly all 12- to 15-year-olds watch television (98.5%) and use computers (91%), but only one quarter of boys and one third of girls meet an American Academy of Pediatrics–recommended limit of 2 hours a day or less for television plus technology use outside of school (Herrick, et al., 2014).

- **Media multitasking** (using more than one form of media at a time) is another prominent technology use feature among teenagers. The much-publicized *Generation M2* study reported that teens and tweens averaged 7 hours and 38 minutes during a typical day using different types of digital and screen media (computers, video games, music players, television). However, media multitasking means these youngsters were actually experiencing 10 hours and 45 minutes of media time daily (Rideout, Foehr, & Roberts, 2010). Those numbers have not declined in the decade since the publication of the *Generation M2* study; in fact, children and adolescents continue to spend enormous amounts of time with digital and screen media at younger and younger ages.

In 2018, the Harris Poll found dramatic shifts in technology use between **Millennials**—those born after 1981—and those K–12 students who were born after 1996. The results are summarized in Table 1.1. Both groups are immersed in learning with technology, but members of Generation Z show greater preferences for visual media and video learning, interactive apps and websites, and, perhaps surprisingly, in-person group activities.

Increasingly, mobile phones are children and teenagers' most widely accessed technology. Growth in phone technology use has been rapid. By 2013, nearly four out of five 12- to 17-year-olds (78% had a cell phone, while almost half (47%)) owned a smartphone (Lenhart, 2015). Teens use their phones when communicating with friends, using apps, and accessing the Internet for information and other educational purposes. One in four teens are "cell-mostly Internet users" who get information for school almost solely by using their phones; more than half of those youngsters download apps for entertainment or educational purposes. A majority of parents believe mobile devices are tools of the future that should be used to enrich and engage students' learning. Although in about one in five households youngsters do not use any mobile or portable devices, by high school only 1 in 10 students is a non–technology user at home (Grunwald Associates LLC, 2013).

Table 1.1 Technology Preferences for Generation Z and Millennial Learners

Generation Z	Millennials
Social Media • YouTube (82%–67%) • Instagram (70%–45%) • Snapchat (69%–32%) • Twitter (43%–34%)	*Social Media* • Facebook (43%–34%)
Online Visual and Video Sites • Watching movies online (43%–27%) • Visiting video sharing sites (66%–55%) • Playing online games (53%–35%) • Sharing pictures, videos, music (66%–56%)	*Online Visual and Video Sites* • No preferences in this category
Tools for Learning • YouTube (59%–55%) • In-person group activities (57–47%) • Learning apps and interactive sites (47%–41%)	*Tools for Learning* • Books (60%–47%)

SOURCE: Pearson. (2018, August). Beyond millennials: The next generation of learners.

Digital Dialog 1.1

Looking at the Harris Poll survey findings in Table 1.1, college students who are planning to become teachers may find their experiences with technology are closer to the older generation of Millennials than the generation of students you will be teaching when you enter the classroom. Consider whether you align more closely with Gen Z or Millennials in the categories of the survey, then connect and comment online about the following questions:

- Based on what you now know about Gen Z and Gen Alpha, what digital tools might you consider using for teaching to engage your students? Explain why.
- Students use technology in so many parts of their lives outside of school. Should they be constantly connected to technology in the classroom? Why or why not?

MyLab Education
Video Example 1.2
In this video, you will learn how technology offers the potential for transformative change in schools. What technologies are you planning to implement in your teaching that are new and different from those you experienced as a student?

MyLab Education Self-Check 1.1

Technology Today

1.2 **Discuss ways teachers utilize digital technologies in their work as educators.**

New digital technologies can become essential teaching and learning tools for beginning teachers or experienced educators by creating learning experiences that would not be possible otherwise. Internet-connected computers, tablets, and smartphones offer unparalleled access to information, interactive games, streaming videos, real-world simulations, social media, online communication and collaboration tools, and many more exciting ways to expand the impact of learning in school for students and teachers.

Every **technology**, from simplest to most complex, ancient to most recent, is a tool, device, or material whose purpose is to solve human problems. Technology is a "practice, a technique, or a device for altering the experience of the world," noted historian Rebecca Solnit (2004, p. 114) in her study of how the telegraph, the railroad, high-speed photography, and motion pictures transformed the American West in the late 19th century. Those technologies altered existing social, cultural, economic, and political patterns by extending the nation's industrial base, displacing native peoples from ancestral lands, changing how people experienced the world, and setting a course for the future.

Creating technological solutions to problems facing humans has been happening since the beginnings of humankind. The wheel, stone tools, and rocks crafted into arrowheads are examples from the ancient past. The technology of writing in the form of written record keeping changed patterns of trade and commerce in the Middle East, Asia, and the Americas thousands of years ago. Beginning in 1450, the printing press transformed European society by making books and newspapers available on a scale never before imagined (Wheeler, 2019). U.S. history is marked by the technological transformations brought about by the cotton gin, interchangeable manufacturing parts, the telegraph and telephone, electricity, television, and most recently, information-processing machines known as computers.

Technologies have continually transformed American education—the first widely used educational textbook, *The New England Primer*, was published in 1690; students in colonial one-room schoolhouses used hornbooks, wooden paddle-shaped devices with reading material pasted on them; the chalkboard dates back to the 1840s; mass-produced paper and lead pencils came into use after 1900; with support from Thomas Edison, among others, teachers started showing educational films as early as 1910; educational radio entered many schools in the 1930s; the first videotape premiered in 1951; the handheld calculator arrived in 1958; and the interactive whiteboard debuted in 1999 (Haran, 2015; Reynolds, 1976).

Importantly, the technologies that became widely used in schools and society before the 1980s were non-digital technologies; that is, they were not connected

Figure 1.2 A Digital Technology Timeline

1980 to 1990	First portable laptop computer (1981) Internet standards for sending and receiving messages (1982) Macintosh computer (1984) Cell phone goes on sale (1984) First one-on-one computing program (1985) Eudora e-mail (1988)
1990 to 2000	PowerPoint released (1990) First digital camera (1991) World Wide Web open to the public (1991) First website published (1991) Mosaic, first widely popular graphical web browser (1993) eBay started (1995) WikiWikiWeb, first wiki (1995) Interactive whiteboards (1997) NetLibrary provides e-books to libraries (1998) Blogs (1999)
2000 to 2010	Microsoft tablet PC (2000) Wikipedia launched (2001) First generation iPod introduced (2001) Skype, iTunes (2003) Facebook (2004) Podcasts online (2004) First YouTube video uploaded (2005) More text messages than telephone calls (2007) iPhone, Twitter, Tumblr, Kindle e-reader (2007) Android smartphone (2008)
2010 to 2020	iPad (2010) Instagram (2010) Digital music outsells CDs for the first time (2011) MOOCs (2012) Game-based learning Digital textbooks Open Education Resources (OERs) 3-D Printing and the maker movement Flipped classrooms Adaptive technologies Digital badges Wearable technologies Augmented reality Virtual reality Mixed reality Adaptive learning Virtual and remote laboratories
Emerging	The Internet of Things (IoT)—devices talking to devices Artificial intelligence (Siri, Twitter bots) Robotics in the classroom Voice-based applications

to computers or the Internet. The shift from non-digital to digital tools marks a modern-day revolution in how technologies are being used in schools. Figure 1.2 shows a timeline of new computer-based educational technologies that have entered schools over the past four decades.

Notice how many of the technologies in Figure 1.2 are very recent developments (i.e., in the past decade), yet it is hard to imagine living or learning without them. As digital technologies become more commonplace, they tend to disappear from our view, as sociologists Bertram Bruce and Maureen Hogan (1998) observed almost two decades ago. People often take everyday technologies for granted, hardly noticing the changes they bring to our lives. Becoming more aware of technology's presence is a crucial first step to understanding its potentials and complexities as educational tools. Not every use of technology is automatically positive or productive. To make the best of technology's possibilities, teachers and students must continually and thoughtfully review and redefine how it is used in schools and society.

Technology changes every aspect of a teacher's work, including lesson planning, recordkeeping, and communicating with students, families, and colleagues.

SOURCE: Shutterstock

Computer Technologies

The modern digital computer is a uniquely powerful form of technology that is changing all aspects of our lives. Before the middle of the 20th century, the word *computer* referred to human beings hired to do work that involved repetitive mathematical computations (Campbell-Kelly, et al., 2013). This type of *computer* was shown, for example, in the 2016 movie *Hidden Figures*, in which the calculations of African American women were essential to launching the first American astronaut into space in 1962.

Today, **computer** refers to an information-processing machine that manipulates data by following instructions of human programmers, millions of times a second, far exceeding human capacity to do the same tasks. Modern computers provide people the ability to store, retrieve, and communicate information in ways never before possible.

The two main components of a computer are hardware and software. **Hardware** refers to the basic machinery and circuitry of a computer. **Software** is the term for computer instructions—a collection of codes that tells the hardware to perform specific functions. Computers have two main types of software. System software is responsible for the overall functioning and control of a computer. It includes the operating system, network operating system, database managers, and teleprocessing (TP) monitor. Application software performs specific functions in specialized ways to produce a variety of services, including word processing, presentation design, music playing, Internet browsing, e-mail management, or movie making, to name a few. You will recognize many of these programs by their commercial names: Microsoft Word, Microsoft PowerPoint, Adobe Acrobat, Adobe Photoshop, Norton Antivirus, and so on. Sometimes programs are bundled together in one large productivity package, such as Microsoft Office Home and Student.

Standard software applications are indispensable tools for every computer user. For example, we cannot imagine writing this book without the speed and other functions of word processing. We are reliant on Microsoft Word's features to organize, draft, revise, and format our chapters. Writers are not alone in their need for computerized tools; accountants need tax preparation software, architects need design programs, physicians need patient data tracking tools, and weather forecasters need programs to provide interactive models of meteorological patterns.

Digital Dialog 1.2

Interviewed in 2012 by researchers from the Pew Internet & American Life Project, more than 1000 education and social policy experts concluded that technology's future impact on people and society will be generally positive (Anderson, 2012). Thinking about the impact of technology today on your own life and society as a whole, comment and connect online about the following questions:

- How might the future impact of technology on the learning behaviors and thinking patterns of students be positive? Negative? Why?
- What technologies do teachers need to use to successfully teach today's students?
- How can educational technologies enable teachers to promote learning success for all students?

From Web 1.0 to Web 2.0/3.0

The Internet in the form of the World Wide Web, observed history podcaster Brian McCullough (2018), "is the reason that computers actually became useful for the average person." The web is essentially a network of networks, more than 1 billion websites linked to one another and accessible through powerful computer-based search engines. While only about 25% of all websites are active, those sites contain an almost infinite amount of information. In 2015, one *Washington Post* newspaper reporter estimated that to print out the entire Internet would take 305.5 billion pages of paper—the equivalent of 212 million copies of Leo Tolstoy's classic novel *War and Peace* (Dewey, 2015). Yet teachers and students and anyone else with an Internet-connected computer can access whatever amount of this information they want to acquire.

The Internet of today is not the Internet that first became publicly available in the early 1990s. **Web 2.0/Web 3.0** denote how the Internet has evolved into a more open medium capable of promoting interaction and collaboration among teachers and students. While the early Internet (Web 1.0) was dominated by content developed by experts, Web 2.0/Web 3.0 are marked by widely shared, frequently changing information provided through easy-to-use Internet websites and mobile phone applications.

Experts do not agree about a precise distinction between Web 2.0 and Web 3.0; in general, Web 2.0 technologies include blogs, wikis, podcasts, social bookmarking and **social networking** tools, inquiry-based educational websites, photo-sharing websites, virtual worlds, and other highly interactive tools and services that are now becoming resources for teaching and learning in schools (Richardson, 2011). Interactive web tools have given rise to what Harvard University Professor Christopher Dede (2008) called **Web 2.0 knowledge**—bottom-up, democratically derived, consensus-driven ideas and information that differ dramatically from the theoretical knowledge created by experts and elites.

As Web 2.0 evolves to Web 3.0 past the year 2025, forecasters say technologies will be more closely networked together as new systems emerge with broadband access speeds 50 to 100 times faster than the average connection today (Rainie, Anderson, & Connolly, 2014). Devices will respond to voice and touch commands; embedded and wearable devices will provide immediate feedback to improve personal well-being and social life; information will be shared seamlessly across the globe, giving everyone wider access to human knowledge—all part of the Internet of Things (Anderson & Rainie, 2014b). Complexities will arise—unforeseen and unintended consequences of technology's growth will create new problems, especially for those groups who are left behind the pace of change (Anderson & Rainie, 2014a).

As the Web evolves into an ever-more expansive component of people's everyday lives, one of the overriding challenges for educators is teaching students the skills to critically analyze and respond to change as technology expands, evolves, and engages them in the next decade and beyond. Tech Tool 1.1 looks at three integral **information and communication technologies** for teaching: tablets, smartphones, and laptops.

Tablets, Smartphones, and Laptops

As a college student, you may own a smartphone as well as a laptop, desktop, or tablet computer. By 2018, 95% of all Americans owned a cell phone; 75% had smartphones; three in four owned a desktop or laptop computer; half had a tablet; one in five had an e-reading device (Pew Research Center, 2018). Mobile and digital technologies provide anywhere, anytime online access to ideas, information, and learning resources—essential features of educational life for teachers and students. The three basic mobile devices include:

Tablets

Tablets are small, powerful machines that use touch-screen controls and Internet access to promote interactive learning among teachers and students who can collaborate on projects, share information, access multimedia resources, compute and calculate numbers, and perform many other learning activities. The Apple iPad (multiple models), Microsoft Surface Pro, Samsung Galaxy Tab S4, and Asus ZenPad are all highly rated tablets. The definition of what is or what is not a tablet is evolving, giving rise to a new term, *phablet*, meaning a device that combines features of a tablet and a mobile phone. Its larger size screen hosts full high definition with superior resolution for online browsing, music listening, photo taking, movie and video viewing, and e-reading.

Smartphones

Smartphones are mobile telephones that perform a range of information communication functions, including Internet access, voice communication, text messaging, and video viewing. As historian Paul Ceruzzi (2012) noted, smartphones blend the functions of technologies from the past—telephone, radio, television, phonograph, camera, and teletype—to create a multifunctional handheld device. Apple's iPhone propelled the development of smartphone technology, and now there are numerous competing models from multiple companies.

The smartphone's popularity opens up many possibilities as a learning technology. First, smartphones support anywhere,

anytime learning. Teachers and students can access a wealth of audio and video educational resources whenever they choose. Second, the portability of a smartphone lets students take course content wherever they go. Third, teachers and students can record their own podcasts and then listen to them on their phones. Although not yet total substitutes for desktops and laptops, smartphones offer on-the-go teacher options such as rapid note taking, quick texting and e-mail communicating, and easy information searching. Like tablets, smartphones run many apps for educational learning.

Laptops

Laptops (also called *notebooks, netbooks,* or *ultrabooks*) weigh between 2 and 8 pounds. Although their lightness is a significant bonus, the computing power of these machines makes them vitally useful for teachers. High-quality laptops offer long battery life, an easy-to-read screen display in all kinds of light, sufficient memory to run multiple applications, and enough processing speed to handle downloading information and processing files. They have enough storage to be filing cabinets and virtual libraries. Ask yourself, "What kind of laptop user am I?" If you are a frequent note taker, you may want to consider battery life. If you do lots of traveling, weight may be your number-one concern. If you store lots of data, memory may be your purchasing focus.

Tablets, smartphones, and laptops run apps, support software, and access interactive websites that can be used for thousands of instructional purposes:

- Supporting learning in every subject area—interactive world maps in social studies, online dictionaries and poetry collections in language arts, calculators and problem-solving activities in math
- Asking students to research existing apps that specifically address the needs of people in local communities
- Inviting students to envision new smartphone apps to explore pressing social or environmental problems.

MyLab Education **Application Exercise 1.1:**
Transforming Technology Tools for Tablets, Smartphones, and Computers

MyLab Education **Self-Check 1.2**

Highly Interactive, Inquiry-Based Teaching and Learning with Technology

1.3 Analyze how 21st century technologies can be used to create highly interactive, inquiry-based learning environments.

In today's technological age, teachers have much more to teach than just the basics of reading, writing, math, and science. To prepare students for productive lives and fulfilling careers, teachers are expected to use technology to convey digital-age skills to students through **highly interactive, inquiry-based learning.** *Highly interactive* means organizing educational activities in which students and teachers are actively involved in using technology to create and evaluate their educational experiences. *Inquiry-based* means preparing, delivering, and assessing lessons differently, helping students to think critically and creatively about the learning they do and the technologies they use. In highly interactive, inquiry-based classrooms, students move from being mainly consumers of ideas and information to becoming creators of knowledge using technology.

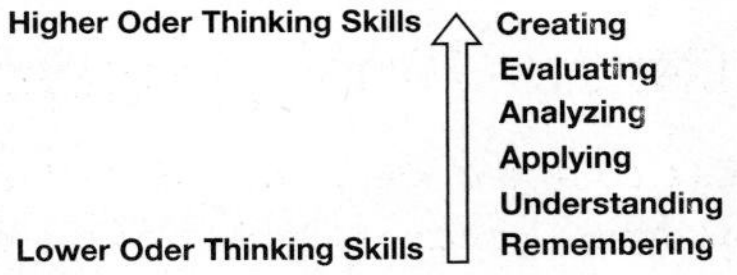

The following ideas and concepts are central to understanding how technology can be used to transform classrooms into centers of interactive teaching and active learning.

Figure 1.3 Bloom's Taxonomy

Higher Oder Thinking Skills — Creating / Evaluating / Analyzing / Applying / Understanding / Remembering — Lower Oder Thinking Skills

Updating Bloom's Taxonomy with Technology

Bloom's taxonomy is a seminal educational classification first presented in 1956, revised in 2002, and re-envisioned for a digital age in 2008 (see Figure 1.3).

Bloom's taxonomy consists of six levels of thinking skills ranging from lower order to higher order. When first proposed, its original thinking levels were knowledge, comprehension, application, analysis, synthesis, and evaluation. The skills are now expressed using action-oriented verbs: remembering, understanding, applying, analyzing, evaluating, and creating (Krathwohl, 2002).

Each thinking skill indicates what students do intellectually at each level. **Lower order thinking** skills involve students recalling and understanding academic information; **higher order thinking** skills involve students applying their understanding of information through analysis, evaluation, and creative actions: Remembering focuses on information recall and recognition. Understanding means deriving meaning from information. Applying involves using what one has remembered or understood in new situations. Analyzing results when learners examine a situation or a problem to arrive at a solution. Evaluating means making an assessment based on set criteria. Creating happens by making something new based on what is being learned (Ormrod, et al., 2017).

Commentators now propose that digital technologies can support different thinking skills; for example, social bookmarking tools can support remembering while podcasting is a form of creating (Churches, 2008). While it is true that technology can support and develop students' higher order thinking skills, the "capacity for transformation is not intrinsic to the technology itself," as Nicholas Burbules and Thomas Callister Jr. (2000, p. 7) noted more than two decades ago. Adding computers to a classroom or requiring students to use digital tools in their assignments is not what will change education. Only as teachers and students adopt new attitudes and behaviors will schools change in meaningful ways. By itself, technology cannot remake schools or learning, but teachers and students using technology creatively and expansively will generate new directions for learning across grade levels and the curriculum.

Technologies can be evaluated in terms of how they promote higher order or lower order thinking by students. For example, technologies can be used in ways that are "highly transformative," "moderately transformative," or "minimally transformative":

- Highly transformative (5–6 stars): The resource is open-ended and allows users to think critically and solve problems using ideas and explorations. The resource emphasizes creating and evaluating, the top two higher order thinking skills on Bloom's taxonomy.

- Moderately transformative (3–4 stars): The resource offers pre-set and guided explorations that structure how users engage with the material. The resource emphasizes analyzing and applying, the middle two higher order thinking skills on Bloom's taxonomy.

- Minimally transformative (1–2 stars): The resource offers mainly drill and practice activities that provide little variety for users. The resource emphasizes remembering and applying, the bottom two lower order thinking skills on Bloom's taxonomy.

Digital tools transform the learning experience in today's classrooms.

SOURCE: Annie Fuller/Pearson Education

There are many useful online resources for learning more about Bloom's taxonomy. Fresno State University has published a collection of action verbs for teachers to use when designing learning activities for each thinking skill. There is an interactive version of the taxonomy available from the Iowa State University Center for Excellence in Learning and Teaching. New Zealand educator Andrew Churches has posted a digital taxonomy connecting specific technology-based activities to each of Bloom's thinking skills.

21st Century Skills

The term **21st century skills** represents the knowledge and understandings that students will need to succeed in our highly technological, information-based society. These skills include the ability to think critically, make informed judgments, solve complex problems, think creatively, communicate and collaborate with others, use information in innovative ways, and take responsibility for one's personal and civic life (Figure 1.4). Each skill propels students from passively receiving information from technology to actively creating knowledge and talents with technology.

Teaching skills is not new; schools have always prepared students for life and work, but not in the same ways for everyone. Looking back at schooling for more than a century, historian Diane Ravitch (2000, p. 14) noted, "The great educational issues of the twentieth century in the United States centered on questions of who was to be educated and what were they to learn." Public schools in the late 19th and 20th centuries focused on preparing working-class and immigrant students for roles as workers in an industrial society, emphasizing the skills and knowledge of vocational education and domestic work (Tyack, 1974; Cremin, 1988). Those from backgrounds of wealth and privilege followed very different educational pathways, from elite schools to positions of leadership in industrial America.

By the mid-1980s, however, the number of U.S. professional, managerial, and technical workers exceeded the number of manufacturing workers for the first time—just

Figure 1.4 A Diagram of 21st Century Skills

SOURCE: Partnership for 21st Century Skills (P21), www.p21.org. Used with permission.

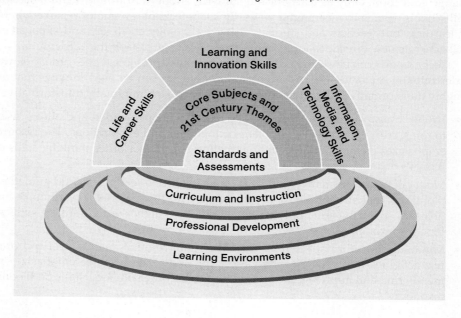

as manufacturing workers had exceeded those who worked on farms for the first time around the turn of the 20th century. Society was then transformed by the computer revolution that reached into every aspect of American life. "Information technology changes everything," declared William E. Halal more than a decade ago, and as "computer power continues to rise exponentially, and artificial intelligence (AI) becomes human-like, all this capacity will soon allow almost any social function to be performed online" (2008, p. 59).

Since that time, many students—particularly those from low-income and non-White families—have not achieved the higher levels of educational attainment needed for life and careers in today's society. Without higher levels of education, they lack the skills needed in an increasingly information- and technology-based society, and they find themselves trapped in low-skill/low-wage jobs. Educational inequality leads to economic inequality. Ideally, 21st century skills result from schools where every student learns the knowledge, competencies, skills, and habits of mind needed for current and future careers and workplaces.

The National Council of Teachers of English (NCTE; 2007, 2008b) has issued its own definition of skills students will need for the future, called **21st century literacies**. To live and work successfully, students must have the basic competencies of reading, writing, and mathematics, as well as an array of technology-based literacies, including proficiency with technology tools, the ability to build relationships and solve problems collaboratively, the knowledge to design and share information, the capacity to analyze and evaluate information from multiple sources, and the capability to handle information in ethical ways. "These literacies—from reading online newspapers to participating in virtual classrooms—are multiple, dynamic, and malleable" (National Council of Teachers of English, 2008b).

There are two key concepts that are essential to understanding 21st century skills: 1) technological pedagogical content knowledge (TPACK), and 2) the ISTE (International Society for Technology in Education) Standards for Students and Educators.

> **MyLab Education**
> **Video Example 1.3**
> In this video, you will learn how one high school is connecting academic learning to the solving of real-world problems. How can technology be used in schools like this to further promote 21st century learning?
> https://edisonhs.fcps.edu/academics/stem

Technological Pedagogical Content Knowledge

Technological pedagogical content knowledge (TPACK) proposes ways 21st century skills can be taught through **21st century technologies** (TPACK & Koehler, 2014). Through TPACK, teachers bring together three different forms of knowledge to produce powerful learning experiences for students:

1. *Content knowledge* includes the essential academic subject matter that teachers must convey to students in elementary or secondary schools.
2. *Pedagogical knowledge* includes all information that teachers know about teaching methods, instructional design, curriculum development, and how different students think and learn.
3. *Technological knowledge* includes knowing how to use multiple types of technologies in teaching, from books, manipulatives, and whiteboards to computer- and Internet-based Web 2.0 tools.

To be successful leaders in today's schools, teachers must blend all three forms of knowledge in ways that meet different instructional and student needs as follows:

- Academic content combined with technology creates technological content knowledge that shows teachers how to use technology to communicate content to students.
- Pedagogical knowledge combined with academic content knowledge becomes pedagogical content knowledge through which teachers understand how to use different methods of teaching to engage students.
- Combining content, pedagogy, and technology produces the technological pedagogical content knowledge that can guide the effective teaching of students with 21st century technology tools.

ISTE Standards for Educators and Students

The International Society for Technology in Education (ISTE) is the leading technology organization in the country, and its educational standards guide the use of technology in K–12 school systems, as well as in college and university teacher preparation programs around the country. ISTE's first standards, National Educational Technology Standards (NETS), were issued in 1998, followed by standards for teachers and administrators in 2000 and 2001. Those early standards focused on students learning basic technology skills, at the time called "computer literacy." Revised standards for students and teachers came out in 2007 and 2008, and those focused on ways to successfully integrate technology into classroom learning.

A decade later, ISTE has refreshed and updated its standards for students and educators once again to stress using technology for highly interactive and inquiry-based teaching and learning. To generate next-generation learning environments, the latest **ISTE Standards for Students** (2016) identify seven roles for students: Empowered Learner, Digital Citizen, Knowledge Constructor, Innovative Designer, Computational Thinker, Creative Communicator, and Global Collaborator. Each of these roles is intended to "empower student voice and ensure that learning is a student-driven process of exploration, creativity and discovery no matter where students or teachers are in the thoughtful integration of technology" (Aglio & Gusky, 2017).

To support its standards for students, **ISTE Standards for Educators** (2017) set forth seven roles for teachers: Learner, Leader, Citizen, Collaborator, Designer, Facilitator, and Analyst. While stating that these roles are not "technology standards" per se, ISTE states that they "set the vision for how educators can use technology to create next-generation learning environments" (quoted in Smith, 2017). The first five chapters of this book are aligned to the ISTE Standards for Educators. The last seven chapters are aligned to the ISTE Standards for Students.

ISTE believes its updated standards for students and teachers "provide a framework for learning, teaching and leading that is amplified by technology" (ISTE Team, 2017). *Amplify* is the key word here. To amplify is to make larger, to expand, to present more broadly and expansively. Just like surround-sound speakers bring the audio experience of a concert, a movie, or a classroom presentation to whole new levels for audiences, ISTE believes that technology can bring the experience of teaching and learning to whole new levels for educators and students. The goal becomes how to achieve these new levels. Technology creates learning experiences that would not be possible without it, providing unparalleled access to information, unprecedented amounts of interactivity, unsurpassed levels of communication, and unmatched capacities for creative self-expressions, along with many more ways to impact education at all grade levels.

In ISTE's vision, technology is not a curriculum add-on or an individual reward that students get only after completing other assignments. Nor is it the "end all/be all" of the instructional process. Rather, technologies function as tools for learning—vehicles for focusing student thinking on important ideas while discovering what they can create or invent through hands-on/minds on activities. Digital tools let teachers and students together create and design, explore and express, imagine and envision—while incorporating ideas and concepts that are part of the required academic curriculum. When using technology in classrooms, said one educator, "it's about the teaching, not the tools" (Stoeckl, 2016).

As a digital age teacher, your goal is to use 21st century technologies to create interactive and inquiry-based learning experiences that teach academic content as well as literacy and learning skills to K–12 students. All the ideas, activities, and materials you use with students, from textbooks to group activities to new technologies, are the instruments of that goal. As a teacher, you are the person who puts these elements into action, blending them in ways that generate exciting, challenging, and memorable learning experiences for students. You can discover how one teacher builds a lesson around the ISTE Standards for Students in this chapter's In Practice.

In Practice

Envisioning New Water Conservation Technologies: An ISTE Standards for Students Learning Activity

Grade Level	Featured Technologies
Upper Elementary and Middle School	Interactive websites, 3-D Modeling Software, 3-D Printers, Presentation Tools

Lesson Outline

The seventh-grade social studies curriculum at the middle school where Irene teaches emphasizes addressing state curriculum standards through thematic teaching, student-centered instruction, and the integration of digital technologies. In a learning activity on water-saving technologies, Irene integrated the latest ISTE Standards for Students—Empowered Learner, Digital Citizen, Knowledge Constructor, Innovative Designer, Computational Thinker, Creative Communicator, Global Collaborator.

To explore Central and South Asia as part of the world geography curriculum, Irene decided to focus on water use and conservation as a core theme through a unit titled "Water Conservation Technologies." The United Nations 2015 World Water Development report forecasts that 40% of the world's population will lack access to usable water by 2030. The goal of Irene's lesson was for students to understand the life-threatening issues faced by people who live in the regions of the world where access to clean water is neither readily found nor easily maintained. Climate (arid lands/rainy followed by dry seasons) and human actions (population growth/pollution/environmental exploitation) dramatically impact the availability and quality of water.

Teaching with Technology

While countries and cities throughout Central and South Asia face severe water shortages every day, the water crisis impacts people in United States and the families in Irene's school community as well. A 2016 U.S. Geological Survey report identified her state as being at high risk of having toxic metals in household pipes leach into drinking water supplies. High levels of lead were also found in more than 1,000 schools around the state. Utilizing the ISTE standards of Knowledge Constructor and Empowered Learner, the students and Irene began the unit by calculating their personal water footprint use with an online tool from the Grace Communications Foundation. The Nature Conservancy estimates that the average water use of an American is equivalent to 32,911 glasses a day—96% of which goes to growing food, making clothes and everyday items, and producing energy. Integrating math learning, students compared their daily use of water with that of people throughout the United States and around the world.

Irene next introduced students to the concept of greywater—water that has been used but is not done being useful thereafter. Water from sinks, washing machines, showers and tubs are common examples of greywater. When one student asked if it were possible to reuse the water the class used to wash hands and flush toilets to reduce overall water consumption, Irene suggested the class design ways for this to happen. Soon, students offered more ideas for how water could be used more efficiently and less wastefully. Leaky pipes that carry water from reservoirs to cities could be repaired or replaced; seawater could be repurposed through desalination; rainwater could be harvested for irrigation; composting toilets could be installed in public facilities.

Implementing the ISTE Innovative Designer and Computational Thinker standards, Irene challenged individuals and small groups to create engineering designs for their water conservation ideas. Students had the option of using physical materials (paper, cardboard, glue, tape, and other supplies) or 3-D modeling software to display their designs. More than a dozen students chose to use Tinkercad, a software program, for their designs, which could then be sent to a local college library where the digital code could be transformed into a hands-on model by a 3-D printer.

Finally, in the roles of ISTE Creative Communicators and Global Collaborators, students shared the results of their projects through different forms of media, including written reports, digital presentations, and short videos. Students' projects were posted on the class website so people locally and globally could access and learn from what the students proposed could be done to improve water safety and availability. Students found the project and its various technology connections personally meaningful to them as learners. One youngster commented: "In school, when we have a project and they give you a set of rules, sometimes these projects don't show any skills that I have. . . . 3-D printing lets you use your imagination." Another said that 3-D modeling "portrayed what we were trying to get across in a different way." Summarizing the full experience from an ISTE Digital Citizen perspective, a third student remarked how "everyone was talking about problems, but no one was talking about solutions." Now an entire class had ideas and proposals to solve real-life problems.

MyLab Education Self Check 1.3

Building a Professional Learning Network

1.4 Organize a professional learning network (PLN) as a technology-using educator.

▶ **MyLab Education**
Video Example 1.4

In this video, long-time educator Rita Pierson describes why every kid needs an adult who believes in them and their potential. How can you use your PLN to become a teacher who is a champion for students?

https://www.ted.com/talks/rita_pierson_every_kid_needs_a_champion?utm_expid=166907-24&utm_referrer=http%3A%2F%2Fwww.ted.com%2F

To become a technology learning and leading educator, you will benefit by organizing a **professional learning network (PLN)**—an anywhere, anytime source of ideas and information that supports and expands your talents and competencies as a teaching professional. A PLN is a multifaceted system of people (e.g., colleagues, Twitter contacts), spaces (e.g., conferences, Facebook groups), and tools (e.g., listservs, information curation sites) that support ongoing learning and professional growth. It serves as a way for you to keep expanding what you know how to do instructionally and professionally with interactive digital tools and educational change ideas (Trust, Carpenter, & Krutka, 2018; Trust, 2012). It directs and connects all the ways you obtain ideas, resources, materials, and connections.

A PLN is an extension of the term *personal learning network*, which has been defined as a "set of connections to people and resources, both offline and online, who enrich our learning" (Richardson & Mancabelli, 2011, p. 2). Personal learning networks include family, friends, and associates with whom we interact during our lives, as well as the media and information sources we use to gain ideas and information. These personal networks evolve dynamically as you meet new people and participate in new experiences.

A professional learning network acknowledges that teachers—like doctors, artists, dancers, scientists, engineers, designers, musicians, and other professionals—are learners for a lifetime. Being a lifelong learner gives teaching vitality and creativity as a profession, and it sustains a career filled with long working hours in schools. Teachers experience joy and accomplishment from teaching students and learning new ideas and information that support their work as educators. A PLN demonstrates your commitment to being an innovative, future-focused teacher, declaring, "I am serious about learning, personally and professionally, and sharing ideas and resources with students and colleagues." It is also a way to demonstrate to superintendents and principals that you possess knowledge, skills, preparation and forward thinking to apply for a job as a full-time classroom teacher. As one college student wrote to us:

> I just wanted to let you know that I included my PLN padlets [a virtual bulletin board] on a job application to a social studies position, and in the past week I had an interview and they just offered me the job! They mentioned that the padlets really helped them get to know my values as a teacher and see all of the skills and resources that I have—I think it really helped me stand out from the crowd. I landed my dream job!!

Your "Must Know About" Technologies

Digital technologies will be central to your work as a teacher and central to the learning of students who are daily users of multiple technology devices. Imagine you are beginning your teaching career next week. What might be your "must know about" technologies for 21st century teaching?

In answering this question, some of you might cite subject specific technologies such as the dual visualization tool TinkerPlots for mathematics teachers, a Google Lens camera-based augmented reality app for science teachers, or iCivics interactive games for social studies teachers. Others will list tools like presentation software, social media, and video-making apps that can be used across the disciplines and the grade levels. Understanding and being able to utilize your "must know about" technologies as teaching and learning tools is a prime reason for creating a PLN.

In 2008 when we asked Michael Flynn, a Massachusetts State Teacher of the Year and winner of a Presidential Award for Excellence in Mathematics Teaching, for his "must know about" technologies, he listed a laptop, an interactive whiteboard, a student participation system with clickers, and a smartphone. He used these tools to create

Table 1.2 Types of Educational Technologies

Physical devices	Online references	Software and apps	Online tools	Social media tools
Computers	The Internet	Word processing	Blogs	Twitter
Smartphones	Web-based maps	Presentation tools	Wikis	Pinterest
Tablets	(e.g., Google Maps)	Animation tools	Multiplayer games	Facebook
Video cameras	Infographics	Spreadsheets	Virtual worlds	Instagram
3-D Printers	Interactive charts	3-D modeling	Wikipedia	Video posting
Audio recorders	Online archives (e.g.,	Digital assistant	Infographic builder	(e.g., YouTube,
Remote control drones	Library of Congress)	(e.g., Siri, Alexa)	Screen capture	Vimeo)
Robotics kits			Survey tools	
			Multimedia messaging	

small-group alternatives to whole-class instruction, to activate student engagement with learning, to differentiate instruction, and to produce interest-building, problem-solving experiences in language arts, math, science, and history. He recognized then that every teacher will be constantly learning to use new technologies throughout their career to continue creating unique, powerful, and transformative learning by students.

Now, more than a decade later, "must know about" technologies are much more than the newest mobile phone, computing machine, or classroom tool. Instructional Technologist Fred Zinn has listed five types of educational technologies that teachers should learn about as teaching and learning tools (see Table 1.2):

Technologies in the five categories may be categorized by one of three levels indicating how they are used by teachers:

- Level 1 (*Old-School Tools*): Teachers are familiar with these technologies and use them regularly.
- Level 2 (*Current Devices*): Teachers may be somewhat familiar with these technologies and/or may need time to learn how to use them effectively.
- Level 3 (*Emerging Technologies*): Teachers are unfamiliar with these technologies and will need time to learn and use them.

In this framework, presentation software (Google Slides, PowerPoint, Keynote) is a Level 1 tool because it has been used regularly in schools for years. By contrast, online survey tools (Google Forms), virtual worlds (Minecraft), or online programming, coding and robotics resources are at Level 2 or Level 3, depending on whether they are part of current or future instructional practices by teachers.

You will be utilizing these five kinds of technologies for multiple purposes:

- *Instructionally* for activities you conduct directly with students, such as class presentations, multimedia demonstrations, and group projects and activities
- *Professionally* for activities you do to support teaching, such as lesson planning, person-to-person communications, and grade and record keeping
- *Interactively* for activities you create that involve students in learning in face-to-face and online settings.

As a new teacher getting ready to enter the teaching job market, you will want to know about and be able to use technologies from all three levels. You will want to be conversant and confident with tools that are considered old-school (Level 1) as well as technologies that are either current or emerging educational practices (Level 2 and Level 3). That way, you are prepared for what is and what will be available in the field of educational technology.

Push and Pull Technologies

The far-reaching influence of a PLN emerges through the ways you use online **technologies**. The web is a vast stream of information where individuals and organizations constantly offer resources and materials to technology users using **push technologies**). From all that available information, people select specific resources

Table 1.3 Robert's Push/Pull Information Flow

Information to the Web (Push)	Information from the Web (Pull)
Teacher-created websites and wikis	Online searches
Teacher-written blog posts	E-mail inquiries and blog post requests
Teacher-made videos and podcasts	Information alerts and updates
Teacher-made presentation slides and notes	Online journal articles
Personal resume and professional portfolio	News headlines sent to smartphones

and materials using **pull technologies**). Learning about the weather is one example of push and pull technologies. Television stations, online organizations, and interested individuals provide (push) weather news to the web every day for people to access (pull) as sources for information.

Teachers continually pull information from the web to expand academic content knowledge, build lesson plans, assess student learning, and stay current with educational trends and policies, and they constantly push information to students, colleagues, families, and school administrators—making themselves information seekers and information providers.

Table 1.3 shows how one history teacher uses push and pull technologies in his professional learning network.

- *Push*: Robert provides educational information to students and colleagues by posting links to blogs, videos, podcasts, and his online professional portfolio on the homepage of his teacher website. He also contributes to wikis for teachers and tutors, making his research available to interested readers worldwide.

- *Pull*: Robert receives ideas and resources from online information searches, professional learning communities, and information alerts in his e-mail from a global network of history teachers using the Diigo social networking site to offer each other links to new curriculum resources.

Like Robert, you can organize the push and pull of information from multiple sources to help construct your professional learning network.

Components of a Professional Learning Network

Building a professional learning network through the push and pull of information establishes three features of your identity as a technology-using educator:

- *Multimedia resume.* Your PLN presents an evolving portrait of your ideas and talents as a teacher. It shows everyone—from a school district's hiring committees to colleagues, families, and students—that you are a 21st century education professional with the knowledge, talents, and values of a technology-using educator.

- *Teaching and learning activities.* Your PLN showcases your teaching skills, your use of interactive technologies to create engaging lessons and deliver lively instruction, and your readiness to conduct thoughtful assessments of student learning. It provides evidence that you use the web to collaborate with students, post assignments, provide feedback, and invite learning to extend beyond the school day.

- *Technology modeling for students.* Your PLN offers students a model for using technology independently, creatively, and appropriately for learning. From the diverse ways that you use multiple technologies professionally, students observe examples of what it means to be technologically literate, ethical, and safe. As they build their own learning networks, students learn firsthand about the roles and responsibilities of engaged citizens in an information-based society who use technology wisely and effectively for everyone's betterment.

In each chapter, you will find a Building Your Professional Learning Network Application Activity that serves as a feature of your PLN. These activities are designed to introduce new strategies and methods to your teaching, helping you to integrate technology into learning. We invite you to join us in exploring how digital technologies can realize the possibilities of change for you as a teacher/leader and for students as learners, problem solvers, and critical thinkers in the world of today and tomorrow. You can also learn more about professional learning networks at PLNs for Educators, an open online course developed by Torrey Trust and students at the University of Massachusetts Amherst, free online at https://blogs.umass.edu/plncourse/.

MyLab Education Application Exercise 1.2:
Building Your PLN—Selecting Professional Pull and Push Resources
In each chapter, you will find a Building Your Professional Learning Network application exercise that serves as a feature of your PLN. These activities are designed to introduce new strategies and methods to your teaching, helping you to integrate technology into learning.

MyLab Education Self-Check 1.4

Chapter Summary

Learning Outcome 1.1

Summarize the changing diversity of American education and the roles of technology in the lives of students and families.

- American schools are increasingly more culturally and linguistically diverse settings.
- Academic achievement gaps, as well as connectivity and participation gaps, continue to serve as barriers to learning for students who are living in poverty, have special educational needs, or are speaking English as a new language.
- Students today grow up immersed in technology, experiencing a "digital childhood" and becoming a generation of technology users in their teens.
- Most 8- to 18-year-olds access some type of digital or screen technology almost every waking hour outside of school.

Learning Outcome 1.2

Discuss ways teachers utilize digital technologies in their work as educators.

- Every technology, from simplest to most complex, ancient to most recent, is a tool, device, or material whose purpose is to solve human problems.
- Technology is producing profound changes in every aspect of modern society, transforming how children and teachers live in, interact with, and understand their world.
- Web 2.0 tools are a new generation of technologies that can be used to create highly interactive, inquiry-based learning experiences at all grade levels.

- To become technology-using educators, teachers must continue to learn about their "must know about" technologies.

Learning Outcome 1.3

Analyze how 21st century technologies can be used to create highly interactive, inquiry-based learning environments.

- Twenty-first century skills represent the knowledge and understandings that students need to live and work in today's digital age.
- Technological pedagogical content knowledge happens when teachers combine grade-level subject matter with technology to produce engaging teaching and learning activities in classrooms.
- The ISTE Standards for Educators and Students show teachers how to integrate 21st century digital resources into all aspects of teaching and learning to create alternatives to traditional educational practices by promoting high levels of interaction, engagement, and collaborative learning.

Learning Outcome 1.4

Organize a professional learning network (PLN) as a technology-using educator.

- As a teacher, your PLN includes your technology skills and talents, the ways you integrate technology in your teaching, and how you model technology use for students.
- A PLN is a way to achieve three essential goals as a teacher: a multimedia resume, a space for learning and teaching resources, and a model of technology use for students.

Key Terms

> **MyLab Education Application Exercise 1.3:**
> *Growing and Leading with Technology: Marco's "PLN Building" Activity*

For Reflection and Discussion

Life Before Computers

One way to understand the role of computers in schools and in society is to imagine what people would do if that technology did not exist. Widespread use of computers is a very recent phenomenon. Ask parents, grandparents, and other family and community members to recall how people did things before we had word processing software, e-mail, online banking and shopping, mobile phones, digital cameras, or other digital devices that have revolutionized our lives. What has changed, and has anything remained the same?

The Hype Cycle for Emerging Technologies

The Hype Cycle for Emerging Technologies, from the technology analytics firm Gartner, projects where various new technologies are on a growth and adoption continuum that ranges from initial appearance to long-term use or obsolescence. The cycle has five stages that play out over 5 years in the life of a new technology: innovation trigger; peak of inflated experiences; trough of disillusionment; slope of enlightenment; and plateau of productivity. According to the cycle, after an exciting new technology emerges in the marketplace, people's expectations rise, often to unrealistic heights, before disillusionment sets in and expectations plummet. The technology then either vanishes from the scene (replaced by a better product) or rebounds from its fall to reach a middle ground where it becomes a productive feature of everyday life. For example, the 2017 Hype Cycle had virtual personal assistants (e.g., Siri, Alexa) and autonomous vehicles (driverless cars) high on the peak of expectations, augmented reality dipping into disillusionment, and virtual reality moving toward mainstream adoption.

Consider the latest new technologies that you have begun using or that you have heard about in the news. What do you think will be the potential hype cycle for each of these tools—both in schools and in society?

Replacing People with Machines

Efforts by states around the country to replace human court reporters—stenographers who record testimonies, arguments, and sidebar discussions during trials—with digital recording equipment represent an example of how technology replaces jobs formerly done by people (Crimaldi, 2018). There are many other examples, including telephone switchboard operators, bank tellers, highway toll collectors, pharmacy technicians, travel agents, film projectionists, receptionists, and cashiers at many stores. As you think about the impacts of technology on people and jobs, consider the following questions:

- In what other everyday activities are machines replacing humans? What advantages and drawbacks do you see when technology restructures jobs formerly done by human workers?
- What jobs and careers are most likely to change because of technology in the next decade? Which ones are least likely to change?
- How might teaching change, and how might it stay the same in a digital age?

Chapter 2
Understanding Educational Technology Issues and Trends

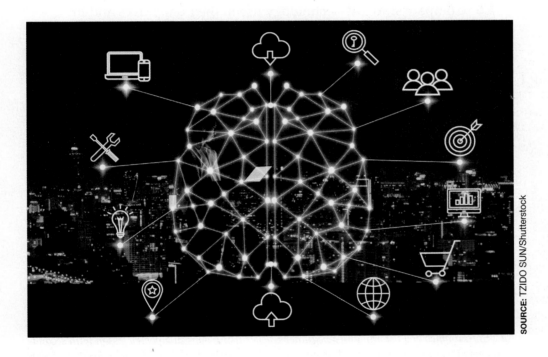

SOURCE: TZIDO SUN/Shutterstock

Chapter Overview

Chapter 2 explores educational technology in K–12 schools through a series of five short surveys about the key issues and trends you will encounter as a technology-using educator. Responding to the surveys will help you consider how technology inspires learning and creativity for students, a goal of the ISTE Standards for Educators and Students.

Following each survey is a brief review explaining how educators and researchers are thinking about technology in schools today. These commentaries address the "Learner" domain of the ISTE Standard for Educators that asks teachers and future teachers to stay current with research that supports improved student learning outcomes and then apply that research to their instructional and professional practices. The questions are designed so teachers can discuss them with students, as well as to establish dialogs about technology and its roles in teaching and learning in schools.

Learning Outcomes

After reading this chapter, you will be able to:

2.1 Assess your motivations for becoming a technology-using teacher.

2.2 Analyze barriers to the use of technology in schools, including digital inequalities, achievement gaps, and online safety and digital privacy issues.

2.3 Describe roles for technology in teaching.

2.4 Evaluate how technology supports different teaching philosophies and instructional methods.

2.5 Compare students' technology use in their daily lives and in schools.

Chapter Learning Goal

Analyze key issues and trends in the field of educational technology while assessing your readiness to become a technology-using educator.

Featured Technologies

Computers

Smartphones

Tablets

Apps

Internet

One-to-one computing

Online educational resources

Three Future Teachers Discuss Technology

Donasha, Max, and Ava, all college students preparing to become teachers, were together in the college library completing an assignment for their educational technology course. They viewed a TED-Ed video of a veteran and a beginner teacher using apps in a poetry lesson with second-graders. Then they consulted online databases to research educational theories for a class presentation incorporating audio, video, and animation. On break, they walked to the café in the lobby. As they waited in line, Donasha read her Twitter feed on her tablet, Max checked texts on his smartphone, and Ava previewed the latest science news with her laptop. Over coffee, they began discussing how they planned to use technology as first-year teachers.

Donasha, an early adopter of technology, had a laptop computer for her own use throughout elementary and high school. As a college student, she now uses a smartphone, a tablet, and a desktop computer, on which she does all her assignments while tracking developments in the medical and educational fields. Based on all of her experiences, Donasha said she is convinced that infusing technology into every curriculum area is unquestionably where teaching is going in the future: "Tablets and smartphones create exciting new opportunities for teaching and learning because kids are able to control parts of their learning environment. Technology offers a bigger invitation to learning than I ever imagined when I started to use it in first grade. There is so much more that I will be able to teach with technology, so I am always learning about how to utilize it with students."

"I like it for my own learning, but I am skeptical about using technology in classrooms," Max countered, explaining that the out-of-date equipment at the school where he is interning is often not working properly and is difficult to schedule for use. "My wariness is not based solely on equipment problems," he explained. "I really think students need to learn how to learn; they should have limited use of computers and videos to figure things out for themselves without

relying on machines. And I do not see the benefit of everyone holding a phone or a tablet all day long instead of reading real books and writing on paper."

Ava admitted that although she is interested in technology as a way to interest students, she feels uncertain about how to use smartphones, tablets, Internet resources, or any of the other emerging technologies as tools for learning. "My concern is that technology changes so rapidly, and the students always know more about all of it than I do," Ava observed. "I realize that there are opportunities for learning using technology, but I wonder how I can learn about them first so I can teach them to students with confidence." Ava anticipated that integrating technology into learning might be a full-time job all by itself and felt nervous about how to do it: "I do not see how I will have time to make technology part of my teaching, unless I can learn more about it first."

Donasha, Max, and Ava are expressing widely held beliefs and uncertainties about the role of technology in schools. Perhaps you have expressed similar views as you think about using technology for learning with students. So have many educators, from new professionals to veteran teachers who have been in the classroom for many years.

To explore the presence of technology in education more fully, we have organized this chapter using a series of five surveys focusing on major issues, developments, and trends in the field of educational technology. There are no right or wrong answers to these surveys. They are intended to challenge your thinking, to encourage you to let new ideas take hold and evolve as you learn more about schools, students, teaching, and technology throughout this book.

Our questions ask you to think in terms of the differences in impact between new and emerging **21st century technologies** and older, more commonplace, and increasingly obsolete educational technologies. Digital technologies for the 21st century feature highly interactive devices and apps that promote active engagement and learning by students.

Handheld devices enable almost anywhere, anytime access to learning and entertainment.

SOURCE: Georgejmclittle/Fotolia

Motivations for Using Technology

2.1 **Assess your motivations for becoming a technology-using teacher.**

How would you classify your interest in using technology as a teacher? Rate each factor listed in Figure 2.1 as a major factor, a minor factor, or not a factor motivating your decision to use digital technology as a teacher.

You may have selected several major factors for using digital technologies as a teacher. Many teachers would agree. In survey after survey, a majority of educators (between two thirds and three fourths of respondents) say they believe that technology facilitates student learning, provides a positive impact on educational processes, allows for more individual and personalized learning, supports project-based learning, and makes daily teacher tasks like grading and student record-keeping easier and more efficient (Dreambox Learning, 2018; Singleton, et al., 2018; Shifflet & Weilbacher, 2015).

You may have chosen technology as a way to develop engaging learning activities for students. Many teachers do too. More than 9 out of 10 Advanced Placement (AP) and National Writing Project (NWP) teachers report using the Internet to locate lesson plans and teaching materials (Purcell, Heaps, Buchanan, & Friedrich, 2013). Most of these teachers receive online alerts about new developments in their teaching field, while younger professionals are more likely than veteran teachers to engage in online discussions with colleagues and to use web-based tools to edit and share their professional work.

→ **Figure 2.1** What Motivates You to Use Digital Technologies as a Teacher?

Motivating Factor	Major Factor	Minor Factor	Not a Factor
Teach my subject field(s)			
Use time more efficiently			
Plan engaging learning activities			
Support students who are lagging behind or advancing quickly			
Let students use new technologies			
Respond to student interests			
Extend learning beyond the classroom			
Differentiate/personalize learning			
Model technology use for colleagues			
Improve my professional evaluation			
Other			

Enhancing Teaching with Technology

Teachers are also motivated to use technology because it can enhance two major aspects of their daily work in schools and classrooms: 1) instructional practices and 2) administrative/professional activities.

- **Instructional practices** are teaching methods used when interacting directly with students. Examples include using videoconferencing tools to bring authors and scientists into the classroom; asking students to design videos, podcasts, and images to showcase their knowledge; using polling tools to quickly collect student responses and engage a class in discussion about a topic; accessing the web for class discussion; using technology for presentations or simulations; having students use tablets and smartphones as part of group projects; and integrating handheld and wireless devices into academic activities.

- **Administrative/professional activities** include all planning, organizing, and record keeping, as well as data-driven analyses and assessment activities teachers perform to support the direct instruction of students. These behind-the-scenes tasks make instructional practices succeed. Examples include maintaining academic records with grading software, creating a class website to communicate with students and families, conducting correspondence through e-mail, doing research using web resources, and writing reports with word processing software.

Some technologies support both instructional practices and administrative/professional activities. E-mail and collaborative documents can be used to provide formative and summative feedback to students about writing and research projects (instructional practices) and to communicate with families about student learning progress in school (administrative/professional activities). A teacher-created blog or website could display notes from class, describe homework assignments, and present project grading rubrics (instructional practices) while providing a publishing format for students' work, visual records of class field trips, or a calendar of upcoming events (administrative/professional activities).

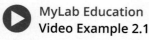

**MyLab Education
Video Example 2.1**

In this video, teachers discuss and demonstrate using technology to enhance and expand teaching and learning. How do you imagine integrating digital technologies as learning tools in your future classroom?

https://www.you-tube.com/watch?time_continue=30&v=qmLEl4QjQ3w

Most teachers, especially recent college graduates, are familiar with writing on computers, corresponding by e-mail and text messages, and keeping records on spreadsheets and databases. They confidently use technology to handle the preparation and support tasks that make up such a large part of a teacher's workday. Nevertheless, those same teachers have less experience integrating technology seamlessly into the day-to-day activities of classroom learning because innovative uses of new tools were not featured either in their own schooling or in their teacher preparation courses. They are therefore less familiar with using technology to differentiate instruction during class time, assess student learning, or teach 21st century skills.

Part of the challenge and excitement of being a digital-age teacher is developing ways to make new and emerging technologies an integral part of classroom teaching and student learning. In the 21st century, professional educators face the ongoing challenge of creating new instructional patterns, building new technology integration models, and setting new standards of technology-based learning in schools. You can explore more about using technology to design engaging classroom learning experiences for students in Chapter 4.

Motivating and Inspiring Students

Perhaps you indicated in the survey in Figure 2.1 that you would like to use technology as a way to motivate and inspire student learning. If so, you have identified one of the greatest challenges in U.S. education today. Students at every grade level feel detached and alienated from school. Teachers see this disengagement in blank and bored faces, defiant and resentful behavior, and let-me-get-this-done-as-quickly-as-I-can responses to classroom activities or homework assignments.

Multiple studies document a growing problem of **student disengagement**. A national Gallup Poll found that as students progress through school, their level of engagement steadily declines, from nearly 8 in 10 engaged at the elementary school level to only 4 in 10 at the high school level (Busteed, 2013). In another survey, teachers and administrators identified engagement and motivation as the number-one key to academic achievement, but only 4 in 10 said most students at their school are highly engaged academically (Education Week, 2014).

Since 2003, Indiana University's High School Survey of Student Engagement (HSSSE) has been documenting patterns of student boredom and alienation. According to the HSSSE:

- Two thirds of high school students report feeling bored in classes every day.
- Half of all high school students spend 4 hours or less a week doing homework or otherwise preparing for their classes; 20% spend 1 hour or less per week.
- More than half of high school students said that outside of class they never discuss academic material or readings with teachers.
- Half of high school students said they never receive prompt feedback from teachers on assignments.
- Just over half of high school students (57%) said they participate frequently in class discussions or ask questions (52%) of their teachers.
- Just over half of high school students indicated that they put "a great deal of effort" into their schoolwork (Yazzie-Mintz, 2010).

Disaffection from and disengagement with school are factors leading to the significant number of students who leave before high school graduation, a pressing issue facing educators today (Balfanz, Bridgeland, Bruce, & Fox, 2013, 2012). While the dropout rate has declined in recent years, about one in five Black and Hispanic students will not earn a high school diploma or a general education development (GED) equivalent (Fry, 2014). Students who experience "graduation gaps" will be disadvantaged financially over their lifetime; a college graduate will make more than double the annual earnings of someone who has less than a high school education. Meanwhile, society as a whole benefits when students complete postsecondary levels of education—college graduates generally enjoy better health, live longer lives, generate greater taxable income, and are more likely to vote in elections and volunteer in local communities than are their less-educated peers.

For many students, one key reason for dropping out is that classes are simply not engaging or stimulating enough to keep them in school. Repetitive modes of instruction and teachers who fail to connect academic material from the textbook to real-world issues and problems leave students unmotivated to do assignments and projects. As a result, absence from school becomes more frequent, propelling an alienating spiral of frustration and failure.

To stay engaged with school, students want better teachers, smaller classes, individualized assistance, a school climate fostering achievement, and a strong relationship with at least one adult in the school believing in them and seeing their potential for educational success. Group projects and lessons that incorporate technology are also among the instructional practices that students find most engaging.

Digital Dialog 2.1

Many educators believe that technology enables the active engagement and rapid feedback that students need for maximum learning but do not consistently receive when teachers emphasize whole-class instruction, individual silent reading, and fill-in-the-blank worksheets. As you consider technology's influence on and importance to student learning, comment and connect online about the following questions:

- How are today's media-immersed students different from the way you were as a learner and from students in the past? How are they the same?
- How might technology address persistent patterns of student boredom and alienation from academic learning in schools?
- How might technology help teachers to accommodate the needs of diverse learners?
- How might teachers combine technology-based and non-technology-based resources within classroom lessons to help students demonstrate competency and reflect on their learning?

Approaches to Student Engagement

Actively engaging students in learning is a prime goal of every approach to teaching. Widely used methods for engaging students include:

1. **One-on-one tutoring** engages students by adapting instruction to each learner's individual needs, interests, and knowledge. Adult examples of tutoring include training for high-risk careers, such as piloting airplanes or controlling a nuclear reactor, or preparing for professions in which high artistry is sought, such as master classes for musicians and dancers or personal coaching for athletes, chess players, or actors.

2. **Small group learning** engages students in working on problems collaboratively and cooperatively in ways that produce high-quality explanations and performances among peers. **Learning groups** can vary in size from pairs, trios, and foursomes to larger learning structures.

3. **Inquiry-based learning** engages students in projects that ask them to do authentic and active work by investigating relevant questions in a subject field. Students gain the analytical ability to use information in a variety of ways through researching hypotheses, collecting data, formulating conclusions, and presenting their findings in oral and written formats.

4. **Metacognitive thinking** engages students by encouraging them to examine their own learning through self-explanation and self-evaluation. As students gain the capacity to question and reflect on their own learning, they improve their performance using the concepts and skills they are learning in school.

Imagine a school in which teachers combine instruction with technology to enact active learning, constructivist approaches, and **brain-based education**. What would that look like? One model is High Tech High (HTH) in San Diego, California. Begun in 2000 as a single charter high school, HTH has grown to become a network of high

Table 2.1 Innovative Learning Characteristics of High Tech High

HTH Learning Principle	Key Characteristics
Personalization	Every student has an advisor who oversees long-term goals and short-term performance.
	Every student creates a personal digital portfolio to document the year's learning.
	The school supports full inclusion of students with special needs.
	Networked wireless laptops and tablets are always available for use.
Adult world connection	Students shadow adults in the community.
	Semester-long internships with local businesses and agencies are part of the curriculum.
	Community service learning projects are where independent study projects begin.
	Small-group learning in technology-based labs and project areas is the norm for all students.
Common intellectual mission	No tracking or ability grouping takes place.
	All learning by students is evaluated using performance assessments based on learning rubrics.
	Teachers work in teams.
	Nearly all graduates go to college.

schools, middle schools, and elementary schools serving thousands of public school students. The school's expansive network reflects its remarkable educational successes. Nearly all HTH graduates go to college. HTH also has its own program for preparing new teachers, operated in collaboration with San Diego State University.

HTH's educational philosophy blends new technologies with innovative constructivist approaches to teaching and learning. Responding to the issues of student disengagement and low academic achievement, HTH offers a rigorous, project-based learning curriculum that involves children and adolescents in every aspect of their education. Three principles of learning guide the curriculum and instruction, with technology integrated seamlessly to support the goals of the school (see Table 2.1). The school's founders believe that these learning principles, which are not routinely found in U.S. schools, form the foundation for the kind of education students need to prepare them for 21st century jobs and professions.

Technology is a constant feature of students' everyday educational experiences at HTH in all subjects. Utilizing technology activates the four core approaches of student engagement highlighted earlier: one-on-one tutoring and learning; small-group activities; inquiry-based teaching; and metacognitive and reflective thinking by students. As students use different tools for different purposes, technology becomes the vehicle through which the school and students connect to the community, and the community connects to the school. Furthermore, technology itself serves as a field of study so that students understand how technology impacts schools and society.

> MyLab Education **Self-Check 2.1**

Barriers to Technology Use

2.2   Analyze barriers to the use of technology in schools, including digital inequalities, achievement gaps, and online safety and digital privacy issues.

What barriers can potentially impede or block your use of technology as a teacher? Figure 2.2 asks you to rate each factor as either a major barrier, a minor barrier, or not a barrier.

Digital Inequalities and Achievement Gaps

Perhaps you cited a lack of access to up-to-date equipment as a major barrier to using technology regularly with students, as many teachers certainly have. It is true that nearly all public schools have Internet access, and the ratio of students to computers has

Figure 2.2 What Impedes Your Use of Technologies as a Teacher?

Impeding Factor	Major Barrier	Minor Barrier	Not a Barrier
Lack of up-to-date classroom technology			
Inadequate Internet/Wi-Fi connections			
Lack of time during class			
Technology does not fit my teaching style			
Have not received training in how to use digital tools			
Technologies change too rapidly			
Intimidated by technology			
Administrators and other teachers do not support using technology			
Concerns about online safety and digital privacy			
Concerns about student distraction or misuse of technology (e.g., cyberbullying)			
Lack of confidence in troubleshooting if classroom or student technology breaks down			

grown to nearly 1:3. Still, K–12 schools have less technology than is the norm in higher education or corporate America, and the educational technology that is available is replaced or updated less often. Small and rural schools in nearly every state lack the fiber optics needed for high-speed Internet—defined by the Federal Communications Commission as at least 100 kilobits (kbps) per second (Fay, 2017). The result is a **connectivity gap** where schools lack the broadband capacities to provide students with access to today's essential digital technologies for learning.

In recent years, a constant squeeze between the need for expanded technological capabilities and declining educational budgets has forced schools to curtail their technology goals. Although there are schools with multiple computers in every classroom—along with a flat-screen television, high-speed Internet access, a digital projector, and a workstation from which an instructor can control what is happening on student screens—in many schools the technology infrastructure remains locked in the past. In those schools, technology is out of date or in poor condition, software is limited, and software and hardware are often incompatible due to differences in computer memory and operating system requirements. By contrast, teachers with multiple computers in a classroom are more likely to use technology as an integral part of classroom learning. Multiple machines make it easier for a teacher to divide a class into smaller groups, with some students using technology while the rest do other activities.

Access to and use of the latest technologies are not distributed evenly throughout society or schools, creating what educators and social scientists used to call digital divides and now refer to as **digital inequalities**. Digital inequalities happen when non-White, immigrant, urban and rural youngsters from low income areas do not have the same level of access to the latest technologies in school or at home as many of their peers.

Digital inequality produces **technology participation gaps** for minority students and those from low income areas. Even though access to technologies such as cable television, mobile phones, and the Internet has increased across all income levels in our society, participation gaps happen when the latest, most expensive technologies

capable of performing complex tasks and functions are primarily found among affluent and White families and schools in wealthy communities. When students do not
have access to the latest technologies, their educational experiences are shortchanged.
Researchers have found, for example, that students are more likely to develop interests
in science, technology, engineering, and math fields when teachers feature up-to-date
digital technology, social media, and student-driven learning as regular components
of classroom learning (Project Tomorrow, 2012b).

Digital Dialog 2.2

Many students from low-income and culturally diverse families lack access to the latest, most powerful technologies outside of school.
Even when schools have new technologies, some students use tools for inquiry-based investigations, experiments, and research projects while other students are confined mostly to online worksheets with drill and practice exercises. As you think about how you will use
technology to reduce digital participation gaps, connect and comment online about the following questions:

- In what ways can integrating technology into classroom instruction and student learning reduce digital participation gaps for students?
- How might you organize classroom instruction to ensure that all students have substantive learning experiences combined with
  formative and summative assessments?
- Do you see Bring Your Own Device/Technology (BYOD/T) programs as a solution to or a continuation of digital divides, digital
  inequalities, and digital participation gaps?

Technology access for students exists along a wide spectrum of experiences
known as a **digital continuum**. Because far fewer low-income households have the
latest technologies or high-speed Internet, students in those households do not have
the same media literacy or learning experiences as their more affluent peers. Lack of
technology access contributes to academic **achievement gaps**, a term that refers to dis-
parities that result when African American, Asian and Pacific Islander, Hispanic, and
Native American students do not succeed academically at the same academic levels as
white students; the term can also be applied to differences in educational results between boys and girls, students from higher- and lower-income families, native English
speakers and students learning English as a new language, and nondisabled students
and students with special educational needs. You can explore more about using technology to address digital inequalities and participation gaps in Chapter 5.

Schedules, Skills, and Supports

For many teachers, and perhaps for you in your responses to the questions in Figure
2.2, a combination of demanding teaching schedules, lack of opportunities to learn
about using technology for teaching, inadequate administrative support, and one's
personal attitudes act as barriers to the integration of technology into classroom learning. These factors impact:

- *Teaching schedules.* Teachers with long block schedules (class periods that last for
  90 to 120 minutes) are more likely to use technology than teachers with shorter
  classes. Longer class periods mean teachers have more time to include digital
  tools as part of daily instruction. Many schools, however, schedule class periods
  of less than an hour, and the time needed to get students from the classroom to
  a computer lab or library and back again makes it difficult to create technology-
  infused activities. Plus, facing a mandate to teach and review large amounts of
  curricular material in preparation for state and national education exams, many
  teachers feel they do not have time to integrate technology into teaching. Teachers
  teaching fewer curriculum topics were twice as likely to have students using computers in class on a regular basis.
- *Technology skills.* Teachers who are technologically skilled integrate technology into classes more frequently than do teachers with fewer technological skills.
  However, most teachers feel they do not have sufficient technical assistance and

support for using equipment and software in the classroom. Teachers familiar with multimedia tools, presentation software, and interactive web materials tend to be active technology-using educators.

- *Organizational support.* Teachers find it more difficult to make technology part of their teaching in schools in which principals do not advocate for technology integration or in which there is no schoolwide emphasis on technology use. Administrators generally set the tone and direction in a school, and teachers find it easier to integrate technology when the principal supports that effort. Professional development for teachers has not kept pace with the changes in technology tools and systems, and educators in low-income schools receive less training than their colleagues in more affluent districts.

- *Personal beliefs.* Teachers need a strongly positive belief in the educational potential of technology in order to spend the time needed to learn new tools to motivate and energize students. Not every teacher has that belief. Some teachers are reluctant to use technology due to worry about excessive screen time for students; others are concerned that students might misuse technology (such as through cyberbullying); still others think technology leads children to become distracted and overly sedentary learners. But even teachers with positive attitudes about technology's usefulness struggle to use it in ways that promote student-centered learning. They experience a disconnect between beliefs and practices in which external factors like lack of access or inadequate professional development override their desire to use more technology regularly in the classroom.

As a teacher, you may encounter one or perhaps multiple obstacles to technology use in your school, and while there are no instant solutions, finding ways around the barriers is central to the job of a teacher. Most educators work in organizations that are underfunded and under-resourced. For years, teachers have compensated by working long hours, spending their own money on materials and supplies, collaborating in informal networks, taking extra courses and workshops, writing grants, and lobbying policy makers for change. Responding to barriers to technology use will require all of these strategies and continuous evaluation of how to integrate technology's potential power for student learning into teaching practices.

Critics of Technology in Schools

Thinking about possible barriers to technology use by teachers, you may have concluded that computers and other digital technologies have not yet generated—and perhaps will never produce—substantive changes in how teaching and learning happens in K–12 schools. Technology critics, notably Stanford University historian Larry Cuban, have raised similar points. Cuban (2018, 2013, 2009, 2003) has argued that computers have been "oversold and underused," with their use featuring mainly:

- Drill-and-practice worksheets but not exploratory learning using software and interactive web materials
- Word processing for publishing but not for writing or other forms of creative self-expression by students
- Accessing the Internet as an encyclopedia of information but not as a tool for learning how to do thoughtful research and critical analysis of online materials
- Smartphones, digital cameras, interactive websites, and handheld or wireless devices barely used as learning tools.

In his most recent book, a study of 41 technology-enriched classrooms in six California Silicon Valley school districts, Cuban (2018, p. 2) found "only occasional instances" of teachers integrating laptops and tablets to create more student-centered classrooms and "scattered cases" of schools using technology to substantively alter how teachers teach and students learn—developments he found "puzzling in their isolation from mainstream practices."

Cuban is hardly alone in expressing concerns about technology's impact on students. Noting the increasing use of screen technologies—television, videos, phones, and tablets—by babies, toddlers, and preschoolers, the Campaign for a Commercial-Free Childhood (CCFC) found few learning benefits and multiple potential risks from increased technology use (CCFC, 2012). The CCFC found evidence of diminished creativity, aggressive behavior, desensitization to violence, and diminished capacity for self-control among preschoolers who were heavy technology consumers.

Other critics worry that children's critical thinking and choice making are being subverted by online commercial marketing that encourages children and families to buy the latest consumer culture items. Many educators recommend that families set screen time limits for children while creating more opportunities for creative play and time to engage in conversations and interactions with adults. Some commentators urge parents to insist that children avoid video games, despite the fact that there is no evidence linking video games to aggressive or violent behavior among youth. In fact, it is adults, not children, who play video games the most.

Some commentators believe that extensive exposure to technology negatively affects users' intellectual development—rewiring brains and making children, adolescents, and adults more demanding of instant results and less able to sustain concentration on complex intellectual tasks (Rosen, 2012, 2010). Nicholas Carr, author of the best-selling book *The Shallows: What the Internet Is Doing to Our Brains*, described his experience before and after the Internet as: "Once I was a scuba diver in the sea of words. Now I zip along the surface like a guy on a Jet Ski" (2011, p. 7). Carr (2015) believes that technology reroutes neural pathways in ways that block thoughtful reflection and deep learning. Yet every new experience—digital, interpersonal, personal—rewires the brain in ways that expand a person's knowledge and capacity for action. More research will be needed to determine just how technology is restructuring how people think and act.

From a different perspective, researchers suggest that teachers and parents should focus more on how children use devices, not solely on how much time they spend with them (Oreo, 2019; Canadian Paediatric Society, 2017). These researchers emphasize the importance of **active screen time** where, rather than passively receiving information from screens (e.g., watching videos or scrolling through social media posts), youngsters are physically or cognitively involved by solving puzzles, thus expending energy and expressing creative ideas. Adults should "mitigate"—not just "minimize"—screen media by watching videos with children, actively curating what programs children are using, and ensuring that youngsters combine screen viewing with active and creative play (Domoff, et al., 2017). These efforts will help children and adolescents to maintain a healthy "digital diet" in which they utilize websites and apps that teach as well as entertain, limit media multitasking when studying, and receive technology guidance and role modeling from parents and teachers.

As a teacher, you will hear competing perspectives about the value of digital tools, and you will need to carefully consider what they mean to your use of technology. Your decisions about technology use will stretch beyond the classroom into the lives of students and families in the community where you are teaching, making your choices important ones for years to come. The book *Plugged In: How Media Attract and Affect Youth* (Valkenberg & Piotrowski, 2017) provides a thoughtful review of evidence about technology's potentials and drawbacks as a learning medium for young students.

Maintaining Online Safety and Digital Privacy

In 2018, the political consulting firm Cambridge Analytica was found to have engaged in mining the data of as many as 87 million Facebook users, vaulting concerns about safety, privacy, and third-party access to personal information to the forefront of public opinion. Facebook subsequently banned the firm from the site while promising to implement new policies to protect the personal information of users. Less well publicized at the time was research by a team of computer scientists and educators who found that some 5,855 of the most popular free third-party apps for children on Android devices were improperly collecting user data (Reyes, et al., 2018). Nearly three in four (73%) of the apps transmitted sensitive data over the Internet; 40% shared information insecurely; and 19% provided private information to third-party services that were not supposed to be involved with apps for children. All in all, more than half of apps appeared to be in violation of Children's Online Privacy Protection Act (COPPA) regulations.

A definition of terms is important to understanding app/website safety and privacy issues. **COPPA** is a federal law that went in effect in 2000 and was updated in 2013 and 2017. COPPA is designed to protect children under age 13 by setting rules that all Internet-connected companies and services are supposed to follow. In theory, the law protects children's identifying information (including name, address, Social Security number, phone number, username, IP addresses, location data, and more).

In practice, COPPA's protections are far from complete. For example, social media sites like Facebook and YouTube are not required to follow COPPA guidelines since they are meant to be used by individuals age 13 and older. Plus, companies can apply to the Federal Trade Commission for "safe harbor" status that certifies they are in compliance with COPPA guidelines. But researchers found that safe-harbor apps were not as safe as claimed—237 apps transmitted personal information to advertisers even though this was prohibited by the terms of service of apps for children (Reyes, et al., 2018).

In addition, in their eagerness to sell products, online companies are not always vigilant in how user data is collected or shared. Many online games specifically marketed to children use a business model called "freemium" in which the game is free, but advertisements and product linkages are embedded within the program. This encourages users to make in-game or in-app purchases to earn more points and rewards. Meanwhile, the games collect data on users that are sold to third-party vendors.

Third-party apps are software applications developed by someone other than the maker of a technology device. Almost everyone has lots of applications on their computer, smartphone, or tablet that were not made by Apple or Android device manufacturers. Third-party apps have access to your data; for example, anytime you log in to a tool using Gmail, the app can access some or all of your Google data. Once given access to your device, third-party apps have it forever—unless you revoke it, a process users should follow for any web services they no longer wish to use. Go to Google Search Permissions to see all the third-party apps you've given permission to via Google.

Granting access to information can present serious problems. Fordham University School of Law researchers revealed the presence of an extensive and under-regulated market for selling the personal data of student computer and smartphone users (Russell, et al., 2018). Noting that there is no federal privacy law governing student data brokers, the researchers found that personal information was being related to student ethnicity, income, lifestyle, and other criteria. One company, noted the research team, had mailing addresses for over 5 million high school students available for sale for commercial purposes (Russell, et al., 2018, p. 2).

Given privacy concerns, educators and parents wonder how children can safely use websites and apps for educational purposes. There are steps that teachers and parents can take to minimize risks to children when they are using websites and apps.

1. Engage in conversations with children about issues of apps, privacy, and online behavior. Children and adolescents will respond favorably to honest talk from adults who give them positive strategies for how to use online materials safely.

2. Utilize the parental software controls available on most computers, smartphones, and tablets to block sites, impose screen time limits, and monitor online activity. Web browsers like Mozilla Firefox, Google Chrome, and Apple Safari also have functions for controlling the content that children can access. Also disable the automatic installation of apps from third-party vendors so you can select materials on a case-by-case basis.

3. Install kid-friendly browsers that provide protected environments for child users, but note that many of these may be too limiting for older youngsters who require access to a wider range of content on the web to complete school assignments.

4. Download apps only from official app stores (Google Play and Apple App Store), where efforts are made to filter out harmful software.

5. Read reviews and ratings from consumer and educational groups like Common Sense Media to locate safe, high-quality educational materials.

6. Purchase apps from trusted web content developers who have a known reputation, make clear the terms of service, offer troubleshooting FAQs, and openly disclose their privacy policies.

7. Closely review the terms of service and privacy policies for any apps and tools that you and your students sign up for. These documents are full of legal jargon and are designed to be hard to read, but understanding them is critical to knowing how your data is collected and used.

MyLab Education Application Exercise 2.1:
Building Your PLN: Examining Apps for Safety and Privacy

MyLab Education Self-Check 2.2

Roles for Technology in Teaching

2.3 Describe roles for technology in teaching.

What are your ideas for using technology in teaching? Choose one answer for each of the potential frequencies listed in Figure 2.3, paying attention to the different roles that technology can play for you as a teacher and for the students you are teaching.

As you think about your responses in Figure 2.3, note that nearly all schools and classrooms have computers and access to the Internet, although many low-income and rural districts lack the newest machines and high-speed broadband connections. You can see the connectedness of communities throughout the country by looking online at a Fixed Broadband Deployment Map from the Federal Communications Commission that shows technologies and broadband speeds available in different geographic locations.

Figure 2.3 How Often Do You Plan to Use the Following Technologies in Teaching?

Technology	All the Time	Regularly	Occasionally	Hardly Ever
Educational apps on smartphones and tablet computers				
Digital presentations (PowerPoint, Prezi, Google Slides)				
Classroom response systems for quizzes and participation (Kahoot!, Poll Everywhere, Quizlet)				
Word processing tools for student writing (Microsoft Office, Google Docs, Open Office)				
Video and video clips (YouTube, Vimeo, TED-Ed, Hulu/Netflix, Internet Archive)				
Interactive learning games (ABCya!, GeoGuessr, Stop Disasters!)				
Academic content curation (G Suite for Education, Diigo, PBworks)				
Back channels (TweetChat, Chatzy)				
Collaborative writing and editing (Google Docs, Evernote, Simplenote, Slack)				
Design and publishing (Photoshop, PageMaker, Adobe Spark, Canva, Haiku Deck, Lucidpress)				
Photo and movie making and editing (iMovie, Final Cut Pro, PicPlayPost, PicMonkey)				
Coding and game making (Scratch, Minecraft, Construct 2, GameMaker Studio)				
Augmented reality and virtual reality (Google Tour Builder, HP Reveal, Quiver, Star Walk, 4D Anatomy)				

What does a technology-integrated classroom look like in practice? In some schools, it is a **smart classroom** equipped with U-shaped workstations or tables featuring laptops or tablets connected to the Internet, a digital projector, a document camera, an interactive whiteboard, lecture capture equipment, videoconferencing, wireless microphones, surround sound speakers, a student response system, a printer, a scanner, and other interactive tools like virtual reality headsets, robotics sets, or augmented reality tech (e.g., MERGE Cube). Many schools, however, lack an up-to-date technology infrastructure, and teachers and students must use older tools. Still, no matter what technologies are available in schools and classrooms, it is important for teachers to think in terms of the kinds of actions and behaviors that will result from the ways students and teachers use the tools they have.

Competency and Confidence with Technology

Your responses in Figure 2.3 may reflect your personal competency and confidence with technology. Throughout the 1990s and early 2000s, teachers mainly used computers for e-mail, word processing, record keeping, and data management, but not regularly for classroom instruction (Project Tomorrow, 2012b). Now, as new digital and mobile technologies become more widely available, teacher attitudes about teaching with technology are changing.

Based on results from a national survey, the Education Week Research Center (2016) has categorized teacher users of technologies as "bulls" and "bears." Bulls are highly confident technology users who tend to push rapidly ahead using new tools in the classroom. Bears are less confident technology users who, while not averse to teaching with technology, tend to take a more wait-and-see attitude toward new tools. Technology-confident teachers are more likely to work in suburban and lower-poverty schools while less technology-confident teachers tend to teach in urban and high-poverty districts. Importantly, less affluent schools tend to have fewer up-to-date machines and more outdated software, which can make it more difficult for teachers to use technology confidently.

A teacher's level of technology confidence impacts how each will use it in teaching. While technology-confident and less technology-confident teachers use wireless connectivity about equally, technology-confident teachers are more likely to use digital and online tools for grading and class record keeping and family/student communication. They are more likely to use laptops, interactive whiteboards, and cell phones with students. More often, they integrate multimedia tools, access digital curricula, conduct web-based assessments of student learning, include educational games, show online videos, and utilize website/content creation tools. On average, tech-confident teachers use technology 50% of the time in class; less tech-confident teachers use technology only 25% of the time.

More and more teachers across the country say they are comfortable using technology and want to use it more than they currently do. They see technology as an indispensable tool for designing and implementing classroom lessons, collaborating with other teachers, and enhancing their own professional development as educators. Teachers who regularly use digital content (e.g., interactive websites, animations, and digital media) report higher levels of student involvement and engagement than teachers who do not (Evans, 2018). Many teachers believe technology promotes "more personalized learning, increased motivation, collaboration and pro-social behavior, and student efficiency and productivity" (Pressey, 2013, p. x). They are less sure that technology can directly improve student academic achievement as measured by standardized test scores.

Advanced Placement (AP) and National Writing Project (NWP) middle school and high school teachers reported integrating technology into all aspects of their professional work, particularly accessing the Internet to locate resources and materials for teaching. More than half say the Internet has had a "major impact" on how they interact with families, other teachers, and students (Purcell, et al., 2013). In addition, three of four AP and NWP teachers ask students to utilize mobile phones in class for learning and to access and submit assignments online.

The AP/NWP study did reveal differences in technology use between younger and older teachers. Teachers under age 35 are more likely to describe themselves as "very confident" with technology while teachers over age 55 were more likely to think that students know more than they do about technology. Younger teachers (45%) were somewhat more likely than older teachers (34%) to have students develop and share work on a school website, wiki, or blog and to have students participate in online discussions or use online collaboration tools like Google Docs (Purcell, et al., 2013).

Digital Dialog 2.3

A dramatic rise in smartphone use among children, teenagers, and adults in recent years poses interesting questions about what might be done educationally with mobile phone technologies. As you consider your use of a smartphone, comment and connect online about the following questions:

- Do you utilize your smartphone to do many of the things you accomplish on a desktop or laptop? What do you do on both?
- What education- and teaching-related activities do you prefer to do using your smartphone—search the Internet, add resources to a social bookmarking site, participate in a video meeting, read information alerts or newsletters, read or tweet about educational topics, take a virtual field trip, or do other activities?
- Do you regard a desktop, laptop, and/or smartphone as essential technologies for teaching? Would you prefer a combination of some of these devices with other technologies?

Teachers Using Technology in Classrooms

Despite positive beliefs about its potential for learning, large numbers of teachers still use technology for limited traditional instructional activities rather than more active and creative learning projects (Education Week, 2017). Survey data from the National Assessment of Education Progress found that nearly 75% of eighth-grade math students never or hardly ever use a computer to research a math topic; only 5% do so weekly, and 1% do so daily. While half to three quarters of those eighth-graders use technology at least once a month to practice or review math for tests, only a fifth to a third (depending on the state) use a graphing program or draw geometric shapes with a digital tool (National Center for Education Statistics, 2018b). Social studies educators use technology less than other educators in other subject areas (Karchmer-Klein, Mouza, Shinas, & Park, 2017). In a survey of 398 grade 6–12 social studies educators, respondents indicated rarely using the following technologies in their practice: social networks, photo sharing, animated tutorials, podcasts, role play/simulation, and microblogging (Kormos, 2019). The most commonly used technologies were documents, videos, class/teacher websites, and classroom management tools. Additionally, over half of social studies teachers never participate in online communities; nearly 40% never assign students online work to be done outside of class; one in four never use video sharing technologies (Kormos, 2019).

Other evidence comes from a Speak Up technology use survey that found just 8% of the California teachers surveyed said they gave digital homework daily or almost daily (18% said they did so weekly) even though three out of four middle school students regularly go to websites and watch videos to learn about a topic of personal interest outside of school (Speak Up, 2017). The Speak Up researchers concluded that students are using the Internet on their own at almost four times the rate at which teachers are assigning Internet-based activities for school-based learning.

In the schools where you will be doing your early field experiences and student teaching, you will likely find a small number of teachers regularly collecting and interpreting data using mobile devices, creating webpages or wikis to display individual or group student writing, asking students to analyze resources found on the Internet, or otherwise building technology into lessons. There also will be teachers who hardly

MyLab Education
Video **Example 2.2**
In this video, you will learn how one school in England used technology to transform learning for students. What features of Essa Academy's innovations would have interested you and propelled your learning in elementary or secondary school?
https://www.youtube.com/watch?v=lPgZCV7T2t8
From 1:25 to 4:01

ever use technology while teaching. As a new teacher, you must determine whether to be a "bull" or a "bear" in how you begin incorporating technology in the classroom while recognizing that your plans will evolve as your ideas and learning expand.

Apps for Teaching and Learning

Perhaps on the Figure 2.3 survey you selected educational apps as a technology you plan to use regularly or all the time when teaching. The word **app**—short for application—refers to a software program that runs on a smartphone or computer. First appearing in 2008, apps have since become an ever-present digital technology. "App" was named the 2010 word of the year by the American Dialect Society. There is now a National App Day every year on December 11. Apple's iconic marketing phrase "There's an app for that!" declares that everyone can use an app to do whatever they need to do. People seem to agree—on average, smartphone owners in the United States use 30 apps a month for about 2.5 hours per day (Perez, 2017).

For teachers and students, apps can be powerfully engaging learning technologies. By combining audio, video, animation, illustration, and text, apps can create multimodal experiences that educate and entertain. Apps function through finger taps, swipes, and pinches that allow users to physically manipulate material on touchscreen devices, generating sensory-based experiences in which users exert choice and control over the learning process. The app Faces iMake lets young artists create pictures on screens, insert graphics, and play music while they draw; in Cleanopolis, students combat climate change in a virtual reality environment; iMovie lets users produce professional-quality movies from videos they record on their tablets or phones, inserting slow-motion, fast-forward and picture-in-picture effects.

There are engaging apps for every subject field at every grade level. Molecules, a free science learning app, provides three-dimensional views of molecules. Users can zoom in and out and move material across the screen. Back in Time uses awe-inspiring graphics to present the history of the earth from prehistory to modern times. None of these learning experiences could happen as readily or as engagingly when presented in less interactive, paper-based formats.

Effective educational apps utilize principles of learning set forth more than 100 years ago by pioneering physician and educator Dr. Maria Montessori (1870–1952). The **Montessori method** is organized around three commanding features to attract and retain the attention of children, adolescents, or adults:

- A point of interest that draws learners to educational materials
- Open-ended explorations that invite learners to return to an activity time and time again to discover new information and skills
- Self-correcting feedback that teaches new learning in nonjudgmental ways (Montessori, 1964).

Montessori's goal was to capture a child's curiosity and desire to learn independently without the need for adult attention and continual instruction. She pioneered hands-on/minds-on educational materials, notably cut-out continent map puzzles that have proportionally sized land masses color-coded to a globe with the same shapes and colors; proportional-length wooden blocks for building a sequential block staircase; and beads that can be threaded on strings by 10s to make flats of 100 and attached to each other to form a cube of 1000.

Apps that integrate all three of the Montessori principles deliver engrossing, challenging, and independent learning experiences for students. These apps have a point of interest that draws users to the material. That point of interest might be a storyline with memorable characters, puzzles or challenges found in a game, or unique creative functions to be accessed on the screen. These apps are open ended so the experience is different each time the app is used. Users learn through feedback that is built in to the structure of the program or by making mistakes and revising their strategies on their own.

Montessori-like apps for learning are available for every subject. Finding the right one for you may take time—there are literally millions of apps available that might

Tech Tool 2.1

APPS for Educators

There are four primary categories of apps that can be used for teaching and learning in schools.

- **Information apps** provide facts, materials, and resources about curriculum topics. The Weather Channel app offers daily and weekly forecasts locally and from around the world; SoundHound and Shazam use sound recognition features to identify musical lyrics from short segments of sound; Today's Document provides a daily primary source of historical importance from the National Archives as a gateway to the study of history. The Library of Congress has two apps, DB Quest and Case Maker, designed to help students explore primary sources related to dramatic moments in United States history.

- **Productivity and communication apps** respond to teachers' daily professional responsibilities and work demands. Next-generation presentation tools like Prezi, Haiku Deck, Emaze, Google Slides, Buncee, and Educreations can be used to combine words, video, sound, and images to create engaging instructional activities for students; iTranslate converts words, phrases, and sentences in more than 80 world languages; Notability and Penultimate offer visual note-taking and idea-generating functions with words, spoken words, sketches, and diagrams; Twitter and Remind provide real-time mobile messaging.

- **Entertainment apps** provide recreation, fun, and learning ranging from online chess to adventure games to viewing sports, listening to music, and watching films and videos. Spotify offers music; Vimeo and Dailymotion access videos and trending topics; and Hulu and Netflix offer movies, television shows, and other programming.

- **Creativity apps** enable users to express ideas and images in new and exciting ways through drawing, filmmaking, comic strip writing, and many other forms of artistry. Verses delivers a touch-screen magnetic poetry writing experience; GarageBand blends sound and words to generate musical creations; Brushes provides a mobile easel and palette for artists; and Shadow Puppet supports digital storytelling.

---

aid or enrich your teaching. The American Association of School Librarians (AASL), Common Sense Media, *Parents* magazine, and other organizations provide yearly listings of the best apps for educators and families. You can also search online using the keywords "best educational apps" to find descriptions and reviews of apps to use for teaching and learning in school. You can also browse for apps at the App Store for Apple devices and Google Play for Android devices. Tech Tool 2.1 offers more insights about apps as an educational tool for teachers and students.

MyLab Education Application Exercise 2.2:
Writing a Brief About an Educational App

MyLab Education Self-Check 2.3

Approaches for Teaching with Technology

2.4 **Evaluate how technology supports different teaching philosophies and instructional methods.**

How frequently will you use different types of teaching approaches in the classroom? Rate the choices in Figure 2.4 as always, regularly, occasionally, rarely, or never.

Considering Your Teaching Philosophy

Your responses in Figure 2.4, however tentative, reflect the reality that every teacher acts on a vision or plan for how she, he, or they will conduct classroom learning. This is your **teaching philosophy**, and it includes essential ideas and basic assumptions about how to teach so students will learn. Broadly speaking, there are two primary types of teaching philosophies:

⤴ **Figure 2.4** How Frequently Will You Use these Instructional Approaches in the Classroom?

Instructional Approach	Always	Regularly	Occasionally	Rarely	Never
Teacher lectures and presentations					
Student small-group work and cooperative learning					
Student presentations and performances					
Multiple choice quizzes and exams					
Online research by students					
Students work alone on self-paced assignments					
Flipped classroom lessons (students review content/lectures online before coming to class)					
Digital presentations and online videos					
Differentiated instruction (tailoring curriculum to learning needs)					
Portfolios, exhibitions, and other alternative assessments					
Student design projects (e.g., creating videos, podcasts, graphics, 3-D models)					
Other (please describe)					

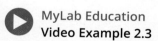

**MyLab Education
Video Example 2.3**

In this video of a high school math class and a high school history class, students learn at their own pace, help each other learn, and use technology in self-initiated ways https://www.edutopia.org/video/student-centered-model-blended-learning

- *Teacher-centered.* Some teachers consider teaching to be the formal conveyance of information from a knowledgeable instructor to novice students. This is sometimes called *teaching as telling.* These teachers use student scores from tests and other quantitative measures to determine who has learned and who has not. Educators who are most firmly committed to **teacher-centered teaching** occupy one end of a teaching philosophy continuum.
- *Student-centered.* At the other end of the teaching philosophy continuum are those who view teaching as orchestrating different experiences for students. They believe the role of the teacher is to create puzzles, ask questions, and engage in conversations with students, which leads the students to learn information and develop skills through interesting activities based on exploration and discovery. **Student-centered teaching** is also called constructivist, progressive, project-based, or problem-based teaching. This chapter's In Practice shows a teacher using technology to facilitate student-centered learning in mathematics.

Teachers in any given school may be more or less teacher-centered or student-centered in their instructional approaches and teaching methods. Figure 2.5 shows four dynamic aspects of teaching philosophies using a series of continuums. In these continuums, inquiry- and discovery-based approaches are on the left side of each scale, and teacher-centered methods are on the right side, as follows:

- *Teacher's role*—from teachers facilitating learning to teachers presenting and explaining academic material
- *Goal of learning*—from students discovering ideas and concepts to students mastering teacher-delivered curriculum content
- *Student motivation*—from students expressing wide-ranging interests and curiosity to students knowing the material in textbooks and curriculum frameworks
- *Classroom organization*—from students engaging in individual and small-group activities to students engaging in mainly whole-class activities.

Figure 2.5 Philosophical Continuums

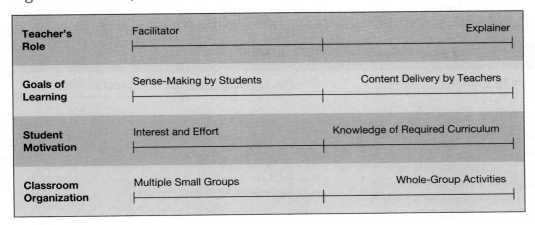

In most cases, teachers adopt elements of both student-centered and teacher-centered ideas while still maintaining a core set of beliefs and behaviors rooted in one approach or the other. Nevertheless, ideas about the best approaches to teaching may vary considerably, even among members of the same high school department, middle school instructional team, or elementary school grade level. When asked, many teachers say they are somewhere in the middle of each of the four continuums in terms of their philosophy. You will have an opportunity to write a draft of your teaching philosophy as part of the Building Your PLN activity in Chapter 5.

Mapping Instruction to the Common Core and the ISTE Standards

You can examine your teaching philosophy in relation to the **Common Core State Standards** and the ISTE Standards for Educators and Students, as well as to their broad visions of 21st century education featuring technology-supported learning environments for every student. Published in 2010 by the National Governors Association and the Council of Chief State School Officers, the Common Core State Standards offer teaching and learning guidelines in English/language arts and mathematics from kindergarten to grade 12. These guidelines are designed to prepare students for college and careers by providing states and school districts with rigorous national standards that will improve educational outcomes for all students.

The Common Core redefines how the core subjects of English/language arts and mathematics are taught in school. In English, the Common Core wants students to become critical readers, writers, and analysts of written texts. Teachers are asked to focus on increasing student understanding of academic language and discipline-specific vocabulary by emphasizing the use of nonfiction texts. Students are asked to analyze written language and use evidence to support their conclusions. In mathematics, the Common Core urges more in-depth study of fewer topics at each grade level while cumulatively building a strong foundation in problem solving and numerical skills. Students are expected to understand mathematics both conceptually and procedurally so they can compute and do mathematical operations and explain how they derive solutions to problems.

Technology, the Internet, and digital media are cornerstones of the Common Core standards, which declare that all 21st century learners must be proficient users of 21st century technologies. The English/language arts standards state that students who are "college and career ready in reading, writing, speaking, listening, and language" should be able to "use technology and digital media strategically and capably." Technology is also a prominent part of the English/language arts standards for writing. Students, the Common Core states, should learn to "use technology, including the Internet, to produce and publish writing and to interact and collaborate with others."

Student-Centered Math Learning with iPads and Online Resources

Grade Level	Featured Technologies
Elementary school	Tablets, laptops, math apps, interactive websites

Lesson Outline

Having decided he wanted to become a teacher, Anders, a college senior and math/science major, took a semester-long "tutoring in schools" course to gain experience in school classrooms. Unsure what grades he eventually wanted to teach, Anders hoped that working with elementary-age students would broaden his understanding of how teaching and learning happens in the grades before middle school. He chose a Title I innovation-designated elementary school near his college campus that offered interactive math learning, online accounts for all students to practice basic skills, and desktop computers for students to use in every classroom.

With his outgoing and inviting personality, Anders quickly became a sought-after tutor in a fourth-grade classroom. One day he heard a group of girls declare that math was their least favorite school subject. "I just stink at math," one of the girls exclaimed. Reflecting on the conversation, Anders recognized that many youngsters, lacking success with mathematical learning, believe that math is a special talent that only some students possess. This attitude, when fixed at an early age, can limit how students—especially girls—think about themselves as learners. He wondered how to promote new mind-sets among the math-averse students in the classroom by proving how effort and hard work can promote success in unfamiliar and challenging math learning.

Anders understood that elementary students need to gain both procedural and conceptual knowledge of mathematical topics to begin mastering the school's grade-by-grade math curriculum. Procedural knowledge refers to the mathematical operations of addition, subtraction, multiplication, and division. Conceptual understandings of place value, fractions, decimals, and other functions explain the underlying processes of math problems and their solutions. Procedural knowledge can be practiced and memorized using worksheets and quizzes, but conceptual knowledge needs to be visualized, analyzed, and discussed before students develop more complete understandings of mathematical situations. Learning the how and the why of math is at the center of the Common Core State Standards, which require multiple approaches to math problem solving, including making models and diagrams as ways to solve math problems.

Teaching with Technology

To build more positive math learning mind-sets while practicing procedural and conceptual math skills, Anders decided to bring five iPads to the classroom for students to use with him before school, during math curriculum time, and as part of afternoon "you-choose" time when students could engage in self-chosen learning activities. The iPads were available to college students who were taking the tutoring course and came loaded with interactive math learning apps, including Zoombinis and Motion Math. Students could also use the iPads to connect to an online math tutoring system called 4MALITY (Four Coach Active Learning Intelligent Tutoring System) featuring strategies for solving math word problems offered by four online coaches with different instructional approaches: a reading coach, a computation coach, a strategic thinking coach, and a visual learning coach.

Anders started by having only girls use the iPads during math learning time. It was the girls who had expressed negative attitudes about math and who rarely chose computers during the afternoon "you-choose" time. The first app was Zoombinis, an online game reissued for tablets in 2015 by its developer, the technology research company TERC. Zoombinis are thumb-sized creatures with five different types of hairstyles, eyes and eyewear, nose colors, and feet and footwear—625 different combinations in all. The Zoombinis have embarked on a long and perilous journey to reclaim their ancestral island home, and game players must maneuver them through a series of obstacles and puzzles that block their progress. As students solve the puzzles facing the Zoombinis, they are using set theory, graphing, algebraic thinking, and theory building—all core concepts for future math learning. What is unique in Zoombinis is that no numbers appear in any of the puzzles. Next, the girls played the original version of Motion Math: Fractions, an app in which game players perceive and estimate fractions by tilting the iPad from side to side by hand to land a bouncing ball on a number line. Students can visual the size of fractions while enjoying the challenge of moving through ever more complex levels of game play. As players' level of knowledge expands, fractions become decimals and percents.

After the girls had opportunities to use the iPads, Anders had each girl choose one boy partner to teach how to play the games. Gradually, everyone in the classroom had opportunities to use the devices, and the teacher added more online math learning resources to the mix. All these math learning apps and online resources functioned differently from drill-and-practice math learning sites. Students were learning by making mistakes in both of the apps. As they made mistakes, the apps let them try again, and gradually students began to think through math problems and situations before selecting an answer choice. Instead of feeling frustrated and ready to give up, students saw value in slowing down, carefully considering possible answer choices, and then confidently choosing the solution that makes the most sense for the problem at hand. In this class, technology resources were the key to a "thinking and checking" approach that would improve their attitudes and their performance as math learners.

The Common Core further states that technology is essential to understanding and doing mathematics "mindfully." Under the general standard of using tools in math learning, students need to "know that technology can enable them to visualize the results of varying assumptions, explore consequences, and compare predictions with data." Technology enables students to solve equations, graph functions, display data, evaluate logarithms, model phenomena, and perform other mathematical operations.

The ISTE standards (discussed in Chapter 1) have been set forth by the International Society for Technology in Education and endorsed by the National Council for Accreditation of Teacher Education (NCATE), many states, and hundreds of teacher education programs in colleges and universities throughout the nation. At the core of the ISTE standards is a belief that technology makes possible new learning experiences that could not happen otherwise.

The role of technology in the Common Core and the ISTE standards is to support teachers and schools as they teach academic content, promote innovative and creative thinking, and prepare students for citizenship in a digital world while also addressing the needs of all learners in equitable ways. Table 2.2 contrasts technology-based learning environments with traditional, non-technology-based learning environments.

In the language of the ISTE standards, teachers inspire student learning and creativity by designing digital-age learning experiences, modeling digital-age work, promoting digital citizenship, and engaging in professional development and leadership in schools. Students are asked to think creatively, communicate and work collaboratively, learn the skills of information research and fluency, think critically while solving problems and making decisions, and practice digital ethics, all while expanding their knowledge of technology operations and concepts.

As a matter of policy and of day-to-day practice, teachers and schools should decrease the traditional practices on the left side of Table 2.2 and increase the emerging styles on the right side. ISTE's call for new learning environments echoes what many progressive education reformers have urged for decades—namely, that schools become places where students are directly involved in learning at every grade level, as shown in the following recommendations:

- Less teacher talk and more adult–student interaction and discussion
- Less individual work by students at their desks and more group work and collaborative projects by students in and out of the classroom
- Less emphasis on tests that measure factual recall of information and more time using assessments that measure student inquiry, problem solving, and critical thinking. You can explore standards-based lesson planning and instructional design further in Chapter 4.

Table 2.2 Transforming Learning Environments with Technology

Traditional Classrooms	Technology-Based Classrooms
Teacher-centered learning	Student-centered learning
Limited non-computer-based technologies (overhead projectors, television, slides)	Multiple computer-based and Internet-accessible technologies
Step-by-step learning following teacher directions and textbook progressions	Flexible and spiral learning based on a combination of teacher directions and student interests
Emphasis on individual work and accomplishments	Emphasis on collaborative work and group achievements
Academic information from noninteractive textbooks and encyclopedias	Academic information from multiple interactive web-based sources
Memorization and recall of information	Creative and critical thinking with application of information to real-world issues and problems
Assessment of learning based on test scores and other standardized measures	Assessment of learning based on digital portfolios and student projects

SOURCE: Chart based on *ISTE Standards for Students*, Second Edition (ISTE, 2007).

MyLab Education Self-Check 2.4

How Students Are Using Technology

2.5 **Compare students' technology use in their daily lives and in schools.**

How are the students you will be teaching using technology for learning in and out of school? Figure 2.6 asks you to rate each of the listed technologies as to whether you think student use is increasing, staying the same, or decreasing.

Student-Initiated vs. Teacher-Chosen Technology Use

Students who have known and used technology throughout their lives interact confidently with old and new devices.

SOURCE: Hurst Photo/Shutterstock

Your answers in Figure 2.6 highlight how children and adolescents develop knowledge about technology in ways that are different from those of older adults who are teachers. A decade ago, Marc Prensky (2012, 2010, 2001) famously classified these two groups as digital natives and digital immigrants. Digital natives were those youngsters who have grown up using interactive technologies and wireless devices. Many teachers, by contrast, were digital immigrants, continuously learning how to integrate new tools into classroom learning environments. When it comes to technology, adults did not share the students' frames of reference.

Researchers are now rethinking the digital native/digital immigrant dichotomy, suggesting that teachers, particularly those who are early adopters of technology, may be more, not less, technologically savvy than students, who primarily use technology for entertainment and recreation (game playing and

Figure 2.6 How Are Students Using Technology for Learning in and out of School?

Technology	Increasing	Staying the Same	Decreasing
Television			
Desktop computers			
Smartphones and tablets			
Video games			
E-mail			
Texting			
YouTube and other videos			
Radio or streaming music (e.g., Spotify)			
Handheld calculators			
E-books			
Digital cameras			
Blogs			
Social media			
Other _____			

listening to music) but lack the skills to use digital tools for academic learning (Wang, et al., 2014). Survey results of more than 325,000 students in 9,000 districts nationwide indicate that not all students are advanced technology users, and not all teachers lack the latest technology knowledge.

A report from Project Tomorrow, "The New Digital Learning Playbook" (Project Tomorrow, 2014a), urges educators to distinguish between **teacher-facilitated technology use** for schoolwork and **student-initiated technology use** for individual learning beyond what is assigned at school. At school, with teacher supervision and at all grade levels, more and more students use digital devices to access information from teacher or school websites, take online tests, and watch teacher-created videos related to class content. One in four elementary students and one in three middle school and high school students use mobile devices provided by their school in their classes.

But there are very different patterns to student-initiated technology use outside of school:

- Nationally, more than 9 out of 10 children and adolescents have access to a computer at home and use the Internet (Center for the Digital Future, 2013).
- Four out of five school-age youngsters send messages or chat online, and more than half share links or forward information using social networks (Lenhart, 2015).
- More youngsters have Wi-Fi access at home (93%) than at school (62%) (Harris Poll, 2014).
- Large numbers of students have mobile phones (89% in grades 9–12, 73% in grades 6–8, and 50% in grades 3–5) as well as access to laptops, tablets, and digital e-readers (Madden, et al., 2013).

MyLab Education
Video Example 2.4
In this video, Chris Lehmann, principal of the Science Leadership Academy, discusses his reasons for utilizing mobile and digital technologies, which are central to students' lives outside of school, as learning tools inside of school. How might these technologies inform and support students' learning in your future classroom?

Students use outside-of-school technologies for academic as well as recreational and entertainment purposes. At the high school level, girls outpace boys in texting with classmates about academic topics, taking photos of assignments and related resources for homework, finding educational videos, and using Facebook, Skype, or iChat to communicate and collaborate with other students about assignments. More girls than boys use technology for written communication, including writing essays and reports, sending e-mails, composing poetry, keeping journals, blogging, and tweeting, although boys do slightly more HTML coding.

What is clear, reports technology researcher danah boyd in *It's Complicated: The Social Lives of Networked Teens* (boyd, 2014), are the profound ways that social media technologies are changing students' lives, although not always in the ways adults expect. Students, particularly teenagers, use technology as a primary means of connecting with others. They see online environments as spaces where they "can gather and socialize broadly with peers in an informal way" (boyd, 2014, p. 5). In these "networked publics" created by social media, young technology users explore issues of identity, friendship, politics, learning, and future plans. For students, connection to others through technology is an essential part of their lives, and they resist efforts by schools and families to curtail their technology use.

The centrality of technology to the lives of students has important implications for current and future teachers:

- *Student perspectives.* Students value the ideas and talents they have learned from digital environments—everything from web navigation to game-based learning to integrating sound, image, and text in multimedia environments. They are less inclined to learn using the traditional school-based literacies of book reading and writing on paper.
- *Teacher actions.* Teachers must think critically and creatively about how to change teaching to accommodate the different technological experiences of students. Teachers' learning experiences have made them familiar with reading books and writing on paper. But reading and writing based on teacher-led activities and whole-group instruction featured in school classrooms are becoming less central in a wired world where learning is available to students anywhere and anytime. Choosing how and when to integrate new technologies into teaching and learning becomes a pedagogical decision made by every teacher.

Learning with Technology to Overcome Digital Disconnects

Five similes describe how students think about the Internet when they are not at school and not under the direction of their teachers:

- Internet as virtual textbook and reference library
- Internet as virtual tutor and study shortcut
- Internet as virtual study group
- Internet as virtual guidance counselor
- Internet as virtual locker, backpack, and notebook.

In each case, youngsters tend to be more comfortable finding information online than they are locating it in books and other print sources or asking adults directly.

Students find many schools lagging far behind their technology experiences and expectations. Sociologists call this a **digital disconnect**, referring to the differences students perceive between themselves—Internet-savvy, social-networked computer users who are able to streamline all types of tasks, in and out of school—and their teachers, whose integration of technology into classroom learning seems painfully slow by comparison (Cortesi, et al., 2014; Project Tomorrow, 2011a, 2011b). A majority of students across the grade levels feel as though they know more about technology than their teachers do (Harris Poll, 2014).

Students want more technology to use in school. In 2011, about one in three students regarded smartphones and MP3 players as essential tools for an engaging classroom, which was double the number of teachers and administrators who considered those important to school learning (CDW Government, 2011). Three years later, a majority of students wanted more access to online sites, more opportunities to use mobile devices in class, more tools and apps to help with homework, and, for one in four survey respondents, more online access to tutors and teachers to support learning. They described the ultimate school as "socially based," "untethered" from print resources, and "digitally rich" (Project Tomorrow, 2014b, p. 11).

Digital Dialog 2.4

Many elementary, middle, and high school students say they want to use technology more often in their school classes. Ask K–12 students you know how they use technology for learning about things that interest them, and then comment and connect online about the following questions:

- What reasons did the students give you? Were you surprised by what they said?
- How might the students' ideas influence your plans for teaching with the Internet, digital games, and other technologies that students view as learning tools?
- What one new technology do you think, if used widely in schools, could change how teaching and learning happen for students?

Many teachers, parents, and school administrators, while acknowledging the importance and value of technology for learning, do not rank mobile devices, digital games, or text-based communications as high a priority as students do (Project Tomorrow, 2014b, p. 13). In general, adults do not share students' view that school learning should be flexible, social, unscripted, and self-directed. Adults stress the need to manage technology within the confines of classroom schedules and information management systems, using firewalls and filters to restrict online access. Students resent these restrictions, wanting to freely use laptops, cell phones, and other mobile devices in class.

As a teacher, your actions will either bridge or extend the digital disconnect that many students perceive between themselves and their schools. When we ask students what makes a teacher effective, they consistently place the following items at or near the top of their lists:

- Challenging students to think
- Using interactive digital technologies
- Giving clear and organized presentations
- Using student-centered teaching methods
- Motivating students to learn
- Giving feedback to students
- Showing enthusiasm for teaching and learning
- Teaching to different ways of thinking
- Asking challenging, thought-provoking questions
- Providing students with new or needed academic skills
- Managing the flow of information so everyone understands the material
- Interacting positively with students.

Technology in the form of computers, the web, educational software and apps, blogs, wikis, and other tools offers ways to achieve all of these items through active learning that makes academic content easy to access and engaging to use. At the same time, students need to learn about issues associated with technology in schools. Information posted online, for example, is not always useful or reliable. Deciphering what is and what is not reliable is part of learning about technology as an educational tool and a part of everyone's daily life. Teaching with technology requires teachers to play a dual role—using technology to teach students and teaching students how to use technology. These dual roles interrelate; one without the other creates incomplete teaching and learning experiences.

MyLab Education Self-Check 2.5

Chapter Summary

Learning Outcome 2.1

Assess your motivations for becoming a technology-using teacher.

- A technology-using teacher is often an innovator and a change agent in schools.
- Many students at all grade levels report feeling disengaged and alienated from school.
- Technology creates many different learning formats that can engage students with academic material.
- Technology supports both the instructional and the administrative/professional work of teaching.

Learning Outcome 2.2

Analyze barriers to the use of technology in schools, including digital inequalities, achievement gaps, and online safety and digital privacy issues.

- Digital inequalities and participation gaps limit access to technology for many students, contributing to academic achievement gaps.

- Tight education budgets and rapidly changing devices, software, and technical systems mean many schools are not up to date technologically and thus do not use technology to its fullest potentials for student learning.
- Teaching schedules, pressure to teach the required curriculum, and teachers' own lack of confidence in their technological skills are also obstacles to technology use in schools.

Learning Outcome 2.3

Describe roles for technology in teaching.

- Most teachers feel increasingly positive about technology and how it supports their work in schools, but want up-to-date equipment and more professional development training in the use of new tools.
- Many future teachers know how to operate computers, search the Internet, create digital presentations, and communicate online, but are less informed about how to use technology to transform teaching and learning for students in schools.

- Critics of technology in education believe it has been oversold and underused in schools, whereas advocates see it as a way to unleash student learning and teacher effectiveness.

Learning Outcome 2.4

Evaluate how technology supports different teaching philosophies and instructional methods.

- A teaching philosophy encompasses an educator's ideas and assumptions about how to teach so students will learn. Teaching philosophies depend more on situations and settings than absolute beliefs, and a teacher's approaches can vary on the continuum of choices from teacher-centered to student-centered.
- The ISTE Standards for Educators and Students and the Common Core State Standards offer a broad vision of a technology-supported, student-centered approach to curriculum and instruction.
- Student-centered classrooms are learning environments where students are asked to think creatively,

communicate and work collaboratively, learn the skills of information research, think critically while solving problems and making decisions, and practice digital ethics and behave as digital citizens.

Learning Outcome 2.5

Compare students' technology use in their daily lives and in schools.

- Children and adolescents develop literacy with technology in ways different from those of many adults.
- Students find many schools lagging far behind their technology experiences and expectations, resulting in a digital disconnect existing between tech-savvy youngsters and more traditional teaching and learning practices.
- A successful technology-using educator is someone who confidently integrates digital resources to create highly interactive, inquiry-based learning for students.

Key Terms

Achievement gaps, p. 31
Active screen time, p. 33
Administrative/professional activities, p. 26
App, p. 38
Brain-based education, p. 28
Common Core State Standards, p. 41
Connectivity gap, p. 30
COPPA (Children's Online Privacy Protection Act), p. 34
Creativity apps, p. 39
Digital continuum, p. 31

Digital disconnect, p. 46
Digital inequalities, p. 30
Entertainment apps, p. 39
Information apps, p. 39
Inquiry-based learning, p. 28
Instructional practices, p. 26
Learning groups, p. 28
Metacognitive thinking, p. 28
Montessori method, p. 38
One-on-one tutoring, p. 28
Productivity and communication apps, p. 39

Smart classroom, p. 36
Student-centered teaching, p. 40
Student-initiated technology use, p. 45
Student disengagement, p. 27
Teacher-centered teaching, p. 40
Teacher-facilitated technology use, p. 45
Teaching philosophy, p. 39
Technology participation gaps, p. 30
Third-party apps, p. 34
21st century technologies, p. 25

> **MyLab Education Application Exercise 2.3:**
> Growing and Leading with Technology: Cherelle's "Using Technology in the Classroom" Activity

For Reflection and Discussion

Personal Experiences with Technology

Our learning experiences play fundamental roles in shaping our understandings about technology. To learn more, interview another college student or a teacher about his or her early experiences with technology. Write a short first-person narrative using the words of the interviewee. These questions can guide your interview:

- At what age did you start regularly using a computer? Were you self-taught? Who or what helped you become fluent with computers and other technologies?

- How do you think your early technology experiences compare with those of K–12 students today? Do you think they differ significantly?
- Is self-teaching the most effective way for students to learn to use technology? Do you think schools should have a technology center where students can engage with new tools and teach themselves? What do you think they might learn?

Meeting 21st Century Educational Challenges with Technology

With funding from the National Science Foundation, a group of computer scientists and educators examined technology's role in meeting the educational challenges of the 21st century. Their *Roadmap for Educational Technology* report identified seven grand challenges facing the field of education:

1. Personalizing education
2. Assessing student learning
3. Supporting social learning
4. Diminishing the boundaries between people and institutions
5. Developing alternative modes of teaching
6. Enhancing the role of teachers, students, parents, and other stakeholders
7. Addressing policy change (Computing Community Consortium, 2010).

How might technology address these grand challenges? For example, how might technology meet the needs of individual learners (challenge 1) or provide teachers with immediate assessments of student learning (challenge 2)?

Apps for Learning

New apps are constantly being developed for tablets and smartphones as people seek online support for everything from recreation to communication to learning. By 2014, there were more than a million apps available for both Apple and Android devices, although as many as half of all apps are never downloaded.

As the next step in developing your professional learning network, begin considering what apps you are currently using and what apps you may want to add to your computer or phone as a new teacher. Here are some questions to get you started:

- What smartphone and tablet apps are you using to support your learning as a college student in a teacher education program?
- How has using apps changed the way you function as a student or as a consumer, if at all?
- Do you view smartphones and tablet apps as tools primarily for teachers or as direct instructional devices for students? How might you use apps in teaching to engage students and support their learning?

Chapter 3
Transforming Learning with Unique, Powerful Technologies

SOURCE: bestfoto77/Shutterstock

Chapter Overview

Chapter 3 discusses how technology generates unique, powerful, and transformative learning in K–12 schools. Transformative learning is a central goal of major national educational technology standards, including the ISTE Standards for Educators, the ISTE Standards for Students, and the Student Outcomes for Learning from the Partnership for 21st Century Skills. As they implement these standards, teachers and students create fundamentally new patterns of teaching and learning in schools that could not happen without the interactive dimensions of computers, the Internet, social media, apps, hand-held devices, and other innovative digital tools.

The chapter addresses the "Facilitator" domain of the ISTE Standard for Educators, which envisions teachers using technology to create and conduct interactive, collaborative, inquiry-driven, and student-centered learning experiences in K–12 classrooms. Transformative technologies enable teachers to create opportunities for students to think critically and solve problems, develop essential digital literacies, communicate and collaborate in print and digital media, express ideas and information creatively, and acquire the attitudes of digital citizens, the core elements of the ISTE Standards for Students.

Learning Outcomes

After reading this chapter, you will be able to:

3.1 Discuss how technology promotes critical thinking and problem solving.

3.2 Analyze the meaning and importance of digital literacies.

3.3 Examine how technology facilitates communication and collaboration.

3.4 Identify how technology enables multiple expressions of creative thinking.

3.5 Explain the meaning and importance of digital citizenship.

Chapter Learning Goal

Explore ways unique, powerful technologies can transform teaching and learning in schools.

Featured Technologies

Online problem-solving environments	Creativity web resources and apps
Immersive and non-immersive games	Digital citizenship web resources and apps
Critical thinking/problem-solving web resources and apps	Multiuser virtual environments (MUVEs)
Information/Internet literacy web resources and apps	Adaptive and intelligent tutors (ITs)
Communication and collaboration web resources and apps	Programming languages

A Parent–Teacher Conference

At a midyear meeting to assess learning progress, a parent and a teacher were discussing one student's learning gains when the parent asked: "Why are you emphasizing technology so much in the classroom activities? I just don't see the value." This parent was skeptical about the role of computers, tablets, videos, digital cameras, and apps for learning in the curriculum. "We limit his use of computers and television time at home. We want him to be able to figure things out on his own, not to become reliant on machines." After pausing momentarily, the parent continued: "What is it that teachers and students can do with technology that cannot be done just as well without it?"

The teacher explained that students gravitate to technology-based instructional activities and that these offer a sense of independence, exploration, curiosity, and dynamic learning. In addition, students teach each other with technology. Children with different knowledge and skills as readers and writers work together as partners, and with new digital tools, the partners support each other's learning.

*Recalling the conversation later, the teacher shared that she understood the importance of the parent's question. She strongly believed that having students use technology for learning is essential to education in the 21st century, so she found digital resources and created interactive technology-based activities to engage students individually and in groups. With focus, enjoyment, and opportunities to teach each other, everyone in the classroom experienced learning in exciting, stimulating, academically challenging ways. What the teacher wanted the parent to understand was that it is **how** technology is used educationally—not whether it is used—that makes the difference in successful learning for students.*

"What can teachers and students do *with* technology that cannot be done just as well *without* it?" is a question that continues to be asked by teachers, parents, college students, university professors, technology developers, educational policy makers, and community members across the country as they explore using digital tools and online resources for learning. In this chapter, we join the conversation, showing that digital technologies—used creatively and thoughtfully—generate **unique, powerful, and transformative learning (UPT)** experiences that do not happen in the same way or at all when non-computer-based materials are used.

Unique. Powerful. Transformative. Each term conveys how digital technology propels academic learning and educational change by directly impacting the attitudes and behaviors of teachers and students.

- *Unique* declares that digital technologies can accomplish what non-computer-based materials cannot—at least not in the same way and with the same learning impacts.
- *Powerful* measures technology's impact on schools and society as substantive in nature and long lasting in duration.
- *Transformative* states that technology alters the ways teachers teach and students learn, making schools more relevant, engaging places for education.

In this chapter, we introduce five categories of UPT learning: 1) critical thinking and problem solving, 2) digital and media literacy, 3) online communication and collaboration, 4) creativity, and 5) digital citizenship. Each type of UPT learning is aligned to one or more parts of the ISTE Standards for Students, the ISTE Standards for Educators, and the **21st Century Student Outcomes for Learning** from the Partnership for 21st Century Skills.

Collectively, UPT learning sets forth a vision of highly interactive, inquiry-based educational approaches that will prepare students for life and work in a technology- and information-based society. The five categories of UPT learning are also core goals in the national standards for the subjects commonly taught in K–12 schools: Communication and digital literacy are part of the standards for English/language arts; creativity is central to Common Core standards for dance, media arts, music, theater, and visual arts; critical thinking and problem solving appear in the standards for mathematics and science education; and digital citizenship connects to the theme of civics ideals and practices in standards for history/social studies education.

Each category of UPT learning shares the following characteristics:

- Applies to every subject area at every grade level
- Emphasizes how technology creates new teaching and learning experiences for students
- Enables educational experiences that would not be possible without them. Students and teachers are able to access and evaluate unparalleled amounts of information; investigate and solve problems individually and collaboratively; communicate locally and globally; and express ideas in multiple creative genres.
- Serves as an invitation for further thinking and discussion about teaching and learning in 21st century schools.

As you think about the core concepts discussed in this chapter and the goals of unique, powerful, and transformative learning, use these focus questions to guide your reading:

1. How can you use technology to support students in becoming critical and creative thinkers?
2. How can you use technology to promote 21st century literacies among students?
3. How can you use technology to develop students' capabilities as effective communicators and collaborators?
4. How can you use technology to promote creative self-expressions by students?
5. How can you use technology to support students in becoming digital citizens?

UPT Learning 1: Thinking Critically and Solving Problems with Technology

3.1   Discuss how technology promotes critical thinking and problem solving.

Critical thinking and **problem solving** are essential skills in a digital world where so many aspects of everyday life are constantly changing as new systems replace older approaches. Think of all the different ways your own life has been changed in just the past decade by the emergence of smartphones, e-commerce, Internet banking, satellite radio, streaming video, and online learning. Students and teachers both need problem-solving mind-sets to be able to flexibly and creatively respond to changing conditions and shifting practices.

Online Problem-Solving Environments and Learning Games

Online learning environments, especially educational games and interactive simulations, develop students' talents as problem solvers and critical thinkers. Game-like environments create "virtual worlds for learning," concluded sociologist and linguist James Paul Gee and colleagues from the Games and Professional Practice Simulations (GAPPS) research group at the University of Wisconsin, Madison (Gee & Hayes, 2010).

From the simplest to the most complex, online games feature problems that must be solved through critical thinking about strategy and results. Action is required, and input from multiple information sources must be used to guide strategies. Learners make mistakes, and they view those mistakes as indicating there is more to learn. **Immersive games** seek to totally involve players in the world of the game. The player enters the game world, encounters puzzles and problems, and must make decisions that have real consequences. To advance through the game and win, players take on roles (known as avatars), and they experience the elements and mysteries of the game world. Many youngsters play in **multiuser virtual environments (MUVEs)**, online communities with thousands of players. They share strategies with other players and can even play together as problem solvers, further fostering the conditions for deep and lasting learning with technology.

Online games succeed as educational tools when they provide in-depth learning experiences in which students connect academic concepts to puzzles and problems they care about solving. iCivics, founded by former Supreme Court Justice Sandra Day O'Connor, has dozens of games designed to put students in problem-solving roles where they learn about their civic rights and responsibilities as citizens in a democratic society. In the game "Do I Have a Right?" student game players assume the role of members of a law firm who must demonstrate their knowledge of constitutional issues. In "Cast Your Vote," game players run a political debate, while in "Crisis of Nations," teams of students must work together to respond to international crises. Other games simulate a presidential debate, serving on a jury, guiding immigrants to citizenship, and deciding the expenses of the federal budget. iCivics demonstrates, as the Federation of American Scientists forecast more than a decade ago, how serious educational games can "improve students' attitudes about learning even difficult subjects" (Federation of American Scientists, 2006, p. 17).

Non-immersive games can also promote problem solving and academic learning. **Non-immersive games** do not have complex storylines with open-ended activities for game players to complete, real-world settings with complex puzzles that must be solved during game play, or opportunities for game

Technology invites critical thinking and problem solving from the youngest ages.

SOURCE: Sakkmesterke/Fotolia

Figure 3.1 Spinners, a Learning Game

SOURCE: Utah State University. Reprinted by permission.

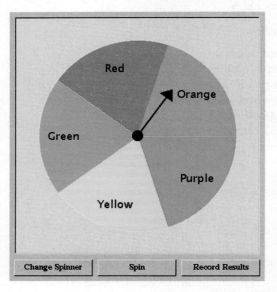

Change Spinner · Spin · Record Results

players to interact with virtual characters as they play the game, but they can be thought-provoking learning experiences in which students have opportunities for replaying the game with different possible outcomes.

Spinners, an online math app for students of all ages from the National Library of Virtual Manipulatives (NLVM) at Utah State University, is an engaging example of a educationally challenging non-immersive game. Designed to teach students about probability, chance, and random choices, Spinners starts with an onscreen circle divided equally into five colored parts labeled red, green, orange, yellow, and purple, with a spinning needle in the middle (see Figure 3.1). A game player pushes "spin," the computer spins the needle, and the color the needle stops at is recorded automatically in a bar graph that is viewed next to the spinner.

Students can spin again and again to see which colors are landed on most and least often. The number of spins for a single turn can be set from 1 to 999. Interactivity and choice expand as students change the colors, numbers, and/or size of the spinner sections, thus weighing possible outcomes in favor of one or more sections. Labels can be changed to the names of friends, television characters, or even answers to questions posed by classmates in a poll.

The Spinners game environment is simple yet engrossing, teaching math concepts as students think critically using the laws of probability. The NLVM features dozens of such interactive math problem-solving games for all grade levels in the areas of number operations, algebra, geometry, measurement, and data analysis.

Whether games are immersive or non-immersive, effective online problem solving has three basic characteristics.

- First, students use technology to accomplish what they cannot as easily do with paper.
- Second, students interact with problems that occur in the real world or problems of personal interest to them.
- Third, students integrate knowledge of technology with academic content to learn and understand the science, math, history, or language arts material that is embedded in the game.

In immersive and non-immersive games as well as other problem-solving environments, the ease and speed of technology enables students to access resources, develop working hypotheses, do experimental trials, and draw conclusions based on data—while behaving and thinking as capable and confident problem solvers.

In Practice

Making and Reading Graphs with Software and Apps

Grade Level	Featured Technologies
Upper elementary, middle, and high school	Internet, tablets, smartphones, and graph-making apps and software

Lesson Outline

To engage middle school students in the higher order thinking skills of creating and evaluating, Briana, a first-year math teacher, decided to add technology to a unit on making and reading graphs. She anticipated that having students design their own surveys and graphs would promote information literacy and mathematical learning while integrating all levels of Bloom's taxonomy more directly into the curriculum. The lesson would also address parts of the Data Analysis and Probability Learning standard from the National Council of Teachers of Mathematics (NCTM).

Students learn about graphs in math and science at many grade levels—pie graphs, bar graphs, line graphs, and pictographs, and in high school, graphs for quadratic equations, linear equations and functions. Graphs display descriptions of measures and amounts. They communicate information concisely to readers in design formats with minimal text. Reading graphs is part of a larger process of teaching students how to read different kinds of informational pictures, symbols, and infographics. A graph is a representation of some part of social reality, and representations require analysis. Graphs offer a different kind of meaning-making experience from written words. It is possible to know the meanings of the words that accompany a graph but still not understand what the graph is showing. Assisting students to comprehend a graph's symbols and structure and how those symbols communicate information is what this learning activity is all about.

Briana's curriculum guide for graphs suggested that teachers have students construct paper graphs, and then collect survey information that can be answered by Yes/No or Either/Or questions. A student's survey question might ask, "Did you finish all of yesterday's homework?" or "Do you view videos to learn?" Students answer the question by putting their name or a symbol for their name on the poster. After this introductory activity, students create their own questions, collect data from survey respondents, and make their own graphs from the answers they receive. In so doing, students compare four types of graphs—pictographs, pie graphs, bar graphs, and line graphs—and analyze how each communicates different types of information. Students decide for themselves which type of graph best delivers the information collected from survey questions.

Teaching with Technology

Briana began by modeling how to pose questions for which survey respondents need to make personally meaningful choices from among the options. "Do you want to be a millionaire?" does not encourage much deep thinking; almost everyone answers yes. Questions that elicit different viewpoints are more thought-provoking: "Would you like to live on a space station for a year?" or "Do you want a job where you travel the world?" are designed to spark conversations about personal preferences and the reasons behind them.

Next, Briana had small groups of students practice creating questions with more than two choices. As an example, for the question, "If you found $100 on the street, would you keep it or give it to someone who needs it more than you?" (Keep/Give), Brianna proposed the following: "If you found $100 on the street, would you keep it, give it to someone who needs it more than you, or share half with someone who needs it and keep half for yourself?" (Keep/Give/Share). Questions with more choices expand the range of ideas that will surface in students' discussions of survey results.

To make the lesson more technology-based, Brianna asked students to collect data using an online Google Form. She posted the students' surveys on Twitter so they could collect and analyze global responses. After the student groups compiled their survey data, members of each group entered the data into one of the following graph-making software programs or tablet computer apps:

- Excel. This spreadsheet program is easy to use and powerful in its data-analysis capabilities. Upper elementary, middle, and high school students can use this tool independently.
- Google Sheets. This easily accessible program allows users to easily make charts from data.
- Graphers (Sunburst Technology) and The Graph Club 2.0 (Tom Snyder Productions). These programs enable K–6 students to enter and easily convert their data into four types of graphs: bar, line, pie, and pictograph.
- TinkerPlots. This data visualization program lets students build their own graph plots and much more. Data entry is easy, and because there is no menu of graphs, students must drag and click around the screen to see their graphs emerge based on their actions.
- Numbers. While not specifically designed for children, this app creates and displays data on spreadsheets. It works on iPads, iPhones, and iPods.
- GeoGebra. This easy-to-use and free graphing calculator features a variety of additional online math tools.
- Desmos Graphing Calculator. This simply designed tool offers video tutorials and online help for users.
- Create a Graph. This free program from the National Center for Education Statistics, an agency of the U.S. Department of Education, provides colorful and visually engaging graphs of all types that can be adjusted for size and ease of reading.

Briana then asked students to choose a graph type they believed would most clearly display their data, letting each group compare how effectively mathematical information is communicated to prospective readers. She asked the class, "Does a pictograph describe the survey results as clearly as a pie graph?" Looking at the data from their questions, students saw that in some cases it would but in other cases it would not.

Once the graphs were completed, Briana had students put all the graphs on individual slides in a Google Slideshow so students could see them presented and analyze them together as a class. Students could also make infographics using their data. Some infographic tools allow users to create interactive charts so when individuals mouse over the chart, more details are provided.

Using different graph formats teaches students how to express mathematical information visually in ordered ways. Graphs and infographics present information in few words because that is their function. Written reports and infographics accompanying the graphics are ways for students to explain the findings using expository or information-sharing sentences. Through data collecting, visual display designing and graph making, students utilize all levels of thinking skills in Bloom's taxonomy while consistently emphasizing the higher order skill of creating knowledge for themselves.

The Role of Feedback

Information technologies also promote critical thinking and problem solving by providing teachers and students an essential element of successful learning—rapid (often nearly instantaneous), self-correcting **feedback** about their efforts. In education, feedback is another term for communication between a learner and an instructor. Feedback is one of the instructional practices that promotes increased learning gains for students (Hattie & Yates, 2014; Hattie, 2013).

Think about a skill or activity that you have been pursuing recently—operating a new smartphone or tablet; performing a physical sport such as golf, ballroom dancing, juggling or rock climbing; or learning how to input information on federal and state tax forms. These activities may be self-taught, learned in a class, or acquired in a small-group or one-on-one setting. Feedback lets you know when you are proceeding correctly and when you are not. Feedback encourages learning from successes and mistakes, both necessary for critical thinking and problem solving.

Interactive software, educational websites, smartphone and tablet apps, online tutoring systems, and even simple learning machines provide rapid electronic feedback to learners. Such feedback not only is of great importance in subjects like mathematics and the sciences, in which posing and solving problems are at the center of the curriculum, but also is essential to virtually every part of school learning. The following list describes more ways that teachers can use technology for feedback:

- Tutoring systems and adaptive learning software
- Live self-paced assignments and assessments (e.g., Classkick or Go Formative)
- Text messaging and real-time chats
- E-mail, online discussion groups, and blogs
- Online polls and quiz games
- Note taking, writing, and editing apps
- Interactive educational websites and games
- Interactive maps and galleries
- Screen casts (audio/video)
- Smart pens.

Programming languages for children and teens are examples of digital materials that promote learning by providing supportive feedback. Scratch, a programming language developed at the Massachusetts Institute of Technology Media Lab, features jigsaw-shaped symbols and icons in place of complex code so students as young as kindergartners can click and drag pieces to make characters move or put a series of events in motion (Johnson, 2007, p. C5). The program provides immediate feedback so that young designers can view, change, and assess the result of their programming decisions. ScratchJr., a programming language for use by younger students, is a space where choices and instant feedback teach as the learner directs the learning (see Table 3.1 for more examples of critical thinking and problem-solving resources). You can explore critical thinking and problem solving with technology further in Chapter 8.

Personalized Learning

The goal of **personalized learning** is to adapt instructional settings and practices so each student can receive individually designed educational experiences. Technology in the form of computerized learning is crucial to this approach. In theory, computers and other digital tools make it possible for every student to have their own teacher, a dramatic contrast to classes where 20 to 30 elementary students (or 80 to 100 middle or high school students) receive similar teaching and are expected to progress at a common pace.

Personalized learning can happen with a creative teacher and 1-to-1 devices where the teacher designs activities like Hyperdocs or inquiry lessons for students to explore at their own pace and creates products to show what they have learned. Technology-based systems gather and display information about student performance in real time so teachers and students can adjust what is happening educationally.

Figure 3.2 MathSpring, an Intelligent Mathematics Tutor

SOURCE: MathSpring screenshot (c) University of Massachusetts Amherst. Reprinted with permission.

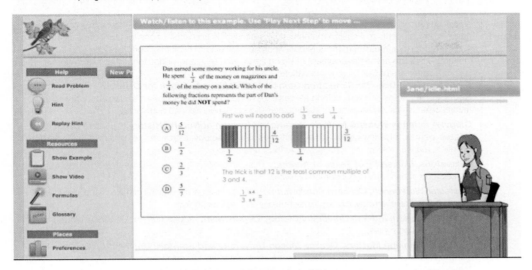

However, not everyone agrees that schools should commit to personalized learning for every student. Researchers warn that there has been little oversight on how personalized learning programs lack safeguards for student privacy. Citing a lack of evidence for the effectiveness of one-to-one technology-driven personalized learning models, researchers further worry that such programs will tie students to a restrictive curriculum that does not promote open-ended explorations of topics or areas of personal interest (Boninger, Molnar, & Saldana, 2019). One UCLA researcher starkly declared that school systems should "refrain from assuming personalized learning is the only model for computers in the classroom" (Enyedy, 2014, p. ii).

Adaptive and intelligent tutoring systems (ITS) are powerful programs that promote personalized learning through computer responses to student actions (Maloy, Razzaq, & Edwards, 2014; EDUCAUSE Learning Initiative, 2013b; Beal, et al., 2010). As students answer questions, the program records their responses and makes predictions about what users know and do not know. Based on these predictions, the program adapts its presentation of content to reflect what a student needs to understand and practice; for example, different questions are asked when a student demonstrates mastery of concepts and procedures than when a student fails to demonstrate knowledge. Like a human tutor, an intelligent tutor can provide the level of information practice students need to understand the material. Figure 3.2 shows a screenshot from Math-Spring, an intelligent mathematics tutor that provides different types of problem-solving assistance to students, including hints, video explanations, a glossary of terms, and an online teacher/coach who offers encouragement and support.

Intelligent tutors with adaptive learning are constructed in a variety of formats, including simulations, games, tutorials, and collaborative learning models. For example, a student might solve fraction problems while learning about endangered species, draw perspective lines overlaid on classic art treasures, or practice procedures for responding to emergency cardiac arrest. Compelling storylines, animated characters, and problem-solving hints are used in these systems to foster student engagement and analytical thinking. Learning is organized within authentic activities and contexts (e.g., students solve math problems to feed and save an endangered species or to protect jungle habitats from deforestation).

As researchers have noted, not all computer-based tutoring systems promote higher order thinking and inquiry-based learning. Many programs still deliver concepts, facts, and findings by directing students to a single correct answer. Some discipline-specific systems often serve as encyclopedic reviews rather than as ways to conduct investigations of problems and cases. In such systems, the computer directs the learning, asks the questions, and evaluates the answers. In contrast, dynamic systems change educational experience dramatically by offering individualized, adaptive, and interactive instruction tailored to student interests and needs by emphasizing problem solving and inquiry-based learning. Intelligent tutors can also be embedded in online or blended learning courses to teach students who do not have face-to-face time with an instructor.

Table 3.1 Web Resources and Apps for Critical Thinking and Problem Solving

Web

- **National Library of Virtual Manipulatives (NLVM), Utah State University.** Interactive web-based games allow students to visualize mathematical relationships and applications for number operations, geometry, algebra, measurement, and data analysis. Link also to *Evolution, JohnKyrk.com*. An engagingly interactive timeline of the development of life on Earth, with links and videos for further explorations; this is part of a larger site of Cell Biology Animations.
- **Stop Disasters! Disaster Simulation Games, United Nations Office for Disaster Reduction.** Online problem-solving games explore how human actions can accelerate or prepare for natural calamities such as wildfires, earthquakes, floods, tsunamis, and hurricanes.
- **Ology: A Science Website for Kids, American Museum of Natural History.** Students explore quizzes, games, interviews, puzzles, and activities in archaeology, astronomy, biodiversity, earth science, genetics, marine biology, paleontology, aquatics, and zoology.
- **eSkeletons, University of Texas at Austin.** This game offers 2-D and 3-D full-color digitized versions of skeletons of human and nonhuman primates.
- **Molecular Workbench, Concord Consortium.** Interactive visual simulations of molecular dynamics are offered in physics, chemistry, biology, biotechnology and nanotechnology.
- **Plants-in-Motion, Indiana University Biology Department.** QuickTime movies show plant growth and reproduction cycles.
- **Historical Thinking Matters, George Mason University and Stanford University.** Student-centered historical investigations of 20th century history topics—Spanish-American War, Scopes Trial, Social Security, and Rosa Parks and the Montgomery Bus Boycott—use primary sources, video introductions, and key questions.
- **iCivics.** These free web-based games teach students about the functions of courts and the law in a democratic society. For example, in the game "Supreme Decision," students serve as law clerks for a Supreme Court justice who must write an opinion in a First Amendment case in which a school district seeks to ban students from wearing music or band logo T-shirts.

Apps

- **Wolfram Alpha.** Answers to factual questions as well as scientific and mathematical calculations are shown in fields ranging from physics to astronomy to history, geography, and technology.
- **Bobo Explores Light.** Bobo the Robot leads readers through investigations of the science of light.
- **Simple Physics.** Students design a structure with minimal or multiple features and then test its strengths and stresses in a competition to see whose idea is the best design for its cost.
- **Question Builder for the iPad.** Elementary school children answer questions from the simple to the abstract by reading and listening to digital material.
- **Brain Pop.** Interactive video series animations showcase experiences from science, social studies, English, math, art, music, health, and engineering. There are quizzes and tests, along with the GameUp feature, which offers a collection of digital learning games that is paired with classroom teaching materials, including standards-based lesson plans. SnapThought, a tool which encourages reflection in key moments in game play, can be found in many of the games.

MyLab Application Exercise 3.1:
Building Your PLN: Web Resources and Apps for Critical Thinking and Problem Solving

MyLab Education Self-Check 3.1

UPT Learning 2: Developing Digital Literacies

3.2 Analyze the meaning and importance of digital literacies.

Technology has revolutionized how people find and use information. Search engines, social media, digital encyclopedias and online databases, smartphone and tablet apps, and other information storage and retrieval systems make it possible to explore all topics digitally. Students and teachers have immediate access to text, photos, audio, and/or video information about the arrival of a hurricane on the coast of Florida, the hearings of a congressional committee, the newly released papers of a famous historical figure, the latest scientific discoveries, or any other inquiry-based topic.

The emergence of computer technology has enlarged the scope of literacies for students and teachers. Consider reading and writing as examples. American schools in the 19th and 20th centuries sought to educate students to read and write, master arithmetic, and know about basic information about history and science—the well-known three R's of "reading, 'riting, 'rithmetic." Reading was regarded as an essentially reflective process, with a person reading a book, magazine, or newspaper and contemplating its meaning (Houston, 2016). Today, pixels replace print on paper, and people read using digital screens where words, images, and data intersect in complex collections of information. Touch screens, websites, and apps encourage individuals to interact with the material on the screen, transforming the reading experience.

Writing also happens differently in a digital world—the Internet, smartphones, laptops, and tablets offer multiple modes for expressing ideas using voice dictation software, texting, picture sending, on-screen keyboard typing, and multiple publishing formats from Facebook and Twitter to websites and blogs. Online writers contribute to the vast array of information now available. Technology can be used to crowdsource ideas and problem-solving strategies for addressing local, national, and international problems. At the same time, literate individuals must be aware of and prepared to resist the spread of viral fake news.

To be a successful member of today's information-based society, students need new digital literacies to understand the Internet, mass media, online information, and the dynamics of multimodal learning. In the words of two English Language Arts educators, students must be able to "critically consume information," share knowledge using different mediums, solve problems collaboratively, "persevere in light of setbacks," and "maintain flexibility" in complex situations (Hicks & Turner, 2013, p. 59).

Information Literacy and the Internet

With unprecedented access to ideas and information comes new requirements to assess the quality of the information teachers and students access online. *Accessing information* refers to the activities of locating and acquiring information. *Assessing information* refers to processes of determining the reliability and usefulness of that information. Knowing how to access and assess information is the foundation for **information literacy**, a term that encompasses the skills of reading and understanding all forms of information, paper and digital.

Information-literate students at every grade level learn how to:

- Identify what information is needed
- Understand how the information is organized
- Identify reliable sources of information for a given topic, question, or issue
- Locate those sources, evaluate the sources critically, and share that information (University of Idaho, 2012).

Information literacy equips students to recognize differences among information sources—what is intended to be persuasive (campaign speeches or product commercials), what is intended to be objective (scientific studies or newspapers), and what is intended to be satirical (news on Comedy Central or in a humor magazine). The sheer volume of images, text, and data from multiple media may overwhelm students who do not know how to evaluate information. The resulting information overload results in confusion about what sources to use or believe. Without ways to analyze or compare and contrast resources, students are left with diminished critical thinking and a lack of understanding of what they find online. One recent study reported that seventh-graders, especially those from economically disadvantaged backgrounds, lack the skills to read and understand academically based online materials, including being able to identify the author or the point of view of digital texts (Leu et al., 2015).

Information literacy includes the skills required to understand how information is presented in online formats, what is known as **digital literacy**. Students tend to assume that what they find online is accurate and relevant (Wineburg, 2018; McGrew, et al., 2018; Steeves, 2014). To demonstrate the complexities of online information presentations, researchers from the Teaching Internet Comprehension to Adolescents (TICA)

MyLab Education
Video Example 3.1
In this video, you will learn why information literacy is a vital skill for students to possess in today's technological society. How can teachers and students become informed decision makers about what does and does not constitute reliable online information?

Figure 3.3 Northwest Tree Octopus

SOURCE: Courtesy of Lyle Zapago, ZAPATOPI.NET. Reprinted with permission.

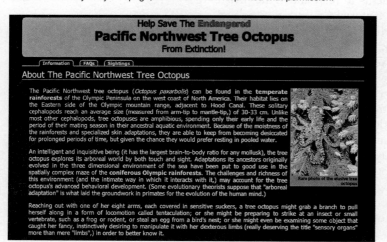

Project, conducted by the University of Connecticut and Clemson University, created a website for the "Northwest Tree Octopus" (see Figure 3.3), a make-believe animal whose existence is threatened by loggers and attacks by its natural predator, the sasquatch. The site's academic-sounding text, authentic-looking photos, and seemingly legitimate contact information made the hoax seem real. When told the site was a hoax, students first had difficulty believing they had been fooled and then were hard pressed to identify the fictitious elements of the online information.

To develop digital literacy, the TICA Project urged greater use of **reciprocal teaching**, an instructional technique designed to improve students' reading comprehension. Reciprocal teaching emphasizes dialog and discussion among teachers and students to explore meaning and identify misconceptions in a written or visual text. When encountering a text, for example a website or other material posted online, teachers begin by reading web material aloud to students, pausing for discussion about the meaning of words, pictures, graphs, and other images. Individually or in small groups, students reread the same material aloud, focusing on critically evaluating what is being said and what might be omitted or obscured. As they summarize and clarify the meaning of a text, students also predict what might be said next and propose ways that information might be presented more clearly or accurately to readers.

Media Literacy and Multimodal Learning

Media literacy, a subset of information literacy, involves students learning to think critically about their experiences with all types of media, from entertainment and social media to commercial advertising and political communications (Ray, Jackson, & Cupaiuolo, 2014b). It means analyzing information across multimodal environments while also having the capabilities to express one's own ideas using multiple digital tools. Large corporate media organizations are powerfully adept at conveying the messages they want people to learn. Media literacy, therefore, includes being able to "replace media programming with ideas of your own" (Potter, 2010, p. xviii).

Media literacy teaches students skills they need to critique and assess the many different types of visual and audio presentations they will encounter in school and society, including pictures, moving images, illustrations, diagrams, charts, and graphs. One fascinating media literacy tool is the Lego Gender Remixer. Select audio from boys or girls commercials and place it over the opposite gender commercial to hear firsthand how much gender plays a role in how products are marketed and perceived.

Like media literacy, visual literacy develops from personal experience as well as from learning how colors, forms, sizes, angles, and images can be used to communicate ideas and information. Designing ways for people to become visually literate has been the focus of information theorist Edward R. Tufte. In his classic book *Envisioning Information* (1990, pp. 9, 12, 33, 35), Tufte observes that although "the world is complex, dynamic, multidimensional, the paper is static, flat." Even though we perceive the world in three-dimensional terms, information is presented to us "in the two-dimensionality of the endless flatlands of paper and video screens." To communicate information most clearly, writers and readers must find ways of "escaping flatland." Tufte notes how consumers are inundated by what he calls "chartjunk"—crowded and cluttered information displays that offer neither clarity nor detail. He urges writers (and, by extension, teachers) to create clear, visually accessible images.

Teachers can teach media literacy using technologies such as:

- WebQuests, Hyperdocs, and other teacher-designed online research projects
- Classroom websites that involve students in their design and maintenance
- Student-created web and multimedia materials

- Student reviews of published websites
- Online newspapers and news broadcasts
- Bookmarking and social bookmarking
- Digital dictionaries
- Multimedia timelines.

Media literacy supports **multimodal learning**, an educational practice at every grade level. Multimodal learning happens as students gain information through different types of visual and digital media, extending learning beyond reading or listening to a presentation about a topic. Before interactive digital technologies, classroom learning meant viewing static charts and graphs shown on an overhead projector, creating diagrams on chalkboards, or watching slideshows or television video clips. Many teachers longed to present lessons featuring multisensory experiences in which students got to see, hear, and touch different learning materials.

Multimodal learning with software programs, tablet apps, interactive websites, online videos, learning games, and digital telescopes and microscopes presents information dynamically, creating a sense of being in a setting, not just viewing it. Teachers can recreate the past, view the present, or envision the future through moving images rather than static words and pictures. Technology reveals the ocean's depths, the immenseness of the solar system, and the structural systems of a human body. Students can view tiny objects such as bacteria, one-celled animals, and insects or vast phenomena such as weather systems, geological landforms, or planets and other extraterrestrial objects. They see things that we would not otherwise be able to see.

An array of learning technologies release students and teachers from the limitations of static images in books and other print-based materials. Animations have the capacity to zoom in and out or to rotate scenes, letting viewers see images from multiple perspectives. Virtual reality environments and social simulations allow students to enter a setting and observe how it works from the inside. In some, the user can affect the environment and determine the course of events. Apps provide three-dimensional images that allow students to see and manipulate objects and models in subject areas as diverse as science, history, geometry, and art. The development of 3-D printing makes it possible to take a scan of an object and then use rubber, plastic, or other materials to produce an actual representation of that object for study in the classroom.

Multimodal materials increase instructional options for teachers and learning options for students. Every time teachers enter a classroom, they must decide what academic content to teach *and* what teaching methods to use. Content and method are directly connected, and each is an integral part of every learning experience. For example, an animation can show young students number operations in ways that photos or illustrations do not. Consider this word problem: "Mr. Dolan bought 9 boxes of erasers with 12 erasers in each box. How many erasers did Mr. Dolan buy?" An animation begins with 9 boxes of 12 erasers opening simultaneously and from each of the boxes march 12 erasers in top hats with twirling canes. The erasers form themselves into 9 groups of 10 erasers and 9 groups of 2 erasers. The animation shows how the use of place value, 9 x 10 and 9 x 2, compute easily to find a total for 9 x 12, and the animation can be viewed multiple times. Students could then make their own animations of other multiplication computations.

Digital Dialog 3.1

Many students become more engaged academically when learning from multimodal presentations. For these learners, an online interactive periodic table of elements communicates meaning more readily than a static paper chart. Thinking about your own learning experiences, connect and comment online about the following questions:

- What types of information do you prefer to learn multimodally and interactively?
- What are recent examples of information that you have learned using online interactive websites or data visualization technologies?
- How do you plan to support students' multimodal learning when you enter the classroom as a teacher?

Technologies that promote learning through multimodal experiences include:

- Online simulations, tutorials, and experiments
- 3-D virtual reality presentations and apps
- Augmented reality apps
- Virtual manipulatives and 3-D digital models (e.g., Smithsonian 3D)
- Real-time data displays and analysis
- Online video clips and streaming video
- Digitized primary sources (photographs, writing, charts, graphs, or maps)
- Vodcasts (video podcasts).

Table 3.2 has resources for promoting students' digital and media literacy development through multimodal learning. You can explore digital literacies further in Chapter 5.

Table 3.2 Web Resources and Apps for Developing Digital Literacies

Web

- ***FactCheck, Annenberg Public Policy Center at the University of Pennsylvania.*** To help students and teachers distinguish credible information from fake and false news, FactCheck provides critical evaluations of news stories, political campaign ads, press releases, policy statements, and politicians' claims; FactCheckED is specifically designed for classroom use. SciCheck.org from the Annenberg Public Policy Center and Fact Checker from the *Washington Post* newspaper are two more excellent fact-checking sites.
- ***American President, Miller Center, University of Virginia.*** Documents, photographs, audio and video recordings, and other materials about all the nation's presidents. See also *The American Presidency, Smithsonian National Museum of American History*.
- ***Visuwords Online Dictionary.*** This website provides interactive word definitions with color schemes and graphics that link related words. Other sites, *Kidswordsmyth* and *Little Explorers Picture Dictionary* provide interactive vocabulary building experiences for younger learners.
- ***Thinkmap Visual Thesaurus.*** This semantic relationship tool invites students to research word meanings and their connections to other words using an online mapping program. Words and their related meanings are displayed in a visual format that can be moved and changed on the screen. (FEE). *Word Hippo* is a comprehensive thesaurus for synonyms and antonyms; *Reverso Speller* is a spell checker, grammar checker and translator.
- ***Rome Reborn Virtual Reality, Flyover Zone Production.*** Students explore history through 3-D virtual reality tours of ancient Rome, digitally reproduced as it was on June 21, CE 320, during its preeminence as the capital of the Roman Empire.
- ***The Valley of the Shadow: Two Communities in the American Civil War, Virginia Center for Digital History.*** Maps, letters and diaries, census and tax records, newspapers, soldiers' records, and other primary source materials from two counties in Virginia and Pennsylvania provide a snapshot of history from before the Civil War to the end of Reconstruction.
- ***Cassini-Huygens Mission to Saturn, California Institute of Technology Jet Propulsion Laboratory.*** This site explores a mission to Saturn, with information about the planet, its moons, and the spacecraft, through images and video. NASA's *Explore Solar System & Beyond* offers images, videos, and teaching resources about the sun, stars and galaxies, black holes, dark matter, and more.
- ***Interactive maps and materials.*** Students have several options, including the National Weather Service (online maps of weather warnings, advisories, and forecasts), Modern Language Association (interactive maps of languages spoken in the United States), National Endowment for the Humanities (interactive gallery of high-quality color reproductions of masterpieces), and PBS (interactive maps to accompany historical and science documentaries).

Apps and e-books

- ***Early Jamestown, Virginia Department of Education's Beyond Textbooks initiative.*** This e-text for elementary and middle school social studies presents the history of colonial Virginia, including relationships between Native Americans and European settlers.
- ***The Fantastic Flying Books of Mr. Morris Lessmore.*** This highly acclaimed graphic novel offers an interactive reading experience in which the pictures animate and the narrator speaks at the touch of your finger.
- ***Word Wagon.*** Mozzarella the mouse and Coco the bird bring words and letter sounds to life in this app for beginning readers of text.
- ***In a World (Drama).*** Students use this app to create movie trailers with their own title and rating, combining text, music, and a voice reading of the script.

MyLab Application Exercise 3.2:
Building Your PLN: Web Resources and Apps for Digital Literacy Learning

MyLab Education Self-Check 3.2

UPT Learning 3: Communicating and Collaborating with Technology

3.3   Examine how technology facilitates communication and collaboration.

Information technologies make possible new patterns of communication and collaboration to help students work together attentively, thoughtfully, and willingly on academic activities. Students are drawn to the dynamism of digital environments in their outside-of-school lives. Viewing movies, television and videos, sending text messages, using cell phones for conversation and communication, surfing the Internet, participating in social media sites and online forums, playing video games, and playing with remote control toys and models mean teachers have ready-made opportunities to use students' technology-centered behaviors to promote school learning. Technologies that promote communication and collaboration include:

- Social networks and social media
- Real-time collaboration tools (e.g., Google Docs/Slides/Sheets/Keep, Padlet, Lino)
- Virtual conversation tools (e.g., Slack, Piazza, Yo Teach!, Vynchronize)
- Online polls and surveys
- Collaborative digital storytelling
- Digital games for learning
- Translation software
- Online posters and website publishing
- Student-friendly programming languages and environments (e.g., Scratch).

Communication and collaboration technologies focus, engage, and motivate students, and of the three, motivation may be the most necessary in educational settings. To motivate learning, philosopher John Dewey (1943) observed, teachers constantly strive to gain the "outer" and "inner" attention of students. Most of the time, educators focus on students' outer attention (for example, requiring students to remain quietly in their seats throughout class or having them copy notes and assignments from the board) while neglecting their inner attention (helping students think deeply about the topics under discussion). But inner attention is where learning truly happens.

Inner attention, said Dewey (1904, p. 148), is the "giving of the mind without reserve or qualification to the subject in hand. It is the first-hand and personal play of mental powers. As such, it is a fundamental condition of mental growth." It takes skillful perception of individual behaviors by teachers as well as engaging and relevant teaching methods to gain students' inner attention. Inner attention, concluded Dewey, "comes fully into being only when the child entertains results in the form of problems or questions, the solution of which he is to seek for himself ... with growing power the child can conceive of the end as something to be found out, discovered; and can control his acts and images so as to help in the inquiry and solution. This is reflective attention proper" (1943, p. 146).

Engaging Students through Active Learning

Communication and collaboration technologies promote **active learning**, the name given to educational activities that activate students' inner and outer attention. Active learning is also known as *discovery learning, learning by doing, inquiry-based learning, design-based learning,* or *hands-on learning.* Each of these terms suggests that students focus on and actively engage in writing, doing experiments, making models, building with blocks and other materials, analyzing documents, or working with other students to design or make something.

Increasing active learning has been recommended by many education reformers. Summarizing what they call a "progressive consensus," researchers Steven Zemelman,

**MyLab Education
Video Example 3.2**
In this video, teachers explain how technology promotes collaboration and cooperation among students. How do you plan to encourage collaboration among students in your future classroom?
https://www.edutopia.org/video/tech-buddies-building-technology-skills-through-peer-teaching

Computers engage students in active learning as they analyze information and solve problems online.

SOURCE: Rob/Fotolia

Harvey Daniels, and Steven Hyde (2012) urge less whole-class teacher-directed instruction, less student passivity, less reliance on standardized tests, and less time spent with textbooks and basal texts or leveled reading books. They report studies showing that student learning flourishes when teachers utilize experiential activities, emphasize higher order thinking, spend time discussing student-chosen fiction and nonfiction books, promote creative and analytical writing, and engage in performance-based evaluations of achievement.

Communication and collaboration technologies promote active learning by offering students multiple ways to interact with readers, listeners, and viewers. Word processing, design, and paint programs and apps give young writers and artists unparalleled ways to express their ideas on screens and online platforms. Social tools like blogs, wikis, texting on phones and tablets, Twitter, Facebook, Instagram, and other online networks and videoconferencing tools allow students to connect with peers and adults locally and around the world. Photo-taking and video-making tools make it possible for individuals and classroom groups to share still and moving images online. These modes of communication not only invite the outer attention but also sustain the inner attention of learners who are actively involved in expressing their ideas and sharing them with diverse audiences.

Digital Writing with Social Technologies

Composing and communicating with technology is known as **digital writing** and supports teachers as they integrate technology directly into how students learn writing across the grade level (Hicks, 2013; National Writing Project, et al., 2010). Digital writing encompasses not only writing using word processing programs like Microsoft Word, but also writing for a website, communicating by e-mail or text messaging, contributing to a blog or a wiki, or expressing one's ideas through another technology-based communication outlet. Even composing text messages that consist of GIFs, bitmojis, or emojis is still a form of digital writing.

In its Read/Write/Think website, the National Council of Teachers of English (NCTE) offers interactive tools to support students' digital writing, including many types of poetry (acrostics, shape poems, and diamante poems) as well as resources for composing fiction and nonfiction stories. We discuss writing with technology further in Chapter 11.

Technology enables teachers and students to communicate and collaborate through social media and digital writing tools, sharing ideas among people who know each other and those who do not. Sending and receiving information digitally combines elements of face-to-face interactions with those that have been traditionally created by letters, postcards, and memos. In other cases, new communication patterns include teachers and students engaging in online discussions of topics using a blog or wiki to post ideas and to read and respond to people's comments.

In addition to its speed, informality, and access to friends, social technologies offer children and adolescents authentic occasions for speaking, reading, and writing. Some youngsters—reluctant communicators within school assignments that offer few choices of topic or genre, no opportunity to deviate from a preset form, and seemingly no relevance to their lives—are eager to talk, read, and write about personally meaningful topics with others using these technologies. In schools, social technologies can support students making choices about what to read and what to write as well as how to write reports, essays, debates, poems, and other written communications. Social technologies encourage communication and collaboration through peer reviewing, collaborative storytelling and script design, and sharing one's work publicly for feedback from readers beyond the teacher and classmates.

Writing digitally features speed and flow as ideas emerge in lighted letters on a screen. From initial free writing and brainstorming to final editing and publishing, writers have different ways to produce their creative work. Digital technology also profoundly affects the vision of those who are designing, calculating, and painting. Once images are present on a screen, surprisingly creative transformations are possible. From simply copying an original image or adding details, color changes, and size modifications to animating the images in a slideshow or movie with sound and text, creative tools and apps inspire new ways to express ideas. Voice, music, songs, theater, and improvisations are all able to be included through video and audio formats.

Groupwork and Cooperative Learning

Groupwork features collaboration among classmates—students work together in pairs, trios, quartets, or other small-sized groups on an assignment or task. In **cooperative learning**, students perform different roles in collaborative activities, such as note taker, writer, artist, researcher, or presenter (Strebe, 2018; Cohen & Lotan, 2014).

Groupwork and cooperative learning decrease the amount of teacher-centered whole-group instruction. Small groups of students do different activities while the teacher moves from group to group checking in, conversing with students, and offering specialized assistance and suggestions and asking clarifying questions. In some schools, groupwork and cooperative learning generate organizational alternatives to the tracking of students by ability groups. This is called "detracking," and it happens when students from all ability and performance levels take the same classes (Watanabe, 2012). In these settings, groupwork and cooperation allow students to support each other's learning through peer teaching and teamwork.

Technology supports groupwork and cooperative learning. "The computer is its own grown-up," one elementary school teacher told us, referring to how technology allows her to create different learning centers throughout the classroom. During morning literacy time in that teacher's classroom, tablets capture and maintain the attention of pairs of six to eight children while she instructs reading, writing, spelling, math, or science with small groups in other parts of the room. When the groups rotate, other students utilize the tablets. Almost any technology can be used collaboratively; small groups can consult interactive websites, play online games, work together filming student-made videos, or use digital tools for science research experiments.

Organized group activities that utilize technology resources creatively provide students with control and responsibility in the learning process. As sociologists Elizabeth Cohen and Rachel Lotan (2014, p. 2) noted: "Delegating authority in an instructional task is making students responsible for specific parts of their work; students are free to accomplish their task in the way they think best, but they are accountable to the teacher for the final product." Groupwork does not let students do a task exclusively by themselves but asks them to make use of the strengths that each student brings to the assignment and, as a collection of learners with different skills, to teach each other and problem-solve creatively when there are open-ended problems at hand.

The ways technology captures students' inner attention and generates active engagement create settings in which learners can work together thoughtfully and productively. In so doing, technology facilitates a vision of education based on the idea that when students communicate and collaborate, they will gain skills and exchange knowledge in ways that create and sustain lasting learning. Web resources for communication and collaboration are listed in Table 3.3. You can explore communication and collaboration with technology further in Chapter 9.

Table 3.3 Web Resources and Apps for Communication and Collaboration

Web

- **G Suite for Education.** This Google product promotes online collaboration between teachers and students as they build shared documents, presentations, spreadsheets, and forms.
- **#edchat, #sschat, #engchat, #scichat, #mathchat.** These are examples of hashtags for online educational conversations that teachers can join using the microblogging site Twitter. There are separate chat feeds for each subject field as well as many others on educational issues and trends.
- **Zoomerang.** This online survey tool allows teachers and students to poll classroom, school, or community members. Other effective poll and survey tools include *Poll Everywhere, Kahoot!* and *Micropoll*.
- **Sutori.** Teachers and students build multimedia timelines by entering their own material or importing content from a variety of learning management systems, including Google Classroom, Moodle, Canvas, PowerSchool, and Blackboard.
- **Google Keep.** This tool organizes information as if you were collaborating virtually on a community whiteboard. Users can see each other working on projects and see how much progress they have made through the process of writing digital sticky notes.
- **MindMeister.** This virtual graphic-based mind-mapping tool can be used collaboratively. Templates and guides are available, and you can add photos and live links to your ideas.
- **Flipgrid.** Students can create their own engaging videos and post them within the library, where their peers can reply to their videos either with comments or their own video creations. Search the Discovery Library for ideas based on topics and various grade levels.
- **Poll Builder, George Mason University Center for History and New Media.** This is a helpful resource for a classroom webpage to obtain people's opinions on questions posed by students and teachers.

Apps

- **Goodreads.** Students and teachers create their own collections of books they have read or intend to read, write reviews, create book groups, and share resources with others. Other web bookmarking tools include *Flipboard, Pinterest, Diigo*, and *Trello*.
- **Skype, Zoom, Google Hangouts.** These platforms offer video and voice calling.
- **Duolingo.** This language learning program allows users to contribute to translating websites and documents as they progress through lessons.
- **Dragon Dictation.** This app produces written text for e-mails, text messages, and personal notes and reminders when you dictate thoughts and ideas to a smartphone.

> **MyLab Education Application Exercise 3.3:**
> Building Your PLN: Web Resources and Apps for Digital Communication and Collaboration
>
> **MyLab Education Self-Check 3.3**

UPT Learning 4: Expressing Creativity with Digital Tools

3.4 Identify how technology enables multiple expressions of creative thinking.

Digital technologies provide teachers and students with easy-to-learn ways to express themselves creatively. Using computer-generated words, pictures, symbols, videos, and music for filmmaking, writing, drawing, and information presentations offers new ways to teach ideas and concepts. **Creativity** may be broadly defined as thinking and acting in ways that generate alternative, fresh approaches to people, presentations, and problems. Expressing ideas creatively is a highly-valued talent in virtually every field from the artistic to the commercial and is one of the core national educational technology standards for students.

Multiple intelligences researcher Howard Gardner located creativity in the actions of historically significant people—Sigmund Freud, Albert Einstein, Pablo Picasso, Igor Stravinsky, T. S. Eliot, Martha Graham, and Mahatma Gandhi—who "solve problems, create products, or raise issues *in a domain* in a way that is initially novel but is eventually accepted in one or more cultural settings" (2011a, p. 116). Social psychologist Mihaly Csikszentmihalyi (2013, 2008) contends that for an idea or contribution to be truly creative, it must pass the test of time and the judgment of many evaluators. The teenage Mozart was uniquely talented, but the society-altering impact of his compositions evolved over time as musical conventions changed profoundly from his influence. In this view, those who are acknowledged to be "creative" are those whose accomplishments enrich life and change the course of history.

By contrast, children and adolescents display their creativity in personal ways within family, school, and after-school environments (Kafai, Peppler, & Chapman, 2009). Some draw, paint, or sculpt; build with blocks or clay; or explore outdoor landscapes or interior mindscapes. Others express themselves through physical movement on bikes, skateboards, rollerblades, or basketball courts. Still others play musical instruments, act in plays, or write stories and poetry. To be creative, children do not need to design, compose, or develop something no one has done before; they may need only to say or do things they have not thought or done before in quite the same way or style. The creative act can be what is new to the individual, not new to the world.

Sir Ken Robinson, internationally known author of highly watched TED Talk "How Schools Kill Creativity," sees creativity as an essential element of school curriculum and a way for teachers and students to challenge the prevailing emphasis on standardized testing. In his view, creative ideas do not just suddenly happen; they emerge, often in unexpected ways from hunches and random experiences, through a process that combines "critical thinking" with "imaginative insights" to generate "fresh ideas" (Robinson & Aronica, 2015).

In his book *Lifelong Kindergarten*, Mitchel Resnick (2017) finds individual creativity emerging when children or adults can engage in what he calls a "creative learning spiral." The spiral begins with imagination and proceeds through stages of "create," "play," "share," "reflect," and back to new forms of imagining—the very activities that young children do in kindergarten, but schools tend to diminish or ignore as students get older. "As children go through the spiral," notes Resnick, "they develop and refine their abilities as creative thinkers. They learn to develop their own ideas, try them out, experiment with alternatives, get input from others, and generate new ideas based on their experiences" (Resnick, 2017, pp. 12–13).

Writers, artists, composers, engineers, and designers, as well as teachers and students, can access a growing number of tools and apps that support the processes of creative thinking, including:

- Creative and expository writing, storytelling, and poetry
- Desktop publishing and online publishing of individual or classroom projects
- Designing, coding, and model building
- Art, music, graphics, and photo editing
- Animation and movie making
- Podcasts and digital movies
- Designing virtual and augmented reality experiences and environments.

Seymour Papert's Vision of Technology Learning Environments

An expansive view of how technology promotes creative self-expression can be found in the writings of MIT professor, mathematician, and artificial intelligence researcher Seymour Papert. In a series of now classic books—*Mindstorms* (1980), *The Children's Machine* (1993), and *The Connected Family* (1996)—he set forth a sweeping vision of teaching and learning transformed by computers. According to Papert, as technology propels active engagement and creative thinking, it creates continuous opportunities for teachers to make children's ideas and questions integral to the learning process.

Papert refers to the "child as builder" with technology as essential tools for constructing new and expansive intellectual understandings. Two groundbreaking ideas, first expressed in *Mindstorms,* have been constants in his books and articles. First, "it is possible to design computers so that learning to communicate can be a natural process, more like learning French by living in France than like trying to learn it through the unnatural process of American foreign-language instruction in classrooms." Second, "learning to communicate with a computer may change the way other learning takes place" (1980, p. 6).

For Papert (1980, pp. 8–10, 179), a fundamental distinction exists between how children learn in nonformal, everyday environments such as the family or the neighborhood and how children learn in the regulated settings of schools. Outside of school, children acquire many skills—for example, learning to talk—"painlessly, successfully, and without organized instruction" through "real participation and playful imitation." However, these same qualities are not found in most schools. As typically arranged, a school classroom is "an artificial and inefficient learning environment."

To connect children to more natural ways of learning math, Papert created learning environments in which children were free to invent and explore what happened when they used Logo computer language to program an electronic turtle to move around a screen in response to a series of commands. Moving the turtle, children are "learning how to exercise control over an exceptionally rich and sophisticated 'micro-world'" (Papert, 1980, p. 12). Turtle geometry introduces concepts of shapes, sizes, angles, spaces, and places in ways that allow children to build "hierarchies of knowledge" on which understandings about the world can be firmly and permanently based. Some of these understandings are mathematical, and some are broader, dealing with learning about learning. Throughout, children explore the basic foundational principle that "in order to learn something, first make sense of it" (Papert, 1980, pp. 60, 63).

For Papert, Logo learning was the foundation of a broader goal, expressed in *The Children's Machine,* through which technology can "create an environment in which all children—whatever their culture, gender or personality—could learn algebra and geometry and spelling and history in ways more like the informal learning of the unschooled toddler or the exceptional child than the educational process followed in schools" (1993, p. 13).

Moving forward, Papert predicted technology will make possible a "megachange in education as far-reaching as what we have seen in medicine, but will do this through a process directly opposite to what has driven change in modern medicine. Medicine has changed by becoming more and more technical in its nature; in education, change will come by using technical means to shuck off the technical nature of school learning" (Papert, 1993, p. 56).

Visual Thinking and Concept Mapping for Creative Thinking

Visual thinking and concept mapping tools let teachers and students organize and outline their ideas visually on desktops, laptops, and tablets. Kidspiration (for elementary school students), Inspiration (for high school students and adults), and InspireData (for middle school and high school students) from Inspiration Software are three flexible visual thinking programs. These tools include graphs, symbols, charts, voice, and other organizing devices that are catalysts for creative self-expression by students.

Original work involves creating something new. When we ask students to create an original piece of writing or drawing, many report experiencing the "terror of the blank page," an overriding discomfort that may include staring at an assignment in frustration, feeling frozen intellectually, or not knowing what to write or draw or where to start. In response, many teachers urge students who feel blocked creatively to begin describing and drawing whatever comes to mind, without editing,

Technology's capability to creatively produce and publish is a way for students to reach audiences around the world.

SOURCE: Annie Fuller/Pearson Education

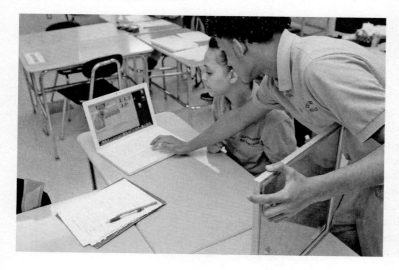

to stimulate their creative imaginations. Expressing ideas verbally and through pictures produces creative momentum. Once started, new ideas often follow quickly, sometimes in smooth sequence, sometimes in a maze of thoughts, connections, and questions.

Some youngsters and teens can express their ideas more easily visually than by putting pencil or pen to paper. Kidspiration and Inspiration have a linear writing mode, a chart- and graph-making mode, and a money-counting mode, as well as colorful graphics and a voice. Each can be used as a brainstorming tool and as a presentation organizer as well. InspireData displays information dynamically using Venn diagrams along with bar, stack, and pie charts. All these products promote creative thinking, offering students countless ways of using the software to express their understanding of curriculum ideas and concepts.

There are many visual thinking and brainstorming tools online, either free or commercially available; even single-purpose tools can be useful for students. NCTE offers Persuasion Map on its Read/Write/Think website, an outlining tool for composing a five-paragraph persuasive essay. The program is activated when a student enters a name and the title of the paper. The next screen asks for a one- or two-sentence thesis statement. The following screen asks for three ideas that support the thesis statement and then for different facts that expand the ideas. With a completed persuasion map, the student has a working outline of the essay minus a summary paragraph. NCTE also offers compare-and-contrast maps, circle plot diagrams, essay organizers, and doodle-drawing makers to support creative writing by students at all grade levels.

MyLab Education
Video Example 3.3
In this video, you will learn how students can use technology to express their ideas through writing. How have you used digital tools to express your own creative ideas in print, video, audio or other mediums?
https://www.youtube.com/watch?v=A54kdrjA8UE

Building and Inventing with Creative Tools

Building, inventing and creating happens when students engage in open-ended investigations of topics and items that interest them. Such learning begins at young ages as preschoolers, kindergartners, and elementary school students play with blocks, puzzles, dolls, LEGOs, balls, paints, and other manipulative materials. Older students build, invent, and create while conducting science experiments, engaging in investigations of historical primary sources, acting in plays and skits, performing their own musical compositions or dance routines, making film or art, and writing creatively.

Efforts to expand creativity in schools include approaches known as Genius Hour and 20% time. **Genius Hour**, an idea made popular by writer Daniel Pink (2011), gives students regular time to work on new ideas, learn new skills, or express themselves in new ways. Some teachers have converted unused spaces into innovation areas with technology where students can pursue their creative visions.

Google embraced the concept of **20% time**, in which employees are encouraged to spend 20% of their week working on projects they think will benefit the company, but the practice has been traced back to the 3M company in the 1950s and the invention of Post-it Notes (Schmidt & Rosenberg, 2014). As in Genius Hour, teachers invite students to spend time working on projects of their own choosing that can be connected to the curriculum or outreach to the community.

Tools for building, inventing, and creating provide students with technology-based environments for interactive and engaging learning. The most effective are those that do not have a single right way to use them. They are open ended, enabling the child to design and direct the outcome. The classic program Kid Pix is an example of building, inventing, and creating that enhances student learning in multiple curricular areas.

Kid Pix was first released for Macintosh computers in 1989 and published by Brøderbund in 1991 as a paint program. It has since evolved into an online multimedia art studio with extensive features. In addition to being able to draw, paint, and make collages on the computer screen, you can import text and images from other files, add sound effects, resize images and other visual materials, record your voice, create a video, and build a slideshow. Young artists and animators use this software continuously to discover new ways to express their ideas creatively.

Much of what elementary school students do on a paper worksheet can be uniquely recreated in Kid Pix.

Kid Pix invites students to make their own books and posters illustrating math facts and concepts. To learn about numbers from 1 to 10 or beyond, kindergarten students can make slideshows of images they draw or print to show these numbers in entertaining displays. The stamp-creator function is a way to display addition, subtraction, multiplication, and division in action. Upper elementary school students can make charts and graphs, write and illustrate word problems, and show visual representations of fractions, decimals, and percentages, and then use Kid Pix to publish their work in slideshows, animations, videos, printed posters, or cartoons. The versatility of Kid Pix for showing one's ideas to others is greater than adults imagine until they see students exploring how many different tools are there for creating their projects. More web resources and apps for creativity are listed in Table 3.4.

Table 3.4 Web Resources and Apps for Creativity

Web
• ***The Bridge Designer by Stephen J. Ressler.*** Using this free educational software package, middle school and high school students try to design the least expensive bridge possible that will pass a simulated load test; users can test the viability of their designs online. Formerly known as the West Point Bridge Designer, this program was used in the West Point Bridge Design Contest from 2001 to 2016.
• ***Stone Soup magazine.*** This site provides a publishing venue for young writers of all ages.
• ***Poetry Writing with Jack Prelutsky, Scholastic.*** This online writing workshop is designed for young poets and features audio clips of the poets reading some of their poems in dramatic, engaging ways.
• ***Educational Uses of Digital Storytelling, University of Houston.*** This site explores strategies for digital storytelling, a form of creative expression produced by combining the art of storytelling with the multimedia tools of graphics, audio, video animation, and web publishing.
• ***Poetry 180: A Poem a Day for American High Schools, Library of Congress.*** Find poems for every day of the school year.
• ***National Day of Writing, National Council of Teachers of English.*** In this annual event, everyone from published authors to students in schools can create and share writing through digital media.
• ***Student Interactives, National Council of Teachers of English.*** This site offers activities for poetry and prose writing, language learning, and practicing organizing, summarizing, inquiry and analysis skills.
• ***Tuxpi.*** This simple online photo editor allows students to upload an image and turn it into art.
• ***BigHugeLabs.*** Students can create magazine covers, mosaics, movie posters, motivational posters, maps, badges, trading cards, and more using this image design tool. *Smithsonian Learning Lab* is a digital archive for more than a million images, recordings and texts that students and teachers can use to create and share their personal learning collections.
• ***Google Spotlight Stories.*** This site features storytelling in virtual reality with interactions between characters and readers.

Apps
• ***Harold and the Purple Crayon.*** In this app based on Crockett Johnson's classic picture book, children express their creativity as they draw Harold's world in purple colors.
• ***Verses.*** Users create magnetic poetry–style poems by arranging the words on the screen.
• ***Story Kit.*** Users build storybooks with pictures, text, drawings, and voices.
• ***Toontastic, Strip Designer, and Pixton.*** These apps allow students to create animated stories and short cartoons with spoken dialogue.
• ***Mindomo, Inspiration, and Kidspiration.*** Students build mind maps—diagrams composed of words, numbers, images, and other items organized around a key idea or problem.
• ***Tinkercad.*** An easy-to-use 3D modeling and design program for students from early elementary grades through high school; online tutorials guide users as they create imaginative designs, shapes and objects.
• ***Silk.*** Users manipulate ribbons of different-colored lights to make digital art and envision fantastical shapes, objects, and creatures.

> **My Lab Application Exercise 3.4:**
> Building Your PLN: Web Resources and Apps for Creativity
>
> **MyLab Education Self-Check 3.4**

UPT Learning 5: Becoming Digital Citizens

3.5 **Explain the meaning and importance of digital citizenship.**

The presence of digital technologies in every aspect of society has given rise to a new term, **digital citizenship**, and with it, a new role for schools in developing students' attitudes and skills as members of a digital society and a global world. Broadly speaking, digital citizenship means that young people become "critical consumers" and "constructive producers" of digital media and information while serving as "social advocates" for a better society (Barron, et al., 2014, p. 23). In schools, teaching digital citizenship means students learn how to use technology productively, honestly, and safely in their current and future lives.

Digital citizenship extends from the broader concept of citizenship, meaning membership and participation in a society or a country. In the United States, every American citizen has legal rights and social responsibilities. Legally, there are protections under the law—freedom of speech, freedom of worship, freedom from unreasonable search and seizure, freedom from unlawful arrest and punishment. Importantly, one person's rights do not include violating someone else's freedoms: "The most stringent protection of free speech would not protect a man falsely shouting fire in a theater and causing a panic," Supreme Court Justice Oliver Wendell Holmes, Jr., famously wrote in 1919.

Citizens have social responsibilities that accompany their individual rights and freedoms. Some responsibilities are mandatory—wage earners must pay taxes, and drivers must be licensed—whereas others are voluntary, such as voting in elections, participating in civic and community organizations, and conducting one's life according to broad ethical principles of honesty, fairness, and compassion.

Digital citizenship extends the rights and responsibilities of citizenship to a person's digital and online experiences. We all have personal freedoms in the digital realm, but those freedoms do not include infringing upon or blocking the rights of others. Just as falsely yelling "fire" in a crowded theater is not protected speech in a public space, an individual may not use technology to harass, intimidate, or otherwise violate the rights of others.

Although the law is still evolving, teachers have broad free speech rights when speaking or writing as private citizens. However, what teachers are allowed to say in the classroom is more limited (American Civil Liberties Union of Washington, 2016). Some school districts specifically prohibit teachers from discussing their personal opinions on political or religious matters in the classroom or on social media. A teacher who does so may face disciplinary action by the school district. Nor can a teacher post negative or derogatory comments about students or use individuals' names in such communications.

A digital citizen has guaranteed legal rights—a person's writing, photos, or graphic designs, when posted online, are subject to copyright protection. This means online users may not download copyrighted material, falsely present another

Digital Dialog 3.2

Digital citizenship means using technology honestly, safely, and in ways that promote the common good, but students often do not understand their responsibilities as users and creators of the information that appears in the digital world. As you think about the importance of teaching digital citizenship, comment and connect online about the following questions:

- In your view, what are a teacher's most effective strategies for leading students to be digital citizens in schools and other educational settings?
- Teaching about digital citizenship now begins in the elementary grades. What types of digital citizenship topics might be age-appropriately explored with elementary-age students?
- What specific steps are you planning to take as a teacher to develop digital citizenship among all students?

person's work as their own, or share confidential information without permission. At the same time, a digital citizen's responsibilities include using technology in safe, responsible, and ethical ways and rejecting exploitive or harmful online practices. Active participation and involvement are crucial to this view of digital citizenship for students. Each student contributes to the community while maintaining strong and committed interest in the principles of freedom, justice, equality, and democracy.

Elements of Digital Citizenship

Educator Mike Ribble (2015) has identified nine elements of digital citizenship that every student should know and organized them around three main parts of schooling—student learning, the school environment, and a student's life outside school (see Figure 3.4).

Teaching digital citizenship is now a required part of many school curricula to help students learn to use technology appropriately and creatively. For example, teachers do not want students copying information from a book or a website and failing to attribute the source, so they instruct students about standard procedures for crediting authors and incorporating quotes into text, and they provide strategies and practices to help students develop personal digital ethics that override the conveniences of copying and plagiarism.

Learning to be a digital citizen has multiple facets and ultimately depends on students voluntarily making the choices that teachers hope they will make in their use of technology. Telling students not to use technology inappropriately or punishing them when they do so is an insufficient approach to teaching digital citizenship. Negative warnings only tell students what not to do; they fail to show what students can or should do. Students need to experience approaches to digital citizenship that put them in roles in which they learn to use technology safely and responsibly. For example, students given responsibilities to create and maintain a class blog or wiki will need to learn about copyright laws and plagiarism because they wrote the material posted on their site. As writers, they see firsthand why copyright laws are designed to protect authors and their ideas. Avoiding plagiarism by acquiring a viewpoint and a style of voice in writing is a skill that students can and will practice if instructed how to do so from a writer's perspective.

Digital citizenship becomes integrated into school classrooms through experiences in which students are connected to the larger society. Community service learning and civic engagement projects are accessible, responsible, real-world ways to involve students with their communities. Students learn about technology by using technology with the guidance and leadership of teachers and adults in the community. The skills and ethics of digital citizenship need to be learned and practiced at every grade level

Figure 3.4 Elements of Digital Citizenship

SOURCE: Based on Ribble, M., & Bailey, G. (2011). *Digital citizenship in schools* (2nd ed.). Washington, DC: International Society for Technology in Education.

Student Learning and Academic Performance	**Access:** Equitable access to latest technologies
	Communication: Open and productive online exchanges of information
	Literacy: Understanding when and how to use digital technologies
School Environment and Student Behavior	**Security:** Actions to ensure personal safety and privacy
	Rights and Responsibilities: Personal rights, freedoms, and restrictions
	Etiquette: Appropriate conduct when using technology
Student Life Outside of the School Environment	**Commerce:** Fair and honest business practices online
	Health and Wellness: Understanding issues of personal health and well-being
	Law: Using technology legally and understanding legal restrictions

and in every subject, as teachers guide students through experiences with technology in both in-class and outside-of-school learning activities.

Digital citizenship learning is strengthened when children and adolescents are directly involved in setting rules about technology use while simultaneously learning strategies for safely using and critically evaluating online materials. Adults can also promote digital citizenship by utilizing parental software controls available on computers, smartphones, and tablets to disable the automatic installation of apps so each resource can be evaluated for its safety and privacy protections. Chapter 6 presents strategies for teaching students how to use the Internet as responsible and informed digital citizens.

Empowering Students to Use Technology Wisely

Teachers involving students in creating the rules for technology use is one democratic way for children and adolescents to learn the meaning and purpose of digital citizenship. In many schools, note educators David Schimmel and Leslie Stellman (2014), adults establish rules without input or participation from students. Sometimes those rules are enforced selectively, in authoritarian ways, where some individuals or groups receive harsher treatment than others. The effect of not including students in rule making is "to unintentionally teach many students to be nonquestioning, nonparticipating, cynical citizens in their classrooms, schools, and communities" (Schimmel, 2003, pp. 17, 18).

Schimmel suggests "collaborative rule making" by teachers and students as a way to promote citizenship education for elementary and secondary students. Only if students are invited into the process of discussing and deciding what rules should be in place will students become invested in them. In this collaborative approach, rules are not framed as imposed restrictions and limitations but as ways students learn about rights and responsibilities as citizens in a democratic society.

Including meaningful opportunities to regularly practice appropriate technology use in class is a second way for students to learn the ethics of digital citizenship. It is expected that teachers will tell students to quote sources, communicate respectfully, maintain personal privacy, and avoid distracting classmates. To get buy-in and enthusiasm for learning with those norms, authentic experiences that demonstrate the reasons for such rules are necessary if students are going to follow them repeatedly and respectfully.

For example, creating a website or blog where students in an English/language arts class can post original stories and poems gives everyone a personally meaningful framework for understanding the importance of copyright rules on the web. Similarly, students who have opportunities to present group projects to classmates experience firsthand the frustration of being ignored if members of the class use cell phones to text or surf the web instead of listening and participating in learning activities. As students create, teach, and publish online, they experience for themselves the importance of digital norms in their classroom and larger community lives.

Civic Engagement and Service Learning with Technology

Civic engagement and service learning projects are mutually beneficial ways for students to learn and practice the values of digital citizenship (National Task Force on Civic Learning and Democratic Engagement, 2012). There are resources for teaching digital citizenship in Table 3.5. **Civic engagement** refers to experiences that students have outside the classroom in which they work for the betterment or improvement of the community. **Service learning** refers to outside-the-classroom experiences that feature both *service* and *learning* in which students work to address community needs while learning and applying academic concepts and skills. For example, students volunteering at a local senior center or food bank are practicing civic engagement. And when those volunteer experiences are connected to academic topics such as the economics of rich and poor, the history of the community, and the stories of people's lives, service becomes a way for students to learn the school curriculum.

When teachers connect service learning and community engagement activities to specific curriculum learning standards, concepts come alive for students in ways that classroom-only learning does not. Students studying ecology in science see issues of sustainability more directly when they are engaged in recycling efforts in a school or community. Similarly, students learning about the U.S. political system understand the importance of elections and voting more directly when they participate in a community-based voter information initiative. Project Soapbox from the Center for Action Civics invites students to compose 2-minute-long speeches on issues important to local or national communities. Speeches can create awareness, propose solutions to problems, or issue calls to individual or collective action. Recording their speeches as videos or podcasts gives students the opportunity to expand the reach of their ideas.

Technology offers ways to enhance and extend civic and service projects in four areas related to this chapter's focus on unique, powerful, and transformative learning:

- *Personal self-reflection.* Student reflection, at the center of both civic engagement and service learning projects, makes sense of students' experiences through talking, writing, drawing, acting in plays or skits, or other means of self-expression. Indeed, an essential part of community experiences is what students learn about themselves as they examine their personal ideas and assumptions in light of new experiences. Word processing, digital photos, video, and other software programs give students engaging electronic tools to use in creating personally meaningful reflections about activities. These technologies enable student choice of many different ways to express their ideas and to learn from everyone's self-expressions.

- *Project documentation.* Technology offers creative ways to document the results of civic and service projects. Video cameras and smartphones enable teachers and students to record events as they happen in community settings. These photos and videos show the impact of projects, giving students ways to recall the experiences at a later time, a needed step in promoting thoughtful reflection about community involvement. Sharing videos, pictures, and reflections on a website or blog also gives the community access to the learning experiences.

- *Service projects in schools and communities.* Student-led cyber teams in schools can support technology use by teachers, other students, or community members. Students might work to integrate technology in classrooms or volunteer with community organizations to assist senior citizens or other individuals in using online resources. Social media also generates new learning as students perform and document their civic engagement/service learning activities. PBS education reporter John Merrow (2012) offers three examples: (1) students chart air quality or water quality measurements throughout the school year and share the results with students in other schools in the community, state, and nation; (2) students map local streets and neighborhoods to monitor littering and trash removal and share results with local officials; and (3) students participate in shared poetry projects by posting videos of their own poems read aloud for other classes to view. Projects can be more informal, such as a school where students post pictures of random acts of kindness on the school's Instagram account (Serico, 2014). In all these cases, students bring new ideas and relevant information to people through online networks, and in so doing, they become engaged members of their communities.

- *Apps for social change.* Apps for social change are emerging as a means of connecting service, engagement, technology, and digital citizenship. Designed for smartphones and tablets, social change–related apps focus on ways that students and community members can contribute to societal improvement and change. Socially responsible apps of note include SeeClickFix, which invites community members to report and monitor neighborhood issues, Catalista for accessing local volunteer opportunities, and Charity Miles, in which users raise money for worthy causes by walking, running, or biking. You can locate more apps by searching online using the keywords "apps for social change."

Table 3.5 Web Resources and Apps for Digital Citizenship

Web

- *American Memory, Library of Congress.* Materials are available from the library's collections under topics as wide-ranging as African American history, immigration and national expansion, religion, the presidency, and sports. A section titled "Today in History" features what happened historically for every day of the year. *America's Story from America's Library* offers short summaries of important people and events to engage students in learning about the past.
- *Civic Online Reasoning, Stanford History Education Group.* Free online learning activities are available for evaluating the reliability of websites and identifying false and misleading claims made on social media.
- *Project Soapbox, Mikva Challenge.* Students write and record two minute speeches about local, national and global issues that concern them; examples can be seen on the project's Vimeo channel.
- *Educational Games, Media Smarts: Canada's Centre for Digital and Media Literacy.* Online games teach students about exploitative marketing, bias, prejudice, netiquette, ways to authenticate information, cybersecurity, and other citizenship-related topics.
- *Media and Technology Resources for Educators, Common Sense Media.* Videos and interactive materials for teachers, families, and students address cyberbullying, digital creation and plagiarism, social networking, cell phone use, and commercialism in the media.
- *Digiteen Project/Digitween Project, Flat Connections.* This site features initiatives for resource and research sharing among global middle school and high school classrooms, as well as local school-based digital citizenship education projects.

Apps

- *Back in Time.* Available in six languages, this app presents a history of the universe and the evolution of life on Earth in a 24-hour clock. The Big Bang begins the first hour, and humans appear in the final second.
- *Today's Document from the National Archives.* An important historical document is posted every day.
- *Professor Garfield Cyberbullying.* Elementary school students learn strategies to deal with bullies.
- *BeSeen.* This app offers approaches for responsible social networking behavior by youth, including managing personal information online.
- *Flipboard, BBC News, and Circa News.* These apps compile the latest news from newspapers, websites, and Twitter and send them to your device; Circa lets you customize the content by selecting your own categories.

Learn more about civic and service initiatives, as well as ways to integrate technology, by visiting the websites of the National Service Learning Clearinghouse (NSLC) and the Community Works Institute. You can explore digital citizenship further in Chapter 6.

MyLab Education **Application Exercise 3.5:**
Building Your PLN: Web Resources and Apps for Digital Citizenship

MyLab Education **Self-Check 3.5**

Chapter Summary

Learning Outcome 3.1

Discuss how technology promotes critical thinking and problem solving.

- Online learning games, virtual worlds, and interactive simulations promote critical thinking and problem solving within the context of activities students find engaging and challenging.
- Rapid feedback from digital technologies supports students' curiosity and desire to learn independently without constant teacher direction.
- Technology can be used to create personalized learning by adjusting the pace and scope of learning to meet the needs of individual students.

Learning Outcome 3.2

Analyze the meaning and importance of digital literacies.

- Internet sites, search engines, and online encyclopedias give teachers and students unparalleled access to information, but students are not skilled at identifying useful and relevant sites and sources online.
- Information literacy includes the ability to locate, evaluate, and use information effectively. **Internet literacy** applies those skills to online information.
- Media literacy and visual literacy include the skills students need to read and assess many types of online visual presentations.

Learning Outcome 3.3

Examine how technology facilitates communication and collaboration.

- Online surveys, digital storytelling, online publishing, discussion boards, and wikis create new patterns of engagement and collaboration for students and teachers.
- Active learning (also called *inquiry-based* or *discovery* learning) refers to the direct involvement of students in educational activities.
- Digital learning involves integrating technology directly into how students learn writing and communication across the grade levels.
- Groupwork and cooperative learning are two ways to promote active learning in classrooms.

Learning Outcome 3.4

Identify how technology enables multiple expressions of creative thinking.

- Word processing, desktop publishing, design tools, digital cameras, digital videos, and podcasts support expressions of creativity by students and teachers.
- Computer pioneer Seymour Papert envisioned schools in which students use technology-based learning environments to express new ideas, create new approaches, and envision new solutions to problems.
- Visual thinking and concept mapping tools let teachers and students organize and outline their ideas visually on desktops, laptops, and tablets.
- Building, inventing, and visualizing tools enable students to engage in open-ended investigations of topics and items that interest them.
- Genius Hour and 20% time approaches create opportunities for new types of creative self-expression and interaction among students.

Learning Outcome 3.5

Explain the meaning and importance of digital citizenship.

- Digital citizenship includes the attitudes and skills students need to use technology creatively, effectively, and appropriately in today's society.
- Digital citizens—teachers and students alike—have rights and responsibilities in the areas of student learning and academic performance, school environment and student behavior, and student life outside the school.

Key Terms

Active learning, p. 63
Adaptive and intelligent tutoring systems (ITS), p. 57
Building, inventing and creating, p. 69
Civic engagement, p. 73
Cooperative learning, p. 65
Creativity, p. 66
Critical thinking, p. 53
Digital citizenship, p. 71
Digital literacy, p. 59
Digital writing, p. 64

Feedback, p. 56
Genius Hour, p. 69
Groupwork, p. 65
Immersive games, p. 53
Information literacy, p. 59
Internet literacy, p. 75
Media literacy, p. 60
Multimodal learning, p. 61
Multiuser virtual environments (MUVEs), p. 53
Non-immersive games, p. 53

Personalized learning, p. 56
Problem solving, p. 53
Reciprocal teaching, p. 60
Service learning, p. 73
20% time, p. 69
21st Century Student Outcomes for Learning, p. 52
Unique, powerful and transforming learning (UPT), p. 52
Visual thinking and concept mapping, p. 68

For Reflection and Discussion

To practice identifying websites, apps, and online tools for the five types of unique, powerful, and transforming learning, review the five types of UPT learning discussed in the chapter. Then, using the accompanying chart, research and add two additional websites or tablet or smartphone apps to each of the five types. As you research web resources and educational apps, choose those you imagine will be useful, either instructionally with students or professionally for developing your own knowledge. Identify those that have a point of interest and instant feedback and invite repeated use for new learning. Limit your search to a specific curriculum topic or include materials that may be useful across the curriculum.

Type of Transformative Learning	Web Resource	Educational App
Critical Thinking and Problem Solving		
Developing Digital Literacies		
Communication and Collaboration		
Creativity		
Digital Citizenship		

Technology's Impact on Teaching

Can digital technologies improve every part of the job of teaching in positive and productive ways? When might technology be unhelpful or even counterproductive? To explore these questions, brainstorm a list of teacher roles and responsibilities and consider how technologies might positively or negatively affect that work. Use the following chart to get started.

Work of a Teacher	Positive Role for Technology
Student record keeping	Online grading software makes record keeping easier.
Interactive learning experiences	Educational software, educational websites, digital cameras, and video resources involve students in learning.
What other areas would you add to the list?	

Work of a Teacher	Negative Role for Technology
Safety and security	Personal privacy can be violated; identity theft might occur.
Academic research	Students might plagiarize from online sources.
What other areas would you add to the list?	

Chapter 4
Designing Instruction with Technology

SOURCE: Rawpixel.com/Shutterstock

Chapter Overview

Chapter 4 discusses how teachers use technology to engage students, teach academic content, and assess student learning as integrated elements of the processes of instructional design and development. We begin by reviewing contemporary theories about learning, including the different approaches of behaviorists, cognitive scientists, and constructivists. Two learning activity development models—student learning objectives and Understanding by Design (UbD)—are explained. We stress the importance of teachers looking through students' eyes to develop learning activities that encourage engagement, participation, curiosity and self-directed learning by individuals and groups. The final section of the chapter introduces test-based, standards-based, and performance-based assessments of student learning. Step-by-step learning plans show ways to apply technology throughout the instructional design/lesson development process.

Focusing on instructional design, planning, and assessment, the chapter addresses the ISTE Standards for Educators of "Designer" and "Analyst." Both ISTE standards focus on ways for teachers to develop student-centered, digital-age learning experiences and instructional assessments.

Learning Outcomes

After reading this chapter, you will be able to:

4.1 Summarize research on the science of learning.

4.2 Compare student-centered and teacher-centered approaches to learning with technology.

4.3 Describe the elements of instructional design using technology, including standards-based content, teaching methods and materials, and student learning assessments.

4.4 Apply the instructional design process in two science learning plans.

Chapter Learning Goal

Integrate technology in planning, delivering, and evaluating learning experiences for students.

Featured Technologies

Instructional design tools	Student-to-expert communication websites
Research resources and apps	Real-time and recorded data websites
Assessment resources and apps	Archival and primary source websites
Grading and record-keeping software and apps	Skills/practice websites
Online academic curriculum standards	Exploration and discovery websites
Online rubrics	

A New Teacher Designs Curriculum

Shortly before starting student teaching at a middle school in her hometown, Christina was hired as a long-term, full-time substitute English teacher at a school in a neighboring town. The unexpected job offer happened rapidly. Christina turned in her application on Friday, was interviewed by the school principal Tuesday, was offered the position Thursday, and was told she would start work the Monday after that. Suddenly, instead of teaching part of the day as a student teacher, she was responsible for a full schedule of planning, instruction, and assessment every day.

Christina soon found that designing instruction for multiple classes was her biggest challenge. She could not create a successful class on the spur of the moment. Although she anticipated many occasions of joyful spontaneity and unexpected learning in the classroom, she realized concrete instructional plans and regular assessments of her students were paramount for success. She marveled at how veteran teachers in the school handled these responsibilities. "My mentor seems to know exactly what to do all the time," Christina remarked about a teacher who had assembled an extensive collection of teaching and learning resources she could implement quickly and smoothly. Years of teaching experience had facilitated the freedom to begin an activity, monitor student responses, and make adjustments as situations changed—all without appearing to have formally planned the action of the day.

When Christina asked her colleague about how she designed instructional activities, the teacher explained that she was constantly assessing learning, observing the effects of every one of her activities on each student's progress and using her observations to inform the next day's or week's plans. Technology, the teacher explained, was her go-to instructional design partner. To organize her ideas, she went online for academic content information, curriculum learning standards, and digital instructional planning templates. She kept notes about student questions on her iPad, and she used grade-keeping software to maintain information about student performance. Technology enabled her to create a broad vision of the curriculum and to sequence daily activities and ongoing student evaluations. Christina began doing the same, discovering links between technology and instructional design that she did not know existed. Soon Christina was using her school desktop and personal tablet in all her work, from planning learning activities to teaching classes to assessing student performance.

Like Christina, as a beginning teacher you too will enter the classroom without the background knowledge that constantly develops from having taught academic topics many times. Consequently, you will need instructional plans and student assessments, and you will need to write them down—both as broad outlines and as specific agendas of who is doing what with which materials. Plans and assessments are indispensable road maps that chart the course and direct the learning for students and teachers.

Designing instruction does not mean you must script every interaction or rigidly adhere to a fixed plan. Effective teachers provide room for spontaneity and time to explore questions and topics that are on students' minds. They recognize that well-designed classes retain structure and direction and that planning allows the leeway to vary an original design and then return to it according to the flow of the class.

In this chapter, we explore how to design instruction using technology, showing how the Internet and digital tools can support teachers in selecting academic content, planning activities, and assessing student learning. We contrast test assessments (also called traditional assessments) and performance assessments (also called alternative or authentic assessments). To consider technology's use in instructional design, focus on the following questions as you read the chapter:

1. What pivotal ideas about the science of learning do you need to know as a teacher?
2. How does technology offer ways for you to actively engage students with learning?
3. What are the essential elements of instructional design?
4. How can you design learning experiences that address standards, utilize the student learning objectives and Understanding by Design (UbD) approaches, and incorporate different ways to evaluate and assess student learning?

Research on the Science of Learning

4.1 Summarize research on the science of learning.

More than two decades ago, researchers from the National Academy of Sciences, National Academy of Engineering, Institute of Medicine, and National Research Council issued *How People Learn: Brain, Mind, Experience, and School,* a book designed to apply the latest research about the science of learning to the issues facing teachers and schools (Donovan & Bransford, 2000). Researchers subsequently completed separate volumes about how students learn history, science, and mathematics, as well as the impacts of culture and learning environments on people's understandings (Donovan & Bransford, 2004a, 2004b, 2004c). The latest book in the series is *How People Learn II: Learners, Contexts, and Cultures,* which incorporates recent research on what influences individual learning (National Academies of Science, Engineering, and Medicine, 2018).

Drawing on work in social psychology, cognitive psychology, anthropology, neuroscience, and technology, the *How People Learn* books explain that humans, from the youngest infants to adults of all ages, are "goal-directed agents who actively seek information" (Donovan & Bransford, 2000, p. 10). "The contemporary view of learning," called **constructivism**, "is that people construct new knowledge and understandings based on what they already know and believe" (Donovan & Bransford, 2000, p. 10; Piaget, 1968).

From the youngest ages, learners use what they already know to learn something new.

SOURCE: Samuel Borges/Fotolia

The initial *How People Learn* report was published at the beginning of education's technology revolution. Its constructivist vision established a framework for how technology can be used to transform the processes of teaching and learning in K–12 schools. At the core of constructivist thinking is the belief that learners construct meaning and knowledge for themselves. Learning does not imply passively receiving new information; substantive, lasting knowledge for a student is created and re-created through active minds-on, hands-on interactions with other people and with educational materials—this makes teachers and students partners in the process of knowledge construction (Costa & Kallick, 2014; Dean, et al., 2012). You can see an example of a constructivist approach to teaching and learning in this chapter's In Practice.

Constructivist Approaches to Learning

To illustrate a constructivist approach to learning, imagine you are teaching elementary school students how the planets revolve around the sun. Apart from simply telling or showing them the facts, how do you make this scientific knowledge important and understandable? Students' everyday experiences suggest that the opposite occurs—as they observe the sky, the sun seems to be moving while they and the earth seem to be standing still. Young students observe a similar phenomenon at night when the moon appears to follow their movements as they ride in a car or walk outside. The idea that the planet we call Earth is moving presents an intellectual and experiential challenge to what students think they know from their acquired knowledge as observant learners.

To start the process of building new conceptual understandings, a constructivist-oriented teacher might take students outside early in the morning on a sunny day and demonstrate how to trace with chalk the shadows of different-sized objects they find around the school's parking lot—signposts, a bench, and a fire hydrant—as well as the tallest and shortest students in the class. Then, in partners, the students trace each other, outlining their shoes first so they can stand in the same spot 1 hour later. When they finish the tracing, they write the time in the outline.

Returning to the same location throughout the day, the students repeat the shadow tracings with a different color of chalk and again record the time in the outline. At noon and on every hour during the afternoon, the class traces the changing shadows, each time using another color of chalk. The multicolored tracings display each shadow's movements and changes in size and shape. Shadows shrink as noon approaches but lengthen again as the afternoon progresses, and all shadows point in the same direction.

Over 3 or 4 days of on-the-hour tracing once in the morning, once at noon, and once more during the afternoon, the students discover that shadows mark the passage of time. The changing shapes in the same locations each day make an outdoor clock, a realization that is quite extraordinary. "So this is how time is measured," exclaimed one youngster. "This is like a sundial," said another. The youngsters are constructing their own new understandings based on the connections between what they are observing (shadows have different sizes and shapes at different times of the day) and something new they had not known (the movement of the planet throughout the day makes shadows change size and move west to east in the same way, day after day).

Learners' inner attention is gained through these experiences, and students wonder about the mysterious puzzle: "What is causing the movement of the shadows, and if it is the earth, why can't we feel the movement?" Answering the question will involve utilizing learning resources: reading the daily newspaper's weather page to track increasing or decreasing seasonal day lengths, spinning tops to simulate planets rotating in their orbits and revolving around the sun, setting up a light source to demonstrate stationary sunshine on a spinning globe revolving around the sun, viewing online simulations and a 24-hour day/night map, and asking students to draw their understanding of what they think is occurring.

To learn about the process of earth's rotation creating day and night, students measure shadows at different times of the day. Such active learning methods bring abstract science concepts to life through real-world observations and experiences.

SOURCE: Cheryl Casey/Fotolia

Walking Back in Time with Technology: A Constructivist Learning Activity

Grade Level	Featured Technologies
Elementary and middle school	Internet, video, and handheld technologies

Lesson Outline

Sharon's "Walking Back in Time with Technology" learning activity uses technology's unique capacities for multimodal and constructivist learning, integrating web, video, audio and interactive choices. Topics that are hard to visualize come to life onscreen, capturing students' attention and inspiring wonder. Digital tools offer learning opportunities that printed materials alone do not. They are open-ended and do not need to be sequential for learning.

The curricular goal of "Walking Back in Time with Technology" is to enable students to visualize vast numbers, learn the geologic time scale, and explore the fossil record of the 4.6 billion–year history of Earth. This interdisciplinary activity integrates standards and concepts from mathematics, science, language arts, social studies and information technology. It optimizes minds-on, hands-on student learning through whole group, small group and individual activities that culminate in constructing and publishing a project with classmates.

Students discover and construct new understandings by choosing one idea or topic and becoming a teaching source for that idea or topic. Choice is a core principal of constructivist teaching and learning. As students construct new knowledge through their own investigations and conversations, information becomes personally meaningful and lastingly remembered.

Teaching with Technology

The activity begins with students viewing online and print-based models of large numbers to visualize the 4.6 billion–year age of Earth. Starting with National Geographic's video, "How Big Is 7 Billion?" students record questions they have about huge numbers. Then they select their own reading choices from a collection of picture books and nonfiction texts that include *Is a Blue Whale the Biggest Thing There Is?*, *Millions, Billions & Trillions: Understanding Big Numbers; Count to a Million: 1,000,000, How Much is a Million?* and other choices. These books provide examples for students to see of how artists and authors construct models to conceptualize the size of a million and a billion—concepts that are difficult to imagine without reference points in our minds. After reading the picture books, students have answers to some of the questions they recorded. To answer others, they ask Siri or Google or go online to see what they can learn. It is amazing to learn that it would take an entire human lifetime for someone to count to a billion by ones and that a million seconds equals 0.032 years, but a billion seconds is 39.69 years.

"Walking Back in Time" continues with Sharon and the students going outside to construct a short-distance model, placing student-made markers on the ground at the points when different life forms appeared in the physical history of Earth. Using a mathematical framework contained in the picture book *Millions of Years Ago* by David Drew, one step equals 10 million years, and 456 steps equal the entire age of Earth. Students begin walking, stopping to mark the first human (½ step), last dinosaur (6 steps), first bird (8½ steps), first mammal (5 steps), first dinosaur (4 steps), first reptile (8 steps), first amphibian (5 steps), first fish (13 steps), first shellfish (5 steps), first jellyfish (10 steps), and first bacterial life (285 steps).

Sharon has a pedometer fitness tracker app on her smartphone to count the steps which she gives to a student. She also counts the steps aloud as students in the roles of documentary photographers and videographers take photos and videos with phones as others place markers on the ground to make the timeline of millions, then billions of years passing. Photos and videos are posted on the class website and class Instagram. Photos of the timeline are displayed in the classroom.

Continuing the activity inside the classroom with apps and online interactive sites, Sharon offers students a visual picture of life on Earth during different time periods in the past. In small groups with iPads, students explore the app, Back in Time, a multimodal resource of photos, videos, explanations, diagrams and information that generates interest by its array of ways to learn. With computers, an equally engaging journey through time is presented in the multilingual science site, Evolution, created by biologist and artist John Kyrk. It offers an interactive online exploration of the passage of time on Earth with links to photos, videos and resources that otherwise would require much teacher time to find and collate. These materials enable journeying back in time, viewing life on Earth eons and eons ago in unique and powerful ways. After review of these resources, students choose a question to ask and begin a study of information to answer it.

As a final assessment, students show what they know by creating interactive infographics, videos, songs with accompanying videos or hand drawn or made models of the topics they investigated. These projects are published and put on display with poems or paragraphs by students that creatively describe aspects of the passage of time since the beginning of the universe.

The students' shadow tracings attest to the importance of the constructivist principles of active learning and metacognitive thinking. Active learning means that students are physically and cognitively involved in the learning process, personally doing something to compare and contrast ideas and information rather than passively sitting as they listen to explanations, view videos, or read about a topic. Metacognitive thinking involves students becoming aware of how to recognize their thinking, a process also known as self-assessment or self-reflection, in which students increase their learning by showing what they know and identifying what they do not know.

Active Learning and Metacognitive Thinking

Active learning and metacognitive thinking have important implications for teaching constructively:

- Teachers must discover and work with the preexisting knowledge and understandings that each student brings to the learning.
- Teachers must teach subject matter in depth, providing many different examples and models of the same concept to construct a foundation of factual knowledge and personal understanding that makes new knowledge memorable.
- Teachers must integrate metacognitive skills into the curriculum in a variety of subject areas (Donovan & Bransford, 2000, pp. 19–21).

A social constructivist approach holds that students' learning develops over time through their individual lived experiences and their collaboration with teachers, families, peers, and communities (Vygotsky, 1978). As reading researcher Frank Smith observed in *The Book of Learning and Forgetting* (1998), students learn from the company they keep. Smith's observation reminds us that learning is a social process that occurs with and from others.

As they develop teaching skills and knowledge of instructional practices, new teachers incorporate a combination of constructivist principles and elements of the following learning theories:

- **Behaviorism** maintains that learning is a set of changes in human behavior created as a response to events in the environment (Skinner, 1965, 1976). Thus, learning is a process of memorizing, demonstrating, and imitating. The teaching implication is that learners should be provided with explicit and planned stimuli—what has been called drill-and-practice methods. Older-style computer instruction and some newer apps and software programs use this principle, presenting text and graphics carefully arranged, planned, and controlled by the machine, not by the learner. The primary objectives of such learning strategies are memory building and information recall. The teacher, or the machine and its software, is the source of knowledge.
- **Cognitivism** holds that learning is influenced by non-observable and internal constructs, such as memory, motivation, perception, attention, and metacognitive skills (Piaget, 1968). Thus, instruction must consider the effects of attention and perception and be based on individual learning needs and differences. Cognitivism often incorporates the "mind as a computer" metaphor in that humans take in information, organize and store it, and retrieve it when needed. Its focus is on program design and interaction and how learners share control of instruction with the technology. The primary objectives of such learning strategies are active transfer of learning, comprehension, and metacognitive skills. The teacher is the coach, facilitator, and partner, supported by technology. Virtual tutorials, online games, puzzles, and simulations in which students draw connections between new information and their mental schema (organizations of information in their minds) are examples of a cognitivist approach.
- **Constructionism**, a term created by computer pioneer Seymour Papert, emphasizes the idea that, as in constructivism, learners build their own knowledge from their ongoing physical experiences in the world (Harel & Papert, 1991). As summarized by two subsequent researchers, constructionism holds that "children don't *get* ideas; they *make* ideas (Resnick, 2017, p. 37). Constructionism is a

decisive contrast to what Papert calls "instructionism" in schools. When students use an adult-created software program, it is an instructional activity, but when students envision and create their own learning games, construction of knowledge happens. Youngsters will invest more time, energy, inner and outer attention, and meaning in knowledge they create for themselves.

Although learning theories are not explicitly identified or referred to in daily instructional plans, the principles of constructivism, behaviorism, cognitivism, and constructionism guide teachers' thinking about curriculum, instruction, and assessment. As you enter the classroom and begin teaching, you will undoubtedly base your instructional approaches and students' use of technology on elements of different learning theories. Technology is a tool that can support your choice of approaches for teaching and learning.

> **MyLab Education Self-Check 4.1**

MyLab Education
Video Example 4.1
In this video, you will observe how the use of technology shifts teaching and learning of math and science. What do you see as the primary educational benefits of real-world learning with technology?

Student-Centered Learning with Technology

4.2   Compare student-centered and teacher-centered approaches to learning with technology.

The new science of learning presents an opposite model to the way teaching occurs in many elementary and secondary schools. This is the difference between teacher-centered and student-centered approaches to teaching and learning. These methodologies have many versions and variations; their central assumptions are summarized in Table 4.1.

Teacher-Centered and Student-Centered Approaches

For more than a century, the predominant teaching method in American schools has featured teachers at chalkboards lecturing and students reading textbooks, completing worksheets, and taking multiple-choice tests and quizzes (Cuban, 2018, 2013, 2009; Cremin, 1988). These instructional practices are called *teacher-centered* (or transmission teaching)—meaning the major focus and energy of a class flows from the teacher to the students.

Teacher-centered instructional methods convey information to students who are expected to learn and use it. In this view, "knowledge is conceived as discrete facts commonly understood by everyone, and knowledge is fixed, something we can all point to and understand in the same way" (Coppola, 2004, p. 19). The goal of the teacher is to "instruct" in the most efficient and effective ways possible so that students will learn the information.

Table 4.1 Contrasting Approaches to Learning

Teacher-Centered Approaches	Student-Centered Approaches
A view that learning is hard	A view that learning is a natural process
Beliefs that some students will learn and others will not	Beliefs that everyone can learn with different methods and materials
Learning happens best when content is presented in small units of instruction	Learning happens best when content is integrated into real-world problem-solving tasks and activities
More whole-group instruction than small-group and one-on-one instruction	More small-group and one-on-one instruction than whole-group instruction
Seatwork by individual students	Cooperative learning and group projects
Discussions focusing on factual recall answers	Class activities and discussions considering many possible solutions to problems
Assessments based largely on worksheets, quizzes, and tests	Assessments based largely on students' projects, performances, presentations and portfolios

Student-centered instructional methods feature students as active participants in all elements of classroom lessons. Students conduct activities and experiments, engage in discussions, and participate in assessing their learning. The goal of student-centered instruction is for teachers and students to work together to investigate problems, pose solutions, and reflect on what they are learning. In student-centered instruction, teachers "stop seeing themselves as curriculum *deliverers* and start seeing themselves as curriculum *creators*" (Wolk, 2008, p. 122).

Student-centered approaches build classroom learning upon the active engagement of students with academic material and real-life situations. Based on a central assumption of constructivist and constructionist approaches, teachers seek to raise questions about students' taken-for-granted and unexamined beliefs and assumptions. As students encounter and work to resolve questions and puzzles, they incorporate new knowledge and understandings into their views and values. The goal of the teacher is to create situations in which students participate in minds-on problem solving and thoughtful reflection about academic experiences. You can explore different types of student-centered websites and apps in Tech Tool 4.1.

Tech Tool 4.1

Types of Educational Websites and Apps

In developing classroom curriculum activities, teachers need access to online digital content that supports student-centered learning. There are thousands and thousands of **educational websites** and **educational apps** developed by colleges and universities, historical and scientific organizations, museums, government agencies, nonprofit organizations, for-profit companies, classroom teachers, and independent researchers. The best of these digital materials offer inquiry-based curricular resources for teachers and creative learning activities for students. For teachers, educational websites are essential tools in creating engaging classroom learning activities for students. These resources enable teachers to a) see how other educators have organized academic content learning for students; b) view models of classroom activities that incorporate focus, curiosity, and self-propelled learning into classroom activities; and c) develop multiple ways to assess student learning outcomes.

To locate materials that will address standards and engage students, you will benefit from a system that organizes the academic content available online. With that goal, we have selected the following six types of websites and apps based on a framework originally proposed by the Center for Innovation in Engineering and Science Education (CIESE) at the Stevens Institute of Technology in New Jersey (2002), to which we added two categories based on our experiences. As you use each category, look for information that is up to date, factually accurate, and presented multimodally through text, audio, video, photos, charts, graphs and interactive simulations or exercises. Interactively engaging sites and apps support students in exploring information on their own and learning through asking questions and doing focused inquiries.

The six types of educational websites and apps include:

Planning and assessment websites and apps offer teaching and assessment plans with step-by-step methods and procedures. Many feature links to interactive activities

or additional resources and curriculum extensions. Students can use these sites as part of classroom activities, their own study resources, or homework assignments. Read/Write/Think from the National Council of Teachers of English (NCTE), Illuminations from the National Council of Teachers of Mathematics (NCTM), teAch-nology.com, and the California Academy of Sciences are examples of planning and assessment websites and apps.

Student-to-expert communication websites and apps feature exchanges of ideas and information between students in K–12 schools and adult experts in colleges, museums, businesses, and other organizations. Ask Dr. Math, Ask Dr. Universe, Ask an Earth Scientist, and Ask Smithsonian are examples of student-to-expert communication websites and apps. Using these sites, K–12 students can formulate questions to send to experts in the field and then receive replies electronically. Students can access experts presenting their ideas online by viewing resources such as TED Talks or listening to TED Radio Hour podcasts. Student-to-expert websites also include telementoring, videoconferencing, and e-tutoring activities. Telementoring often involves students learning about career opportunities from professionals in different fields, whereas e-tutoring focuses on help with homework and class projects.

Real-time and recorded data websites and apps include information about scientific, governmental, economic, and mathematical topics. Rutgers University Coastal Ocean Observation Lab (RUCOOL), HubbleSite from the Hubble Space Telescope, statistics about the world from Worldometers, and iNaturalist are examples of real-time and recorded data websites and apps. Like virtual field trips, real-time and recorded data sites provide opportunities for students to enter a setting as involved observers, learning about science or other subjects as if they were physically present at a remote location.

Teachers

The Library of Congress offers classroom materials and professional development to help teachers effectively use primary sources from the Library's vast digital collections in their teaching.

Find Library of Congress lesson plans and more that meet Common Core standards, state content standards, and the standards of national organizations.

Search Our Classroom Materials by Standards ○ Common Core ○ State Content ○ Organizations

Classroom Materials

Civics Interactives
Congress, Civic Participation, and Primary Sources projects

Teaching World War I with Primary Sources
Idea Book for Educators from HISTORY

Alexander Hamilton
Primary Source Set

Baseball Across a Changing Nation
Primary Source Set

Archival and primary source websites and apps allow students to conduct historical investigations by accessing primary and archival source materials from museums, libraries, and other organizations. The Library of Congress, the Smithsonian, the Gilder Lehrman Institute of American History, and the Digital Public Library of America are examples of archival and primary source websites and apps. Some sites provide mostly static informational materials; others offer activities that guide students in the use of the materials. These sources include print-based materials as well as online images, photographs, and video.

Concept/skills practice websites and apps offer subject-specific review and practice activities for students at all grade levels. Khan Academy, the National Library of Virtual Manipulatives (NLVM), and PhET Science Simulations are examples of concept and skills practice websites and apps. Many teachers use these sites as learning tools, assigning small groups to classroom computers while the teacher works directly with other students.

Exploration and discovery websites and apps provide opportunities for students to engage in online explorations of topics of interest. OLogy, Pixar in a Box, Molecular Workbench, Visible Body: Human Anatomy, and National Geographic Kids are examples of exploration and discovery websites and apps. These sites feature interactivity, self-correcting, never-dull learning, and exploratory appeal. Students do not passively read or view online material; they respond to it through interactive learning activities using critical and creative thinking.

MyLab Education **Application Exercise 4.1:**
Exploring Educational Websites and Apps

Locating High-Quality Websites and Apps

Locating high-quality, student-centered materials within the vastness of the Internet is not easy given the amount of material available in any subject area. More than 20 years ago, Seymour Papert, co-inventor of the computer programming language Logo, concluded one way to identify high-quality software is to recognize its opposite. In Papert's view, low-quality software has three main characteristics: 1) the computer dictates the activity; 2) competition, stereotyping, or violence is present; and 3) quick reactions are favored over sustained thinking and problem solving (1996, pp. 55–56). In deciding which software to buy for learning, Papert believes adults should first answer the following question: "Will the child program the computer or will the computer program the child?" (1996, p. 56).

Evaluating software, websites, and apps is essential to understanding what happens when students use them. Computers can become infected with **badware**, a type of invasive software that fundamentally disregards a user's choice or control over how their devices will be used. Also known as adware, malware, spyware, and stealth dialers, badware enters people's devices without their knowledge and disrupts normal operations by allowing pop-up ads, redirecting web searches, working against anti-spyware programs, and modifying other functions to make it easier for commercial product ads and other unwanted images to appear on the user's screen. StopBadware is a nonprofit software consumer watchdog organization with corporate support from companies like Google and Mozilla. It serves as a "neighborhood watch campaign" whose goal is to identify and negate destructive, manipulative, or unscrupulous software that can harm people and machines. (Consumer Reports WebWatch is an unpaid special advisor to the organization.)

Numerous other organizations have online resources to assist teachers in selecting the best software, websites, and apps.

- **Common Sense Media.** In 2012, the San Francisco–based nonprofit organization Common Sense Media launched its Learning Ratings Initiative to inform teachers, families, and students about the learning potential of websites, video games, and mobile apps. Sites, games, and apps are evaluated for age-appropriateness and academic content with outcomes rated on a scale of best, good, fair, or not for learning. Highly rated programs feature active engagement, learning centered on concepts and deep understanding, helpful feedback, and support for extended experiences.

- **Edudemic.** This website offers reviews for a wide selection of educational technology resources, including laptops, mobile phones, tablets, mobile apps, and web-based tools. Reviews and ratings are contributed by users of the website.

- **Entertainment Software Rating Board (ESRB).** Established in 1994, ESRB is an independent evaluation group that assesses and rates new pieces of software every year. Like the ratings that accompany motion pictures, ESRB symbols provide buyers with a way to determine the appropriate age level of a program using six basic categories: EC (Early Childhood, ages 3 and up); E (Everyone, ages 6 and up); E10+ (Everyone 10 and Older, ages 10 and up); T and Older (Teen, ages 13 and up); M (Mature, ages 17 and up); and AO (Adults Only, ages 18 and up). There is also a Rating Pending designation for software that is currently under review.

- **Webby Awards.** Sponsored by the International Academy of Digital Arts and Sciences, Webbys honor outstanding work in website design and development; the award categories most relevant to teachers are education, family/parenting, politics, science, art, and social activism.

- **American Association of School Librarians (AASL).** Every year, the AASL produces a listing of the "Best Websites for Teaching and Learning" and "Best Apps for Teaching and Learning," including awards in multiple categories: organizing and managing, content resources, curriculum collaboration, media sharing, digital storytelling, social networking, and communication.

- **Websites for Educators.** Educational weblinks are maintained by the Gutman Library at the Harvard University Graduate School of Education.

- **Online Tools for Teaching and Learning.** This database of digital tools for enriching teaching and learning was designed and updated by undergraduate and graduate students at the UMass Amherst College of Education. Each tool page features a tool snapshot with an overview of privacy, cost, accessibility, ease of use, learning theory, and ISTE Standard addressed, as well as tutorials for learning how to use the tool, examples of using the tool in different subjects and at different SAMR levels, and related research articles.

MyLab Education Self-Check 4.2

Elements of Instructional Design

4.3 Describe the elements of instructional design using technology, including standards-based content, teaching methods and materials, and student learning assessments.

MyLab Education
Video Example 4.2
In this video, an elementary class and teacher are engaged in a science activity identifying insects in a game using the whiteboard. What does the white board provide in the learning that interests students? From 4:54–6:05.

Instructional design refers to all the activities that teachers do to create, teach, and evaluate learning activities with students. In designing learning for students, teachers make decisions about three interrelated elements of classroom instruction (see Figure 4.1):

- Academic content (what to teach)
- Teaching goals, methods, and procedures (how to teach)
- Learning assessments (how to know what students have learned).

Instructional design answers the content, methods, and assessment questions faced by every teacher deciding what to do academically and instructionally during the school week. These lesson development decisions are part of what gives teaching its immense joy—the process of continually creating new learning experiences for students—and its intrinsic frustrations—the reality that there is always more academic content to teach than time to teach it.

Every teacher is an instructional designer, responsible for organizing, delivering, and assessing learning activities with students in the classroom. Designing lessons combines teaching and learning, the two interconnected dimensions of every educational experience. Teaching refers to the work of a teacher, and learning refers to the actions of a student, although in a class setting more than one adult often has instructional responsibilities, and many students collectively are the learners.

Every instructional activity can be seen from the perspective of either teacher or student. As shown in the left-hand side of Figure 4.2, every teacher makes decisions about what instructional practices or pedagogical approaches to use in a lesson. These approaches achieve high impact (they make a real difference) when they feature multiple media that engage students in problem-solving and inquiry-based activities.

Figure 4.1 Elements of Lesson Development

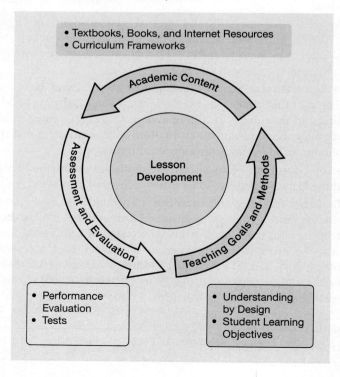

Figure 4.2 Teaching and Learning in Classrooms

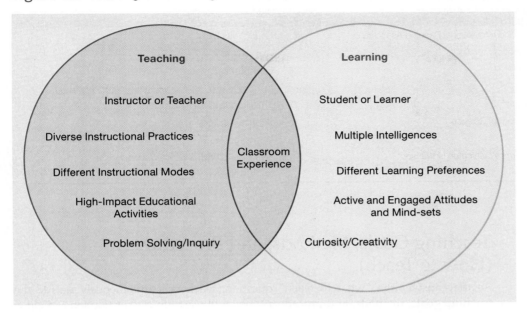

However, a teacher does not make these choices in isolation. The right-hand side of Figure 4.2 shows that teacher activities are focused on students who bring different learning preferences to every lesson. Teachers seek to create experiences in which students use their natural creativity and curiosity to propel learning. Effective lesson development thus always encompasses both the teacher and student view of the classroom experience.

Academic Content (What to Teach)

Every time they teach, teachers make choices about **academic content**—the facts, concepts, ideas, skills, and understandings they intend to share with students. This is the "what to teach" choice facing every teacher. School system guidelines, state and national curriculum frameworks, and the Common Core State Standards mainly define—and in some cases mandate—what academic content will be taught. However, because no local or national standard spells out everything to teach about any given topic, classroom teachers must choose what will be explored by and discussed with students each day.

Before computers and the Internet, teachers answered the "What do I teach today?" query by working with other teachers, consulting school curriculum guides, reading professional books and journals, and gathering materials from libraries and school resources. Today, teachers have online access to detailed and proven teaching and learning materials whose resources provide ongoing lesson development ideas for every teaching situation. Digital content available on the Internet includes a vast collection of curriculum resources and information. Using Internet search engines, online databases and encyclopedias, blogs, wikis, and other technology tools, teachers and students gain access to multiple ways to research and retrieve information.

Professional educational organizations (such as the National Council of Teachers of English or the National Science Teachers Association), as well as colleges, universities, museums, foundations, and media groups, maintain subject-specific websites in English/language arts, humanities, mathematics, arts, geography, economics, history, science, family literacy, and many other topics (see Table 4.2). These storehouses include curriculum ideas and standards-based instructional plans, arranged by grade level and subject matter and searchable by keywords.

Table 4.2 Subject Area Teaching and Learning Resources

Educational Organization	Website Name
National Council of Teachers of English and International Reading Association	Read/Write/Think
National Council of Teachers of Mathematics	Illuminations
National Endowment for the Humanities	EDSITEment
National Geographic Society	Xpeditions and National Geographic Education
Smithsonian Museum of American History	Smithsonian's History Explorer
American Association for the Advancement of Science	Science NetLinks
National Center for Family Literacy	Wonderopolis
Center for History and New Media, George Washington University	National History Education Clearinghouse
National Science Teachers Association	NGSS@NSTA

Teaching Goals, Methods, and Procedures (How to Teach)

As they answer the "what to teach" question, teachers simultaneously decide the **teaching goals, methods, and procedures** they will use with classes (Larson & Keiper, 2012). *Goals* are the reasons a lesson is being taught. *Methods* are the instructional strategies teachers use to convey academic content to students—large groups or small groups, discussions, lectures, role-plays, simulations, case studies, inquiry-based activities, creative writing, learning and reflection journals, drill-and-practice exercises, design projects, online tutors, or learning games. *Procedures* are the scheduling and grouping of students by teachers during a lesson along with the decision of how much time to spend on each activity.

Teachers combine goals, methods, and procedures into formats for daily learning. Sometimes curriculum content dictates these formats; sometimes the goals, methods, and procedures dictate the choice of content. Either way, content, goals, methods, and procedures mutually support each other in a dynamic instructional design process. Technology enhances teaching goals, methods, and procedures in a variety of ways by offering the following:

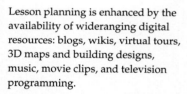

Lesson planning is enhanced by the availability of wideranging digital resources: blogs, wikis, virtual tours, 3D maps and building designs, music, movie clips, and television programming.

SOURCE: Annie Fuller/Pearson Education

- Presentation software
- Visual thinking tools
- Infographic, diagram, and chart-making tools
- Website and multimedia production tools and apps
- Threaded online discussions, social media, and e-mail
- Blogs, wikis, and podcasts

- Interactive software
- WebQuests and HyperDocs
- Intelligent tutoring systems
- Digital cameras and video-making software and apps
- Assistive technologies.

One way to begin to infuse technology into your teaching goals is to use Allan Carrington's Pedagogy Wheel, a graphic organizer that combines several different domains of pedagogical thinking from Bloom's taxonomy with popular technology apps and suggests the specific educational purposes they can provide. Teachers can design their pedagogical goals and teaching activities by using the Bloom's taxonomy domains and Substitution, Augmentation,

Modification, Redefinition (SAMR) areas on the grid. Subcategories within each area suggest action verbs, activities, and apps, along with the capabilities and attributes the learners will acquire by the end of the lesson or activity. The SAMR approach is discussed more fully in Chapter 5.

Learning Assessments (Knowing What Students Have Learned)

Learning assessments occur before, during, and after instructional activities, and enable teachers to evaluate student knowledge, understanding, and performance. These can be **summative assessments** (summarizing what students have learned at the end of a lesson), **formative assessments** (happening as a lesson unfolds), or diagnostic assessments (preceding a lesson to measure what students already know). The purpose of these learning assessments is to help teachers determine who is learning easily and confidently and who needs individualized assistance, differentiated teaching methods, or alternative learning experiences.

Five interconnected factors contribute to how teachers think about assessment:

1. *Personal experiences being assessed.* Teachers tend to teach the way they were taught and assess the way they were assessed. Beginning teachers must unlearn the impulse to make lecturing their predominant mode of instruction. Similarly, teachers who took many multiple-choice tests and quizzes throughout elementary, middle, and high school often assume these tests are the best way to measure students' learning. Teachers may not readily envision using portfolios, creative writing, groupwork, daily conversations, or other performance assessment tools with students if these techniques were not part of their own experiences as K–12 or college students.

2. *Standardized testing.* A steep rise in **standardized testing** began with passage of the 2001 federal No Child Left Behind (NCLB) law, which requires all states to have a student learning assessment test. Students in states who have adopted the Common Core State Standards take one of the following tests: Partnership for Assessment of Readiness for College and Careers (PARCC), Smarter Balanced Assessment Consortium (SBAC), or a state-developed exam. Standardized testing is an enormous enterprise in this country. FairTest, a testing industry watchdog group, estimates that 100 million standardized tests are administered annually to K–12 students. Students take tests from kindergarten through high school, in some districts as often as twice a month, totaling as many as 20 different assessments a year (Center for American Progress, 2014). To learn more, consult *Education Week* magazine's yearly survey of state testing practices.

3. *High-stakes tests.* Exams where grade-level promotion or school graduation depends on achieving a passing score are considered to be **high-stakes tests**. Elementary school children take yearly tests in reading, writing, mathematics, and speech and language; middle and high school students have ongoing tests of their language arts, mathematics, science, and history proficiencies. With the amount of time required for preparation and administration, testing is a contentious issue. Some parents and teachers worry that students are being over-tested while learning experiences are shrinking; others contend that well-constructed test assessments provide essential information about individual learning progress while promoting higher standards for all, regardless of youngsters' differences of language or family income. In a climate of test score accountability, teachers may conclude that the only assessments of consequence are those that rank students according to numerical scores on local, state, and national exams. There is evidence that the testing landscape is changing. In 2017, FairTest reported the following impacts of assessment reform campaigns on national high-stakes testing:

   - States with high school exit exams dropped from 25 to 13 since 2012, while various states cut tests for kindergarten as well. Districts across the nation, including locales with many students of color and low-income families, ended their tests.
   - Seven states halted the use of student scores to judge teachers.
   - Ten states now allow parents to opt their children out of some or all exams.

MyLab Education

Video Example 4.3

In this video, a teacher describes how she conducts assessments of student learning by listening to and talking with students while they are engaged in a class activity. How many different assessment ideas do you plan to use when you are evaluating the learning of students?

- Increasing implementation of performance assessments by states and districts. New Hampshire's pioneering program now involves half the state's districts (FairTest, 2017).

4. *Teacher tests.* Tests for teachers contribute to how teachers think about assessment. Most states require new teachers to pass a test before they earn a teaching license. Many states use Praxis, an exam developed by the Educational Testing Service (ETS), whereas other states use customized teacher exams from Pearson Education. The goal of teacher tests is to ensure that anyone receiving a license to teach has the competencies needed to do the work, as demonstrated by passing scores in reading, writing, and knowledge of academic content fields. New teachers might assume that students must be assessed in the ways they themselves were assessed and that passing a standardized test is the only truly valid assessment format.

5. *Misconceptions about assessment.* Many new teachers focus attention on choosing academic content and designing engaging learning experiences (because both seem paramount to planning lessons) while assessment is left until the activity's completion. We see this pattern repeated over and over as beginning teachers submit plans containing engaging instructional ideas but underdeveloped or misconceived methods for assessment. Not surprisingly, new teachers are unsure about or unaware of ways they might assess students' learning as part of teaching activities.

Assessment can be done using multiple-choice and short answer tests, essays and other written tasks, oral discussions, teacher observations and conversations, students teaching each other, class participation, and student-made projects, portfolios, and performances—all of which provide evidence of what students have learned and are able to do. Technology tools available to support the assessment and evaluation process include the following:

- Online tests, trivia games, and quizzes
- Grade-keeping software and learning management systems
- Digital portfolios and design tools
- Student response systems
- Online surveys
- Learning performance rubrics.

MyLab Education Self-Check 4.3

Instructional Design in Action: Two Science Learning Plans

4.4 Apply the instructional design process in two science learning plans.

To illustrate the process of instructional design using technology, we present case studies of two science learning activities: "Ecological Footprints" for high school and "Rainscapes Show the Water Cycle" for elementary school. Each demonstrates ways to use technology to address the "what to teach," "how to teach," and "how to know what students have learned" questions.

Ecological Footprints: A High School Biology Learning Activity	Rainscapes Show the Water Cycle: An Elementary School Science Learning Activity
This learning activity shows students the impact that modern lifestyles, including their own, exert on environmental resources. Every group of people leaves a lasting impact on the environment through natural resource consumption and waste accumulation—their "ecological footprint." As students research environmental and ecological issues online and document their personal ecological footprints, they can assess the current and potential future impact of human lifestyles on the world's natural resources. The lesson challenges every student to identify ways to live on the planet without harming it.	This learning activity introduces students in grades 1 through 6 to the water cycle (also known as the hydrologic cycle), including the science concepts of evaporation, transpiration, condensation, and precipitation. These processes are essential to life on Earth, which is possible because of the presence of freshwater. By studying the water cycle using online resources and videos as well as hands-on science experiments, children see demonstrations of how water is naturally recycled from Earth's surfaces to the atmosphere and back again, changing from liquid to gas and back to liquid.

Identifying Curriculum Frameworks and Learning Standards

Curriculum frameworks and learning standards guide teachers in choosing what academic content to teach. Virtually every academic discipline taught in elementary and secondary schools has national, state, and local standards for teachers to follow in planning their curriculum (see Table 4.3 for a list of national curriculum standards for the major subjects taught in K–12 schools).

Most national standards are issued by a **discipline-based professional organization** such as the National Council of Teachers of English (NCTE), the National Council of Teachers of Mathematics (NCTM), or the National Association for the Education of Young Children (NAEYC). The goal of professional organizations is to support educators at all levels in teaching academic subjects to students. Many professional organizations have also issued position statements affirming the centrality of technology in their teaching field; for example, "Strategic Use of Technology in Teaching and Learning Mathematics" from the National Council of Teachers of Mathematics (2015) or "Beliefs for Integrating Technology into the English Language Arts Classroom" from the National Council of Teachers of English (2018).

The curriculum frameworks most directly applicable to the "Ecological Footprints" and "Rainscapes" lessons are the Next Generation Science Standards from the National Science Teachers Association, ISTE Standards for Students, and

Table 4.3 National Curriculum Standards for Major Academic Subjects

Teaching Field	Professional Organization	National Standards for Teachers
English/language arts and mathematics	National Governors Association and Council of Chief State School Officers (CCSSO)	Common Core State Standards
Computer science	Computer Science Teachers Association International Society for Technology in Education (ISTE)	K–12 Computer Science Standards ISTE Standards for Computer Science Educators
English	National Council of Teachers of English (NCTE)/International Reading Association (IRA)	Standards for the English Language Arts
Science	National Science Teachers Association (NSTA)	Next Generation Science Standards (NGSS)
Mathematics	National Council of Teachers of Mathematics (NCTM)	Principles and Standards for School Mathematics
Social studies	National Council for the Social Studies (NCSS)	National Curriculum Standards for Social Studies: A Framework for Teaching, Learning, and Assessment
Elementary education	Association for Childhood Education International (ACEI)	Elementary Education Standards
Early childhood education	National Association for the Education of Young Children (NAEYC)	The 10 NAEYC Program Standards
Foreign languages	American Council on Teaching of Foreign Languages (ACTFL)	World-Readiness Standards for Learning Languages
Special education	Council for Exceptional Children (CEC)	Special Educator Professional Preparation Standards
English as a second language	Teachers of English to Speakers of Other Languages (TESOL)	TESOL/CAEP Standards for P–12 Teacher Education Programs
Dance, media arts, music, theater, and visual arts	National Coalition for Core Arts Standards (NCCAS)	National Core Arts Standards
Health/physical education	American Alliance for Health, Physical Education, Recreation, and Dance (AAHPERD)/American Association for Health Education (AAHE)/Society of Health and Physical Educators (SHAPE)	National Health Education Standards National Standards & Grade Level Outcomes for K–12 Physical Education
Gifted and talented education	National Association for Gifted Children	National Standards in Gifted and Talented Education
Sexuality education	American Association for Health Education/American School Health Association/National Education Association Health Information Network/Society of State Leaders of Health and Physical Education	National Sexuality Education Standards: Core Content and Skills, K–12
Reading	International Reading Association (IRA)	Standards for Reading Professionals
Educational computing and technology	International Society for Technology in Education (ISTE)	ISTE Standards for Educators and Students
Social justice	Teaching Tolerance	Social Justice Standards

Figure 4.3 Common Core Science and Technical Subjects Standards for Two Science Learning Activities

Ecological Footprints	Rainscapes
Follow precisely a multistep procedure when carrying out experiments, taking measurements, or performing technical tasks. Compare and contrast the information gained from experiments, simulations, video, or multimedia sources with that gained from reading a text on the same topic. Determine the meaning of symbols, key terms, and other domain-specific words and phrases as they are used in a specific scientific or technical context relevant to grades 9–12 texts and topics.	Follow precisely a multistep procedure when carrying out experiments, taking measurements, or performing technical tasks. Compare and contrast a firsthand and secondhand account of the same event or topic; describe the differences in focus and the information provided. Interpret information presented visually, orally, or quantitatively (e.g., in charts, graphs, diagrams, timelines, animations, or interactive elements on webpages) and explain how the information contributes to an understanding of the text in which it appears.

SOURCE: Common Core State Standards. Retrieved from http://www.corestandards.org/ELA-Literacy/.

the Common Core State Standards for Science and Technical Subjects (see Figure 4.3). Environmental topics are also included in the framework of the National Council for the Social Studies (NCSS).

In planning what to teach, many teachers list the ideas, information, and skills they want students to learn. In every case, there are questions about what to include and what to omit from any list, stemming from the reality that there is so much information in every curriculum area that students potentially need to learn. Every teacher must make decisions about what topics to explore in detail, what to teach broadly, and topics to mention in passing. Student needs and interests, available time, and accessible materials influence teacher decisions. But even after choosing topics that are grade-level appropriate, there is still more material to teach than there is time to teach it.

National curriculum standards and the Common Core focus the "what to teach" question on specific topics and skills but leave considerable discretion about how to teach that content. State and local frameworks may direct you to specific resources, but you will still have to make decisions about what academic content to emphasize and which teaching methods to use in class. And as you make these decisions, you will also need to consider the third essential aspect of lesson development: learning assessments.

Choosing an Approach to Lesson Development

Teachers' goals, methods, and procedures determine the structure of learning for whole-group, small-group, and one-on-one instruction. Organizing goals, methods and procedures into instructional activities for students is known as lesson or learning planning, and more broadly, **lesson development**. Lesson development typically follows one of two approaches: student learning objectives or Understanding by Design (UbD).

Digital Dialog 4.1

Almost every school district uses curriculum standards and frameworks to guide teaching and learning at every grade level. Local standards are often based on the national standards listed in Table 4.3. After reviewing the national standards for the subject and grade level you plan to teach, connect and comment online about the following questions:

- How do you think educational standards can support your work as a teacher?
- What elements of the day-to-day work of a teacher are not addressed in the standards?
- As a matter of educational policy, do you think that teachers should be required to follow common national standards or standards set at the state or local level? What are the classroom implications of each of these policies?

Figure 4.4 Student Learning Objectives for Two Science Learning Activities

Ecological Footprints	Rainscapes
Student Learning Objectives	**Student Learning Objectives**
Students will be able to:	*Students will be able to:*
Calculate an ecological footprint.	Draw a diagram of the water cycle and its essential processes or act out the water cycle during a class simulation.
Connect the ecological impacts of their lifestyles with ways to reduce these impacts.	Identify evaporation, condensation, transpiration and precipitation as phases of the water cycle.
Discuss the ecological impacts of human actions in developed and third-world societies to define the concepts of "sustainability" and "sustainable growth."	Discuss the future consequences of changing water amounts on Earth, from lack created by drought to overabundance from melting polar ice, rising sea levels, or drastically changing weather patterns.
Offer insights into global ramifications of wealth and poverty through the comparison of ecological footprints of rich and poor nations.	
Are there other objectives you would add?	**Are there other objectives you would add?**

SOURCE: *NETS for Students: National Educational Technology Standards for Students*, Second Edition. Copyright (c) 2007 by ISTE (International Society for Technology in Education). www.iste.org. All rights reserved.

Student Learning Objectives. You may be familiar with **student learning objectives**; most planning, assessment, and teaching methods courses introduce this framework. Student learning objectives are the intended or planned outcomes of instructional activities, not the activities themselves. Learning objectives:

- tell *who*
- is going to do *what*
- *when* and
- *how much* or *how often* and
- how it will be *measured* or *evaluated*.

Student learning objectives emphasize outcomes—specifically, what students will be able to do after the lesson is taught. Using these learning statements, a teacher identifies teaching methods, writes a lesson procedure, and states what forms of assessment will be used to measure student performance. Examples of student learning objective statements for the "Ecological Footprints" and "Rainscapes" lesson activities are shown in Figure 4.4.

Understanding by Design. **Understanding by Design (UbD)** (also called *backward design*) is an approach to curriculum development explained in a series of books by educators Grant Wiggins and Jay McTighe (2013, 2005). UbD has three main components:

- *Stage 1: Identify desired results (enduring understandings and essential questions).* To provide a frame for student exploration of a topic, the teacher identifies the learning activity's enduring understandings and its essential questions. **Enduring understandings** are the big ideas or relevant information that students will remember long after the activity has been taught. **Essential questions** are a way to organize the topics that students examine in an activity.
- *Stage 2: Determine acceptable evidence (assessment strategies).* The teacher decides what kinds of evidence will show that students have learned the material and can articulate information and ideas about the enduring understandings and essential questions. Evidence includes papers, performances, or other products that students create using the new knowledge they have learned. Decisions about assessment thus precede the writing of objectives and procedures for the activity.
- *Stage 3: Plan learning experiences and instruction (objectives and methods).* Many of the same elements found in a student learning objectives approach are present in a UbD learning plan. The teacher chooses learning objectives, identifies teaching methods, and crafts a plan for how an activity will be conducted.

The key ideas of the two science learning activities, stated in terms of enduring understandings, are shown in Figure 4.5. You may also consult the Lesson Plan Generator (LPG) website at San Diego State University, which guides teachers through instructional planning using a UbD approach.

Figure 4.5 Enduring Understandings for Two Science Learning Activities

Ecological Footprints	Rainscapes
Enduring Understandings	**Enduring Understandings**
Human behaviors change our planet's ecological balance, sometimes damaging the environment in dangerous, hard-to-fix ways. For the sustainability of the planet, people must learn to live in ways that do not compromise the ability of future generations to meet their needs. People face choices about how much space and resources are required for humans to live the way they choose to live. There are crucial decisions about how much space and resources other species on Earth require if they are to survive.	The water cycle is an essential component to life on Earth. Without freshwater, life is not possible. Different environmental conditions— for example, temperature, ocean currents, drought, and floods— create different outcomes in the cycle. Because only 1% of Earth's water is available for consumption, water-wasting or water-conserving behaviors by people influence how much fresh, unpolluted water will be available in the future.
What other enduring understandings would you add?	**What other enduring understandings would you add?**

Selecting Test or Performance Assessments

What makes assessment of student learning an exceedingly complex activity is the fact that it is almost impossible for a teacher to accurately determine what students are learning without talking to each one individually. Yet teachers must conduct assessments of entire classes and of each individual student in those classes. To evaluate student learning, teachers utilize the following types of assessments: test assessments; standards-based assessments; and performance assessments.

TEST ASSESSMENTS. Some educators believe that **test assessments** best determine what a student knows or is able to do academically. Test scores in the form of numbers on a scale are used to represent knowledge proficiency. In theory, because all the students in a class are taking the same test, it is possible to compare student performance and develop instructional plans for those who are struggling academically. Figure 4.6 shows test assessments for the "Ecological Footprints" and "Rainscapes" science lessons.

Teachers need to know about three basic kinds of test assessments:

- **Norm-referenced tests** compare students' performance to that of other students of the same grade or age. Test takers are ranked according to how high or low they

Figure 4.6 Test Assessments for Two Science Learning Activities

Ecological Footprints	Rainscapes
Test-Based Assessments	**Test-Based Assessments**
Exam Question Which of the following steps will reduce the impact of the U.S. ecological footprint on the environment? a. Recycling of paper and waste b. Water conservation c. Driving 55 miles an hour d. All of the above	**Exam Question** Which of the following terms is *not* part of the water cycle? a. Precipitation b. Conservation c. Evaporation d. Condensation
Quiz Question Ecology is the scientific study of a. interrelations between living things and the environment b. living organisms c. Earth's seas and oceans d. the planet Earth	**Quiz Question** Which of these conditions is necessary for the rainscape to work as a model for the water cycle? a. Enclosed container b. Plants c. Moisture in the container d. All of the above
Short Answer Test Question What are the characteristics of the ecological footprints of humans living in modern industrial and technological societies?	**Short Answer Test Question** What process occurs to make condensation at the top of the rainscape container?
What other test-based assessments would you add?	**What other test-based assessments would you add?**

score in comparison to the norms set by the larger group. The results typically follow a bell-shaped curve, with small numbers at the high end, small numbers at the low end, and a large number in the middle. Many of the tests schools administer are norm-referenced, including such national exams as the Iowa Comprehensive Test of Basic Skills; the Metropolitan, Stanford, and California Achievement Tests; and Tests of Academic Proficiency. An IQ test is a norm-referenced test, as are others that place student results on rank-ordered scales to determine school readiness, developmental levels, or reading or math proficiency.

- **Criterion-referenced tests** compare students' performance, not to other students, but to specific objectives or standards. Test takers are evaluated according to personal performance, and because the criterion-referenced test scores are not arranged on a bell-shaped curve, it is possible for many students to score well or poorly depending on what they know about the questions on the test. A driver's license exam is a criterion-referenced test, as are the informal quizzes or tests that teachers create to check students' recall or application of specific academic material. The National Assessment of Educational Progress (NAEP) and the Partnership for Assessment of Readiness for College and Careers (PARCC) are examples of criterion-referenced tests in education.

Critics of the growth of testing in K–12 schools argue that a reliance on standardized assessments has changed the nature of teaching, narrowing the curriculum and limiting student learning (National Council of Teachers of English, 2014b). They express growing concern that art, music, physical education, world languages, and history/social studies are being crowded out or eliminated from many school curriculums by an emphasis on preparing for and taking tests in English, math, and science. It has been estimated that teachers lose up to 100 hours of instructional time a year to test preparation and test taking (Nelson, 2013). Critics also cite the negative impact of high-stakes testing on low-income and minority students and English language learners, who tend to receive lower scores and then face more limited career options as a result.

Some education reformers support standards-based testing as a means of countering inconsistencies in how teachers evaluate students. They contend that there is enormous variability among teachers regarding what they teach and how effectively they teach it. For example, one child might have a teacher who is highly knowledgeable in math, whereas another child's teacher might be less knowledgeable in math, yet both students receive high math grades. "What does a grade really mean in such a situation?" reformers ask, because there is no common measure of what each child knows or can do mathematically. To eliminate such variations, standards-referenced measures are used to compare every student against broad national achievement norms.

STANDARDS-BASED ASSESSMENTS. **Standards-based assessments** (or *standards-referenced testing*) start with national, state, or district curriculum frameworks that specify what students are expected to know and be able to do at each grade level. Tests are then used to assess the performance of students relative to those national, state, or district expectations. Test takers in a subject area or academic skill are then grouped in terms of their scores on the standards test as advanced, basic, needing improvement, or failing. Statewide standards establish what high school students are supposed to know or do, usually in English/language arts and mathematics but in some cases in science and history as well. The tests determine who has reached basic competency according to the standards. A declining number of states (12, down from 29 in the 1990s) require students to pass a standardized test to receive a high school diploma while eight states have recently mandated that students must pass a civic exam to graduate (FairTest, 2017).

Standards-based grading (SBG) is a variation of standardized-based assessment. Instead of using a traditional numerical scale (A = 90% to 100%; B = 80% to 89%), SBG evaluates students on which skills they have mastered or accomplished relative to particular learning standards. Ratings are based on accomplishment with the top score being Advanced, followed by Target, Acceptable, and Unacceptable. SBG has similarities to performance assessment, which is explained in the next section of the chapter.

Opponents of standards-referenced testing see the situation in exactly opposite terms. Rather than trying to remove the teacher from the process, they believe it is essential to prepare teachers to develop their own assessments based on state learning standards and student performance in the classroom. It is the teacher, after all, who is the primary conductor of the curriculum. That teacher knows what was taught, how it was taught, and under what conditions the students are most likely to engage with activities and demonstrate what they have learned. For these reasons, individual teachers should be taught how to create tests to evaluate students—not test writers who work for testing companies far removed from the day-to-day worlds of classroom learning.

Standards-based assessment is now a reality for college students preparing to become teachers. Over the past decade, major professional educational organizations have issued national standards for teachers and programs that prepare teachers for licensure. Many colleges and universities, notably those accredited by the National Council for Accreditation of Teacher Education (NCATE), have incorporated these national standards into teacher preparation programs. Teacher candidates must demonstrate they have met the standards for their field before being recommended for a teacher license.

PERFORMANCE ASSESSMENTS. Many educators believe that **performance assessments** (sometimes called *alternative* or *authentic assessments* or *performance evaluations*) more accurately measure student learning. Figure 4.7 presents examples of performance assessments for the "Ecological Footprints" and "Rainscapes" lessons.

Performance assessments measure what someone can do in a certain activity within the context of that activity. A baseball player with a .300 batting average (3 hits in every 10 at bats) is considered to be an outstanding performer at the major league level of that sport. Skydivers who are part of a team executing complex aerial maneuvers together strive for a world-class level of performance based on the scores given by judges. A small business owner who successfully expands her network of coffee shops is performing above expectations in a highly competitive business field. In each of these cases—batting average, aerial formations, and profit margin—performance is measured in tangible terms. Completed products, performances, publications, and presentations by students offer tangible evidence of knowledge and skills learned. As a new teacher, you will find both test and performance assessments useful to document what each student knows and still needs to learn.

Figure 4.7 Performance Assessments for Two Science Learning Activities

Ecological Footprints	Rainscapes
Performance-Based Assessments	**Performance-Based Assessments**
Discussion Question Which type of farming produces the largest yields that serve the most people while creating the smallest ecological footprints—organic farmers or large agribusinesses? Which type of farming should be supported by governmental policy, and why?	**Discussion Question** Discuss how you acted like a scientist in this lesson. What do you think scientists actually do in their work?
Performance Task Using writing, drawing, and math, describe your own ecological footprint or that of your family or neighborhood. Provide a detailed description of what resources are used and for what purposes. Make concrete proposals for reducing the wasteful use of resources.	**Performance Task** Using writing and drawing, explain how a rainscape works as a model of the water cycle. • Working in small groups, construct three rainscapes from the same materials. Place each rainscape in a different part of the room so they all receive different amounts of sunlight. Put one under a box or behind a cardboard or paper screen to shade it from windows. • Working in the same small groups, observe the three rainscapes daily, spending a few minutes at each to compare and contrast what is happening. • Each day groups return to their rainscape to record the daily observations and to photograph the containers. • At the end of the week, each group shares its recorded information, highlighting any observable differences found in its rainscapes.
Technology Project Once you have assembled your ecological footprint analysis and proposals for change, create a technology-based format for communicating this information to other people. You could use a digital presentation format as a way to present your findings, or you could create a website, blog, or other educational networking site devoted to ecological topics as a way to get more people involved in sustainability issues. Explain how the technology you are using provides an effective way for you to communicate information and achieve your goals.	**Technology Project** Photograph or draw each day's observations of the water cycle. Then create a slideshow to demonstrate the actions of the water cycle.
What other performance-based assessments would you add?	**What other performance-based assessments would you add?**

Performance assessment is not the same as standards-based assessment. Tests may be involved, but these assessments primarily include educational activities other than tests. For example, a high school student in an art or design class might be evaluated on a portfolio of drawings and sketches rather than a test of artistic knowledge. In the same way, new teacher candidates in a college or university program cannot receive a teacher license without being evaluated on their performance in the classroom during student teaching where they are assessed by how successfully they develop and deliver the curriculum, manage learning time, communicate with students, and handle the many other responsibilities of a full-time teacher.

Rubrics are a key performance assessment approach. Rubrics use known-in-advance criteria to guide how students create and teachers evaluate educational activities and materials. Students know what is expected of them when they begin an assignment, and they can strive to perform at the high levels of a rubric. Teachers can then use the criteria set forth in a rubric to assess how successfully students performed on the assignment. To help ensure that everyone understands what is expected, teachers and students can construct rubrics collaboratively to guide the assessment of performance-based learning activities.

Classroom teachers often use performance assessments to evaluate student work, in part because planning what or how to teach can begin with a performance assessment, before a lesson or unit is begun. Rather than giving a multiple-choice test, they ask for a product, performance, or presentation as a way for students to show what they have learned in addition to what they already know. For example, to assess what students know about data analysis and statistics, a high school math teacher might ask students to investigate the data plans offered to individuals, small businesses, and large firms by major cell phone companies. Students would then prepare a written report or digital presentation featuring cost/benefit calculations that include line plots and equations detailing rate changes in cents per minute, with results for all companies explained in the report. Students find this performance-based assignment personally relevant because they are interested in mobile phone rates and they have opportunities to demonstrate their knowledge of mathematical concepts and number operations.

As with other parts of the lesson development process, technology serves as a constant feature of how teachers assess student learning using performance assessments. Teachers can use tablets or smartphones to record ongoing learning activities in the classroom, take photos of student work, keep track of student participation during class discussions, and assess student contributions to a classroom blog or wiki. Students can use technology to create their own videos, podcasts, digital presentations, 3-D models, Scratch programs, augmented or virtual reality experiences, blogs, or written and artistic work for teachers to assess. Table 4.4 offers more examples of web resources and apps for assessing student learning.

Throughout the instructional design/lesson development process, technology is more than a tool for planning, delivering, and evaluating academic assignments and presentations. It is a means for creating broad new approaches to schooling. Technology has the power to enhance everyone's understanding of the goals and

Digital Dialog 4.2

Multiple-choice tests and quizzes are often-used approaches to educational assessment. Many teachers want to have more performance-based ways to evaluate students. As you recall your own experiences with evaluation and assessment, comment and connect online about the following questions:

- Do you consider multiple-choice tests a way to show all you have learned about a topic? What are the strengths and shortcomings of this form of assessment for students?
- What skills and talents might be completely evaluated by paper-and-pencil tests? What skills and talents are demonstratively evaluated by performance-based measures?
- What kinds of performance-based assessments did you engage in as a student? What performance-based assessments do you envision using with students you teach?

Table 4.4 Web Resources and Apps for Student Assessment

Web

- **RubiStar.** RubiStar provides a set of templates for teachers to use as written or to customize to fit the parameters of an assignment. Rubrics are provided in six areas: multimedia, products, experiments, oral projects, research and writing, and work skills. Two types of rating scales are available: numerical (4, 3, 2, and 1) and descriptive (excellent, good, satisfactory, and needs improvement). Each rubric you make in RubiStar is saved to its own URL so you can access it at any time.
- **QuizStar.** QuizStar provides software for multiple-choice, true/false, and short answer quizzes with multiple options, including reviewing results by class, student, or question. Multiple data formats can be generated that are compatible with conventional data-processing programs.

Apps

- **Classdroid.** This free open-source app manages student grading and interfaces with most classroom or school blogs.
- **Quizlet Live.** Work in teams to match ideas and concepts much like you would using digital flashcards.
- **Teacher's Assistant Pro.** This software keeps track of grades as well as students' classroom behaviors and interactions. The software works with text, phone, or e-mail interfaces to easily communicate data with families.
- **Essay Grader.** Preset comments applicable for responding to student essays are offered, but teachers can add their own personalized comments as well. The goal is to give teachers a digital alternative to writing individual comments on dozens of student papers.
- **Easy Assessment.** This assessment tool incorporates personalized rubrics, video, and photo-taking features into one grading system, making it a useful accompaniment to portfolio-based teaching.
- **Android for Academics.** Functions are available for tracking attendance and grading as well as for building student performance rubrics.
- **Plickers.** Poll your class for answers as they use a "paper clicker," that your device will scan (like a barcode) to check for understanding. Poll results are delivered directly to your device and make the data collection easy to evaluate.
- **Recap Video Response and Reflection for Education.** Once the teacher poses a question, the students can answer either via written response, a video, chat groups, or e-mail. Various levels and channels of communication can be tailored to fit the needs of the classroom and students who dialogue within this application.
- **Socrative.** This student response system interacts with mobile devices and the web. Student answers can be aggregated and formatted into reports that are e-mailed or formatted in a web-based spreadsheet. Multiple-choice questions are graded automatically by the system.
- **Nearpod.** Software allows teachers to broadcast interactive slideshows and presentations about a variety of different topics to students' tablets and smartphones. Quizzes, tests, polls, and other assessments based on the presentations can be deployed from the teacher's machine to individual devices. Formal and informal data can be assessed through online reports.
- **Spiral.** Multiple assessment tools can all be found in one assessment hub, including Quickfire, a rapid check-in with the class system; Discuss, a presentation tool that can be used collaboratively; and Clip, which enhances video with quiz and test features.

You can see more examples of assessment-centered tools by visiting the site "Online Tools for Teaching and Learning" developed by Professor Torrey Trust at the University of Massachusetts Amherst, free online. https://blogs.umass.edu/onlinetools/

objectives of education. It helps teachers and students gain ideas and information from the required curriculum, but it also promotes higher order and critical thinking, visual learning, problem solving, communication, creative self-expression, different approaches to learning, and individual self-reflection and personal assessment—all topics to be explored in the next chapters of this book.

> **MyLab Education Application Exercise 4.2:**
> Building Your PLN: *Using Technology to Design a Classroom Learning Activity*
>
> **MyLab Education Self-Check 4.4**

Chapter Summary

Learning Outcome 4.1

Summarize research on the science of learning.

- Constructivist approaches to teaching and learning emphasize active student engagement and a focus on metacognitive thinking to create student-centered educational settings.

- Teachers and schools organize teaching and learning around the following learning theories: behaviorism, cognitivism, constructivism, and constructionism.

- Technology can be used creatively to redefine and fundamentally change how teaching and learning are conducted in K–12 schools while supporting each of the major learning theories.

Learning Outcome 4.2

Compare student-centered and teacher-centered approaches to learning with technology.

- Teacher-centered methods convey information to students, who are expected to learn and use it.
- Student-centered (also called learner-centered) instruction features students as active participants in all elements of classroom lessons, working together with teachers and other students to investigate problems, propose solutions, and reflect on what they are learning.
- There are six main types of educational websites and apps: 1) instructional plan, 2) student-to-expert communication, 3) real-time and recorded data, 4) archival and primary sources, 5) skills/practice, and 6) exploration and discovery.

Learning Outcome 4.3

Describe the elements of instructional design using technology, including standards-based content, teaching methods and materials, and student learning assessments.

- Successful learning by students is the overall goal of instructional design.
- Instructional design includes three essential decisions by teachers: 1) content: what to teach; 2) methods: how to teach; 3) learning assessments: how to know what students have learned.

- Technology supports teachers in implementing the three aspects of instructional design and lesson development.
- Technology helps teachers locate and plan engaging learning experiences and instructional activities through online planning templates and websites.
- Teachers use test and performance assessments to measure the knowledge of students before, during, and after lessons.

Learning Outcome 4.4

Apply the instructional design process in two science learning plans.

- National, state, and local curriculum frameworks and the Common Core Standards define the academic content teachers present to students.
- Student learning objectives emphasize specific skills and information that students will know and be able to use.
- Understanding by Design (UbD) emphasizes enduring understandings and essential questions that students should be able to answer.
- Technology offers multiple ways to conduct learning assessments, from tests and quizzes to digital portfolios and student writing.
- Proponents of standardized tests contend that these tests accurately measure student performance and encourage schools to reform educational practices. Critics believe that standardized tests measure only a limited amount of student knowledge and restrict schools to delivering a more narrow curriculum based on teaching to the test.
- Performance evaluation assesses how students perform when asked to complete specific tasks or assignments and present evidence of their learning.

Key Terms

Academic content, p. 89
Archival and primary source websites and apps, p. 86
Badware, p. 87
Behaviorism, p. 83
Cognitivism, p. 83
Concepts/skills practice websites and apps, p. 86
Constructionism, p. 83
Constructivism, p. 80
Criterion-referenced tests, p. 97
Discipline-based professional organizations, p. 93
Educational apps, p. 85

Educational websites, p. 85
Enduring understandings, p. 95
Essential questions, p. 95
Exploration and discovery websites and apps, p. 86
Formative assessments, p. 91
High-stakes tests, p. 91
Instructional design, p. 88
Learning assessments, p. 91
Lesson development, p. 94
Norm-referenced tests, p. 96
Performance assessments, p. 98
Planning and assessment websites and apps, p. 85

Real-time and recorded data websites and apps, p. 85
Rubrics, p. 99
Standardized testing, p. 91
Standards-based assessments, p. 97
Student-to-expert communication websites and apps, p. 85
Student learning objectives, p. 95
Summative assessments, p. 91
Teaching goals, methods, and procedures, p. 90
Test assessments, p. 96
Understanding by Design (UbD), p. 95

MyLab Education Application Exercise 4.3:
Growing and Leading with Technology: *Tony's "Planets in the Solar System"
Learning Activity*

For Reflection and Discussion

Comparing Lesson Development Approaches

After reviewing the "Ecological Footprints" and "Rainscapes Show the Water Cycle" instructional design plans in the chapter, choose a topic to teach and outline a learning activity using the student learning objectives and Understanding by Design approaches, and then answer the following questions:

- How do these lesson development frameworks differ? How are they the same?
- What do you perceive may be advantages and drawbacks of each approach?
- Which format would you find most helpful for planning a 3-day math, science, or literature lesson?
- Do you think one approach is more effective in one subject area or another?

Your Experiences with Performance Evaluation

Digital presentations can combine text, audio, and video; can be performance evaluations; and can be included in e-portfolios of student learning.

SOURCE: Annie Fuller/Pearson Education

Most of us have experienced performance evaluations in some area of our lives. Athletes know the final score determines who wins or loses a game or meet. Musicians recognize the importance of audience reaction. Employees realize that their jobs depend on meeting the expectations of supervisors. However, performance assessments are less common in many classrooms where test assessments are emphasized. Recalling your own experiences of being assessed in school, respond to the following questions:

- What forms of assessment did you find most helpful and least helpful to your learning?
- What knowledge might be best assessed by a test?
- What knowledge might be best assessed through performances, portfolios, and presentations?

Taking Tests on Computers

Researchers have found that test scores on standardized tests are lower for some students when they take exams on computers versus taking them in paper and pencil formats. Why do you think this would be the case? One answer to the question is that lower-scoring students are less familiar with using technology based on their home and school experiences. To address the problem, researchers urge that teachers require students to use technology for school assignments to develop what have been called "facilitative" computer skills like keyboarding and using word processing—both necessary ingredients for taking tests on computers. Do you agree? Why or why not? What other steps might you take to improve student performance on computer-based tests?

Technology and Curriculum Frameworks

National curriculum frameworks from the National Council of Teachers of English (NCTE), National Council of Teachers of Mathematics (NCTM), National Science Teachers Association (NSTA), National Council for the Social Studies (NCSS), Association for Childhood Education International (ACEI), International Society for Technology in Education (ISTE), and Common Core State Standards all include references for how teachers and students should use technology. These curriculum frameworks are available online at each organization's website.

Choose one organization's framework and examine its technology learning expectations for teachers and students. Compare these expectations for use of technology at the grade levels you plan to teach with those in your state's curriculum frameworks for English/language arts, mathematics, the sciences, history/social studies, or educational technology. What similarities and differences do you find? State curriculum frameworks are available online at each state department of education's website.

Chapter 5

Applying Technology as Teacher Leaders and Innovators

SOURCE: sdecoret/Shutterstock

Chapter Overview

Chapter 5 discusses technology integration and educational change as ways for technology-using teachers to become instructional leaders and innovators in schools. Issues and strategies for infusing technology into classroom instruction and professional work are discussed along with ways for teachers to address the digital divide, digital inequality, and the participation gap—all factors that disproportionately impact diverse students and those from low-income families. The contrasting concepts of "informate" and "automate" establish a framework for teachers to use in redefining how learning happens through innovative uses of technology in teaching. The chapter concludes with steps for current and future teachers to take to become technology-using leaders in schools.

The chapter incorporates ISTE Standards for Educators of "Collaborator" and "Citizen," through which teachers demonstrate leadership by integrating technology equitably and effectively across the curriculum while role modeling for students, families, and colleagues the skills and dispositions of technology-using educators and citizens.

Learning Outcomes

After reading this chapter, you will be able to:

5.1 Identify technology integration stages and challenges.

5.2 Discuss the dynamics of digital inequalities and the participation gap.

5.3 Analyze technology's role in educational change and flipped learning in schools.

5.4 Demonstrate ways teachers can become technology-leading educators in schools.

Chapter Learning Goal

Develop strategies for successfully utilizing technology and creating change in schools as a teacher leader.

Featured Technologies

One-to-one computing

Bring your own device/technology (BYOD/T) programs

SAMR Technology Integration Model

Flipped classrooms

Interactive digital textbooks

Mindtools

Digital badges

Wearable technologies

Three New Teachers Become Leaders with Technology

Starting their first year as full-time teachers, Whitney, Randall, and Tim found that their schools had widely different educational technology resources. Whitney joined the faculty of an independent school that gave every student a tablet to use in and outside of class. Randall was hired by a public high school in which every classroom had five Internet-connected desktops, along with an overhead projector and a screen. Tim's elementary school had one computer in each room, limited access to laptops on a rolling cart, and 40 minutes of class time scheduled weekly in the building's computer lab.

Using what they had, Whitney, Randall, and Tim integrated technology into daily lessons and individual activities for students. With a tablet for every student, Whitney found it easy to design online learning activities in which small groups of students explored multimodal material and shared knowledge with classmates. Wanting academic learning to continue even after the bell rang, she gave assignments featuring online resources related to the next class for students to do outside of class. In this way, everyone was using technology for learning activities.

Even without tablets for each student, Randall and Tim utilized technology for daily curriculum and instruction. Randall found clips from multiple online documentaries and podcasts and used his Twitter account to post assignments and share resources with the students. In class, students accessed interactive web resources to learn about units of study. Tim connected the classroom's desktop computer to online weather radar and climate information, and he reserved laptops with graph-making software to record data for the students' yearlong study of seasonal change.

As new teachers, each felt compelled to do more to create classrooms and schools with technology. Continuing her long-term interests in educational policy, Whitney began advocating for more equitable technology funding for schools serving low-income communities. Randall joined a regional International Society for Technology in Education (ISTE) organization to serve on committees planning educational conferences. Tim volunteered to be on his school's teacher professional development committee so he could focus on role modeling and peer teaching for colleagues interested in more expansive uses of technology. Each began to see themselves as teachers who were technology innovators and leaders concerned with classroom-based and system-wide educational equity and change.

The learning goal for this chapter is how to become a technology-using teacher innovator and leader, a role Whitney, Randall, and Tim achieved by redesigning school learning environments through technology integration while working and advocating for educational equity and change. **Technology integration** refers to ways teachers make technology integral to their instructional and professional work. **Educational change** refers to how educators create new patterns of teaching and learning in schools. Redesigned school learning environments feature technology-based instructional activities—groupwork and cooperative learning, one/two/three time rotations, one-to-one computing or bring your own device/technology (BYOD/T) programs, digital textbooks, flipped learning, and computers as mindtools. Achieving technology integration and educational change requires teachers to adopt action-oriented mind-sets that welcome opportunities to explore how curriculum and instruction can be shaped using technology tools.

Teachers become technology leaders by the ways they utilize interactive websites, apps, learning games, blogs, wikis, cameras, podcasts, assistive technologies, digital portfolios, and other tools discussed in this book to create exciting and relevant learning in student-centered classrooms in elementary, middle, and high schools. Indeed, making learning environments more student-centered involves using digital technologies in open and participatory ways.

Interactive digital tools and technologies have the potential to be **disruptive innovations** that alter existing patterns of teaching and learning in schools (Horn & Staker, 2015). Indeed, as two forward-thinking educators forecast near the end of the 21st century's first decade, "There are deep incompatibilities between the demands of the new technologies and the traditional classroom" (Collins & Halverson, 2009, p. 6). Digital technologies disrupt long-held educational practices; for example, when everyone has instant online access to knowledge, teachers and textbooks are no longer the sole sources of information.

Not everyone, however, embraces the use of new digital tools in schools. In the book *Disruptive Classroom Technologies*, educator Sonny Magana (2017) asks why, in this digital age, so many school systems still continue to use analog tools and drill and practice worksheets as primary teaching and learning approaches. His answer is that people fear the new, and to overcome that fear, they must become knowledgeable about and capable of managing educational change—an essential step in establishing oneself as a technology-leading educator. Other researchers have concluded that teachers' core beliefs and attitudes are critical influences in their use of technology—teachers with a student-centered approach to teaching are more likely to integrate new technologies than are educators who adopt more teacher-centered practices (Ertmer, et al., 2012).

As you read the chapter, consider the following questions about technology and change:

1. How can teachers go about integrating technology into school and classroom learning?
2. How can you use technology to counter digital inequality and the participation gap?
3. How can you engage in technology-based changes in school organizational patterns and learning cultures?
4. What steps can you take to become a technology-leading teacher?

Integrating Technology into Teaching

5.1   Identify technology integration stages and challenges.

Teachers tend to respond to the changes and challenges of technology integration by following the pattern of the **Rogers innovation curve**, a model developed to show

how individuals in business and management respond to change (ValueBased Management.net, 2011; Rogers, 2003). Rogers's model proposes that for every new idea or organizational innovation there is always a small percentage of innovators and early adopters who are followed by a sizeable majority of other individuals who sooner or later will adopt new practices. There is also a small group of individuals who generally avoid or resist change.

Applying the Rogers innovation curve to schools reveals that there are teachers who respond to technology as follows:

- A small group of innovators will eagerly integrate the latest new technologies into their teaching.

- A larger group of skeptical, cautious, and undecided observers will want to wait and see the results of new approaches before using them in their teaching.

- A small number of change resisters will lag behind the pace of new developments.

Students and teachers share ideas for using the latest tools in school.

SOURCE: Goodluz/Fotolia

K–12 students, by contrast, are eager to use new technologies; more than one in three students across the grade levels say they are "among the first people to check out a new electronic device or gadget" (Harris Poll, 2014). As one middle school student told us after happily and rapidly learning to use 3-D modeling software for a class project, "Now I can build something and show people what I am thinking."

As a teacher you will be constantly making decisions about whether to lead, follow, or stay behind education's evolving technological innovation curve. You may choose to be an eager innovator, a cautious adopter who waits to see if change makes sense, or a leader in one area (utilizing 3-D modeling and printing) with a wait-and-see approach in another (using social media to interact with classrooms around the world). Now—before you enter the classroom—is a time to carefully think through your technology-using decisions, drawing on information from courses you take, skills you learn, and perspectives you adopt related to technology and teaching.

To fully and successfully integrate technology into teaching, you must become a teacher who:

- *Makes informed choices.* Placing student learning at the center of the curriculum, teachers decide how to utilize technology's assets in the fast-paced environment and differentiated learning demands of a modern school. This means choosing between a variety of approaches: technology as a centerpiece of instruction, technology as a small part of a lesson, or no technology at all.

- *Explores technology's multiple dimensions.* In using technology for classroom learning, teachers help students to analyze the role of computers and other tools in schools and society. This makes the social, political, and economic impacts of technology regular topics for classroom discussion in science, history, mathematics, and language arts.

- *Promotes educational change.* At the classroom level, teachers use technology as a "disruptive" force. Its presence is an invitation to rethink the way things are and the way things might be, and to implement new patterns of curriculum and instruction that make it possible for every student to reach her or his full learning potential.

- *Engages in continual learning.* Teachers constantly gain new knowledge and expertise and apply those perspectives to classroom teaching and personal/professional learning. This process of ongoing learning establishes a teacher's practice as an educator committed to using technology for educational change.

Inclusion or Infusion

Technology use in schools follows one of two broad directions: inclusion or infusion. **Inclusion** means that digital technologies are mainly used for transferring information and practicing skills. Inclusion might take the form of scheduling every class into a computer lab for weekly instruction. Technology use in a classroom might occur during recess or when students who have finished written work or other assignments have free time.

Infusion means that digital technologies are features of teaching and learning in all academic subjects at all grade levels as ongoing parts of the day-to-day educational experiences of students. Infusion might involve equipping every classroom with multiple machines for academic instruction, or it could mean a single device or pair of machines are designated integral parts of daily lessons as students engage regularly in online research, word processing, game-based learning, portfolio development, and other technology-based interactive activities.

Infusing technology in teaching practices offers opportunities for teachers and students to use new tools in new ways for new learning. Ongoing involvement with technology increases student motivation and engagement, which also expands everyone's ideas and opportunities for creative self-expression. Your choices about how to use technology are significant because they help shape larger patterns of classroom organization, student interest in learning, and technology integration in schools today.

MyLab Education
Video Example 5.1
In this video, students begin their school day by opening their laptops and beginning their academic work. How does this classroom demonstrate infusion—not just inclusion—of technology?

The SAMR Model

Assessing where you are as a technology-using educator and making choices to advance your skills and competencies is a first step in integrating technology in teaching. More than a decade ago, Marc Prensky (2005) famously described technology integration as a process of moving from "dabbling" to "doing old things in old ways" to "doing old things in new ways" to "doing new things in new ways."

Observations of organizational change using technology from the seminal 1995 Apple Classrooms of Tomorrow (ACOT) Project to the **SAMR Model of Technology Integration** (Substitution, Augmentation, Modification, Redefinition) developed by Reuben Puentedura (2014) show a prevailing pattern in how teachers go about integrating technology into classroom-based teaching and learning practices (see Table 5.1). At the **entry stage** or **substitution stage**, teachers initiate using technology-based materials to replace non-technology-based materials, as when students answer questions for homework online instead of on paper. At the **adoption stage** or **augmentation stage**, teachers include technology in ways that slightly modify non-tech learning. This level of technology integration promotes modest changes in curriculum and instruction, as when students take online quizzes and get immediate feedback.

At the **adaptation/appropriation stage** or **modification stage**, teachers are using technology to enrich and facilitate learning experiences for students—for instance, struggling writers might use speech-to-text tools to get their ideas on paper before

Table 5.1 Two Technology Integration Models

Stages of Technology Integration	Apple Classrooms of Tomorrow (ACOT) Project	Substitution, Augmentation, Modification, Redefinition (SAMR) Model
Teachers are learning new skills and understandings and beginning to use technology for teaching.	Entry	Substitution
Teachers are using technology without making significant changes to regular teaching practices.	Adoption	Augmentation
Teachers are more fully and confidently using technology both in the classroom and for their own professional work.	Adaptation and Appropriation	Modification
Teachers are exploring new ways to creatively use technology in and out of the classroom.	Invention	Redefinition

working on revisions. This is followed by the **invention stage** or **redefinition stage**, in which teachers use technology to individualize and differentiate instruction, create student focus and interest, and extend learning investigations beyond what is possible in a paper-only environment.

The SAMR model has been criticized as lacking clear evidence of its stages. Some educators contend that teachers can move up the SAMR scale, but not really change the substance of their teaching practices. A fill-in-the-blank paper worksheet is still a worksheet when it is done as a digital activity (Hamilton, Rosenberg, & Akcaoglu, 2016). Similarly, a lecture is still a mostly passive learning experience for students whether it is done with or without PowerPoint presentation slides.

Advocates of the SAMR model find that its simplicity helps teachers analyze and reflect upon their current uses of technology and identify ways to create more innovative technology-rich lessons. For instance, teachers might examine a recent lesson using technology and identify where their use of technology fits on the SAMR model. Then, they could explore ways to shift their use of technology higher on the SAMR scale.

Indeed, when teachers integrate digital tools into daily classroom learning, students are able to:

- Explore and present information dynamically
- Act in ways that are increasingly socially aware and confident
- Communicate differently
- Become self-starters
- Share knowledge spontaneously
- Have a positive orientation toward the future.

However, technology by itself may not improve students' academic achievement as measured by standardized test scores. Reviewing dozens of studies of technology use with at-risk high school students, Stanford University researchers found that to positively impact student learning, technology had to be used in three specific ways: 1) interactively, 2) promoting exploration and creation rather than rote memorization, and 3) in combination with teacher support and social interactions with other students (Darling-Hammond, Zielezinski, & Goldman, 2014). These outcomes, the researchers noted, are particularly clear where students have one-to-one access to technology.

As the International Society for Technology in Education (ISTE) documented nearly a decade ago, the following conditions must be in place for technology to positively influence student learning while promoting meaningful change in schools (International Society for Technology in Education, 2008b, pp. 7–8):

1. There must be professional development for teachers.
2. Technology use must be aligned to curriculum standards.
3. Technology must be integrated into daily learning, not used as an add-on to instruction.
4. Students need individualized feedback, and teachers need to differentiate technology use to match personal learning needs.
5. Students need opportunities to use technology collaboratively.
6. Technology must support project-based learning and include real-world simulations.
7. Leadership and support for technology must be present from all of those involved in a school, including teachers, administrators, family members, and students themselves.

Factors Impacting Technology Integration

The following factors impact teachers' efforts to integrate technology into teaching and learning:

1. *Teaching style.* A teacher's instructional style affects how technology is integrated into classroom activities. It can be difficult for educators with a teacher-centered approach to step aside and allow students some control of classroom learning

using technology. They may be unsure how to organize small-group activities and uncomfortable if questions arise they cannot answer.

2. *Professional development.* In addition, technology integration is supported when teachers receive regular professional training, ongoing support from school administrators, and sufficient resources to make change happen smoothly. Teachers also benefit when given time to share ideas and strategies with colleagues before undertaking technology integrations by themselves.

3. *Unwillingness to change favorite lesson plans.* Some teachers have favorite lesson plans and curriculum activities that they are eager to repeat with every new class. If these plans were developed without technology, a busy teacher may lack the time and knowledge to discover how to integrate technological resources into them. Here again, ongoing professional development support is crucial to informing teachers as they infuse more technology into learning activities.

4. *Lack of awareness of technology resources.* When a district realigns its curriculum to meet the requirements of state or national frameworks and assessment tests, a teacher may be faced with teaching units that are all new. Teachers may not know of resources available online or in apps for teaching academic content. This can be especially true when they begin teaching a subject or a grade level they have not taught before. Infusing technology requires time and energy to organize new lesson plans and curriculum units and discover tools that can be interesting and challenging curriculum materials.

5. *Rewards and punishments.* Recognizing that students gravitate toward digital devices, many teachers use technology as a behavior management tool. Students who follow directions or finish assignments are offered technology use as a reward; students who misbehave or fail to complete assignments are denied technology. Such inequitable practices create classroom dynamics in which students who do not or cannot meet the goals set for using technology give up trying to achieve them, becoming distanced from academic learning while losing the positive feelings of personal accomplishment as a successful learner.

6. *Overreliance on one or two tools.* Some teachers, responding to school system expectations or mandates to integrate technology, make one or two tools a constant feature of learning. In such instances, the technology may deprive students of interactive instructional options when there is no real reason to do so. Students may watch videos instead of researching a topic or conducting hands-on investigations. Viewing short video segments makes sense instructionally, particularly when the videos are interspersed with other activities, but regularly viewing videos from beginning to end replaces the opportunity for students to engage in group discussions, express ideas through writing and drawing, or use hands-on manipulatives for learning.

7. *Separating students by ability groups.* In some schools, technology is used to divide students according to test scores or perceived readiness to do certain academic activities. Students with higher rankings are given one kind of technology-based experience, while those with lower rankings get another kind. Dividing a class according to perceived ability means that in most situations, highly ranked and lower-ranked students are rarely together for the same learning activities. This practice reinforces a sense of academic haves and have-nots and neglects the reality that using technology can make all the students in a class productive problem solvers and peer teachers. By letting individuals with different knowledge and skills work together, teachers give students opportunities to discover aspects of each other's learning potentials that are not shown when classes are grouped by perceived ability.

MyLab Education **Self-Check 5.1**

Addressing Digital Inequalities and the Participation Gap

5.2   Discuss the dynamics of digital inequalities and the participation gap.

Differences in access to technology, broadly known as **digital inequality** continue to be a persistent and pervasive educational issue. Digital inequality is a contrast of technological haves and have-nots. Older individuals, those living in lower-income households, those with less than a high school education, those living in rural areas or urban centers, those with disabilities, and individuals who speak home languages other than English are more likely to be among the technological have-nots (Rainie, 2013). In education, African American and Latino youngsters, as well as many White students from low-income households and students with disabilities, tend to have more limited home and school access to desktop or laptop computers, the Internet, broadband at home, and mobile phone connectivity than do their more affluent peers (U.S. Department of Commerce, 2013; Ragnedda & Muschert, 2013).

New technologies have given new dimensions to digital inequality. As more and more families acquire smartphones, e-readers, tablets, and high-speed Internet, students living in higher-income households (more than $75,000 a year) have strikingly different experiences with technology than everyone else. Those students are more likely to use the Internet every day, more likely to own multiple Internet-ready devices, and more likely to get news and conduct business online (Ray, Jackson, & Cupaiuolo, 2014a). They are constantly learning new ways to use the latest technologies, and that knowledge lets them use digital tools confidently at school.

By contrast, youngsters in lower-income households are more likely to use mobile phone technology to access social media, listen to music, and conduct other online activities. Mobile technology growth among non-Whites has increased dramatically in recent years, although Whites still have greater home broadband access and own more desktop machines. Phones provide easy Internet access, but mobile technology imposes key limitations on users. Many school-related learning activities are not easily done on a phone (writing papers, analyzing materials, recording data); thus, users tend to emphasize accessing the web for entertainment more than for education.

Entering a classroom, you will likely find students who have had markedly different experiences with technology based on family income or racial/ethnic background. Those with reduced access to multiple technologies at home or in school are educationally disadvantaged because they are less able to use and learn from the latest tools. Integrating technology into teaching means finding ways to expand the technology experiences of all students.

A Digital Inequality Perspective

A digital inequality perspective holds that simply adding more technology to homes or schools will not, in and of itself, address differences in access among social groups. More technology does not always solve the kinds of problems that technology itself helps to create.

Marc Warschauer (2011, 2003), a professor at the University of California, Irvine, adopts a **social informatics** analysis in which technology's impacts are considered within the context of larger social, economic, and political realities, as well as social and racial differences. In theory, families with children who lack the latest technology might access the Internet and have high-quality learning experiences in libraries that are technologically well equipped, open nights and weekends, and located in schools or community centers. But if municipal, state, and federal budget cuts reduce library funding and hours of operation, and if the library or community center is accessed mainly by public transportation and the schedule includes few options for coming and going, then government policies extend rather than minimize digital separation between social groups.

In a series of books spanning more than a decade, Henry Jenkins, a professor at the Massachusetts Institute of Technology, has analyzed how lack of access to new technology creates a digital participation gap (Jenkins, Ford, & Green, 2013; Jenkins, 2006). There are great differences "between what students with 24/7 access can do and what students can do when their own access is through the public library or a school computer" (Long, 2008). Without access to the latest technologies, students fall behind their peers in online skills and competencies, becoming bystanders in society's participatory media culture. They lack regular opportunities to navigate the Internet, play web-based learning games, and engage in online problem-solving activities, which diminishes their media and technology literacies.

Digital Dialog 5.1

Many students from low-income and culturally diverse families lack access to the latest, most powerful technologies outside of school. As you think about how you will use technology to reduce these digital participation gaps, comment and connect online about the following questions:

- In what ways can integrating technology into classroom instruction and student learning reduce digital participation gaps for students?
- How might you organize classroom instruction to ensure that all students have substantive learning experiences with technology?
- Do you see bring your own device/technology (BYOD/T) programs as a solution to or a continuation of digital divides, digital inequalities, and digital participation gaps?

Viewing technology access in systemic terms reveals complex issues related to the types of learning experiences that students have in and outside of school. Adding computers to schools might actually extend digital inequality rather than reduce it based on teaching and learning practices. In many schools, some students use technology for inquiry-based investigations, experiments, and research projects, while other students are confined to mostly online worksheets with drill-and-practice exercises. Often, it is the economically advantaged youngsters who regularly engage in more intellectually challenging activities—a consequence of tracking by test scores that label some as talented and gifted and others as lacking proficiency in basic skills. If students from low-income and minority households are unable to use the latest technologies or engage in challenging curricular activities, then access during school to updated technologies will not reduce an inequality of educational outcomes.

How can schools support the integration of technology into teaching while also responding to digital inequality and the participation gap? To answer this question, many schools are changing the structure of classroom learning to provide regular access to technology for all students in similarly interesting ways. The following strategies demonstrate efforts to shorten the amount of time teachers and students spend in large-group instruction to make time for more highly interactive, technology-based learning experiences for individuals and small groups.

One-to-One Computing and BYOD/T Programs

One-to-one (or 1:1) computing means all students in a grade, school, or district have or own computing devices, usually laptops or tablets. All over the country, schools and districts have implemented 1:1 programs. Maine's Learning Technology Initiative (MLTI), the nation's largest, has provided laptops for every middle school student since 2001. It now includes every middle school and high school teacher statewide, offers funds to help high schools provide computing devices to students, and plans to ensure every middle school student's household has the option of home Internet access.

The growth of 1:1 programs has been propelled by three factors.

1. *New devices.* Manufacturers continue to introduce powerful, lower-cost, ultraportable computing devices—tablets, laptops, smartphones, and e-readers. For less than $500, these mobile devices offer considerable memory, Wi-Fi capabilities, and many other features that support teaching and learning in schools—although they have slower processors and more limited battery time than more expensive devices sold to the general public. In 2018, Microsoft announced the release of the Surface Go, a laptop for classrooms designed to compete with Apple's iPad as well as Google Chromebooks, the current industry leader in sales to schools across the nation.

2. *Use in higher education.* More and more colleges and universities now require or strongly encourage first-year students to have a laptop or tablet when they enter school. Even when purchasing a laptop or tablet is not required, many instructors expect students to have access to portable computing resources. Most college students themselves own multiple technology devices, including smartphones, laptop computers, video game consoles, tablet computers and desktop computers.

3. *Impacts on Student Learning.* One-to-one computing programs have been shown to positively affect student learning—in specific ways and under certain conditions. In more than 100 studies of laptop programs, researchers have found increases in students' school attendance, homework completion, teamwork in the classroom, engagement with writing and the writing process, and motivation to learn (Singleton, et al., 2018; Zheng, et al., 2016). As with every new idea, there is a caveat: Giving every student a computing device does not by itself improve learning outcomes. For positive results to occur, teachers must want to engage with and support the program; technical support and professional development are necessary; and technology must be directly connected to the academic curriculum. Accordingly, not all one-to-one programs have realized successful outcomes or generated improvement of student achievement as measured by standardized tests. More use, creative ideas and research are needed to determine how one-to-one computing devices can best facilitate student learning in schools.

Bring your own device/technology (BYOD/T) programs are another initiative designed to support all students in using technology at school. BYOD/T means that students either bring whatever technology they have at home to school for use in daily learning experiences, or have the option to buy or rent an inexpensive laptop from a local reseller. In theory, this allows schools to greatly increase technology use in classrooms even when they cannot afford to purchase laptops for every student. According to the Digital Districts survey from the Center for Digital Education, more than half of all school districts (56%) have implemented BYOD/T programs, including 84% of high schools and 74% of middle schools (Schaffhauser, 2014).

In theory, one-to-one computing and BYOD/T programs reduce digital inequalities by providing every student with their own device to use for learning. Ideally, technology at school paired with interactive learning opportunities and expansive curricular resources compensates for the lack of access outside of school that students from non-White and low-income households experience in homes and community settings. Such initiatives are a prominent feature of education across the nation; Figure 5.1 shows the different ways, based on 2014 survey results, that schools provide technology to students.

Providing every student with a personal computing device—laptop or tablet—has the potential to transform classroom learning. Teacher lectures, textbook assignments, and drill and practice worksheets are no longer the main materials used or the focus of in-class activities. Teachers and students spend class time in a workshop-like setting in which individuals and small groups explore topics in interactive and multimodal ways using a variety of technology-based and paper resources. Students might do lab experiments, visit interactive websites, and develop and present group projects with video, audio, and animation. While students are engaged in groupwork or individual investigations, teachers meet with those who need academic tutoring support or accelerated learning. By observing the hands-on, minds-on learning students do during class, teachers can better understand and more quickly respond to individual learning needs.

Not everyone agrees that access to learning is supported by giving students more technology. Critics contend that BYOD/T programs perpetuate rather than overcome digital inequalities among students and families. Some students will be able to bring

By giving every student access to their own technology, one-to-one computing and Bring Your Own Device/Technology programs promote active learning and engaging explorations of academic topics.

SOURCE: Rob/Fotolia

Figure 5.1 Providing Computers to Students

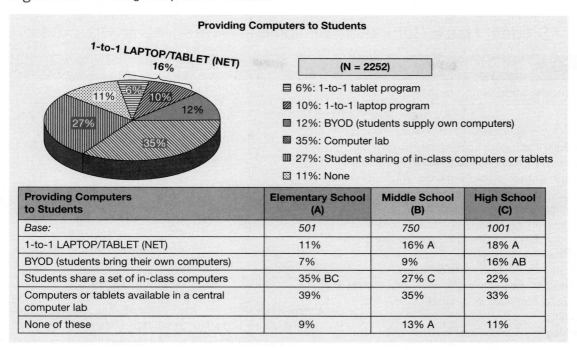

Providing Computers to Students

1-to-1 LAPTOP/TABLET (NET)
16%

(N = 2252)

- 6%: 1-to-1 tablet program
- 10%: 1-to-1 laptop program
- 12%: BYOD (students supply own computers)
- 35%: Computer lab
- 27%: Student sharing of in-class computers or tablets
- 11%: None

Providing Computers to Students	Elementary School (A)	Middle School (B)	High School (C)
Base:	*501*	*750*	*1001*
1-to-1 LAPTOP/TABLET (NET)	11%	16% A	18% A
BYOD (students bring their own computers)	7%	9%	16% AB
Students share a set of in-class computers	35% BC	27% C	22%
Computers or tablets available in a central computer lab	39%	35%	33%
None of these	9%	13% A	11%

the latest smartphones or laptops to school, whereas others will be able to access only older devices with limited technological capabilities; thus, no real change to the digital divide between students will occur.

There are other concerns as well. Faulty Wi-Fi is a huge problem in many buildings. Teachers also worry they will not know how to use or troubleshoot all the different types of technology that students might bring to school. Some Internet networks that support personal technology tools, including 3G and 4G devices, will not run through school web filters. Finally, because one-to-one and BYOD/T are relatively new approaches, districts are still drafting legal policies related to school liability. For example, districts may or may not be held responsible for the information accessed through students' own devices while at school. This chapter's In Practice shows how one new teacher integrated one-to-one tablets into daily instruction.

One/Two/Three Time

One/two/three time is an instructional mode that uses technology to redesign how learning happens in a classroom. An instructional mode is a "way of structuring students' learning environment for teaching purposes" (Peelle, 2001). One/two/three time arrangements split a class of students into three smaller groups that rotate through a series of distinct learning experiences—one or two of which involve using technology for problem solving and information gathering.

Dividing whole classes into smaller learning groups challenges traditional instructional practices. As educational architect Prakash Nair (2014) has noted, most school classrooms built in the past century facilitate only two basic learning modalities—teacher lectures and student presentations—even though extensive research has found that students learn in a variety of action-oriented, exploratory ways through team-based learning, roundtable discussions, peer-to-peer tutoring, online research, purposeful play, and movement. One/two/three time activities reconfigure longstanding arrangements of rows and desks from which the entire class of students interacts mainly with a single teacher into a series of smaller "learning studios" where different kinds of activities are organized around small-group, student-centered learning communities. All students, especially those who have less access to technology outside of school, are able to use computers for learning on a regular basis.

MyLab Education
Video Example 5.2
In this video, you will see a teacher setting up a one/two/three time learning station model that uses technology-based and paper-based materials. How do small groups and learning centers change the educational experience for students?

When Every Student Has a Computer: Teaching in a One-to-One Classroom

Grade Level	Featured Technology
Elementary, middle, and high school	Tablets

Lesson Outline

Beginning a year-long internship as part of her college's teaching license program, Kirsti was surprised to find she would be teaching in a school where all the students had their own laptop computers. A regular technology user herself, Kirsti brought a laptop, smartphone, and smartwatch with her to her college classes every day, using these devices continuously for note-taking, academic assignments, and personal communications. Still, even with all this personal technology experience, Kirsti was unsure about how to organize and conduct classes with middle schoolers, each of whom had a computer they were expected to use every day for academic learning.

In her college technology education class, Kirsti had read viewpoints from debates about the use of computers and tablets in K–12 classrooms. Proponents envision students using personal technologies for inquiry-based, personalized learning experiences. Critics worry about too much screen time, as well as a growing dependence on technological tools to solve problems. Finding no consensus as to whether computers for every student would be a revolutionary practice or an ongoing distraction when used as part of daily learning, Kirsti began planning how she would teach in a school were students use computer technology for academic learning in a one-to-one classroom.

Technology in Teaching

Hearing students say they want to use technology for learning in class prompted Kirsti's first step, designing a "digital game plan" so everyone could share ideas for ways to integrate computers and online resources into daily lessons. Kirsti thought it was essential to initiate these discussions to create engaging, relevant learning experiences while making common ground with students about technology rules and practices.

Students welcomed the opportunity to voice their views, telling Kirsti about their past frustrations with slow-loading machines, repetitive PowerPoint presentations, and time-wasting trips to the computer lab, where the technology was not always working. As part of that discussion, Kirsti asked students to imagine their ideal technology-integrated school: "What technologies would they include, and why?" While the students brainstormed in small groups, she circulated through the room, listening to conversations in process. Students' lists featured technologies from their outside-of-school lives: social media, mobile phones, and video- and photo-sharing tools. Kirsti wrote a list that included a teacher website for

posting student work and class assignments, as well as a large flat-screen display with improved audio and video capabilities.

Kirsti and the students then viewed a slideshow of educational technology innovations from the past to the present: the chalkboard from the 1840s; mass-produced paper and pencils that came into use after 1900; the first videotape, which premiered in 1951; the handheld calculator that arrived in 1958; and the interactive whiteboard that debuted in 1999, as well as current technologies like YouTube, Facebook, and Instagram. Technology is always evolving, the class concluded, and its impact on learning and teaching depends on how it is used for learning by students and teachers.

Next, students drafted rules and procedures for ways to use technologies for learning. They agreed that computers and phones would be used daily, but only with full participation and no one disrupting learning. They decided that Kirsti would schedule regular times for technology use and that phones would have ringers turned off and be clearly visible on desks when not part of an activity. Kirsti agreed to include video and audio materials in daily learning activities and to offer games and simulations that students could access to practice academic concepts. She suggested that students submit photos and short videos with their written paper assignments as additional ways for them to document their learning.

Next, Kirsti and the students began searching for interactive resources that would help everyone experience in new ways academic concepts they were learning in geography class. They watched videos, simulations, animations, and virtual reality presentations, exploring different parts of the world using Google Expeditions. They learned about the devastation of war through a virtual tour of the Syrian city of Aleppo; they listened to stories and songs from Uluru-Kata Tjuta National Park in Australia; they visited United Nations–designed world heritage sites, some of which are threatened by war or neglect.

Kirsti quickly realized that regular computer use and the integration of multimedia materials energized the process of learning by increasing student interest and informing their ideas for discussions. She decided to include more active technology-integrated learning by individuals and small groups so students would benefit from using computers in class. The result was a technology-integrated classroom where students felt committed to their use of rules and where Kirsti felt committed to integrating a wide variety of tools that enabled students to write, create, and share ideas for learning and teaching each other.

One/two/three time learning centers, initially a feature of small group learning activities in elementary school classrooms, now extend into middle school and high school classes to facilitate the goal of using technology to help teachers move away from a reliance on whole-class instruction and to help learners feel energized by and interested in academic learning experiences.

During one/two/three time formats, the computer is an always-available teacher, ready for smaller learning groups to use games, simulations, WikiQuests, Hyperdocs, and other creative tools as interactive learning experiences. Whole-class activities are replaced by smaller working groups, giving teachers time to offer students individualized instruction or extra skills practice. Since there are never enough adults to put someone with every group, technology facilitates one/two/three time arrangements, letting the teacher plan activities that children and teens can do independently.

Interactive Digital Textbooks

Digital textbooks integrate technology into the teaching of academic material. They offer interactive learning resources in different situations: when students are in a one-to-one setting, when a teacher is using a smartboard or projector to show web material on a large screen, when students are completing homework or other outside-of-class projects, and when students are taking an online class.

Depending on the book, digital texts provide a range of multimodal resources for readers, including interactive word definitions or glossaries, audio narration, on-screen note taking, color highlighting of key terms, self-check quizzes, in-book application exercises, and in some cases, embedded multimedia in the form of video, music, and graphics. Each of these features supports the reading experience for students who do not have access to the latest technologies at home, particularly youngsters who are learning English as a new language or who have special educational needs. As engaged readers of digital texts, students and teachers are able to choose from an array of resources to find those that best fit individual learning needs. There is more about digital books and open educational resources (OERs) in Chapter 6's Tech Tool on Open Textbooks, Tools and Courses.

Because of the spiraling cost of educational materials, changing from paper to digital textbooks is now a national education priority. The average college student spends more than $1,200 a year on books and related course materials; elementary and secondary schools are unable to meet the costs of replacing outdated textbooks. In response and as school districts around the country shift to digital textbooks and online curriculum materials, educational organizations are providing free digital resources (also called *open educational resources*) to schools. The California Learning Resource Network (CLRN) has a huge collection of resources for K–12 schools; follow the free textbooks link to get more information. The Open Education Group at Brigham Young University has online textbooks for middle school and high school science classes, while Multimedia Educational Resource for Learning and Online Teaching (MERLOT) has more than 2,500 textbooks, websites, and lessons for teachers to use. The CK-12 Foundation offers free "FlexBooks" that align math and science content to state curriculum standards.

MyLab Education Self-Check 5.2

Technology and Educational Change

5.3 Analyze technology's role in educational change and flipped learning in schools.

Even with digital devices in wide use throughout society, many schools remain technology-limited settings. Therefore, when you integrate technology into classroom instruction, student assignments, professional communications, and other aspects of teaching, you create educational change. As with many other technological changes that are unfolding in society, the integration of digital tools in schools is new and complex and does not always achieve its intended outcomes.

To understand the connections between technology integration and educational change, we discuss four concepts important to a technology-using educator: a) the culture of schools, b) computers as mindtools, c) informating and automating as types of change, and d) flipped learning in technology-based classrooms.

Technology and the Culture of Schools

Technology's capacities to transform teaching and learning can be sidetracked or stymied by the organizational culture of schools. In a series of influential books beginning with *The Culture of the School and the Problem of Change*, sociologist Seymour Sarason has described how organizational cultures affect change. In Sarason's view, most educational change efforts—whether they involve technology or not—follow a predictable pattern. As a result, in education, "the more things change, the more they remain the same" (Sarason, 1982, p. 116).

The pattern is set in motion when policy makers propose top-down changes to existing systems. Much fanfare accompanies these pronouncements. Expectations are raised, meetings and training workshops are held, and consultants are brought in to facilitate communication between administrators and teachers. You may recall a time of top-down, district-wide change when you were in elementary or secondary school. Perhaps your school system adopted a new reading series, revised its approach to math teaching, or rearranged the order of science topics in the curriculum. As top-down initiatives, these change ideas were mandated by administrators, not planned and developed by teachers at the building and classroom level.

From the start, teachers often fail to embrace top-down mandates for change—in part because they were not consulted or involved in the design of plans for change. According to Sarason, when innovative ideas, no matter how sensible or needed, are imposed from the top, they fail to alter the "behavioral and programmatic regularities of schools." In other words, ideas for change do not become part of the culture of the school. Teachers do not embrace the change as something helpful to their regular way of doing things. Lacking teacher "buy-in," the change idea loses momentum and then fades away, only to be replaced by another new reform idea.

Sarason's conclusions raise a key question: If substantive change in schools can be sidetracked by top-down administrative mandates and lack of input from stakeholders, how do teachers create unique, powerful, and transforming learning experiences with technology? His answer is clear: It is not a lack of new ideas that blocks change in schools. Rather, successful change ideas in educational organizations must flow upward from teachers, students, parents, and community members, not downward from administrators and policy makers. Those most affected by a change must be directly involved in making change happen. As a technology-using educator in a school, you will be at the forefront of making change happen, often through small, incremental steps as you integrate new tools and new approaches into curriculum and instruction.

Digital Dialog 5.2

Despite technology's enormous potential for teaching and learning, many schools and classrooms remain technologically out of date. As you think about what you would be able to do as a teacher with limited and/or outdated technology, comment and connect online about the following questions:

- What teaching and learning activities might you do with only one Internet-accessible machine and a large screen for student viewing?
- What teaching and learning activities might you do by taking students to a computer lab or bringing a rolling cart of laptops to the classroom?

Tech Tool 5.1

Mindtools for Learning *with* Technology

Mindtools, a term coined by computer educator David Jonassen (2010, 2005, 2000), offers a far-reaching perspective about how technology can create substantive change in schools. Mindtools enable students and teachers to use technology to create intellectual partnerships, extending academic learning and critical thinking in new and creative ways.

A mindtools approach is dramatically different from ways technology has historically been used for learning. When computers first appeared in schools, the dominant focus was on what Jonassen calls "learning *from* computers." Computer-assisted drill-and-practice instruction, simple educational games, and word processing that was faster than typewriting were all examples of learning *from* computers. This practice of learning from technology continues today in many classrooms where students passively receive PowerPoint presentations of information.

As technology became more common in schools, a second focus emerged, what Jonassen characterized as "learning

about computers." Many teachers and administrators connect learning about computers with the term **computer literacy** or knowing names, functions, and procedures of hardware and software. Computer-literate students do more than learn from computers. But still they may not be interactive users who create new ideas and solve problems with technology.

Jonassen proposes an expansive type of technology use, "learning *with* computers," in which digital devices function as mindtools. Mindtools support the "construction of knowledge, exploration, and discovery, learning by doing, interactive communication, and personal reflection" (Jonassen, 2000, p. 9). As teachers and students learn *with* computers, they access different kinds of multimodal learning resources—including video, audio, and adaptive online tutorials. They further use technology as creators of their own games, simulations, apps, and other experiences designed to meet learning goals and academic interests. Inquiry-based teaching and learning happen as technology is viewed and used as mindtools.

MyLab Education Application Exercise 5.1:
Learning *from* versus Learning *with* Technology

Automate and Informate

The terms **automate** and **informate** further illustrate the distinction between students learning *from* technology and students learning *with* technology. As explained by technology educator Alan November (2012, 2009), automating happens when a new technology essentially re-creates existing practices, usually at greater speed and sometimes with greater efficiency. In an organization or business, "the work remains the same, the locus of control remains the same, the time and place remain the same, and relationships remain the same. The same processes solve the same problems" (November, 2009, p. 2). Automating is much like the substitution level of the SAMR model discussed earlier in the chapter.

Automating also happens when individuals use technology to make a change to improve their daily lives. A fitness enthusiast who formerly estimated distance by driving a car around her running route can automate her calculations by wearing a small pedometer on a belt or sleeve. A teacher who used to write paper-based student report cards can automate the grade-keeping process by submitting the same information using a database program, a website, or an app. In these examples, technology does not fundamentally change the practice of tracking personal fitness or evaluating student academic progress.

Informating occurs when technology fundamentally redesigns and refines an activity. The concept comes from Shoshona Zuboff's classic book *In the Age of the Smart Machine* (1989), published at the beginning of the computer revolution when American companies were struggling to integrate new technologies into business practices. At the time, as computers replaced mechanical typewriters, corporate communications were transformed as written materials could be shared within and outside an organization. On the manufacturing side, computers not only began controlling equipment, but keeping track of what had been produced—jobs formerly done by human workers. In short, the informating capacity of technology can produce "radical change as it alters the intrinsic character of work" (Zuboff, 1989, p. 11).

As an everyday life example, consider how **wearable technologies** allow a fitness enthusiast to informate her running routes and related workout routines with clothing and accessories whose built-in devices track physical activities—a bracelet monitors heart rate, number of steps taken, and sleep patterns; shirts, headbands, and socks have stress-measuring sensors in the fabrics; and running shoes include built-in mechanisms that send data in real time to a smartphone or tablet. While running, walking, or exercising, she can read the information (or hear it through ear buds) while listening to music playlists specifically customized to her pace and interests. She can access data and send messages through her smartwatch. Having real-time information substantively restructures the health and exercise experience.

In school settings, instead of producing a static online report card as an end-of-the term evaluation of academic performance, teachers—along with family members, guidance counselors, and students themselves—can utilize social media and data visualization technologies to create ongoing digital assessments of learning progress throughout the school year. Interactive technology enables everyone to set goals, chart activities, note achievements, identify areas for learning improvement, and create instructional modifications based on immediate needs. A standards-based report card format connects student performance to specific skills and competencies. Students themselves can compile their own learning narratives, describing what they have learned and archiving examples in digital portfolios. Family members can offer feedback and responses as well. In this way, a formerly passive evaluation procedure in the hands of the teacher is informated by a technology-based interactive system of feedback and change that enables students and families to interact as partners in the process of documenting learning.

Importantly, the same technology can be used one way to automate and another way to informate. Consider a TV remote control device. At first glance, a remote appears only to automate the use of a television set by letting a viewer change channels, program a DVR, and adjust sound remotely instead of by hand. Yet a TV remote can informate the experience as well. A viewer can use it to channel-surf among networks and shows, avoid commercials, view previously recorded programs in any order, and put current shows on pause while performing other tasks. When used with a "smart" television (a TV with Internet-connected technologies), the remote can direct such functions as streaming media content, apps and games, gesture and voice control, and web browsing—all on a large screen. Television's largely passive experience is made interactive as viewers exert greater choice and control over what is being watched.

Digital technologies can automate or informate learning, depending on how they are used by teachers and students. That is, they can function as routine tools or as expansive mindtools. The challenge facing every teacher is finding the ways to ensure that students use technology actively and creatively, not passively and traditionally.

Flipped Learning in Student-Centered Classrooms

Flipped learning is a technology integration approach in which digital tools dramatically reposition how education happens inside and outside of schools (Bergmann & Sams, 2014). A model of schooling that has dominated education in the United States for more than 100 years—teacher as transmitter of knowledge, students as receivers of information—is redesigned by the capacity of digital technologies to reach and teach different ages simultaneously and individually. Classrooms become highly interactive, student-centered learning environments where teachers guide students "as they apply concepts and engage creatively in the subject matter" (Sophia Learning, 2014).

A flipped classroom explicitly decreases teacher-centered approaches to curriculum and instruction, as activities that used to happen in the classroom now happen outside it and activities that used to happen outside the classroom now happen inside it (see Figure 5.2). Common in-class activities such as listening to teacher lectures, taking notes, completing worksheets, and viewing presentations take place before class as

Figure 5.2 Traditional and Flipped Classrooms

	Traditional Classroom	Flipped Classroom
What happens during class	Teacher-led instruction with whole groups, small groups, and individuals	Student-led activities with whole groups, small groups, and individuals
	Students as learners	Students as teachers and learners
	Teacher comes ready to teach by imparting information or directing activities	Students come prepared to learn by doing activities and adding to online information
What happens outside of class	Students do homework using paper worksheets and writing prompts	Students watch videos or pencasts or listen to podcasts of teacher presentations
	Reading assignments come from paper textbooks	Reading assignments come from online textbooks or interactive web resources

students view videos and read text on computers or other mobile devices. Face-to-face class time is then devoted to interactive learning activities such as completing individual research, working on group projects, using web tools and apps, and meeting with teachers for tutoring assistance.

Flipping the classroom changes everyone's roles and responsibilities. The teacher is no longer the sole director of what and how students learn, pivoting from dispenser of information to manager of individual and group learning experiences. At the same time, students shift from acting as passive recipients of curriculum to becoming active researchers, analyzers, and presenters of ideas and information. Teachers and students use new technologies for learning regularly.

Flipped learning is on the rise in schools. In 2014, according to one national survey, 78% of teachers reported they had flipped a lesson, up from just 48% two years earlier. Nearly half (45%) said they flip classes once or twice a week. Overwhelmingly, the teachers reported greater engagement and improved academic performance among students, particularly youngsters with special educational needs, English language learners, individuals from low-income households, and students taking Advanced Placement classes (Sophia Learning, 2014).

Flipping would not be possible without technology's capacity to create anywhere, anytime learning. In the past, teachers used class time to teach material presented in the textbook, employing a variety of traditional methods. Now, teachers can shift much of the information presentation function to outside-of-school time. For homework, students go online to listen to audio or engage with interactive videos related to the class topic. Students can also view PowerPoint slides or other presentation formats of class material, complete assignments using interactive digital materials, and post comments on topic-related discussion boards. Using interactive video tools, like TED-Ed and Ed Puzzle, teachers can immediately assess whether students understand parts or all of the topic and prepare their lessons for the next class accordingly.

Flipped learning happens when teachers create multimodal lessons for students to do outside the classroom so group work, projects, and other problem-solving activities can be accomplished during the class period.

SOURCE: Goodluz/Fotolia

There are drawbacks and complexities to flipped learning as an approach to educational change. First, students from low-income households, rural areas or remote places may not have up-to-date computers or high-speed Internet access at home, making it difficult for them to complete the outside-of-class activities needed to flip in-class learning. Teachers need to be sure that everyone has the learning materials, either by providing paper copies or by designating in-class time to access materials online.

Second, assigning text-heavy readings as the outside-of-class component of flipped learning can disadvantage students who are learning English as a new language, students with special educational needs or who are not reading on grade level. Teachers need to be sure that learning materials can be accessed in languages other than English and be read aloud by screen reading software at different levels of reading competence.

Third, some students may not finish doing the outside-of-class activities before coming to the in-person class, thus lacking the background information needed to fully participate in learning activities. Teachers need to consistently monitor student engagement and participation in both the in-class and outside-of-class components of flipped learning, including helping students to develop new homework completion routines so that preparation is done before class, not after it.

Finally, flipped learning in K–12 schools may not look the way it does in college courses where professors put lectures and other course materials online, and in-class time features team-based learning experiences for students. At elementary, middle, and high school levels, a teacher may only occasionally flip learning experiences, asking students to do assignments outside of class in preparation for project-based learning activities in class. Or a teacher may flip learning experiences by limiting teacher-directed activities in favor of students working together and teaching each other about a topic.

Successfully using technology to build a student-centered flipped classroom provides ongoing experiential learning for teachers and students. There is no single best formula for what to do. This is mainly because technology is not evenly distributed among schools. For every teacher with multiple connected technologies, there are many teachers with only a single machine in a classroom or whose access to technology is limited to the school's computer lab. Some instructional activities that need a multiple-device classroom are not doable in a classroom with a single machine. Similarly, lessons that involve students in a computer lab once or twice a week may not easily fit the desires of teachers to use technology every day.

Involving Students in Technology Rule-Making

Students are rarely asked for their thoughts and suggestions about almost all aspects of school life—from daily schedules and teaching approaches to homework, discipline policies, and to ways to use technology for learning. In the words of Hofstra University researcher Roberto Joseph, students have been "silenced and excluded" from educational decision-making change processes (2006, p. 35). As a result, students experience school as routines and regulations imposed on them by adults, not as ongoing opportunities to share learning and grow and develop as people.

There are so many reasons why it makes sense for students to become active partners in deciding the rules about how technology will be used in schools and classrooms. First, groups who are left out of a change process may resent and resist intended reforms. Giving students a substantive voice in reform makes it more likely that they will support a change they helped to design. Second, teachers gain valuable insights about student motivation and behavior when they listen considerately to the ideas and concerns of children and adolescents. Few teachers succeed in managing classroom behaviors by constantly imposing rules on students. Involving students addresses developmental needs of young people to collaborate in forming consensus regarding issues of change. When students find that their voices are heard, they feel positive about themselves, and those positive feelings contribute to more productive behavior in schools.

Inviting students to build a "digital game plan" is one way for teachers to involve students in deciding how technology will be used in classrooms. A digital game plan is a set of rules and agreements about technology use that evolves based on discussions between students and teachers. Teachers can begin by asking students to imagine what technologies they would like to include in an ideal technology-integrated school. Most student lists will have technologies from their outside-of-school lives: social media, smartphones, video- and photo-sharing tools. Teachers, too, add their technology choices to the list. Next, students list the technologies available to them in school as well as their rules and procedures for how they want to use them for learning.

A digital game plan process will involve discussion and compromise. A teacher and students might agree that using smartphones for learning can happen as part of some activities, but only with full participation where no one disrupts the focus of learning. They might further agree that when not in use as part of a lesson, phones would be turned off and clearly visible on desks. A teacher and students might agree that video and audio materials will be a regular part of lessons, but everyone must be active viewers of the material. Similarly, they could agree that students can submit photos and short videos along with written papers as ways to complete assignments. Once in place, the digital game plan can continue to evolve democratically throughout the school year.

Students are natural partners for teachers and administrators when investigating ideas that involve technology. In surprising ways, students are technology experts, particularly when experts are defined as individuals who work with information on a daily basis, who exchange knowledge with others in the field, and who are constantly updating their skills with the newest tools in the field. What some students may lack are the sophistication and maturity developed with experience and the ability to reflect on how to use new tools to communicate information in fair and accurate ways. This is where teachers hold a key position for successful change, contributing guidance and wisdom, confirming that every voice matters, and showing how the ideas of younger and older individuals can be synthesized to produce learning outcomes welcomed by all.

Using the Technology You Have: Change Strategies for Teachers

As a teacher, you need to constantly consider how to integrate technology to achieve maximum learning within a class time and setting. By looking at what other teachers are doing, by asking students what they have experienced, and by being curious about the most effective ways to maximize the potential of learning tools, you can be informed and inventive with uses of technology.

As an activity, in a school where you are teaching, tutoring, or visiting for a college class, examine the availability of technology across the four dimensions of technology-equipped classrooms shown in Figure 5.3. Looking at the four dimensions focuses attention on the following key points:

- Classrooms without technology are becoming less common, but there are still schools where access to technology occurs mainly in the school library.
- In many schools, a teacher has a single computer, usually on a rolling cart or a desk. Students can access multiple machines only in the library or a computer lab. Alternatively, the school may have laptops or tablets on rolling carts, moving between the classrooms. Labs or rolling cart machines must be reserved and may or may not be available on any given day.

Figure 5.3 Four Dimensions of Technology-Equipped Classrooms

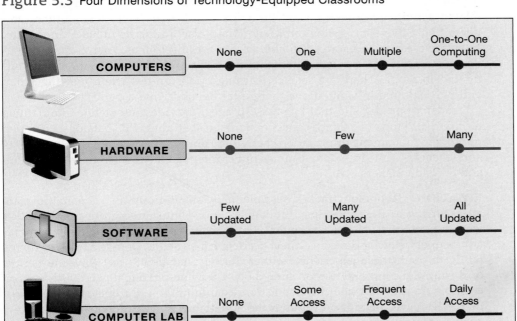

- Even where there is regular access to technology, there may or may not be up-to-date software or digital projectors, interactive whiteboards, digital cameras, and other tools to integrate into lesson activities.
- Newer or recently refurbished schools often feature multiple computers in a classroom, including one for the teacher and two or more machines for students. There are a number of advantages to these arrangements. First, multiple computers mean the teacher can conduct small-group activities and does not have to rely on moving the class to a computer lab or reserving a rolling cart or machines. Second, funding supporting new or refurbished schools often means the software is up to date and readily available. These classrooms tend to have other technologies as well, such as whiteboards and document cameras.

Despite constraints in equipment and schedules, a single desktop, laptop, or tablet can successfully transform teaching and learning in flipped, student-centered classrooms. Thinking creatively about using the technology is what makes possible interactive multimodal experiences for students. Here are strategies for integrating technology in classrooms with a single device or multiple machines.

INFORMATION With steady Wi-Fi connectivity, technology in a classroom is an always-on-call librarian and tutor for individuals, pairs, or small groups. Students have access to educational information anytime through online dictionaries, thesauri, maps, weather pages, video links, story read-alouds, math games, science demonstrations, and varieties of writing formats. Weather information, for example, is constantly updated online, making checking any weather site or the weather page of *USA Today* a reading comprehension activity. Similarly, news sites offer current and archived reports for student reporting, synopsizing, and tweeting. Maps at Google Earth, the National Geographic website, and other sources offer up-to-date information interactively and in different formats. Online dictionaries can speak words aloud, translate them into other languages, and display synonyms and definitions. More interactive and engaging than static texts, all these materials offer students—both native English speakers and English language learners—images, links, and related information that assist academic learning.

INTERACTION Technology in a classroom enables interaction with countless digital learning resources. Online read-alouds are just one example. For example, Canadian children's book author Robert Munsch reads his own stories on his website in as delightful a style as one could wish for. Poetry read-alouds and related activities are featured on the websites of many children's authors and poets. Shel Silverstein's site is an invitation to read and write in black and white. Interactive experiences are available across the disciplines. At other sites, students can receive interactive math tutoring, with resources that are almost unlimited in scope. There are science learning opportunities when viewing video and participating in simulations that go far beyond what a paper text can offer. Edheads, a popular site that engages all ages, provides interactive simulations teaching all kinds of science concepts. For social studies, PBS catalogs extensive photo and document information, activities, and primary sources for students and teachers, while interactive games put students in the roles of historical actors and decision makers.

ROTATION Technology makes possible many small-group instructional formats all occurring at the same time. Students, divided into three groups, accomplish learning activities at the computer, complete independent work with minimal adult supervision, and receive direct academic instruction from the teacher. By rotating through these experiences either during a single 40- to 80-minute period or during the course of two or three days, everyone participates in all three. For example, in a high school history lesson examining how European countries replaced China as a world power after the mid-15th century, students in groups can analyze computer-based historical world maps, complete a map assignment using a selection of paper atlases, and discuss readings about the topic with the teacher.

In more technology-limited schools, teachers can include digital materials in the rotations by:

- Creating small-group assignments (partners or trios) in which students use a mobile device for web access.
- Using a tablet to display visual images or video clips while the teacher and students read aloud a story or discuss information about a topic.
- Giving an assignment and asking students to share the use of a tablet or smartphone, a desktop machine, and paper-based materials such as a textbook, picture books, or readings to create presentations. When all are finished, students compare and contrast what they learned from using the various devices (Bennett, 2012).

MyLab Education Self-Check 5.3

Becoming a Technology-Leading Teacher

5.4   Demonstrate ways teachers can become technology-leading educators in schools.

MyLab Education
Video Example 5.3
In this video, you will learn what dispositions and attitudes one middle school principal looks for when hiring new teachers. What steps are you taking to become an impactful teacher who many schools will want to hire?

Leadership is highly valued in our society; the media is filled with stories about the importance of leaders. In business, politics, sports, and entertainment, leaders are hailed as keys to organizational success—the president leads the country, a CEO leads a company, and a point guard leads a basketball team. Leaders are important to successful schools, and while most people think of principals and superintendents as the key educational leaders, teachers, too, have vital leadership roles to play in shaping what happens for students as learners.

Being a leader connotes taking charge of people or situations to generate positive activities and meaningful change. A teacher is not in charge of a school district's curriculum, organizational budget, or day-to-day operation. Individual teachers seem to have minimal impact on educational policy, locally or nationally. Many teachers have told us they feel powerless to effect change in educational systems.

Leadership, however, is not exclusively measured by someone's position of power or status within an organization's hierarchy. Teachers are inherently leaders in classrooms. They are the ones who make education happen for students. Curriculum standards and academic concepts remain abstract until a teacher creates learning experiences that give those ideas meaning for students. Every day, through countless actions and interactions, teachers lead the education of students.

So how do college students who are just entering the teaching profession become educational leaders? Here are strategies for becoming a technology-leading teacher in a school.

Building Your Digital Reputation

Your **digital reputation** (also called an *online or web presence*) is an online archive about you—written by you and by others about you (Lowenthal, Dunlap, & Stitson, 2016). It consists of the materials that someone would find when searching for your name on the Internet. In today's digital age, all of us have a digital reputation—especially college students who are regular participants on numerous social networks such as Twitter, Facebook, Instagram, YouTube, LinkedIn, Pinterest, and more. As author Erik Qualman (2014) has stated, "We don't have a choice whether we *do* social media, the question is how well we *do* it."

A well-managed digital reputation offers many advantages to a new teacher's professional career. Students, families, colleagues, administrators, and prospective employers may seek you out to learn from—and possibly even collaborate with—you. You might be invited to present at school district workshops or educational conferences, join a grant writing or research team, or author a blog post or article based on your areas of expertise. It is as if your resume is instantly available for people to see and review. Your digital reputation declares, "I am an engaged, dynamic, connected teacher and leader who will make an outstanding resource to students and colleagues and a creative member of a school and community."

> **MyLab Education Application Exercise 5.2:**
> Building Your PLN: Managing Your Digital Reputation as a Teacher

Tracking Technology Trends

Technology is never stagnant—new developments race ahead and change how people interact digitally. Some technologies prosper briefly and fade into obsolescence, only to emerge again in new ways. In 2008, Polaroid Corporation announced that it would no longer make instant film; instant cameras with self-developing film, which had been a groundbreaking technology in the 1950s, were now considered to be a relic of the past. But now instant picture technology is again part of the future. Digital cameras print and store photos that can be distributed globally through sites like Instagram, which has become a vast social network with millions of daily users.

Staying up to date with technology is essential if teachers are to understand what students are experiencing technologically. Teachers do not need to be trendy, just trend-conscious. Teaching students to be critical consumers of Internet content and the impacts of technological change is just one way technology-using teachers can utilize their knowledge of trends to inform what they do in the classroom.

Resources for tracking technology trends include:

- **7 Things You Should Know About . . . Briefs** is a series of short summaries focusing on new and emerging educational technologies written by the EDUCAUSE Learning Initiative, a nonprofit organization of more than 2,200 colleges, universities, and educational and corporate groups. Each brief answers seven questions about a new technology: 1) What is it? 2) Who's doing it? 3) How does it work? 4) Why is it significant? 5) What are the downsides? 6) Where is it going? and 7) What are the implications for teaching and learning?

- **Trendsandissues.com** is a biweekly podcast series focusing on the latest topics in instructional design, educational technology, and the learning sciences. Each podcast episode is about 15 minutes long and an easy way to stay up to date on technological developments.

- **Pew Research Internet Project** is the online home for the extensive trend-tracking efforts of the Pew Internet & American Life Project, a nonpartisan, nonprofit fact tank funded by the Pew Charitable Trusts. Pew Internet has more than a decade of data on technology trends and conducts ongoing research on such topics as teens, broadband, health, social networking, mobile devices, and the digital divide. You can sign up to receive free online newsletters, research alerts, and RSS feeds through e-mail.

- **EDUCAUSE Higher Education Horizon Report** offers yearly forecasts about educational technology trends and developments. Begun in 2004 as the NMC Higher Education Horizon Report and conducted since 2018 by EDUCAUSE, this report examines technologies that are likely to enter mainstream use during the next five years. Each technology is discussed in terms of likely time frames to widespread adoption: short term (one year or less), mid-term (two to three years), and long term (four to five years). Makerspaces (short term), adaptive learning technologies (mid-term), and robotics (longer term) were highlighted in the 2018 report.

- **Envisioning** is an independent Brazilian-based research foundation that reports on what academic researchers, computer designers, hackers, and coders are saying about education and the future of technology throughout the world.

- **Imagining the Internet: A History and Forecast** has thousands of pages on the history and future of the digital world available at an online site maintained by the Elon University School of Communications. The site includes recent survey data and learning materials for teachers and students.

- **The Scout Report** is an online weekly publication exploring the latest technological developments in STEM and humanities from researchers and educators at the University of Wisconsin–Madison.

- **Center for the Digital Future** at the University of Southern California's Annenberg School for Communication and Journalism issues yearly reports of its long-term study of the impacts of digital technology on American society.

Grant Writing and Crowdfunding

One of the biggest realities in teaching is that teachers do not have all the resources they need to teach effectively. In many underfunded schools, textbooks and technology may be out of date, and other teaching materials may be unavailable at the time teachers need them. A technology-leading teacher constantly looks to fill gaps that exist in a school's resources by writing grants to outside organizations.

Writing educational grants, like every other teaching skill, is something you learn how to do. It requires writing for a purpose with clarity and precision. It often means networking with others. Many organizations—whether they are government agencies, corporate foundations, private philanthropies, or local businesses—support educational projects that relate to that organization's mission and goals. The Digital Wish Program matches your classroom wish list with donors. Across the country, Computer Recycling Center (CRC) collect used computer equipment and refurbishes computers for reuse in schools. The U.S. Department of Education maintains a clearinghouse of funding information called Find Grants. The website TEACH.com provides grant seeking and writing advice for teachers.

Successful grant writers focus requests for support around the priorities of funding sources. Companies that do business on the Internet have a compelling reason to support projects where teachers and students access online materials using laptops, smartphones, or tablets. Government agencies give grants to support specific policies such as projects that improve learning for students with special educational needs or immigrants learning English as a new language. You can use Google or other search engines to locate organizations interested in supporting education. THE Journal Insider e-newsletter and GetEdFunding feature listings of grants for education.

Crowdfunding—a term for using the Internet to do fundraising—is another way that technology helps teachers tell people and organizations what resources and materials they need for their school. Crowdfunding websites like DonorsChoose, Adopt a Classroom, Kickstarter, and PeerBackers give teachers and schools a place to post online profiles of themselves and the projects they want to fund. *Education Week* magazine reported that funds raised by educators on DonorsChoose reached $159.9 million in 2018 (Schwartz, 2019). Clearly, a compelling presentation of need using videos and pictures posted online can attract the attention of organizations and individuals interested in supporting education.

Teacher crowdfunding has become a contested topic in some school districts, where the practice has been questioned or banned by administrators. Critics contend that there is potential for misuse of funds when teachers raise money but do not fully account for it within school budgets. Advocates maintain that teachers never have enough resources to support their classroom activities and should be encouraged to pursue donations. In an effort to develop helpful regulations, the American Association of School Administrators (AASA) has partnered with DonorsChoose to issue a crowdfunding best practices toolkit featuring suggestions for successful and equitable fundraising activities.

Because not every need will be met by a large monetary grant from an agency or foundation or by crowdfunding efforts, many teachers build small-scale partnerships with businesses, human service agencies, and charities. Local agencies, for example, may be able to provide online access to students during after-school clubs, thereby giving students more time to explore learning games and websites. As a teacher, you can establish such school/agency connections through community networking with local leaders and organizations.

Working with Technology-Using Colleagues and Organizations

Technology-leading teachers recognize that effective technology integration in schools is a team effort. You need partners and allies with whom you can share ideas and create projects. Some schools have computer teachers, technology liaisons, or e-learning coaches whose job it is to help classroom teachers use technology effectively. Other teachers may be interested in collaborating online, either in the school, the district, the region, or the country.

There may be staff members in your school who you do not yet recognize as technology-using colleagues. Many schools have specialists, such as a reading coach or math coach whose job it is to improve performance in core academic subjects. These individuals often see technology as a valuable way to improve student learning, so they have a genuine reason to work with you. The same is true for special education teachers, teacher aides, and paraprofessionals, all of whom may have technology-related skills and will be happy to share that knowledge with you and your students. Talking to everyone in your school about their interests is one way you may find partners for technology projects.

To widen the network of supportive colleagues and to find new ideas about teaching and learning, technology-leading teachers join professional organizations. These groups, operating at the state and national level, will expand what you know and can do with technology. The International Society for Technology in Education (ISTE) is a leading professional organization for technology-using teachers. You will also want to know about the Association for the Advancement of Computing in Education (AACE) and the Association for Education Communications and Technology (AECT). All these technology organizations produce regular newsletters and hold national conferences.

ISTE has affiliated technology education organizations throughout the United States, including Computer-Using Educators, Inc. (CUE), a nonprofit organization located in California. Regional computer-using educator organizations include the Massachusetts Computer-Using Educators (MassCUE), which serves all the states in New England and the Northeast; Louisiana Association of Computer-Using Educators (LACUE); Computer-Using Educators of Nevada (CUENV); Midwest Education Technology Council; Northwest Council for Computer Education; New York Association for Computers and Technologies in Education (NYSCATE); and Texas Computer Education Association (TCEA). You can find a complete list at the ISTE website in its affiliate directory.

There are also professional organizations for different subject fields that have ideas for using technology with students, including the International Reading Association (IRA), National Council of Teachers of English (NCTE), National Council of Teachers of Mathematics (NCTM), National Science Teachers Association (NSTA), National Council for the Social Studies (NCSS), American Council on Teaching Foreign Languages (ACTFL), and National Association for the Education of Young Children (NAEYC).

Earning Digital Badges

Digital badges have emerged as a new technology-based way for teachers and students to document and share educational skills and achievements. **Digital badges** are online credentials that describe what someone has accomplished through projects, programs, courses, and other learning and enrichment activities (EDUCAUSE Learning Initiative, 2012b). The idea for digital badges first gained popularity as part of massive open online courses (MOOCs); those who complete an online course receive digital recognition. Now people can earn badges symbolizing learning for many different types of skill and competency-building activities—in school and in the community.

Badges serve as a way for individuals to achieve recognition for accomplishments that fall outside conventional systems of credit courses, professional licenses, and career-related certifications. A teacher may have expertise in a particular area—programming or game-based learning—but never have taken a credit course about those topics. By demonstrating competency through projects and activities, that individual can earn digital badge recognition. University of Wisconsin researcher

Michael Olneck (2012) calls digital badges an "insurgent credential," in that individuals are not bound by or reliant upon formal educational institutions to document meaningful achievements and accomplishments.

Schools, employers, community organizations, and individuals award badges after someone has successfully demonstrated meeting the criteria for a particular skill or competency. Each badge includes "information about when and how it was earned and who issued it" (Alliance for Excellent Education, 2013). The Mozilla Foundation, in collaboration with the MacArthur Foundation and Humanities, Arts, Science, and Technology Alliance and Collaboratory (HASTAC), has established Open Badges, an online system where individuals earn recognition and then share their accomplishments publicly using an Open Badges backpack.

In theory, individuals complete multiple activities to fill their backpacks with recognitions and credentials. Teachers might earn badges for developing new professional skills in grant writing, curriculum development, teaching English language learners, peer mentoring, student evaluation, Common Core implementation, and other new learning activities. Students, too, can collect badges showing they have completed substantive learning experiences, such as completing Advanced Placement (AP) classes, participating in community-based internships, and engaging in self-chosen activities from songwriting to architectural design.

The uses of digital badges in education continue to expand. Schools are beginning to build digital recognition into courses where earning badges supplements or even replaces tests as a method for student learning assessment. As a teacher, you may be receiving or granting badges in a digital recognition program; in both roles you will be demonstrating leadership as a technology-using educator. Make sure to upload your digital badges to your PLN/e-portfolio and share them on your social media sites to strengthen your digital reputation.

Celebrating Digital Learning Day

Supporting teachers in becoming technology leaders is one of the primary goals of Digital Learning Day, a technology-learning initiative sponsored by the Alliance for Excellent Education in Washington, D.C. (see Figure 5.4). The first Digital Learning Day was held on February 1, 2012. More than 30 states and the District of Columbia held digital learning ceremonies and events.

Digital Learning Day recommends three core strategies to promote greater awareness about the impacts of digital learning in schools. You can use these strategies to guide your own technology leadership efforts:

- *Start a conversation in person or online about technology and education.* As you express your ideas about technology, you develop a voice as a technology-using educator.

- *Try new teaching strategies and educational technology tools on a regular basis.* Using new approaches puts you in a continuous learning mode and prevents you from becoming stagnant as a professional learner.

- *Showcase innovative practices using social media.* By letting other teachers, students, and families know about your digital learning efforts, you become part of a wider community of people committed to using technology for teaching and learning.

Everyone benefits from seeing models for how to use technology creatively and from recognition of their efforts to integrate technology in schools. As someone new to the profession, you can be a leader in both areas while also being a member of groups dedicated to improving learning for everyone using technology.

Figure 5.4 Digital Learning Day Logo

DIGIT▲L LEARNING DAY

SOURCE: Digital Learning Day. Reproduced by permission from Alliance for Excellent Education.

Adopting a Technology-Leading Mind-set

A technology-leading teacher possesses a technology-leading mind-set—a willingness to continuously investigate how digital technologies can be used to transform teaching and learning in schools through creative and critical thinking. Many times it may not be immediately apparent how to integrate technology into educational activities, as when students have limited access during the school day. At other times, you may not be familiar with the technology tools you want to use, such as Prezi or screencasting as alternatives to PowerPoint. It is easier professionally to create networks of technology tutors by involving students who will teach each other than it is for you to be teaching everyone.

Teachers with a technology-leading mind-set demonstrate curiosity and perseverance, which is why they continue exploring technology's use in schools. They recognize that even glitches and setbacks are part of the learning process that everyone experiences with new tools and new approaches. They use in-school and outside-of-school professional networks to maintain their enthusiasm and momentum for change. Ultimately, they realize that one never finishes the quest of becoming a teacher. There is always more to learn, to try, to do and redo, to add to one's repertoire of knowledge and interests. One enormous upside of technology is how it keeps you and students learning, growing, and leading together.

Becoming an Advocate for Equity and Change

Beyond integrating technology into how teaching and learning happen in a classroom, technology-leading educators can also become advocates for equity and change at the school, district, state, and national levels. An advocate is someone who forcefully and persuasively works to improve society through action and change. Many people believe advocacy is their civic duty or responsibility. After all, making sure that the voice of the people is heard is essential to a democratic society.

Being a technology advocate as a teacher means working for greater funding and support for educational technology. It means contacting school committee members, local government officials, and state and national legislators to urge action on technology-related issues and policies. It means joining committees at the local, state, and national level to help shape a strong vision of technology use in education. It means being well-informed about key educational issues and being prepared to discuss them with many different groups, from students and colleagues to families and other community members.

ISTE (2019) has identified the following policy priorities: educator preparation and professional development; broadband Internet for learning; student privacy and security; digital citizenship; higher education modernization; and computer science and computational thinking. As a teacher leader, you could advocate for any of these topics or focus on another area that is a high priority in your community. The key is to become and stay involved and to pursue your vision of how together, everyone can achieve more success.

MyLab Education Self-Check 5.4

Chapter Summary

Learning Outcome 5.1

Identify technology integration stages and challenges.

- In every organization, there are a small number of innovators, a large majority of followers, and a small number of people who lag behind change.

- While technology enables teachers to create transforming learning experiences for students and teachers, not every learning activity needs to feature digital tools.

- There are five technology integration stages: entry, adoption, adaptation, appropriation, and invention.

- Key technology integration challenges include: 1) unwillingness to change favorite lesson plans to include technology, 2) reluctance to use technology when teaching new lesson plans, 3) using technology as a student reward or punishment, 4) using technology as an add-on to other activities, and 5) using technology as a way to separate students by ability groups.

Learning Outcome 5.2

Discuss the dynamics of digital inequalities and the participation gap.

- *Digital inequality* is the term used to explain students' lack of access to technology based on their socioeconomic status.
- A participation gap means that many students of color as well as students who are living in poverty, who have special educational needs, or who are learning English as a new language do not have the same opportunities to use the newest technologies for learning as do their more affluent peers.
- One-to-one computing, bring your own device/technology (BYOD/T) programs, one/two/three time instructional formats, and interactive digital textbooks are approaches for addressing digital inequalities and the participation gap.
- The growth of 1:1 programs has been propelled by three factors: new devices, use in higher education, and impacts on student learning.

Learning Outcome 5.3

Analyze technology's role in educational change and flipped learning in schools.

- A technology's educational change potential is determined by the needs and imaginations of teachers and students, mediated by the realities of school organizational goals and priorities.
- Learning *from*, *about*, and *with* computers and learning to automate and informate are ways for teachers to think about the goals they want to achieve when using technology.

- Flipped classrooms are an instructional model in which the teacher's role changes from dispenser of information to manager of individual and group learning experiences using technology.
- Teachers need to prepare to use whatever technologies they have in their classrooms. Ideally, they will have up-to-date tools in Internet-accessible classrooms, but in many schools, teachers must use machines with older software programs and limited Internet access.
- A single desktop or tablet, connected to a digital projector or an interactive whiteboard, can make student learning interactive and impactful.

Learning Outcome 5.4

Demonstrate ways that teachers can become technology-leading educators in schools.

- Teachers who use technology in schools have the potential to become technology-leading educators.
- Leadership as a technology-using educator happens through the ways teachers collaborate with students to integrate methods, materials, and technologies for learning.
- To demonstrate technology leadership, teachers keep track of new developments in the fields of educational technology, write grants, work with technology-using colleagues, join professional organizations, involve students in implementing new technologies in the classroom, and adopt a technology-leading mind-set.

Key Terms

Adaptation/appropriation stage, p. 107
Adoption stage, p. 107
Augmentation stage, p. 107
Automate, p. 117
Bring your own device/technology (BYOD/T), p. 112
Computer literacy, p. 117
Crowdfunding, p. 125
Digital badges, p. 126
Digital inequality, p. 110
Digital textbooks, p. 115
Digital reputation, p. 123
Disruptive innovations, p. 105
Educational change, p. 105
Entry stage, p. 107
Flipped learning, p. 118

Inclusion, p. 107
Informate, p. 117
Infusion, p. 107
Invention stage, p. 108
Mindtools, p. 117
Modification stage, p. 107
One-to-one (or 1:1) computing, p. 111
One/two/three time, p. 113
Redefinition stage, p. 108
Rogers innovation curve, p. 105
SAMR Model of Technology Integration, p. 107
Social informatics, p. 110
Substitution stage, p. 107
Technology integration, p. 105
Wearable technologies, p. 118

> MyLab Education Application Exercise 5.3:
> **Growing and Leading with Technology:** Kate's "Becoming a Technology Leader in Her First Teaching Job"

For Reflection and Discussion

Integrating Technology into Your Teaching

Mindtools is a term for people, as David Jonassen (2005) noted, developing new patterns and approaches *with*, not *from*, technology. Consider the technologies you or your friends use daily—smartphones, digital video cameras, ATMs, high-definition television, or other tools and devices.

- How have these technologies changed your everyday activities compared to when you were younger?
- What new patterns or approaches have you adopted as a result of your technology use in high school or college?
- Which of these technologies do you define as mindtools, and why do you think of them as such?

Now consider the technologies you plan to use in teaching—laptops or tablets, interactive educational websites, blogs and wikis, handheld and wireless devices, and other tools.

- How might these technologies change education from what a teacher would do if the technologies were not present?
- Which of these technologies do you define as mindtools, and why do you think of them as such?

Digital vs. Paper Note-Taking

To compare the experience of taking notes digitally using laptops or phones with hand-writing notes with paper and pens, conduct the following experiment in your college classes this semester.

1. Take notes digitally for an entire week in one of your courses.
2. Continue the experiment by taking notes the next week in the same class using paper and pens.
3. After utilizing these note-taking systems, write a paragraph response to the following two questions:
   - What advantages and drawbacks did you experience with each system?
   - How can teachers incorporate digital note-taking in BYOD/T classrooms?

Chapter 6
Teaching Information Literacy and Digital Citizenship

SOURCE: Cathy Yeulet/123RF

Chapter Overview

Chapter 6 examines how teachers and students can collaboratively develop the 21st century skills of information literacy and digital citizenship. We begin by defining information literacy, then explore the problems associated with the spread of fake and false news, and conclude with background information about ways to use Internet search engines to research and retrieve information. Next, we look at evaluation tools that identify purpose, slant, and bias in online materials. Wikipedia is reviewed as one of the websites often visited by teachers and students. Then, we explain the importance of students becoming digital citizens who are ethical users of technology, including how teachers can address plagiarism and cheating when students do not understand the meaning and purpose of copyright and fair use. The chapter concludes with a Technology Transformation Learning Plan focused on building information literacy skills, "From Text Sets to Media Sets: Researching Historical Biographies of Women Scientists Online."

By exploring search engines, web-based information, and digital citizenship, this chapter responds to the ISTE Standard for Students: Digital Citizen and Knowledge Constructor, which expects students to learn the essential elements of information literacy, including how to successfully search for information online while critically evaluating reliable vs. unreliable digital sources. As digital citizens and knowledge constructors, students are further expected to learn how to engage in the appropriate, responsible, and ethical treatment of online information, to cite sources and materials when conducting online research, and to stand up against bullying and cyberbullying behaviors.

Learning Outcomes

After reading this chapter, you will be able to:

6.1 Explain the meanings of literacy in an information age for teachers and students.

6.2 Analyze the challenges of online information, including uncovering fake news and utilizing Wikipedia.

6.3 Identify strategies for researching and retrieving online information, including open educational resources and public domain materials

6.4 Discuss ways teachers and students can use technology as digital citizens.

Chapter Learning Goal

Teach students how to research and critically evaluate online information as responsible digital citizens

Featured Technologies

Search engines and databases

Open educational resources (OERs)

Public domain materials

Open access e-books and e-textbooks

Visual search tools

Web evaluation resources

Note-taking tools and apps

Wikipedia and online encyclopedias

Wikimedia Commons

Plagiarism prevention tools

A Library of Unimaginable Size

Imagine that the world's largest library is located beside your house, apartment, or school. In your lifetime, visiting daily, you will not be able to see, read, or hear all that it contains. In actual physical space, this place is the Library of Congress in Washington, D.C. It contains 167 million items requiring more than 838 miles of bookshelves to hold them. Its collection includes 39 million books and print materials, 72 million manuscripts, 14.8 million photographs, 5.5 million maps, 8.1 million pieces of sheet music, and 3.6 million sound recordings. Twelve thousand items are added to the collections every working day (Library of Congress, 2018).

The resources of the Library of Congress are miniscule in comparison with the amount of materials that a teacher or student can access online with an Internet-connected digital device. The World Wide Web turned 25 years old March 12, 2014, the anniversary of Tim Berners-Lee's famous paper outlining a worldwide information management system of a networked system of computers (Fox & Rainie, 2014). Today, the vastness of the Internet is far greater than most of us can imagine. Nearly 4 billion people worldwide use the Internet, accessing almost 2 billion websites. Every day people conduct billions of Google searches, send millions of tweets, upload millions of Instagram photos, make millions of voice calls on WhatsApp, view billions of videos on YouTube, and send billions of e-mails. You can watch the numbers change in real time by going to the website Internet Live Stats (http://www.internetlivestats.com/). Most Americans see all this instantly accessible online information as strongly positive, helping them learn, stay informed, and share ideas and information with friends and colleagues (Purcell & Rainie, 2014).

The Internet has fundamentally altered what it means to live and learn in our society. Students at all grade levels are engaged in networked learning using digital devices. Most high school and middle school students (over 90%) have access to a smartphone, and nearly half say

they are online "almost constantly." Computer access at home, however, is substantially lower for youngsters in low-income households, resulting in a critical form of digital inequality known as the homework gap. For example, just three in four youngsters in homes with an annual income of $30,000 or less have computer access, compared to households with an annual income of $75,000 or more, where nearly every youngster (96%) has computer access (Anderson & Jiang, 2018).

The Internet is interwoven into the educational lives of students. Two-thirds of 3- to 18-year-olds use the Internet at school (National Center for Education Statistics, 2018b). Given a research topic or homework assignment or question of personal interest, students turn to Google or another search engine to find resources. Many use social media to discuss schoolwork and learning with peers. Students tell adults that they want opportunities for more digital learning in schools. Access to the Internet has also shifted how teachers prepare lessons, teach classes, and assess students. More and more educators are using digital tools to implement innovative approaches like flipped classrooms, blended learning, self-publishing, and use of serious learning for learning. The enormity of change is racing forward and will continue through our lifetimes.

This chapter highlights how teachers and students can utilize the vast worldwide network of the Internet while building the mindsets and mindfulness of digitally literate citizens. The Internet has been called "this generation's defining technology for literacy and learning" (Leu, 2008). Never in human history have so many people been able to find so much information so readily. Students and teachers go online to learn about a topic with videos, podcasts, and written text. However, this library of virtually endless quantity includes much material of questionable quality. Teachers and students must act as online search experts, fact-checkers, and information analysts.

Learning to locate and use online information is part of a broader set of values and behaviors new to our technology-based society: digital citizenship. Nearly instantaneous information access, social networking, and online publishing mean that students and teachers have important rights and responsibilities as users and creators of online materials. To safeguard these rights, they need to learn how to live and act as "digital citizens of character and integrity" in an information age (Ribble, 2015). We explore these multiple dimensions of the Internet, information literacy, and digital citizenship by focusing on the following questions:

1. What does it mean to be a digitally literate teacher and student in schools and society?
2. How can you and the students thoughtfully evaluate online information resources, including fake and false news and Wikipedia?
3. What do you and the students need to know about search engines, Internet searching, and open educational resources (OERs)?
4. How can you help students learn about digital ethics, bullying and cyberbullying prevention, copyright protection, plagiarism, and fair use of information?

Literacy in an Information Age

6.1 **Explain the meanings of literacy in an information age for teachers and students.**

Teachers and students have a constant need for accurate, relevant, and engaging educational information. Information enables teachers to develop lively curricula, update academic knowledge, and assist students to answer their questions. Students require information to write papers and compose essays, prepare for exams, develop personal interests, and propel their quests for knowledge. Information is the currency of learning in and out of schools.

Acquiring information once meant (and, for some, still means) using a library, reading books and magazines, taking classes in school, and attending conferences and presentations. Now the search for information is dominated by the Internet. Three in four American adults (77%) go online every day, and 25% of them do so "almost constantly" (Perrin & Jiang, 2018). Once online, they engage in a vast range of digital

MyLab Education
Video Example 6.1
In this video, you will learn how a networked classroom connects students around the world—locally, nationally, and internationally. What other ways are technologies expanding how students experience the world and communicate with each other?

activities, including sending e-mail; reading online news, weather, and financial reports; locating health information; engaging in civic and political activities; shopping; banking; social networking; researching jobs, businesses, housing, and schools; playing games; watching and uploading videos; listening to music; sending tweets; and creating and uploading content to blogs, wikis, and websites.

Becoming Digitally Literate

Immediately accessible online information means teachers and students must acquire new literacies related to the digital world. In the past, when books and other printed materials were the primary means of communicating knowledge, literacy meant learning to read and write. The reading and writing of print remain essential skills and understandings in the 21st century, but in addition, everyone must be able to process information that comes through computers, the Internet, and social media. In today's world, multiple digital literacies have joined print literacy as the basis for what it means to be an educated person.

According to the American Library Association's widely accepted definition, a digitally literate person is someone who knows how to "find, understand, evaluate, create, and communicate digital information in a wide variety of formats" using many different technologies. Additionally, a digitally literate person uses information in ethically appropriate ways that promote learning and maintain privacy while knowing how to "communicate and collaborate with peers, colleagues, family, and on occasion, the general public" as members of a "vibrant, informed, and engaged community" (Visser, 2012).

Digital literacy includes multiple types of literacy. There is information literacy, defined by the Association of College & Research Libraries (2014) as "the skills needed to find, retrieve, analyze and use information." Information literacy includes knowing how to *access* information (locate resources and materials on the web) and *assess* information (evaluate the accuracy, quality, and usefulness of what is found among the web's boundless resources).

Media literacy, introduced in Chapter 3, is another essential dimension of digital literacy for teachers and students. It includes "the capacity to access, analyze, evaluate, and communicate messages in a wide variety of forms," including the media students access when watching television, reading newspapers, and using the web, as well as the media they themselves create when posting to a blog or wiki, texting, e-mailing, or writing in multiple genres (National Council of Teachers of English, 2008a).

Digital literacy includes other literacies as well. History teachers teach historical literacy and civic literacy; math teachers emphasize computational, coding, and data literacies; science teachers focus on scientific literacy; art teachers address visual literacy. All these literacies are vitally important in today's society where teachers and students constantly access and communicate information using digital devices and online sources. In a digital age, every teacher is constantly learning and teaching multiple literacies.

Gaining Fluency with Technology

Ideally, learning about digital literacy begins in the early grades and continues through college. Presently, many college and elementary, middle, and high school students do not demonstrate knowledgeable digital literacy skills, tending to rely on Google searches or Wikipedia when doing research while underutilizing government and university websites, scholarly databases, or the assistance of research librarians. As naïve or unschooled consumers of online information, they assign credibility to material on the Internet without checking or verifying when it was published and by whom for what purpose.

A national survey of Internet users from all age groups found widely varying knowledge about technology, its history, and its important concepts (Smith, A., 2014). Teenage users tended to know the most about social media terms and conventions (e.g., the meaning of hashtag or CAPTCHA); college graduates knew the latest technologies (e.g., Twitter and wikis). But across the age groups only one in three knew what year the iPhone was introduced, while less than half knew that a company can have a privacy policy without keeping all your information private. These patterns further reinforce the importance of digital literacy as an essential skill in our technology-based society. As University of Wisconsin Professor James Paul Gee (2007, p. 19) declared more than a decade ago, "In the modern world, print literacy is not enough."

IT (information technology) fluency is a core goal for teachers and students who are learning about technology. Broadly defined, *fluency* means approaching a task or a topic as an expert would. Someone who is fluent understands things from the inside and speaks the language of the field. Fluency means learning academic content from the perspective of people performing work in real-world settings. Through the use of interactive websites, simulations and animations, learning games, video materials, and other technologies, students view science as scientists, history as historians, and language as writers. Similarly, students learn about technology as engineers, analysts, researchers, inventors, and other professional, managerial, and technical workers who use it in their careers.

IT fluency in schools begins with the use of digital technologies by teachers and students in all subject areas at all grade levels. According to the International Society for Technology in Education (ISTE), the learning goal is for students to be able to use diverse technologies to effectively locate and critically evaluate information from all types of digital and non-digital sources. IT-fluent students also know how to use information to supplement and extend what they already know about a topic. In today's world, students do not lack information; they lack the experience to understand and analyze that information in relevant and meaningful ways.

Connecting learning fluency with technology lets children and adolescents practice creative thinking by investigating, analyzing, comparing, and choosing. Computer pioneer Seymour Papert (1996, pp. 28, 29) said "the word *fluent* expresses the most important aspect of the kind of knowledge children should have about technology." Fluency develops not by focusing students' practice on finding a right answer or recalling the right method to complete exercises in books, worksheets, or multiple-choice tests. Fluency develops by creatively thinking, puzzling and revising important-to-the-learner, technology-based activities in real-world settings where actions and choices have meaningful consequences. Students learn by making mistakes, figuring things out, and constantly asking questions that experts, peers and teachers help answer.

Note-Taking Tools and Apps

Writing notes to recall information and expand ideas located during information searches is an essential digital literacy skill for teachers and students. Notes summarize key ideas, concepts, and themes about a topic. Using notes, teachers and students can review what others have said and formulate their own interpretations or analyses to present in class. Middle school and high school students are expected to take notes on readings from textbooks, online sources, and teacher lectures to understand and review class material and prepare for exams.

Writing notes by hand on paper takes time, especially when recording quotes with correct citations. If paper materials are lost or misplaced, rewriting them doubles time consumption. **Note-taking tools and apps** are online technologies that organize and expedite note taking. They transfer the work of writing, filing, and organizing to a computer, enabling users to type notes and save them to the cloud.

Digital note taking has advantages and drawbacks for students. Its major advantage is that information can be recorded and retrieved quickly. With the work of writing, filing, and organizing paper materials transferred to a digital space, notes are available for anywhere/anytime review. While paper materials can get lost or damaged, digital notes can be saved to the cloud.

But researchers are questioning whether note taking on a laptop results in better or improved learning for the note taker, observing that laptop note takers can be more easily distracted, especially if they are multitasking when taking notes by e-mailing friends or checking out entertainment options and sports results (Dynarski, 2017; Mueller & Oppenheimer, 2014). Digital note takers appear to process information differently from those taking notes using paper and pen. While typing on a keyboard lets the writer record information quickly, the extra time that hand writers take to form letters and words may allow them to process ideas more directly and remember them longer—resulting in better performance on tests and other assessments. Still, for those who labor to write or whose handwriting is unreadable by others, digital note taking may supersede all other considerations.

Learning to engage in digital note taking can also be useful to students in one-to-one and BYOD/T classrooms. While many college students take in-class notes on their laptops, tablets, or phones almost every day in class, most elementary, middle school, and high school students have had much less experience taking notes. They are not used to identifying and recording important ideas and concepts from the stream of information they receive in class from teachers, peers, and multimedia materials. By recording ideas and information digitally, younger students get more opportunity to utilize a computing device as a central part of the educational process while simultaneously practicing the skills of synthesizing information and recording it for later recall and review. Some teachers might vary the note-taking experience by having students record information using handheld devices some of the time and paper and pens at other times. Teachers can then review student notes and make suggestions for improving future note taking.

Evernote, a cloud-based note-taking program, makes materials accessible from an Internet-connected desktop, laptop, smartphone, or tablet. The ability to access notes from multiple devices is a valuable time saver for teachers, who spend much of the day moving quickly from class to class. When locating material, you can enter it into your phone or tablet and return to it later when you sit down with your computer. As an online and offline application, Evernote collects different types of data, storing pictures, text, web clippings, and photos within easily organized files. You can share your notebooks by sending live links to your friends and colleagues, and you can tag your notes to search all your notebooks by keyword. Evernote also lets you collect from e-mail materials made by colleagues or virtual student teams. Notes of meetings, sketches and drawings, and text materials can be organized by using the camera on your laptop, tablet, or smartphone. Once you take the snapshot, the software will recognize the text inside the photo of the document and allow that text to be searched by the app.

OneNote, a commercial software program and app for either Mac or PC computers, is a multifaceted electronic note-taking option. OneNote serves as a digital notebook for multiple notebooks or binders that can house different types of data with the click of a mouse or push of a button. Notability is a similarly well-regarded note-taking tool that includes many features for teachers. For example, you can do voice editing of student writing by marking changes on a document and describing them orally. The student can then replay the comments as they review your proposed revisions to the writing.

You can also use the word processing and audio-recording features of Microsoft Word for note taking. Open a Word document and select the notebook layout view. Once this option is selected, a recorder will appear and indicate it is "standing by." Press the red recording button, and the machine starts recording a teacher lecture or class discussion. As you take notes, the program will leave audio markers so you can go back and listen to the audio again by simply clicking on your written comments. Writing one or two keywords is enough to generate an audio marker so you can concentrate on what is being said rather than writing extensive notes.

This tool provides students and teachers with a common notebook that can be used for warm-ups, note taking, class work, and homework. PDFs and Word documents can be placed in the notebook. With a stylus, you can annotate these inserted documents, eliminating the need for all paper. Notebooks can be organized by tab, page, sub-page, or section. There are mobile Windows, Mac, iPad, and web versions, making the tool accessible from anywhere.

There are diversified research and note-taking apps for the iPhone, iPad, and Android tablet and smartphone devices. Any.Do is a list-making app to get things done. It is mobile or web based and has the capability to merge with your Gmail or Google Chrome account. You can designate lists for "today," "tomorrow," "next 7 days," and "sometime." The app will prompt you at the same time daily to check your to-do list and increase productivity.

MyLab Education Self-Check 6.1.

Internet Information Challenges and Responses

6.2 **Analyze the challenges of online information, including uncovering fake news and utilizing Wikipedia.**

The Internet, where information is easily created and widely and rapidly disseminated, poses multiple challenges for teachers and students. Quantity does not equal quality, so an Internet searcher often must sift through pages of poorly written or factually wrong information to find valid data. Editors or experts do not check most postings, and it can be difficult to verify the credentials of a website's author. In the digital age, teachers and students need to understand the types of information found online, the growing problem of fake and false news, and how best to use Wikipedia as an online source.

Knowing where and how to find accurate data is important. Teachers must oversee choices of Internet sites to best serve the ages and learning needs of students.

SOURCE: Pressmaster/Fotolia

Four Types of Online Information

In an older but still relevant framework, researchers Nicholas C. Burbules and Thomas A. Callister, Jr. summarized "troublesome" online content under four categories:

- **Misinformation** describes content that is "false, out of date, or incomplete in a misleading way" (Burbules & Callister, 2000, p. 96). Such information is everywhere on the Internet but sometimes hard to identify. *Disinformation* is a particular type of misinformation in which "knowingly false or malicious" material is posted online, often from unknown or unidentified authors, in an attempt to discredit individuals or organizations. A widespread type of misinformation is phishing, in which cybercriminals pose as legitimate online businesses to steal money from unsuspecting consumers.

- **Malinformation** is what reasonable people might consider "bad" or harmful information and includes "sexual images or material, potentially dangerous or damaging information, political views from militant fringe groups, and so on" (Burbules & Callister, 2000, p. 98).

- **Messed-up information** is "poorly organized and presented" material such as long lists of data without synthesis or context, webpages marked by "gratuitous logos or other graphics that distract or clutter," or discussion boards and blogs that feature rambling text without a clear focus or topic (Burbules & Callister, 2000, p. 100). There may be so much messed-up information about a topic that a reader is confused by the data or unable to make sense of them.

- **Mostly useless information** includes trivial, mundane, or eccentric topics and interests.

MyLab Education
Video Example 6.2
In this video, you will learn how teachers are helping students to assess what is reliable information on the Internet. How might Wikipedia be used as a valuable starting point for evaluating online material?

Many school organizations seek to control online access through one of the following information management and control strategies: censorship, filtering software, partitions, and critical reading. Each approach has instructional implications for teachers and students.

- **Censorship** means that material deemed offensive is banned from a school. But banning material is a notoriously slippery slope. Standards of what is inappropriate or indecent shift over time, and in a society dedicated to freedom of speech and expression, a legitimate concern exists whenever a single individual or organization has the power to decide what to censor from view. Every year, the American Library Association conducts Banned Books Week to raise public consciousness about the dangers of censorship in a free society.

- **Filtering software**, required in schools receiving federal funds under the Children's Internet Protection Act (CIPA) of 2000, attempts to block material by identifying objectionable keywords or phrases. Schools often adopt this method of content control, much to the dismay of teachers who are blocked from accessing online materials and many adolescents who feel that blocking material from classrooms and libraries conflicts with their desire to discuss issues of sexuality, race, and youth culture. Filtering software usually blocks YouTube and social media sites, so students are unable to do activities like exchanging tweets with a book author or engaging in an online chat with academic experts in various fields.

- **Partitions**, like filtering, "restrict access only through pages (archives or 'portals' as they are sometimes called) that are themselves lists of approved sites" (Burbules & Callister, 2000, p. 110). Teachers might partition material using a web-based bookmarking tool such as Portaportal. In effect, teachers create a boundaried space within the larger Internet by limiting where students go online during a class activity or homework assignment. Many schools use Internet content providers that edit online content in advance. Burbules and Callister liken large-scale organizational partitions to "gated communities" that shelter homeowners from "external threats and inconveniences" (Burbules & Callister, 2000, p. 111). They wonder about the accountability of those who decide what information to allow in and what to rule out. An individual teacher or librarian is directly accountable to students and families, but a large corporate provider is detached from the wishes, needs, and interests of local communities.

- **Critical reading** involves teaching students how to read online material and decide for themselves its usefulness or appropriateness. Educators Mark Baildon and James Damico (2011) have used the terms *excavation* and *elevation* to define ways for students to identify and avoid undesirable, illegal, or inappropriate online content. *Excavation* means carefully analyzing an Internet text to identify its main ideas, guiding assumptions, and use of sources and images. *Elevation* refers to locating a source within a larger historical and contemporary discussion of a topic. Many schools teach critical thinking skills, and students apply those skills to assess the quality of works of literature, historical documents, science experiments, or mathematical proofs. Critical reading extends critical thinking to an analysis of media images, expanding how students can become information-literate members of schools and society.

This chapter's In Practice presents an example of how a teacher uses web resources to expand students' knowledge of science and history.

Uncovering Fake and False News

Digital and media literacy includes teaching students how to uncover and reject fake and false news. **Fake and false news** has been defined as "sources that intentionally fabricate information, disseminate deceptive content, or grossly distort actual news reports" (Penn State University Libraries, 2018). In a book published by the American Library Association, information science professor Nicole A. Cooke (2018) characterized fake news as material "expressly disseminated for the sake of earning money from clicks and views, and it is also used to mislead and misinform." Philosopher Lee McIntyre concluded that fake news "is not the abandonment of facts, but a corruption of the process by which facts are credibly gathered and reliability used to shape one's beliefs about reality" (McIntyre, 2018, p. 11).

Today's digital-age students are ill-prepared to assess the credibility of the information they receive on their smartphones, tablets, and computers. They tend to accept as factual whatever they find online. Having not acquired the skills they need to be close and critical readers of written text or visual images, they tend to skim over the surface of online materials, concluding that if something looks academic, it must be reasonable and reliable (Wineburg, et al., 2016; Kahne & Bowyer, 2017; Coiro, et al., 2015). As naive consumers of information, they are easily distracted by flashy clickbait headlines, regardless of their accuracy.

Students from middle school to college who use the Internet and social media with ease still struggle to distinguish credible from false information. In studies conducted by Sam Wineburg and the History Education Group at Stanford University, few students realized the difference between an actual news story and a piece of sponsored content (material paid for by advertisers); few could decide whether an unattributed photograph was digitally altered or depicted an actual scene; few could explain why a tweet might or might not provide reliable information about a topic (Wineburg, et al., 2016).

It is true that fake and false news has been used for commercial and political purposes throughout American history. The authors of pre–Revolutionary War broadsides stretched the truth to support pro-colonist or pro-England points of view. In a 1782 newspaper article written during the Revolutionary War, Benjamin Franklin falsely accused Native Americans allied with the British of committing atrocities against New England colonists.

Newspapers in early America exploited the truth for commercial gain. In the Great Moon Hoax of 1835, the *New York Sun* reported false discoveries of an advanced civilization living on the moon. Papers also took decidedly different positions on local events. Researching the history of two scandalous murder cases in New York City in the 1830s and 1840s, Columbia University professor Andie Tucher (1994) found that the so-called "penny press" was far from objective in its reporting—one paper accused a man of murder while the other proclaimed his innocence. According to Tucher, "Different newspapers had different audiences, so journalists catered to the tastes and sympathies of their particular readership" (quoted in NPR *Hidden Brain*, 2018).

Later in the 19th century, newspaper publisher William Randolph Hearst exploited the sinking of the battleship *Maine* in Havana harbor in 1898 to fuel the start of the Spanish-American War. Radio and television also served as vehicles for false stories in the 20th century. Orson Wells' 1938 *War of the Worlds* radio broadcast had many people believing that aliens were successfully attacking Earth, while the U.S. Army's optimistic assessments of military progress during the Vietnam War have since become known as the "Five O'clock Follies" for their level of misinformation about what was actually happening.

What is different today is how the sheer volume of news available from multiple social media platforms makes it difficult for anyone to easily distinguish the credible from what is distorted or totally false. Importantly, misinformation tends to spread much faster than truth on social media platforms. When Massachusetts Institute of Technology (MIT) researchers looked at 126,000 stories that had been tweeted by 3 million people some 4.5 million times between 2006 and 2017, they found "it took the truth about six times as long as falsehood to reach 1,500 people" (Vosoughi, Roy, & Aral, 2018). Adding to the problem is that "social bots" (automated information distribution programs) are able to spread questionable content incredibly quickly to large numbers of social media accounts before fact-checkers can assess the accuracy or inaccuracy of the claims (Shao, et al., 2018).

Digital Dialog 6.1

Findings by MIT researchers that falsehoods travel "farther, faster, and deeper than truth" on social media have raised great concerns among educators, who wonder how best to respond to all kinds of misinformation online. As you think about your own future role as a teacher combating fake and false news with your students, comment and connect online about the following questions:

- What occasions of fake or false news have you encountered recently on social media?
- What strategies do you use to distinguish between true and false online information?
- How would you go about teaching students to be careful and critical consumers of information they read, view, or listen to on various social media platforms?

Educators agree that building students' media literacy and false news detection skills needs to involve continual practice in carefully reading and analyzing types of written, numerical, and visual information. Just urging students to be critical readers will not motivate them to act as information-checking detectives who welcome the challenge of determining fake from true. Students need to understand that people can and do put anything online, sometimes with the purposes disguised; critical readers have both power and responsibility to distinguish real information from fake and false news.

Utilizing Wikipedia: An Online Encyclopedia

SOURCE: Public Domain Image, Wikimedia Commons

Wikipedia is an online encyclopedia with a worldwide collection of authors and readers. A truly massive undertaking, in 2018 Wikipedia's English language version had more than 3.5 billion pages—more than double its size since 2005—creating a body of information 60 times greater than the next-largest encyclopedia (Wikimedia Foundation, 2018b). It consistently ranks among the most visited sites on the web. Almost every teacher and student uses Wikipedia at one time or another for educational purposes. To track Wikipedia's continuing growth, search the site for "Wikipedia Statistics" to find usage information about all 293 language versions of the encyclopedia.

Wikipedia also offers a more language-accessible version called Simple English Wikipedia. Contributors are invited to write and edit entries in the clearest and most concise language possible. In addition to text, both Wikipedia and Simple English Wikipedia have pop-up definitions and pictures for selected terms, letting the sites serve as both a dictionary and a pictionary while adding a multimodal component to reading and learning. Through its contributor collaboration and language accessibility, Wikipedia and Simple English Wikipedia are examples of how the audience, not the product or software, is used as the key to organizing a resource accessible to all.

In theory, anyone can contribute to Wikipedia by adding a new listing or revising an existing one. In practice, relatively few people contribute to the site. A small paid staff and a group of volunteers known as Wikipedians write and edit articles. Wikipedia listed about 121,000 active Wikipedians as of July 2018. In contrast to a print encyclopedia written by experts, Wikipedia seeks to make the presentation of knowledge an open and participatory process by inviting everyone to be part of the writing. Wikimedia believes that high levels of information accuracy will emerge from the interchange of ideas and information generated by multiple contributors.

Articles on Wikipedia are expected to honor three basic core content principles: 1) the content must be "verifiable"—meaning the information is reliable and truthful; 2) contributors cannot post original research; and 3) all articles must be written from a "neutral point of view." Using these principles, Wikipedia strives to be factually accurate and to correct errors and omissions in a timely manner. When disagreements arise, the site's policy is to "present what the various sources say, giving each side its due weight." Moreover, "any material lacking a reliable source directly supporting it may be removed" (Wikimedia Foundation, 2018c). YouTube now adds "fact check" boxes containing information from Wikipedia next to videos posted by climate change deniers.

You can disagree with what has been posted on Wikipedia through its dispute resolution process. Readers who find entries that are not neutral—factually or conceptually—can request dispute resolution through a series of steps, including posting their concerns on the article's page. The dispute is resolved when: 1) the information in an entry is modified, 2) the information in an entry is expanded to include all competing points of view about a topic, or 3) the person who initiated the dispute is unable to substantiate the claims of bias. In the last case, the entry remains as it was before the dispute began.

Many people, librarians and teachers among them, distrust Wikipedia. Since recognized experts do not serve as referees of the knowledge selection process, these critics contend the reliability of information cannot be ensured. However, since Wikipedia's origin in 2001, growth in the number of readers and contributors, along with the validity and currency of its entries, has made Wikipedia a widely established information source. Many educators now echo the words of one anthropology professor who noted that "I not only approve of the use of Wikipedia but also strongly encourage my students to edit it and help it grow" (Jemielniak, 2014, p. 1).

Despite its popularity and policies, Wikipedia lacks diversity in its coverage of topics related to women, people of color, and members of the LGBTQ community. Noting that 87% of those editing Wikipedia are men, the site itself has taken steps to add more contributions from diverse contributors about multicultural topics (Wikimedia Foundation, 2018a). Wikipedia now has an LBGT Studies project to expand the number of entries on lesbian, gay, bisexual, transgender, and queer studies. Pursuing the goal of diversity, faculty and students at many colleges and universities have organized edit-a-thons designed to add to and improve Wikipedia's information about the accomplishments of women in mathematics, science, and technology—sometimes holding these events on Ada Lovelace Day to honor the early 19th century mathematician and computer pioneer who wrote the first algorithm for a computer program a century before there were such machines. An edit-a-thon in 2017 sponsored by the Museum of Modern Art added or expanded Wikipedia's entries for more than 6,500 women artists.

Teachers initiating conversations with students about Wikipedia could use any of the following strategies.

COMPARE WIKIPEDIA WITH OTHER ONLINE ENCYCLOPEDIAS   Ask students to assess how Wikipedia differs from online encyclopedias such as Microsoft Encarta or Encyclopedia Britannica Online or other websites such as How Stuff Works and InfoPlease. Many of those resources consist of mostly fixed bodies of information and change only with a new edition. By comparison, Wikipedia is dynamic; its information is updated and changes (unless a selection is closed by the review board).

To inform the comparison, teachers can explain that other online encyclopedias are written and edited by scholars in different fields of knowledge, whereas Internet readers who may or may not be experts in a field of study write and edit Wikipedia entries. When experts create the entries, there is no way for users to disagree with the content, but Wikipedia users may challenge entries by placing text under dispute. Students can then review Citizendium, an alternative to Wikipedia that invites readers to contribute articles that are then reviewed and revised by a team of content editors. Contributors to Citizendium must include their real names, and articles that are not approved appear with a disclaimer to that effect.

FACT-CHECK WIKIPEDIA ENTRIES   Elementary, middle school, or high school students can fact-check Wikipedia entries, comparing information found in articles about a topic being studied in class and verifying those facts using non-Wikipedia sources. If errors are found, students may submit their revisions to the site. While fact-checking, students may investigate the voices, perspectives, and points of view underrepresented in Wikipedia and in traditional encyclopedias as well. Students locating omissions can propose new material to expand an entry. You can find strategies for evaluating Wikipedia's material in Michael A. Caulfield's open source online book, *Web Literacy for Student Fact-Checkers* (Caulfield, 2017).

ROLE-PLAY ENCYCLOPEDIA DEVELOPMENT   Students can personally experience the complexities of encyclopedia development by participating in a class simulation. Choosing topics that students nominate because they either know them well or have studied them recently, small groups collaborate in writing and illustrating a factual, non-biased entry about a topic (just like experts do who write encyclopedia entries). Multiple entries by different groups about the same topic are perfectly fine.

Groups do not divulge details of their work to protect their decision making and their thinking processes. On the day entries are shown in print for class consideration, criticism, and revision, everyone has opportunities to comment. It is informative and interesting to note the similarities or differences of other entries. The process of information creation demonstrates the complexities of writing entries for encyclopedias, including whether different authors are inclusive and expansive with their information or write in an easy-to-understand style. Composing the entries and discussing decision and design issues familiarizes students with the process of how online information is created and evaluated.

In Practice

Researching Extinction Events in Biology Class: A Web Search Learning Activity

Grade Level	Featured Technology
Upper elementary, middle school, and high school	Internet websites

Lesson Outline

As an introductory learning activity for the ninth-graders in her Introduction to Biology class, Stacy asked the students to research online what life forms survived the last major extinction event—the Cretaceous-Paleogene extinction that occurred 66 million years ago and resulted in the elimination of three-quarters of all animal and plant species, including the dinosaurs. She had recently read Elizabeth Kolbert's Pulitzer Prize–winning book, *The Sixth Extinction*, which explains how our current world is in the middle of a massive planet-wide die-off of species due to unchecked human activities. Stacy wanted to connect the current vanishings of plants and animals to what happened in the past as a theme for the biological investigations she and students would conduct in the class.

This was an opportunity to teach students how to conduct online research into important scientific and academic topics. The concept of extinction—a species disappearing forever—would arouse students' interest and curiosity. Stacy recognized that locating information, assessing its credibility, and presenting it through their own writing and drawing with correctly cited sources are skills that students need to acquire and practice as they move forward in school and into future careers as information-literate digital citizens.

Teaching with Technology

Stacy knew from past experiences that when given an online research assignment, students usually access a single online source such as Wikipedia or some other site that appears at the top of the page of search results. While these sites may contain useful information and resources for further investigation, they are not a one-stop source for learning. Some sites contain factual errors, deliberate misinformation, and dubious scientific claims that are not obvious to young students.

Stacey opened the learning by defining "extinction" and "de-extinction." *Extinction* refers to the elimination of species due to natural occurrences or human activities. Natural occurrences include volcanic eruptions, wildfires, and the buildup of carbon dioxide that contributed to the most severe extinction event, the Great Dying that happened

252 million years ago. Human activities involve the harm that people do to plants and animals, such as how over-fishing or hunting have nearly eliminated the Atlantic bluefin tuna and the American buffalo. *De-extinction* refers to the intensely debated efforts to bring back extinct species through genetic engineering.

Then, the students began brainstorming possible key terms to enter in online search engines as part of the search for information. Small groups listed terms on whiteboards or poster paper to display to the class. With all the lists in view, each small group could use terms from any of them to facilitate their searches, such as "major extinction events," "last major extinction event," and "what species survived each mass extinction." Group members used computers to put the terms in different search engines, comparing results from Google, Bing, Yahoo, DuckDuckGo, WolframAlpha, and Ask.com.

From their online searches, each group recorded sources of information they found and from which search engines. In addition to the results the students found, Stacey had her own list of recommended, reliable sources: American Museum of Natural History, *Smithsonian Magazine, National Geographic,* NPR (National Public Radio), *Science Friday,* PBS, (Public Broadcasting Service) and the biology section of Phys.org as potential sites from which to begin gathering information. With expansive sources, and the possibility of finding more material that could be cited from other universities, museums, and science-based sources, Stacy asked each group to begin their research looking at not only text-based materials, but videos from YouTube as well as charts, graphs, pictures, and other visual images.

When groups finished their research, students from each group presented the information, role-playing scientists at a conference. A lively discussion followed about each group's findings. Stacy then reviewed with students what they knew about Internet searching, the importance of locating information from reputable sources such as museums and historical organizations, and the use of more than one source about a topic. Everyone in the class now knew how to initiate searches online for information about topics of interest with expanded choices of sites they had not previously known.

MyLab Education **Self-Check 6.2.**

Researching and Retrieving Online Information

6.3 **Identify strategies for researching and retrieving online information, including open educational resources and public domain materials.**

The Internet has transformed how teachers and students research and retrieve information. In the past, teachers and students used library card catalogs and other paper resources to locate information in books and periodicals. In today's digital age, **information research and retrieval** happens online within the "world's largest and linked document collection," the opposite of paper-based library searches, where users look for information "within smaller, more controlled, nonlinked collections" (Langville & Meyer, 2012, p. 5).

To locate information online, computer users type **keywords** (short descriptions of the information one is seeking) into search engines. Google is the most well-known and most often used search resource. When Stanford University students Larry Page and Sergey Brin founded Google in 1998, they revolutionized searching by ranking sites using keywords, site popularity status, and how often a site is cross-listed with other sites. In a PBS Online interview, Brin described Google's page ranking as a process through which webpages interact with one another as if they were people discussing a topic of interest. In effect, Google's technology asks: "What does one page say about another page? And what do other pages say about that one? And kind of reputation building around the whole web, translated into mathematics" (quoted in Michels, 2002).

Researchers have now demonstrated that search engines like Google do not necessarily produce unbiased or neutral results. In her book *Algorithms of Oppression*, Safiya Umoja Noble (2018), argues that software code designed by mostly white men influences how people search (e.g., by offering to fill in the search query) and what they find (e.g., by determining the ranking of search results). A disregard for marginalized groups in American society distorts how search results portray women and people of color. Racial and gender discrimination, Noble concludes, is "embedded in computer code and, increasingly, in artificial intelligence technologies that we are reliant on, by choice or not" (2018, p. 1).

Nearly all students assume researching means going to Google to get information (Purcell, et al., 2012). Students also go to Wikipedia, YouTube, or other social media sites, as well as ask their peers. Less than 2 in 10 consult librarians or print books for information. Some users prefer a search engine other than Google when searching for videos, directions, or products, but for general searches, Google remains the top choice. You and individual or groups of students can preview different search tools to find which provides best results for maps, social media, shopping, and travel, health, and political information.

To teach students the procedures and ethics of online searching, Google launched Search Education in 2012. The site includes lesson plans organized by level of search expertise and coded to the ISTE Standards for Students, the Common Core Standards, and the American Association of School Librarians. Search Education includes "Google a Day" puzzles, which challenge students to discover reliable information about history, geography, science and culture based on clues and hints provided at the site. Its first puzzle stated: "Two future presidents signed me; two did not. What document am I?" (The answer is the Constitution—George Washington and James Madison signed; John Adams and Thomas Jefferson who were out of the country did not sign.) Google offers "Be Internet Awesome," a digital citizenship and safety curriculum with media literacy learning activities for children and adolescents.

Despite the impressive utility of its tools, Google's reach into people's privacy is a troubling development for some observers. In *The Filter Bubble: What the Internet Is Hiding from You,* political activist Eli Pariser (2011) suggests that the process of searching for information online is a much more problematic activity than is commonly assumed. Google's technology builds an increasingly detailed profile of each user. After several searches that establish a baseline of personal interests and patterns, the technology predicts what search results someone will find most useful.

MyLab Education
Video Example 6.3
In this video, a teacher describes how she uses the vast digital library of the Internet to find information for classroom learning. What other ways might teachers and students collaboratively locate online information?

These personalized searches mean that different people will get different results even with the same keywords. A search on climate change, for instance, may produce different results for an environmental activist and an oil company executive based on their respective search histories. In Pariser's view, "there is no standard Google anymore" (2011, p. 2).

Personalized search advocates cite the usefulness of receiving specific information more quickly and efficiently. Consumers do not have to wade through less relevant sites because technology has done that work for them, so a person knows where to get the latest products and services that best fit their needs. But critics worry that personalization distorts democracy's need for widely available shared information so citizens can make informed political decisions and choices. Google's personalized searches may be directing voters and community members to materials that reinforce already established views and perspectives, distorting the broad civic dialogues among the competing viewpoints that a democratic society needs to function fairly.

Using Search Engines Effectively

A **search engine** is a software program that uses networks of computers to retrieve information from the Internet. The remarkable aspect of a search engine is its speed, propelling an Internet-connected device instantaneously through millions of webpages to locate topic-related websites. Anyone who has typed a keyword or phrase into a search box on a desktop, laptop, tablet, or smartphone and received tens of thousands of results knows how amazingly fast and potentially confusing online searching can be.

Overwhelmingly, Google is the most widely used search site (generating some 3.5 billion searches a day in 2018), followed by YouTube, Amazon, Facebook, and Bing—all of which are used more than such alternative search engines as DuckDuckGo, Ask, or Dogpile. Such general-purpose search engines locate information quickly and easily, but teachers and students benefit from tools like databases that allow them to directly access resources on academic topics with readily useful learning materials.

Internet search engines offer multi-modal information; display the text in original documents, books, magazines, blogs, and wikis; and include television and radio as sources of accessible materials.

SOURCE: Annie Fuller/Pearson Education

A **database** is a collection of information organized around specific topics and easily searchable by users. There are databases for almost every conceivable topic. Film viewers can learn about old movies from the Turner Classic Movies (TCM) database; baseball fans can gather statistical data about their favorite players from a database maintained by the Society for American Baseball Research (SABR); people who like to travel can learn about people and places around the world by consulting the Columbia Gazetteer of the World database. Individuals can create their own databases, as when an amateur chef builds a favorite recipe database.

Specialized search sites and databases are often more useful to teachers and students than what is found by typing keywords into a general search engine. Table 6.1 lists selected specialized search resources and databases for teachers.

Search engines have limitations in classroom teaching situations. In response to a query, massive search engines will return thousands of potentially relevant webpage selections. The question, "Why do volcanoes form near oceans?" will produce returns ranging from elementary-level science sites for children to U.S. Geological Survey links on geochemistry and satellite imagery intended for scientific specialists.

As a teacher, you must sort through masses of material to find what is relevant and age-appropriate for the class curriculum. Such sorting may take considerable time, and it can be tempting to choose whatever sites appear at the top of the search engine's list. But the most popular (meaning the most often visited) sites may not be the best

Table 6.1 Specialized Search Resources and Databases for Teachers

Search Engine/Database	Specialized Use
Citizendium	An encyclopedia with entries attributed to authors who wrote them to generate more focused and relevant search results
PsycINFO (Psychological Abstracts)	More than 3 million resources from the fields of psychology, behavioral science, and mental health
Webopedia	Computer and Internet definitions
Artcyclopedia	Works of art and famous artists from history and the present
Library of Congress American Memory	Primary source documents and exhibits on U.S. history
The National Archives Experience: Digital Vaults	Access to digital records from U.S. history and society
University of Texas at Austin Perry-Castañeda Library Map Collection	Online maps from the United States and the world
Open Library	A site whose long-term goal is to create one webpage for every book ever published
Educational Resources Information Center (ERIC)	More than a million education-related journal articles, books, conference papers, and technical reports
Web of Science	Materials from science, social science, and the arts and humanities
MacTutor History of Mathematics Archive	People and topics from the history of mathematics

match for classroom use. So teachers must review and select websites for learning and teach students about using the web as well.

The following strategies will help show students how to use search engines. This chapter's Technology Transformation Learning Plan, "From Text Sets to Media Sets," show these learning strategies in action.

INTRODUCE SEARCH SITES DESIGNED FOR STUDENTS   Search engines designed for students are relevant sources of age-appropriate curriculum resources. When students are able to read and understand the materials they find online, they learn how to access and assess the information independently. Table 6.2 provides a list of general and specialized Internet search tools for students. The general search sites conduct searches of all topics; the specialized search sites conduct searches within a specific information topic or category.

The Children and Technology Committee of the Association of Library Service to Children (ALSC) has specific criteria for evaluating whether a website communicates effectively to children. You can also find strategies for using search engines, evaluating webpages, and explaining Internet jargon in *Finding Information on the Internet: A Tutorial*, a free online resource from the University of California, Berkeley Library.

USE VISUAL SEARCH TOOLS   Typing keywords into any search engine will produce a list of relevant URLs. Google offers a variety of resource options with the standard URL list. These search options change over time: Presently, choices include images, news, maps, videos, applications, and books.

ENSURE SAFE ONLINE EXPERIENCES FOR STUDENTS   To ensure safe online experiences, teachers can preselect sites for students to visit. The bookmarking tool Portaportal limits students to only the sites you want them to view. If preselecting sites is not possible, several companies offer software packages to restrict where children go online. It lets adults control what sites students access online. Net Nanny and netTrekker are software programs that monitor, block, and report sites visited. These programs act as filters to prevent objectionable content from being viewed and are

Table 6.2 Kid-Safe Search Tools for Students

General Search Resources	Description
Kidtopia	For preschool and elementary students, this site indexes only educator-approved resources.
Kiddle and *KidRex*	*Kiddle* provides safe web, image, and video searching from Google; *KidRex*, also from Google, identifies websites with content geared to children.
KidsClick!	From the School of Library and Information Science at Kent State University, this site enables searches by keyword, digital media, and major topics of interest to children and adolescents.
SweetSearch	Locates only resources approved for Internet research experts.
Search-22	This single portal for 22 kid- and family-safe search engines sorts data from a variety of sites and combines the results into one database. See also Wacky Safe from Microsoft, as well as Safe Search Kids, available as an app.
Specialized Search Resources	
Kids.gov	This site provides searches and categories for governmental and nongovernmental services.
NASA Kids Club	Site provides news, missions, and multimedia about the National Aeronautics and Space Administration (NASA).
The Why Files: The Science behind the News	The Institute of Science and the University of Wisconsin–Madison present weekly science news stories and a Google-supported news story search feature.
U.S. Patent and Trademark Office Kids' Pages	The U.S. Patent and Trademark Office presents trading cards about famous inventors.
Time for Kids	This site searches news from around the world.
Smithsonian Education	The Smithsonian's collections for kids are featured online.
International Children's Digital Library	Find books in English and other native languages from around the world.

available for a monthly or yearly subscription fee. The American Library Association has assembled a collection of online safety and security resources for children titled "Especially for Young People and Their Parents." The site includes rules and suggestions for online safety and security, search resources designed for young people, and educational websites for families and teachers.

Evaluating Web Resources

Most search engines locate thousands and thousands of resources on virtually every academic topic. Most middle school and high school students assume that online search results produce fair and unbiased information, but that is not always the case. The following strategies are designed to teach students to evaluate the different types of information resources they will encounter online.

START WITH "WHO, WHAT, WHEN, WHY, AND HOW" AS WEB EVALUATION CRITERIA Most libraries, large and small, post specific criteria for evaluating web resources on their websites. Their lists commonly ask teachers and students to examine five attributes of web resources—Who, What, When, Why, and How.

- "Who" identifies the author of the site. Teachers and students must determine the authority or credibility of whoever has created this online material, including whether the author has the credentials and qualifications to produce web material on this topic.
- "What" measures the accuracy or reliability of the content. Teachers and students must determine whether the information is well researched and objective in its presentation.
- "When" assesses whether information is up to date. Teachers and students must assess whether the material posted on the site contains current facts and information.

- "Why" asks whether material is fair and unbiased. Teachers and students must assess whether the site is an objective presentation of information or primarily a one-sided presentation whose purpose is commercial (to sell products) or ideological (to promote a specific viewpoint or political position).

- "How" evaluates the ease of use and clarity of the information presented. Teachers and students must decide whether readers and viewers can easily navigate the site to access information.

High-quality sites generate informative, reliable, user-friendly content free from advertisements and commercial messages that clearly shows the author's credentials and the site's purpose.

PROVIDE WEB RESEARCH GUIDELINES AND PROCEDURES   Teaching students web research guidelines shows them how to become well-informed, thoughtful web users. Figure 6.1 offers web research guidelines for students. Students benefit from having a step-by-step process to follow for their web research. First, students begin their searches with straightforward, fact-based questions to establish a foundation of verifiable information on which to begin further study. For example, a science teacher teaching about hurricanes might ask students to research what was the most destructive hurricane in U.S. history. Locating answers to that question would lead to distinctions between the deadliest hurricane (the Great Galveston Hurricane of 1900) and the most devastating storm (Hurricane Katrina in 2005). Once known facts are in place, students can then proceed to investigate in depth the causes and consequences of events.

HAVE STUDENTS IDENTIFY THE URL AND DOMAIN NAME   Most students probably realize that every Internet address—or **uniform resource locator (URL)**—has a designation at the end, but they may not know why. This URL ending, known as a **top-level domain name (TLD)**, indicates the purpose and goal of an online site. The domain name system began in 1985. There are now over 1,500 TLDs in the United States, the most widely used of which include:

.**com** indicates a site that has a commercial purpose.

.**biz** is an extension of the .com domain name for individuals and companies whose goal is to either sell their site's contents or promote the sale of products mentioned or advertised on the site.

.**org** is for noncommercial organizations.

.**gov** is reserved for governmental agency sites.

.**net** means the site is a network provider.

.**edu** designates accredited postsecondary institutions (colleges and universities).

Figure 6.1 Web Research Guidelines

1	Limit a search to avoid unnecessary surfing and remain focused on your topic.
2	Determine the purpose of the site. Look for potential or hidden bias by answering the questions: "Who created this site, and why?"
3	Always check the credentials of authors whose writing appears on the web. People who publish on the web are not all experts in a field. Before citing information, determine whether the author is a reliable and credible source.
4	To determine the reliability of a website, cross-reference (check the facts with another source) your research.
5	Evaluate the site and its content before downloading information.
6	Credit web authors for their words and ideas using proper citations. While it is easy to copy other people's words and ideas from a website, this practice is no different from copying directly from a book—it is plagiarism.
7	Keep a log of all the sites you visit for the assignment. Bookmark or highlight your favorites.
8	Share useful ideas and information to help others with their research.
9	List all websites in correct form for every assignment. Websites are like books. If you use them, you must be able to document them and share with others how and where to locate the information.

.mil is for military organizations.

.info is for organizations providing general information.

.k12 is for schools in the United States (**.sch** is used by schools outside the United States).

.br (Brazil), **.ca** (Canada), **.in** (India), and **.il** (Israel) are examples of country code web addresses in other countries in the world.

Have students consult international sources of information when researching topics for school. News organizations and individual commentators often have different views from U.S. media sites reporting important events. You can follow the expansion of domain suffixes at the website of the Internet Corporation for Assigned Names and Numbers (ICANN).

The expansion of top-level domain names has led to a troubling new practice called Internet or IP Address Spoofing. This form of spoofing happens when someone creates a false domain name to impersonate a real one, generally with malicious or fraudulent intent. Adding just one or two look-alike characters to an Internet address is enough to divert traffic from real sites to bogus ones, creating real threats to computer users who are not fluent readers, who are learning to speak English as a new language, or who are just unwary about what they have typed into their device.

HAVE STUDENTS GO BEYOND THE FIRST PAGE OF SEARCH RESULTS   When doing research, students, whether in college or elementary and secondary schools, tend to choose sites appearing at the top of a page of search results, even when the content is not directly relevant to the topic they are researching. However, deciding to only consult the first couple of resources on a page of search results may not produce a reliable source for use in the classroom. To expand students' web search strategies, teachers can require them to go beyond the first page of search results to locate academic and news resources on a topic.

HAVE STUDENTS EVALUATE COGNITIVE LOAD   The ways online information is presented, known as **cognitive load**, either supports or restricts understanding and learning by readers and viewers. Some multimedia or information-rich websites offer too much information, distracting learners from the main ideas. To evaluate cognitive load, researchers from the University of Hawaii, Honolulu, have proposed six questions for students and teachers to ask when examining sites:

1. Is there an overload of information being presented?
2. Are the visuals used to enhance the text presented?
3. Do the graphics take over the webpage?
4. Are there a lot of media techniques used?
5. Is the information organized and clearly presented?
6. Does the site equally meet the needs of visual, auditory, and kinesthetic learners?

Iding, M., & Klemm, E. B. (2005). Pre-service teachers critically evaluate scientific information on the World Wide Web: What makes information believable? Computers in the Schools, 22(1/2), 7–17. Used with permission.

These questions help students see how websites that are selling products and services present cognitive load differently from sites that are dedicated to communicating scientific or historical information with no advertising or product promotion. Evaluating information presentation sharpens students' critical analysis skills and gives them knowledge to make informed choices about what are high-quality websites.

Open Educational Resources and Public Domain Materials

Increasingly, teachers and students are searching online for **open educational resources (OERs)**, what the United Nations Educational, Scientific and Cultural Organization (2017) has defined as "any type of educational materials that are in the public domain or introduced with an open license." In short, OER means "you may freely use and reuse, without charge" (OER Commons, 2015). It must be noted that "open" does not always mean free to use as one's own. Books in a library and most materials on the Web can be freely accessed, but they are not fully open, while OERs are explicitly free and open for use.

OERs are part of a broader movement toward **open education** that seeks to remove barriers to education by reducing costs and increasing access to high-quality teaching and learning resources. OERs include textbooks, journal articles, learning plans, audio and video materials, animations, podcasts, simulations, classroom exercises, assessments, and presentations, as well as courses and programs that are made available so teachers and students can freely use them.

Open educational resources carry licenses that include a set of permissions given by the creator(s) of the material to anyone who accesses them, organized around what educator David Wiley (n.d.) has called the "5 Rs of Openness." The 5 Rs give OER users the rights to: retain (make, own and control copies of the content); reuse (use content in a wide range of ways); revise (adapt, modify, alter the content); remix (combine content with other content to create something new); and redistribute (share content, revisions, and remixes with others).

For a teacher, collecting, bookmarking, and saving OERs greatly expands the range of materials students can use in the classroom. OERs offer ways to promote "peak learning experiences" in which students use information to engage in "application, analysis, decision-making and problem-solving" (Shank, 2014, p. 8). There is evidence that OERs improve students' academic performance. One large-scale study involving over 21,000 college undergraduates found that use of OERs increased end-of-course grades while decreasing the number of Ds, Fs, and class withdrawal for all students, including Pell Grant recipients, part-time students, and historically underserved diverse populations (Colvard, Watson, & Park, 2018).

OERs represent an alternative to commercial textbooks—materials that have long been as much a part of most schools as desks, chairs, and boards at the front of the room. Pre-K–12 publishers annually earn nearly $3 billion in sales of educational materials, much of that from textbook adoptions by states and school districts. As a student, you are undoubtedly well acquainted with textbooks—their length, complexity, and costs. The Center for Open Education at the University of Minnesota estimates college students spend $1,200 annually on textbooks and related course materials. Efforts are underway to address these expenses: More than 600 institutions of higher education nationwide are part of an open education network committed to reducing costs while utilizing free resources for course readings and learning activities.

In 2009, California began its free digital textbook initiative, while Oregon's Virtual School District made open educational resources available to teachers and students statewide. Utah began one of the earliest open textbook projects in 2012; that same year, the Washington State Legislature mandated the development of open courseware aligned to the Common Core standards. Many other states, including Virginia, Texas, Maine, and Maryland, also have open initiatives underway. You can keep track of the latest developments with the OER State Policy Tracker from the Scholarly Publishing and Academic Resources Coalition (SPARC), online. https://sparcopen.org/our-work/state-policy-tracking/

Just about every type of educational material is available as an open resource— textbooks, course readings, learning games, simulations, animations, lesson plans, worksheets, tests and quizzes, videos, audio recordings, lecture notes, and much more. And because the authors of these materials have not retained their ownership rights, teachers and students may use them and, in some cases, edit and repost them on school websites, blogs, and other online sources. Tech Tool 6.1 presents a listing of open access books, platforms, and courses.

To help teachers put this growing landscape of resources to use, the U.S. Department of Education launched #GoOpen, an initiative to invite educators to use OER licensed materials. #GoOpen districts pledge to integrate open licensed resources into their districts: 1) identifying a district #GoOpen team who will work to develop a strategy for the implementation of openly licensed educational materials; 2) committing to replace at least one textbook with openly licensed educational materials in the next year; 3) documenting and sharing their implementation process.

OERs support **Open Educational Practices (OEPs)**, also known as *open pedagogy* or *OER-enabled pedagogies*. OEPs create an intersection between learning, teaching, technology, and social justice. They promote direct student involvement in the teaching and learning process. Students from younger grades through high school can be involved in choosing, adapting, or remixing academic content; they can help adapt and create OERs to share with students in other schools; they can critique materials they find in paper and online sources; they can build their own collections of learning materials (what are known as cyberinfrastructures).

Teachers working with students to create OER learning resources is an example of an open educational practice. Beginning with the challenge, "Why consume information when you can create it?" teachers invite students to develop open materials that

---

Tech Tool 6.1

Open Access Textbooks, Materials and Courses

Open access textbooks are textbooks that have been published with licenses that let teachers and students freely use, adapt, and distribute the material for educational purposes. They provide relevant curriculum resources for teachers and engaging learning experiences for students. Not all open access textbooks offer interactive features, but those that do provide readers with unique educational experiences. Readers can access the text on a computer, tablet, or smartphone. Depending on the book, readers will find numerous interactive features that expand the text into multimodal learning experiences: 1) live links to video, audio, and print resources; 2) interactive search and navigation features; 3) embedded quizzes and application exercises for self-paced learning; and 4) capacity to create study notes on a page while visually highlighting important concepts.

OpenStax at Rice University offers online textbooks for college courses in math (Prealgebra, Algebra, Calculus, Statistics), science (Anatomy & Physiology, Astronomy, Biology, Chemistry, Physics), humanities (U.S. History), and social science (American Government, Economics, Psychology, Sociology). Although the books are designed for college courses, middle school and high school teachers and students will find many useful resources.

Additional free to use open textbooks include:

- Directory of Open Access Books is a clearinghouse created to make open access texts easy to find.
- College Open Textbooks is a peer-reviewed source for almost 800 textbooks serving advanced high school, two-year and four-year institutions.
- Open Textbook Library is sponsored by the Center for Open Education and the Open Textbook Network. Most of this library's resources fall under a Creative Commons license, so they can be edited and adapted to fit the needs of your curriculum.
- OER Commons is a vast online library of free and open educational materials featuring more than 500 content providers from around the world; Wikimedia Commons is an extensive database of images and other visual materials for use in classroom lessons and homework assignments;

LibriVox has audio recordings of literature, poetry, and nonfiction materials in the public domain available in their entirety or a chapter a day from iTunes—the site's long-term goal is to make all public domain books available free in audio formats.

There are two other types of open access materials to guide teachers and students through finding and categorizing OER and public domain resources: 1) open access tools and 2) open access courses.

Open Access Materials

- The Mason OER Metafinder from George Mason University is a tool for finding open resources; it searches multiple databases, including OER Commons, and locates online courses, presentations slides, simulations, images and other resources.
- Pixabay lets you locate royalty- and attribute-free downloadable images and share your own images with people around the globe.
- PicJumbo has free stock photos for any type of use with a user-friendly search engine. No attribution is needed.
- Copyright and Intellectual Property Toolkit is a University of Pittsburgh database connecting users to artwork and images that can be found in the public domain.

Open Access Courses

- LearningSpace from Open University hosts Creative Commons licensed materials and offers learning categories that include "Brush Up on Skills" and "Earn While You Learn" digital badges.
- Open Courseware is a higher education search engine with an Educator Portal K–12 and Featured Courses area. Resources include exams, texts, and video lectures.
- Open Culture offers over 1,000 free courses from all over the world organized by topic, title, and faculty.

As with any resource, open educational and public domain materials vary. In terms of quality and usefulness, teachers and students need to assess the materials to determine appropriateness to their curriculum needs.

other teachers and students can use in their classes. Students could research science and history topics or information about well-known and lesser-known writers and their works. They could create interactive maps of community settings, write informational materials about how to use new digital tools, or respond to other issues and problems in their community. Once the research is done, students can design a website and post their materials online where it can be freely accessed by educators.

Public domain materials are another category of open educational resources in that they are either ineligible for copyright or their original copyright has expired. As the U.S. Copyright Office has explained, the "public domain is not a place" but a status that is assigned to written or visual publications. Materials in the public domain may be freely used without the permission of the former copyright owner.

In general, works published in the United States before 1923 are in the public domain, as are materials produced by the U.S. government (laws, judicial opinions, and legislative reports and documents). Words, numbers, names, symbols, and signs are not subject to copyright—nor are scientific principles and mathematical formulas (University of California, 2003). Under current law, no new works could enter the public domain until 2019. Even when using public domain materials, teachers and students are required to cite the material appropriately with footnotes and references.

Notable OER and public domain resources include materials from the Library of Congress, the National Archives, government agencies, museums, universities, and not-for-profit organizations. Additionally, Smithsonian Education has primary source documents and interview clips with professionals from many different fields. While not all are Creative Commons, TED Talks where researchers and educators share ideas in 18-minute long videos can be a surprising, entertaining, up to date classroom resource. Khan Academy videos are not necessarily OER, but some, not all, are open licensed. They cannot be downloaded or remixed, only watched and embedded on other websites.

> MyLab Education **Application Exercise 6.1:**
> Exploring the Interactive Features of an OER e-Textbook
>
> MyLab Education **Self-Check 6.3**

Using Technology as Digital Citizens

6.4   Discuss ways teachers and students can use technology as digital citizens.

Teaching students to think and act as digital citizens has become an essential part of school curriculum throughout the United States. Digital citizenship is a broad concept; it includes multiple aspects of appropriate technology use, as identified by (Common Sense Education, 2015):

- *Digital footprint and reputation* (the information that exists online about an individual; for more, see Chapter 5)
- *Digital relationships and communications* (ways in which people share ideas and information electronically; for more, see Chapter 9)
- *Privacy and security* (protections that exist to maintain an individual's information in online spaces; for more, see Chapter 2)
- *Internet safety* (rights, responsibilities, norms and expectations for proper conduct in online settings; for more, see Chapter 3)
- *Cyberbullying and digital drama* (using computers and social media to harass or demean others; for more, see the following section of Chapter 6)
- *Creative credit and copyright* (rules for how an author's work can be used online while avoiding wrongfully using someone else's words or ideas as one's own; for more, see the following section of Chapter 6)
- *Information literacy* (using search engines and other tools to do digital research and critically assess information from the Internet; for more, see the following section of Chapter 6).

MyLab Education
Video Example 6.4
In this video, you will learn how copyright and fair use are as important with digital materials as they are with paper sources. How do you plan to help students learn to cite sources and produce original work?

Acting as a digital citizen requires individuals to adopt ethical habits of mind while engaging in safe, responsible online behaviors that harm no one, themselves included. Digital citizenship may be usefully thought of as values and norms that students learn to adopt, with teachers as coaches providing different types of experiences to define and practice how to behave collectively and individually in the classroom and outside of school.

To promote digital citizenship, many schools adopt **acceptable use policies (AUPs)**—rules for technology use and consequences of ignoring them. Common penalties for violating acceptable use rules include loss of cell phones, detention, or suspension from school. However, as educators Mike Ribble and Gerald Bailey (2011, p. 9) remind teachers, "Rules do not teach students what is appropriate and why, and instead simply define the uses that are restricted in the school setting."

Beyond being told what not to do, students need to learn why to be responsible users of technology in schools and communities. Students need a framework of digital ethics and values that explains how to live and act in a digital world as a way to consider their choices seriously before making them. In schools, students encounter the realities of appropriate and inappropriate technology use, giving teachers real-life examples for the teaching and learning of digital values.

Copyright, Fair Use, and Creative Commons

Immense amounts of instantly accessible online information require teachers and students to learn about copyright and fair use guidelines. Violations of copyright rules occur inadvertently and unintentionally, but no educator wants students to deliberately copy another person's work without permission or attribution. Here are key concepts for teachers and students to understand:

COPYRIGHT   Have you ever created anything that holds a copyright? Copyright can be tricky, but let's simplify it a bit. Have you ever taken a photograph with your phone? Then, yes, you have created something that holds a copyright. Unlike a patent, which you have to submit to the government, you own the copyright to anything you create the second it is created if it is captured or written down. **Copyright** is a legal protection given by the laws of the United States to a person's creative "literary, dramatic, musical, or artistic works" (U.S. Copyright Office, 2011). Software code, too, is copyrightable. Copyright establishes that creative material is owned by its creator and cannot be used by others without the original author's permission. One goal of copyright is protecting the commercial interests of authors who want to sell their work in the marketplace, but copyright is also intended to support the ongoing free expression of ideas and images in a democratic society. Individuals who create materials for everyone to enjoy are duly recognized for their efforts through copyright protection. You can learn more at "Copyright Basics" from the U.S. Copyright Office at the Library of Congress.

FAIR USE AND CREATIVE COMMONS   The doctrine of **fair use** allows teachers and students to freely use limited amounts of copyrighted material for educational or research purposes. Fair use is based on four principles: 1) purpose and character of the use; 2) nature of the copyrighted work; 3) amount of material being used in relation to the entire work; and 4) impact on the potential market for the material (Harvell, 2018). Fair use involves judgment calls—teachers and students should not use so much of a copyrighted work that they impact the author or copyright holder's ability to distribute or sell the material.

Broadly speaking, fair use allows teachers to make multiple copies of material for educational use with students, although technically copying an entire chapter of a textbook and sharing it with a class is copyright infringement. The Technology, Education, and Copyright Harmonization (TEACH) Act of 2002 extended the concept of fair use to distance education and online learning settings, but laws leave the line between fair use and copyright infringement intentionally vague. In theory, use of copyrighted material by teachers and students should be brief, spontaneous, and occasional rather than systematic. Using someone else's material throughout the school year without permission or attribution is not protected. Students and teachers must be careful about how they use and distribute material. Posting someone else's work (for example, any image taken from a Google image search) on school or classroom websites without permission is distributing that material beyond the boundaries of fair use.

Creative Commons is a process by which authors keep their copyright but allow other people to copy, use, or modify the materials, provided users credit the author in a way the author specifies through one of four Creative Commons licenses (Attribution, Share-Alike, Non-Commercial, and Non-Derivative). Wikimedia Commons, sponsored by the Wikimedia Foundation, is one comprehensive source of public domain and freely licensed photographs, videos, sound recordings, and other visual media covering just about every educational topic, available in dozens of different languages, all under Creative Commons licenses. You can use images and other media from Wikimedia Commons if you give proper attribution and comply with the Creative Commons license selected for the material. See "How to Give Attribution" from the Creative Commons website to learn more.

Wikimedia Commons offers an ever-growing collection of resources for teachers and students who want to include visual materials with classroom lessons or homework assignments. There are photographic reproductions of works by artists, well known and obscure, that expand the teaching of any subject area. If teachers want images of famous people, historical events, or modern-day topics, they can type in a keyword search term and receive an impressive range of resources. For example, "William Shakespeare" as a search term returns hundreds of images, including the title pages from the first printings of his works, an 1849 painting by John Gilbert featuring scenes from several plays, an 1864 poster stamp featuring a side image of the playwright, a poster for the 2008 season of Shakespeare by the Sea in Los Angeles, and a modern-day photograph of Shakespeare's birthplace in Stratford-upon-Avon, England.

Wikimedia Commons features a Picture of the Day and Media of the Day on its home page; votes by users of the site determine the best pictures of the year. Pictures of the Day include live links, offering multiple instructional possibilities. When the Picture of the Day featured photos of the almost-finished Eiffel Tower in 1888, the live link brought teachers and students to a World War II order by Adolf Hitler to General Dietrich von Choltitz to demolish the tower and burn the city, an order the general defied, saving Paris and its priceless historical and architectural treasures from destruction. Because its vast resource files include explicit images, Wikimedia Commons must be previewed and used with discretion by teachers.

STRATEGIES FOR USING PUBLIC DOMAIN AND CREATIVE COMMONS MATERIALS There are basic rules for teachers and students to follow when dealing with public domain and Creative Commons materials:

- Taking someone's pictures or information and using them as your own is a violation of the copyright laws of the United States. If you find online information that you wish to use for a digital presentation, wiki, blog, or other teaching format and it is not in the public domain, you must seek and get permission from its author.

- If you find website information that is in the public domain, that information is usable without infringing copyright laws. In addition, if you find websites that have Creative Commons licenses, you are welcome to use the information posted on those sites if you abide by the Creative Commons license rules for the material.

- Contact the rightsholder if you are unsure about the status of material you want to use. Here is a sample letter we used when adding an image of the Massachusetts state constitution to a wiki for history students and teachers.

Hello,

We are writing to inquire if we can use an image of the Massachusetts Constitution from your website [insert URL here]. We have searched the Internet for a picture of this document but were unable to find one from a government website. We are creating an educational wiki, and this image would be a useful source for us. Thank you for your consideration of our request.

Plagiarism and Cheating

Plagiarism is the direct copying and misrepresentation of someone else's work as one's own. Quoting or copying someone else's words—written or spoken—without attribution is dishonest, whether in publishing, schools, colleges, or society. **Cheating** involves gaining information without permission before or during tests or sending information about a test to other students before or during an exam.

Rapid access to online information has given students digital tools for plagiarizing and cheating (Bain, 2015). Some students use the Internet to plagiarize an assignment, in some cases by submitting papers written and posted online by others as their own work. Other students cheat on tests by saving information from notes and textbooks on their cell phones, texting pictures of exam questions to friends, or using phones to search the Internet when teachers are not looking.

Three primary factors contribute to these forms of plagiarism and cheating in schools.

1. *The web.* The Internet is a vast, unregulated marketplace in which term papers are for sale or available free to students, and entire texts of articles and books are posted online from which information can be easily copied without citing the author during a test or in an assignment.

2. *High-stakes testing.* The nation's current emphasis on test results, high grades, and intense competition for college placement creates a context that makes plagiarism seem conducive to achieving high grades.

3. *Student misunderstandings.* Students may venture over the line of academic dishonesty without realizing they have done so (Cleary, 2017; Dee & Jacob, 2012). They may assume that if information is on the Internet, it is free to use and they incorporate it without citing sources. Alternately, they may not understand how to correctly cite an online or paper source or may be confused about what to cite and what to credit as their own ideas. For instance, students in a web design class thought that they could use any image from a Google Image search on their website if they "cited" it—but this is still copyright infringement. At other times, when teachers ask students to write about topics that experts have already explained in books and articles, youngsters may feel intimidated, realizing their content knowledge and writing style cannot approximate that of academic sources. They think, "I'll just copy what I found so I will be sure to be right."

Teachers employ different strategies to identify papers that contain uncited material, including searching the Internet themselves to find the original sources. Some type a sentence that might be plagiarized into a search engine to see if the original source turns up. Many school systems subscribe to plagiarism detection services, such as Turnitin and iThenticate, which electronically scan student work to identify text copied directly from other sources. Google for Education has a feature called Originality Reports that identifies text that should have a citation.

Critics of plagiarism detection systems contend that these services cause undue anxiety, fear, and stress for students who worry that their own unique words and original compositions might be plagiarized by accident. These critics urge teachers to spend more time teaching students how to write clear and appropriately cited papers. Additionally, two researchers have taken issue with Turnitin's business model, saying that by incorporating student essays into its database, the company is profiting, although legally, from the work of uncompensated student authors (Morris & Stommel, 2017).

Rather than focusing on the outcomes for students who plagiarize material, there are strategies for teachers to use before students submit their work. Writing more than 20 years ago, educator Jamie McKenzie 1998) identified seven still-relevant ways for teachers to combat plagiarism and cheating while teaching important research and thinking skills: 1) distinguish between different levels or types of research; 2) discourage "trivial pursuits" and fact-based assignments; 3) emphasize essential questions for students to explore in their research; 4) require students to provide written responses in their own words; 5) collect information and references about key topics; 6) stress citation ethics; and 7) assess student progress throughout the whole research process.

McKenzie's strategies, which apply to both paper and online learning, emphasize that the way teachers construct assignments determines how likely students are to plagiarize. If an assignment asks students solely to find already established facts (for example, "Describe the climate of the Gobi Desert" or "List the characteristics of each of the planets in the solar system"), it is easy and quick to copy sentences and phrases verbatim from books or websites.

When asked to locate information and analyze the material, students have fewer ready-made opportunities to copy other people's work. McKenzie recommends that instead of asking "why" something happened in the past, teachers ask students to consider "why various outcomes did not occur." Or students might be asked to present multiple strategies for solving a math or science problem or to compose a poem or a story from different points of view than the one they are reading. The goal is for students to "become producers of insights and ideas rather than mere consumers" of the information they locate during their research.

Standing Up against Bullying and Cyberbullying

Bullying is "unwanted aggressive behavior" by one person toward another; in and out of schools, it can involve threats, rumors, physical assaults, and exclusions (StopBullying.gov, 2014). In contrast with face-to-face verbal or physical threats and intimidations, **cyberbullying** is a form of bullying in which the bully uses mobile phones, text messages, chat rooms, e-mail, and webcams to communicate negative and harmful messages. Many times, victims do not know who is sending bullying messages. Instead, anonymous threats suddenly appear on their phones or computer screens. The issue has become so pervasive that almost every state has passed laws addressing cyberbullying, cyberstalking, and cyberharassment. You can find state-by-state information regarding cyber laws on the National Council of State Legislatures website.

Bullying and cyberbullying are significant problems in schools. "From Teasing to Torment," a 2016 national report by the Gay, Lesbian & Straight Education Network (GLSEN) found that despite efforts to create safe educational environments, large numbers of secondary school students continue to hear high levels of biased language from other students, and sometimes from teachers and other adults. Additionally, a sizeable number of youngsters say they feel unsafe at school, experiencing bullying and harassment based on physical appearance, gender expression, race/ethnicity, or academic ability (Kosciw, et al., 2018; Greytak, et al., 2016).

A U.S. Department of Justice study reported that nearly one in three students say they have been bullied at school; 1 in 10 say they have been cyberbullied (Robers, et al., 2014). Between 10%-20% of school-age students admit to engaging in some form of harmful technology use, including cyberbullying (Patchin & Hinduja, 2012). A study by the Children's Hospital of Pittsburgh found that two in five teenagers in dating relationships experienced cyber abuse that included threatening comments, rumor spreading, or unwanted sexual advances (Dick, McCauley, & Jones, et al., 2014).

Bullies and cyberbullies target girls who, more than boys, are called names, made fun of or insulted, made the victim of false rumors, or deliberately excluded from peer group activities. Girls are also more likely to have hurtful information posted about them online or to receive harassing text messages. Both girls and boys engage in bullying and cyberbullying activities, although girls tend to spread rumors online while boys are more likely to post harmful pictures (Patchin & Hinduja, 2012, p. 20).

Bullying and cyberbullying can have a negative and lasting impact on students' academic performance and personal self-esteem. Consequences for victims include depression, anxiety, low self-esteem, poor school performance, and suicidal tendencies (Williams & Peguero, 2011; Patchin & Hinduja, 2016). Student victims of cyberbullying have been found to be twice as likely to smoke, drink, and use marijuana (National Center on Addiction and Substance Abuse at Columbia University, 2011). Lesbian, gay, bisexual, and transgender students are at greater risk of being bullied in schools and online and are two to three times more likely to be verbally threatened or physically harassed because of their gender expression (GLSEN, 2013). Almost half of all LGBT youth surveyed had skipped at least one class or an entire day of school in the past month because of fear for their safety at school (Greytak, Kosciw, & Diaz, 2009).

Many schools and teachers have a zero tolerance policy toward hateful or abusive language in the classroom, and this prohibition can be extended to online communications. But zero tolerance alone does not stop bullying and cyberbullying. Students need to understand the negative consequences of bullying in any form and then choose to avoid participating in such behaviors. Teachers play crucial roles in creating safe spaces for students within schools (Meyer & Sansfacon, 2014). By their words and actions they demonstrate convincingly how harmful to everyone it is when any individual or group is singled out because they do not conform to perceived norms or expectations.

Strategies for building safe and supportive school cultures include:

- Peer mentoring of younger students by older students to counteract bullying by having both age groups learn to respect and care about one another.
- Promoting empathy and compassion among students in schools to encourage peer group disapproval of bullying and to improve the overall climate and safety of a school (Eyman, 2009).
- Providing ongoing support for all students within a learning community to build mind-sets among youngsters that emphasize wise choices for using technology. Schools in which teachers and peers purposefully support each other create "up-stander" behavior where individuals and groups intervene to prevent negative actions. Unlike bystanders, who watch from the sidelines, upstanders create a climate of peaceful conflict resolution and mutual respect among adults and students.
- Participating in Teen Tech Week, an annual event sponsored by the American Library Association every March, to teach the importance of ethical technology use. Related initiatives include No Name Calling Week, sponsored by the Gay, Lesbian & Straight Education Network (GLSEN) and Safer Internet Day, held in February in 140 countries worldwide. All these activities are designed to raise awareness of and change attitudes about the practice and prevention of bullying and cyberbullying.

Digital Dialog 6.2

Many students are online by third grade, and increasing numbers of them have their own mobile phone by middle school. Grades 3 through 8 also are when bullying and cyberbullying emerge as serious issues in schools. As you consider the roles of teachers in dealing with bullying and cyberbullying, comment and connect online about the following questions:

- In your view, why do bullying and cyberbullying occur, and how might teachers help students to examine their causes and eliminate their hurtful behaviors from schools?
- At what age do you think teaching empathy toward others and respectful communication should begin in schools? Do you know of or have you participated in activities that are effective bullying and cyberbullying prevention strategies?
- As a teacher, what are you planning to do to create safe classrooms, corridors, and play spaces for all students?

Resources for combating bullying and cyberbullying are available from the following organizations:

- Cyberbullying Research Center
- Safe Schools Coalition
- CyberSmart Curriculum
- BeatBullying.org
- National Organization for Women (NOW)
- Teaching Tolerance, a website from the Southern Poverty Law Center
- Gay, Lesbian & Straight Education Network (GLSEN)

> **MyLab Education Application Exercise 6.2:**
>
> **MyLab Education Self-Check 6.4:**
> Building Your PLN: Exploring the Multiple Dimensions of Digital Citizenship

Technology Transformation Learning Plan

From Text Sets to Media Sets

Researching Historical Biographies of Women Scientists Online

Grade(s)	Upper elementary, middle, and high school
Subject(s)	History/social studies or English/language arts or science
Key Goal/Enduring Understanding	Students cannot gain a full picture of the lives of historical individuals—famous figures or ordinary people—solely by reading one or two sources. Biographical research that includes multiple types of information from different perspectives creates a more complete presentation of a person's life and times.
Essential Question	How can technology enable middle and high school students to investigate and document the lives of historical figures using multiple sources?

Academic Discipline Learning Standards	**National Council for the Social Studies (NCSS):** *Expectations for Excellence: Curriculum Standards for the Social Studies*
	    Theme III: People, Places, and Environment
	    Theme IV: Individual Development and Identity
	    Theme XI: Global Connections
	National Council of Teachers of English (NCTE): *Standards for the English Language Arts*
	    Standard 8: Using Technology to Research and Communicate Information

Learning Objectives	Students will know how and be able to: • Demonstrate the value and application of essential questions to guide research about history and society • Apply an organized note-taking system for gathering information from diverse sources and record properly formatted bibliographic references • Analyze the differences among facts, opinions, and inferences in written and online sources of information • Use the Internet and video equipment technology to produce informative historical biographies about famous and unknown people
Technology Uses	The lesson utilizes the Internet, social bookmarking, and wiki technologies for investigating and publishing students' historical research.

Minimal Technology	**Infusion of Technology**
Students consult a librarian and/or online catalog to locate information about historical figures.	Students use search engines and databases to locate information about historical figures.
Students take notes on paper notecards or teacher-generated worksheets.	Students use digital note-taking tools.
Students write historical biography reports and present them orally to the class.	Students assemble a collection of historical biography websites using social bookmarking and publish these resources digitally on a class website, blog, or wiki.

Evaluation	• Journal entries describing online research findings • Digitally archived list of websites used by each student, including online biographies, primary source materials, books, media, and other resources • Individual and group participation in researching, writing, and presenting findings • Student performance rubrics completed at the level of exemplary or very useful

Learning Plan Description	**Learning Focus**
	
	"From Text Sets to Media Sets" utilizes websites, social bookmarking tools, and a class wiki, blog, or website to diversify student research sources and enable presentation of historical biography media sets. This lesson, intended for upper elementary, middle, or high school classes as part of a history/social studies or language arts curriculum, is equally useful to science and math teachers exploring contributions of scientists and mathematicians or historical discoveries and ideas in these fields.
	
	    Teaching about the lives of historical figures is a regular part of most school curricula: U.S. presidents in social studies classes, prominent writers and artists in English classes, and notable biologists, chemists, mathematicians, and computer scientists in math and science classes. Stories about famous people are featured in textbooks and state or local curriculum materials.
	
	    But famous and powerful people, most often men, are not the only history-making individuals for students to explore. Important discoveries and great changes in every academic field can be traced to women who are not mentioned or are little recognized in textbooks. Examples include:

(continued)

**Learning Plan
Description**
(*continued*)

- Mary Anning, who, in 1810 at the age of 12, discovered the first Jurassic-age ichthyosaurus fossil on a beach at Lyme Regis, England, which launched her lifelong career as a paleontologist at a time when women were not recognized for their work in science, no one realized what these fossils were, and the term *dinosaur* had not yet been created. As a self-taught, impoverished woman in the new field of geology and paleontology, her work remained largely unknown and uncredited during her lifetime and for 100 years thereafter.
- Caroline Herschel, who as the first woman to discover a comet, received a gold medal from the Royal Astronomical Society honoring her lifetime of work as an astronomer.
- Beatrix Potter, author, illustrator, and inventor of children's hand-sized Peter Rabbit books, did important research about the specialized study of mycology (fungi) that was never published, nor was she allowed entry into the prestigious all-male Linnean Society of natural history researchers.
- Grace Hopper, an early 20th century contributor to the field of computer science, became a rear admiral in the U.S. Navy and invented the language for computers called COBALT.
- Hedy Lamarr, a Hollywood film actress known as the most beautiful woman in the world, who with modern music composer George Antheil, collaboratively invented and patented the device that introduced the application of frequency hopping to stop the jamming of messages between submarines in 1942 during World War II. Its use today in technologies throughout the world—cell phone networks, Bluetooth, GPS and other information systems—is a result of Lamarr's math and science knowledge and her inventive mind.
- Ada Lovelace, a 19th century scholar and pioneer in thematic computing, invented the first algorithm, the conception of a computer language, in 1843. Her work is honored every October as part of the international Ada Lovelace Day celebration of women in science, technology, engineering, and math.

The list of little-known women advancers of knowledge goes on and on—individuals who made history but are not featured in the history books. In this lesson, students practice the skills of information and media literacy. They construct historical biographies of famous and little-known individuals from web-based information sources and present their findings on a classroom wiki, blog, or website. In so doing, they use multiple digital media to demonstrate new forms of digital-age reading and writing. This process has been called "media interactivity," in which writers "bring multiple media into play with one another as part of a single, overall composing process" (Ranker, 2010, p. 37).

Learning Design—Minimal Technology

A minimal technology version of a historical biography lesson begins with students choosing or being assigned individuals to investigate. Students proceed by following guidelines provided by the teacher. After completing the assignment, students write a summary of the person's life and accomplishments, noting the individual's importance in the fields of history, literature, math, or science/engineering.

Students use a search engine or online library database to locate biographical information in this minimal technology version of the lesson. These information sources constitute a *text set*. Text sets, usually books or other text-based materials about a person's life, may also include information available online at websites such as Wikipedia, Biography, or About.

Students use text-based resources to generate a written biographical summary of a person. Their reports may differ little from a summary of information found online or in a general history book. Students present their reports in class as part of a discussion that summarizes the lesson and what everyone has learned about different historical people. The teacher grades student reports, assessing the quality of research resources and the clarity of the written presentations.

Learning Activities Using Technology

A teacher can open the learning activity with this announcement: "Today we are going to learn about women scientists in history who have done extraordinary things that make them both *influential* and *consequential* to our lives today. You may or may not recognize their names, but the accomplishments of each will be surprising."

Groups of students are then given the names of historically significant women in science to research using online resources and social bookmarking tools, in combination with wikis, blogs, and websites, to transform how students think of doing historical research and presenting their findings to others. Here are the steps to follow:

1. *Change the research process from text set to media set.* Teachers begin a technology-transformed history biography lesson plan by redefining the Internet search process. Instead of locating text-based information sites about a historical figure (a text set), students find multimedia resources—different forms of information presentation that become a *media set*. A media set includes web-based video, audio, and interactive multimedia resources, as well as text-based materials.
2. *Locate a range of resources for a media set.* A goal for students when assembling a media set is to locate a range of resources about the life and times of a historical figure. In contrast to a written biographical report, a media set offers a collage of viewpoints about the person. A media set for paleontologist Mary Anning might include a biography from the Women in Science website of the San Diego Supercomputer Center; a timeline of her life from England's National History Museum; drawings of fossils she found in her discoveries; a video of the cliffs at Lyme Regis, England, where she discovered her first fossil as a child; and an evocative picture book biography about her life, *Mary Anning and the Sea Dragon* by author Jeannine Atkins.

3. *Ask students to analyze their media set resources.* Have students pair up and analyze each other's curated media sets, evaluating how the range of resources informs their knowledge about the persons they are researching. It is likely that by locating multiple media resources, students will discover interesting stories or details that comprise important themes, accomplishments, and struggles in addition to the names, dates, and places of that life. Mary Anning tried to practice science in a male-only field that neither recognized women as equals nor appreciated the vast importance of their discoveries. The frustrations of not receiving recognition or monetary compensation for important achievements may be more clearly understood through a wide-angle view of a media set.

4. *Assemble media set resources around common topics or themes.* Working together, teachers and students create groups of resources about historical figures, transforming paper text sets into digital media sets.

5. *Publish student research on a class wiki, blog, or website.* When the research is completed, students publish their media sets on a Google Doc or Site, wiki, or virtual bulletin/whiteboard (e.g., Padlet, Wakelet, Webjets.io). Students can add a short commentary explaining their conclusions about the historical significance and lasting impacts of the person they researched. They could also create their own media to add to the media set (e.g., a remix video, an annotated image, a history trailer).

Analysis and Extensions

1. Describe two features you find useful about this learning activity.
2. How widely do you think information technology has been integrated into the students' research?
3. Name two areas for extension or revision of this learning activity.
4. How might students become involved in designing, enacting, and evaluating their technology use in the experience?

Chapter Summary

Learning Outcome 6.1

Explain the meanings of literacy in an information age for teachers and students.

- Instantly available online information has created the need for teachers and students to learn how to carefully *access* and critically *assess* the resources and materials they find on the web.

- Teaching students how to do Internet research is a necessary element of information literacy.

- Fake and false news includes efforts to present misleading or totally untrue information as straightforward and accurate facts.

- Open educational resources (OERs) and public domain materials are low-cost or no-cost resources for teachers and students to use for academic learning.

Learning Outcome 6.2

Analyze the challenges of online information, including uncovering fake news and utilizing Wikipedia.

- Four types of information problems are found on the web: 1) misinformation, 2) malinformation, 3) messed-up information, and 4) mostly useless information.

- Wikipedia offers opportunities to teach students ways to evaluate the quality of information found on the web.

- High-quality online information meets five criteria: 1) authority, 2) accuracy, 3) currency, 4) objectivity, and 5) coverage.

- Paying attention to URLs, discussing cognitive load, using lesson and learning plan sites selectively, and giving clear web research guidelines are important strategies for teaching Internet information evaluation to students.

Learning Outcome 6.3

Identify strategies for researching and retrieving online information, including open educational resources and public domain materials.

- Search engines enable teachers and students to access online information by locating webpages that have been linked to their database.

- Online information searching, or Internet information research and retrieval, means knowing how to locate and analyze information from the web.

- Specialized search resources narrow the sweep of searches to more educationally relevant materials.

- Digital note taking offers teachers and students new ways to record and save the information they locate online.

- Search resources designed for students provide age-appropriate information and information literacy learning experiences.

Learning Outcome 6.4

Discuss ways teachers and students can use technology as digital citizens.

- Digital ethics include the ways teachers and students should use technology appropriately.

- Copyright laws are designed to protect authors and artists; fair use guidelines enable teachers and students to use copyrighted material for educational purposes;

public domain materials can be used without infringing on copyright.

- Plagiarism is the act of directly copying or misrepresenting someone else's work as one's own; people plagiarize both intentionally and unintentionally.

- The ways teachers structure classroom and homework assignments can significantly reduce or even avoid situations in which students might plagiarize.

- Cyberbullying involves the use of computers, cell phones, or other technologies in ways that threaten or harm others.

- Building a classroom culture that has zero tolerance for hateful or abusive language and behavior is an essential step in combating cyberbullying and other harmful uses of technology.

Key Terms

Acceptable use policies (AUPs), p. 152
Bullying, p. 155
Censorship, p. 137
Cheating, p. 154
Cognitive load, p. 148
Copyright, p. 152
Creative Commons, p. 153
Critical reading, p. 138
Cyberbullying, p. 155
Database, p. 144
Fair use, p. 152
Fake and false news, p. 138
Filtering software, p. 138
Information research and retrieval, p. 143
Information technology (IT) fluency, p. 135
Keywords, p. 143

Malinformation, p. 137
Messed-up information, p. 137
Misinformation, p. 137
Mostly useless information, p. 137
Note-taking tools and apps, p. 135
Open access textbooks, p. 150
Open education, p. 149
Open educational practices (OEPs), p. 150
Open educational resources (OERs), p. 148
Partitions, p. 138
Plagiarism, p. 154
Public domain, p. 151
Search engine, p. 144
top-level domain name (TLD), p. 147
uniform resource locator (URL), p. 147
Wikipedia, p. 140

MyLab Education Application Exercise 6.3
Growing and Leading with Technology: Erich's "Researching the First Thanksgiving" Learning Activity

---

For Reflection and Discussion

Developing Effective Search Strategies

From planning learning activities to answering students' questions, effective search strategies will make a difference in how successfully you can find the resources you need to teach and inspire students. To develop effective search strategies, answer the following questions:

- How do you begin researching a new topic online? What search strategies do you employ? How do you keep track of the results of your searches?

- Which of the most popular search engines give the clearest information results when you are seeking academic and educational resources and information?

- Examining search results, what differences did you find in the kinds of information on sites designated .org, .com, .gov, or .net?

Evaluating Wikipedia

Using Wikipedia to examine a topic in your teaching field or one of your college education classes, consider the following questions:

- How do your college textbook and Wikipedia discuss the same topic? Do they repeat the same information or complement each other with different facts and illustrations? Does each source provide full and accurate representation of women, people of color, and LGBTQ topics?

- What are the strengths and weaknesses of the Wikipedia entry? Would you suggest putting the Wikipedia entry under dispute? If you could, would you suggest putting the textbook's treatment of the same topic under dispute?

- Which source, textbook, Wikipedia or do you evaluate as more accessible to K–12 student readers?

Chapter 7
Engaging in Virtual Learning with Online Resources

SOURCE: Legend_art/Shutterstock

Chapter Overview

Chapter 7 explores how teachers and students can utilize the online learning resources provided by educational websites, apps, and other digital materials. The first half of the chapter introduces social bookmarking, cloud computing, learning management systems (LMS), information alerts, and e-newsletters as ways to curate learning resources. We focus on developing lessons aligned to local, state, and national curriculum frameworks. In the second half of the chapter, virtual schools, online and blended learning, massive open online courses (MOOCs), and WebQuests/HyperDocs are discussed as virtual learning alternatives to face-to-face classroom instruction. We also examine different types of educational websites and apps—including virtual and augmented reality tools—that support exploratory learning in online settings. The chapter concludes with a Technology Transformation Learning Plan titled "Weather Station WebQuest."

With its focus on using digital tools to curate and utilize online information, the chapter addresses the ISTE Standard for Students: Global Communicator, in which students learn how to use digital technologies to connect with and learn from people and places—locally and globally—through online and offline experiences.

Learning Outcomes

After reading this chapter, you will be able to:

7.1 Describe technologies for curating digital content, including bookmarking, social bookmarking, cloud computing, Google tools, and learning management systems.

7.2 Organize web resources to address curriculum standards utilizing information alerts, e-newsletters, RSS feeds, standards connectors, and inquiry-based WebQuests/HyperDocs.

7.3 Analyze the advantages and drawbacks of online learning and virtual schools.

7.4 Utilize exploratory learning websites and apps, virtual and augmented reality, and virtual field trips for online and offline learning.

Chapter Learning Goal:

Use web-based information curation tools, digital content, and inquiry-based and exploratory learning websites and apps to develop online learning experiences.

Featured Technologies

Bookmarking tools	Standards connector
Cloud computing	WebQuests/HyperDocs
Social bookmarking tools	Virtual reality (VR) and augmented reality (AR)
Google tools for educators and students	Virtual field trips
Google geographic tools	Virtual schools
Information alerts, e-newsletters, RSS feeds	Massive open online courses (MOOCs)
Learning management systems (LMS)	

What a Student Teacher Discovers about the Web

Like many college students preparing for a career in education, Brian was enthusiastically looking forward to his year of student teaching. But the demands were much greater than he anticipated. The school day is a long one, and a teacher must be well organized, highly focused, and able to juggle multiple responsibilities at the same time. Brian was teaching two classes, U.S. history and Native American history. The Native American history course was new, so there were no curriculum plans to follow or revise. Working with his cooperating teacher to build the course from its beginning was exciting yet stressful. Simultaneously, Brian was taking college courses that required written reflections on teaching experiences and learning plans that integrated active learning instructional methods with historical content. Psychologically and physically fatigued by the end of the second month of student teaching, Brian wondered, "Am I going to be able to keep this pace for the rest of the school year?"

At this point, following suggestions of other students in the teacher license program, Brian found the Internet to be a time-saving resource, a surprise that he would not have previously predicted. At the beginning of his graduate work, Brian was dismissive of many of the ideas and tools presented in his educational technology course, thinking them too far removed from the realities of the classroom and his daily work. But as the demands of student teaching grew and the other practicum students displayed their growing collection of online resources, Brian turned to the web to help him find teaching ideas and resources.

He started by seeking digital content for teaching Native American history. As his research grew, he was surprised to find a wealth of information in the form of primary sources, videos, interactive websites, historical biographies, and engaging lesson plans. Social bookmarking became an everyday tool for storing resources and locating student-friendly materials in sites identified by other teachers. Using social bookmarking tags, he began aligning resources to the state's history/social studies curriculum framework, a step required by the school district and his college's teacher license program.

Brian wanted to find ways for students to experience history through lively, interactive, and thought-provoking experiences. His choice for opening new units was showing video clips about history topics from the viewpoints and perspectives of Native Americans. Reserving the school's iPad cart regularly, he asked students to collaborate in small groups to find online information from websites he had preselected. Students enjoyed these online learning experiences, expressing new interest in history study. Using online resources to inform his teaching allowed Brian to effectively manage his resources, re-energize his instruction, and successfully engage students in learning.

Teaching might be better named constant learning; that is what the job requires. As a teacher, you are always expanding your knowledge to design engaging learning experiences for students—the goal of ISTE's "Learner" Standard for Educators, which connects directly to this chapter's focus on teaching students to become global communicators. Gaining new knowledge to communicate to students is one of teaching's great joys. An English teacher we know finished an eight-year quest to read a biography of every U.S. president since George Washington. Learning about presidents and the times in which they lived was a way for him to contextualize the literary efforts of writers and poets during different periods of history. While reading the books, he listened to interviews online with the biographers, viewed videos of conversations with reviewers, and bookmarked selections of these to acquaint students with what he learned.

Another colleague, an elementary school teacher who specializes in teaching young children to read and write, constantly searches for new science information that will intrigue, amaze, and engage young minds, giving them reasons to read about, experiment with, and write about their own questions. Through new picture books, online science sources, podcasts, photos and videos, she helps students understand that science is done by people of all ages and that adult scientists investigate questions they find interesting and puzzling, producing research and breakthrough discoveries.

For teachers, the Internet is unparalleled as an immediately accessible source of virtual learning and **digital content**, which refers to information that is stored and transmitted digitally. Teachers can use virtual learning and digital content to teach the school curriculum and assist students to pursue individual interests. Any device with Internet access enables a teacher to investigate any number of sites about topics of personal or professional interest, locating relevant information and enriching class activities. An Internet search opens doors to a library or bookstore, museum or collection, interview, or newscast. In addition to expanding personal and professional knowledge, searching the Internet informs teachers about local, state, and national curriculum frameworks and ideas for teaching them.

The web also promotes innovative approaches to virtual learning, including virtual schools, blended learning, and web resources for exploratory and inquiry-based learning, topics we discuss in this chapter. As you explore the multiple dimensions of virtual learning, consider the following questions:

1. How can you and students utilize information management technologies to support teaching and learning in schools?
2. How can you organize digital resources to support teaching academic concepts, curriculum frameworks, and learning standards?

3. What are the advantages and complexities of online learning, virtual schools, WebQuests/HyperDocs, virtual field trips, and videoconferencing?

4. How can you use educational websites and apps, including virtual reality (VR) and augmented reality (AR), to provide interactive and exploratory learning experiences for students?

Curating Information with Technology

7.1 **Describe technologies for curating digital content, including bookmarking, social bookmarking, cloud computing, Google tools, and learning management systems.**

Teachers want efficient ways to organize large amounts of educational information they find online. As one teacher candidate recently told us, "With an inbox that is always filled, I never have the time to organize it. I need a sorter and a sifter to help me." Technology makes it possible to easily and efficiently organize online resources.

Content curation is the process of locating, evaluating, and saving educational information for your use. Every teacher is to some degree a content curator—a librarian of one's own resources—who saves learning plans, teaching ideas, student learning materials, tests and quizzes, and more for use and reuse in the classroom. The need to curate information is not a new phenomenon connected to the computer age. Before the computer revolution, teachers saved educational information in paper form with file folders, notebooks, bins, drawers, and organizing systems.

Since the invention of writing, scholars have sought to create systems to "store, sort, select, and summarize" information (Blair, 2010). The 18th century *Siku Quanshu* (The Complete Library in Four Sections) of China consisted of 800 million words in 79,000 chapters and 36 volumes—an amount of written information exceeded only by Wikipedia when it passed the billion-word mark in 2010. Our grandparents and great-grandparents, living and working during the 19th and early to mid-20th century, also needed to manage the information they encountered in their daily existence. Their lives, organized around the cycles of seasonal change for those who worked on farms or the patterns of 8- to 10-hour shifts for those employed in firms and factories, required information to be recalled, used, revised, and taught to others. Over time with faster travel and audio connections available, radio, television, newspapers, and magazines accelerated the pace of change, although not as rapidly as what occurs today with technology-driven information flows.

Today's speed of news and discoveries further complicates information curation in education. Textbooks are quickly out of date, but school systems usually do not have money to replace them as often as they change. So the need for information curation is immense. Now, with technology, social bookmarking tools, and cloud storage of information, content curation is accomplished with a computer, tablet, or smartphone, allowing entry to your personally curated digital library of educational materials from anywhere.

Increasingly, part of the job of teachers is using digital technologies to curate and then create—in partnership with students—learning materials that are reliable, relevant, engaging, and timely. Researcher Torrey Trust (2017, pp. 106–107) has identified four content curation roles for teachers in online environments: 1) Contemplator, an active browser of educational information; 2) Curator, someone who collects and organizes educational information; 3) Crowdsourcer, a person who posts requests for educational information; and 4) Contributor, an individual who shares educational links, resources, and knowledge.

As you begin your career as a teacher, you will probably play each of these content curation roles more than once, both in online and face-to-face environments. With that in mind, what follows are brief descriptions of tools for curating digital content as a teacher.

MyLab Education
Video Example 7.1
In this video, a teacher helps students to search for, collect, and utilize information using digital tools. How does collaborating with students inform how you will manage digital information as a teacher?

Bookmarking, Social Bookmarking, and Cloud Computing

Bookmarking refers to the capability of a computer, through a web browser, to remember websites. Using a bookmark, you can electronically catalog and subsequently access webpages with just one simple command. A baseball fan might bookmark the website of a favorite team, as well as sites devoted to everything from baseball scores to inside information about trades, draft choices, contract negotiations, and online leagues. The latest news about baseball is only a click or a tap away.

Cloud computing means using the Internet, rather than a personal computer or local network, to store and retrieve files (New York State School Boards Association, 2010). A teacher's materials can reside on the web ("the cloud") to be accessed anywhere, anytime from an Internet-capable computer, smartphone, or tablet. Google Docs and Dropbox are two popular cloud-based digital tools. Each allows you to curate and organize content in the cloud and share this content with students through a URL. One added advantage is that the resources you store in the cloud can be opened simultaneously by multiple people, allowing you to collaborate with students and colleagues in real time while on individual desktops.

Digital Dialog 7.1

Developing curriculum, instruction, and assessment for students and documenting one's own development as an educator means that new teachers must locate and save different types of information. Thinking about how you will use technology to organize the varied educational information, comment and connect online about the following questions:

- How do you manage the information you need for your college courses and school teaching assignments in the most time-efficient ways?
- What types of record-keeping systems do you utilize for keeping track of information from paper and digital sources? Is there a difference in how you sort and store the two?
- What strategies do you use to avoid information overload and confusion?

Social bookmarking expands the concept of bookmarking from one user at one device to a community of users on many devices. Instead of a private resource library seen by one person, social bookmarks create a public list that can be viewed by many readers. You may also choose to keep all or some of your bookmarks private. You can see how one teacher uses social bookmarking in this chapter's In Practice.

In social bookmarking, you create **tags** for your online resources. A tag is a keyword or phrase that identifies a resource so it can be easily found during a digital search. For example, a resource about the life and times of civil rights pioneer Jackie Robinson might be tagged as "baseball," "civil rights," "integration," "Brooklyn Dodgers" and "African American history."

Social bookmarking happens within the framework of online groups where members decide to share bookmarked resources with each other. The advantages of joining an educational social bookmarking group are immense. You can post your bookmarks publicly, providing the other members of the group with your saved resources. In exchange, you can access the resources everyone else has posted on the site. Such a system is a **folksonomy** in which users with similar interests, rather than a panel of experts, generate the content. Teachers thus become part of a community of educational users who are continually identifying resources about school curriculum. Social bookmarking tools for curating academic content and instructional resources are listed in Tech Tool 7.1 and outlined in Table 7.1.

Teachers can plan and share resources with colleagues around the globe using social bookmarking sites.

SOURCE: Annie Fuller/Pearson Education.

Tech Tool 7.1

Social Bookmarking Tools and Apps

Social bookmarking is a time-saving, immediately useful information curation approach, and it is not just a technology for teachers. Social bookmarking can be used to establish classroom learning communities around areas of academic interest and study. Students can share sites they find on curriculum topics while adding tags and comments. A teacher can serve as the organizer and moderator of the group. Here are some of the most popular social bookmarking tools for supporting teaching and learning in schools.

Tagged resources in social bookmarking sites like Flipboard and Diigo can be grouped together in **tag clouds**. In this way, teachers and students assemble learning activities, interactive websites, podcasts and videos, and biographies of important individuals into collections that can be easily located by their tags. Tag clouds offer new ways to search and sort information. Instead of using Google to generate a list of sites that then must be reviewed to determine their usefulness, you can consult the tags and tag bundles assembled by others. This is a time saver if you need access to information and want resources that users have liked and saved. You can follow other social bookmarkers whose collections you find interesting and relevant to your teaching and learning. Every time someone you follow adds resources, you are notified. Joining is free, and membership enables you to curate your own resource collections.

Table 7.1 Social Bookmarking Resources and Apps

Diigo	Diigo (pronounced DEE-go and short for Digest of Internet Information Groups and Other Stuff) allows you to bookmark sites, highlight portions of webpages, add sticky notes, tag the sites, and easily share resources. Once you embed highlights or bookmarks, your notations appear every time you open the page. Diigo is free online with registration.
Pinterest	Pinterest offers a visual collection of favorite ideas and content with a social media twist. Create virtual "pinboards" by posting content, categorizing them, and sharing them with Pinterest "followers." Pinterest is especially popular with elementary school teachers as they share classroom setup designs, crafts, and other multidimensional ideas.
Symbaloo and LiveBinders	These are popular social bookmarking tools for K–12 teachers.
Padlet/Webjets.io	Virtual bulletin boards allow users to curate information.
Bitly	Popularized by its ability to shorten a URL for easy sharing, Bilty also offers a Bitlink account where you can categorize, organize, and search your links inside this user-friendly platform.
Flipboard	If you are focusing on aesthetics, choose Flipboard to organize your bookmark links as if they were published in a multimedia magazine. This format may attract the attention of students who like seeing their resources represented as images.
Gooru	Using this all-inclusive platform starts by gathering your own subject-related content archives or adapting the resources from the collaborative library. Your collection of web resources can be turned into actual lessons where students find a specific "Study" section to access weblinks, videos, and resources woven into activities within the collection.
Goodreads	Organize your favorite books online, creating shelves of titles by topic while viewing the selections of more than 85 million readers worldwide. Goodreads offers multifaceted resources for teachers and students. Begin by selecting books that you have read, intend to read, or want to remember, and then place them on online bookshelves. You add titles to your shelves by searching through Amazon.com by author name or book title or by entering the author and title manually. Once the book titles are entered, you can rate them (one to five stars according to criteria that you define), sort the selections (by title, author, or rating), connect with friends who share similar interests, and, if you desire, join or start a book group. Most importantly, your library is always with you, ready to be accessed for instructional activities rather than bookmarked and available solely on your personal device. Goodreads is free online with registration.

> **MyLab Education Application Exercise 7.1:**
> Assembling a Social Bookmarking Collection

Google Tools for Teachers and Students

Through its GSuite for Education, Google provides a wide-ranging collection of information curation resources for teachers and students. Each of the tools in the suite support multi-user collaboration and sharing (via URL or e-mail). All files are saved in the cloud (online). All edits are saved automatically (there's no file→ save button). In Google Docs, Drive, and Sheets you can access various versions of a file under a historical timeline. Membership to Google Apps for Education includes access to a Gmail account, an intranet of Google tools, an ad-free workspace, enhanced security, and the following features:

- Google Drive—a cloud space for creating, saving, and organizing Google files (e.g., Docs, Sheets, Slides, Forms)

- Google Docs—a word processing tool that supports collaborative writing and editing and discussion-based commenting
- Google Forms—a data collection/survey tool that is used for pre-lesson or formative assessments, student interest surveys, or class projects
- Google Sheets—a spreadsheet tool for collecting and analyzing data (similar to Excel)
- Google Slides—a presentation tool, similar to PowerPoint, that allows multiple individuals to develop slides at the same time; it's easy to embed YouTube and Google Drive videos directly into slides, making this tool excellent for collaborative group presentations and projects
- Google Sites—a space for creating custom, professional-looking websites; it can be used for designing a collaborative class website or showcasing student projects and is compatible with the other Google productivity tools
- Google Calendar—a virtual calendar that makes it easy to set up and organize group meetings or parent conferences
- Google Classroom—a learning management system for educators in which teachers can build class rosters, share assignments, assign grades, and provide feedback within Classroom
- Google Hangouts—a virtual conferencing tool
- Google Keep—a virtual, multimodal note-taking and to-do list tool

Beyond the GSuite for Education, there are Google geographic tools, resources that teachers at every grade level are incorporating in their practice. Students can take virtual journeys throughout their community or across the country to visit places of current or historical interest. Google's geographic discovery tools are widely used in science and social studies classes at all grade levels.

Google Earth, first released as a downloadable free web tool in 2005, is an interactive globe composed of photographs by satellites and aircraft of virtually every location in the world (updated by Google on a rolling basis). Users zoom down from the sky to explore landmarks, places, and points of interest for study. Google Earth includes the moon, sky, and Mars, as well as enhanced 3-D modeling, time-lapse animations, large image overlaps with greater details, and added layers of information (such as the Rumsey Historical Maps folder). Google Earth is viewable in a browser without needing to be downloaded.

Google Earth journeys offer unique opportunities for thoughtful conversations between teachers and students. "Are you surprised that there is so much water in the area?" a local teacher asked students as they scanned the area around their school. The visual presentation of lakes and rivers was an opportunity to discuss the importance of water to people's lives, a science standard in the environmental curriculum.

Google Maps enable users to view locations using a map (which gives a pictorial view of roads and rivers), satellite (which shows the same area photographically and offers ways to journey throughout the solar system), or hybrid view (which reveals traffic, photos, weather, and video images as visual overlays). Maps invite creative searches of places all over the nation and world, from large sections to specific locations. Google Street View lets students and teachers look at famous sites and geographic locations as well as specific addresses or areas. You can transition to Street View from *Google Maps.*

Google Tour Builder and Tour Creator are new digital tools that allow individuals to generate their own interactive maps or virtual reality journeys. Through Tour Builder, students can create multimodal maps of their summer vacations or map out the places they want the characters in the books they author to go. Tour Creator takes 360-degree photos (e.g., from the Google Street View app) and turns them into interactive virtual reality experiences that can be viewed with Google Cardboard. In an English class, students might visit places where the action in a novel occurs, providing a visual connection between the story world and the actual world (as an example, see Google Lit Trips—Frankenstein).

Google Sky examines the solar system—planets, stars, and constellations—from the Hubble Space Telescope with a sky map app that allows you to see which stars, planets, and constellations are above you. Google Moon has images of the moon along with locations and video footage of lunar landings. You can view moon elevations and charts blended with the images of the moon. Google SketchUp is a tool that allows users to design 3-D models of buildings and place them on a map to see what they would look like once constructed. You can select different options to see how historical places have changed over the years, go underwater to view ocean shipwrecks, or use 3D Warehouse, which has three-dimensional models of real and imagined places.

You may also want to utilize the following Google resources and tools:

- Google MyMaps—a digital map tool that allows you and the students to generate your own interactive maps (good for mapping characters' journeys in books or creating a classroom community map)
- Google Scholar—a web search engine for scholarly readings
- Google Groups—similar to an e-mail list serv, Google Groups offers ways to communicate with students and colleagues, post information, and conduct online discussions
- Search Education—resources for using the Google search engine
- Map Education—information about Google Earth, Google Maps, and SketchUp, a 3D model-making tool
- Book Search—allows teachers and students to locate in-print, out-of-print, and public domain book titles in the search engine's database
- Blogger—lets teachers and students create a personal blog and share academic work, class notes, and pictures online
- Picasa—lets teachers and students find, edit, and share pictures online
- Handwrite—lets teachers and students write search terms with a finger on a mobile device

In Practice

Exploring Social Change Movements with Social Bookmarking Tools

Grade Level	Featured Technologies
Upper elementary, middle, and high school	Internet, social bookmarking tools

Learning Plan Outline

During a unit about American political action, eighth-grade students in Lucas's history classes research America's social change movements from 1800 to the early 1900s. For this activity, Lucas introduces online social bookmarking resources, technology tools that can expand students' knowledge of how to find and use information from the Internet. Only Lucas uses these tools before the study begins, so this information is new to everybody.

To open the learning activities, Lucas explains, "Today, as we begin research, I am inviting you to access my resource collection, saved to a cloud and open to everyone using a device with Internet access. Each of you will create your own free account to save resources to the cloud so you and your group will be able to see all of each other's research. We will be making our own library of web materials about our topics of study. We will all become librarians."

"This technology, called social bookmarking," adds Lucas, "lets people bookmark online sources to create a collection of materials that others can use and save to their individual libraries. You will find my account easily; it is under my name. Using your name for your account helps others find you online."

Teaching with Technology

Lucas shows the class his files, saved to Diigo, each resource marked with one or more tags with some of them assembled in folders. For example, he shows an immigration infographic, "Who Is Coming to America?" tagged with "immigration," "migration," "infographic," "Central America," and "Asia." He writes a short synopsis of this resource for others to read. He shows more immigration resources collected in a tag bundle because they all relate to a single topic. When students or colleagues open the tag bundle, all the resources appear one under the other. Lastly, Lucas demonstrates how to follow him and other social bookmarkers: "When someone you follow saves a resource, you get an immediate notice," he explains. "If you want to, you can add that resource to your collection."

Lucas wants students to know different ways to identify and assess online resources in addition to Googling a topic. He wants them to be able to easily save resources and find them again to share with others in the research group. He also hopes students will begin following him and each other—something the students are happy to do—making social bookmarking a regularly used learning tool among the members of the class.

In Diigo, account holders choose keywords to search the files of all users of the site to see what is tagged and stored about a topic. When the name of Harriet Tubman, a Civil War–era African American abolitionist, is entered into Diigo, all entries tagged "Harriet Tubman" will be shown. This is one of the most useful aspects of social bookmarking—a student or teacher can access a personal library of saved URLs while simultaneously utilizing the efforts of other social bookmarkers who have contributed resources about the same topic.

Students may also begin their searches with Wikipedia, where they will find many entries to investigate while discovering keywords that they might not have originally thought of as potential search terms. Through social bookmarking, students can search the Diigo community using those keywords, accessing saved resources under such tags as "women," "change makers," "abolitionism," "abolitionists," "19th century abolition," and "anti-slavery."

The students enjoy learning and using social bookmarking, especially liking sharing resources and following each other. The American social change activity concludes with each group's research published online with a bibliography of resources compiled from those saved in students' accounts. For Lucas and the students, the history of 19th century social reform occasions use of a new online research tool for learning.

Learning Management Systems

A **learning management system** (LMS) is a digital platform or cloud-based system for supporting the delivery of in-person, online, or blended educational learning experiences. Used in all types of educational settings, from public schools and higher education to corporate training programs, an LMS functions as an "online extension of, or replacement for, the classroom" (Foreman, 2017). You are probably using an LMS for one or more of your college or university courses, and you will likely be using one when you begin teaching in a K–12 school.

Learning management systems function as a one-stop home base for teachers as they organize academic experiences for students. On an LMS, instructors post assignments and reading, viewing, or listening materials; send information alerts to everyone in a class or relay private messages to individual students; post rubrics for grading; and maintain constantly updated records of student performance. Students are able to access class materials, submit papers, and take tests and quizzes while monitoring their academic progress online. Teachers and students use an LMS to communicate with one another digitally, including web conferencing and contributing to a class discussion board.

Moodle is one of the most widely used learning management systems in both higher education and K–12 schools because of its easy-to-use features, and, as an open-source program, it is free with no licensing fees to commercial and non-commercial organizations. In addition to Moodle, others widely used in K–12 are Canvas, Google Classroom, Pearson SuccessNet, and Schoology; Blackboard, Canvas, Schoology, and Brightspace are popular in higher education.

Teachers' use of an LMS depends on the structure of the class they are teaching. A fully online class will use an LMS to manage all aspects of the educational experience, while a class that meets in person every day may only post supplementary and review material in its online LMS space. More and more teachers across the grade levels are thinking in terms of blended learning experiences for students; that is, there are important in-person and online activities for students to complete to achieve maximum educational impact. In a blended approach, student learning experiences do not end when an in-person class is over for the day. Using an LMS, students continue their learning by viewing videos, engaging in projects with classmates using collaborative cloud-based tools like Google Docs, doing additional reading, writing papers, and taking quizzes online.

MyLab Education Self-Check 7.1

Organizing Web Resources to Address Standards

7.2 **Organize web resources to address curriculum standards utilizing information alerts, e-newsletters, RSS feeds, standards connectors, and inquiry-based WebQuests.**

Almost every state and school system has adopted academic curriculum frameworks for teachers and students specifying the scope of each subject at each grade level. Ideally, standards serve as the floor, the beginning, not the ceiling, the end point of the structures of learning that teachers build with students. Information alerts, e-newsletters, RSS feeds, standards connectors, and WebQuests are useful ways to identify and organize web resources to address curriculum standards.

Information Alerts, e-Newsletters, and RSS Feeds

An **information alert** is a digital notice that new information about a topic has just become available in an online publication format. Information alerts provide teachers and students with a convenient system of receiving online announcements about educational topics and learning resources.

Google Alerts, a free service for those with a Google account, is one information alert option. You enter a keyword, and the search engine automatically sends you an email whenever there are new results for your term. A teacher might get information alerts about a topic (planets discovered outside the solar system, water on Mars), a new teaching methodology (AR and VR), relevant scholarly research, or a current educational issue (unequal funding of public schools).

Google Alerts can be a time saver. Rather than searching yourself, Google Alerts searches for you, generating five types of notices: articles in newspapers and other news outlets, videos, new blog posts, discussions, and books. You decide how often you want to receive updates and for how long. Google Scholar Alerts serves as a way to keep track of the latest research in one's teaching fields and areas of educational interest.

Like information alerts, **e-newsletters** appear in your e-mail on a regular basis once you sign up to receive them. Many organizations offer educationally themed selections. Poetry and surprising historical and cultural information are the topics of an e-newsletter from the podcast "The Writer's Almanac," in which author, storyteller, and radio host Garrison Keillor reads a poem aloud each day and briefly discusses events and writers connected to that day of the year. The *Sesame Street* e-newsletter, published weekly, includes games, puzzles, and websites about topics that families will find interesting. ASCD SmartBrief and SmartBrief on EdTech are resources for up to date educational trends and news. The Daily Skimm is a free newsletter that appears in your email Monday-Friday if you subscribe. You can connect through social media and its app as well. The scope of its news is current politics and world affairs and historical information that informs history teaching.

RSS feeds, short for Really Simple Syndication, give subscribers access to information via e-mail or an app (e.g., Flipboard) rather than requiring the reader to visit a particular site to check for updated news. Updates are sent via a "feed reader." News sites, blogs, political campaigns, and many other organizations use RSS feeds to make information available through e-mail or information curation apps. The *New York Times*, Yahoo! News: Technology, BBC News, and the *Washington Post* are widely accessed RSS feeds. Educators' blogs, such as Richard Byrne's FreeTech4Teachers, can be subscribed to via an RSS reader, and you can get the latest posts in your e-mail inbox. You can receive RSS feeds through your web browser by subscribing to an RSS feed organizer. Some popular web-based RSS readers include Panda and NewsBlur.

Building a Standards Connector

A **standards connector** is a collection of web resources aligned to curriculum frameworks—organized in a way that allows easy access for teaching and learning within different subject fields. A history standards connector has multimodal resources catalogued by historical time periods and standards. Similarly, a math, science, or English/language arts standards connector has interactive resources categorized by topics and standards. You can build your own standards connector as a new teacher using resources that schools have assembled for staff and student use or that a teacher or group of teachers has created. Students can be contributors as well—inviting their participation creates an inclusive learning experience for everyone.

A standards connector can also serve as a way for teachers to share resources with other teachers. Technology researcher Torrey Trust (2017) has labeled this type of colleague-to-colleague information sharing a "peer-to-peer professional development network" (PDN). A PDN serves as a virtual space for collecting and distributing knowledge. It is a uniquely teacher-driven form of professional development in which teacher participants determine how and what information will be shared. Each PDN thus continually evolves through the actions of its members.

One model for a standards connector for teaching and learning can be found in resourcesforhistoryteachers, a free education wiki founded and edited by University of Massachusetts Amherst faculty member Robert Maloy. Since 2006, college students and practicing teachers have been contributing online resources to this wiki, each aligned to the Massachusetts History & Social Science Curriculum Framework and the national Advanced Placement (AP) themes for U.S. history, world history, American government, and art history (Trust & Maloy, 2018; Maloy & LaRoche, 2015). The wiki features multicultural and multimodal resources drawn from universities, historical organizations, and independent sources to address learning standards for all grade levels.

To build a standards connector, you need access to the Internet and one of the data management or social bookmarking technologies discussed earlier in this chapter (such as Pinterest or Diigo) or a personal or classroom website or wiki on which to post resources. These steps follow:

- As you search online for curriculum materials, connect curriculum frameworks that you need to teach with websites featuring resources for specific learning standards. Locating one or two interactive or attention-getting multimodal sites for each framework topic provides a starting point; you can add others later based on your own research and that of students.

- Bookmark your online resources using Flipboard or Diigo to create a collection of web resources that you can share with students, other teachers, and interested educators. The process is quick and creative. Record the URL, title, and a brief summary of each web resource you want to save.

- "Tag" the resource using a set of keywords that you select to help you remember what the resource is about. This is the creative part. You are using your own organizing categories for your own purposes, and your tag system should include the learning standards you are expected to teach students. Creating keyword tags lets you and the students efficiently search your collection of resources.

Figure 7.1 shows a tag cloud based on one history teacher's system of tag terms. The largest tag terms in bold font are the most often cited items in this teacher's classification system. The terms cited less often are smaller and not bold. Because this teacher is particularly interested in the history of African Americans and women, these are among the bolded terms. The teacher has also included the letter and number of the state learning standards as a keyword term.

Social bookmarking is not the only way to collect and maintain information for a standards connector. Table 7.2 shows a list of resources for teaching middle school physical science topics that one teacher placed on her class blog. By listing required frameworks on one side of a webpage and web resources on the other side, teacher and students are able to directly connect the web resources to the learning standard being studied.

Figure 7.1 A History Teacher's Social Bookmarking Tags

Table 7.2 Sample Standards Connector—Physical Science (Grades 6–8)

Learning Standard	Web Resources
Properties of Matter	Your Weight on Other Worlds The Internet Plasma Physics Education Experience
Elements, Compounds, and Mixtures	States of Matter BBC K52 Bitesize Science

Curating Standards-Based Academic Content

Every teacher—and every college student entering a career in education—has a constant need for new academic information. Discoveries, developments, issues, trends, and topics in one's teaching field(s) are all potential material for instructional lessons with students and interactions with colleagues. Whether you plan to work with younger learners in early childhood or elementary schools or specialize in one of the upper-grade academic subjects, becoming a teacher means it is essential to stay informed as best you can of just about anything and everything related to teaching, learning, technology, and schooling.

It is challenging to stay fresh and up to date. There are vast amounts of information instantaneously available online. How do you decide what to pay attention to right now, what to set aside for later consideration, and what to ignore altogether? As college students, you are used to having professors direct you to learning resources through course syllabi, textbooks, and reading lists. How do you locate important information and resources on your own once courses are complete and you enter the world of work?

Many teachers think in terms of establishing a set of "go-to" content sources that they read, listen to, and view regularly to learn more about topics in their teaching fields and at the grade levels they teach. A science teacher, for example, might subscribe to the Science Friday and Cosmos and Culture podcasts from National Public Radio (NPR) to get summaries of the latest research. To gain perspectives on new instructional approaches, that same teacher might find #formativechat, #edugladiators, #weteachun, #engagechat, and other hashtags and Twitter chats valuable sources of student-engaging learning plans. A math teacher might make youcubed, Stanford University Professor Jo Boaler's highly regarded blog, a go-to resource while a history teacher might add Today's Document from the National Archives to a collection of social studies–related smartphone apps. Many of these go-to examples feature open educational resources and public domain materials.

Successful content curation as a teacher involves three key activities: 1) locating up-to-date, reliable information from online sources; 2) connecting that information to subject area and grade level curriculum standards; and 3) saving the information you find using an organized, easily accessible, cloud-based digital storage system. All steps can be done by yourself, but are greatly enhanced when undertaken as part of a community of similarly interested content curators. Here is how to do so:

First, you may already be using Pinterest, Flipboard, Reddit, or another information sharing tool to access and share photos, videos, and other materials of personal interest to you and friends. You can expand the use of these tools by following other teachers who are using these sites. Look online for "best teacher pages" or "educators to follow" and see if you find someone who matches your interest and approach.

Second, professional educational organizations such as the National Council of Teachers of English (NCTE), National Council of Teachers of Mathematics (NCTM), National Science Teachers Association (NSTA), and International Society for Technology in Education (ISTE) are another source of new ideas and information for teachers. You can visit their websites, read their professional journals and magazines, and connect with them through social media.

Third, as discussed earlier in this chapter, social bookmarking tools are time-saving, immediately useful content curation resources. Instead of trying to locate high-quality resources by yourself, you join a community of technology-using educators who are interested in the same topics and questions. As you share web resources to a social bookmarking site, you support the work of all the other members of the group, just as they support you by sharing their resources with everyone in the community.

Common Sense Education maintains a listing of the best apps and websites for content curation. For more ideas and strategies about content curation, go to "Trends & Issues in Instructional Design, Educational Technology & Learning Science," a web resource maintained by technology educators Abbie Brown and Tim Green.

MyLab Education Application Exercise 7.2:
Curating Multimedia Standards-based Content

Designing Inquiry-Based Learning Using WebQuests and HyperDocs

WebQuests are online inquiries and explorations for students, designed and guided by teachers. HyperDocs are a series of online learning experiences that emerge from one central document or hub (Highfill, Hilton, & Landis, 2016). While a WebQuest is not a HyperDoc, both formats enable students to proceed through a playlist of interactive online and in-person experiences having some choice and direction of the learning. Neither functions as an online worksheet; both promote discovery learning with multimodal resources.

In inquiry-based WebQuests and HyperDocs, students follow a digital map or take an online tour, moving from one web resource to the next to gather information and learn about a topic. In a paper environment, a student might read articles or selections from books and then write a paper or a report; with WebQuests and HyperDocs, the academic information is digital. Students visit sites preselected by a teacher and, based on their explorations and investigations, prepare individual or group presentations to share with classmates. "Weather Station WebQuest," this chapter's Technology Transformation Learning Plan, uses a WebQuest to show the learning method in action and the same topic can be explored with hyperdocs as well.

By featuring multimodal and multicultural materials, WebQuests and HyperDocs broaden students' academic knowledge and instructional experiences. Multimodal websites feature reading, viewing, listening, and interactive activities so students read text, view videos, listen to audio materials, and interact with online resources to explore topics in depth. Multicultural websites explore the hidden histories and untold stories of women, African Americans, Latinos, Native Americans, Asian Americans, and LGBTQ individuals who have been historically left out of or marginalized in many textbooks and curriculum frameworks. The contributions of unknown people to all curricular topics from fashion design to writing, physics and chemistry to painting, medicine to poetry, mathematics to history are in online resources.

WebQuests and HyperDocs offer immersive learning experiences that combine the appeal of technology use, the game qualities of an adventure quest, and the satisfaction of conducting an inquiry, discovering new information, or solving a problem. Similar to a scavenger hunt where one moves from place to place adding items to a collection, students visit an online site to complete an activity before going to discover a new activity on another site. To make these experiences engaging and interesting, a variety of activities provide different ways of learning. Otherwise students will lose momentum if sites and accompanying activities require lengthy reading of text to complete a worksheet or viewing a complete video to compose a summary or answer questions about it.

By design, WebQuests or HyperDocs should incorporate the attributes of innovative thinking to be springboards for learning the Internet literacy skills of information retrieval and analysis. Most WebQuests include the following five steps which can be used or modified for HyperDoc activities:

1. *Stage setting.* An introduction by the teacher builds curiosity and a sense of anticipation before students begin.
2. *Task.* Multimodal activities that students will do or create are listed.

Figure 7.2 QuestGarden Logo

SOURCE: Reprinted by permission of Bernard J. Dodge.

QuestGarden

where great WebQuests grow

3. *Process.* Specific instructions students follow throughout the quest are explained.
4. *Evaluation.* Assessments by the teacher (and possibly the students) determine if everyone achieved the requirements of a quest.
5. *Conclusion.* A summary of key understandings and learning goals is shared by students.

For teachers, designing a successful WebQuest means answering four questions:

1. What will interest the students, and what are they capable of doing independently?
2. What are the primary ideas you wish to teach?
3. How will students at different skill levels help each other learn together?
4. Is technology integrated seamlessly into the assignment?

WebQuest and hyperdoc activities are designed for student learning success. Students who do not have independent reading skills will not engage with densely packed text. Students who zone out when listening will not recall information in a long podcast or an unexciting video.

To promote success for all, WebQuests or HyperDocs might use a cooperative learning model in which different students do different tasks. A student who is not an accomplished reader may be a talented artist who can put the information from websites into an interesting visual summary for other students to see. Another student may be a confident oral communicator who can record a podcast narrating the findings of the activity. Giving different roles to members of a WebQuest or hyperdoc team or letting students choose roles provides teachers with a way to use everyone's individual talents. Students can be part of a research team, a writing team, a graphic design team, or a video or podcast production team.

Interactive presentation software, PowerPoint, Prezi, Haiku Deck, or PowToon or presentation apps such as Educreations or Knowmia offer visual ways to construct WebQuests/HyperDocs. Online sites can be placed in a digital presentation in which colorful graphics and interactive elements draw students' attention to their tasks. For more information about creating your own WebQuests, go to the QuestGarden website developed by Professor Bernie Dodge and his colleagues and students at San Diego State University (see Figure 7.2).

MyLab Education **Self-Check 7.2**

Online Learning and Virtual Schools

7.3 Analyze the advantages and drawbacks of online learning and virtual schools.

Online learning and virtual schools are among the most discussed and hotly debated topics in education today. **Online learning** (or *distance learning*) refers to the delivery of educational experiences through digital technologies. **Virtual schools** are educational organizations that teach students and confer degrees through online learning. In many virtual school programs, students never enter a brick-and-mortar school building, taking all classes and exams online instead (Cuban, 2012). More and more schools are moving toward educational programs that feature a **blended learning** (or *hybrid learning*) model, a combination of "clicks and bricks" where students' face-to-face interactions with teachers in school buildings (the bricks) are paired with computer-based online coursework and testing (the clicks).

Online and blended learning has become a huge educational enterprise. Already well established in higher education—half of all college students take at least one online course—online learning in K–12 schools grew to the point that by 2013 nearly every state had considered some form of virtual school legislation. Nationally, students in all 50 states plus the District of Columbia have access to online learning. In 2015–2016, there were 278,511 students enrolled in virtual schools and 36,605 students attending blended schools. Thirty-four states had full-time virtual schools and 21 states had blended schools (Molnar, et.al., 2017).

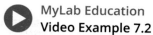

MyLab Education
Video Example 7.2
In this video, students and family members describe their experiences in a virtual school. How do you think virtual schools create viable alternatives to traditional schooling?
https://www.gcvs.org/testimonials/

Digital Dialog 7.2

Numerous states and school districts require students to take at least one online learning course to graduate from high school. Reflect on your own experiences with face-to-face and online learning as you comment and connect online about the following questions:

- Do you think requiring all students to take online courses is an option you would have welcomed in high school? Why or why not?
- How might online courses and virtual learning better prepare students for future jobs and careers?
- How might blended learning (courses taught partially in person and partially online) be a help to students in comparison to an entirely in-person or entirely online experience?

In addition to those attending fully online virtual schools, many students take one or more online courses as part of their regular K–12 education while a smaller number attend full-time blended schools where the program of study includes face-to-face and online courses. The growth of online learning is evident in higher education as well. The Babson Survey Research Group notes that the number of graduates and undergraduates taking at least one distance or online course between 2012 and 2016 has increased by 17.2% (Seaman, Allen, & Seaman, 2018). You can learn more about virtual education trends and developments by reading a report by the Colorado-based Evergreen Education Group called "Keeping Pace with K–12 Online and Blended Learning."

Budget constraints facing school systems and the needs of students and families continue to drive the growth of online learning in K–12 settings. Financially, many smaller public schools cannot offer advanced courses in specialized subjects (e.g., physics, advanced mathematics, the histories of different regions and cultures) because there are not enough students to justify hiring someone to teach them. These students can be served online, where youngsters from many different communities enroll in the same course together. From a family perspective, many youngsters want the convenience and flexibility of virtual schooling and its anywhere, anytime online learning formats. Freed from the fixed schedule of a typical public school day, students can proceed at their own pace and still have time to pursue outside-of-school interests or jobs in the community.

Debates over Virtual Schools

Virtual schools are an intensely debated educational policy. Proponents see online learning as a way to prepare students for careers in technology fields. High school students enrolled in virtual schools are more likely to take online tests, access online databases, post self-created content, listen to podcasts, post to blogs, conduct virtual experiments, and watch teacher-created videos than students in traditional schools (Project Tomorrow, 2014a).

When they first opened, virtual schools attracted mainly students from home-schooling families. Now, advocates stress that many different types of students are pursuing online learning, including youngsters with medical conditions or other constraints on mobility, gifted and talented children seeking advanced studies, and students who want alternatives to traditional in-school environments. Virtual schools give students more time to pursue their interests in sports or the arts. They also provide options for students who want a change from their local educational environment or do not feel safe at school because of bullying or harassment.

Critics of virtual schools cite low test scores, lack of full-time teachers and the isolating nature of the online experience as major drawbacks to this educational approach (Heinrich, Darling-Aduana, Good, & Huiping, 2019; Ahn & McEachin, 2017; Babiak, Patton, Price, & Roberts, 2017). They contend that students in virtual schools have less social interaction with peers, have fewer opportunities to learn together collectively, and receive smaller amounts of individual attention from instructors. In their view, the benefits of elementary and secondary education are broader than the efficient transfer of information through technology. Students need to have opportunities for group collaboration and cooperation that schools provide through face-to-face classes and extracurricular activities.

The role of for-profit companies is another troubling issue for many observers of virtual schools. The overwhelming majority of virtual school students (as many as 8 out of 10) attend schools run by for-profit companies, including K12 Inc., the nation's largest virtual school provider, and Connections Learning, another major for-profit virtual school company. Nonprofit organizations, states, individual school districts, and colleges and universities all deliver online schooling.

From a business standpoint, operating a virtual school can be a profitable enterprise. The school controls costs by limiting teacher salaries and having no transportation or building expenses with all courses delivered online. On balance, fewer buildings, lower maintenance needs, and minimal transportation costs make virtual schools less expensive to operate than regular K–12 schools. Not often publicized, but important to budgets, virtual schools employ fewer teachers at generally lower salaries with fewer employment benefits. These actions contribute to a potential high profit margin for virtual school companies.

There is worry that the profit incentive can compromise educational quality. In 2014, the National Collegiate Athletic Association (NCAA) announced it would no longer accept credits awarded by 24 virtual schools operated by K12, Inc., because the schools' curriculum failed to meet the organization's requirements for nontraditional courses (Ravitch, 2014b). In this analysis, some for-profit virtual schools may not be spending the funds needed to provide students with a full range of educational resources and materials.

Online student performance on standardized tests is also a concern for educators. Studies have found that virtual schools managed by for-profit educational management organizations (EMOs) had more than twice as many students per teacher than brick-and-mortar schools. The on-time graduation data show that between 2015 and 2016 the graduation rate of full-time virtual and blended schools was about half the national average of 82.3% (Molnar, et al., 2017).

The ongoing role of virtual schools in the nation's educational system is evolving. Virtual schooling has strong political support in many states among legislators and parents who are frustrated by what they see as the slow pace of education reform in public schools. For these supporters, virtual schools are an immediately effective way to educate students. Opponents worry that for-profit companies are undermining public education by drawing resources and support away from already underfunded public schools, even as they see the benefits of combining face-to-face with online learning. You will likely be part of public policy decisions about virtual schools in the future, both as a teacher and as a voter.

Massive Open Online Courses (MOOCs)

Depending how you define what a MOOC is and what it does, **massive open online courses** either a) originated in 2008 when Stephen Downes and George Siemens deployed an online course through Siemen's teaching at the University of Manitoba with over 23,000 participants from around the world, or b) were launched in 2011 when Sebastian Thrun deployed a free web-based course on artificial intelligence, attracting 160,000 followers. MOOCs are designed to teach large numbers of people online, often with little or no restrictions on who or how many people can enroll in a course. In a MOOC, students perform much like they do in any online course—by watching lectures, completing assigned readings, writing papers, and taking quizzes and exams—there are just many more students in the course (EDUCAUSE Learning Initiative, 2013a).

Some of the most popular MOOC providers—Coursera, edX, Future Learn, XuetangX and Udacity—collectively serve several million students throughout the world. In 2014, 40% of MOOC students were from developing countries and 38% were from the United States. Among institutions of higher education, Harvard University and Duke University, as well as the Massachusetts Institute of Technology (MIT), host hundreds of courses in a variety of subject areas.

MOOCs are also making their way into K–12 education as a way for students to access educational experiences in areas typically not available at their school; about one in six MOOC participants is in high school. Students in Ohio, Florida, and Massachusetts, for example, have participated in computer science, advanced biology, and physics courses. Brown University developed a pre-college engineering course that had 2,000 participants in 2013 (Wilhelm, 2013). edX, an online learning organization created by Harvard University and MIT, is offering Advanced Placement exam preparation courses for high school students. MOOCs also offer creative professional development opportunities for teachers.

MOOC innovations present challenges as well as concerns. First is the issue of student retention and engagement as participants are expected to independently keep pace with the class. The average completion rate of MOOCs in higher education is around 10% (Ha, 2014). Public school officials concede that they will need to closely monitor participation in MOOCs to ensure that students are getting the maximum benefit from the experience and completing the coursework and that the perspectives of male and female students are balanced. Second, so far MOOCs have reached only a select group of students. To date, about three of every four enrolled people in MOOCs are adults who have a four-year college degree or higher education. The average student age is 26, and most participants are men (Selingo, 2014). Educators will need to find ways for more students to access the resources provided by MOOCs. You can track the latest MOOC developments at the website Class Central.

Interactive Videoconferencing

Interactive videoconferencing is a powerful learning technology offering real-time access to people and places that students are unable to visit. Videoconferencing tools such as Skype, Google Hangouts, FaceTime, or WhatsApp turn a computer into a telephone and a videoconference at the same time. With video calling, users make free phone calls over the Internet and make low-cost calls between a computer and a landline or cell phone. It is possible to see the party you are talking with, whether in the next town, across the country, or around the world. One exciting example is "Exploring by the Seat of Your Pants," an organization that uses Google Hangouts to connect classrooms with researchers, scientists, and explorers. Students communicate with individuals who are doing research in some of the world's most remote and challenging locations.

Skype's popularity is so enormous that it has become its own verb in the language, as in the sentence "Let's Skype tomorrow." Millions of people worldwide use this technology; Microsoft spent $8.5 billion to acquire Skype in 2011. Skype's basic service is free, but more enhanced services are available for a fee. And as of 2018, you can communicate with up to 24 users at once. Skype is not the only video calling option for teachers and schools. Google Talk offers free video and audio chatting and domestic phone calls for those with a Gmail account and an Android phone. Apple has FaceTime, which enables individuals with an iPad, iPhone, iPod Touch, or Mac to engage in video communications with one another. Zoom has become a popular videoconferencing tool for online courses, higher education settings, and businesses.

Interactive videoconferencing enables students to communicate with scientists, historians, writers, and other experts from all over the nation, extending the classroom far beyond the local community.

SOURCE: Tatyana Glodskih\Fotolia.

Videoconferencing achieves online interactivity between students (the "near site") and the people or places the class is visiting electronically (the "far site"). Successful conferences make participants at each site feel involved and invested in the experience. Classroom teachers can create connections with other teachers, schools, and organizations worldwide. "Skype in the Classroom" is a clearinghouse of information related to its educational uses. Teachers can find partner classes organized by geographic location as well as subject areas and themes by searching its vast collections. "Learning about Ocean Animals," "Portuguese for Beginners," "Lego Robotics," and "Science of the Rainforest" are just some of the topics available on the website. Teachers can sign their classes up to participate in a "Mystery Skype," with a classroom located in a different state, county, city, or country. During "Mystery Skype," students from each classroom try to figure out where the other students are located, using a series of Yes/No questions (like the 20 Questions game) and exploration of information on maps and digital tools.

The online learning benefits for students are multifaceted. Videoconferencing is a way for students to learn about other people and cultures, practice their language and communication skills, and gain information about academic topics from experts and professionals in many fields. Participating in a video conversation generates high levels of engagement and makes the content more memorable and relevant.

> **MyLab Education Self-Check 7.3**

Exploratory Learning with Websites and Apps

7.4 Utilize exploratory learning websites and apps, virtual and augmented reality, and virtual field trips for online and offline learning.

Exploratory learning means that students delve into a topic or a concept on their own or with small groups of peers to build connections between what they already know and new or unfamiliar knowledge they are about to learn. Like explorers and researchers in fields as different as medicine or archaeology, students learn through their encounters with the unknown. They assemble new understandings from their experiences and apply that knowledge to future encounters. For students, exploration happens when playing an online game for the first time, trying a new writing genre, solving an unfamiliar math problem, or learning a new scientific process.

MyLab Education
Video Example 7.3
In this video, students utilize a virtual chemistry lab instead of mixing chemicals by hand. How do you plan to use online technology to explore academic concepts interactively with students?

Features of Exploratory Learning Resources

Students at every grade level benefit from opportunities to explore online materials in novel, interesting, and potentially surprising ways. Rather than simply presenting academic material, exploratory educational websites and apps engage emotion, heighten interest, and inspire creativity in learners through:

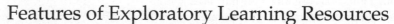

- *Interactivity.* Students interact with online content by viewing simulations or demonstrations, conducting searches, responding to questions, analyzing data, or posting responses. Interactive sites provide information, but each student constructs knowledge for themselves through how they use the site in ways that would not be possible without the technology.

- *Exploration.* Students explore questions and topics by proceeding through the site in a nonlinear rather than a linear fashion. Instead of being restricted to a straightforward presentation of information, students can chart their own paths through the website, pursuing different topics and interests each time they visit.

- *Engagement.* Students engage with website material through compelling storylines, interesting characters, perplexing mysteries, creative thinking, or novel concepts or ideas. A student is thus drawn to the online material in ways that could not happen with information presented in a text-based, less interactive format or in a one-right-answer quiz or flashcard game.

The following examples of exploratory learning websites and apps from social studies, English/language arts, mathematics, and science show interactivity, exploration, and engagement in action as students and teachers explore curriculum topics.

MYSTERIES OF ÇATALHÖYÜK! AN ARCHAEOLOGICAL INVESTIGATION.   This site from the Science Museum of Minnesota (see Figure 7.3) opens dramatically: "Right now in Turkey at a place called Çatalhöyük, people are asking questions: Is this the first city, and why did people start living there? What is the meaning of these murals? What were they eating for dinner 10,000 years ago?"

The site explores these fascinating archaeological and historical questions by recording the process and results of an actual archeological dig. Çatalhöyük (pronounced "cha-tal hay OOK"), located in central Turkey, means "forked mound," in reference to the large earth mounds that were created as successive generations of people built and rebuilt the town. It contains the ruins of a nearly 10,000-year-old town, one of the ancient world's largest human settlements, with more than 10,000 inhabitants. It is being excavated and studied by an international team of archaeologists and anthropologists, and their findings are revolutionizing how we think about life in the ancient past. The mural paintings at Çatalhöyük are the oldest in the world on human-made structures. The city itself was estimated to be more than 50 soccer fields in length, a remarkable development at a time when humans were thought to have lived only in small bands of hunters and gatherers. Students and teachers see how the mounds were formed, make a Neolithic dinner, play an excavation game, go on virtual tours, or explore one of the city's clay brick homes. Key archaeological findings are presented as interactive stories titled "Çatalhöyük Comics." A short movie highlights the work of archaeologists who dig deeply to uncover the distant past.

FAVORITE POEM PROJECT.   Founded by former Poet Laureate Robert Pinsky, the Favorite Poem Project features five- to six-minute video documentaries of young, teenage, middle-age, and older Americans from diverse occupations and backgrounds reciting their favorite poems. The project is now maintained as a partnership between Boston University and the Library of Congress. Its videos are compelling—a young boy dressed in his Little League uniform discusses his love of baseball and recites "Casey at the Bat" by Ernest Lawrence Thayer as he stands in the batter's box and on the pitcher's mound at a ball field; a Boston construction worker pauses from his manual labor job to recite Walt Whitman's "Song of Myself" while wondering how one poem reveals new thoughts with each return to it; a sister reminisces about her brother each Thanksgiving, reciting "Laminations" by Louise Gluck. These videos change the poetic experience for students who see firsthand that poetry is a spoken art form in which words and phrases need to be heard as well as read and experienced emotionally. Students can video themselves performing a favorite poem or reciting one of their own.

Figure 7.3 Mysteries of Çatalhöyük! Screenshot

SOURCE: Reprinted with permission of the Science Museum of Minnesota.

NATIONAL LIBRARY OF VIRTUAL MANIPULATIVES (NLVM).   Created by mathematicians and instructional designers at Utah State University, NLVM is a collection of interactive web-based games and tutorials to help K–12 students learn mathematical concepts. The site receives tens of thousands of visitors per day from people around the world.

NLVM includes activities and games for all grade levels, connected to the major math education standards set forth by the National Council of Teachers of Math (NCTM): numbers and operations, algebra, geometry, measurement, data analysis and probability, problem solving, reasoning, and proof. Activities are free at every grade level. To access the site without a Java enabled web browser is fee-based, with licenses for a single computer, and discounts available to school districts that buy multiple licenses.

As an interactive and exploratory resource, NLVM responds to the ongoing national problem of student disengagement and low academic performance in math. In general, students become disengaged from math when they cannot understand the connections between relationships and operations. In other words, they cannot visualize how to work out the math in their heads.

NLVM creates virtual settings where students manipulate objects with the click of a mouse to comprehend how actions change mathematical relationships. In classrooms, teachers often use physical objects as manipulatives for students to move with their own hands to visualize concepts. In NLVM, the objects are digital, but the purpose is the same. To learn about percents and fractions, for example, NLVM has a money game where virtual coins serve as manipulatives. Counting the coins, students learn that 10 pennies is 100% of one dime and 5 dimes is 50 percent of one dollar. The concept of a fraction as part of a whole becomes visible and practiced through the student's own actions. From a constructivist perspective, students create personal meaning by using coins, exchanging denominations, and exploring relationships rather than listening to a teacher explain monetary equivalences. And this is only one of almost 100 choices that put learning opportunities into students' hands.

MUSEUM IN A BOX (MIAB).   As a way to make museum collections more accessible to schools around the world, Museum in a Box (MiaB) was begun by an educational start-up company located in London, England, that pioneered using 3-D printing to fill boxes with small replicas of 3-D printed art, postcards, and other objects. Now museums and other organizations are adopting this approach. The Smithsonian Libraries have Museum in a Box projects; so does the National Aeronautics and Space Administration (NASA), which has dozens of activities about the science of flight. To create a Museum in a Box, organizations digitize small 3-D versions of artifacts and place them in a physical box. Each box comes equipped with Raspberry Pi technology that lets organizations virtually share audio information and additional resources about the materials. Students and teachers can combine hands-on and virtual learning to create museum-like experiences without ever leaving the classroom. The longer-term goal is to make the experience even more original by having students curate their own collections of objects and information.

Virtual Reality and Augmented Reality

Virtual reality (VR) is a computer-generated, 3-D environment that generates a "near-reality" experience for students and teachers (Virtual Reality Society, 2017). The digital environment is not real, but computer users participate in it as if it were real. VR is being used to train new employees, aid in patients' recovery from injuries, practice surgery or other medical procedures, and test out the effectiveness of architectural designs—just to name a few of the emerging applications of this powerful technology.

There are emerging educational uses as well. In one preliminary study, University of Maryland researchers found that volunteers using a head-mounted VR display had much better information recall of different sets of faces of famous people than those using a desktop computer. The researchers concluded that "if memory recall could be enhanced through immersively experiencing the environment in which the information was learned," then virtual environments show great promise as a teaching and learning tool (Krokos, Plaisant, & Varshney, 2018).

The Google Expeditions virtual reality platform takes computer users on 3-D tours to places all around the world. Google Tour Creator lets teachers and students create their own virtual tours using images from Google Street View as well as their own 360-degree photos. Once assembled, teacher- and student-made virtual tours can be published in Poly, Google's free virtual reality library. Google Cardboard, which transforms a smartphone into a virtual reality headset, is an easy and inexpensive way to get started making virtual tours.

Augmented reality (AR) is an enhanced version of reality in which technology adds information, images, and virtual objects to real-world scenes to create new, artificial environments (The Franklin Institute, 2018). You may be familiar with augmented reality from your experiences as a consumer and a customer, using apps to find your way through a busy airport, redesigning rooms in a home or apartment, trying out different eyeglasses and cosmetics, or watching the flight of a ball or the speed of a player at a televised sporting event.

Virtual and augmented reality are two points on an immersion spectrum ranging from light augmentation (AR) to full immersion (VR). It is the immersiveness of the experience that creates the illusion of reality for students and teacher—the more real it seems, the more real it will be treated. Virtual and augmented reality examples in K–12 schools include students visiting the tomb of an ancient Egyptian pharaoh, witnessing the horrors of World War I trench warfare, journeying to the moon with the Apollo 11 astronauts, exploring the inner workings of the human body, observing the lava flows of an active volcano, recreating scenes from classic literature and more. Tools like MERGE Cube can be used to bring learning experiences to the palm of your hand through AR and VR. By holding the MERGE Cube in your hand and using a connected AR app on your phone or VR headset, you can manipulate objects like famous sculptures, the solar system, and human anatomy.

Virtual Field Trips

Virtual field trips (also called *virtual tours*) take students to places all over the world without ever leaving the classroom or school computer lab. Such trips can expand the worldviews of students immediately, as Stanford University researchers showed by having high school students experience coral reef destruction caused by increased levels of ocean acidification. Students experienced the simulation as a pink coral living underwater whose environment was degraded over time under the acidic water. When the coral was tested weeks later, students gained a heightened awareness of environmental change and showed they retained scientific concepts taught during the activity (Markowitz, et al., 2018).

Virtual field trips are a flexible teaching approach. With multiple devices and Internet access, groups of students may go on a virtual trip while other students meet with the teacher or work independently on projects. With one device connected to an interactive whiteboard, the whole class can visit places all around the world.

Virtual field trips, virtual tour apps, and virtual reality environments are widely available for use at all grade levels. National Geographic National Parks is a free app that offers detailed information and images about the most frequently visited national parks. Chimani National Parks and Oh, Ranger! ParkFinder are two other options for connecting online experiences to math, science, and geography topics. Park Wildlife Field Guide offers information about plants and animals found in each location. The National Park Service has introduced Bent's Old Fort, a site on the Santa Fe Trail in Colorado, reconstructed in the game Minecraft as a fully immersive 3-D virtual reality experience.

Teachers and students can access UNESCO World Heritage, an app that presents more than 900 world heritage sites around the world. Museums offer virtual field trip apps such as The Art of Life from the J. Paul Getty Museum and World Aquariums, which offers tours of 50 different sites worldwide. Smithsonian Mobile has an online guide to all its museums. Google Earth includes an impressive collection of virtual tours, including famous cathedrals, castles and palaces, art museums, skyscrapers, libraries, and other historic sites from around the world. In addition, many museums, science centers, and other educational organizations have developed online field trip and virtual tour programs that do not require human-to-human interaction, so no reservation is needed.

More locations for virtual field trips and tours include Colonial Williamsburg, Roman Colosseum, Palace of Versailles, Great Wall of China, Sistine Chapel, Hagia Sophia, Mount Vernon Virtual Mansion Tour, Baseball Hall of Fame, USS Arizona Battleship Memorial, Cleveland Museum of Art, National Gallery of Art, Lake Michigan Science Research Center, U.S. Capitol Building, Virtual Gettysburg Interactive Battlefield, and Fossil Halls at the American Museum of Natural History.

MyLab Education Self-Check 7.4

Technology Transformation Learning Plan

Weather Station WebQuest

Investigating Science Using Interactive Web Resources

Grade(s)	Elementary and middle school
Subject(s)	Science/social studies
Key Goal/Enduring Understanding	Weather is a naturally occurring phenomenon that may appear unpredictable but is actually a group of interconnected elements that can be studied, understood, and predicted.
Essential Question	What types of patterns do we see in weather, and how can we use those patterns to make our own weather predictions?
Academic Discipline Learning Standards	**National Science Teachers Association:** *Next Generation Science Standards* Earth and Space Sciences Earth and Human Activity **National Council for the Social Studies**: *Curriculum and Content Area Standards* **Theme III:** People, Places, and Environment **Theme VIII:** Science, Technology, and Society
Learning Objectives	Students will know how and be able to: • Recognize patterns in weather • Use tools that simulate weather patterns • Disseminate weather-related information using web-based tools • Make predictions about future weather based on weather pattern data
Technology Uses	Students begin by using paper-based tools for recording, analyzing, and publishing weather data, and then move to technologies that offer online data, multimedia simulations, digital mapping, and other information.

Minimal Technology	Infusion of Technology
Students describe weather patterns using paper-based recording systems.	Students use web-based charts, graphics, and other online tools to investigate, simulate, and teach about weather patterns.
Students read books that describe weather patterns and weather-related concepts.	Students observe, document, and communicate weather patterns using web-based multimedia tools.
Students create poster displays of weather data.	Students create digital displays of weather data.
Students give poster board presentations.	Students create interactive presentations with software or apps.
Students perform live skits in front of the class.	Students record digital videos of class performances for viewing and reviewing.
Students hand-create weather logs, charts, graphs, and maps.	Students create digital weather logs, charts, graphs, and maps.

Evaluation	Students are evaluated on the creative design and the completeness of their weather projects, including how they record, analyze, and present their findings.
Learning Plan Description	**Learning Focus** "Weather Station WebQuest" capitalizes on students' interest in weather forecasting and weather reporting and the effects of climate change to teach the processes of scientific inquiry and investigation. This experience, conducted in upper elementary and middle school classrooms, is part of the study of the environment, ecology, or geology. Students investigate how weather, a seemingly predictable daily event, in fact follows not only patterns in nature but also changes in temperature and climate. Viewing teacher-selected interactive web resources, students explore different aspects of weather phenomena. When they are finished with the WebQuest or HyperDoc, students prepare a presentation or a video explaining what they learned and featuring further questions to investigate.

Using interactive educational websites, "Weather Station WebQuest" demonstrates the power of the Internet as a teaching and learning environment. The academic content of this learning plan blends ideas and information gained from two sources: the latest Internet resources and students' eyewitness observations of weather phenomena, the most ancient of learning tools. Students learn ways to record eyewitness observations as scientific data and to create interesting group presentations using apps and online tools.

This learning plan addresses standards from the National Science Teachers Association (NSTA) and the International Society for Technology in Education (ISTE). Students learn about the processes of scientific inquiry as applied to the study of the earth and the environment, as well as ways to use technological tools for writing and publishing.

Learning Plan Design—Minimal Technology

A weather study using minimal technology might utilize any or all of the following:

- Going outdoors to experience the elements that create weather—sunshine, wind, precipitation, or clouds—recording them on a graph, and describing them in writing and pictures
- Reading fiction and nonfiction books about weather
- Recording visible weather phenomena daily on a monthly calendar
- Reading the local daily weather report in the newspaper
- Writing a weather report for cities in the United States after learning to read the charts and graphs of *USA Today*'s weather page, which show temperatures and weather in all 50 states and in major cities around the world
- Reading a classroom thermometer showing the indoor/outdoor temperatures
- Mounting a commercial or student-made weather station—thermometers, wind cups (anemometers), barometers, rain gauges—for observations of outside conditions
- Showing videos or online photos of weather phenomena
- Displaying student-made cloud and weather pictures and photos, weather charts, and weather symbols reporting daily weather

Learning Activities Using Technology

The teacher constructs the WebQuest/HyperDoc by selecting websites, designing or adapting activities, and structuring learning to feature students' questions as well as to utilize multimodal resources that add interest and surprise.

1. *Search for web resources.* Search engines, teacher planning sites, and resources from national weather information and science museums will help locate resources that will appeal to a range of students. Third- and fourth-graders appreciate interactivity and visually oriented sites without large amounts of text that may be above their reading level. Pair individuals or small groups with adult guides (teacher aides, parent volunteers, college tutors) to help students navigate and interpret more complex material. Giving attention to historical and multicultural information for this study, picture books provide learning opportunities that online sources do not. A multicultural resource for learning the history of weather predictors includes writers of almanacs, the world's first predictors of weather, seasonal phenomenon, and sky and star motions. One of the famous writers of an almanac for the eastern colonies of the United States is Benjamin Banneker, a free African who wrote Benjamin Banneker's Almanac annually 1792-1797, sending a copy to Thomas Jefferson who sent it on to France to the highest scientific organization there. In addition to writing his almanacs, Banneker was a surveyor and a key part of the designers of the layout of Washington, D.C., for the United States capital. Picture book biographies tell of his many inventions and huge intellectual talents.

    The first peoples of America were the most skilled, knowledgeable weather watchers and forecasters of yearly patterns in nature throughout the American continents. American Indians developed their skills as astronomers and agrarians, engineers and conservationists. Their nations lived with, built for, and used sophisticated information about sky and stars, seasonal occurrence, weather patterns, growing conditions and when to prepare for changes in weather. Adult resources to acquaint teachers with information to convey to students are available in texts and online resources.

2. *Choose interactive websites.* An effective WebQuest/HyperDoc incorporates three to five websites whose interactivity focuses attention and inspires conversations between students and with adults. A WebQuest/HyperDoc does not replace hands-on learning or personal reading experiences; it provides interactive virtual explorations of ideas and concepts. Students cannot feel the wind blowing from a screen, which is why they go outside on a windy day. On the other hand, to access visual images and real-time information about weather around the world, students need online technologies.

3. *Sequence the websites or make student choice a viable way to move through the resources.* The flow of a WebQuest/HyperDoc may be either a planned sequence of sites or a choice of where to begin and where to proceed after that. Variety is inviting. If the first site shows video clips, the next might contain diagrams, and the last might be a web activity to be completed by the students. Here are some interactive resources:
    - *Web Weather for Kids.* Explore how weather can affect and interrupt people's daily routines. By reading personal narratives of extraordinary events, students learn about individuals who have experienced out-of-the-ordinary weather. *Ball of Lightning!* by Enrique (Henry) J. Coll details the experiences of a Canadian who had a ball of fire fly through his front door. Ask students who have had experiences of unusual weather to describe them orally or in writing. Those who have not can create a fictional description of unusual weather. You can use the book *Cloudy with a Chance of Meatballs* by Judi and Ron Barrett as an example.

(continued)

- *Interactive Weather Maker.* Experiment with changing weather conditions by sliding temperature and humidity gauges up and down. While the students move the gauges, they observe how a small house and its surroundings are affected by the climate change they are creating. After using this site, students can write weather recipes for a snowstorm, windstorm, and rainstorm.
- *The National Oceanic and Atmospheric Administration (NOAA).* Research local weather by typing in your ZIP code and then studying maps by zooming in on different regions. Use the tabs across the top of the page to navigate among geographical forecasts, national maps, radar, rivers, air quality, satellite, and climate reports at a glance. Students can write weather reports for different cities or towns in your state, including temperature, humidity, wind speed, barometer readings, dew point, and visibility.
- *Edheads Weather.* Predict weather changes and report weather conditions using underground weather caves.

4. *Choose how to evaluate student performance.* Construct rubrics together with students to evaluate written work, final projects, or group work. Students may work in pairs to provide insights and conversation that produces questions, ideas, and enjoyment of learning.

5. *Set the stage.* Ask the class if anyone has tried an online treasure hunt for learning, a quest in a virtual space where students can access information about all kinds of weather. The introduction or opener may assign a role: "You have been hired by News Station Channel 3 to be a guest meteorologist. The station wants viewers to know more about how to recognize and simulate weather patterns, predict future weather based on weather pattern data, and disseminate weather-related information using web-based tools."

6. *Clearly demonstrate what students will do.* Let students know what to do during the WebQuest/HyperDoc by either writing the directions or including a short video explanation of the process. WebQuest/HyperDoc tasks are generally project-based and require building or inventing something new. There can be a problem to be solved or an issue to be debated inside the task. Display in the class and online the learning procedures, grading rubrics, and expected outcomes of the activity.

7. *Prepare a digital presentation.* Once students finish, they can choose how to use technology to share what they have learned. A presentation, video, and written posts on a classroom website or blog are a few ways to display information about weather patterns and predictions.

Analysis and Extensions
1. Describe two features you find interesting in this learning plan.
2. How widely has technology been integrated into the learning plan?
3. Name two areas for extension or revision of this learning plan.
4. How might students become involved in designing, using, and evaluating their technology use in the learning plan?

Chapter Summary

Learning Outcome 7.1

Describe technologies for curating digital content, including bookmarking, social bookmarking, cloud computing, Google tools, and learning management systems.

- **Information management** is the process of organizing, storing, and administering the academic materials and curriculum resources used by teachers and students in schools.

- Digital content is academic information delivered using Internet technologies.

- Social bookmarking happens when groups of interested people share their weblinks on a public site using tools such as Bitly or Diigo.

- Cloud computing refers to storing personal files on the web; Google tools offer multiple ways to manage online materials; learning management systems (LMS) are digital platforms or cloud-based systems for the delivery of in-person, online, or blended educational learning experiences.

Learning Outcome 7.2

Organize web resources to address curriculum standards utilizing information alerts, e-newsletters, RSS feeds, standards connectors, and inquiry-based WebQuests.

- Teachers can locate local, state, and national curriculum standards online.

- Information alerts are digital notices of new educational developments.

- A standards connector organizes and stores web-based materials for teaching curriculum learning standards.

- Inquiry-based WebQuests/HyperDocs are virtual journeys in which students visit a group of preselected websites to explore academic topics by accessing text, picture, audio, and video resources.

Learning Outcome 7.3

Analyze the advantages and drawbacks of online learning and virtual schools.

- Online learning is the delivery of educational experiences with computers and other technologies through organizations known as virtual schools.

- Blended or hybrid learning involves a combination of face-to-face and online learning.

- Advocates cite the advantages of delivering academic instruction outside the confines of a school day and at less cost to school system budgets.

- Critics cite the loss of in-person student–teacher communication and limited opportunities for students to interact with other students.

- Massive open online courses (MOOCs) are designed to teach large numbers of people online, often with little or no restrictions on who or how many people can enroll in a course.

- Interactive videoconferencing enables students, teachers, and academic experts in different places to converse electronically in real time.

Learning Outcome 7.4

Apply exploratory learning websites and apps, virtual and augmented reality, and virtual field trips for online and offline learning.

- Exploratory learning websites and apps provide digital content specifically designed to support K–12 curriculum learning.

- Exploratory learning websites and apps engage students through stories, images, graphics, characters, mysteries, and important issues.

- Virtual reality (VR) and augmented reality (AR) create interactive digital environments for student learning.

- Virtual field trips provide opportunities for students to explore their own questions about academic topics in a nonlinear, self-directed manner.

Key Terms

Augmented reality (AR), p. 181
Blended learning, p. 175
Bookmarking, p. 165
Cloud computing, p. 165
Content curation, p. 164
Digital content, p. 163
e-newsletters, p. 170
Exploratory learning, p. 178
Folksonomy, p. 165

Information alert, p. 170
Information management, p. 184
Interactive videoconferencing, p. 177
Learning management systems (LMS), p. 169
Massive open online courses (MOOCs), p. 176
Online learning, p. 174
RSS feeds, p. 170

Social bookmarking, p. 165
Standards connector, p. 170
Tags, p. 165
Tag clouds, p. 166
Virtual reality (VR), p. 180
Virtual field trips, p. 181
Virtual schools, p. 174
WebQuests/HyperDocs, p. 173

MyLab Education Application Exercise 7.3:
Growing and Leading with Technology: Irene and Stacy's "Thinking Globally, Acting Locally" Learning Activity

---

For Reflection and Discussion

Curating Educational Information

As you reflect on the strategies you use to locate, organize and store educational information, answer the following questions:

How have you been locating, organizing, and storing information as a student and/or as a teacher license candidate (e.g., saving paper copies of materials, bookmarking websites on your computer, going to the library when you need information, joining a social bookmarking site)?

How do you now plan to locate, organize, and store education and teaching-related information in the future?

Using HyperDocs as a Teacher

HyperDocs are ways for teachers to create online learning experiences for individuals, small groups, and entire classes

(Highfill, Hilton, & Landis, 2016). To create a HyperDoc lesson, teachers arrange digital content in a sequence of live link activities that emphasize problem solving and inquiry-based learning by students. There can be links to podcasts, videos, and infographics, as well as text-based sources. Teacher Jennifer Gonzalez (2016) refers to the links embedded in a HyperDoc as a "playlist" of learning activities. Students make their way through the playlist, checking in with teachers who monitor and support their progress. As you think about the idea of HyperDocs, what sequence of online learning activities would you construct for a topic in your teaching field? Begin constructing a playlist of experiences for students. What interactive, multimodal resources are you using? How will you check in with students to best support their learning?

Chapter 8

Solving Problems and Designing Solutions Through Coding, Makerspaces, and Serious Gaming

SOURCE: Alex Traksel/Shutterstock

Chapter Overview

Chapter 8 examines how interactive **educational software** and apps, coding, makerspaces, and 3-D printing, along with digital learning games, support and promote **problem solving** and inquiry-based learning by K–12 students. We begin by defining problem solving before turning to the importance of teaching students computational thinking, coding, and robotics. Next, we introduce digital learning games and game-based learning as instructional choices for teachers and students, followed by an overview of makerspaces, the Maker Movement, and 3-D modeling and printing. The chapter concludes with a Technology Transformation Learning Plan titled "Recreating Precontact First American Homes with Makerspaces and 3-D Printing."

Through its focus on inquiry-based learning and problem solving, the chapter responds to ISTE Standards for Students: Computational Thinker and Innovative Designer. Using coding, 3-D printing, serious games, and other technologies, students engage in the design process, address real-world problems, and develop the ability to work with complex, open-ended challenges while practicing the steps of problem solving from initial designs to trials and experiments to workable solutions. They develop the skills to pursue their curiosities and interests through data collection and data analysis, algorithmic thinking, and the clear presentation of findings and solutions.

Learning Outcomes

After reading this chapter, you will be able to:

8.1 Explain how technology promotes problem solving among students.

8.2 Analyze computational thinking in coding and robotics.

8.3 Apply digital games, educational simulations, virtual reality, and virtual worlds as learning resources for teachers and students.

8.4 Utilize makerspaces, the Maker Movement, and 3-D modeling and printing as instructional resources in schools.

Chapter Learning Goal

Use physical and digital technologies, including apps, 3-D printers, digital games, and simulations, to promote problem solving and inquiry-based learning.

Featured Technologies

Makerspaces

3-D modeling and printing

Digital games

Virtual worlds

Visual-thinking and concept-mapping software and apps

Coding apps and websites

Robotics

Data collection tools

Interactive simulation games

Afternoons at Engineering School

Kindergarteners to sixth-graders at a nearby elementary school eagerly await Thursdays when as part of the after-school program, they can choose to attend "Engineering School." This weekly opportunity to explore science, technology, engineering, and math (STEM) concepts in an informal, self-choice setting is the idea of two college undergraduates, Emily and Marissa, who are preparing for careers in education. As part of their undergraduate learning, the two want to see how different ways of learning contribute to children's self-confident, self-directed inquiries. They chose engineering as their weekly topic to invite elementary students, especially girls, to engage in math and science activities different from classroom curriculums. Engineering School offers hands-on and digital materials with which to experiment and create. Emily and Marissa observe how kids' individual curiosity and creativity lead to design, building, and sharing materials and ideas with others.

Engineering School begins with experiments in flight, folding and flying paper airplanes of children's own designs. Beyond the challenge of configuring flat 2-D pieces of paper into 3-D objects that can glide, students experience how engineers use the scientific method to design models, test their prototypes in real-world conditions, and revise their creations based on the results of experimental trials. Mistakes help students ask questions of each other and try new ideas or folding techniques to get the planes to lift and fly. Marissa reminds them, "If your plane had even a moment in the air, it was a success; it wasn't a failure. Now let's try to keep it in the air longer. Let's make some changes and see what happens."

After Flight School, students learn Origami to create 3-D boxes and animals. Children fold paper into parts or fractions using symmetry to make triangles, squares, and rectangles, shapes that emerge when the paper is being folded. Kids see the geometry. They find that multiplication, the repetition of doing the same thing over many times, affects the growth of their skills as folders. By practicing the folding of boxes with different sizes of paper, precision and attention to the folding process develops. Practice makes efforts easier and the boxes look professional. Children teach each other, assuring one another that they made the same mistakes and that redoing improved the results.

Then children access online resources for design, using TinkerCAD, a 3-D modeling program, to create a digital version of what they want to make. They build a model of a personal nameplate or one of their original designs that is then sent to the local college library, where the children's creations are transformed into tangible objects by a 3-D printer.

They also design and build with good junk: scraps and left over materials, packing that would be thrown away, boxes and cleaned plastic food containers, sticks and bottle tops, straws and pipe cleaners. These free materials inspire creative projects that youngsters design for their own pleasure. "See this purse?" a child said to Emily, "I designed it! I'm a designer."

In an environment where youngsters feel comfortable exploring new ideas, utilizing their creativity, taking risks, and learning through design-based thinking, students evaluate their models, ask other students about their creations and confidently exchange ideas. What Emily and Marissa observed through the experiences at Engineering School is children gaining confidence in themselves as problem solvers and technology users. Expecting to make mistakes, to change their minds and revise their projects, children engaged in habits of real-life scientists, engineers, and inventors. They tried, retried, and assisted each other with their designs.

Students' engagement with math, science, and technology at Engineering School introduce this chapter's learning goal of ways to promote problem solving and inquiry-based thinking through coding, robotics, digital games, makerspaces, and 3-D printing. Problem solving and inquiry-based learning refer to educational activities in which students ask questions, make predictions, test theories, and revise ideas based on data and evidence (Pratt, 2012; National Science Teachers Association, 2003). These are the same methods used by scientists, mathematicians, historians, and other professionals to conduct research, make discoveries, and advance human knowledge. In this chapter, we examine how teachers can place problem solving and inquiry-based learning at the center of curriculum and instruction by focusing on the following questions:

1. How can you use technology to promote problem solving among students?
2. How can you use computational thinking, coding, and robotics as inquiry-based learning experiences for students in classrooms?
3. How can you and the students use serious digital games and interactive simulation materials as learning resources?
4. How can you support students as inventors through makerspaces and 3-D modeling and printing?

Teaching Problem Solving

8.1. Explain how technology promotes problem solving among students.

In teaching problem solving, teachers use real-world situations and issues to actively stimulate students' wonder and curiosity. In history class, students might examine primary source documents—personal letters, government documents, census data, news stories, photos, paintings, and other materials—to explore causes and outcomes of historic events. In this way, they "do" history, reasoning about historical dynamics while contextualizing the study of the names, dates, and places of the past. In science, math, and English classes, as students undertake inquiry-based learning activities, they simulate the work of professionals in those fields. Children and adolescents are natural inquirers who ask questions about every imaginable subject. Incorporating students' personal interests makes problem solving an engaging instructional approach to learning at every grade.

Problem-Based Learning

Problems must be questions worth answering to attain students' attention, observed educator David Jonassen (2010). This quality is missing from too many school assignments in the minds of a majority of students who are constantly wondering why they would possibly need to know or care about the topics. Jonassen urges teachers to create activities that arise from real-life problems as they are what interest and inspire students. **Problem-based learning** (or *inquiry-guided learning*) is a common term for such assignments. Students investigate issues and questions for which there is no one right or predetermined answer using a process of asking questions, assembling evidence, drawing conclusions, and evaluating the results.

Technology presents new ways for students to pose and solve problems.

SOURCE: Lucky Dragon/Fotolia.

As students grapple with open-ended problems, they exercise critical thinking skills, a willingness to take risks, mental self-discipline, and a creative approach to everyday challenges. Instead of promoting acceptance of hasty or ill-informed conclusions, either based on first impressions or resulting from little forethought, problem solving and inquiry-based learning require students to follow a well-known approach proposed by George Polya (2009) for solving mathematical problems. The essential steps in Polya's framework include:

- *Understanding the problem.* Students identify the type of question they are being asked, what the question is asking them to do, and what they already know that can help them solve the problem.

- *Using problem-solving strategies.* Students implement problem-solving strategies; in math these would include computational approaches, separating a problem into sequenced steps, connecting given information to something they know, deducing further ideas, and deciding whether a chosen strategy will lead to a solution of the problem.

- *Checking results.* Students determine whether they have solved a problem correctly or if they should try to solve the problem a second time (after getting an incorrect answer) by reassessing what is being asked in the question, eliminating now obviously wrong answers, or rechecking their computations and procedures.

Most importantly, notes Jonassen, students must encounter problems that are not easily solved. In school, students typically encounter well-structured problems that include all the information needed to solve them without need of inquiry and curiosity as learning stimuli. These problems, "organized in a predictive and prescriptive way," have a single correct answer and follow a "preferred, prescribed solution process" (Jonassen, 2010, p. 6).

But the social, economic, and political situations of real life rarely, if ever, have well-structured problems. Problems in society are complicated, messy, and stubborn and often require trade-offs and compromises to resolve, making them **ill-structured problems** because there is no simple formula to follow to resolve them (Simon, 1973).

Ill-structured problems offer complex learning opportunities for students. Ill structured does not mean that a problem needs to be fixed or changed; it means students must use higher order thinking—analyzing, applying, comparing, and creating to find possible solutions. In facing such problems, students learn to define issues precisely, consider a wide number of possible solutions, evaluate the pros and cons of

MyLab Education

Video Example 8.1

In this video, a teacher challenges students to decide whether toys can be used to illustrate science concepts. How does the teacher introduce the concept of problem solving to the students?

each approach, decide on the most viable course of action, and reassess their strategy based on results. Such actions develop a flexible mind-set and the creative ability to continually shift strategies when situations change and new evidence appears. This chapter's In Practice shows how one teacher uses online resources to teach problem solving to upper elementary and middle school students.

In Practice

Stop Disasters! Teaching Problem Solving with a Simulation Game

Grade Level	Featured Technologies
Elementary and middle school	Tablets and online games

Learning Plan Outline

To teach problem solving in a middle school social studies world geography class, Lauren decides to use simulation games to engage students, many of whom are avid online game and video game players. A gamer herself, she recognizes the invitations of games. Players are transported into visually appealing virtual environments where their decisions and actions determine the outcomes of events. For students, game playing creates intense interest, concentration and willingness to continue playing to achieve a goal.

Lauren read James Paul Gee's book *What Video Games Have to Teach Us about Learning and Literacy* to investigate the uses of games that combine the engaging elements of game play with academic topics and concepts to create memorable learning experiences for students. As part of an environmental science and geography unit, Lauren introduced *Stop Disasters!*, a group of free online simulation games from the United Nations International Strategy for Disaster Reduction (ISDR; see Figure 8.1). *Stop Disasters!* focuses on the preparedness for and prevention of environmental catastrophes in five different regions of the world: tsunami (South Pacific), hurricane (east and west coasts of North America), wildfire (interior of North America), earthquake (Asia and Indian Ocean), and flood (Europe and Asia). The ISDR developed these games to educate students about the causes and effects humans exert on their environment.

Teaching with Technology

As students begin, the program informs them that there is a huge natural event coming with the possibility of catastrophic damage and loss of hundreds of human lives (see Figure 8.1). Game players have 15 minutes to try to reduce the natural disaster's impact on the local population.

As a real-world simulation, the process of disaster-reduction planning is multilayered, requiring students to address problems by making difficult choices. Preparation for hurricanes and tsunamis means building seawalls, securing boats, and constructing safer buildings with sturdier materials. All of these activities cost money, and limited funds diminish quickly with each new expense. Time is also of the essence. A hurricane/tsunami probability bar keeps moving steadily toward total disaster as players race the clock to respond.

In the game, students decide multiple economic and social options, and every decision has a reasonable counter-decision to consider. Building seawalls will protect low-lying areas, but these structures will change the view of the beach, making it less likely that investors will build luxury beachside hotels to attract high-end tourists and provide jobs for the local population. There is a question of constant balance between economic development and ecological defense as game players consider the trade-offs between loss of lives and loss of prosperity.

Stop Disasters! illustrates how simulation games generate highly engaging learning experiences for students. Each decision has real-world consequences, and the games can be played multiple times to see how different choices create different results. Through this interactive digital simulation, Lauren observed students involved in ill-structured problem considerations—posing substantive questions, trying possible solutions, and assessing the effect of their decisions on people and settings. The game provides essential problem solving skills within the science and social studies curriculum that reflect current life situations.

Figure 8.1 Stop Disasters! Digital Learning Game Screenshot

SOURCE: From United Nations International Strategy for Disaster Reduction. Reprinted by Permission of UNISDR.

There are a growing number of tools for teaching problem solving to students. Software programs and apps, learning games, and intelligent tutoring programs provide challenging problems for students to solve. Using technology, students may consider multiple possible solutions and then receive immediate feedback about their ideas. Digital games offer an environment in which trial and error are part of the experience. Think about the last digital game you played—did you make it to the end without failing? Probably not. Games are built on the idea of trying new strategies until you reach the next level, and then figuring out the best way to advance to the end. Failure is part of learning through gaming. When playing digital games, students can try, fail, and try again without worrying about the consequence of getting a lower grade (unless you assign students grades based on their game level achievement, which we do not recommend). In games, students have the opportunity to try without fearing failure and utilize mistakes as ways to learn.

Problem-solving activities may be simple or complex, depending on the assignment, and as a result, students will utilize either surface or in-depth thinking. A math facts drill-and-practice program to review or memorize basic computation facts (2 times 2 is always 4) requires little creativity or complexity, but a design project built in Scratch, a programming language for designers of all ages, requires students to apply creative thinking, computational thinking, and problem-solving strategies from beginning to end.

MyLab Education Self-Check 8.1

Computational Thinking, Coding, and Robotics

8.2   Analyze computational thinking in coding and robotics.

In today's digital age, there is growing awareness that students will need to know how to think computationally. **Computational thinking** involves knowing how to use data, models, simulations, and algorithmic thinking to formulate and solve problems (Computer Science Teachers Association, 2011). As computational thinkers, students engage in "solving problems, designing systems, and understanding human behavior" in ways that utilize "concepts fundamental to computer science" (Center for Computational Thinking, 2012). The national K–12 Computer Science Standards propose teaching computational thinking as a core skill beginning in elementary school. In 2018, ISTE also released standards for computer science educators.

Learning to Code

Computational thinking can be developed when students learn to code. **Coding** is the act of programming a computer using written instructions. Through coding, students learn how to control or direct what they do with a computer or robot. From envisioning a project to writing instructions for a computer to follow, making certain actions and sequences happen, and revising or changing those instructions as needed, students practice how to read and write code to see their creative ideas appear on screen. Mathematical concepts and applications are integral to the design process—multiplying whole and decimal numbers, measuring straight lines, creating angles and turns in degrees, and utilizing fractions. This understanding of mathematics has applications in all sciences, engineering, design animation, movie making, and most relevantly, in using the language of code for students' own purposes.

Coding languages for non–computer programmers first appeared in schools in the 1970s, propelled by the work of Seymour Papert, who in 1967 with Daniel G. Bobrow, Wally Feurzeig, and Cynthia Solomon created the programming language Logo for children to use to control the actions of an onscreen turtle. Derived from the Greek word *logos*, Logo translates as "speech" or "thought."

Table 8.1 Coding Programs and Apps

Scratch, Scratch Jr.	Programming languages enable younger (Scratch Jr.) and older (Scratch) students to solve problems by making and learning from mistakes. These free resources invite creating and playing with coding to make games, videos, and animations. Almost anything is possible here.
Daisy the Dinosaur	In this app, young coders make Daisy move, jump, spin, turn, grow, shrink, and roll in response to commands while mastering the basic steps and moving on to programming responses of "if/when" statements.
Kodable Pro	This programming app for elementary school students offers short but engaging puzzle challenges that increase in complexity as children demonstrate their skill and understanding of sequencing and programming logic.
The Foos	This iPad app is designed for easy learning at the beginning levels. Elementary, middle, and high school students can create code to direct many options. CodeSpark Academy is an online version of the app.
Hour of Code	Coding is combined with opportunities to do all kinds of activities in this free site. Players can choose their own activities to learn to code, create their own games and designs, and move from using blocks for commands to learning programming languages.

Today, learning to code does not require programming knowledge. Instead, programs for learning to code, like Scratch, and Scratch Jr., utilize **object-oriented programming** in which students create a virtual object and make it do things in response to programmed instructions. A student might create a ball and program it to fall and bounce back up repeatedly as an animation. The ball's movement demonstrates the concepts of velocity and negative velocity and invites students to discover other ways to program a ball's movement.

In these open-ended online coding apps or online sites, students learn to code by creating code to make something happen. Each young coder has the freedom to explore, design, experiment, revise, start over, and try again. Engaging directly in the thinking and problem-solving process of coding offers students experiences that memorizing key terms or completing pre-set exercises within an online program does not do. Learning to code by coding teaches computational thinking, an approach to solving problems that is based around organizing and analyzing data, representing that data abstractly, and creating solutions using algorithms (another term for an ordered sequence of steps). Table 8.1 includes coding apps for all ages.

Learning to code also supports the development of the 21st century skills of critical thinking, creativity, communication, and collaboration among students. Critical thinking and creativity are needed to arrange symbols and text into a meaningful code. Communication is fostered when the code works as planned and produces its intended result for others to see. Collaboration happens when young coders work together to create code or when young coders remix a predesigned code that someone else created (e.g., the Scratch community).

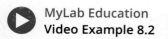

MyLab Education
Video Example 8.2

In this video, high school students use coding in the study of literature. How can you envision using coding to involve students in problem solving and critical thinking?

https://www.youtube.com/watch?v=AxsZouCwnPc

Coding for All Students

Many educators believe that coding and programming are a worldwide language that students need to know to participate effectively in the global economy (Edutopia, 2013). In 2014, Britain began teaching coding to all students in state primary and secondary schools to develop thoughtfully reflecting, learning from making mistakes, and maintaining persistence when using math and physics concepts. Through creating code, students see the application of their efforts demonstrated before their eyes; they regard the activity as relevant, interesting, and worth doing again and again.

In the United States, analysts predict that by 2020 there will be a need for 1.4 million computing jobs (DeNisco, 2014). However, as of 2015, only 25 states counted computer science classes toward high school graduation in math or science and fewer than 5% of American college students graduated with a degree in computer science. In 2013, only 30,000 high school students nationwide took the Advanced Placement (AP) computer science test; fewer than 20% were women, while only 8% were Hispanic and 3% were African American. In 11 states, no African American or Hispanic students took the AP computer science test (Ericson, 2014).

To increase the number of students majoring in computer science, coding can be taught in the early grades as part of reading, writing, science, social studies, art, and math, enabling students to learn computer science concepts by constructing simple programs, seeing the results, revising the codes, and enjoying the experience. Coding should continue throughout middle and high school where students, girls and boys, have choices of in-depth computer science and math/science learning experiences. To introduce computer programming to upper elementary, middle, and high school students, in 2014, the organization Code.org released *Code with Anna and Elsa*, a coding tutorial using characters from the Disney movie *Frozen*. Code.org continues to release new games and activities each year offering interesting choices for all ages to learn coding.

Other computational thinking and coding resources for students are available online from the following organizations: Girls Who Code, Technology Education and Literacy in Schools (TEALS), Code with Google, and the Carnegie Mellon University Center for Computational Thinking. Teachers and students can visit the Coding in the Classroom series at Edutopia and participate in the annual Hour of Code campaign, initiated to publicize and involve students in coding as part of Computer Science Education Week—held each December to recognize the birthday of U.S. Navy Rear Admiral Grace Hopper, a 20th century computer pioneer. In Hour of Code, students learn coding online by playing with Angry Bird characters, creating greeting cards, programming an app, or completing a variety of other projects. Table 8.1 lists more digital learning environments that offer open-ended, self-correcting opportunities for elementary, middle, and high school and college students to learn to code.

> **MyLab Education Application Exercise 8.1**

Robotics in the Classroom

Robotics is the study of how humans can make smart machines called robots do things that are difficult, dangerous, or even impossible for humans to do on their own. Robots are everywhere in our society—building cars, exploring the oceans and outer space, helping to perform surgeries, cleaning homes, maintaining farmlands, filling prescriptions at the pharmacy, defusing bombs, reviewing thousands of pages of documents in short amounts of time, dispensing money at ATMs, and doing many other previously human-performed jobs. It is estimated that there will be 18 million industrial robots globally by 2035 performing the work of 100 million U.S. workers—an output equal to the world's entire current manufacturing production (Chen & Moenius, 2017).

Robots have three main parts: 1) a "controller," a computer that receives instructions from human programmers; 2) "mechanical parts," movable pieces powered by air, water, or electricity; and 3) "sensors," devices that tell a robot about its environment (Science Trek, 2019). Teaching robotics to students offers ways for youngsters to understand how these three components work together to perform automated tasks.

Educators cite at least five reasons for teaching robotics in schools beginning in the early grades and continuing through high school: 1) teaching programming, especially when done in conjunction with other learning-to-code activities; 2) increasing creative thinking as students envision how to use their robotic designs; 3) introducing youngsters to fields and future jobs and careers in science, technology, engineering, and math; 4) showing children and teens the process of drafting, building, and revising that is integral to the design process, as initial designs usually do not work as planned; and 5) promoting inclusive learning experiences for girls and boys, students with special educational needs, and youngsters learning English as a new language (Lynch, 2017).

Robotic toys and building kits are engrossing tools for classroom learning. The plastic brick maker Lego has been designing robotics and robotics kits for more than three decades. Lego introduced its first computer-controlled product in 1986, and its Intelligent Brick and Robotics Invention System was launched in 1998. Lego

Mindstorms NXT, a programmable robotics kit, arrived in 2006 and has been upgraded to Lego Mindstorms EV3 since then. Lego Boost Creative Toolbox lets young builders download a free app to their computer or smartphone and then program different robot toys, including Vernie (who moves and talks); Frankie the Cat (an interactive pet); and Guitar 400 (a musical instrument with sound effects). Elementary-age students will also enjoy littleBits Star Wars Droid Inventor Kit, while older students can use UBTech's Jimu Robot, Meccano MeccaSpider, and Wonder Workshop Cue CleverBot.

In 2019, Lego introduced a collection of brightly colored multifaceted pieces with design plans for learning coding and robotics called Spike Prime. The pieces are a tool kit to accommodate design thinking, the process of building, trying, making mistakes and trying again.

Lego products offer many creative learning features, but they can be expensive. So are robot toys from other manufacturers. You can find cheaper but still highly rated robots by searching online for "top robot kits for kids" or "build your own robot kits." Resources for learning more about teaching robotics include robotics-based lessons and activities from the Center for K12 STEM Education at the New York University Tandon School of Engineering; a robotics teaching resources website from the University of Southern California; and the KOOV Educator Kit from SONY with sensors, switches, motors, wheels, LEDs, and other building blocks and accessories. You can learn about the history of robots from the roboworld website at the Carnegie Science Center in Pittsburg, Pennsylvania.

MyLab Education Self-Check 8.2

Digital Games and Game-Based Learning

8.3 Apply digital games, educational simulations, virtual reality, and virtual worlds as learning resources for teachers and students.

Mention games and gaming, and most educators, parents, and students think of **computer- and web-based games** that people play for entertainment. But educators are increasingly drawn to educational impacts of **game-based learning** that combine the challenges of game play with specific academic content teachers need to teach and students need to learn.

Gaming is a huge and growing industry, reaching into nearly every home and many schools for four main reasons:

- Games are readily available on a variety of platforms. Internet- or browser-based games and apps can be played on any Internet-connected device, including smartphones and tablets, while **desktop-based games** are permanently downloaded to your desktop or laptop or to a stand-alone or handheld game console. Many Internet-based games are free to play, whereas desktop games and apps are commercial products you purchase.

- Manufacturers promote interest in games across age groups and grade levels by creating highly publicized connections between games and commercial products, television shows, and movies. Symbols of the gaming culture appear on pencils, purses, notebooks, clothing, backpacks, playing cards, stuffed animals, figurines, and logos marketed to young consumers.

- Action and adventure narratives with alluring characters and fast-paced play make games attractive to adults and children alike. While the majority of adult game players are young men, ages 18–29, 4 in 10 women and 2 in 10 Americans over age 65 say they play games on occasion (Brown, 2017). Among teenagers, nearly all boys and over 80% of girls play video games (Anderson & Jiang, 2018). Game playing has given rise to gaming groups, and membership in them is linked to a perception of social success for some youngsters.

- **Gamification**, the "application of game elements to non-gaming situations, often to motivate or influence behavior," has become part of the way people do business in many sectors of the economy (EDUCAUSE Learning Initiative, 2011b). Companies use gamification as part of reward systems through which customers earn points for purchases and accomplishments. The game structure is designed to build brand loyalty and motivate customers to keep buying that company's products. In schools, teachers use gamification when they give individual or group recognition and rewards for assignments done in class or for homework. *Jeopardy!*-style quiz games to review academic material before a test are a popular form of gamification in schools.

Games in Schools

The availability of tablets and the growth of apps for learning have made it possible for many schools to provide students with their own computing devices during class time and to purchase relatively inexpensive learning games for handheld machines. Three out of four teachers use digital games for instruction; just over half have students play games weekly as part of the regular school curriculum (Takeuchi & Vaala, 2014). These teachers report that game play, particularly in mathematics, improves student skills while acknowledging that it can be difficult to find games that align to local, state, and national learning standards. Interestingly, fewer than 1 in 10 teachers said they received training in digital game integration as part of their preservice teacher education courses.

At the same time, educational learning games are a growing segment of the game field, ranging from relatively simple programs where students select a choice to answer a question to highly interactive and dynamic multimedia experiences where users interact with a complex digital environment. In a single-user or in multiuser format, game players encounter obstacles to overcome or problems to solve. There is visual feedback of each player's actions, and there are rewards for successful accomplishments.

Digital Dialog 8.1

Digital games, immensely popular among today's students, are powerful learning experiences for teaching academic content. As you think about your own experiences playing or watching friends or siblings playing video games and web-based games, comment and connect online about the following questions:

- What are the learning behaviors used and practiced when youngsters choose and play games that they like?
- What educational purposes might be part of games that go "against the grain" of competition by emphasizing cooperation, creative problem solving, and peaceful solutions to problems?

There are sharp debates among educators about the impacts of game play for children and adolescents, especially when games are used to promote educational learning. Critics contend that playing a game can override the importance of academic material when students become more concerned with winning and losing rather than learning (Anderson & Rainie, 2012; Quitney & Rainie, 2012). And although gaming can be engaging and motivating for students, critics see hyper-competitiveness discouraging noncompetitive students who regard themselves as unsuccessful game players. In win/lose game situations, noncompetitive youngsters can be distanced from, not drawn to, the learning activity.

There is also concern about the value of earning rewards as a way to measure success in a game. Education reformer Alfie Kohn (2011) has consistently criticized giving external rewards to children, contending that prizes, stickers, or points teach youngsters to seek a tangible product rather than to become engaged with learning as a personally satisfying experience. Game players, perhaps because the systems provide them, seek these symbols as measures of success.

Tech Tool 8.1

Digital Games, Simulations, and Interactive Activities

Educationally effective digital games, simulations, and interactive activities possess several common attributes:

- Open-ended activities, often with complex storylines and multiple avenues for exploration
- Memorable, age-appropriate virtual characters who interact with students as learning companions in the activity
- Real-world settings that include complex puzzles to be solved
- Activities that can be done multiple times with different possible outcomes
- Engaging graphics to draw students' attention and the capacity for users to choose how and when to access different learning spaces
- Academic skills, concepts, and ideas embedded in the activity so students are learning while they are playing or doing

computational skills. Dynamic online tools offer new ways to think about the concepts of mathematics that are difficult to understand without manipulating variables that affect sizes, shapes, outcomes, graphs and x–y axes. In so doing, game play becomes one way to help address a persistent "algebra gateway" that near the end of middle school separates mathematical haves from mathematical have-nots who are disproportionately African American, Latino, and female.

The popular digital game *Zoombinis*, first released in 1996 in Europe and then in the United States in 2001, teaches critical thinking, mathematical problem solving, and conceptual thinking to elementary students ages 5 to 12 without using numbers. Zoombinis are thumb-sized creatures with five different types of hairstyles, eyes/eyewear, nose colors, and feet/footwear—625 different possible combinations—who have embarked on a long and perilous journey to reclaim their ancestral island home. Using set theory, graphing, algebraic thinking, and theory building, game players must maneuver the Zoombinis through a series of obstacles and puzzles that block their journey. There are three entries in the Zoombinis series—Zoombinis Logical Journey, Zoombinis Mountain Rescue, and Zoombinis Island Odyssey. The technology research organization TERC has reissued Zoombinis Logical Journey as an app for tablets and online (see Figure 8.2 for a screenshot).

You can learn more about the impacts of games, simulations, and interactives in a science and social studies classroom in this chapter's In Practice: Stop Disasters! Teaching Problem Solving with a Simulation Game.

Digital games involve actions that build focus, persistence, flexible problem solving, and collaborative information sharing.
SOURCE: © Jovannig/Fotolia.

The educational importance of digital games, simulations, and interactive activities was forecast more than a decade ago by a group of Arizona State University researchers who noted that in well-constructed, academically based digital activities, "students act as investigative reporters, environmental scientists, and historians who resolve meaningful dilemmas" (Barab, Gresalfi, & Arici, 2009, p. 76). These researchers saw the potential of games to generate transformational play in which students use their knowledge and insights to solve problems by making decisions. Being able to analyze a problem and make choices to solve it can transform both the play space and the player.

The influence of learning games, simulations, and interactives extends across subject fields. In math, for example, games and simulations offer open-ended, self-correcting opportunities to practice

Figure 8.2 Pizza Pass Screenshot from Zoombinis

There is growing examination and some strong endorsement of games being used instructionally in schools. "The theory of learning in good video games fits well with what I believe to be the best sorts of science instruction in school," famously noted James Paul Gee, a professor of reading at the University of Wisconsin and an early proponent of using games for educational purposes (2007, p. 7). Similarly, teacher and game user Jeremiah McCall has stated that games promote learning across the curriculum, noting that historical games are "superior tools for learning about historical context, historical systems, and historical limitations" (2011, p. 12).

Gee's and McCall's conclusions have been supported by more than a decade of research identifying valuable educational outcomes for students from video and computer game play (Takeuchi & Vaala, 2014; Bogost, 2011; Federation of American Scientists, 2006; Houssart & Sams, 2008; Prensky, 2006). After reviewing the literature on gaming, three American Psychological Association researchers concluded that "video games provide youth with immersive and compelling social, cognitive, and emotional experiences" and that such "experiences may have the potential to enhance mental health and well-being in children and adolescents" (Granic, Lobel, & Engels, 2014, p. 66).

As a new teacher, you are inextricably part of these debates, and your actions as a technology-using educator will contribute to shaping the terms and outcomes of these ongoing discussions. You can learn about the history of gaming over the past 30 years from The Video Game Revolution, a PBS website that provides an overview of games and gaming and their place in contemporary culture.

MyLab Education Application Exercise 8.2:
Exploring a Digital Game for Learning

Serious Games and Online Simulations

Serious games (also known as *digital games for learning*) are computer- and web-based games and apps that have been designed with educational goals in mind (Honey & Hilton, 2011). A national survey by the Joan Ganz Cooney Center at Sesame Workshop found growing use of educational-based digital games by teachers, with one third of elementary school educators utilizing them two to four times a week to increase interest, motivation, and engagement in learning and to more readily convey academic material to students (Millstone, 2012).

Emphasis on serious digital games for learning began in 2006, when the Federation of American Scientists convened a Summit on Educational Games. Participants concluded that game players are mastering skills essential for careers in a 21st century information society: strategic thinking, interpretive analysis, problem solving, the ability to form and carry out plans, and adaptive responses to rapid change.

Some serious digital games specifically address higher order thinking skills by asking students to analyze, evaluate, and/or create as central elements of game play. Such games are open-ended where more than one outcome or result is possible based on the choices and decisions made by game players. Students learn from the consequences of their actions within the game, seeing how choices can produce alternative results, such as when more investment in disaster preparedness minimizes the destructive impacts of hurricanes in the game Stop Disasters!

Game playing offers new ways to connect students with academic content. For many youngsters, taking classes in school and playing games outside of school are vastly different experiences, and those differences point the way toward revolutionary change in how teaching and learning happen in K–12 education. Games are active, challenging, and demanding of focus and concentration to solve problems in innovative ways. You can learn more ways to use serious educational games at the Connected Learning Alliance website which in its collections has the games and resources from the Institute of Play, a non-profit design studio in New York City (2008-2019), whose games designers created games for learning through play.

Online **simulation games** place students in computer-generated representations of real-world situations and settings. In many simulations, game players must make decisions and choices that have meaningful consequences within the game. For example, in a public health crisis simulation, students—acting as research scientists and investigators—must collect information about possible causes, form

Table 8.2 Digital Games for Science, Math, History/Social Studies, and English/Language Arts

Digital Games for Science	
Nobel Prize Games	Educational games are based on Nobel Prize–awarded achievements in the fields of physics, chemistry, medicine, peace, and economics. (Free)
Edheads	Multiple science simulations are offered for elementary and middle school students. Virtual Hip Replacement presents a step-by-step animated simulation of hip replacement surgery in which the game player performs the procedure by clicking and moving the mouse to utilize operating room tools. Other simulations include designing a cell phone, doing heart repairs and transplants, and performing aortic aneurysm surgery. (Free and Paid)
PhET	Free, award-winning, interactive science and math simulations (or sims) are presented in game-like formats emphasizing exploring, discovering, and problem solving; sims are developed at the University of Colorado, and there are sims for physics, biology, chemistry, earth science, and math. (Free)
ABZU, An Aquatic Mystery	Imagine you are a diver exploring the ocean, and as you come in contact with sea creatures and ancient civilizations, you must figure out how to rejuvenate polluted areas and restore a balanced ocean habitat. (Fee)
Digital Games for Math	
Math 4: The River Raft Challenge	To enter the school raft race, you must help Carl and his friends build a winning entry by solving a series of math puzzles and challenges in this graphic comic-like website from Learn Alberta, an initiative of the government of Alberta, Canada. (Free)
Science Game Center	Science games involve math concepts for learning all topics and for all ages. The ways students think about math are extended through the play of the science choices. There is an option to leave a game review. (Free and Paid)
Zoombinis	The three original games in the Zoombinis series—Zoombinis Logical Journey, Zoombinis Mountain Rescue, and Zoombinis Island Odyssey—teach critical thinking, mathematical problem solving, and conceptual thinking to elementary students ages 5 to 12 without using numbers or the traditional operations of addition, subtraction, multiplication, or division. Only Zoombinis Logical Journey has been newly released for play. (Paid)
Digital Games for History/Social Studies	
iCivics	This collection of games teaches students about their rights and responsibilities as democratic citizens. Do I Have a Right? simulates decision making in a law firm that specializes in constitutional rights. Win the White House involves students in managing a successful campaign for the presidency. (Free)
Democracy 3	This political policy simulator invites game players to practice being president or prime minister. Work to pass policies in the areas of the economy, welfare, foreign policy, public services, tax, transportation, and law while keeping your voters happy. (Fee)
GeoGuessr	Photos from Google Street View transport students to unknown places around the globe. Reading the pictures for clues to the location, game players then guess where they are in the world. There are options to locate the photos to just the United States, famous national and international places, or U.S. cities and European stadiums. (Free). A fee-based upgrade, GeoGuessr Pro, lets players create their own maps. (Fee)
Stop Disasters!	Online simulations from the United Nations International Strategy for Disaster Reduction (ISDR) focus on the environmental threats facing different parts of the world: tsunamis (South Pacific), hurricanes (east and west coasts of North America), wildfires (interior of North America); earthquakes (Asia and Indian Ocean), and floods (Europe and Asia). Game players must make disaster-reduction planning decisions under the demands of limited budgets and economic trade-offs. (Free)
Civilization VI: Rise and Fall	Players develop strategies to become the ruler of the world as they navigate scenarios that are based on historical fiction in one of the most popular strategy games on the market. (Fee)
Digital Games for English/Language Arts	
80 Days	This problem-solving travel and adventure narrative game is based on Jules Verne's classic science fiction novel, *Around the World in 80 Days*. Game players act as a valet to Phileas Frog, whose goal is to circumnavigate the globe in just 80 days. To win the race, one must carefully manage money, maintain safety, and outsmart other players. (Fee)
Dave Morris' Frankenstein	In this interactive app-based adaptation of Mary Shelley's classic novel, readers choose what to read and pose questions to the story's narrator. (Fee)
Minecraft: Story Mode	Favorite television shows are rendered in game formats where game players' choices and actions determine the telling of the story. (Fee)

and test hypotheses, conduct experiments to test their ideas, and make recommendations while submitting research reports based on their findings. Effective simulations feature **stealth learning** where students, without realizing they are learning, encounter essential academic information by being inside the activities of the game. This chapter's In Practice depicts one teacher using simulation games in the classroom.

Simulation games utilize different amounts of time to play. There are shorter-length simulations for every grade level: PhET from the University of Colorado Boulder presents chemistry simulations, National Library of Virtual Manipulatives (NLVM) from Utah State University offers math simulations, and GeoGames from the National Geographic Society provides engaging ways to study people and places around the world. Zoombinis and Lure of the Labyrinth, two online math adventure games, offers problems to solve using pre-algebra skills.

Among simulations that take longer to play and need to be downloaded to your desktop, Sid Meier's Civilization series has middle and high school–level players compete to build viable societies through exploration, war, diplomacy, and the innovative application of new technologies (from the wheel and the alphabet to nuclear power and spaceflight). SimCity (first launched in 1989) lets game players create a variety of cities and cultures—from law-abiding to lawless. In Restaurant Empire and Restaurant Empire II, players help Chef Armand LeBoeuf build and manage multiple restaurants in Paris, Rome, and Los Angeles by hiring staff, ensuring the food quality, creating interior designs, and choosing popular dishes, all with the goal of acquiring new customers and high-quality ratings.

Selected free-to-play digital games and simulations are presented in Table 8.2. Resources for finding more games can be found at the following websites: Common Sense Media, Games for Change, *PC Gamer* magazine, Larry Ferlazzo's Websites of the Day, Gaming the Past: Historical Simulations in the Classroom, and TERC for math and science games and projects.

Virtual Reality and Virtual Worlds

Virtual reality (VR) is a lifelike simulation of a three-dimensional environment that can be explored and interacted with by students and teachers through software and hardware. While immersed in a virtual world, a person often has an online identity as an **avatar** that walks, runs, or flies within the virtual space. Some virtual worlds include sound, fragrance, and temperature variations, adding multiple layers of sensory input into the experience. Students can conduct three-dimensional frog dissection experiments, fly a computer-generated airplane, do virtual hip replacements or other surgeries, and experience traveling online to other regions of the world. Virtual simulations are available in areas of science, math, history, and English.

With the advent of Samsung Gear's virtual reality headset, the Oculus Rift, these modestly priced software "development kits" were released into the open market in 2014 to give software engineers a chance to tinker with and co-create virtual content before the rollout of the formal version the following year. VR development kits have proven to be popular with members of the general public seeking their own virtual reality experiences. With new research and development on the rise, the future of virtual reality as a tool for teaching and learning is increasingly viable.

Many popular computer games are organized around **virtual worlds**, defined as computer-based environments where users adopt online avatars and interact with other game players using those identities. Virtual worlds, however, do not always have a game structure with formal rules, specific outcomes, or defined winners and losers. Virtual worlds can be compelling learning environments for children as well as adolescents. Anytime students are playing online in virtual worlds, advertising, adjacent sites and distractions are present that adults may not want kids and teens to be participating in.

Many software programs, learning games, and mobile apps feature "edutainment" (entertainment and education combined in the same tool) as the format for presenting academic information to students. As you consider games and apps for use in a classroom, comment and connect online about the following questions:

- How are the elements of game play—problem solving, competition and reward, self-correcting feedback, interesting storyline, collaboration, discovery—useful to students' learning of academic content?
- What are ways you might combine entertainment, edutainment, and education to develop exciting, problem-based learning experiences for students with technology tools?

Evaluating Games for Learning

For a teacher, one way to evaluate the learning dimensions of digital games is by identifying their educational purpose and goals on two continuums of game experiences (see Figure 8.4). The vertical line presents Bloom's taxonomy of thinking skills arranged bottom to top from lower order to higher order. Remembering and understanding (lower order thinking skills) emphasize recall of factual information. Creating and evaluating (higher order skills) require using information for analysis and action. The horizontal line represents a game's learning goals, ranging left to right from "entertain" to "edutain" to "educate."

- *Entertainment games* are played without explicit educational problem-solving or inquiry-learning goals in mind. Such games include fighting and first-person shooter action, as well as simple games involving chance and probability.
- *Edutainment games* highlight the fun of game play to attract and sustain the interests of learners. Game designers seek to blend the excitement of point scoring and competition with the entertainment of engaging graphics for teaching academic content. Such games include problem solving and inquiry-based learning as part of game play.
- *Educational games* are activities that have clear academic learning goals as the basis of game play. These games promote higher levels of problem solving and inquiry-based learning by immersing game players in more complex situations where problems must be solved using inquiry methods and imaginative thinking.

You can place digital games and smartphone and tablet apps on the chart based on the learning goals and thinking skills they emphasize within game play. An entertainment-based game requiring strategies on the part of players can be placed closer to the left end of the horizontal line, but higher up on the vertical line next to analyzing, evaluating, or creating (Game A on chart in Figure 8.3). At the same time, an academic game that emphasizes mostly factual recall of information would be placed at the right side of the horizontal line but lower on the vertical line opposite remembering or understanding (Game B on chart).

Figure 8.3 Computer and Video Evaluation Continuums

	Entertain	Edutain	Educate
Creating			
Evaluating			
Analyzing		Game A	
Applying			
Understanding			
Remembering			Game B

Examining learning goals and thinking skills determines whether a game promotes higher order or lower order thinking. In general, most educators agree that higher order thinking games include the following elements:

- Complex storylines with open-ended activities for game players to complete
- Meaningful, age-appropriate characters who become learning companions for game players
- Real-world settings that include complex puzzles to be solved during game play
- Opportunities for game players to interact with virtual characters as they play the game
- Opportunities for replaying the game with different possible outcomes
- Interesting and engaging graphics and the capacity for game players to zoom in and out of different game spaces

In games that feature higher order thinking, students have dynamic experiences in which they think creatively and critically while finding new and challenging experiences each time they play the game.

MyLab Education **Self-Check 8.3**

Makerspaces, 3-D Printing, and Students as Inventors

8.4 Utilize makerspaces, the Maker Movement, and 3-D modeling and printing as instructional resources in schools.

Makerspaces are physical or digital places where people design, experiment, and revise their creations. Educator Laura Fleming (2018) sees "a makerspace as a metaphor for a unique learning environment that encourages tinkering, play, and open-ended exploration for all." In these constructivist settings, makers—young and old—experience the power of building physical objects using their own ideas, imagination, creativity, and problem-solving skills (Hatch, 2013). Makers learn by doing as they discover the tools and materials they need for their creations and by sharing what they make—receiving recognition and support from communities of like-minded builders, designers, and artists.

Makerspaces have led to the development of the **Maker Movement**, a growing effort to provide hands-on, minds-on opportunities for elementary, middle, and high school students to engage in problem solving with technology (Martinez & Stager, 2014). Featuring a do-it-yourself (DIY) approach to objects and systems, "makers" craft electronics, robotics, and smart materials while working within groups of collaborative problem solvers who share plans, prototypes, and resources in person and online.

As the contemporary Maker Movement and makerspaces have evolved, people have been creating and sharing products with broader and broader audiences. Fabrication, physical computing, and computer programming are the technologies in common, both in the world market and in the learning spaces of the Maker Movement. Sometimes, the efforts of many makers culminate in Maker Fairs where builders showcase what they have done and how they did it.

Makerspaces are being introduced into schools, libraries, after-school programs, and youth centers around the country so children and adolescents can create, express, develop, expand, make, and share designs and products from their creative imaginations. "Making can be anything to anyone," declared teacher Nicholas Provenzano (2016, p. 1), citing the freedom and potential of what students and adults can learn through processes of making. The excitement of the Maker Movement comes from how it connects directly to an "innately human desire to make things with our hands and our brains, using tools ... using materials provided by nature and by science, and using language" (Fleming, 2015, p. 2). As two middle school educators noted,

Table 8.3 Inexpensive Materials for a Classroom Makerspace

Empty Cardboard Cereal Boxes	Pre-Cut Cardboard Pieces
Small, Large, and Craft Scissors	Play-Doh
Corks	Different Lengths of String
Glue Sticks and Glue Guns	Scotch Tape and Multicolored Duct Tape
Empty Plastic Containers	Popsicle Sticks and Toothpicks
Legos	Cubelets (color coded magnetic pieces)
GoldieBlox kits	Keva Structures (solid wood building pieces)
K'Nex	Copper Foil Tape
Rubber Bands	Pipe Cleaners
Poster Board	Magnets
Paint Swatches	Cotton Balls
Paper Bags	Buttons
Rectangles, Squares, Ovals, and Circles of Magazine Pages Cut into Shapes	Packaging from Cookies, Muffins, Plastic That Is in Fractioned Compartments

the Maker Movement brings new life to "the best, but oft-forgotten learner-centered teaching practices" (Martinez & Stager, 2014). Classroom, library, or school-based makerspaces encourage tinkering, where students discover multiple ways to solve a problem or create a product that connects to science, technology, engineering, and math standards.

While the concept of a makerspace was re-energized by new technologies like 3-D printers and fabrication tools, not all makerspaces have to be high tech. Makerspaces can be low tech or use a mix of low- and high-tech materials and tools. Many teachers are creating their own mini-makerspaces in the classroom from inexpensive and recycled materials (see Table 8.3). One easy way to start a makerspace in your classroom is to ask students to find "junk" (e.g., unused items, recycled materials, broken objects like old umbrellas) to bring to school and to put these into a bin for "making time" or a making activity.

Another way to inform your knowledge of the Maker Movement would be to take a tour of some of the online maker repositories, such as Instructables, where you can find directions for making things from a square-meter vegetable garden on wheels to a turtle house to an electromechanical insect/flapping oscillator. Following step-by-step instructions, you can make, share, and collaborate with other makers in the Instructables community.

Maker-Based Learning

In schools, makerspaces and the Maker Movement promote **maker-based learning** (Hsu, Baldwin, & Ching, 2017), an approach consisting of three main parts: Makers, those who are creating and building; Makerspaces, spaces and places with lots of supplies and tools for makers to use; and Making, the act of building and learning with materials and technologies. Widely regarded as the province of science and math classes, maker-based learning can dramatically enliven learning about people, places, communities, and societies in humanities and social studies classes.

Makerspaces and maker-based learning offer an opportunity to talk with students about the history of inventions and inventors. Every invention is an effort to solve a problem or improve upon an existing situation. Science and technology are ongoing processes of research and discovery for the betterment of people's lives. Many inventions emerge by accident or through a fortuitous set of circumstances. The Slinky toy happened when the tension springs inventor Richard Jones was making for a power monitoring meter fell on the floor and started bouncing around from place to place. The drug penicillin began the process of creation when Sir Alexander Fleming noticed a mold dissolving bacteria in a Petri dish he had accidentally left sitting on the laboratory counter for two weeks. The message is clear: Keep creating and inventing with an open mind and an active imagination, and who knows what might happen.

Children and adolescents are constantly seeking to change and improve the world around them through their actions and inventions. The 2017 winner of the Discovery Education 3M Young Scientist Challenge is an 11-year-old girl who, inspired by the water emergency in Flint, Michigan, invented a portable device to test for lead in drinking water. Her mentor at the 3M company said the girl, Gitanjali Rao, has a "passion for making a difference through her innovation" (Newsela, 2017).

Learning about inventions leads to learning about the inventors who created them, particularly women and people of color whose achievements are often missing from textbooks and curriculum guides. There is Margaret Knight, known as "the lady Edison," who received 27 patents in her life, including ones for shoe-manufacturing machines and an internal combustion engine; Stephanie Kwolek, a chemist working for the DuPont Company, who created a fiber material that was later made into Kevlar, used today on military helmets, bulletproof vests, and fiber-optic cables; and Grace Hopper, a digital technology pioneer who was the sole woman assigned to the operating crew of the groundbreaking Harvard Mark I computer in 1944—a machine that weighed 5 tons and filled an entire room.

You can learn more about women inventors by visiting the 20th Century Scientific Developments page on the *resourcesforhistoryteachers* wiki; more about the long history of African American inventors, including Benjamin Banneker, Henry Blair, Elijah McCoy, Garrett Morgan, and Granville Woods, Louis Latimer, Miriam Benjamin, Marie Ban Brittan Brown, Mary and Mildred Davidson can be found on the wiki's African American Inventors page." Use a search function on the wiki's main page. http://resourcesforhistoryteachers.pbworks.com/w/page/123820173/FrontPage

To expand learning about technology and inventions, teachers and students could research the lives of diverse inventors. Online research can be followed by a makerspace activity where students create a 3-D model that represents a woman, LGBTQ individual, or person of color who shaped the fields of science, technology, engineering, or math.

3-D Printing and How It Works

3-D printing is a remarkable, almost science fiction–like process in which physical and digital worlds combine to create actual objects from computer-based files and plans. 3-D printing has been called the "third industrial revolution" because it allows anyone to build anything they can imagine. 3-D printers are being used in numerous professions and fields, including medicine, graphic design, fashion, art, construction, engineering, and the food industry. A 3-D printer is a machine that constructs tangible objects from blueprints that users have entered into a digital 3-D modeling program. 3-D printing began in the 1980s when American inventor Charles Hull received a patent for a 3-D printer, but the technology has been in wide use only since 2010. The first-ever 3-D portrait of President Barack Obama using the 3-D printing process went on display at the Smithsonian in December 2014.

Broadly defined, 3-D printing is the "process of creating an object using a machine that puts down material layer by layer in three dimensions until the desired object is formed" (EDUCAUSE Learning Initiative, 2012a). In a 3-D printing project, users design what they want to create using a 3-D modeling program, such as Blender, SketchUp, TinkerCAD, or they select an already constructed design from an online database, such as Thingiverse, Remix 3D, or 3D Warehouse. The object is then created (printed) by a special machine using plastic, metal, or other materials. The applications of this technology are vast, extending from manufacturing and sales to medicine, food, and scientific exploration.

Most consumer-based 3-D printers use coded instructions to build three-dimensional solid plastic objects out of polylactic acid, a corn-based bioplastic material. This material is fed into the printer and heated so it becomes pliable, and then the printer "builds" an object layer upon layer until the intended design emerges (Winter, 2014). Used for years in highly technical fields from aerospace engineering to reconstruction surgery, 3-D printing is now producing toys, jewelry, and countless other everyday objects. Educators are forecasting 3-D printers in every K–12 classroom, giving young engineers and scientists the opportunity to create physical representations of their ideas and designs.

▶ **MyLab Education**
Video Example 8.3
This video shows the first ever presidential portrait made with a 3-D printer. How do you plan to utilize 3-D modeling and printing as a teacher?
https://obamawhitehouse.archives.gov/blog/2014/12/02/new-video-provides-behind-scenes-look-first-3d-printed-presidential-portraits

Table 8.4. Overview of 3D Printing 4 Teaching & Learning Projects

School	Subject	Grade Level	Student-Designed 3-D Objects
1	Science	8	DNA Molecules
2	Science	10	Small Dragons Displaying Different Genetic Characteristics
3	Social Studies	8	Monuments to Honor Individuals Who Have Been Left Out of Textbooks
4	Social Studies	8	Models of Different Types of First American Dwellings
5	Social Studies	8	New Water Conservation Technologies to Address Shortages Through Conservation
6	Social Studies	8	Game Pieces for an American Revolution Board Game
7	Art	11–12	Architectural Monuments

Learning through 3-D Modeling and Printing

The 3D Printing 4 Teaching & Learning Project, a technology education initiative led by the College of Education at the University of Massachusetts Amherst in partnership with local K–12 teachers, demonstrates how students can learn through 3-D modeling and printing. In that project, several hundred students in classes and their teachers engaged in 3-D modeling and printing through classroom-based activities that link required curriculum content with the use of 3-D technology (Maloy, et al., 2017). Students created and printed a wide variety of science, math, and historical models, including genetically modified dragons, monuments for people whose accomplishments have been lost or neglected in history, DNA modules, and replicas of First American dwellings (see Table 8.4).

Creating 3-D projects enables students to build their own artifacts and representations as part of classroom-based learning, forging concrete connections between their own actions and the academic concepts they are learning in class. As products of individual creativity and imagination, 3-D objects have direct relevance for the students who make them. A 3-D model representing a science concept, a mathematical expression, a dramatic event in history, or an important character from literature encourages student designers to combine factual knowledge with larger conceptual frameworks.

Holding the 3-D objects they designed and printed, students see a direct representation of what they learned and a potential stimulus to learn more. Educators who use 3-D printing in their practice have identified multiple impacts on student learning, specifically in the areas of 21st century skills. Trust and Maloy (2017) found that educators perceive that 3-D printing projects help students develop 3-D modeling, creative thinking, technological literacy, problem solving, perseverance, self-directed learning, and critical thinking skills, among others.

The Water Conservation Technology designs from the 3D Printing 4 Teaching & Learning Project show the integration of 3-D technologies into learning. Water use is a commonly taught middle school science and social studies curriculum topic. In science classes, water provides a lens through which students learn about the interrelationships of earth systems (including evaporation, condensation, transpiration and precipitation) while in social studies classes students explore the impacts of human activity on water as a natural resource. In most science and social studies curriculums are learning standards that invite students to design systems and solutions to protect clean water, ecosystems, and human health and well-being.

The teacher began the water conservation activity by asking students to calculate their personal water footprint so they could compare their water use with that of people throughout the United States and around the world. An online water footprint calculator from Grace Communications let everyone estimate personal daily water use. Focusing on each student's personal water footprint reinforced the idea that water scarcity can be the result of climate (there are regions of the world with rainy and dry seasons) and human activity (waste, pollution, deforestation, and other factors).

After the class learned about the concept of "grey water"—water that has been used but is not finished being useful—students brainstormed and designed new water-saving technologies; for example, repurposing the water used to wash hands and to flush toilets, designing new pipes that resist leaking, and developing more efficient systems for desalinating sea water. Next, using the 3-D modeling software program TinkerCAD, students converted their paper-based ideas to digital designs for 3-D printing. The 3-D printed objects were parts of class presentations and the final assessment.

Producing physical objects from computer files, 3-D printing is a rapidly expanding technology that schools are purchasing and teachers are utilizing to integrate student projects into academic curriculums. In theory, students and teachers at every grade level can design and print objects for academic learning. In practice, however, not everyone is convinced of the usefulness of 3-D printing projects. Teachers and administrators wonder about the time required to include 3-D projects into learning activities given the amount of the curriculum that students must know to succeed on high-stakes achievement tests. Creative connections between teaching content while integrating online design and student problem solving is new and just beginning to develop.

MyLab Education Self-Check 8.4

Technology Transformation Learning Plan

Recreating Pre-Contact First American Houses with a Makerspace and 3-D Printing

Grade(s)	**5 to 12**
Subject(s)	**History/Social Studies and Science**
Key Learning Goal/Enduring Understanding	**Building 3-D Models of the homes of indigenous peoples of North America before the arrival of Europeans shows how the First Americans adapted to their natural environments in ways that still have meaning and relevance today.**
Essential Question	**How did Indigenous peoples adapt their homes to the environments in which they lived?**
Academic Discipline Learning Standards	AP United States History: Key Concept 1.1—As native populations migrated and settled across the vast expanse of North America over time, they developed distinct and increasingly complex societies by adapting to and transforming their diverse environments. Next Generation Science Standards: Earth and Human Activity—Make a claim about the merit of a design solution that reduces the impacts of a weather-related hazard. ISTE Standards for Students: Knowledge Constructor—Students critically curate a variety of resources using digital tools to construct knowledge, produce creative artifacts, and make meaningful learning experiences for themselves and others.
Learning Objectives	Students will know and be able to: • Describe how First Americans built houses to utilize different environmental and climate conditions • Construct historically accurate models of different First American houses with hands-on and digital materials
Technology Uses	Minimal Technology: • Students create models of First American houses out of paper and other physical materials. • Students use the Internet to locate information about First American nations and the kinds of housing that developed in different environmental conditions. Infusion of Technology: • Students create digital models of First American houses using a 3-D modeling program like TinkerCAD or SketchUp. • Students create short video presentations summarizing what they have learned about First American housing as cultural, engineering, and scientific accomplishments. • Students propose other sustainable energy structures that might be created using the principles found in First American dwellings (such as passive solar design).
Evaluation	The learning plan uses performance-based evaluation through multimodal activities, including creating hands-on and digital models, utilizing historically accurate information, and making digital presentations to share with classmates and post on a class website or blog.

(continued)

Learning Plan Description

Learning Focus

"Recreating Pre-Contact First American Houses with a Makerspace and 3-D Printing" invites students to use physical and digital materials to build replicas of the kinds of dwellings that the indigenous peoples of North America designed and lived in before contact with European settlers. It shows how native people made use of natural resources, sustainable energy concepts, and design-based thinking in adapting living structures to different climates and seasons of the year. For example, the Anasazi people of Colorado made use of passive solar design in constructing south-facing cliff villages, while Eskimo people of the Canadian Arctic designed domed snow houses called igloos using a circular flow of convection that pushed warm air up to where people live and cold air down and out at the base of the structure.

In the learning experience, students research and build replicas of different types of First American dwellings using hands-on materials. They next convert their designs to a digital format so their online models can be 3-D printed into physical artifacts to show as parts of in-class or online presentations. This plan can be taught in upper elementary, middle, or high schools as part of the history/social studies or science curriculum.

Learning Design—Minimal Technology

A minimal technology version of the learning experience begins with each group of students choosing a type of a type of First American dwelling. Students research the type and create a model structure of the dwelling using art and scrap materials for the design process: paper, glue, scissors, pipe cleaners, clay, tape, markers, Legos, good junk—boxes, small containers, bottle caps, coffee stirrers, paper cups, packaging and other common building items. Students use the Internet to learn about the environmental conditions that produce the materials, designs, and weather- and climate-friendly aspects of the dwelling. They list these factors on posters to display with the models they make. Once the models are built, groups present their information orally in class.

Learning Activities Using Technology

Ask students if they can define the following two terms: Makerspace and 3-D printing. In recent semesters, few of the undergraduates or graduates in our college courses had ever participated in a makerspace in school.

Ask students to individually draw a First American dwelling that they learned about in school without disclosing what they are drawing. Once everyone is finished, have students in small groups show their drawings and list the different types of structures drawn. Half of the students in our college course, Tutoring in Schools, represent teepees to answer the question, even though only nomadic tribes of Plains Indians lived in these structures. Indigenous peoples lived in wigwams, longhouses, tepees, adobe houses, chickees, earthen houses, plank houses, wattle and daub houses, grass houses, pueblos, igloos, and other dwellings, crafted to fit the environmental resources present in different regions of North America. For historical background, link to the website Native American Housing from the Gilder Lehrman Institute of American History, a resource that includes Native American Regions and Housing Maps: online at https://www.gilderlehrman.org/content/native-american-housing

As with the minimal technology version of the lesson, in a makerspace, students begin by choosing a type of First American dwelling. They research it and create a model structure of the dwelling using arts and scrap and good junk materials for the design process. They access the Internet to learn about the environmental conditions that produce the materials, designs, and weather- and climate-friendly aspects of the dwelling. They list these on poster papers to display the models they make.

Next, they use a 3-D modeling software program such as TinkerCAD to create a digital version of their physical model. Students work in pairs or trios to help each other with the design and modeling process. The students' designs are then sent to a 3-D printer, which produces a physical model of the dwelling.

Students complete the learning by creating a multimedia digital presentation of their dwelling construction process using pictures, video, and hand drawn materials.

Analysis and Extensions

Students might create a slideshow of the newest items being made by 3-D printing. These could include a 3-D printed automobile, 3-D printed foods, 3-D printed medical innovations, and 3-D printed Origami folding templates for solving science problems, among many other items. ScienceDaily.com reports new developments in 3-D printing materials and purposes.

For further extension, visit the homepage of the Mashantucket Pequot Museum, which features a large-scale replica of a Pequot village. To make this learning plan applicable to the early elementary grades, choose two indigenous dwellings—one original to the area where the students live and one in an opposite or different temperate or environmental region. Youngsters then choose one of the two dwellings they want to learn about, construct and 3-D print model with the help of a teacher or tutor, and teach what they have learned to classmates.

Chapter Summary

Learning Outcome 8.1

Explain how technology promotes problem solving among students.

- To engage students in academic learning, problem solving and inquiry-based learning incorporate real-world issues and situations.
- A problem-solving framework asks students to: 1) understand the problem, 2) use solving strategies, and 3) check answers or results.

- Many real-world problems are ill-structured and defy straightforward cause/effect solutions.

Learning Outcome 8.2

Analyze computational thinking in coding and robotics.

- Computational thinking involves knowing how to use data, models, simulations, and algorithmic thinking to formulate and solve problems.

- Coding is the act of programming a computer using written instructions.
- Object-oriented programming happens when students create a virtual object and make it do things in response to programmed instructions.
- Teaching robotics in conjunction with coding increases creative thinking, introduces students to future careers, shows the workings of the design process, and promotes inclusive learning experiences for girls and boys.

Learning Outcome 8.3

Apply digital games, educational simulations, virtual reality, and virtual worlds as learning resources for teachers and students.

- Students play computer, video, and web-based games regularly for entertainment, but the educational uses of games are becoming an increasing focus of classroom teaching.
- Some educators and psychologists dismiss games as having little educational value, whereas other researchers believe game playing supports the development of wide varieties of intellectual skills, focus, persistence, and achievement of goals.

- Digital games for learning are a category of educationally themed games incorporating active learning, sustained concentration and focus, and innovative approaches to problem solving as habits of game play.
- As a teaching and learning tool, virtual reality (VR) makes lifelike recreations of real-world settings where students can conduct experiments and solve problems.

Learning Outcome 8.4

Utilize makerspaces, the Maker Movement, and 3-D modeling and printing as instructional resources in schools.

- Makerspaces are physical or digital places where people design, experiment, and revise their creations.
- Maker-based learning consists of makers, makerspaces, and making—the act of creating things with materials and technologies.
- 3-D printing is the process of creating physical objects from computer-based designs and files.
- 3-D projects enable students to build their own artifacts and representations as they forge connections between their own actions as designers and builders and the academic concepts they are learning.

Key Terms

Avatar, p. 199
Coding, p. 191
Computational thinking, p. 191
Computer- and web-based games, p. 194
Desktop-based games, p. 194
Educational software, p. 186
Game-based learning, p. 194
Gamification, p. 194

Ill-structured problems, p. 189
Maker-based learning, p. 202
Maker Movement, p. 201
Makerspaces, p. 201
Object-oriented programming, p. 192
Problem-based learning, p. 189
Problem solving, p. 186
Robotics, p. 193

Serious games, p. 197
Simulation game, p. 198
Stealth learning, p. 199
3-D printing, p. 203
Virtual reality (VR), p. 199
Virtual worlds, p. 199
Visual-thinking and concept-mapping software, p. 187

> **Application Exercise 8.3**
> Growing and Leading with Technology: Sharon's "Inventions and Technologies" Learning Activity

For Reflection and Discussion

Experiences with Coding

As teaching children to code becomes a growing educational movement, recall your own experiences with coding as an elementary, middle, and high school student and discuss the following questions:

- What were your coding experiences, if any, in school?
- What thinking skills were you developing as you tried the one-hour learn to code tutorial activities offered free online by the organization Code.org?
- Why might coding be a required subject for every public school student?

Online Math Problem-Solving Sites

Develop a list of interactive online math problem-solving resources to use with elementary and secondary school students when tutoring or teaching in local schools. These resources include online math dictionaries to support students in learning key math terms and concepts, as well as learning sites where students can practice math problem-solving skills. Bookmark sites that are free for educators, do not display advertisements for commercial products, and offer open-ended and engaging activities so students do not have the same experience every time they visit the site.

- How would you determine whether a site is engaging and interesting for students' learning?
- Are there characteristics you think are essential in determining the usefulness of an online math learning resource?

Robotics for Learning

To learn more about how to use robotics as a teacher, complete the following activities:

1. Overview different types of robots and kits.
2. Explore lessons and learning activities from teachers who use robots in their classroom.

3. Identify three ways to incorporate robotics into the classroom (or create a mini lesson to incorporate robotics and computational thinking into the classroom).

Composing and Calculating

Composing refers to writing, *calculating* to mathematics. Because writing and mathematics are core parts of every school curriculum, every student is expected to gain increasing levels of proficiency in each area from elementary through secondary school. Digital resources from word processing and spreadsheet programs to learning games serve as essential tools for teaching and learning.

Look at a desktop, laptop, or tablet computer in a school where you are teaching or doing a pre–student teaching field experience to see what educational programs and learning resources are installed for teacher and student use. As you review the resources, consider these questions:

- Are there educational programs and learning resources that are new to you?
- After exploring two or three of the resources, how do you rate their effectiveness as learning activities?
- What new resources would you recommend, and why would you recommend them?

Chapter 9
Communicating and Collaborating with Social Technologies

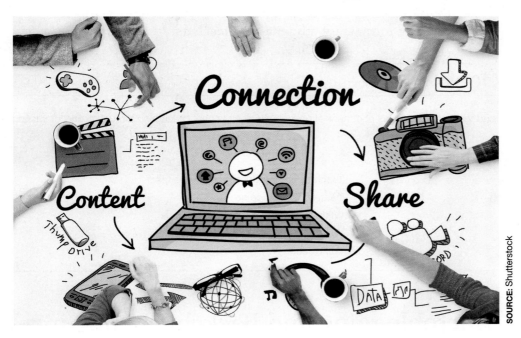

SOURCE: Shutterstock

Chapter Overview

Chapter 9 addresses ways teachers and students can use social technologies to share ideas and information in classrooms and online learning environments. The chapter opens by exploring synchronous and asynchronous communications as ways for teachers and students to interact online. Next we discuss e-mail, texting, and Twitter, popular forms of everyday communication that offer wide educational learning and networking opportunities. Then, we examine blogs and wikis—notably those developed collaboratively by teachers and students—as highly interactive formats for gaining and sharing academic information through collaborative learning. The chapter concludes with a Technology Transformation Learning Plan, "Blogging the News from Room 145."

The chapter responds to the ISTE Standard for Students of Creative Communicator by showing teachers and students how to use social media technologies to communicate ideas and information to many different readers and listeners. It also addresses the Global Communicator standard, in which students use collaborative technologies to interact with peers, teachers, experts, and communities in digital environments.

Learning Outcomes

After reading this chapter, you will be able to:

9.1 Explain the roles of digital communications as teaching and learning technologies.

9.2 Examine e-mail, texting, and Twitter as educational networking tools for teachers and students.

9.3 Analyze how to utilize blogs for student and classroom learning.

9.4 Employ wikis and Google Sites as collaborative project-based learning formats for students and teachers.

Chapter Learning Goal

Use blogs, wikis, Twitter, and classroom and teacher websites as communication technologies to enhance learning through online interaction and collaboration.

Featured Technologies

Blogs

E-mail

Texting

Online discussion boards

Social networks for educators

Teacher- and student-made websites

Twitter/microblogging

Wikis

Wikitexts

WikiQuests

Microblogging and Backchanneling in a High School Classroom

In his first year as a full-time teacher, Joe began using microblogging and backchanneling to increase participation in classroom learning and to connect with students online. A daily Twitter user, he sent tweets to students as reminders about class topics and assignments. While tweets informed students of due dates and upcoming events, Joe found that he was using Twitter more than the students were. He wanted to make his Twitter account an active and desirable online destination for students.

The first strategy for making his Twitter feed a visited location was to post class content online by linking in-class Prezi presentations to his online feed. Students could view these presentations after class on their mobile devices at any time and review material before exams. Joe observed that this helped students who had difficulty taking notes in class: "Instead of trying to focus on viewing the presentation and taking notes while listening to my voice, they could concentrate on hearing the main points and reviewing presentations later for note taking."

Then, Joe began tweeting about each day's lesson before and after class. If the plan was to read or view an important primary source, he tweeted a link to that speech or document. Hearing or previewing different resources, Joe concluded, "allows students a more complete understanding of the document; how something is said is almost as important as what is said." Next, he began tweeting answers to student questions that he could not answer during class. "By posting information and resources on my Twitter account," Joe noted, "I am acknowledging students' contributions to our discussions and encouraging them to investigate the questions they have."

At midyear he introduced a microblogging backchannel tool called Yo Teach! to establish real-time, behind-the-scenes digital conversations during class. Recognizing that every classroom has communication backchannels—students talking to each other informally and not always about the curriculum topics being studied—Joe decided to see what this might accomplish for learning. Yo Teach! lets students compose short, academically focused comments on their smartphones or laptops to display either on Joe's computer or on a large screen when he connects his machine to a digital projector or a smartboard. Importantly, students can respond to and teach each other without Joe intervening, although he can also join the conversations.

Backchanneling produced two unpredicted learning outcomes. First, the opportunity to post a comment enabled students to ask clarifying questions both to Joe and to each other. These comments served as opportunities to consider questions students wanted to discuss, improving communication and enlarging students' understanding.

Second, everyone discovered ways for students to use backchannels to take on different roles and perspectives, increasing their involvement and engagement. Playing the roles of members of the 1787 Constitutional Convention, students commented on the plans for the new constitution. In another class, students acting as presidential advisors discussed the future of Cuba and the Philippines after the Spanish-American War. In a third class, students debated different strategies for ending World War II with Japan. As Joe observed, "It was surprising and enlightening to see students engaging with historical texts and one another, challenging opinions, and having a dialogue about primary sources and historical interpretations using this communication backchannel."

Joe's story illustrates just some of the ways social media technologies are changing how teachers and students communicate with one another in K–12 schools. To further illuminate these developments, think about the ways your own patterns of communication have changed in the past few years. Most of you own a mobile phone, engage in text messaging, and communicate through multiple social networks. You may participate in online communities, read blogs, view videos or other multimedia presentations, shop online, play games on phones and tablets, and use technology to locate information about everything from the weather to entertainment to politics. As author Will Richardson forecast nearly a decade ago, "This tectonic shift of connections has huge significance for the way we think about our roles as educators, our classrooms, and, most important, our own personal learning" (2011, p. 12).

In this chapter, you will explore ways to change and extend communication with students by focusing on the following questions:

1. How can social media and communication technologies generate positive learning experiences for teachers and students?
2. How can you utilize e-mail, texting, and Twitter to foster information exchanges with and among students?
3. What are effective uses of blogs for improving learning for students?
4. How can you use wikis to foster collaborative and team-based learning among teachers and students?

Digital Communications between Teachers and Students

9.1 Explain the roles of digital communications as teaching and learning technologies.

Digital communication—the rapid exchange of information between people using digital devices—happens when teachers integrate social technologies into their in-school instructional practices and their outside-the-classroom professional activities.

MyLab Education
Video Example 9.1
In this video, teachers discuss how students can create digital sites to share information about school projects with wider audiences. How will you foster creative online self-expression and digital communications by students?

Table 9.1 compares social technologies commonly found in schools and discussed in this chapter, including:

- **E-mail** (short for *electronic mail*), **messaging**, and **texting** are three different types of digital communication that can happen between friends, between teachers and students or family members, and between administrative and educational personnel.
- Teacher **blogs** are publicly accessible sites written by teachers (sometimes with students) that are regularly updated to communicate information about academic classes and educational topics to family members, as well as to school and educational personnel.
- **Microblogging** (for example, on **Twitter**) happens when teachers and students use a limited number of words and symbols to share ideas and information.
- **Online discussions** are digital forums in which teachers and students discuss educational topics. Online discussions are components of many teacher websites and blogs, as well as course and learning management systems used by schools.
- **Wikis**, meaning "quick" or "rapidly" in Hawaiian, and **Google Sites** are websites that teachers and students create and edit together by reading and revising each other's ideas and comments. These sites can also be places where teachers post links and resources for students to explore.
- **Backchannels** are synchronous chat rooms that allow students to discuss and exchange information during presentations and projects.

E-mail, texting, Twitter, discussion boards, blogs, backchannels, and wikis might be components of any communication system you create when you start teaching. This chapter's In Practice illustrates how one teacher is teaching writing and poetry using a variety of social media and communication technologies. With social media and communication technologies evolving and generating new ways to communicate, you will continually compare, contrast, and select the tools that meet your own and students' needs.

Table 9.1 Comparison of Digital Communication Technologies

Type of Communication Technology	Purpose	Author	Audience	Uses by Teachers
Texting	Delivering short communication between two or more individuals	Individual	Individual or group	Communicating with colleagues or with students
E-mail	Sending and receiving messages over the Internet	Individual	Individual or group	Communicating with students and families. Communicating with other teachers or a broader community through a Listserv (group e-mail)
Discussion board	Exchange of ideas and information about a topic, usually moderated by a teacher	Group	Group	Online discussions of academic material
Teacher/class blog	Providing materials and resources related to an academic class or learning activity; online journal, including teacher and student information and reflections	Individual	Group	Information for students and families. Publishing student work. Sharing personal reflections on teaching. Sharing learning resources with students. Professional teaching portfolio
Wiki/Google Site	Webpages created by a collaborative group of writers and designers	Group	Group	Group projects by students. Group projects among teachers
Backchannel	Exchanging information among audience members in a presentation or project group members	Group	Group	Peer teaching; information exchanges; digital Socratic Seminar

Synchronous and Asynchronous Communications

Social technologies offer a choice between synchronous and asynchronous communications.

- **Synchronous communications** occur in real time—mobile phone conversations, instant messaging, virtual conferencing, or in-person meetings. There is little or no wait time for a reply to statements.
- **Asynchronous communications** involve time delays—e-mail messages, online discussions, tweets, or blogs. Communicators wait for replies to their statements, as people do when sending a letter or postcard through postal mail.

As a teacher, you employ both synchronous and asynchronous forms of communication while conveying information to students. A classroom discussion happens synchronously when students and teachers ask and respond to questions in face-to-face interactions. Comments and grades written on student assignments are delivered asynchronously when they are returned to students. In digital environments, synchronous and asynchronous communication modes achieve the goals of communicating information.

In Practice

Writing with Social Technologies

Grade Level	Featured Technologies
Middle and high school	Twitter, blogs, wikis, laptops, and tablets

Lesson Outline

Ashley, a middle school language arts teacher, emphasizes creative writing and composing poetry as ways for students to learn the craft of writing through expressing personal thoughts and ideas. An avid writer since her own middle school days, she wants to convey to students the power of written self-expression. Ashley tells students how words communicate, letting writers create joy, offer comfort, express inner feelings, influence political policies, and build connections among people. She relates her story of developing a love of writing as a student in middle school and how the experience propelled her to become a teacher of writing.

Teaching with Technology

Writing with different technologies is at the core of Ashley's language arts curriculum. Students are constantly writing, putting pen to paper and fingers to keyboards while conversing about their style and purpose as writers. Ashley has students try out different communication technologies and then analyze them to identify which tools to use for what purposes as a writer. Blogs give writers the opportunity to express personal viewpoints to readers and invite readers to respond to a post. Wikis and Google Sites are built from everyone's collaborative participation as writers and editors. Texting and Twitter allow people to send short messages while maintaining regular connections as friends or colleagues. As the school year progresses, students actively experience each communication technology from the viewpoints of both writers and readers.

To teach the rules of written language use, Ashley asks students to investigate the roles of writing conventions—spelling, punctuation, capitalization, sentence structure, and paragraphing—and explain their purposes in different texts. 'Role before rule' is the way Ashley describes how conventions assist reading comprehension in all genres of writing. An example of ever-evolving roles of conventions is writers creating and using new spelling for texting. These quick communications utilize informal language, abbreviations of words and phrases, emojis and picture symbols to create shared understandings among writers and readers. A class assignment, college admission essay, or job application, by contrast, requires formal language with standard conventions and grammar to communicate to the intended audience.

Ashley utilizes a website, designed with each year's classes, to post student writing. Publishing on the website gives students a reason and a purpose to practice incorporating standard conventions and to access word processing tools like spelling and grammar checkers, dictionaries and thesauruses, and the track changes function for revising and editing. Technology tools make writing easier and provide formats for different expressions of expository, creative, and persuasive writing.

To understand how writing flows from initial ideas to published material, Ashley's students learn how to critique written communications and suggest changes to make the text easier to understand or more interesting to read. They see how writers use punctuation marks—periods, commas, and question and exclamation marks—as stop signs for readers and how quotation marks show dialogue among the characters of a story. They recognize how a paragraph, with a topic sentence followed by supporting details, communicates a main idea in a length that readers can clearly understand. They discover that the rules of writing support the goals of writers and that different technologies make possible an incredibly wide array of shared communications.

Integrating Digital Communications into Teaching

Teachers use digital communications and social media for professional work in several ways.

TEACHING BEYOND THE SCHOOL DAY   Teachers will tell you time is the most important element of the school day—there is never enough of it to teach everything that students need to know or teachers want to explore. "If I could increase the time I spend teaching," many say, "students would learn so much more."

A digital communication system is a time-stretching option to continue learning when the school day finishes. On a classroom website or teaching blog, teachers post class notes, student questions, homework assignments, writing ideas,

Figure 9.1 Teacher Pencast Posted on a Chemistry Class Website

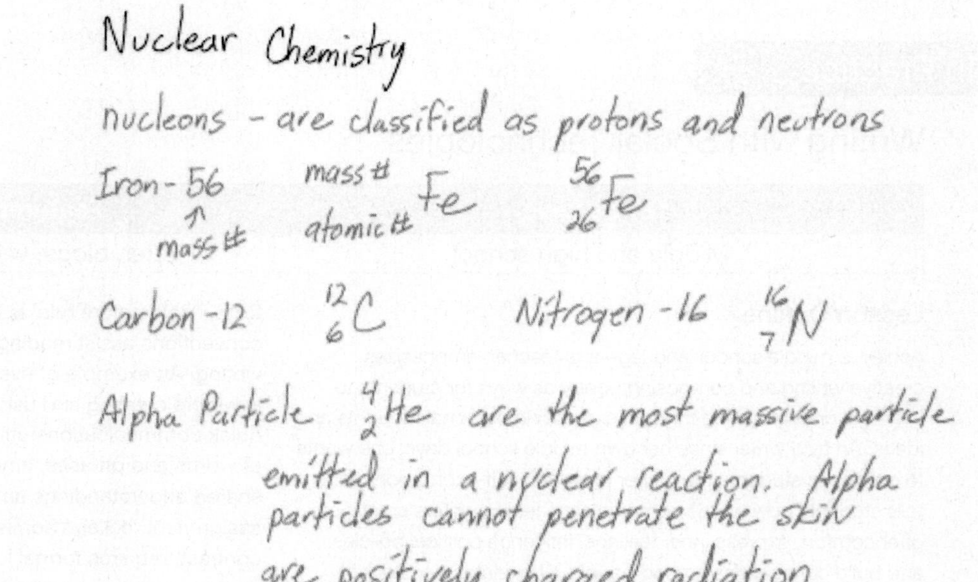

Nuclear Chemistry

nucleons – are classified as protons and neutrons

Iron-56   mass # $^{56}_{26}Fe$ $^{56}_{26}Fe$
  ↑ mass #   atomic #

Carbon -12 $^{12}_{6}C$ Nitrogen -16 $^{16}_{7}N$

Alpha Particle $^{4}_{2}He$ are the most massive particle emitted in a nuclear reaction. Alpha particles cannot penetrate the skin are positively charged radiation

Beta Particle $^{0}_{-1}e$ or $^{0}_{-1}\beta$
 – negatively charged radiation
 – travels a lot farther than Alpha radiatio
 – is not as massive as alpha radiation.
 – so high energy $^{0}_{-1}\beta$ particles can penetrate the skin

Gamma Particles $^{0}_{0}\gamma$
   – Very penetrating and are only blocked

7:27 / 18:05

SOURCE: Reprinted by permission of Shawn E. Sheehan, Easthampton High School.

weblinks for research, suggestions for further reading, experiments to try, or other activities to do outside of class. E-mail and discussion boards promote exchanges of ideas among class members. Teaching occurs digitally as students read and review what you post to connect in-school learning with outside-of-school activities. The process becomes interactive as students respond by submitting their own ideas, inquiries, and homework. Digital exchanges connect student learning inside and outside of school.

Sharing information digitally substantively alters the learning experience for students. Figure 9.1 shows a "pencast" of material about the study of atomic structures that a high school chemistry teacher posted for student review. In a pencast, notes appear on the screen, line by line, as students listen to and view the teacher's digitally recorded presentation. This teacher is "flipping" the classroom experience with online viewing of lectures as homework to create more time for in-class problem-solving activities and science labs.

ENGAGING STUDENTS   Making academic learning interesting and engaging is essential to student success and to your teaching. Lectures or teacher-led discussions, accompanied by worksheets and tests, sustain the interest of some students only some of the time. Most students want to learn by trying out and doing something through active minds-on, hands-on learning. As multiple intelligences researcher Howard Gardner (2011b) noted, many teachers' instructional methods emphasize linguistic and logical-mathematical intelligences, leaving students who do not learn easily in those ways unfulfilled and feeling less smart and less capable than they are. When teachers expand the methods for learning, they assist students in enjoying and connecting with academic classroom learning. Using web-based materials and activities puts students in the position of "doing" activities and projects in math, science, history, and language arts instead of watching or listening as teachers demonstrate or talk about these subjects.

Online learning diversifies how you create levels of student engagement. Post online items from class activities for review—lesson plans, lecture notes, discussion questions, practice worksheets, ideas for further study, or student-written materials. Pose thought-provoking questions and offer simulations and serious games that require students to take part in individual and group discussions and presentations, both online and in class. Ask students to share online materials they created—notes, songs, podcasts, or videos—for review before an exam and to aid recall of information students might have forgotten or missed in class.

SHARING INFORMATION WITH FAMILIES   A teacher's digital communication system opens a continuous flow of information between the classroom and students' families and caregivers and with other teachers and school administrators. Many educators report that Internet-based family–school communication helps student achievement. As a teacher, it is essential to provide information to families about class assignments, grading policies, upcoming activities, homework, and other topics online in an easily updatable format because families are integral promoters of students' success. If the pages include an embedded language translation app, more families will be able to understand and respond to the information.

Posting information on a teacher or school website frees time for instruction because teachers spend less time explaining assignments, due dates, and other administrative matters. Students, parents, and caregivers read on a website answers to their questions, schedules of assignments and exams, and dates of school activities. Everyone receives the information in the same way, minimizing confusion and doubt as students and adults both locate information online. Teacher

Smartphones, with web access and apps for learning math, science, history, and language arts, function as handheld computers.

SOURCE: Michaeljung/Fotolia.

colleagues and building administrators also benefit, seeing information being communicated to students and families in ways that are consistent with the mission and goals of a school.

BUILDING LEARNING COMMUNITIES   Digital communications invite students to actively participate in a community of learners who are exploring topics of interest. As students read your posts, contribute their own ideas, and respond to what everyone else has said and done, a framework for collaborative learning is created. In such educational networks curated by a teacher, students feel like they are part of activities and conversations. From a learning standpoint, the impact of collaborative learning communities can be surprisingly powerful. Children "learn from the company they keep," noted literacy educator Frank Smith (1998) of the ways that peers, families, and schools shape thinking, values, and goals. Students keeping company with you and following other experts in a field through online social networks, enlarge their academic study and accomplishment.

PROVIDING AUTHENTIC AUDIENCES FOR STUDENT WRITERS   A digital communication system opens multiple possibilities for students to write to you and to each other. Paradoxically, teenagers—and younger students—write eagerly and expressively for their own pleasure outside of school. Nearly 90% of 12- to 17-year-olds write text messages or post comments on social networking sites, although a majority of those teens do not think of their personal digital communications as "real" writing (Lenhart, 2012a, 2012b). Journal writing for their own purposes is another favorite outside-of-school writing activity for many youngsters.

When assigned topics to write about, those same students respond with reluctance or disinterest. School writing assignments connote composing in a prescribed manner including conventions of written language, appropriate grammar, and correct spelling that many young writers are not confident using. The most recent national writing assessment, the first done completely on laptop computers, found only one in four students performing at a proficient level, with one in five scoring below basic. Girls outperformed boys, and Asian and White youngsters outpaced Hispanic, African American, and Native American students at the eighth- and 12th-grade levels. By contrast, many of these students confidently write online to friends, practicing what seems easier to do and less constrained by adult rules and expectations.

No matter what subjects or grade levels you teach, you will be a teacher of writing and a teacher of communication. Every curriculum area requires students to write, whether it is an interpretive essay, a science report, an explanation of how to solve a math problem, or a historical analysis. Similarly, every subject requires students to use different forms of written expression to communicate what they know and have learned academically. This requirement may be accomplished through tests and quizzes but also through student-created papers, presentations, portfolios, and performances in paper and digital formats. In every case, students are practicing how to clearly convey their ideas to others through written language.

Central to self-expression and civic participation, writing is used by students to "connect the dots in their knowledge" (National Commission on Writing in America's Schools and Colleges, 2003, p. 14). Writing, accompanied by verbal and artistic communication, allows students to express facts and information that would otherwise remain in the mind of the individual. Synchronous and asynchronous communication technologies create new opportunities for teaching writing in schools, letting students utilize behaviors they want to practice—communicating textually through social media—while offering teachers instructional opportunities that were not in existence even 10 years ago.

PUBLISHING STUDENT WORK   A digital communication system can invite students to publish and display work done in the classroom or at home. Class activities and assignments acquire relevance and meaning when students realize that their work is going to be seen by a broader audience. Students want to create something for others to see, listen to, or read. Every year, school science fairs, poetry readings, history projects, music and dance performances, art exhibitions, and dramatic plays generate interest and energy from students. Participants enjoy doing the work because the activity is meaningful to them and because there is an audience who is going to see the result. Using your communication network to display the products, performances, and publications generates interest and anticipation for students and families.

Classroom newspapers or newsletters that teachers once produced with the school's copy machine become a new experience when published online because:

- Production is immediate. All visual and textual material can be arranged and rearranged easily, scanned into a PDF, and posted. The results are visually interesting, and students' artwork is preserved.

- Students' self-expressions gain permanence beyond paper copies that may be lost, ripped, or discarded before they are viewed by family members or friends.

- Opportunities to be involved in the process of creating, maintaining, and sharing news are open to even the youngest students. "Our class online newsletter is a work-together, everyone-learns-from-each-other concept," said one second-grade teacher who once spent two hours weekly producing a paper newsletter for families. Now, students and teachers create online interactive multimedia news features by adding video, screencasts, audio, and hyperlinks to external resources. A school trip to a farm, for example, might include video of students milking cows, links to the farm's website, and an interactive calendar page where families can sign up for the next field trip.

MyLab Education **Self-Check 9.1**

Social Networking for Educators

9.2 **Examine e-mail, texting, and Twitter as educational networking tools for teachers and students.**

A social network has been defined as a "set of relations among network members" (Rainie & Wellman, 2012, p. 21). Through **social networking**, individuals can share information, ideas, resources, and media with networks of people. These networks might be people you already know, like your friends on Facebook or a Voxer or GroupMe chat among colleagues, or people you haven't met in person, but can still learn from, like other educators on Twitter or Edmodo.

There are a number of different social networking tools, including e-mail, texting, Facebook, Instagram, Snapchat, Twitter, Pinterest, Tumblr, WeChat, QQ, Weibo, Reddit, YouTube, and LinkedIn. These tools provide numerous opportunities for informal, formal, and serendipitous communication and learning. For example, you might have come across an article about climate change posted by your friend on Facebook or Instagram even though you didn't go to Facebook or Instagram to learn about climate change. You went to connect with your friends, but then you discovered new information. This type of serendipitous learning can happen on a social networking site, and it can support your personal and professional growth.

Many teachers engage in educational and professional social networking. There are numerous social networking spaces for connecting with and learning from other educators, including Instagram; Twitter (e.g., #edugladiators, #weteachun, #engagechat, #masterychat, #learnlap, #betheone, #whatisschool); Reddit (e.g., r/edtech); Facebook groups and pages; Voxer, WeChat, and GroupMe group conversations; Pinterest boards; and LinkedIn groups. You may also join networks sponsored by educational organizations such as the Discovery Education Network, PBS: Learning Media Teachers, Scholastic, and International Society for Technology in Education (ISTE), or you may access educational networks such as Edmodo or EducatorsCONNECT. A social network may be private (only invited people can join) or public (open to anyone), giving teachers choices of groups to join and topics to discuss online. Once you are connected, there are many productive uses of social networking as an educator:

- Teacher-to-teacher discussions about curriculum and instruction
- Sharing lesson plans, resources, activity ideas, success stories, and digital tools
- Forming book groups and literature circles
- Linking with educational policy and reform organizations
- Exchanging information about educational research
- Collaborative lesson planning or learning activity design
- Peer teaching about new technologies and digital tools
- Group editing of projects and writing

Researchers Torrey Trust, Jeffrey Carpenter and Daniel Krutka (2016) found that educators who use social technologies to expand their professional learning networks (PLN) beyond their local contexts and communities are able to expand their practice in a number of ways—from affective growth (emotional support, risk taking, confidence), to social growth (overcoming isolation, discovering diverse perspectives), to cognitive growth (exploring new ideas and resources; reflecting on practice), to identity growth (shifting to a teacher-learner/leader). As a new teacher, it can be valuable to cultivate a PLN that will support your ongoing learning and professional growth. Identify people to connect with and spaces to join that you can turn to when you need new ideas, support, feedback, or digital tools. Engage in ongoing reflection and evaluation of your PLN to identify whether it is extending your thinking and learning or just serving as an echo chamber (it's helpful to have motivational support, but having people who can extend your thinking will make you a more creative and innovative educator).

As an undergraduate or graduate student, you are probably using one or several social networks such as Facebook, Instagram, Snapchat, Twitter, Pinterest, Tumblr, and LinkedIn, and you will likely continue to use them when you enter the classroom as a full-time teacher. Here we look at four important social technologies that teachers can use for educational communications: e-mail, texting, Twitter, and online discussions.

Communicating Using E-mail and Texting

E-mail and texting have become so widespread that most of us take them for granted even though they are relatively new to history. For school-age youngsters, text messaging is the predominant form of online communication; they increasingly prefer texting to talking on a telephone. Girls send more text messages than boys, but girls and boys alike believe it is important for them to have up-to-date phone technology to participate in digital communications with peers.

When text messaging, writers use **textspeak** (also called *textese*), a collection of symbols, letters, numbers, and abbreviations that make possible quick communication

Digital Dialog 9.1

Teenagers text more than any other segment of the population. Now even elementary school–age children are using mobile phones to send text messages. As you think about the growth of texting among children and adolescents, comment and connect online about the following questions:

- What features do you think make texting such a popular communication activity among young people?
- In what ways might texting, with its improvised spelling and short messages, promote the development of children's and adolescents' reading and writing skills? Has texting affected your own writing skills either positively or negatively?
- Are there changes you think teachers should make to curriculum and instruction because of the texting behaviors of students?

on mobile phones and other devices. In textspeak, standard language conventions are replaced by textisms: contractions (*tmrw* or *2moro* for "tomorrow"), acronyms (*brb* for "be right back"), word shortenings (*xam* for "exam"), homophones (*2day* for "today"), emoticons (for smiling), and word lengthening or capitalizing with repeating letters (*sooooo* or *NO*) to create emphasis (Verheijen, 2013). Here is a sample in textspeak followed by a standard English translation in italics:

Hey, Wuz ^? Nm here. U look gr8 2day wht R U doing 2moro?

(*Hey, what's up? Not much here. You look great today. What are you doing tomorrow?*)

Nvm. I don't care. Lol, jk brb ok.

(*Never mind. I don't care. Laugh out loud, just kidding. Be right back. Okay.*)

Do u know wht 4 HW? Me neither. w/e will fail 2gether.

(*Do you know what the homework is? Me neither. Whatever, we'll fail together.*)

Texting is a fascinating topic for educational research. While some adults regard texting as a distortion of skillful writing and communication, current researchers believe that youngsters' use of textisms positively, not negatively, relates to gains in reading proficiency among elementary and middle school students. Many text message terms are based on phonetic abbreviations of words. Through texting, students have opportunities to develop phonological awareness, use of printed words, and standard literacy in English. More research will continue to inform these conclusions as texting expands and adds new spellings and terms.

With texting's immense popularity, some teachers view text messaging as a method to strengthen classroom learning communities while teaching academic content. One way to do this in English and history classes is to explore texting word use and spelling patterns with students. Examining how words are spelled informally makes students more aware of the patterns of word sounds and the structures of standard word spellings. English words had no single standard spelling until 1806 with the publication of America's first dictionary, Noah Webster's *A Compendious Dictionary of the English Language*. Prior to that, writers spelled words as they chose and readers used context to understand these individual spellings. The motivation for Webster to establish standard spellings of words in daily use in America was an avowed determination to distinguish and differentiate American English from British English, creating spellings, pronunciations and definitions that would represent this nation.

The use of codes and ciphers offers another example of how words and their spellings affect the course of history. Codes are intended to obscure the meanings of words except to those who can decipher them. The Choctaw Code Talkers, who transmitted telephone messages in their native language, were important to the success of the U.S. Army in World War I. The breaking of the German Enigma code by Alan Turing and other mathematicians at Bletchley Park, England, and the achievements of the Navajo Code Talkers who used their primary language to encode messages that the Japanese military could not decipher were two developments that helped the Allies win World War II.

Here are more strategies for teachers using e-mail and texting to disseminate information and connect with students.

USE E-MAIL OR MESSAGING APPS FOR OFFICIAL COMMUNICATIONS E-mail has advantages over texting as a communication tool for teachers because its built-in record-keeping system maintains a copy of what you e-mail and what is e-mailed back to you. It provides accountability for writers. E-mail allows you, the teacher, to take the time to craft a reply or message that fits the situation at hand, check spelling and revise the language prior to sending. As an alternative to e-mail, many teachers and schools use messaging apps to send reminders to students and families about assignment due dates, upcoming tests, field trips and other information. Popular school communication apps—Talking Points, Remind, Bloomz, Class Dojo—offer language translations and options for sharing files and links.

When using e-mail or messaging apps for student and family communication, teachers need to be sure to:

- Use password-protected sites and never tell passwords to anyone else.
- Have multiple e-mail accounts—conduct school communication in one and personal communication in another.
- Maintain an archival record of communications received and sent, and back up the files on a portable USB drive or to the cloud.
- Employ the basic rules of e-mail etiquette in writing professional communications. Having a clear subject line, copying only those who need to be included, avoiding informal language, and proofreading before sending will all help ensure that the information is understood by readers.

OPEN E-MAIL CONNECTIONS TO LIBRARIES, MUSEUMS, AND UNIVERSITIES Libraries, museums, universities, and other educational organizations offer e-mail resources that are useful to teachers and students. Students can ask questions and receive responses from experts at sites like "Ask a Historian" from the National History Education Clearinghouse and "Ask an Earth Scientist" from the University of Hawaii. Educational and community organizations provide e-mail resources to schools as well. When using e-mail for learning, assist students to formulate thoughtful questions to include in their online correspondence. Time is often required for an organization to reply to a request, so students may not receive an immediate response.

HOLD ONLINE OFFICE HOURS Some teachers schedule online office hours—regular times when they answer questions and discuss assignments. These arrangements function like telephone or online homework hotlines, using e-mail or, in some instances, text messaging. Before a big exam is one popular time for such conversations, and many students like this because responses to their specific questions are quickly received.

For more on how teachers can incorporate e-mail, texting, and other social technologies into the classroom to assist students' learning and use of these tools, see the position paper "Beliefs for Integrating Technology into the English Language Arts Classroom" on the website of the National Council of Teachers of English (NCTE).

Teaching and Learning with Twitter

Twitter is a social networking site where individuals share small segments of information (called **tweets**) with friends and colleagues known as "followers" while exploring topics of interest, organized by **hashtags** (e.g., #education; #girlswhocode; #isteconnects). Twitter is a form of microblogging because each post, or tweet, is limited to 280 characters in English. Twitter users say a lot in a few characters, especially when they utilize text language abbreviations, images, GIFs, emojis, and other symbols as part of their writing.

Launched in 2006, Twitter has expanded tremendously—monthly use has grown from 6 million in 2008 to over 328 million midway through 2017 (Wolfe, 2018). Politicians, advertisers, sports stars, and celebrities have all recognized the advantages of sending messages to fans, customers, and constituents. In 2019, the singer-songwriter Katy Perry had close to 108 million followers, making her the most followed Twitter user in the world. At the same time, it is estimated that two thirds of all tweets are generated by automated accounts (or "bots," a word that is short for web robot) rather than actual human writers (Wojcik, et al., 2018).

As a corporate policy, Twitter gives the accounts of world leaders a special unblocked status, asserting that no matter how controversial, these views must be shared as a matter of public policy (Twitter, 2018). In 2010, the Library of Congress started archiving public tweets. By 2013, it had gathered over 170 billion messages. In December

2017, the Library of Congress announced that it would collect only a select number of tweets (Library of Congress, 2018).

A hybrid form of communication, Twitter brings together elements of blogging, social networking, and text messaging (EDUCAUSE Learning Initiative, 2007). Tweeters share information about personal interests and activities (blogging) with followers (social networking) using written language interspersed with symbols and invented spelling (text messaging). This combination of conciseness and interest is quite compelling for many people who use technology to stay in touch all the time. Teachers can use Twitter to introduce academic material, get students engaged in conversations, maximize full class participation, and offer opportunities for creative writing and self-expression. It is a convenient tool for synchronous or asynchronous educational communications, gathering backchannel information from students, and even conducting educational research.

Teachers can send (push) school-related information to students and families, including academic learning resources and administrative information. Teachers can tweet about upcoming due dates for papers and exams, or send out changes to a schedule or promote selected hashtags that provide multiple perspectives on topics. Twitter is a fast way to provide information, and its brevity means students and families are more likely to read what has been sent. Tech Tool 9.1 discusses how teachers can use the social networking and microblogging platform Twitter, and its Application Exercise focuses on using Twitter instructionally with students.

Twitter has become a controversial platform for the spread of fake and false news and hate speech. Twitter itself has acknowledged that more than 50,000 Russia-linked accounts posted material about the 2016 U.S. presidential election—and has removed them from the site. Small numbers of users are apparently responsible for most harmful posts on Twitter. The company has also stated it intends to prohibit "dehumanizing speech" on the site. Researchers found less than 0.1% of Twitter users accounting for sharing nearly 80% of fake and false news during the 2016 election. Those engaged in tweeting fake news were overwhelmingly older, conservative politically leaning individuals (Grinberg, et al., 2019).

Tech Tool 9.1

Using Twitter for Professional Learning

Twitter is a digital-age form of professional development and social networking for educators—a way to stay up to date in one's academic field, staying aware of what is happening in the field of technology, and connecting with colleagues near and far.

One great advantage is that teachers can follow other teachers using hashtags (#) to organize information around similar topics. You can search hashtags (e.g., #edchat, #edtech, and #ukedchat) for general conversations about education or instructional technology. You can also look for conversations in specific subject areas, such as #scichat and #scitalk for science, #engchat and #engtalk for English/language arts, #mathchat for math, #nchat for new teachers, and so on. The site Science Pond provides a discipline-based listing of scientists on Twitter. Cybraryman has curated an extensive list of educational Twitter hashtags.

As with any social media tool, teachers must measure the risks and complexities of online communications. All tweets need to be professional in nature and without personal information. You may want to post an avatar or bitmoji instead of your picture on your site to further ensure privacy. When asking students to use Twitter to write tweets, due to Family Educational Rights and Privacy Act (FERPA) regulations, to maintain online safety, students should not be required to post with their real names or use a class hashtag.

Be aware that many school districts are limiting the use of Twitter, Facebook, and other social media, and some of these proposals are quite controversial. Many school administrators, however, are supportive of social media use and want to work with teachers and policy makers to establish a middle ground where communication can happen safely and effectively.

MyLab Education Application Exercise 9.1:
Using Twitter with Students

Strategies for Moderating Online Discussions

Online discussions are another way for teachers and students to use social technologies educationally. In online discussions, students learn skills essential to their lives and future careers, including how to communicate points of view, appreciate different perspectives, dialogue and disagree with others respectfully, and consider issues and topics by reading multiple viewpoints (Hostetler, 2012).

Effective online discussions require a teacher to be a moderator, guiding a process encompassing the emotions, beliefs, understandings, and conceptualizations of students. Your role is somewhat like trying to drive a car from the back seat. You guide the driver with comments and directions while you do not have direct control of the wheel. The following suggestions will help you become a successful leader of online discussions.

FOCUS ON ISSUES THAT HAVE MEANING TO STUDENTS Student enthusiasm and interest in online discussions are high when the topics are of personal importance or related to their lives and current issues. Ask students what interests them about a topic, and use that information to craft questions for them to address in the online setting. Have students suggest resources representing diverse viewpoints on the issues they find important.

STRESS ACTIVE, THOUGHTFUL PARTICIPATION You will face two main issues in teaching students how to be active, thoughtful participants in online discussions. First, conflicting ideas may appear in written comments, just as they occur in face-to-face conversations. Students may post judgmental or personally disparaging remarks about other students' opinions or beliefs. Second, student responses will vary in length: Some will compose one- or two-sentence posts, others will write wordy but general comments, and still others will write detailed points that advance the flow of ideas and help the members of the class think about the topics under consideration.

To address these issues, before beginning discussions, ask students to help set formal online commenting guidelines about how they will contribute thoughts, ideas, and viewpoints, while also explaining how you will oversee online communications. Discussing the effects of demeaning or disparaging comments on the conversation is essential. Limiting response lengths to one to three paragraphs or to 100 to 200 words to encourage clarity teaches students why they must reflect on and revise their written text before posting to present their ideas clearly to others.

Encouraging student participation in online discussions can build community and result in thoughtful, articulate responses when students understand the rules and roles of acceptable and appropriate online conduct. When this happens, teachers and students alike discover new knowledge and new ideas by communicating in written dialogues.

Learn your district's appropriate use policies before setting up your blog for online discussions. Decide what type of filters may be required for the blog or what filters may already be in place at your school. You may need to check with your technology department in advance to be sure your site will work in collaboration with the school system's network configurations. In some cases you may want to use an Intranet or closed network service by which your blog is accessible only within the school district's classrooms.

PROVIDE THOUGHTFUL AND SUPPORTIVE FEEDBACK Students need thoughtful and supportive feedback from teachers and peers to make any learning situation successful, including online discussions. Powerful connections happen when students exchange ideas and information with other people who give feedback on what has been written. There is an intellectual connection—one's ideas are being expressed and discussed—as well as the added emotional connection of reading what someone says in response to your statements. And there is the possibility of changes in thinking as students reconsider their ideas based on the feedback they receive from others. When feedback is thoughtful and supportive, writers and readers both benefit. Writers recognize that they have an interested audience for their ideas and the opportunity to get valuable feedback about those ideas. They are not just writing for the teacher. Readers learn from the comments of peers, becoming aware of how important it is to take everyone's ideas seriously because when it is their turn to write, they too will expect to receive thoughtful responses.

CHOOSE LANGUAGE THOUGHTFULLY   A teacher's use of language is crucial to maintaining productive online discussions while modeling for students how to conduct themselves in both digital and in-person conversations. Your responses will inspire students to continue sharing thoughts or dissuade them from doing so. The statement "That's wrong!" will make it less likely that a student will respond eagerly the next time a question is asked. Whereas the response "If you knew someone would dispute your idea, how would you state it so they would consider it?" acts as a conversation starter for the group. As a teacher, you want to phrase comments to affirm students' intentions even if comments are not expected in response to a question. Bland affirmations—"Good job" or "Nice comment"—will provide students with little learning and cause them to dismiss your responses as inconsequential, insincere, or disinterested. Statements such as "I find that interesting," "I had not thought of that," "Thank you for mentioning it" or "What else are you thinking about this?" all confirm that your attention is on what the student is saying.

ESTABLISH ETIQUETTE FOR ONLINE COMMUNICATION   In unmoderated online discussions, it is easy for some students to dominate the conversation. As the discussion leader, your role is to engage everyone and bring forth ideas from all students, including those who are participating the least. Rules for online conduct, devised together with students, protect individual differences and promote civility in the expression of opposing opinions. Posting the online discussion policies that a class has collectively created makes each student responsible for playing by the rules, just as in sports. One statement might be sufficient to keep the dialogue focused on the topic: "As in face-to-face interactions in class, students will refrain from judging others' views as wrong or ridiculous. Disagreeing and stating why is acceptable as long as no one is disparaged through name calling, negative labeling, or put-downs." Students can rephrase this idea in their own words to communicate their expectations.

DEVELOP AN ONLINE READING RESPONSE FORM FOR STUDENTS   Teachers at the middle and high school levels may ask students to post their responses to outside-of-class assignments on an online discussion board. Asking students to provide unfocused comments can produce statements lacking clarity, detail, or analysis. At the same time, making an online reading reaction entry too formal (in the style of a research paper with footnotes and citations) detracts from the ideas and analyses that many students would compose to post. Figure 9.2 provides a template for an online reading response form. Consider how you might use this form or a variation of it with students.

Figure 9.2 Online Reading Response Form

Name: _____

Class: _____   Date: _____

Title of the Reading: _____

1   Describe the professional and personal background of the author.

2   Consider the big themes we have been discussing in class. Select one of those themes, identify it, and write a paragraph summarizing what the reading tells you about the theme. Use at least two quotations of at least a sentence in length from the reading to explain your thoughts.

3   List several adjectives that best describe your opinion of the reading and its usefulness for this course.

4   Assign the reading a letter grade, from A to F, with A indicating a highly favorable rating and F a failure. Comment about the criteria you used to establish the grade.

MyLab Education Self-Check 9.2

Blogs for Teachers and Students

9.3   Analyze how to utilize blogs for student and classroom learning.

Using free or inexpensive online tools, teachers can design blogs to interest and teach students. Blog technology makes it easy to maintain a current, updated site with resources on the homepage, such as live links to other websites, an archive of past postings, a podcast list, a Twitter feed, a place to publish student work, and an online discussion forum. **Teacher or classroom-made blogs** have become part of the educational resources of every subject area and all grade levels. As one principal told a teacher candidate from our program during a job interview: "Your blog is impressive. It was a deciding factor in our wanting to hire you."

What we are calling a *teacher blog* reflects the evolving nature of online communications by teachers. When computers first became widely established in schools, teachers created online teacher or classroom websites. Students, families, and colleagues accessed these sites through a large school system site, and the teacher/classroom site, like the school site, tended to emphasize the administrative side of the classroom experience, displaying class schedules, a calendar of events and assignments, and occasional postings by the teacher. Some teachers still use this mostly static site model. But because of the large variety of communication tools now available, teachers are transforming static websites into updated blogs to publicize educational activities in three ways:

- First, a teacher blog focuses on students' growth, accomplishments, and projects. It may also include a teacher's biographical information, with highlights of professional accomplishments and interests.

- Second, the blog serves as an online journal where teachers post resources and materials related to education and learning to create a channel for online communications with students and other educators.

- Third, the blog conveys pertinent information about class assignments, dates for exams, and schedules of school events as ways to invite students, families, and colleagues to be knowledgeable of the ongoing processes of school and classroom learning.

Figure 9.3 Teacher's Biology Class Blog Page

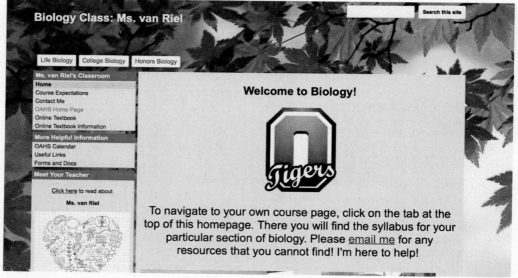

SOURCE: Helen van Riel and Oliver Ames High School.

Figure 9.3 shows a blog developed for a biology class, including links to learning materials, course expectations, and informative sites for all to visit. The teacher's blog site also has links to videos and the teacher's Twitter feed.

Creating a Teacher Blog

Blogging is a popular online activity for journalists, entertainers, sportswriters, political commentators, and other professionals sharing news about the latest happenings in their fields. Elected officials at every political level use blogs to connect with constituents and to promote greater citizen interest in government (Congressional Management Foundation, 2014). Artists, songwriters, musicians, and other performers blog to share ideas and inspire new projects. Advertisers and manufacturers blog to inform customers of the latest developments and new products. Individuals use blogs to share their interests in such diverse topics as cooking, knitting, yoga, exercise, homeschooling, and fashion.

Teachers use blogs as key communication tools in the following areas:

- *Student–family communication.* Teachers can establish school and classroom connections to students and families through a blog. Posting information online invites families to view and respond to parts of their children's education. Blogs take the classroom out into the world by creating opportunities for students, teachers, and family members to discuss ideas, share experiences, and present points of view.
- *Professional networking.* Blogs enable teachers to communicate with other teachers, connecting them professionally with colleagues while sharing ideas about curriculum, technology, and issues in the classroom. Teachers share plans, learning activities, student work, and instructional ideas. Dr. Jackie Gerstein User Generated Education site, an exemplar professional blog, is a virtual portal of ideas and resources that features innovative pedagogical strategies, student projects, and standards-based activities. Blogs provide a format for other educators to add comments in the form of feedback or encouragement.

Blogs also create new instructional formats for teachers. English teachers have students examine the literacy practices of bloggers as part of learning how to analyze language in online settings. Social studies and science teachers have students access and analyze the differing points of view on news-related blogs as part of class and homework assignments. This chapter's Technology Transformation Learning Plan, "Blogging the News from Room 145," shows how to integrate blogs into elementary school classroom learning activities.

As you think about creating a teacher blog, your choices range from costly design-your-own-site software programs to less-expensive preassembled commercial sites and open-source resources that offer free-to-use templates to teachers and schools. You decide which option will work best for you and why. You might choose a commercially available blog builder such as Wix. A commercially available program has the added features of being password protected and offering you a ready-made publication portal

Digital Dialog 9.2

As blogs and wikis have become widely established online sources of information, teachers have begun using these technologies to communicate with students, colleagues, contacts in their professional learning networks, and families. Considering your own experiences as a reader and/or a writer of blogs or wikis, comment and connect online about the following questions:

- What would be the main purpose for your blog as a teacher?
- Who will be the audience for your blog or wiki—students, other teachers, parents and family members, the general public, or some combination of these groups?
- As a teacher, how might you utilize students' use of mobile phones, apps, text messages and blogs?

for your site on the Internet. Alternatively, Blogger, available for free from Google, has an interface that is easy to navigate and produces a professional-looking site.

Many teachers and schools prefer open-source systems like WordPress because they are free of charge and fairly easy to use. *Ease of use* means that such programs may not offer some of the more advanced features found in communication software programs or commercial sites. Open-source programs generally are not password protected, which may be a drawback to their use in schools. These tools also have limited functionality without paying for upgraded plans.

Teachers can also incorporate blogging features in a free, open-source online learning management systems (LMS) such as Moodle or Edmodo, which provide e-mail, online discussion boards, instant messaging, and discussion forums for school districts and individual classrooms. Learning management systems also offer numerous different administrative functions, including grade record keeping and posting, selective content releases, and various filtering options.

Design Decisions for Blogging Teachers

There are four key design decisions in building a teacher blog: content posting, reader response, audience, and authorship. Each of these decisions will help determine how effectively a teacher blog achieves your teaching and learning goals. You, the designer, decide how you want your blog to function as a teaching and learning experience.

- *Content posting* is what and how often new content appears on your site. Posting material at the beginning of the school year and never updating it results in a static site that users will not often return to view. Posting multimodal, interactive content regularly makes a site a dynamic viewing experience. You decide how often you want to post new material on your site. New postings are easy to upload; older postings are easy to find by date and topic.
- *Reader response* is the participation of readers who read or listen to the blog material. You, the designer, decide how you want to receive comments from your audience. On many teacher blogs, comments from readers are posted for all to read, so students view each other's comments and offer their own replies. The conversation flows among the readers while the teacher/blogger guides discussion by adding comments. On other blogs, information flows from teacher to students and back, limiting the online conversations students have with each other. In either blog type, frequent postings invite students to express their views regularly as new material becomes available.
- *Audience* is who may access a site. You decide whether to limit access to a small group (the students in a course) or to extend it to anyone online (all Internet users) or another choice in between these two.
- *Authorship* is who creates content on a site: a single author or multiple authors. You decide if you alone or also students will author the material.

Creating a blog makes you, the teacher, the person in charge of making decisions for content posting, reader response, audience, and authorship. Figure 9.4 shows different design options for teachers.

- Teacher A, the single author of a site open to all Internet users, posts to the site regularly but does not invite readers to offer comments about the material. His site is shown at the right end of content posting and audience, and at the left end of reader response and authorship.
- Teacher B includes students as creators of the content monthly when new assignments are posted. Access is restricted to the members of each class by password protection because she requires every student to respond to online posts as part of how the site is used instructionally.
- Teacher C updates posts on her site every week. She is the primary but not the exclusive author of the site, as students are given class credit for adding material to the site. As a regular assignment, students read and respond to questions, read informational postings, and locate digital resources. Access is limited to the members of each class.

Figure 9.4 Teacher Blog Design Decisions

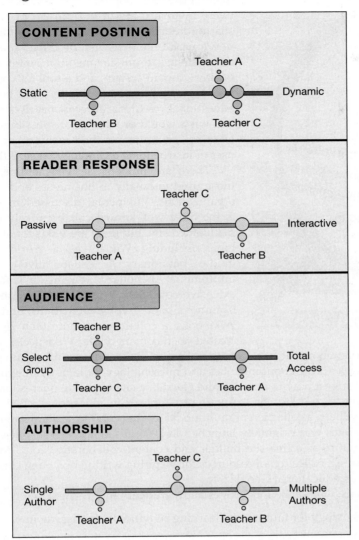

The choices of the teacher blogs outlined in Figure 9.4 are not absolute. Bloggers continuously redesign the functions and features of their blogs. You join that ongoing technology construction process as you decide the purpose and role of blogs in your digital communications as a teacher.

MyLab Education Self-Check 9.3

Wikis and Google Sites for Collaborative Project-Based Learning

9.4 **Employ wikis and Google Sites as collaborative project-based learning formats for students and teachers.**

A wiki is a website collaboratively edited and maintained by a group of people. Google Sites is a real-time collaborative website design tool that is easy to use and expansive in its applications. Both wikis and Google Sites give teachers and students engaging options for collaborative project-based learning at all grade levels.

Wiki
/wi-ky/

def: A website that can often be [edited] by any user via a browser and contains collaborative informa[tion on] one or many subjects.

Teachers post calenders, homework, reminders, information, and review materials through class blogs, newsletters, wikis, and websites.

SOURCE: Stuart Miles/Fotolia

Wikis offer dynamic ways for students and teachers to share resources with classmates and wider online audiences.

SOURCE: alexmat46/Fotolia.

First appearing in the mid-1990s, wikis have maintained their popularity based on how they actively involve users in the process of creating and sharing information online. Ward Cunningham, the developer of the first wiki, described it as composition system, a discussion medium, an information repository, a mail system, and a tool for collaboration. Looking at all the ways this tool can be used, one educational researcher forecast nearly a decade ago that wikis would provide "more possibilities of open learning environments than many other traditional uses of instructional technology" (Lee, 2012, p. 90).

There are millions of wikis online, including those used internally in businesses and educational organizations. Wikipedia (discussed in Chapter 6) is the most well-known collaboratively edited and maintained site, but there are wikis for almost every topic, including WikiTravel, a worldwide travel guide; Wiktionary, a collaboratively developed multilingual dictionary; Wikimedia Commons, an extensive collection of public domain and Creative Commons photographs, animations, and drawings; Wikibooks, a collection of more than 25,000 jointly created open-content books; Wikispecies, a directory of information about all forms of life; MicrobeWiki, student- and scientist-authored resources for learning about microbes and microbiology; WikiHow, an effort to create the world's largest how-to manual; and Curriki, a site featuring open-source curriculum materials for K–12 teachers. Another example of an educational wiki is resourcesforhistoryteachers, a collection of multimodal teaching and learning resources.

Google Sites was originally launched in 2006 as Google Classic Sites. It was redesigned in 2016 as a free site builder and content collaboration tool. Bookcase for Young Writers, a collection of resources for inspiring writing by young children, is an example of an educational Google Site.

In schools, wikis and Google Sites allow students and teachers to:

- Use technology for multimodal learning activities in the classroom
- Collaborate with peers and colleagues in school, in the community, and around the world
- Synthesize and explain content they are learning through writing and different forms of multimedia expression
- Publish writing and other creative or scientific work in all disciplines
- Receive feedback about their learning both inside and outside the classroom

Wikis and Google Sites support intensive student-to-student and student-to-teacher collaboration in three ways (Maloy & Malinowski, 2017). First, through collective writing and editing, each tool promotes high levels of student-to-student and student-to-teacher interactions. Users must work together because no one individual has all the information needed for the site. When every group member contributes material on a regular basis, a wiki can grow from its initial postings to become a frequently updated source of information.

Second, collaborative editing technology keeps track of the online writing and editing process in ways that allow everyone to see what has been added, what has been changed, and who is making those contributions. Teachers and students can follow the content development process to know who has made what changes or additions to the site. Figure 9.5 shows a sample page from resourcesforhistoryteachers, a wiki created and maintained by history/social studies teachers and students. The text highlighted in green shows new contributions to the page. Text that has been deleted from the page is displayed in red. Being able to review revisions—material that has been added or deleted—enables everyone to follow the process of wiki development. Students see text becoming focused and more clear as it is edited, while a teacher sees which students are adding and revising in the text.

Third, creating a wiki or a Google Site is easy. PBWorks, Wikia (also known as Fandom), Moodle, and EditMe offer templates for teachers and students to use in building customized wikis. These site-building services for educators typically include a free basic site that displays some advertising, with options to upgrade features and eliminate ads for a small annual fee. TiddlyWiki, a free open-source tool, lets teachers and students make a wiki to display short writing activities such as book reports, research journals, and class notes.

Despite these advantages, wikis in schools have proven easy to create but difficult to sustain. Most wikis start with a high degree of initial interest, but then fade into disuse for lack of collaborative contributions. Those wikis that continue beyond a few months mainly deliver academic and administrative information to students who are receivers but not creators of information. There are a small but important number of

---

Figure 9.5 Page from resourcesforhistoryteachers Wiki

Key Concept 1.1 Big Geography and the Peopling of the Earth

I . Archeological evidence indicates that during the Paleolithic Era, hunting-foraging bands of humans gradually migrated from their origin in East Africa to Eurasia, Australia and the Americas, adapting their technology and cultures to new climate regions (AP World History Standards).

History, Geography and Time ⏃provides an introduction to big geography.

Archaic Human Culture ⏃presents information on Paleolithic tool technology.

History of the World in 7 Minutes provides a quick video. Presented and created by World History for All of Us.

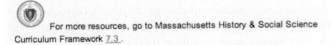
Migration Map of Early Humans

🛡 For more resources, go to Massachusetts History & Social Science Curriculum Framework 7.3 .

A. Early civilizations developed monumental architecture and urban planning.

[Teach one illustrative example of *monumental architecture and urban* **planning** *(such as ziggurats, pyramids, temples, defensive* , either from the list that follows or an example of your choice: Ziggurats, Pyramids, Temples, Defensive walls, street Streets and roads, or sewage Sewage and water systems). systems]

For more, see Massachusetts Grade 7.10

B. Elites, both political and religious, promoted arts and artisanship (such as sculpture, painting, wall

[Teach one illustrative example of *arts and artisanship* , either from the list that follows or an example of your choice: Sculpture, Painting, Wall decorations, or elaborate weaving). Elaborate weaving]

C. Systems of record keeping (such as cuneiform, hieroglyphs, pictographs, alphabets, or quipu) arose independently in all early civilizations and subsequently were diffused.

[Teach one illustrative example of *systems of record keeping* , either from the list that follows or an example of your choice: Cuneiform, Hieroglyphs, Pictographs, Alphabets, Quipu]

MyLab Education
Video Example 9.2
In this video, you will learn how wikis serve as a collaborative learning platform for teachers and students. How might you go about using wikis collaboratively with students?

wikis where students create and post their own multimedia presentations of what they are learning (Reich, Murnane, & Willett, 2012). Those sites show how wikis can function as highly interactive learning environments for students and teachers.

Project-Based and Team-Based Learning

Wikis and Google Sites support **project-based learning (PBL)** and **team-based learning (TBL)**, two student-centered instructional approaches in which teams of learners collaborate to solve problems while discovering academic concepts and constructing knowledge. PBL and TBL environments shift the role of the teacher from expert-in-charge to facilitator of peer-to-peer interactions, social learning, and technology use (Hrynchak & Batty, 2012). Teachers learn with students just as students learn with teachers. The goal for both is to create active learning environments in which students take responsibility for their own learning while getting ongoing feedback and support from teachers.

PBL rests on the idea that students learn by working together on activities that connect the academic curriculum to real-world problems and issues. In small groups, students do in-depth explorations of a topic over a sustained period of time. To begin, students, with their teacher, develop a compelling question to investigate. A social studies class might conduct an investigation about whether a historic site in the community should be preserved or torn down to make way for new commercial developments. Science students might explore the advantages and drawbacks of alternative energy sources, including solar, wind, and biomass. When the project is complete, students share what they have learned with classmates, members of the school, and wider audiences of families and community members using print and digital communications.

In TBL, students do assignments outside of class (as in a flipped classroom model) and then interact during class in small groups to research topics, design solutions, and publish findings, all the while learning from each other's thinking as collaborative problem solvers. At the college level, many TBL classrooms feature Internet-accessible laptop computers on circular tables, flat-screen monitors connected to a central instructional station, a digital projector, a document camera, lecture capture equipment, and other interactive tools—all to generate collaborative learning using technology.

TBL and PBL mirror the way information is created in society, where no one individual can know enough to singularly solve complex social, economic, and technological problems. Working together to develop a wiki becomes a way for students to understand the processes by which knowledge is generated, evaluated, and revised by groups of individuals in business, government, education, and other fields. As members of teams, students become active constructors rather than passive receivers of academic knowledge. In this way, wikis are an example of educator Marc Prensky's (2010, p. xv) vision of technology-driven educational change: "The digital technology now coming, more or less rapidly, into our classrooms—if used properly—can help make our students' learning real, engaging, and useful for their future."

Addressing Educational Standards Collaboratively

Almost every school uses a set of local, state, or national curriculum frameworks to organize teaching and learning, so most teachers are guided by a standards-based curriculum. Teachers and students can use wikis to help them address curriculum frameworks by assembling a **standards wiki**—a collection of class notes and multimodal Internet resources corresponding to specific learning standards.

A standards wiki can be a team-based or project-based learning activity for teachers and students. Figure 9.6 shows the homepage of one wiki.resourcesforenglishteachers .pb.works.com. The site provides resources for teaching standards from the Massachusetts English Language Arts and Literacy Curriculum Framework, including recommended books for middle grade students to read. The wiki has sections for American literature, world literature, seventh-grade language arts, poetry, and the teaching of writing.

For a seventh-grade unit on folktales, the teacher created individual pages for several of *Grimm's Fairy Tales*, including the original text of what were at the time decidedly more gruesome and dark-in-tone stories than recent film adaptations. Students then wrote their own versions of "Cinderella," "Hansel and Gretel," and "Little Red Riding

Figure 9.6

Welcome to
Resources for English Teachers

**A site featuring interactive multimodal resources and lesson activities
for teachers and students created by teachers and students**

Adventures of Ulysses, Apollonio di Giovanni, 1460

SOURCE: Image identified as public domain on Wikimedia Commons
https://commons.wikimedia.org/w/index.php?search=adventures+of+ulysses&title=Special%3ASearch&go=Go&ns
0=1&ns6=1&ns12=1&ns14=1&ns100=1&ns106=1#/media/File:Adventures_of_Ulysses_02.jpg

Hood" by either Disneyfying the tale (eliminating negative imagery and replacing it with a light and happy mood and plot) or fracturing the tale (creating variations and changes in characters, setting, and outcome). Once posted on the wiki, other students and teachers could go to the *Grimm's Fairy Tales* pages, read the new versions that students had written, and add their own contributions and resources. The result is a collaboratively developed and maintained collection of students' creative writing of folktales.

More examples of standards-based wiki projects include:

- Science Fair, National History Day, and other project-based learning activities
- Student-developed texts and open-content source books
- Student-created movies and podcasts
- Literature circles and book discussion groups
- Teacher-to-teacher projects and information exchanges

Wikitexts and WikiQuests

Wikis shift the dynamics of the teaching and learning experience in K–12 classrooms. Instead of reading a textbook, answering questions on worksheets, or reviewing flashcards, students become directly involved in creating knowledge by helping to construct an educational wikitext or by participating in online WikiQuests.

A **wikitext** is a collection of free digital resources compiled by teachers and students for learning academic material. The wikitext is an interactive instructional model. Students are in decision-making roles, becoming "not only readers and writers, but also editors and collaborators" (Richardson, 2010, p. 6). With a heightened sense of engagement as students participate in collaboratively building wiki pages, they come to see curriculum content as meaningful topics rather than information for a test.

An early model for a collaboratively written wikitext originated in a foundations of education course taught at Old Dominion University. Professor Dwight Allen and his graduate teaching assistants selected 77 topics from foundations of education textbooks to include in a student-written wikitext. Each student wrote a 1,000-word essay about one topic, citing five or more references from both scholarly and popular sources. A "sidebar addendum," composed for each entry, describes how traditional textbooks explain the topic, letting readers compare and contrast a textbook style entry with the wikitext. Students created five multiple-choice questions and one essay question to accompany each wikitext entry. Members of the class then rated each of the entries, and those that were most highly rated were posted online as the final product of the coursework.

Creating a wikitext places students into the role of content creators, not exclusively content receivers. They could make a wikitext to review academic content instead of rereading textbook information. For students, there is the added incentive of wanting to read what they and their classmates have written online. Professor Allen's students reported spending more time interacting with the wikitext than they did with textbooks for other classes. The collaborative writing and editing invited their personal interest and attention.

Engaging in WikiQuests offers students a different way to use wikis for collaborative learning. A **WikiQuest** is an interactive learning activity that makes a wikispace the primary research library for an online search. Teachers post multimodal materials on a wiki for students to read, hear, and view—in class or for homework. Like a WebQuest or HyperDoc, a WikiQuest has an introduction, a series of tasks to complete, and a summary activity. A high school student told us, "I like to do homework online where I listen to and watch things instead of only reading." A WikiQuest's blend of readings, videos, and audio sources inspires class discussions and includes a variety of facts and information learned in the multimodal online resources.

As an interactive learning strategy using digital technology, a WikiQuest's experiences cannot be replicated using textbooks or other static paper sources. Online, students can read an overview of a topic, see photographs, peruse original sources, view videos, play digital games, watch historic news footage and hear podcasts with stories and personal narratives or music and entertainment associated with the topic. Students can access resources such as websites from university faculty and departments, libraries, historical and scientific organizations, government agencies, and scholars and researchers that they are unlikely to find when searching the web on their own.

WikiQuests can be parts of a hybrid or blended teaching model combining face-to-face instruction with online learning. One statewide study involving more than 8,000 students in 10 Pennsylvania school districts indicated that on standardized exams, those who participated in a hybrid approach—a combination of small-group work, direct teacher instruction, and individual learning with digital content—markedly outperformed peers who received traditional instruction in non-hybrid classrooms (Hybrid Learning Institute, 2014). These results were found across all subjects and grade levels, suggesting that blended learning—integrating digital resources with in-person instruction—is a promising approach to improving educational learning outcomes.

Successful WikiQuests depend on a few resources. First, teachers need to have access to a broad collection of interactive learning resources for students. Then teachers must decide what students will do when they access materials in learning quests. In constructing a WikiQuest with students, one history teacher, wanting students to access and assess resources to check for accuracy, interest, and multimodal learning, asks everyone in the class to read, hear, and view several types of resources and respond to the following questions:

- Who produced the source? When? Is the source trustworthy?
- What is the perspective of the source? Is there more than one perspective?
- How would you summarize the main points of the source?
- How does the source relate to class notes, discussions, and readings or provide new information?
- Using facts, observations, and background knowledge, what is the essential question answered by the source?

The WikiQuest process where students—individually or in small learning groups—read, listen to, and view different types of online materials can be done in conjunction with reading a textbook and discussing teacher-presented information. On its own or in combination with other learning experiences, a WikiQuest offers multimodal learning materials that open opportunities for teachers to expand students' ideas about how to learn and challenge long-held assumptions about the teacher needing to have all the answers.

Using Wikis and Google Sites with Students

Wikis and Google Sites are flexible learning technologies that can be adapted across subject fields and grade levels. Teachers and students can create a new collaborative site or revise and enlarge an existing one. The following strategies will help you use these tools with students.

CHOOSE STUDENT ROLES   Deciding on student roles is important to whatever format you use to organize wiki projects in the classroom. Teachers commonly choose between two approaches: 1) a group of three to five students contribute to a single project, such as a science research project or math problem solutions, or 2) students produce individual projects for others to read and respond to, such as a review of different authors and genres in English class. Each of the formats has different advantages. Working together as a team, students can support and extend each other's learning, but not all group members will contribute equally to the common goal. With everyone in a class responsible for an individual project, each student accomplishes the assigned work but without the element of collaboration. You can choose the format that works best for your purpose or alternate between them at different times to promote academic learning.

PAIR WITH TEXTBOOKS   Creating a wiki or Google Site to accompany a textbook lets the textbook be a starting point rather than an ending point for classroom learning. As they research and post material to the wiki that adds to and extends what is contained in the textbook, students see firsthand that there is always more information and new materials to discover about a topic, and they become active participants in building new knowledge. An elementary school geography class, for example, might read in the textbook about different types of rocks and landforms, and then post pictures and examples of those geological features on the class wiki. Similarly, students in an English class might learn about different poetry genres in their textbook, and then post short videos on a class wiki of themselves reading their own poems. In each case, students expand what is being learned while making new resources available for classmates and others to read, hear, or view online.

WATCH FOR INAPPROPRIATE OR PLAGIARIZED MATERIAL   In addition to collaborating with students in wiki development, teachers are editors of online content who must ensure that students do not post inappropriate or plagiarized material on a class wiki, either purposefully or unknowingly. It is possible to set the preferences of a wiki so that only the teacher has final control over what material is made public and what is not. It is also possible to lock pages so only the teacher/editor can change them. Such features of wiki technology allow teachers to carefully monitor what is posted online while also teaching students about the importance of including clear, accurate, and fair materials.

PROVIDE ASSESSMENT CRITERIA FOR STUDENT WORK   Writing for a wiki represents a new and different form of academic work for teachers and students. As such, it is different from grading with the typical criteria for class assignments. Students need a definition and description of what is expected of them beforehand so they recognize what they must do to receive a passing grade. The sample wiki project evaluation form (Figure 9.7) outlines specific areas for high school students to refer to in developing postings for an informational wiki on community health issues for a science class. Groups of students were expected to create a wiki page entry and to present their findings in an oral presentation to the class. This form can be modified to fit different classroom and subject areas.

Figure 9.7 Sample Wiki Project Evaluation Form

Components of Wiki Assignment	Criteria for Evaluation
Group participants	Contributions of each member
Introduction	General information clearly identified
Resources	Accurate and relevant articles and data
Clarity	Information clearly presented on wiki and in class
Citations	APA format followed
Summary	Complete summary provided
Writing	Standard spelling, grammar, and paragraphs
Oral presentation	Engaging and informative

MyLab Education Application Exercise 9.2:
Creating a Multimodal Educational Wiki Page

MyLab Education Self-Check 9.4

Technology Transformation Learning Plan

Blogging the News from Room 145

Reading and Writing Using Web Communication Tools

Grade(s)	Elementary and middle school
Subject(s)	English/language arts
Key Goal/Enduring Understanding	People share the news by broadcasting on television or radio, publishing in newspapers, posting on the Internet, or using other communication media. Without these sources, news would travel slowly through written or face-to-face communications. For more than 200 years, print newspapers served as a format for delivering the news to mass audiences. Today, blogs provide personal ways to share news with interested readers and viewers.
Essential Question	How can a classroom blog publish news about student learning and school activities to audiences of families, students, and teachers?
Academic Discipline Learning Standard	**National Council of Teachers of English (NCTE):** *Standards for the English Language Arts*: **Standard 4**
Learning Objectives	Students will know and be able to: • Record in writing or through audio or video brief news reports about academic learning activities to post on a classroom blog • Compose captions for photos, graphs, and drawings to post on a classroom blog • Download photos from digital cameras, insert video clips, and scan text and illustrations to a classroom blog • Write in different genres, including factual news reports, entertainment reviews, announcements, comics, opinion pieces, and advertisements
Technology Uses	The lesson uses word processing software, scanners, and a class blog as key technology tools.

Minimal Technology	Infusion of Technology
Students read and view newspapers and television to find examples of news reporting.	Students read and view websites and blogs, as well as newspapers and television, to find examples of news reporting.
Students write news reports using paper and pencil, markers, and crayons.	Students write and design multimodal news reports using word processing software and multimedia production tools.
Students share classroom news through a paper-based newspaper. Families read the classroom newspaper but typically do not respond to what they read.	Students share classroom news through a web-based blog. Families read the classroom newspaper and use the interactive capabilities of the blog to respond to what they read.

Evaluation	This plan incorporates multiple forms of evaluation, including rubrics based on English/language arts standards for different writing genres and technology standards for web-based publication.
Learning Plan Description	**Learning Focus** "Blogging the News from Room 145" uses word processing software, digital files, scanners, and a class blog for students to share their academic and creative news with an audience of family members, other students, and teachers. The experience demonstrates the differences between the older media of newspapers and television and the new media of websites and blogs. This learning plan addresses two realities of classroom teaching. First, students are newsmakers. Every day they are learning something new—writing, drawing, calculating, observing, and analyzing in math, science, history, and language arts. In many schools, the news about day-to-day student learning is rarely shared with anyone other than the classroom teacher. Family members, other students and teachers, and even students themselves fail to note the compelling learning experiences that are happening all the time in school. They take for granted what is truly extraordinary—the changes occurring in themselves. Second, many teachers write a weekly classroom newsletter summarizing the learning activities of students. These newsletters may be paper documents shared with families, school administrators, other teachers, and the students themselves. Students are sometimes not directly involved in the process of printing these classroom newsletters for various audiences. In this plan, to learn about news writing, Internet communication technologies, and the role of an audience in the writing process, students are directly involved in creating, designing, posting, and publishing the learning news from the classroom. Unlike a school newspaper written and copied on paper, then distributed by hand, a classroom news blog provides an easily updatable, regularly evolving electronic record of what is happening academically in a classroom.

A classroom news blog invites readers—family members as well as other teachers and students—to write back to student bloggers, just as newspapers invite readers to "talk back" to the paper by e-mailing reporters, columnists, and editors. A class news blog gives readers the opportunity to comment about and participate in students' learning experiences while giving students the experience of an online, interactive exchange with readers.

Learning Design—Minimal Technology

A minimal technology version of this lesson plan features a classroom newspaper copied on paper and assembled by hand for distribution to students and their families. Students assist in designing, copying, and collating each publication. Classroom newspapers contain photography, writing, and drawing by students along with a letter to families written by the teacher. The work of newspaper production, including layout, copying, and distribution, can be a labor-intensive activity for teachers and students.

Learning Activities Using Technology

Blogs transform the ways that teachers and students can communicate with families and other community members. Here are the steps to follow:

1. *Choose topics or categories for your news blog.* As you begin building a blog, decide with students what categories you will feature on it. Categories, like the table of contents in a book, organize material into easily identifiable areas. Readers can consult the categories as a way to navigate around the site and locate material they want to read or view.

2. *Use a newspaper as a model.* One way to guide students in deciding what categories to include in their blog is to use a local or national newspaper as a model for how to create different sections for readers. Most newspapers have feature stories, an entertainment section, sports pages, an editorial page with a place for letters to the editor, opinion columns, comics, product advertisements, help wanted listings, and other categories. A classroom blog might include similar categories, inviting students to write material for their choices or feature student-invented categories.

3. *Include academic curriculum topics in your blog.* Including major academic curriculum topics is an informative way to choose categories for a classroom blog. An elementary school class might have sections for mathematics, science, history, and language arts, as well as special features that the students decide to include. A middle or high school class might organize by major subtopics in one curriculum area—a class on U.S. government could have separate sections for the presidency, Congress, the Supreme Court, political parties, and the electoral politics.

4. *Give roles to students.* Giving students meaningful roles is essential to the successful publishing of your news blog. Writers, artists, editors, designers, and webmasters are needed. Rotate students through each of the roles so that everyone has an opportunity to experience each function. As the blog develops over time with the addition of new topics, students can choose different roles.

5. *Organize curriculum teams.* Establish student teams for each curriculum area—math reporters, science reporters, history reporters, and language arts reporters. Team members then have separate roles within the team, such as writers, editors, designers, and webmasters. Ideally, all the students will serve in more than one curriculum area team during the year. Collectively, team members decide what material they want to post on the blog. The writers are then responsible for creating initial drafts, while the editors and designers ensure that the posts are clearly written and artistically finished. The webmasters have the responsibility for posting final copy on the blog.

6. *Encourage talking back to your blog.* Once material has been posted, there are more opportunities for exciting learning when readers (other students or members of students' families) respond in writing to what they have read. When readers "talk back" to your blog, students receive feedback about their work and can respond to the reader responses as well. Such exchanges between student writers and outside readers expand the instructional use of blogs.

   To prepare readers to avoid writing "Nice job!" or "Good work!" statements that offer no substantive feedback to students and fail to establish a basis for further communication, provide response starters to be completed by readers, such as:
   1. The way the blog is laid out is _____
   2. When I saw the illustrations, I thought _____
   3. I was surprised to learn that _____
   4. The story reminded me of _____

7. *Teach about old and new media.* News, by definition, is information that is shared with people who want to know it. People read newspapers, watch television, listen to radio, use RSS feeds, receive information alerts, and scan the Internet to learn about what is happening in their community, nation, and world. News reporters are writers who record the news in words and pictures and share it through multiple forms of media. *Old media* refers to pre-computer sources of information such as newspapers, magazines, and television. These sources have traditionally provided information for users to consume. *New media* refers to Internet-based sources of information such as websites, blogs, wikis, streaming video, and more that allow anyone to create news. A classroom blog teaches the differences and similarities between old and new media by having students compose text for public consumption and upload classroom news to the web for broad audience viewing.

Analysis and Extensions

1. Describe two features you find useful about this learning plan.
2. How widely has technology been integrated into the plan?
3. Name two areas for extension or revision of this plan.
4. How might students be involved in designing, using, and evaluating the technology in the plan?

Chapter Summary

Learning Outcome 9.1

Explain the roles of digital communications as teaching and learning technologies.

- Social networking technologies connect teachers with students, promote teacher/student communications, and extend academic learning beyond the confines of regular school days.
- Teachers make decisions and choices about the types of digital communication systems they intend to use professionally.
- Synchronous communications happen in real time (as in a phone call or a face-to-face conversation).
- Asynchronous communications include a delay between responses (as in e-mail correspondence, a response to a blog post, and a delivery of a letter through postal mail).
- Teachers use digital communications for: 1) teaching, 2) information sharing, 3) community building, 4) publishing student work, and 5) energizing student writing.

Learning Outcome 9.2

Examine e-mail, texting, and Twitter as educational networking tools for teachers and students.

- Teachers use e-mail as a way to communicate with students, families, and professional colleagues.
- Teachers can use text messaging for teaching about writing and how informal language can be best used.
- Twitter is a microblogging tool that facilitates short communications between teachers and students, colleagues, families, and professional groups.

- Following other educators and educational organizations on Twitter provides teachers with ongoing access to instructional ideas and teaching resources.

Learning Outcome 9.3

Analyze how to utilize blogs for student and classroom learning.

- Teacher blogs are a current way for teachers to communicate with students, families, and colleagues.
- Teacher blogs have three goals: 1) sharing teaching and learning resources, 2) communicating with students and colleagues, and 3) posting class information.
- Teachers use blogs to promote student learning, establish home–school communications, and engage in networking with other educators.
- Options for creating a teaching blog include: 1) a do-it-yourself option, 2) a commercially available option, or 3) an open-source option.

Learning Outcome 9.4

Employ wikis and Google Sites as collaborative project-based learning formats for students and teachers.

- Wikis are webpages collaboratively created and maintained by multiple computer users.
- Wikis become project-based and team-based learning environments in which teachers and students work together to investigate topics and share information.
- A wikitext is an online resource that teachers and students create together as part of a class study of a topic.
- A WikiQuest is a learning activity for students that uses resources within one or more wikis.

Key Terms

Asynchronous communications, p. 213
Blogs, p. 212
E-mail, p. 212
Hashtags, p. 220
Messaging, p. 212
Microblogging, p. 212
Online discussions, p. 212
Project-based learning (PBL), p. 230
Social networking, p. 217
Standards wiki, p. 230

Synchronous communications, p. 213
Teacher or classroom-made blogs, p. 224
Team-based learning (TBL), p. 230
Texting, p. 212
Textspeak, p. 218
Tweets, p. 220
Twitter, p. 212
Wikis, p. 212
Wikitext, p. 231
WikiQuest, p. 232

MyLab Education Application Exercise 9.3:
Brook's "Who Came Down That Road?" Learning Activity

For Reflection and Discussion

Online Homework Assignments for Students

Social media gives teachers and students new ways to design and complete homework assignments. State your reactions to the following assignments by teachers in upper elementary school or middle/high school settings for science or history classes, where reading about current events is a focus of the learning experience for students.

Assignment 1: After reading an article from the class reading list, respond with an online posting on a class blog or discussion board about the article's main ideas or key themes.

- List potential advantages and drawbacks you recognize with this assignment.
- Are students likely to invest time and energy on this assignment? Why or why not?

Assignment 2: Write a draft of a news report, letter to the editor, or review of an article from the class reading list. Post it online so three other students can respond to your ideas. Revise the paper based on the comments you receive before submitting it for a final grade. Please read and respond to two entries by class members to whom you have not given feedback within the past month.

- List potential advantages and drawbacks you recognize with this assignment.
- Are students likely to invest time and energy in this assignment? Why or why not?

Texting and Microblogging

Texting enjoys enormous popularity among adolescents today; microblogging using Twitter is done more by college-age students and adults under 50. As you answer the following questions, consider where you think these social media technologies are headed in the future.

- How can texting and microblogging—called *communication technologies* because they connect people digitally—best be used as educational technologies?
- How would you compare and contrast the information-sharing effects of texting and microblogging today with other historical communication revolutions, such as the printing press, telephone, and television?
- What roles might texting or microblogging have for classroom teaching and academic learning in your future classroom?

Creating Social Networks

As a teacher, you can use social media to access a wide variety of social and educational networks, including those for collaborative bookmarking (Diigo), news and information (PopUrls and Digg), online communications (Facebook and Twitter), and content-driven communities (Wikipedia, TED Talks). As a next step in creating and constructing your professional learning network, you can begin building your social networks as a way of communicating with students and other educators.

Start with Twitter, the microblogging site that features a growing number of educationally themed conversations. Search #edchat or #edtech for general conversations, or look for conversations in a specific subject area, such as #scichat or #scitalk for science, #engchat or #engtalk for English/language arts, or #history for social studies.

Next, take a tour of three other social networking sites for educators on the Internet. Here are some examples to get you started:

Selected Social Networks for Educators

Edudemic	http://edudemic.com
Pinterest for Educators	http://pinterest.com/all/?category=education
Classroom 2.0	www.classroom20.com
Edutopia	www.edutopia.org
ISTE Community	www.iste-community.org
K12 Advantage	www.k12advantage.com/forums/content.php

Once you complete your tour, choose one social network to try in the context of your teaching environment. After you have used this network for a week or two, write a review summarizing its advantages for teachers as a source for curriculum ideas, instructional practices, and assessment strategies.

Chapter 10
Expressing Creativity with Multimedia Technologies

SOURCE: Lenka Horavova/Shutterstock

Chapter Overview

Chapter 10 focuses on presenting and sharing information using multimedia technologies. We highlight free and low-cost digital tools and apps that students and teachers can use for presentations, videos, podcasts, images, infographics, and other multimodal content. Presentation software and apps, video-editing tools, digital cameras, digital storytelling and digital art programs, photo-editing and movie-making apps, and podcasts/vodcasts are explained as expansive ways for teachers and students to express learning across the curriculum. The chapter concludes with a Technology Transformation Learning Plan, "The Shortest Motion Picture You Can Make in Words," showing students incorporating digital cameras, smartphones, and tablets in writing poetry.

The chapter incorporates the ISTE Standards for Students of Innovative Designer and Creative Communicator where teachers support students in utilizing multimedia digital tools to design and express creative ideas and materials. The goal is to provide students with many options and choices for presenting ideas and information to readers and viewers.

Learning Outcomes

After reading this chapter, you will be able to:

10.1 Apply multimedia technologies as interactive tools for teaching and learning.

10.2 Explore presentation software, podcasts, and next-generation presentation tools.

10.3 Incorporate videos to enhance learning in the classroom.

10.4 Utilize photo-taking and movie-making tools to create memorable learning experiences.

Chapter Learning Goal

Utilize multimedia technologies innovatively and creatively to open access to learning for all students.

Featured Technologies

Animations

PowerPoint

Next-generation presentation tools and apps

Screencasting

Video sharing (e.g., YouTube, Vimeo, Ted-Ed)

Streaming video

Common Craft–style video

Digital cameras

Digital projectors and document cameras

Digital storytelling and art tools

Photo-taking and movie-making apps

Photo and video editing apps

Projection apps

Interactive video

Podcasts and vodcasts

Lights, Camera, History

"Lights, camera, history!" announced fifth-grade moviemakers, who, with classmates, a digital video camera, and the combined talents of everyone as writers and performers, were filming short videos about the indigenous peoples of the Americas, European voyages of exploration, the Boston Tea Party, Paul Revere's ride, and the writing of the Constitution to enliven the history curriculum.

In the initial video, students created scenes about Christopher Columbus: his birth, appearance before the king and queen of Spain, voyage across the Atlantic to the Americas with landfall in the Caribbean, encounter with indigenous peoples, and return to Spain. Writing the narration of each scene, incorporating historical facts with their own creative retelling of events, students made simple costumes and props, rehearsed lines, and staged skits before digitally recording the performance. To include families, the teacher posted the videos on Vimeo, an online video-hosting site.

All students played roles in the production—a scene setter introduced each skit to the camera, a stage manager maintained quiet on the set, a camera operator recorded the action, the teacher or a student coached the volume of the actors' voices, a technician ensured that the power cords remained connected to the electrical outlet, the stage crew moved materials between scenes, and the actors played the parts and improvised when lines were forgotten.

Students enthusiastically assumed roles as performers, stage crew, and audience. Roles were practiced earnestly and performed in character. The students were eager and willing to try other types of writing for filming as well, such as commercials for historically themed products and places. There were humorous outtakes and trailers to view. After the year ended, the teacher shared that making videos had not only helped the students learn history but also promoted a spirit of participation and teamwork that lasted in the group after the skits were completed.

Fifth-graders making history videos introduce this chapter's learning goal about how teachers and students can use multimedia technologies to express creativity and present educational information. Powerful and lasting learning happens when education involves a continual two-way process of information creation and presentation among teachers and students.

- Teachers provide ideas and information to students through storytelling, conversations, presentations, discussions, and interactive instructional methods.
- Students provide ideas and information to teachers through verbal and written responses, creative writing, group projects, and other forms of interaction and self-expression.

In this chapter, you can explore the roles of multimedia technologies in learning by focusing on the following questions:

1. What is multimedia technology, and how can you use it to create and share visual information in your teaching?
2. How can you make digital presentations dynamic, maximizing teaching methods and learning impact?
3. How can you use video resources in novel ways while inviting students to contribute their ideas for learning?
4. How can students use digital cameras, tablets, smartphones, and photo-taking and movie-making software and apps as learning tools?

Multimedia Technologies for Multimodal Learning

10.1 Apply multimedia technologies as interactive tools for teaching and learning.

We live in a media-filled world. It surrounds us and occupies large portions of our daily lives. A 2018 Nielsen survey found U. S. adults spend nearly 11 hours a day interacting with media from television and radio to computers, smartphones and game consoles. According to the National Association for Media Literacy Education, media "refers to all electronic or digital means and print or artistic visuals used to transmit messages." This includes print media (books, magazines, newspapers), broadcast media (television, streaming music, movies, radio), social media (e-mail, texting, social networking, Twitter), and "digital media" (apps, websites, software). Digital media has been defined as "a blend of technology and content" (Centre for Digital Media, 2019).

There have been huge shifts in people's use of media during the past two decades from passive consumption (watching TV, listening to the radio, reading newspapers) to active creation and distribution of ideas, images, and information using digital tools and online platforms. Today's digital tools afford anyone the opportunity to become a media creator, but not everyone can do so because of the digital divide that limits access to the latest technologies for many low-income and culturally/ethnically/linguistically diverse people. Teachers and schools therefore have an important role to play in providing students with opportunities to learn from and learn with media. To fulfill this role, educators use multimedia technologies for production and distribution of teacher- and student-created information.

Multimedia technologies offer dynamic ways to create and share information in schools. **Multimedia** means multiple ways of communicating through more than one medium of expression—words (spoken and printed text) pictures (photos, graphs, charts, illustrations) visuals (infographics, video material), and other forms of expression.

Multimedia technologies use words and pictures as well as sound, voice, video, and animation to teach and learn in creative, engaging, and memorable ways. Multimedia is a part of a larger goal of **media synergy** in which video, digital, and print materials—combined with in-person instruction—build technology-based learning environments for students.

Multimodal learning happens when teachers design educational experiences for students that utilize different ways of learning, including auditory, visual, and tactile. Multimodal learning experiences can combine spoken words with visual materials, written text with audio presentations, or online simulations with hands-on student model-building. After reviewing a decade of research on learning, one group of researchers found: "Students engaged in learning that incorporates multimodal designs, on average, outperform students who learn using traditional approaches with single modes" (Metiri Group, 2008, p. 13).

Multimedia technologies make multimodal learning possible. Teachers can employ educational websites, videos, television programs, interactive learning apps, podcasts/vodcasts, and musical and theatrical performances to present information interactively. Educational multimedia begins with the assumption that students will find learning more interesting if multiple modes of learning are used for classroom instruction. Single-mode learning means that students receive information in one form, often via a teacher talking or showing presentation slides.

It is true that teachers have used multimodal learning for years by showing images on overhead projectors, presenting DVDs and other videos, and teaching with textbooks that have embedded images. Now, digital technologies let teachers utilize multiple learning formats such as short mini-presentations, viewing segments of online videos, listening to online podcasts, and using educational games and virtual reality simulations—all within a single class. Students can complete online assignments before coming to school so that their classes can then be organized as learning workshops featuring small group activities and direct teacher-to-student interactions. Students can also access course material and communicate directly with teachers using a variety of devices, including computers, tablets, and smartphones.

Figure 10.1 shows the learning gains for basic and higher order skills within interactive and non-interactive media environments. Gains are measured against how

MyLab Education
Video Example 10.1
In this video, a teacher describes different ways she integrates multimedia technologies into her teaching. How do you plan to utilize multimedia tools as a teacher?

Figure 10.1 Impact of Multimodal Learning

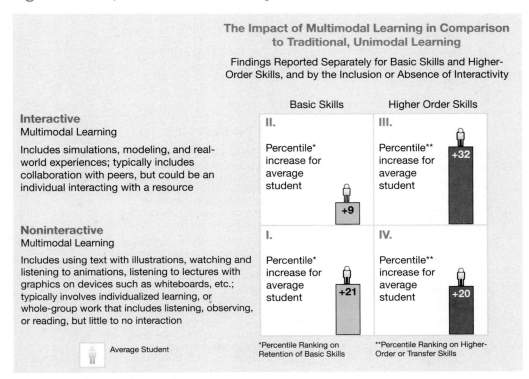

SOURCE: Courtesy of Metiri Group, LLC.

students perform in traditional, single-mode learning situations. While non-interactive multimodal learning produced gains (Boxes I and IV, reading texts with illustrations or hearing lectures while viewing graphics), interactive multimodal situations produced the largest gains (Box III, simulations, modeling, and student-to-student interactions). The report's authors concluded that multimedia, especially highly interactive digital technologies, produce increased teaching and learning outcomes in schools.

Teacher-centered teaching models utilize single media and minimal interaction among students in a class. For example, in a biology class, a teacher may show a video clip but not continue from that introduction to science-based websites or student-made movies of science events as further illuminations of the topic. In an English class, a teacher might play an audiotape or show a video of poets reading aloud but not invite students to recite poems they have composed. When teachers incorporate multiple interactive media using words, pictures, sound, and animation to present educational information, they enable students to take "advantage of the full capacity of humans for processing information" (Mayer, 2009, p. 6).

Minimal and Multimedia Classroom Technologies

Understanding the potential of multimedia technologies begins by examining their impact on teaching and learning in a classroom. Table 10.1 lists the educational or instructional technologies found in two classrooms: an older, minimal technology classroom and a newer technology-integrated classroom. The minimal technology classroom reflects how schools looked technologically before the computer revolution—and how some still look today. The technologies were helpful but limited in the resources and content they could deliver.

Imagine how a teacher in the minimal technology classroom might introduce the water cycle and its processes of precipitation, evaporation, transpiration, and condensation (see Figure 10.2). Using hands-on materials, students—individually, in pairs, or in small groups—add water to glass jars or plastic bottles to observe what happens. Over a day or two the water cycle evolves in those closed containers. To explain the phases of the cycle, a teacher might display a poster of the water cycle; draw an illustration on a chalkboard, a whiteboard, an overhead projector, or chart paper; or ask students to draw the process. Or a teacher might use a timed slideshow or a short video of material from YouTube.

In a technology-integrated classroom, using digital tools and multimedia technologies enriches student learning experiences in the following ways:

- Students can interact with (watch, pause, replay) dynamic presentations on the scientific processes featuring text and animations, as well as create their own to show to peers.

Table 10.1 Instructional Technologies in Two Classrooms

Minimal technology classroom	<ul><li>Less than one computer per every 5 students</li><li>Whiteboard or chalkboard</li><li>Photocopies of material from print sources (books, magazines, etc.)</li><li>Overhead projector and screen</li><li>Television with a VCR or a CD player</li><li>Handheld microphone</li></ul>
Computer technology classroom	<ul><li>One-to-one computers, laptops, or tablets with Internet access for every student</li><li>Software and apps with multimedia applications<ul><li>Multiple screens for projecting images to and from students</li><li>Emerging technologies (e.g., 3-D printers, virtual reality headsets)</li></ul></li><li>Interactive whiteboard</li><li>Digital projector, document camera, and screen</li><li>Surround sound amplification system<ul><li>Digital tools for multimedia production—video cameras, audio recorders, green screens, microphones</li></ul></li></ul>

Figure 10.2 Water Cycle Diagram

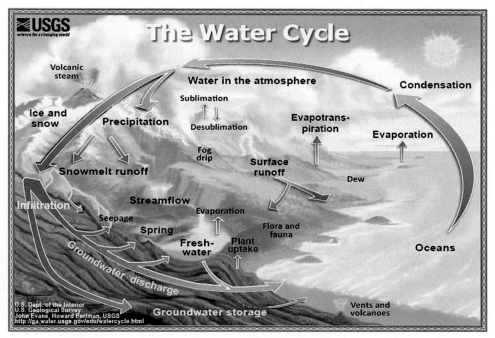

SOURCE: U.S. Geological Survey (http://ga.water.usgs.gov/edu/watercycle.html).

- Students, individually or in small groups, can curate a collection of websites and multimodal materials about the water cycle and share their collections via social media.

- Students' experiments with the water cycle could be filmed with digital cameras or smartphones and the photos or videos shown to the entire class, posted on a class website, or uploaded to a class Instagram account.

A technology-integrated approach combines the resources of the minimal classroom approach—hands-on experiments with the containers of water, teacher and student conversations, and small or large groups that might include singing water songs, reading about water, or acting out the water cycle—with students using digital tools to create graphic displays of the stages of the water cycle while documenting what they are learning in print and video.

Digital Projectors, Document Cameras, and Projection Apps

Digital projectors, document cameras, and projection apps are multimedia technologies that can convert a small computer screen into a classroom-theater-like learning environment, changing the educational experience for teachers and students. Many K–12 classrooms are equipped with a digital projector and a document camera; projection apps and wireless technologies give teachers added flexibility in how to transmit information from tablets to screens and whiteboards.

A **digital projector** (also known as a *multimedia projector*) projects images from a computer to a large screen or other external viewing surface as a springboard for class discussion, analysis, writing, and further study. The teacher chooses the length of time images are viewed. A teacher may freeze the displayed image, zoom in and out, or show a blank screen.

Document cameras project pictures, images, graphs, or text onto a large screen or whiteboard. When a teacher wants to share pages of a book being read aloud to the class but there are not enough copies of the book for every student, the document camera allows everyone to see the images and the text. Document cameras also display science graphs, mathematical calculations, historical documents, photos, and illustrations. Teachers can ask students to find their favorite object from their backpack, select their most prized science photo on their phone or tablet, or bring in an object (e.g., a rock with multiple layers, different types of tree leaves) and project these for the entire class to see. A small desktop document camera costs less than $100.

Projection apps display material from tablets and smartphones, giving teachers flexibility in how they show material to students. The field of information projection is evolving rapidly; researchers are now developing heads-up display technologies (HUDs) to project images on windows, automobile windshields, and eyeglasses. While these technologies are not immediately applicable to schools, teachers have a growing array of projection options including apps that send web content from a tablet to a projector, apps that turn tablets into interactive whiteboards, and apps that transmit images wirelessly so teachers can physically move around the room while controlling what students see on a large screen. Apple TV is one of the more popular technologies found in schools—it allows you to project anything on your iPad or iPhone to a TV. You will want to experiment with different projection apps to see which ones connect with your devices and work best in the classroom setting.

Other Digital Tools: e-Books and e-Readers

E-books and e-readers, technologies that students are eager to use, offer multimodal ways for students to explore and design content. An **e-book** (or *electronic book*) is a book that can be read digitally using an **e-reader**, a lightweight, portable electronic device that lets users access online versions of books, magazines, newspapers, and other print materials. Amazon's Kindle, Sony Reader, Kobo Aura ONE, and Barnes & Noble's Nook are popular e-readers. With high-resolution display technology to project text on screens with a minimum of glare and eyestrain and with long battery life, they are easy to use out in the world, in school, and at home.

e-book apps for tablets and smartphones, include Amazon Kindle, Media 365 Book Reader, Moon+ Reader, Bookari e-Book Reader, Nook, Prestigio Book Reader, and Google Play Books. Each tailors reading experiences to an individual. Features let a reader select print fonts and sizes, decide the number of words displayed on a page, and set amounts and shades of backlighting. There is dictionary access and note taking storage. These differentiations enhance comprehension and enjoyment for many readers.

E-readers provide a dictionary, highlighter, and the capability to send notes digitally as well as choices of text size, font style, screen brightness, and display of single or double pages.

SOURCE: Bloomicon/Shutterstock

Publishers are making college course materials available with e-book packages that include embedded videos, interactive glossaries, pop-up assessment quizzes, collaborative annotations and note taking, and other digital enhancements. Accelerating the interactive e-book trend, California, one of the largest textbook markets in the nation, has mandated that all college course texts must be available electronically. There are also a wide variety of free e-books and classic novels available for teachers and students. Project Gutenberg offers more than 59,000 titles of fiction, nonfiction, and poetry in many languages, all in the public domain.

In education, e-books are part of a broader trend among publishers to make fiction and nonfiction books available in digital as well as paper editions. While overall book readership has remained stable for many years (adults read on average four books a year), e-book reading has expanded. Most popular with young adults, e-book reading is also on the rise among adults, particularly those ages 50 to 64; about one in three adult readers access books using an e-reader. Interestingly, e-book readers overwhelmingly also read print books, but a majority of print book readers do not read e-books (Zickuhr & Rainie, 2014).

The availability of e-books is changing the reading habits of younger learners. One nationwide survey found that e-book readership among children and adolescents has doubled since 2010, and half of those who responded said they would read more books for fun with access to an e-reader. Youngsters identified e-books as better when traveling and for reading alone while paper texts were better at bedtime and for sharing with friends. The survey also found that as children get older, entering middle and high school, they read fewer books for fun or for school. Parents believe children spend too much time with video games and social networking sites. They think children and teenagers should be reading more books in both print and e-book formats (Scholastic, 2015).

The effect of e-books on student literacy learning is part of a larger debate about the current state of reading in today's society. To achieve highly, students must be able to read with skill and confidence in multiple subject areas. Students who engage in reading—particularly self-chosen leisure reading—do better in school in comprehension, vocabulary development, language use, general knowledge, empathy toward others, and personal self-confidence (International Reading Association, 2014).

Many educators agree that e-reading can provide a powerful experience through which students learn the skills of web navigation, information synthesis, and digital text analysis as they spend time reading. Digital texts offer intellectual opportunities that students can use for both online and print reading. Depending on the format, e-readers provide multimodal applications to engage students, including printed words on brightly lit screens, text-to-speech and human voice narration, word highlighting to learn word meanings and pronunciation, interactive glossaries, and record-your-own-voice functions so students can listen to themselves reading the text (Dalton, 2014).

MyLab Education **Self-Check 10.1**

Podcasts and Presentation Tools

10.2 **Explore presentation software, podcasts, and next-generation presentation tools.**

Podcast, a term that combines the words *iPod* and *broadcast*, is an audio recording distributed and accessed online using free software such as iTunes. The software needed to download a podcast is known as a **podcatcher**. A podcast that includes video as well as audio is a **vodcast**.

First appearing in 2004, podcasts are a popular and still growing form of multimedia communication. In 2017, one research group found that 26% of Americans (some 73 million people) said they have listened to at least one podcast in the past month (Edison Research, 2017). In 2018, there were over 500,000 active podcast shows with 18.5 million episodes available in more than 100 languages (Locker, 2018). In schools, podcasts/vodcasts have gained popularity as part of the teaching method of flipped classrooms in which students explore content through audio or video files outside of school and then participate in group experiments, activities, and projects that expand their knowledge of the academic content during class. Many teachers listen to podcasts while commuting to school, working out at the gym, or doing weekend chores as ways to catch up on a subject or new instructional ideas.

There are numerous educational benefits to using podcasts in the classroom. Students can listen anywhere and anytime to presentations of academic material. Reviewing material at their own pace is helpful to all learners and especially those with hearing difficulties or other educational challenges or students who may have been absent from class. Students learning English as a new language can hear the language spoken while learning vocabulary. Many podcasts have a written transcript or synopsis online. Reading these supports learning new vocabulary words and understanding concepts.

Teachers can record and then listen to their class presentations to self-assess and improve how they present information and facilitate discussions. Students can design podcast projects individually or in groups: assembling oral history interviews into a podcast, reading aloud to produce a collection of audiobooks, scripting an audio tour of student exhibits, and creating personal reflections of their learning throughout a school year.

Locating Educational Podcasts

Educational podcasts and vodcasts are everywhere on the web. Major news organizations provide opinion pieces, columns, and current events. Members of Congress, political candidates, and special interest organizations regularly post speeches and policy statements. Authors, scientists, and leading experts discuss their latest research and creative work. *This American Life* and *StoryCorps* are two of the most widely heard podcasts on PBS, and each has a section for teachers on its website. *RadioLab, Science Friday, BrainsOn!, Wow in the World, How I Built This,* and *Last Week in Tech* are engaging science, engineering, and design podcasts. Literary podcasts such as *The Children's Book Podcast, Picturebooking, All the Wonders, The Yarn, Book Club for Kids, Curious City,* and *Storynory* offer information through conversation to interest readers young and old. Students and teachers seeking history information will enjoy *The Story, Revisionist History, The Rest of the Story, The Memory Palace, Philosophize This!,* and *Stuff You Missed in History Class.* Popular podcasts for teachers include *TED Radio Hour, Cult of Pedagogy, Every Classroom Matters,* and *Moving at the Speed of Creativity.*

To find education podcasts, you may:

- Search Apple's iTunes Store or iTunesU by keyword, author, or title or by using the terms *education* and *podcasts.*
- Go to a specific educational, news, science, or historical organization website and find out what podcasts it offers for download. The Education Podcast Network maintains an inventory of podcast programming for teachers.
- Check the directories on iTunes/Apple Podcasts, Spotify, Google Play Music, Podcast Pickle, or Podcast Ready.
- Find podcasts from National Public Radio (NPR) highlighting topics and events in education from around the world and follow them on Twitter or Facebook. *Teacher Created Materials* is a standards-based podcasting resource for teachers who upload podcasts relevant to a wide variety of topics and accompany these with student handouts. *Gamers Advance Meaningful Education* (GAME) offers podcasts for educators interested in teaching and learning games. *Nerdy Cast* follows pop culture and technology as they relate to teaching and learning. *alt.Latino* features music and conversation about Latinx arts and culture.

You will find more ideas for using podcasts with students in Tech Tool 10.1.

Tech Tool 10.1

Creating Podcasts with Students

In 2018, the *New York Times* held its first-ever Student Podcast Contest (New York Times Learning Network, 2018). The 675 entries included fiction and nonfiction stories, utilized spoken words and music, and were judged on how student podcasters integrated the following three main components of an audio production:

- Content (how conversations, storytelling, and/or interviewing were used to entertain or inform listeners)
- Flow (if the broadcast had a beginning, middle, and end that created a complete listening experience)
- Editing (whether sound, including spoken words, music, sound effects, and environmental noise blended to make compelling listening)

Teachers can use the model provided by the *Times* to work with students in producing their own podcasts. Begin any podcast project by asking students "What do you want to talk about?" and "How do you want to offer that information?" (Ramirez, 2016). As students answer these inquiries, their presentation will come into

focus, especially if they have been listening to podcasts by other podcasters, including other students. They can make decisions about how to blend voices, music, sounds, and other elements to create a memorable listening experience.

Producing a successful podcast requires: 1) a voice recording microphone or digital voice recorder, 2) audio recording software, and 3) a site for posting and distributing podcasts.

Voice Recording Microphone or Digital Voice Recorder

Teachers and students can record voices and store material using:

- Computer with a built-in microphone
- Voice recording device
- Digital video camera
- Microphone attached to a recording device

The choice for voice recording depends on the situation—a single voice needs one microphone. When capturing multiple student voices, a digital voice recorder may be the most appropriate tool. Digital voice recorders, available from various manufacturers, range in price, with inexpensive models available for less than $50. A USB flash drive that is also a voice recorder is an inexpensive and effective alternative.

Audio Editing Software

With a completed recording, you can edit out unwanted or distracting material with editing software such as GarageBand or Audacity (a free open-source application for both Mac and PC machines) or digital tools such as 123Apps, Twisted Wave, or Beautiful Audio Editor. These programs import your voice recordings, allow you to edit them and add sound effects and background music (e.g., from the YouTube Audio Library), and provide multiple ways to export the files for sharing.

Site for Posting and Distributing Podcasts

Distribute podcasts to listeners by posting them online in one of the following ways.

1. Using a free online platform such as Anchor, SoundCloud, or Spotify to produce and distribute your podcasts.

2. Listing your podcast on iTunes means anyone can subscribe and listen from the site.
3. Podomatic is a free and easy-to-use podcast posting site with audio- and video-sharing capabilities and customizable podcast pages for you to design as you like. It also has an audience statistics feature to track the number of listeners who have tuned in during the past few days and weeks.
4. You may also be able to post podcasts on the Internet server of a school system or a college or university nearby so people can access them through the school's website. Putting podcasts on your teacher website or blog is another way to distribute them online.
5. Using a portable speaker with Bluetooth, satellite, or wireless capability, you can wirelessly broadcast podcasts from speakers in the classroom. Tablets and smartphones are ready made for this because they are Bluetooth enabled. Wireless speakers create learning environments free from multiple cables and power cords and the need for power outlets. Portable speakers with built-in rechargeable batteries make setting up a sound system easy to do in a variety of situations for indoor and outdoor learning environments.

MyLab Education Application Exercise 10.1:
Selecting a Podcast Learning Source for Students

Presentation Software

Presentation software are multimedia tools that display information in a variety of formats. Prezi, Haiku Deck, Google Slides, Powtoon, and PowerPoint are some popular options. These tools enable teachers and students to share information using materials beyond their own voice by combining text, audio, video, images, and moving graphics to create memorable and engaging presentations.

With millions of copies in circulation, **PowerPoint** is widely used in schools. For teachers who must continually present information in ways that will engage and inspire students, knowing the advantages and limitations of using PowerPoint and other presentation software is essential. With presentation software, you can make slideshows of academic material that include text, pictures, charts, graphs, audio, video, and animations. Live weblinks and interactive polls can be inserted as well. Presentations can be made shorter or longer simply by masking some of the slides so they do not show or unmasking them so they do. To help you remember what to say during a presentation, you can embed notes on your slides visible only on your device. Slides can be printed as a handout or put on a class website where students can view them whenever they want. Slides can be linked to other slides, which offers a chance for interactive learning such as a choose-your-own-adventure exploration of material or a *Jeopardy!*-style game show.

By loading text, data, and images into presentation software, teachers produce visual information featuring colorful graphics and pop-up or slide-in windows and have a choice of other myriad techniques to transition from slide to slide. Moving beyond the basics, teachers can transform still photographs and scanned images into movie-like viewing experiences by adding narration features and text. Or teachers can take multiple images or drawings and turn them into a stop-motion animation by putting one image/drawing on each slide and quickly moving through all the slides. Figure 10.3 shows a slide that combines color, graphics, and text to summarize students' responses to four coaches in an online math tutor.

Figure 10.3 PowerPoint Slide from a Teacher Presentation

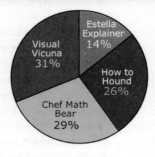
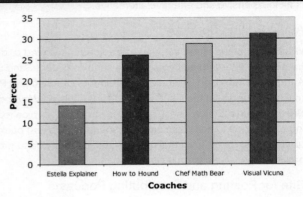

SOURCE: Reprinted with permission from Katelyn Sassorossi.

Tufte's Critique of PowerPoint

While PowerPoint's features can be helpful for teachers and learners at every grade level, there are critiques about the results of its use. Table 10.2 presents a comparison of the advantages and disadvantages of PowerPoint and other presentation software and apps.

Perhaps the most well-known critique of PowerPoint was set forth more than a decade ago by information theorist Edward R. Tufte in the pamphlet *The Cognitive Style of PowerPoint*. Tufte argued that common uses of PowerPoint are "presenter-oriented" and "not content-oriented, not audience-oriented" (Tufte, 2006, p. 4). PowerPoint's preset presentation templates, he said, "often weaken verbal and spatial reasoning" and "corrupt statistical reasoning" (Tufte, 2006, p. 3).

In Tufte's view, the standard features of PowerPoint software create a "distinctive, definite, well-enforced, and widely practiced cognitive style that is contrary to serious thinking" (Tufte, 2006, p. 26). Colorful decorations, what Tufte calls "Phluff," signal a form of information presentation akin to a commercial sales pitch rather than a thoughtful discussion and analysis. Likening PowerPoint to a prescription drug whose side effects outweigh its helpful promise, Tufte concludes that the system's unintended consequences include "making us stupid, degrading the quality and credibility of our communications, turning us into bores, wasting our colleagues' time" (Tufte, 2006, p. 24).

According to Tufte, an overreliance on bullet points for PowerPoint slides reduces key ideas to simplistic phrases. In many presentations, slides contain no

Table 10.2 Advantages and Disadvantages of PowerPoint

Advantages	Disadvantages
Provides short summaries of key points in a lecture or reading assignment	Cannot take the place of more in-depth discussions and analysis
Gives a visual dimension to class presentations	Students may "tune out" during a PowerPoint presentation
Easy to use and available on most school computers	Teachers need to spend time entering the material before showing it
Text can be combined with pictures, charts, graphs, and other images in interesting and entertaining ways	Computer screens may contain so much information that students become distracted from main ideas
What other advantages would you add?	*What other disadvantages would you add?*

more than 40 words, about "8 seconds of silent reading material" that are often read aloud by the teacher or presenter. The narrative flow of the presentation is broken into small fragments and delivered in a hierarchical speaker-to-audience format similar to the ways large bureaucratic organizations communicate information, but without accompanying activities that make the material memorable for viewers.

Students sarcastically refer to unimaginative digital presentations as "death by PowerPoint." These unchanging presentations are essentially old-style "chalk and talk" lectures in digital form. The challenge for every teacher employing this format is to find ways for students to engage with the PowerPoint presentation through interaction rather than passive viewing. This might mean inserting digital presentations of text, images, graphs, interactive polls, or video clips at regular intervals during small-group discussions or asking students to analyze and understand a topic as part of learning activities.

Using PowerPoint more dynamically can help create student-engaging interactive learning activities. For an activity on the 16th century Columbian Exchange of plants, animals, and diseases between the continents of the Old World and the New World, a teacher can frontload a small-group learning experience and then backfill historical information using presentation software with graphics and visuals rather than text-heavy bullet points.

To begin, the class views a slide displaying foods consumed everywhere in the world today, including corn, potatoes, chocolate, peanuts, beans, squash, peppers, vanilla, tomatoes, sunflowers, and rice. Groups of students locate the international historical origins of one of the foods using web resources and place a picture of it on a world map denoting the origin. The teacher can integrate additional information using online websites, interactive maps, and a short quiz about Columbus from the American Myths section of the National History Education Clearinghouse. Students finish this experience by making two or three of their own PowerPoint slides showing a food, its origin, and text they choose to add to the slideshow.

Digital Dialog 10.1

Edward Tufte's critique of PowerPoint asks presenters to rethink how the elements of digital presentations affect audiences. As you reflect about your own experiences viewing or creating digital presentations, comment and connect online about the following questions:

- What factors make interesting and memorable presentations? What makes a presentation uninteresting and forgettable?
- In your experience, do digital presentations promote or hinder class discussions? Describe any positive or negative effects you have noticed.
- What strategies will you use to make digital presentations engaging and interactive, memorable, and lively for student audiences?

Next-Generation Presentation Tools and Apps

Next-generation presentation tools and apps provide interactive and visually engaging ways to produce educational presentations (EDUCAUSE Learning Initiative, 2010a). Teachers and students can use these tools to create educational presentations and digital storytelling projects. Popular next-generation tools include:

- Prezi creates visual displays using nonlinear approaches to information presentation. Slides can be directed to zoom in and out, occupy different parts of the screen, show animations, and emphasize key points over supporting details. Prezi Next offers nine languages to make the displays.
- Buncee and Emaze can be used to design visually appealing multimodal presentations. Both tools offer a library of templates and resources to choose from when building presentations.

- Animoto enables teachers and students to use video clips, pictures, sound, and text to expand how information is presented and received.
- Glogster invites teachers and students to make digital posters (called *glogs*) that combine images, sounds, and graphics with text. Digital posters are shared via e-mail or posted on a class website or teacher blog. Students may need assistance with image uploading the first time they try, but most features of combining and displaying information in an online poster are easy to learn.
- Thinglink is an interactive image or video design tool. Text, visuals, and videos can be embedded within an image or video to enrich the viewing experience and add more opportunities for learning about the content.
- Adobe Spark is an online tool and app for making dynamic presentations using simple graphics, drawings, voice, and background music. Adobe templates include "Promote an Idea," "Tell a Story," and "Teach a Lesson," among others. Teachers and students can share their videos with a wide variety of audiences either by posting them on Facebook and Twitter or by e-mailing or texting them to interested readers and viewers. Visme and Haiku Deck are two more options to consider.

Designing Memorable Presentations

Information presentation design is the arrangement of written and pictorial information so readers and viewers can easily and clearly understand content and context. Information presentation design is a subset of **graphic design**, the process of arranging type and images to communicate information visually.

In educational settings, every learning plan and instructional activity is an occasion for making decisions about information presentation design. Used as intended, presentation tools communicate ideas, concepts, and information in unique and novel ways to students. These tools highlight academic content so students remember it, ask questions about it, and express interest in learning it. Two questions to ask when using PowerPoint or any other presentation software or app include:

- Who is my audience?
- What do I want my audience to know or remember?

Without a focus on audience and memorable learning, it is easy to become distracted by the mechanics of making the presentation. Lots of moving and colorful images, supported by sound and video, may not promote attention to learning. To be successful, students need to be engaged by a presentation so they can explain its main ideas and supporting details in their own words. Digital presentations succeed as a teaching tool when the visual experience arouses students' curiosity and emotional involvement and promotes active discussion, writing, and reflection about the content. Here are strategies for creating interactive and engaging presentations.

USE IMAGES TO GENERATE DISCUSSION   Students respond with curiosity when visual images creatively convey academic content. For example, a history teacher presenting slides of primary source materials can pair images of documents with speech bubbles summarizing historical information in current language. The juxtaposition of historic with contemporary creates a humorous and memorable image for students to recall. Alternatively, for a lesson about the writing of the Constitution, when considering the key Federalists—Alexander Hamilton, John Jay, and James Madison, authors of the Federalist Papers—and key Anti-Federalists—George Clinton, Elbridge Gerry, Edmund Randolph and George Mason—a teacher might show portraits of these men next to empty speech bubbles. The students compose text for each portrait to express a perspective about the rights and responsibilities of citizens.

PROMOTE VISUAL ANALYSIS   Historian, researcher, and educator Marla R. Miller provides a memorable use of visual displays to promote audience discussion in presentations about women and work in colonial U.S. society. The first slide she displays is a portrait of a Puritan woman and child from the mid-1660s. Miller asks the audience, "What do you see?" After conversing about the items and individuals in the portrait, she shows a second slide with surprising changes. Miller explains that curators at the Worcester (Massachusetts) Art Museum using digital analysis discovered that the original portrait was deliberately altered sometime between 1671 and 1674. Elements suggesting a more upper-class lifestyle (expensive black dress fabric and a book, connoting leisure time) were painted over to present a more austere appearance in keeping with Puritan beliefs of the proper way to live a religious life. Seeing both original and revised portraits side by side invites the audience to consider possible motivations for repainting parts. Using presentation technology to compare the two images makes possible a fascinating lesson based on a heretofore-untold story of the portrait's existence.

DISPLAY QUESTIONS OR COMMENTS FOR SHORT WRITING ASSIGNMENTS High school teachers and college instructors often assign prompts for students to practice writing succinct, thoughtful responses to topics introduced in class. One creative structure is composing a 50-word sentence to communicate the main idea of the topic. Students and teachers find this individualized, open-ended way to communicate thoughts and ideas challenging and interesting as the creative aspect of composing is influenced by a word limit. This format is not time consuming to write or to read. Displaying 50-word sentences in presentation software is an efficient way to publish and discuss different styles for achieving clear messages in shorter texts.

STORYBOARD PRESENTATIONS IN ADVANCE The intent of visual presentations is to gain and maintain audience attention. As students view slides, the teacher provides essential facts, tells stories, asks discussion questions, and explains concepts, thereby clarifying the goal or purpose of the lesson. **Storyboarding** is essential to designing interesting arrangements of information with visual tools. First, identify what you want students to know from the presentation. Then, develop learning assessments and activities to assist students in achieving the learning objective. Finally, identify multimodal content that can enrich students' understanding of the topic. It's also helpful to outline what you want to include: time for questions, discussion, and learning activities. Subtract this amount from your total presentation time to establish the direction of your planning before you create slides or choose video segments or construct the presentation. The storyboarding process inspires rather than restricts inventive thinking and assists fitting all that you have planned into the allotted time.

USE SCREENCASTING TO PRESENT MATERIAL **Screencasting** involves a digital recording of a computer screen with voiceover narration. Annotations, enhanced graphics, and other interactive media are used for explanation. Online educational presentations use this format to show a process or communicate strategies and information visually with audio explanations.

With free or inexpensive, easy-to-use drag-and-drop screencast apps such as Educreations, or digital tools such as Screencastify or Screencast-o-matic, teachers and students can create screencasts. These presentations with graphics, video clips, and audio are an alternate way to explain ideas and concepts. Because screencasts may be public or private, teachers can design curriculum for a wide variety of audiences. From desktops, laptops, smartphones, and tablets, students and families can access screencasts and course content in homes, libraries, and community settings.

As with any presentation software or app, screencasting tools depend on creative decisions about timing, use of video or photos, voiceover narration, and the inclusion of music and text. Many of these apps let you or the students draw or write on the screen as others watch.

MyLab Education **Self-Check 10.2**

MyLab Education
Video Example 10.2
In this lesson, fifth-graders and a teacher create their own videos to document in-class science experiments. How would you envision using student- and teacher-made video in the classroom?

Video in the Classroom

10.3   Incorporate videos to enhance learning in the classroom.

Videos, widely used in classroom teaching, offer ways to present information multimodally and redirect the method of instruction from teacher to screen for portions of class time. Teachers across grade levels believe that video content, when integrated with other methods, invites participation in learning. Showing video segments between two and five minutes in length, interspersed with conversation and student work, is more idea-generating and thought-provoking than asking students to watch an entire video without pause. See in this chapter's In Practice, how one teacher uses interactive video viewing as an instructional strategy.

Video is a popular teaching tool at all grade levels for three reasons:

- *Student interest.* Students have been raised in a culture where screen media are a constant presence (Rideout, 2014). Their responses to video differ from those to printed text or teacher talk. Visual images are often most vividly remembered in the long term. Many teenagers participate in video chats using Skype, iChat, Google Hangouts, or FaceTime; record and upload materials to the web; and watch streaming video online.

- *Abundance of resources.* High-quality video materials for teaching and learning proliferate and the sources exponentially expand. Videos offer endless ways to learn. TED talks about all topics, Pixar in a Box connecting Pixar movies with math and science, read alouds of picture books by actors in the Screen Actors Guild for Storyline Online are a few. Others are everywhere, including at the sites of museums and educational organizations (see Tech Tool 9.3). Teachers can locate videos related to almost any curriculum topic, including: 1) Mathematics in Movies curated by Harvard University mathematician Oliver Knill, which features short clips from popular movies that illuminate math concepts; 2) the Caldecott/Newbery Literature video series of award-winning children's books; and 3) National Geographic's science and technology videos.

- *Unique learning experiences.* High-quality videos provide dramatic and memorable learning experiences that would not be possible in any other format. A study of Shakespeare's plays can feature a read-aloud of the text in an English class with inserts of video segments from famous performances and adaptations. A scene may be viewed from multiple video sources to compare how different actors and directors interpret the material. Science topics too can be explored with *Bill Nye, The Science Guy* or, for older students, *Nova*. Videos from educational television programs—*Dinosaur Train, Charlie and Lola* (Disney Junior), *Creative Galaxy, Wild Kratts, Cat in the Hat Knows a Lot About That!*, and *Word World*—support reading, math, vocabulary building, problem solving, and intellectual development.

To see some of the ways videos can be used instructionally, imagine a high school English teacher using Marc Antony's funeral oration from Shakespeare's play *Julius Caesar* to teach students about the uses of persuasive language. The funeral oration that begins "Friends, Romans, countrymen, lend me your ears" shows a speaker using indirect language and cool passion to persuade the crowd that those who assassinated Caesar were neither noble nor trustworthy. That teacher could show students video clips of the funeral oration being performed on stage or film by trained actors whose voice, attitude, and stage presence re-create the power and the irony of the words. Experienced virtually, an on-screen oratory depicts drama compellingly in context rather than isolating the lines of the speech from the actions that caused them. Seeing a speech performed shows students how speakers use language to inform, persuade, and entertain readers and listeners.

The teacher could then read the speech aloud in a purposefully bland tone of voice, asking the students if anyone felt moved or even interested in what was being said and expanding the study of persuasive language to include famous speeches in American history from the online site American Rhetoric, such as Dr. Martin Luther

The Doomsday Seed Vault: Viewing Video Interactively

Grade Level	Featured Technology
Elementary and middle school	Streaming video

Lesson Outline

Sharon's "Doomsday Seed Vault" learning activity responds to national science and social studies standards that ask teachers and students to address issues surrounding catastrophic environmental change. Today, human actions endanger the planet, locally and globally, through greenhouse gas emissions, pandemics, nuclear accidents, oil spills, and other calamities. There are grave threats from natural events humans cannot anticipate like earthquakes, tidal waves, and droughts. If mass destruction events were to occur, people would no longer be able to grow the food necessary for survival. The domestication of wild plants for food began 10,000 years ago. Today, with some 50,000 edible plants, 60% of the world's food intake comes from just three: rice, maize, and wheat. Scientists and policy makers worry that without precautionary actions, manmade or natural disasters could gravely threaten the world's food supply.

The teaching tool for the lesson is a 12-minute video clip from CBS television's weekly news show, *60 Minutes,* in a video uploaded to Vimeo. Reporter Scott Pelley visits the Svalbard Global Seed Vault housed at a remote location in the Barents Sea where scientist and seed bank founder Cary Fowler and other scientists are storing seeds for all the world's crops to protect them in case of mass destruction on the planet. In 2014, the so-called Doomsday Seed Vault had more than 800,000 seeds with room for 4.5 million. Seed groups are securely enclosed in plastic bags, cataloged, and transported deep into the ground in the vault.

Interactive video viewing, a method in which the video is paused at specified times for students to respond to questions and offer comments, is used to create a lasting impression from this lesson. Simply screening a video from start to finish without interruption will not engage students in thoughtful analysis and reflection, nor will asking students to view a video by themselves outside of class as a homework assignment. Students need to experience collective surprise to create personal interest in the topic and make its recall intellectually and emotionally memorable.

Teaching with Technology

To begin this experience, Sharon keeps secret the purpose of the seed vault structure and its contents. Introducing the video on a big screen, she shows a photo of the building as students hear the audio introduction of this mystery but do not see the narrator speaking.

"At the top of the world, 700 miles from the Arctic Circle," Sharon recaps the narration for students, "is a building so strong that it can withstand any catastrophe—earthquake, nuclear war, an asteroid from space colliding with the earth.

Underground, chilled to below freezing, is a storage space for something. We're investigating what this something might be." The class is intently engaged, wondering where and what this place is.

"We're gaining information to determine what this is all about," explains Sharon, "so get ready for a trip to the coldest place you could imagine." Then students view the first three minutes of the Doomsday Seed Vault video.

Pausing at three minutes, Sharon asks the first question: "What do you think is stored in this building? What is so precious, so important, so vital that it cannot be lost or destroyed, no matter what happens on earth?"

In pairs and trios, students discuss their ideas, listing items they think might be the contents of the building to solve the mystery: *Money, weapons, medicine, water, cells, food,* and *books* are among the answers. Occasionally *plants* or *seeds* appear on a list. Each group shares aloud 3 items they proposed. No group may repeat an item already announced and all groups contribute.

"OK, let's see if we identified the purpose," replies Sharon, continuing the video viewing. Throughout the rest of the video, she interjects questions for a class discussion that require students to think and consider ideas to apply to the information they are learning as they view.

- At five minutes, she asks the second question: "How many kinds of apple do you think existed 100 years ago in the United States? How many named varieties of apples distinct to individual family farms?" Again, students discuss and write their estimates on the whiteboard for all to see. When the video resumes, the class learns that in the mid-1800s, there were more than 7,000 named varieties of apples grown on family farms throughout America. Most supermarkets today sell only 8 to 10 types that have been deemed commercially viable by the apple-producing industry. The guesses on the whiteboard range from lows of 25 or 50 to highs of 2000-5000. Everyone is astonished by the contrast of their estimates with the actual figure and that sparks conversation about what happened to all the other varieties.
- At just past eight minutes, Sharon pauses the video and asks, "Where in the world might some of the unstable places for food production be found?" Students ask what is meant by unstable? The discussion begins with individuals contributing ideas to the definition of that word. Political instability, weather, human error, equipment failure result in threats to food and food supplies and is one of the reasons why there are an estimated 1 billion undernourished people in the world, one seventh of the total human population.

- At 10 minutes 40 seconds, pausing the video, Sharon asks the final question for consideration: "What might be possible *perfect storm conditions* in the world that could threaten the world's food supply? List three items you think contribute to this." More lists are made and shared. The video continues and students learn that population, pollution, and climate change all contribute to the conditions.

At the video's end, a summative class conversation leads to a question introducing the second part of the learning activity: "Where is it that people are experiencing hunger today?" The lesson continues with the pairs and trios examining an interactive online food map provided by the United Nations' World Food Programme that shows which countries are facing the most severe food shortage and malnutrition threats. Students are surprised, sometimes amazed, by what they find.

Interactive video viewing that makes academic material compellingly interesting—topically, and geographically—is the key to the universal appeal of the Doomsday Seed Vault learning plan. "There are few disengaged students when interactive video-viewing is part of an experience because students interact; they don't just watch," explains Sharon. This plan generates collaborative effort through dialogue and solving a mystery to engage interest across the range of learners in every class.

King's "I Have a Dream" speech delivered at the March on Washington for Jobs and Freedom, August 28, 1963. Students could write and perform their own persuasive speeches about local or national issues they believe need to be changed while classmates could tweet or blog responses to the speeches, giving everyone more opportunities to analyze the power of spoken words and visual images to evoke emotions and change viewpoints among listeners and viewers.

YouTube, Common Craft, and Streaming Video

YouTube is a video-hosting and -sharing website where people upload videos they have made and view those made by others. One of the most widely recognized sites in the world, YouTube reported that more than 300 hours of video are uploaded every minute by millions of people, including teachers who have their own channels on YouTube where they post their video materials, and students who make YouTube a central part of their media lives. In a Harris Poll survey, 59% of Generation Zers claim that YouTube is their preferred way of learning, 55% said that YouTube has "contributed to their education," and 47% claimed they spend three or more hours daily on the site (Pearson, 2018).

Searching YouTube's "Education" channel locates videos for viewing in regular or flipped classrooms. In 2014, YouTube made freely available to the public thousands of music videos from its Music Vault Channel. In addition, the Smithsonian, Library of Congress, National Archives, National Geographic, Animal Planet, Computer History Museum, National Writing Project, and other educational organizations and universities from around the world have channels for use by students and educators (Clare, 2013). Table 10.3 highlights additional sources of video materials for classroom use, available to schools for free or on a subscription basis.

There are other video-hosting and -sharing sites offering informative and interesting resources for teachers and students. Vimeo, a smaller alternative for independent, noncommercial filmmakers, does not post commercially made videos. Teachers can search for resources or upload their own videos to this site. Net Flix, Hulu, Amazon Prime, and others allow browsing of television shows and movies and are resources for finding recently aired television programming. SchoolTube offers free and appropriate videos created for in-class viewing by teachers and students.

Streaming video is the simultaneous transfer of video, voice, and data from one computer to another. Material is sent over the Internet, displayed as it arrives, and played using software applications such as Windows Media Player or QuickTime Player. YouTube, Hulu, other Internet television services, and numerous other providers offer streaming media.

Common Craft, TED-Ed, and Khan Academy are video libraries featuring short films about educational topics and concepts—all made without showing people's

Table 10.3 Video Resources for Teachers and Students

PBS Learning Media	PBS programs offer fascinating information in visually engaging formats. Many videos have accompanying websites that provide lesson plans, interactive timelines, additional resource materials, and other features to enhance video viewing in the classroom. PBS Learning Media features digital resources aligned to the Common Core as well as information on K–12 technology research, media literacy strategies, and a blog on how technology and Internet culture are affecting teaching and learning in schools.
TeacherTube	TeacherTube, launched in March 2007, provides free online space for sharing instructionally and educationally themed videos made by teachers and students. Videos of the day are displayed on the main page, and teachers and students can search by topics as well. The site's categories are educator friendly, featuring "Most Recent," "Most Discussed," and "Top Rated" videos. Its New Page notifies users of promising video clips recently added to the site.
The Futures Channel	The Futures Channel is a collection of short videos related to jobs, careers, and future opportunities in the areas of mathematics, science, technology, and engineering. Videos show people using their knowledge of math and science working in fields as diverse as design, theater, dance, farming, zoology, marketing, and research. Lesson plans and student activities accompany the videos. A selection of titles is made freely available each week, and the whole catalog is reasonably priced for purchase by schools or teachers.
SnagFilms	SnagFilms is a free online streaming source of movies, television shows, and educational documentary films for multiple subject areas and grade levels. With contributions from PBS, National Geographic, Sundance films, and award winning documentaries, movies are arranged in topics that make it easy to find resources.
Chicago Video Project	Chicago Video Project (CVP) promotes social and economic justice through video projects that give voice to stories of everyday people. Examples of these include challenges facing public housing residents, the Illinois Campaign for Political Reform educating people about the state's campaign finance system, and information about consumer protection from AARP Midwest chapters.
TED-Ed	The TED-Ed website invites teachers to expand their lesson plans utilizing the TED video archive series. TED-Ed showcases self-nominated expert teachers who have been selected to collaborate on and publish multimedia lesson plans for the global audience. TED-Ed also features a contributor area where visitors can publish their curriculum featuring educational videos found on YouTube.
Big Think	Big Think is a collection of video interviews with experts in a variety of fields. Renowned bloggers are also featured on this site. With information organized by topic, including 21st Century Living, Earth and Beyond, Extreme Biology, Power and Influence, and Inventing the Future, it is easy to navigate and browse the site. The podcast resources here are also with experts in the field and will interest high school students.
MIT+K12	Through MIT+K12, college students at the Massachusetts Institute of Technology make and post science videos for use in schools. These videos are posted to their YouTube site and some of them are available partnering with Khan Academy for online science and math learning experiences.
Discovery Education	If you work in a district with a Discovery Education subscription, you can watch, stream, and curate thousands of multimodal resources, including numerous videos.

faces. In **Common Craft–style videos**, the camera focuses on words, numbers, images, or paper cutouts that move around on a whiteboard or white background to pictorially show information. Khan Academy uses screencasting to create its videos. Viewers listen to a narrator as they watch the explanation in action. Teachers and students can produce their own videos using Common Craft–style or screencasting approaches to communicate ideas using minimal materials. With no faces appearing, there are no privacy issues to posting videos online.

Digital Dialog 10.2

When teachers utilize videos as teaching tools, not all students focus full attention on viewing. As you think about your own experiences as a viewer of television, movies, and videos, comment and connect online about the following questions:

- What may be the learning advantages of using short video segments (three to six minutes in length) rather than longer selections?
- Would you want students to view an entire video before asking them to process their ideas through group discussion or written reflection, or would you stop to discuss what is occurring in the video at different points throughout the viewing? What are the reasons for your decision?
- Do you think students attend to and remember more from videos they help create or commercially made videos they see?

Some schools block YouTube, attempting to keep objectionable online content from children's and teenagers' view. In response, YouTube has made educational materials available in non-blocked formats, including YouTube Education and YouTube Teachers with videos aligned to the Common Core. Two web tools, QuietTube and ViewPure, can be used to remove distracting ads and inappropriate comments from YouTube videos. Designed to reduce cognitive overload for students with learning disabilities, these tools support focused learning for all.

Using Video with Students

To enliven and extend the video-viewing experience for students, consider the following:

PAUSE AND REPLAY FOR VIDEO REVIEWING Pausing or replaying video segments engages students in ongoing discussions about what they are viewing, making the experience interactive. Inserting these conversational opportunities ensures that students contribute their own ideas, observations, and interpretations to the discussion. Also, if an idea or concept is not understood or goes past quickly when first viewed, pausing or replaying for review enables clarification, questions, reflections, and understandings to occur.

ASK STUDENTS TO WRITE RESPONSES While viewing video, students can take notes or write reactions to what they are watching to share their thoughts through written text, hand-drawn pictures, or other symbols while teachers read student comments, extending the interactive nature of writing and reflection. Video Not.es is a free digital tool that allows students to take time-stamped notes while watching YouTube videos and saves their notes in a Google Document that can be shared easily with peers and the teacher. By pairing different modes of learning—video viewing and expressive writing—teachers promote student reasoning and concept development.

INTEGRATE SHORT VIDEO SEGMENTS AND STUDENT RESPONSES INTO LESSONS Watching an entire movie, video, or television show without pause, even when the content is of high quality and interesting, is a passive experience. Sitting and staring at a screen without formal opportunities to interact with others about ideas invites tuning out mentally and losing focus academically. Promoting discussion and analysis is easier when teachers show scenes or sections and ask students to discuss or write comments or tweet them to a class hashtag.

MODIFY THE USE OF SOUND OR PICTURES The National Teacher Training Institute (NTTI) suggests that teachers disable the original soundtrack and record their own voiceover to accompany images, choosing vocabulary, sentence structures, and music that match student learning needs and interests. A variation is to turn off the visual display, letting students respond imaginatively to the narration, creating pictures in their minds to replace unseen images on the darkened screen. Experiencing videos in new ways provides opportunities for students to question and discuss topics and to inquire about meanings of words and terms they do not know.

UTILIZE INTERACTIVE VIDEOS TO STIMULATE INTERACTION AND LEARNING An **Interactive video** is the embedding of questions, quizzes, or dialogues in YouTube or other educational videos. TED-Ed, Ed Puzzle, and PlayPosit allow you to embed a variety of questions and prompts into videos from YouTube, Vimeo, or other online sources. Vizia and Ed Puzzle are easy-to-use video quiz tools. Vialogues and Vibby embed commenting and conversations directly into videos. Using these web tools or apps, teachers insert questions in a video, and students pause their viewing to respond. In so doing, students experience video viewing as a real-time learning tool. Using some of these tools, teachers can also insert feedback to questions for students' reading after composing their responses—as we do in the Application Exercises in each chapter in this book.

CREATE YOUR OWN VIDEO CHANNEL AS A TEACHER   By creating one or more personal video channels, teachers can build a library of preselected materials for classroom use. It is relatively easy to find Internet videos. The major challenge will be locating school-accessible, content-specific, curriculum-enhancing educational resources to enrich learning. Many schools, worried about inappropriate online material, block access to video-sharing sites, thus limiting their use by teachers and students.

Teachers can use the Teacher and Education Channels on YouTube, Creative Commons–licensed videos, and YouTube video editor to assemble a library of educational video resources. Teachers can also post video material they make or that students make in classes. Another source of material is YouTube channels created by other teachers, which you can find by searching online for lists of "top teacher YouTube channels."

MyLab Education **Application Exercise 10.2:**
Creating a Teacher Channel for Video Resources

MyLab Education **Self-Check 10.3**

Photo Taking and Movie Making

10.4   **Utilize photo-taking and movie-making tools to create memorable learning experiences.**

The new generation of digital media technologies invites students and teachers to be creators, editors, and publishers of educational materials in every subject area and at every grade level for the following reasons:

- *Engaging learning.* In their daily lives, students are immersed in media, from the videos and pictures they take themselves to the movies they watch on television, in movie theaters, or online. The popularity of YouTube is evidence of just how extensively creating and viewing visual media interest youth today. In school, photos and movies expand the range of teaching materials beyond the teacher's voice by including multiple types of media in the classroom. Seeing and discussing images as part of a lesson helps students concentrate on the main ideas a teacher is trying to communicate.

- *Documenting learning.* Photos and videos provide dynamic ways for students to re-member learning activities. Without photographic records, memories fade, leaving teachers and students recalling events through oral conversation and written records. With photographs and videos, it is possible to revisit a learning activity in an immediate sensory fashion. Students and teachers see and hear what happened, refreshing memories and building new learning while reflecting on their past experiences.

- *Involving students.* Students can be involved in all phases of photo taking and movie making, including:
    1. Filming: Using cameras to create still or moving images
    2. Acting: Being filmed as part of learning activities
    3. Editing: Crafting the film into interesting visual presentations
    4. Viewing: Seeing and responding to what has been produced

- *Creating information.* The processes of taking photos and making movies let students become creators of visual content. For more than a century people have been taking pictures, making movies, and distributing their creative efforts to viewers. Today's smartphones and tablets enable students to do the same in and outside the classroom and in so doing learn not only academic subject matter but also the creative possibilities of digital photo-taking and movie-making technology. One example is the Dear Photograph blog, begun when the site's author held a photograph from the present in front of a place from the past and took a snapshot of the two images one over the other. Inspiring hundreds of submissions, the Dear Photograph site encourages readers to compare images from their own present lives with places that are historically or personally significant to them.

Photo Sharing with Students and Families

Teachers and students can inexpensively photograph or video any instructional activity in any subject area. Students will care more about what is being recorded when they are in the photos, make the videos, or contribute to the scripting and acting of the scenes. And because cameras and smartphones have become available in various forms, even young children know how to use them and are happy to be part of the creative process. Photographs and short video clips can be imported into presentations, websites, e-books, bulletin boards, class newspapers, screensavers, website or blog posts, online slides, and picture books or photo montages of science experiments, art projects, and other student-made constructions indoors or out.

Photo sharing encompasses posting and storing photos online, participating in online communities of photo enthusiasts, and commenting about photos taken by others. Photos with Creative Commons licenses can be used and shared for educational purposes such as making cards, posters, photobooks, slideshows, calendars, postage stamps, and visuals for online presentations.

Individuals and institutions post photos for others' enjoyment and use. Small local historical sites, national libraries, and museums of all sizes (including the Smithsonian) make historical, artistic, and scientific documents and photos available. Flickr, the online photo-sharing site and app, has features to enhance content and add interest to instruction at every grade level. In a section called The Commons, Flickr compiles galleries of uploaded photos about notable topics or events (such as the Supermoon viewed around the world August 7, 2014) so they can be used freely by teachers, students, and families.

Instagram, the web-based photo, video, and social networking application, allows teachers and students to take digital photos, edit them, and share them via other social networking applications. Teachers can take pictures of students' work and upload them to a private Instagram account to be shared with families. Instagram is one of the most popular social media applications among middle and high school students. Because this is a photo application on a public channel, set your classroom account to "private" so you can screen "followers" who sign up to request access.

Teachers can use Instagram to showcase classroom learning activities. One popular teaching strategy involves students archiving images related to the concepts they are learning in a course or on field trips. Other photo activities include story chains based on a primary image that a leader uploads and the followers or other classmates continue as they post comments to the photo. Online tutoring occurs when images of formulas from science and math classrooms are paired with explanations and tutorials. Both teachers and students can capture notes and assignments to share with the learning communities who have access to the account.

Snapchat is another popular social media tool that supports photo and video making and sharing. Teachers and students can capture images or short videos, add location filters or stickers, and send them to one another for viewing.

Figure 10.4 Page from a Student's Alphabet Book

SOURCE: Reprinted by permission from Oliver Richards.

Literacy Learning with Handheld Devices

Child-made alphabet books and concept books are two classroom projects through which digital photographs and short videos promote literacy learning among preschool through middle school students.

ALPHABETS AND ALPHABET BOOKS Kindergarten, first-grade, and second-grade students can make and illustrate their own **alphabets and alphabet books** using photographs and hand-drawn illustrations as they learn spelling patterns, letter sounds, vocabulary words, and text reading skills. A page from a student's alphabet book is shown in Figure 10.4.

One of these alphabet projects features photos of students holding objects of their choice from home or school to illustrate letter sounds, display the spelling of students' names, and explain the possessive apostrophe: Monique's Eiffel **T**ower (T/t), Yehrin's **o**cean liner (O/o), and Ava's **g**lobe (G/g). Students pose holding their object, and photos are printed as a classroom alphabet, a class book, or on card stock for alphabet sorting. Or photos can be posted on a virtual bulletin board such as Pinterest, Padlet, Google Drawing, or Webjets.io.

Each photograph is a template with a student's name, a possessive apostrophe, and a noun with a bolded letter to connect its sound to the item the child displays in the photo. This personal approach to teaching multiple written language conventions can be utilized repeatedly by changing the photos to teach verbs; for example, Yehrin **j**umps rope, Ava **thr**ows a ball, and Monique **d**ances on the rug.

Written language concepts of capital letters, nouns, verbs, and apostrophe usage are the focus of discussions throughout the process of making the alphabet display. Photographs draw attention and remain memorable because students and classmates are featured. These digital photographs can be classroom computer screensavers or displayed in a digital photo frame where children see themselves and pause to read the screen as they walk past.

Middle or high school students in math, chemistry, biology, physics or language classes where learning new vocabulary is important and necessary, can make alphabets for display and change them frequently. Taking photos of objects, hand drawing illustrations, or making short videos to upload to a virtual alphabet board all are interesting ways to use alphabet making to older students' advantage. Their own creations are memorable, might be funny, and easily stored online for review.

CONCEPT AND INFORMATION BOOKS   As resources for readers of text, young and old, and for introducing vocabulary with English language learners, concept and information books utilize digital photography to promote literacy learning and amusement while gaining knowledge. **Concept and information books** display photographs about a single topic or idea for students' learning parts of speech, shapes, sizes, colors, numbers, fractions, opposites, patterns, words, letters, continents, bones in the body, or whatever is the curriculum topic.

Jan and Stan Berenstain's classic concept book for beginning text readers, *Inside Outside Upside Down* (1997), is the inspiration for a student-made version of the book. After hearing or reading the story aloud, children can pose for digital photographs to illustrate their own text. A huge plastic tub or cardboard box accommodates three or four children inside, outside, underneath, and beside it. To illustrate the words *upside down*, students hold the tub or box over their heads and torsos, with legs and feet visible underneath, and the photo is turned upside down when it is printed.

Staging and posing the photographs reveal the meanings of words and concepts. Popping into and climbing out of the container, holding it above their heads, and standing beside or inside making funny faces for the camera keep the activity fun. Student-made concept books can be read side by side with the original, comparing the illustrations and reading both for enjoyment and to produce understanding of the concept or information.

As with alphabet books adapted to older students' learning, concept books can be adapted as a way to learn and publish information about a topic or new concept. Students are infinitely creative. Books or pages they design might include short videos, animations or songs.

Digital Storytelling and Digital Art

Recording digital stories and creating digital art are instructional approaches that attract learners of all ages to drawing, acting, filming, and editing while promoting academic learning. This chapter's Technology Transformation Learning Plan, "The Shortest Motion Picture You Can Make in Words," offers ideas for writing poetry using cameras, smartphones, and tablets.

DIGITAL STORYTELLING   **Digital storytelling** refers to ways that written text, audio, and video imagery can be combined to make unique presentations connecting to history/social studies and English/language arts curricula. In history, students can assemble oral histories, personal memories, and life stories from people throughout the school and the community. In language arts, digital storytelling offers ways to teach about personal narrative, biography, and autobiography as well as fiction and nonfiction writing.

StoryCenter (formerly the Center for Digital Storytelling) in Berkeley, California, is devoted to supporting individuals and organizations using digital media to tell personal stories. Its slogan is "Listen Deeply/Tell Stories." You may learn more from co-founder Joe Lambert's book *Digital Storytelling: Capturing Lives, Creating Community* (2018). There are storytelling resources at the University of Houston's Educational Uses of Digital Storytelling. *StoryCorps*—heard through podcasts and on National Public Radio—has examples, tools, evaluation criteria, and links to creative resources.

There are numerous web-based storytelling tools that can be used easily by teachers and students, including Powtoon, Pixton, Storyboard That, Google Slides, Sutori, and TimelineJS. Combining geography and storytelling, Google Tour Builder uses images from Google Earth as an organizing framework for student- and teacher-constructed fiction or nonfiction journeys. The site displays a map with specific locations to visit. At each location, tour builders embed text, photo, and video content related to the story they are telling.

For example, students and teachers using Google Tour Builder could offer readers and viewers a three-continent map tour about the history of chocolate. The story begins in Central America, where chocolate was a favored drink of Mesoamericans before the arrival of Europeans. Spanish conquerors brought chocolate to Europe, where 18th century "chocolate houses" served it as a favored drink of elite members of French and English society. The invention of the cocoa press during the Industrial Revolution made possible production of solid chocolate bars in 1847, milk chocolate in 1875, and pralines or filled chocolates in the early 20th century. Today, 40% of the world's cocoa beans are grown in Cote d'Ivoire on Africa's west coast.

Choose Your Own Adventure e-Stories are another engaging form of digital storytelling in which students can be readers or creators. In Choose Your Own Adventure stories, readers become characters in an adventure and must make choices that affect the plot and outcome of a story. In making decisions about the outcome of a story, students function both as readers and as agents of action exercising imaginative and creative influence over the course of events. There are engaging story building apps and websites for students of all ages, notably Google Forms, Google Slides, PowerPoint, and Twine. Story or movie creators can craft, edit, and visualize their stories and share them online.

DIGITAL ART   Art education, long regarded as essential learning for K–12 students, has suffered extensive cutbacks in many schools due to budget shortfalls and growing emphasis on student scores on high-stakes achievement tests. Yet art has been shown to support brain development; add to knowledge of reading, writing, and mathematics; expand capacities for creative thinking; and, when integrated with other classroom subjects, reduce dropout rates and lower achievement gaps (President's Committee on the Arts and the Humanities, 2011).

Technology brings new possibilities to art education, notably in digital art. **Digital art** refers to artistic expressions that happen through online or computer-based environments. Creating art digitally offers students opportunities to explore their creativity using tools they enjoy. NGAkids Art Zone, a website from the National Gallery of Art in Washington, D.C., has free interactive resources for students of all ages (see Figure 10.5). The National Gallery also has an iPad

Figure 10.5 NGA Kids: Digital Art in Classrooms

SOURCE: The NGAKids Jungle interactive was programmed by Al Jarnow of Protozone, Inc., and designed in collaboration with the National Gallery of Art, © 2008 National Gallery of Art, Washington, D.C.

app featuring portrait, landscape, seascape, still life, collage, and abstract modules. The interface enables users of all ages to manipulate color, texture, and scale in creating unique pieces of art in many different formats.

Recording Classroom Learning with Digital Technologies

Digital cameras and smartphones produce instant-view pictures *and* videos with recorded sound at no cost, making these devices ideal technologies for classroom teaching and learning. If you do not like the results of what has been photographed or filmed, instantly delete to photo or video again. Then, after downloading the video into a video/photo-editing program, teachers and students can do what filmmakers do—edit together clips, add transitions, add music and sound effects, incorporate still images, add title screens, crop images, change sizes, add words, include speech bubbles, and make slideshows; with digital recorders, students and teachers become videographers and video editors. Picture taking apps enable all kinds of interesting, entertaining, creative options: adding speech bubbles, changing color palettes, cropping out items and dropping in others, adding sound, using effects. Endless creative ideas are possible.

Many schools have digital cameras for classroom use, and teachers regularly use smartphones to record interesting events happening in the classroom or outside of school. These devices record video and audio, which can be downloaded to a computer or uploaded to a video-sharing website. An inexpensive small digital camera is an attention-focusing choice for preschool and K-12 students.

From a curriculum standpoint, making digital videos with students is a way to produce enthusiasm for academic learning. A class determining the distance students can long-jump could measure distances using rulers or tape measures and record them in graphs, charts, written descriptions, and student-made photographs; with video cameras, those same students might record an entire jump from beginning to end and even add a slow-motion effect to watch the minute details of the jump. They could include in the filming different jumping techniques, overall distances, and comic or factual commercials and then share results in a presentation that dynamically reveals successful long jumps in action. Video supports and expands the learning process as students formulate research-based conclusions and explanations to the actions they view and review together.

The topic of seasonal change offers a ready-made opportunity for using class-made video to support students across the grade levels as they collect data and formulate conclusions based on their research. The school year in many communities in the United States begins as summer becomes fall and ends when spring becomes summer. Weather patterns, animal migrations, agricultural activities, and many other aspects of daily life change seasonally, almost unnoticed unless teachers and students actively view and record what they. Students in every grade can record all sorts of natural phenomena, from changing shadow lengths at different times of the year to the effects of different seasons on plants, animals, and people. The camera captures subtle and dramatic changes in nature for viewing and reviewing, comparing and contrasting present with past.

Student- and teacher-made videos document smaller-scale science investigations, too, recording action in real time for students to see. Students constructing ramps and chutes with wooden blocks that propel marbles or toy cars on speedy journeys across the classroom are the kinds of experiments that, filmed in real time, can be reviewed repeatedly by those who want to relive the motion and the excitement of the experiments.

Students can also create digital videos on the playground using cameras or smartphones to capture daily moments, important milestones, or events they want to share with friends and family members. One youngster's videos titled "Skateboarding," "Jokes," and "Friends" showed her range of interests at school recess and during after-school time. The skateboarding video documented her attempts at mastering different jumps. It featured special-effects background music and close-ups of the skateboard from every conceivable angle.

MyLab Education
Video Example 10.3
In this video, a teacher explains to fourth-graders the importance of storyboarding before they create digital presentations about the water cycle. How will you help students integrate video, audio, pictures, and text into their digital presentations?

Digital video-editing software is also an engaging tool for changing the ordinary to the extraordinary. Digital video-editing software lets teachers and students edit their videos, deleting unwanted material and adding transitions, songs, sound effects, titles, text, voiceovers, and special effects. Editing enables creative shaping or manipulating of video images as students produce a finished film. iMovie for Macs and MovieMaker for PCs are widely used video-editing software programs. There are also online tools and apps such as WeVideo, YouTube Studio, or Clips for editing videos.

The following strategies offer ways for teachers and students to record classroom learning activities.

RECORD CLASSROOM ACTIVITIES WHILE THEY HAPPEN   Utilize digital video or photos to capture daily activities in the classroom and school. The archive of events that accrues will enable students to design many short films, photo albums, flip books, documenting daily learning that can be published in different ways for family nights, class viewing, and posting on a class website. Record or photo anything students are learning or producing—plays, poetry readings, math games, outdoor events or science experiments in action. Combine snippets of filmed action to create a short but broad picture of classroom activity over a day or a week, giving importance to the work that students are doing and to the changes in learning they are experiencing.

ENCOURAGE, EDIT, AND PUBLISH STUDENT WRITING   A middle school teacher we know uses iMovie software to publish students' written stories. The idea arose when she recognized that students' stories lacked dramatic elements of characters, storyline, setting, and tension. To help them develop these elements, she encouraged students to extemporaneously stage their stories with class members volunteering to be actors. As some students performed, others filmed. Once a story was filmed with cameras from two different angles, everyone watched the videos and commented on a list of features: character development, interest in the story, vividness of the setting, strength of emotions, and dramatic tension. Then the teacher showed either a video of live actors or an animation or cartoon of an interesting story where students saw unique characters, a vivid setting, and a point of tension to be resolved. In discussing the differences between their stories and the videos, they became aware of the power of word choices. The students revised their stories to add more action, excitement, or suspense and included more description of events by reimagining how the characters might look, sound, and interact. Their revisions revealed the knowledge they gained: attention to detail and dramatic elements, devices used to interest the audience, and a polished telling were now visible in their stories.

UTILIZE THE KEN BURNS EFFECT   A unique feature of digital software is its capacity to produce the filming style known as the **Ken Burns effect**, where still photographs seem to move on the screen. This technique, a hallmark of Burns' documentary films, including *The Civil War, Baseball, Jazz, Prohibition*, and *The Roosevelts*, zooms into and recedes out of a photograph or moves from the left side to the right, from the top to the bottom, or from a small object in the center outward to a full-frame view before fading in transition to the next scene. This style of creating motion with single photos offers wide creative choices for students, including recording narration to accompany photos, inserting short interviews of students or community members, and editing these features into the footage of a science experiment, math activity, history simulation, geography bee, skit, radio show, or any other learning event.

TEACH THE PROCESSES OF FILMMAKING   To increase knowledge of movie making and video editing, teach students about the processes of filmmaking and digital production. Students can learn by doing in the classroom what professional movie makers combine on the set of a cinematic production, including placement of the actors, lighting, camera angles, audio elements, and transitions between scenes. Production 101, an online course by television producer Michael J. Trinklen, is one potential starting point. The author of the 1990s PBS documentaries about the Gold Rush and the Oregon Trail, Trinklen has been twice nominated for Emmy Awards. Creator Academy from YouTube Creators is another resource for teachers and students who want to learn how the pros make quality videos.

As part of teaching filmmaking to students, create a video production area in the classroom. Having a video camera with both a table and floor mount on tripods makes this digital video recording studio quick to assemble and take down. Duct tape the legs of the tripod securely to the floor to ensure stability for younger students. Lightweight durable video cameras with batteries can film in the production area or be transported to wherever the action is happening. Smartphone cameras are easy for everyone to use, even younger students.

CREATE ANIMATIONS WITH STUDENTS   Animations are films where individual drawings, paintings, illustrations or photos of 3D objects—each slightly differently from the one before it—are photographed frame by frame and then projected in rapid succession to create the illusion of a moving picture. Children see animations in media all the time from short gifs (a few seconds in length) to cartoons (such as *Dinosaur Train, Martha Speaks,* or *Dora the Explorer*) to feature-length movies (including the *Toy Story* series from Pixar). Before computers, illustrators hand-drew each single image before combining them in a movie. Walt Disney's classic 1937 movie *Snow White and the Seven Dwarfs* required 50,000 individually hand-drawn illustrations.

Software and apps make it possible for students and teachers to animate their own stories using computers, tablets, and smartphones. Free apps like ABCya! Animate It! and Toontastic let children and teens select the tools, colors, sizes, and shapes they want to use to draw images on a computer screen. In Toontastic 3D, children can animate their own stories by moving their characters around the screen with their fingertips. Puppet Pals HD Director's Pass is a cartoon creator app with many different themes and characters that allows students to star in their own cartoon. With Flip Boom Doodle animation software, young children can create fun animations and share them on YouTube, Facebook, or another social media platform. Students can create professional-quality animations with Powtoon or use stop motion animation apps such as Stop Motion Animation to bring a series of images to life on a screen.

MyLab Education Self-Check 10.4

Technology Transformation Learning Plan

The Shortest Motion Picture You Can Make in Words

Writing Poetry with Cameras, Smartphones, or Tablets

Grade(s)	Grades 2 to 12
Subject(s)	Language arts and science
Key Goal/Enduring Understanding	Just as a microscope in a laboratory enables scientists to see small things in minute detail, poets compose short poems to describe common moments in imaginative, expressive language, making the ordinary a highlighted event.
Essential Question	How can words and digital photos and video create short poems about occurrences in everyday life?

Academic Discipline Learning Standards	National Council of Teachers of English: *NCTE/IRA Standards for the English Language Arts* Standards 4 and 12
	Common Core State Standards: *English Language Arts*
	    CCSS.ELA-Literacy.W.4.3: Write narratives to develop real or imagined experiences or events using effective technique, descriptive details, and clear event sequences.
	    CCSS.ELA-Literacy.W.4.6: With some guidance and support from adults, use technology, including the Internet, to produce and publish writing as well as to interact and collaborate with others.

Learning Objectives	Students will know and be able to: • Utilize central features of haiku—brevity and precise words—to create original short poems • Use digital cameras and smartphones to view ordinary events as ideas for poems • Publish short poems in digital formats

Technology Uses

The lesson features digital cameras, smartphones, or tablets with video-editing software to inspire the composing and publishing of concise, expressive poems.

Minimal Technology	Infusion of Technology
Students make notes about and create drawings of scenes in the natural world or around the school.	Students take photographs and/or brief videos of scenes in the natural world or movement in the school using digital cameras, smartphones, or tablets.
Students display photos so they can write poems from visual images.	Students display digital photos or video clips using Windows Media Player and digital editing software to inspire writing poems.
Students publish their poems on poster board or classroom bulletin boards.	Students publish their poems with photos or video clips on a classroom website, blog, or wiki.

Evaluation

This learning experience uses multiple forms of evaluation, including a rubric to record use of technology and a checklist to record elements of descriptive and imaginative language in the poems.

Learning Plan Description

Learning Focus

"The Shortest Motion Picture You Can Make in Words" utilizes digital video cameras, smartphones, or tablets and movie-making software to provide visually what will become written haiku poems featuring imaginative language that describes scenes or events from daily life in a few precise words. The goal is to convey the action and meaning of an event as if seeing it firsthand by activating a vivid picture in a reader's or listener's imagination. The lesson can be taught in elementary, middle or high school as part of the language arts or science curriculum.

Haiku poets compose deliberately crafted word pictures. Classic Japanese haiku have three lines of verse totaling 17 syllables (five syllables in the first line, seven syllables in the second, and five syllables in the third). In this learning with technology, a haiku is defined cinematically where the poet "uses only as many words as can be easily spoken in one breath" to focus the reader's imagination "on one small happening in the busy world around us" (Merrill & Solbert, 1969, p. 7).

Scientists, like poets, pay close attention to details in their professional work, producing clear and accurate observations as they test hypotheses and do research. Included as parts of science study, short haiku poems are a creative linguistic way for students to practice close observation skills while describing events in the natural world in descriptive, imaginative language.

Learning Plan Design—Minimal Technology

A minimal technology version of the experience begins with a read-aloud of haiku poems. Students close their eyes to hear how a poem creates a "short motion picture in words." Photographs and drawings capture moments frozen in time (in a portrait, a landscape, or a still-life drawing) and require words from a viewer's imagination to create a sense of motion. Motion pictures communicate through pictures that move. Haiku poems use visual imagery of language to describe and make movement.

After hearing haiku poems read aloud to imagine each as a mini-movie, students discuss their perceptions of how language choices convey images to a reader's imagination. Lists of verbs, adjectives, and nouns are made to help young writers choose combinations that poetically describe a moment in time.

Students compose, read aloud, and revise poems. With paper, markers, crayons, scissors, glue sticks, and magazine illustrations and photographs, they construct unique poem presentations in picture frames, collage designs, or comic formats.

They also make flipbooks based on their poems. Flipbooks put nouns—pictures of something or someone—into motion as the viewer flips the pages. In flipbooks, the nouns move as if animated. At a simple level, a flipbook is a technology that puts static images in motion. Publishing their own flipbooks is a way to learn how to animate drawings to make a mini-movie.

Learning Plan Activities Using Technology

Writing haiku poems using digital camera technology adds a new element to students' poetry learning experience. Beginning with read alouds of haiku to familiarize the concept of the shortest movies you can make in words, the digital technologies are used in the following ways:

1. *Go on a poetry hike.* Students take a "poetry hike"—a multisensory activity for inspiring poetry writing. Outdoors presents an endless panorama of nature in motion that young writers can describe in haiku-like short poems. Teachers and students can hike across the schoolyard, through the neighborhood, in the countryside, or up and down city streets in search of inspiration. Even from inside a school building, looking through windows and doorways, students are observing the world outside.

2. *Use digital camera technology.* Digital video cameras, smartphones, or tablets enable young poets to film short motion pictures themselves. On a Haiku poetry hike, motion and movement are everywhere, depending on what students observe. There is the wide-angle view from the schoolyard on a clear day—clouds racing across the sky, cars and trucks rolling down a street in the city or a road in the countryside, people walking. Available also is a microscopic perspective of a spot in nature that is active—ants scurrying in and out of an anthill, snow or rain falling, birds flying from ground to nests, snow melting on pavement, leaves moving on wind currents. Everywhere there are moments to record digitally and describe poetically.

3. *Create short video segments.* Each student should be limited to 10 to 20 seconds of camera time, so a choice of what to film is finite and motion and movement are clearly happening. Beautiful vistas or imposing stationary objects, while interesting visually, are not in motion, so they are harder for youngsters to describe in a short movie format. Ask students to stand quietly before filming to experience the physical feel of 15 seconds elapsing. This is not a long time. Explain that it is half the amount of time of a typical television commercial and a precise measure of a moment in time.

4. *Write the poems.* Before writing, compare the differences between filming and composing. Poetry hike videos have motion but no words. A viewer must provide words from her or his imagination to accompany the film. Written short poems, by contrast, have words but no moving visual images. A poet's word choices provide the image of pictures in motion in readers' imaginations. Video enables young poets to revisit and reenter scenes that they are writing about poetically. Before composing, students view the filmed scenes so they know which of their videos they want to write about. After viewing and before writing, the class discusses possibilities for poets' language choices and how parts of speech make a moving picture in words. After composing their poems, young writers view their videos again to see if their poems convey the images, the moment in time, they see. The poems serve as a narration of the video just as the video serves as the inspiration for the poems.

5. *Publish the poems.* Poems can be published in a format for students and families to view and read. Young poets could also be recorded reading the poems in their own voices. A more elaborate publishing idea is inspired by "Moving Pictures: American Art and Early Film, 1880–1910," an exhibit showcasing early U.S. filmmaking mounted at the Williams College Museum of Art. In the exhibit, some of the first motion pictures made in the United States in the late 19th and early 20th centuries were shown on flat-screen televisions next to artists' renditions of the same scenes. A huge painting of Niagara Falls hung silently next to a movie of the water roaring and rushing over the falls, mesmerizing in its power. Student videos could be juxtaposed next to their poems to create a uniquely memorable visual experience.

Analysis and Extensions
1. Describe two features you find useful about this lesson.
2. How widely has technology been integrated into the lesson?
3. Name two areas for extension or revision of this lesson.
4. How might students become involved in designing, using, and evaluating their technology use in the lesson?

Chapter Summary

Learning Outcome 10.1

Apply multimedia technologies as interactive tools for teaching and learning.

- Multimedia learning involves use of multiple media (text, data, voice, picture, and video) to communicate information and ideas.
- Schools have largely utilized single-medium, non-interactive forms of information presentation while today's multimedia technologies can generate dynamic learning experiences for students.
- A multimedia classroom lets teachers integrate multiple technologies, including digital projectors, document cameras and projection apps, and e-books and e-readers, into daily teaching and learning.

Learning Outcome 10.2

Explore presentation software, podcasts, and next-generation presentation tools.

- PowerPoint and other presentation software are some of the most widely used computer applications, enabling teachers and students to present information in visually engaging ways.
- PowerPoint has been criticized for oversimplifying complex material and creating uninteresting linear presentations, which has led to the development of new ways to make digital presentations interactive and creatively interesting.
- Next-generation presentation software can heighten student attention when teachers utilize two key information presentation design principles: 1) active participation rather than passive viewing and 2) emphasizing what students should leave class experiences knowing or remembering.
- Podcasts are online audio recordings that can be accessed by computers, smartphones, or portable media players. Vodcasts are podcasts that include video and audio.
- Teacher- and student-made podcasts and vodcasts generate opportunities for learning through listening or viewing presentations, discussions, demonstrations, and summaries.

Learning Outcome 10.3

Incorporate videos to enhance learning in the classroom.

- Videos, including those from video-sharing sites like YouTube, are widely used teaching tools that convey academic information in visually memorable ways.
- Video viewing can be a largely passive experience unless teachers create opportunities for students to interact with and respond to onscreen material.

- Strategies for interactive video viewing include using the pause and rewind buttons to view, review, and converse about what students see and hear; asking students to write responses to what they see and hear; varying the viewing experience by occasionally turning off the sound or the picture; and creating immersive videos to promote interaction and learning.

Learning Outcome 10.4

Utilize photo-taking and movie-making tools to create memorable learning experiences.

- Students become directly involved in information presentation by using digital cameras and smartphones in classroom projects and homework activities.

- Photo taking and movie making promote engagement with learning by involving students in filming, acting, editing, and publishing.
- Students at all grade levels can learn academic content by making their own digital picture books and digital videos.
- Instructional uses of photo taking and movie making include recording classroom events while they are unfolding, using student-made videos to generate student writing, and creating a photo and video production area in the classroom.

Key Terms

> **MyLab Education Application Exercise 10.3:**
> Drew's "Physics of Projectile Motion" Learning Activity

For Reflection and Discussion

Teaching Media-Immersed Students

Beginning as early as 6 months and continuing through high school, children and teenagers interact regularly with multiple technologies and media, creating new experiences whose psychological and sociological impacts are still being documented. As you enter classrooms filled with students who have grown up using media technologies, consider these questions:

- How are you going to organize instructional strategies to capture and maintain the attention of students?
- How often do you plan to use media technologies in each class? Every day? Occasionally? Rarely? What factors will help you make your decisions?
- How will you select technologies and use them to promote learning and sustained effort?

Multimedia Presentation Strategies

You are part of a group of teachers who are presenting short descriptions of learning activities happening in classrooms. Each presentation uses technology in similar ways. After half of the presenters have finished, the audience has begun to lose interest.

- How might multimedia technologies be used to make presentations more individualized and different?
- How would you utilize media as part of a short presentation about an educational idea that interests you and make it unique and memorable for others?

Chapter 11
Differentiating Instruction with Technology

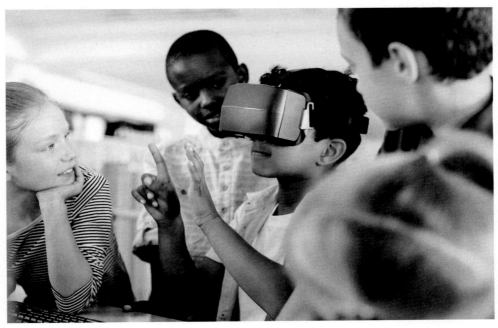

SOURCE: Rido/Shutterstock

Chapter Overview

Chapter 11 examines how digital technologies expand learning opportunities by differentiating instruction for students, including students with special educational needs, students who are learning English as a new language, and students who come from diverse cultural and socioeconomic backgrounds. We begin by defining differentiated instruction (DI) and universal design for learning (UDL) and how technology supports multicultural education and multilingual learning for students. Next, we offer a review of assistive technologies, including handheld spellers, speech-to-text software, and text-to-speech software. We then focus on strategies for integrating technology into the teaching of writing to encourage all students to express ideas and information using written language. The chapter concludes with "Measuring Shadows," a Technology Transformation Learning Plan showing a differentiated science learning approach in action.

The chapter integrates the ISTE Standards for Students: Global Collaborator. The technologies and tools, ideas, and strategies presented here support students and teachers from diverse backgrounds, languages, and cultures in working together to achieve learning goals.

Learning Outcomes

After reading this chapter, you will be able to:

11.1 Demonstrate how teachers use technology to differentiate instruction (DI) and implement universal design for learning (UDL).

11.2 Discuss how technology differentiates learning of culturally and linguistically diverse students.

11.3 Explain how assistive technologies increase opportunities for successful student learning.

11.4 Analyze the roles for technology in a writing process for young writers.

Chapter Learning Goal

Use digital technologies to differentiate instruction and promote learning success for all students, including culturally and linguistically diverse learners, students with special educational needs, and young writers from preschool to high school.

Featured Technologies

Assistive technologies and apps

Online translation tools and apps

Multilingual learning resources

Digitally accessible materials and assignments

Universal design for learning (UDL) resources

Interactive whiteboards

Word clouds

Handheld spellers and dictionaries

Text-to-speech software and apps

Translators and translation apps

Speech-to-text software and apps

A Teacher's Dilemma

As part of his science teacher education program, Shane is taking a course titled "Work of the Middle and High School Teacher." The course includes readings about education and fieldwork in local school classrooms. For Shane, the course has presented a strikingly different perspective about the role of teachers and the complexities of teaching in school organizations.

Shane had always thought of teaching in personal terms. He enjoyed learning science and tutoring younger students. But now he has come to face-to-face with wider realities of the teaching profession. First, there never seem to be enough hours in a school day for teachers to do all they want or need to do educationally for each individual learner. Second, schools are increasingly diverse environments with students from widely divergent social and economic backgrounds, speaking multiple languages, and hoping for acceptance in a social community. Third, across the grade levels there is no single teaching method or approach that will ensure educational success for all students.

As part of this wider view of teaching, Shane realizes that teachers face an overarching dilemma—how to meet the learning needs of every individual in a class even though collectively those students often have very different interests, backgrounds, and life experiences. Striving to find the most effective ways to teach every student is a fundamental reality of the work of every teacher at every grade level.

As Shane has discovered, in every class—depending on the topic of study and individual levels of interest and engagement—there are students who:

- Require the continuity of a teacher's presence along with daily routines, while others prefer flexible learning settings where they can work independently on personal interests some of the time
- Prefer to hear instructions and see demonstrations before trying a new activity because they do not want to make mistakes and appear foolish in front of peers, while others would rather try a new activity first and learn from their mistakes
- Learn by reading texts and expressing ideas in writing, while others depend on visual images with auditory cues to understand and remember new concepts

Trying to balance the varied needs of individual learners within classroom groups is part of what imbues the field of teaching with creativity, excitement, and constant challenge. It can be immensely satisfying for a teacher to design a class incorporating different techniques and activities and see learning happen successfully for all students. It can also be deeply frustrating when a teacher has students who are not succeeding academically because their learning needs and interests vary widely from their peers.

In this chapter, we explore differentiated instruction (DI), and universal design for learning (UDL), two common frameworks for adapting curriculum and instruction to accommodate the needs of students. Often associated with instructional changes for students with special educational needs, gifted and talented learners, or multilingual speakers, DI and UDL can benefit all students by differentiating classroom activities to accommodate multiple learning needs and preferences.

In schools today, technology generates never-before-possible DI and UDL options for teachers and students. Here is one example: Schools have historically been print-bound institutions, and before the digital revolution it was not easy for teachers to modify or manipulate printed text for diverse learners. Digital media make it possible to display academic material in different ways—on touch screens, through videos and animations, or with speech, sound, and pictures. Resources can be hyperlinked to other sources of information and processed at a pace and in a mode that suit learners. No longer reliant on one or two instructional approaches, students have more opportunities to achieve academic success.

As you read this chapter and see how technology can support teachers in addressing the needs of culturally and linguistically diverse students, individuals with special educational needs, and student writers at every grade level, consider the following questions:

1. How can you implement DI and UDL into daily classroom activities?
2. How can technology engage and inspire self-directed learning for culturally and linguistically diverse students?
3. How can you use assistive technologies to support all learners in universally designed classrooms?
4. How does technology promote learning and literacy success for students within a writing process fit for young writers?

Differentiated Instruction and Universal Design for Learning

11.1 Demonstrate how teachers use technology to differentiate instruction (DI) and implement universal design for learning (UDL).

Minimizing disability and maximizing opportunity are keys to using differentiated instruction and universal design for learning to adapt teaching strategies and classroom environments to the needs of all learners (Hehir & Katzman, 2012). The goal is to create **accommodations** through which students have more than one way to access the curriculum. For example, if a student is struggling to learn a topic in mathematics, differentiations and accommodations might include individual or small-group tutoring, use of math websites and apps that utilize interactive teaching approaches, and self-paced exams with no time limit to complete the problems. By offering resources that support specific learning needs, these approaches offer students ways to complete the same assignments as the other members of the class.

Accommodation is different from **modification**, where some students receive less substantive instructional or curricular experiences than other students. Modification in mathematics might involve having students complete fewer math problems or receive assignments that contain less reading and calculating. Allowing a student to do less than their regular education peers minimizes that student's academic experience.

Differentiated Instruction

MyLab Education
Video Example 11.1
In this video, a teacher describes how she differentiates teaching and learning in the classroom. What are additional ways for teachers to differentiate learning for students?

Differentiated instruction (DI) is an instructional approach in which teachers make accommodations to address the learning needs of individual students (Tomlinson, 2017, 2014). When engaging in DI, a teacher intentionally adjusts curriculum content, instructional methods, assessment approaches, and/or the classroom environment to assist students' academic learning. For instance, students might be given the option to read a book, watch a video, listen to a podcast, play an online game, or participate in a hands-on experiment to gain knowledge about an academic concept or skill. Differentiated learning experiences are intended to increase interest and provide attainable challenges by customizing, as much as possible, academic learning to students' learning needs. This chapter's Technology Transformation Learning Plan, "Measuring Shadows," shows a differentiated learning approach in action.

Student learning differences arise in four areas, notes DI advocate Carol Ann Tomlinson (2014):

- *Readiness:* How prior experiences prepare students to learn new academic material
- *Interest:* How much students are curious about or committed to learning the curricula in school
- *Learning profile:* How students optimally learn in formal or informal situations
- *Affect:* How students think of themselves as learners and how they regard the school as a place for their learning

The teacher's challenge is finding the time, resources, and tools to differentiate instruction in ways that engage students' multiple learning preferences, interest them in what school is teaching, and let them experience school as a place of successful learning.

Some students come to school with individual education plans (IEPs) specifying the adaptations, modifications, and supports they must have as part of daily classroom instruction. No one teacher has the time to design individualized daily curricula for every student. However, teachers can vary how information is shared and explored by combining spoken words, visual images, video segments, and hands-on materials to engage individuals differently within a larger classroom group.

Differentiating learning activities increase minds-on learning, engaging students' curiosity and creative thinking while offering ways for them to fully participate in class activities. A teacher might lengthen or shorten the time that students work together on projects to keep the class moving without anyone losing attention or focus. She might split the class into small groups of different sizes to work directly with some while the others work independently or in pairs. Then she changes the groups so students have learning experiences with her and by themselves. Each of these steps differentiates the learning. These methods enhance students' perspectives about learning while engaging everyone as fully as possible throughout the class period.

Differentiating Learning for Women's History Month

Grade Level	Featured Technologies
Elementary and middle school	Tablets, smartphones and online resources

Lesson Outline

During Women's History Month in March, Haley decided to teach middle school students about important women change makers by differentiating learning using online resources. She told her classes that differentiated learning means students learn multimodally using multiple forms of online media—reading printed text, viewing pictures and images, watching videos, listening to podcasts, interacting with online resources, and expressing ideas orally and in writing. When students are seeking information multimodally, they explore topics interactively, participating in an experience that is new for most of them.

Haley's primary objective was to demonstrate how and why it is important to present academic information in more than one way. Following the insights of educational researchers (Rohrer & Pashler, 2012), Haley rejected the incorrect theories that students have a fixed or rigid learning style (such as right brain vs. left brain or assuming someone is a stronger visual, auditory or hands-on learner) and therefore teachers should tailor learning to that style. Rather, Haley believed that information presentations should be differentiated so everyone reads, views, listens, interacts, and writes, and by experiencing multiple modes of presentation, students expand how they learn, gaining confidence and the ability to understand material in new ways.

Teaching with Technology

Combining in-class activities and outside-of-school assignments, Haley asked students to locate four multimodal resources they found interesting to use to introduce a woman from the list of change-makers in history, science, or mathematics:

The Rocket Girls	Beatrix Potter	Rosa Parks	Mae Jemison
Margaret Sanger	Dolores Huerta	Ada Lovelace	Grace Hopper
Rachel Carson	Elizabeth Blackwell	Jane Goodall	Ruth Bader Ginsburg
Emily Warren Roebling	Rosalind Franklin	Marie Curie	Jerrie Cobb and the Mercury 13

Possible online multimodal resources include:

- Video clips
- Audio materials, including podcasts
- Pictures and images
- Interactive websites
- Learning games
- Text-based materials

For each resource they located, students annotated the category. This page was part of their written record for the activity.

Video Resource	Describe the Resource Here
Interactive Web Resource	Describe the Resource Here
Biography Resource	Describe the Resource Here
Lesson Plan Resource	Describe the Resource Here
Text-Based Resource	Describe the Resource Here

To aid students' searches for attention-capturing multimodal resources, Haley suggested they:

- Start with National Public Radio (NPR, for podcasts and audio interviews) and PBS (for video) and use online sites from universities, historical organizations, museums, government agencies and other academic sources.
- Minimize the use of .com sites that have lots of ads and clickbait distractions
- Go to Wikimedia Commons or CreativeCommons.org for Creative Commons photographs and other media.
- Examine the accuracy of the information presented, identify any biases that might shape the information that is shared, and recognize who or what group is presenting the information.
- Look for video sources on TeacherTube or material posted by academic organizations.
- Locate brief biographies, picture books or chapter books, of change makers that can be read to or by elementary, middle, and high school students.
- Consult the *New York Times* and other major newspapers that publish online obituaries to find little known information about a person's life.

As part of the research of multimodal resources, students created a page for each change-maker in a Google slides presentation for the class. Students finished the learning activity by choosing two women to learn about and to compose written comments identifying which resources they found most interesting, most surprising, most memorable and why. Students told Haley that the Women's History Month differentiated learning activity gave them an entirely new way to look at the historical people they were learning about in their history, English, science, and math classes. They could see, hear, and interact with as well as read about a person's life and times, making that individual and her accomplishments more real to them as students than if they had only read an entry in a book or gained information in Wikipedia.

Universal Design for Learning

Universal design, a concept from the field of architecture, is at the center of a widely used approach to serving all students. In building design and construction, a curb cut is an example of universal design because the ramp enables wheelchairs to roll from sidewalk to street, pedestrians to walk without a step to climb, and delivery persons to move large loads smoothly from the curbside to the sidewalk without lifting a handcart.

Universal design for learning (UDL) is the application of universal design principles from architecture and public access to educational settings. UDL applies recent advances in understanding how the brain processes information to the design of a curriculum that can accommodate broad student needs (Hall, Meyer, & Rose, 2012). The Center for Applied Special Technology (2006) has defined UDL as:

- *Multiple means of representation*, to give learners various ways of acquiring information and knowledge
- *Multiple means of expression*, to provide learners alternatives for demonstrating what they know
- *Multiple means of engagement*, to tap into learners' interests, offer appropriate challenges, and increase motivation

The purpose of applying universal design principles in schools is to create teaching and learning situations that serve the needs of the widest range of students without diminishing or reducing opportunities for anyone (Hehir & Katzman, 2012). By emphasizing highly flexible instructional goals, strategies, and materials, UDL minimizes or eliminates potential barriers to learning, thereby increasing equitable learning opportunities for all students. For example, a teacher might use PowerPoint or presentation software to display vocabulary words and definitions on a screen for all students to see so a student needing hearing supports can read the information while the teacher discusses the terms. Although the teacher's instructional plan supports the learning of a student with a hearing impairment, regular education students also have the advantage of reading the material while hearing the terms repeated in conversation.

Similarly, a UDL math activity about the concept of probability might open with a choice of two learning options: student-written and -acted skits to introduce concepts or a series of games that utilize probability principles. Students choose which activity they most want to do first and then groups engage in their choice of learning activity. To teach each other, students perform the skits for the class, and the game players explain and demonstrate the games. By engaging the whole class in thought-provoking and choice-driven learning experiences, the teacher ensures that the theme of the unit is enjoyed by everyone.

Ideas, information, and model lessons for using differentiated instruction and UDL to meet the wide variations of individual learners are available from the Center for Applied Special Technology (CAST), a nonprofit organization located in Wakefield, Massachusetts. CAST boasts nearly three decades of researching and field-testing successful approaches to UDL. On its website, cast.org, CAST provides resources under Free Learning Tools that demonstrate ways to implement UDL in the classroom, including the following:

- The UDL EXCHANGE lets teachers share resources aligned to the Common Core standards and edit and make their own plans according to UDL principles.
- The UDL Book Builder lets teachers explore genres of children's and young adult books and then create their own accessible digital books for diverse learners.
- UDL Editions uses digital media with animated coaches to provide different levels of language and conceptual learning support for students reading classic literature such as Abraham Lincoln's Gettysburg Address, Shakespeare's "Sonnet XVIII," and Jack London's novel *The Call of the Wild*.
- UDL Studio assists teachers to make materials that offer different kinds of learning supports for students.

Digital Dialog 11.1

Teachers, in differentiating learning experiences for individual students, find that planning is essential. As you think about differentiated instruction, comment and connect online about the following questions:

- How have you seen teachers differentiate instruction?
- Think about the last time you learned something new—practicing a musical instrument, playing a video game, speaking a new language, putting together a resume. How did you go about learning? Did you watch a video or listen to a podcast? Ask a friend? Learn through trial and error? Take notes? Observe a group of people? Join an online discussion?
- Given that learning can happen in many ways for many different subject areas, how do you envision organizing teaching activities to support the learning needs of diverse students? How will you differentiate methods for learning?

AccessIT from the National Center on Accessible Information Technology in Education at the University of Washington is another resource, featuring a searchable database of questions and answers about the uses of digital technology. You can also get ideas and information from the National Assistive Technology in Education (NATE) network and the National Association of Special Education Teachers (NASET).

Designing Successful Learning Experiences

Every teacher is an instructional designer, making decisions about all aspects of classroom learning environments from seating arrangements to instructional activities. To promote universal design and learning success, no aspect of the classroom environment is too inconsequential or insignificant to consider. Any aspect of the classroom may make the difference in students maintaining or losing interest in what is being taught, and when interest is lost, so is the motivation to focus and learn.

There are two main areas for designing successful learning experiences for students with diverse learning needs—including students on IEPs and 504 plans: 1) changes in the classroom environment and 2) changes in how the curriculum is delivered. There are low-tech, mid-tech, and high-tech digital accommodations for you to consider as ways to differentiate instruction and fulfill the goals of universal design for learning:

- **Low-tech accommodations** refer to changes that do not utilize digital materials.
- **Mid-tech accommodations** involve substantive shifts in organization and delivery of curriculum that may include the use of digital materials.
- **High-tech accommodations** introduce changes associated with the integration of digital technologies in the classroom.

Tables 11.1 and 11.2 illustrate ways to differentiate classroom organization and teaching methods using low-tech, mid-tech, and high-tech tools.

Creating curriculum materials that are both accessible and engaging for all learners is a continual work in progress for teachers. Ideally, integrating multiple methods and materials for one learner or a small group of learners will also benefit the entire class. In their role as teacher/instructional designer, teachers can use digital and non-digital technologies to modify both the classroom environment and ways the curriculum is delivered. When using technologies to create accommodations for students, it is helpful to begin making low- and mid-tech accommodations and then move on to high-tech ones. No matter where or what you teach, you will be able to influence choice of seating arrangements, whiteboard use, displays on walls and partitions, and reading and writing materials. Additionally, you will be able to organize how the content is delivered, including small or large student groups, student demonstrations or teacher lectures, and use of hands-on and technology-based manipulatives.

MyLab Application Exercise 11.1:
Creating Low-Tech/Mid-Tech/High-Tech Accommodations

Table 11.1 Classroom Organization Tools

Technology Tool	Low-Tech	Mid-Tech	High-Tech
Chairs and desks	Provide desks and chairs with adjustable heights and widths for different-sized students. Use gripping shelf paper to cover the seat to prevent small students from slipping out of chairs.	Provide specially designed seat cushions or "positioning aids" for students who need them or who are more comfortable with them.	Provide alternative seating, beanbag chairs, exercise balls, or stools or standing desk or counters. **Apps** Smart Seat
Whiteboards, chalkboards, chart paper	Write in colors visible to individuals who may be colorblind that do not fade with daylight exposure. Ignore yellow, pink, and light pastel colors for display. Offer a hard copy of printed material or text for students who find copying from the board a challenge.	Use audio recordings made by classmates of notes written on the board or chart paper. Students can access these audio recordings and listen to notes or directions via headphones.	Use an interactive whiteboard that offers a printout of notes and directions and allows the font to be enlarged. **Apps** ShowMe and Educreations
Pencils, pens, paper, scissors	Provide a variety of different writing tools (markers, pencils, and crayons) in assorted sizes with different types of pencil grippers. Provide different-sized writing paper, including poster-sized with lines and no lines; provide correction tape or fluid or stick-on name tags to correct errors on paper. Provide scissors that cut easily left- or right-handed. Use audio recordings that can be transcribed into words and provide dictionaries, thesauri, and magnification tools.	Provide word processing software with spell-checking and grammar correction tools that are developmentally appropriate. Provide different-textured papers with raised lines that can be seen or felt by the writer, and small portable whiteboards. Use magnification software.	Provide a tablet with a writing stylus and software that translates handwritten words into typed text. Provide speech-to-text software that records student voices as text documents. Use word prediction software, speech-to-text software, and enhanced keyboards. **Apps** Instapaper
Reading materials	Provide book-highlighting tape, different sizes of Post-it Notes, and copies of books for all readers in a group.	Provide audiobooks or recordings of books by the teacher or students, and interactive books.	Provide interactive audiobooks with word-by-word highlighting and built-in dictionaries. Use text-to-speech software. **Apps** Audible.com TextGrabber

Digitally Accessible Learning Assignments

Accessibility in education means that every student, using digital or print materials, can access and utilize the learning resources they need to succeed academically. For teachers, achieving accessibility for all students means selecting accessible books, videos, and other learning materials; crafting accessible in-class and outside-of-school learning activities; and using accessible digital technologies in classes and other learning situations.

Accessibility is often thought of in terms of ramps that allow entrance to sidewalks and buildings or assistive devices that allow individuals who need assistance in seeing or hearing to read and write in everyday situations. But, noted technology educator Kel Smith, "accessibility is a concept that can also be applied to *any* condition—physical, mental or cognitive—that prevents equivalent use of a product or service" (2013, p. 4). Digital tools are a key to providing a range of accessibility options and choices for all students.

Students with visual and/or hearing impairments benefit from assistive technologies such as screen readers or closed captions to understand academic material; students learning English as a new language can utilize translation tools with voice pronunciation or websites that provide resources in more than one language; nonfluent readers are aided by visual as well as text-based learning materials; individuals with hearing loss are supported when they receive digital copies of teacher presentations. As a teacher, you must create learning assignments that are accessible to all students in your classes (Smith & Stahl, 2016).

When designing or selecting online resources for students, you can use the Web Content Accessibility Guidelines (WCAG). These are standards for making online content and tools accessible to all web users. Designed to support the experiences of individuals with disabilities, the guidelines help ensure that all web readers can easily

Table 11.2 Classroom Teaching Methods

Instructional Method	Low-Tech	Mid-Tech	High-Tech
Teacher lectures to the whole class.	Teacher uses large charts for ease of viewing information and a machine to amplify voices for ease of hearing information.	Teacher uses presentation software to project information onto a screen. Teacher also uses a classroom amplifier to project voices throughout the entire room.	Teacher uses a personal response system to create an interactive lecture format or self-made vodcasts to provide students with video presentations that are accessible online. **Apps** Socrative
Teacher demonstrates academic concepts.	Teacher uses manipulative materials and provides written directions to accompany oral directions.	Teacher offers digital simulations of manipulative materials to provide a different kind of view or practice.	Teacher makes available video and website resources that simulate or re-create an idea, concept, or phenomenon. **Apps** MIT OpenCourseWare PhET (interactive science simulations) ScreenChomp (screencasting) Educreations (screencasting)
Students manipulate hands-on materials to solve problems.	Students use physical materials for experimentation.	Students use a digital simulation of the same experiment, manipulating variables in a virtual environment.	Students use digital tools to access materials that are unavailable for real-time use in classroom experiments and activities. **Apps** Virtual Manipulatives!
Students learn independently.	Students learn independently at a desk or table.	Students learn independently by completing tasks (e.g., watching a video selected by the teacher) on a computer	Students learn independently using a digital device to look up information in multimodal formats, engage in online design-based activities, and share their work with the teacher for feedback. **Apps** Three Ring
Students learn in small groups	Students share a computer and each assumes a different role in researching, testing, documenting, and presenting conclusions.	Students use collaborative software while researching, testing, documenting, and presenting conclusions.	Students learn collaboratively with classmates and individuals outside the school, including researchers, scholars, and professionals in various fields with whom they connect on social media. **Apps & Tools** Twitter Padlet Flipgrid
Students teach each other in peer-teaching activities.	Students work together to research topics or solve problems presented and submitted on a paper worksheet, and present their findings orally to classmates.	Students work in small groups to create videos that educate their peers about a mathematical process, writing technique, scientific approach, or historical evaluation strategy.	Students provide suggested edits and comments on peers' Google Docs. They engage in ongoing conversations through the commenting feature.

understand online text, images, sounds, and other materials. The standards are part of the W3C Web Accessibility Initiative of the World Wide Web Consortium, an international organization whose host institutions include the Massachusetts Institute of Technology (MIT), ERCIM (in France), Kelo University (Japan), and Beihang University (China). The initial guidelines (WCAG 2.0) were published in 2008; additional standards (WCAG 2.1) appeared in 2018.

WCAG standards are organized around four principles of accessibility. Web content must be:

- *Perceivable:* Users must be able to perceive the information, meaning that closed captions should be embedded in videos, alternative text should be used to describe images, fonts should be able to be enlarged, and transcripts should be provided for audio files.
- *Operable:* Users must be able to operate online interfaces, including ensuring that all materials can be accessed from a keyboard and readers can easily navigate a site.
- *Understandable:* Users must be able to understand information and interfaces, including text that can be read clearly and web pages that function in predictable ways.

- *Robust:* Users must be able to continue to access information even as technologies change so that assistive technologies still function when computers and smartphones upgrade their operating systems.

Teachers can use WCAG as a framework for both online and offline documents and assignments. Materials created in ways that hinder accessibility disadvantage many students, including those with special educational needs, those learning English as a new language, and students not comfortable asking questions.

There are online tools to help ensure that a teacher's instructional materials and assignments are accessible and understandable for students. The WAVE Accessibility Tool developed by the Center for Persons with Disability at Utah State University is a free web service or browser extension for determining the accessibility of online content. Juicy Studio and Readability Formulas have free-to-use tools for assessing the readability of web content. GrackleDocs can be used to examine the accessibility of Google Docs, Slides, and Sheets. Hemingway Editor can assist teachers in improving the readability of text for websites and documents.

> MyLab Education **Self-Check 11.1**

Technology and Diverse Learners

11.2 Discuss how technology differentiates learning of culturally and linguistically diverse students.

Students from different backgrounds and experiences need culturally, ethnically, and linguistically relevant teaching to be successful learners during school and later in their careers. This includes children who live in poverty, who have special educational needs, or are multilingual learners. New and engaging technologies can help teachers design and differentiate instruction to transform classrooms into places of learning and excitement where everyone's ideas and perspectives contribute to the educational process.

Culturally Responsive Teaching in 21st Century Schools

MyLab Education
Video Example 11.2
In this video, two teachers describe how they integrate the cultures and languages of students into the classroom. What are more ways you can affirm the diversity of students as a teacher?

Culturally responsive teaching, as defined by Gloria Ladson-Billings (2009), is the integration of the cultures, histories, backgrounds, and languages of students into all aspects of school environments and classroom activities. Its goal is full and equitable access to education for all students (Research Alliance for New York City Schools, 2016). Culturally responsive teaching has also been called **multicultural education**—a term describing how teachers use learning activities to affirm the diversity of student interests, needs, and talents present in every classroom (Nieto & Bode, 2018; Nieto, 2013).

Culturally responsive teaching and multicultural education honor the realities and diversities of 21st century school populations. Both are based on the principle "that all students—regardless of their gender, social class, and ethnic, racial, or cultural characteristics—should have an equal opportunity to learn in school," and it includes "programs and practices related to educational equity, women, ethnic groups, language minorities, low-income groups, and people with disabilities" (Banks & McGee, 2015, pp. 3, 7).

Culturally responsive educators organize teaching and learning to achieve multiple outcomes simultaneously—providing students information about individuals and groups who are different from them while offering all students opportunities to locate themselves and their histories and cultures within the school curriculum. "America is a nation peopled by the world," observed historian Ronald Takaki (2012, p. 3). For Takaki, an inclusive curriculum is a more accurate curriculum because it confirms that our society has always been diverse and connects the story of the United States to the accomplishments and struggles of all peoples—regardless of sex, gender, race, age, sexual orientation, or socioeconomic status.

Technology differentiates culturally responsive teaching and multicultural learning in the following ways.

REVEALING UNKNOWN HISTORIES AND UNTOLD STORIES   Online resources enable teachers to integrate the unknown histories and untold stories of diverse peoples and cultures into every subject area. Unknown histories and untold stories are those individuals, groups, and events that have been largely neglected or totally omitted from mainstream textbooks and school system–purchased curriculum materials. Students become more interested in and are more likely to embrace the study of history, language arts, math, and science when the experiences of diverse people are integrated into the larger historical narrative (Loewen, 2018, 2009; Takaki, 2012). To help tell these stories, Beacon Press has published *An African American and Latinx History of the United States* (Ortiz, 2018); *An Indigenous People's History of the United States* (Dunbar-Ortiz, 2014); *A Disability History of the United States* (Nielsen, 2012); and *A Queer History of the United States* (Bronski, 2011). Students can read about pioneering achievements of women scientists and mathematicians in *Power in Numbers: The Rebel Women of Mathematics* (Williams, 2018); *Hidden Figures: The American Dream and the Untold Story of the Black Women Mathematicians Who Helped Win the Space Race* (Shetterly, 2016); *Code Girls: The Untold Story of the American Women Code Breakers of World War II* (Mundy, 2017); and *Rise of the Rocket Girls: The Women Who Propelled Us, from Missiles to the Moon and Mars* (Holt, 2016). Book-length multicultural histories and herstories offer insights about the contributions and leadership of unheralded individuals in different fields. In addition, there are interactive websites, online videos, and web-based primary source materials that can bring to the forefront the stories of individuals and groups whose names are rarely—or never—included in traditional textbooks and mandated curriculum frameworks. When teachers integrate online materials about diverse peoples into classroom instruction, students gain an inclusive view of the past, the present, and their own future place in life and society.

SUPPORTING CULTURALLY RESPONSIVE CURRICULUM AND INSTRUCTION   Students of all ages benefit when they can access multiculturally-themed digital content that links academic material to the issues and concerns they are experiencing in their daily lives. Technology also allows students to connect with wider communities of individuals and groups online. The work of remembering information, applying formulas, and writing essays is made more meaningful when those activities connect to real-world situations and people. This is very important for diverse students, many of whom struggle in school when they do not find curricular connections between what they are learning and what they are experiencing in their families and communities. Making teaching and learning culturally relevant requires changing what is taught and how it is taught. As the civil rights pioneer and mathematics reform educator Dr. Robert P. Moses (2002) pointed out nearly two decades ago, students have a greater chance of achieving academic success when math assignments are embedded in situations they are familiar with (calculating the distance between subway stops to learn algebra concepts, for example) than when answering worksheet problems that have no relationship to their daily experiences.

EXPANDING TEACHING METHODS AND APPROACHES   In many schools, diverse students face the stress of feeling isolated from other students in the building. These separations are reinforced when teaching methods emphasize whole-class or large-group instruction along with competitively graded assignments. Without small-group learning opportunities or project-based activities, students do not get to know each other in ways that are different from their daily peer group experiences. When school cultures do little to promote cross-cultural understandings, some students find themselves on their own, without a group affiliation, struggling with academic work or feeling alienated from classmates. In her classic book *"Why Are All the Black Kids Sitting Together in the Cafeteria?" and Other Conversations About Race*, psychologist Beverly Daniel Tatum

(2003) found students seeking out members of their own ethnicity, race, or gender to establish and maintain a sense of personal identity. Technology helps teachers implement teaching and learning activities in which students work together across cultural, racial, language, and gender boundaries on common projects and, in so doing, promote new understandings and images of each other. Creating class websites and blogs, collaborating in teams with student participation systems, and doing research and projects together using laptops or tablets are examples of how changing teaching methods can promote mutual respect while honoring differences and diversities among students.

CONNECTING CLASSROOMS WITH COMMUNITIES AND CULTURES   Schools become separated from the broader society around them by teaching a narrow curriculum on a tight schedule. Under these conditions, teachers and students tend to address the wider communities and cultures only on specific occasions—for example, during Black History, Hispanic Heritage, Asian Pacific American Heritage, or Native American Heritage Month. Yet students learn about people and cultures when schools celebrate the achievements and struggles of culturally different students and families throughout the year and across the curriculum as teachers expand learning beyond the walls of the school to include students and families locally, nationally, and internationally. Technology invites multicultural learning when students access newspapers and online news feeds from around the world, take virtual field trips to international locations, translate materials from one language to another, and communicate with teachers, students, and schools in other places (e.g., Mystery Skype, ePals, global collaboration projects). Cultures, languages, and daily activities can become features of curriculum integrated throughout the year and are better understood when technology assists everyone's learning.

Using Technology with Linguistically Diverse Learners

The United States is a multilingual as well as a multicultural nation. There are at least 350 different languages spoken in U.S. homes (U.S. Census Bureau, 2015). In the nation's major metropolitan areas, people speak well over 100 languages in their homes (see Figure 11.1). Suburban and rural areas are also experiencing increasing language diversity. In addition, there are 150 different Native North American languages spoken throughout the country. The result is that more and more K–12 school classrooms are becoming **superdiverse** settings where five or more languages are spoken (Baker & Paez, 2018).

The following technologies support education for students in diverse and superdiverse classrooms, including students learning English as a new language as well as native English speakers who are studying world languages. In addition, you can learn about language learning with online dictionaries in Tech Tool 11.1.

SPELLING, PRONUNCIATION, AND GRAMMAR APPS   Tools for all ages, these apps provide word meanings and spellings for students speaking English as a new language, students with hearing impairments, non-fluent readers, and English speakers who are learning another language. When mobile devices are used by readers and writers, they can locate correct spellings, listen to words spoken aloud, and check the accuracy of their spelling independently. Headphones and volume controls let students use these tools without disturbing others. Students can see and hear words they may not know or be able to pronounce correctly.

Spelling and pronunciation apps convert spoken words into correctly spelled text. They can also convert printed text into audio versions of the spelled word so that readers and writers can hear how to pronounce words. Multiple companies have developed **handheld speller and dictionary** tools—language resources for elementary, middle and high school students and for teachers who want a professional reference tool—including Easy Spelling Aid, ProWritingAid, Grammarly, and Merriam-Webster Word Central.

Figure 11.1. Number of Languages Spoken in the 15 Largest Metro Areas

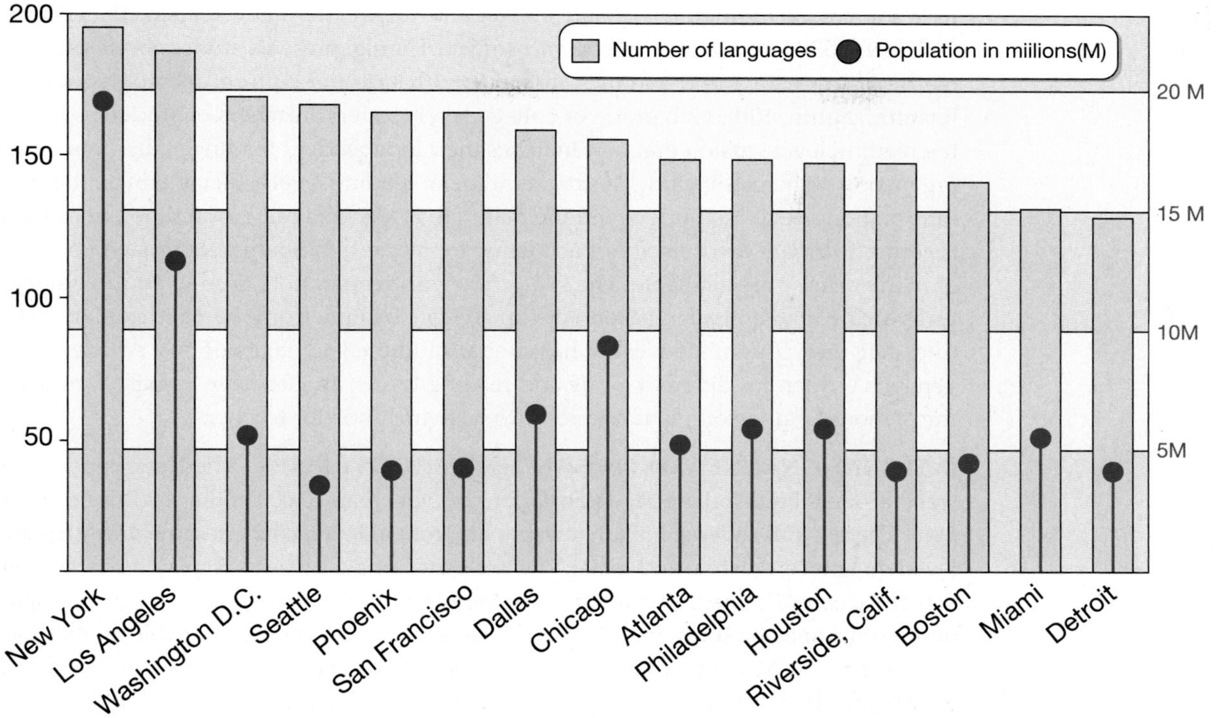

Digital Dialog 11.2

Online dictionaries and translation apps are becoming more commonly used by teens and adults in their daily lives. Many educators and students view these technologies as readily available teaching resources, increasing users' knowledge with each experience, making them indispensable learning tools. As you reflect about your own experiences with online dictionaries and translation apps, comment and connect online about the following questions:

- Do you use online dictionaries or translation apps for your learning? Would you have gained knowledge as quickly or as easily without access to them?
- How might online dictionaries or translation apps support achievement for students with different learning needs, as well as regular education students? How do these tools enable teachers to differentiate instruction for learners?
- What are the arguments for and against students using online dictionaries or translation apps when taking tests and quizzes? How would you explain what these tools might enable students to do academically?

MULTILINGUAL WEB RESOURCES   Increasing numbers of websites provide content and materials in multiple languages. Wikipedia, for example, has articles in nearly 300 languages, although the largest volume of material is in English, German, French, and Dutch. Simple English Wikipedia offers resources from Wikipedia that are adapted to students who are still developing fluency as readers and writers. The mathematics site National Library of Virtual Manipulatives (NLVM) presents games and instructions in English, Spanish, French, and Chinese; Khan Academy's resources are available in more than 30 languages, including English, Spanish, French, and Brazilian Portuguese. Museums, historical associations, governmental agencies, and other organizations now have multilingual content as a way of broadening access to information for more readers and listeners. Easy Spelling Aid, mentioned in the spelling and dictionary apps, also translates into many languages.

ONLINE READING RESOURCES   More and more online sites are offering students the option to access texts at different reading levels. Newsela draws content from multiple sources, including *The Washington Post* and *The Guardian* newspapers, the History Channel, PBS NewsHour, and the Smithsonian. The site presents stories about science/math, government and economics, money, health, arts and culture, and sports written for fifth, eighth, 10th, 12th grade or college level readers. Teachers or students choose the reading level version that best matches their independent reading skills. Newsela's organizing principles include: 1) articles at lower reading levels still contain all the core information needed to understand the material; 2) teachers can group different articles together to create text sets about academic topics; and 3) Spanish-language versions of many articles are available. The site is free with registration, though additional features are available in a fee-based version. Tween Tribune from the Smithsonian Institute, delivered free online weekly, has similar multiple language options: Articles have versions written for different grade and reading levels; articles have Spanish language translations; and lesson plans and resources are included for teachers.

INTERNATIONAL NEWSPAPERS AND INTERACTIVE MAPS   The Newspaper Map website offers English-language translations of more than 10,000 of the world's newspapers. There is full coverage of all newspapers from a dozen countries, including Spain, Sweden, France, Austria, and Israel. The site uses Google Maps to display its choices on a interactive world map. Zoom out to see the entire world or zoom in to locate newspapers from a specific continent or region. Newspaper Map is also available as a smartphone app. The Modern Language Association (MLA) offers another inviting resource, an interactive online map of languages spoken in the United States. Using census data to display the locations and the number of speakers of more than 300 languages, this map zooms in from an entire country or region to a state, local community, or ZIP code to view languages spoken there. The number of college and university students speaking languages other than English is also available at this site.

ENGLISH LANGUAGE WORD ORIGINS   Investigating the origins of words is easy with informative online resources. The United States, a multilingual society from its founding, constantly adds words from diverse cultures and languages into common language use. Wikipedia maintains an ongoing list of "loanwords" or "borrowings"—a source of the origins of English vocabulary to consult and discuss. You can learn more from Philip P. Durkin's book *Borrowed Words: A History of Loanwords in English* (2014). An interactive section of the Children's University of Manchester (England) website features a world languages map with students speaking their home languages along with word origin games and linguistic information. Publishers are continually adding new words to their online and paper dictionaries—850 new words were added to the Merriam-Webster dictionary in 2018 alone. Words continue to come not only from popular culture ("welp," meaning disappointment; "binge-watch," meaning viewing multiple episodes of a show in succession), but from people and places from around the world, a process Merriam-Webster refers to as "wanderwort" from the German words meaning "wander" and "word." Teachers and students can follow the evolution of words entering the dictionary by searching for "new words added to the dictionary" and then tracing their origins in different cultures and languages.

DUAL LANGUAGE PICTURE BOOKS AND YOUNG ADULT LITERATURE   Book publishers are making more materials available to young readers in different languages, issuing the same story in side-by-side languages. Available on Kindle and other e-reading devices, there are classic picture books in bilingual formats such as Eric Carle's *The Very Hungry Caterpillar/La oruga muy hambrienta* or Margaret Wise Brown's *Goodnight Moon/Buenas Noches, Luna,* as well as newer fiction, nonfiction, and poetry titles for elementary, middle, and high school readers. There are listings of bilingual children's books in the publication *School Library Journal.* Also search for dual language children's books at the social bookmarking site *Goodreads.*

Figure 11.2 Scientific Revolution Word Cloud

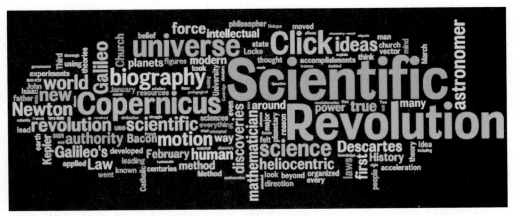

SOURCE: Reprinted by permission of Allison Evans.

WORD CLOUDS Generated by software programs that count the words most frequently used in a document and display them in a nonlinear pictorial image, **word clouds** present written text in a varied and surprising format. Figure 11.2 is a word cloud from a teacher's webpage about the Scientific Revolution in world history with the most frequently used terms appearing in the larger size fonts—prepositions, conjunctions, and other small words are omitted. Some educators dismiss word clouds as overly simplistic ways to present text or summarize data, contending that they could not substitute for in-depth analyses of topics. However, when used as entry points, discussion openers, or graphic organizers, word clouds are effective teaching strategies for both fluent and less fluent readers. A cloud's presentation is an outline of content. Students can compare different documents for common themes and main concepts—before, during, or after reading or listening to a text. Words can be displayed horizontally or vertically, and the number of words displayed can be adjusted from just one to five, 10, or the maximum of 300. Students can word cloud the text of papers or stories they have written, changing the color and font of their document to see it in different shapes and sizes. Wordle is one of the most popular word cloud choices, but there are many other options. Tagxedo creates elaborate word cloud patterns in the shapes of animals, famous people, or geographic maps. ABCya! is a simplified cloud maker. Word Sift links a word in a text to an interactive thesaurus with photos and emojis, and makes a word cloud of the text.

DIGITAL TRANSLATORS Online tools or apps for converting words and phrases from one language to another are known as **digital translators**. Google Translate, with two-way translations of more than 100 world languages and available as a free website and smartphone or tablet app, is now the most widely used online language translation tool—it translates 100 billion words a day. Translations of words, sentences, and webpages are easy and quick to obtain. Widely spoken languages—English, Spanish, Chinese, French, Arabic, and Japanese—are available along with many others, including Swahili, Haitian Creole, Latin, and Russian. Newly added languages are Kurdish, Hawaiian, Samoan, and Xhosa. Google envisions its site as a "universal translator," and according to one reviewer, "Google Translate versions sounded more fluid and natural than the translations in online phrasebooks" (Brown, 2011).

Online translators make notes, assignments, and written materials in English available in other languages—a necessary consideration with speakers of multiple languages in a class. Many teachers use translation tools as a place to begin conversations with students about what they are reading and writing. Translators help identify unfamiliar English words and academic concepts and provide their definitions and pronunciations. Teachers can then expand on how new words and concepts are being used within the context of daily learning activities. Teachers can also create translated versions of materials they are sending home to families whose first language is not English.

More teacher- and student-friendly translation tools include:

- Presentation Translator from Microsoft provides live, subtitled captions for PowerPoint presentations. As a teacher presents information, the program's translation function displays subtitles in more than 60 different languages. Students can receive the presentation on their smartphone, tablet, or computer.
- iTranslate Voice 2 lets a student or teacher say a word, phrase, or sentence and hear its translation in more than 40 languages. The original program, iTranslate, has 80 languages and composes text translations without a voice option.
- Sound of Text uses the text-to-speech engine from Google Translate to enable users to type 100 characters and hear the text read in dozens of languages. Users can download the audio file so they can listen multiple times to improve their use of the language.
- iVoice converts spoken words into different languages.
- Word Lens Translator receives a picture of a word or phrase from your phone or tablet camera and provides an instant translation.
- Skype Translator makes it possible for English and Spanish speakers to converse in one language and hear audio and view text translated into the other language. It also enables instant message translations in 40 languages.
- The Translate Me app converts more than 60 languages and supports SMS text messaging translation.
- Tap toTranslate allows you to embed a pop-up window in your browser so that when you translate a word or paragraph, you stay on one page and see both languages.
- Duolingo, a popular app for students and adults, embeds vocabulary and language lessons in self-paced levels of a game-like structure of earning points and regularly taking verbal quizzes to assess what vocabulary you have learned.

Tech Tool 11.1

Language Learning with Interactive Online Dictionaries

A schoolteacher, Samuel Johnson Jr. (no relation to the British lexicographer Samuel Johnson), compiled the first American dictionary in 1798, which was followed in 1806 by Noah Webster's celebrated *A Compendious Dictionary for the English Language*. Two Springfield, Massachusetts, booksellers, George and Charles Merriam, secured the rights to Webster's *An American Dictionary of the English Language* in 1843. Their company, now known as Merriam-Webster, has been publishing dictionaries ever since.

Many students and teachers think of dictionaries as paper-based resources, as they have been for more than 200 years, but online dictionaries and dictionary apps are powerful technologies for learning. Visual dictionaries, for example, can be effective tools for language learning because they offer students more than one way to understand words and their meanings. Instead of just reading a text-based definition of a word, visual tools provide a multimodal learning experience in which students can connect pictures and other images with the written word.

Here are several interactive online dictionaries that are invaluable resources for students and teachers:

- Visuwords, available free online, generates word clouds of terms related to a main term. Search for "education," and the site provides visual links to "learning," "activity," "school," "lesson," and "homework," to name just some of the connected terms.
- Graph Words, another free online program, displays words in graphical word clouds with different explanations of parts of speech and word origins.
- Thinkmap Visual Thesaurus provides graphical word clouds, games, and vocabulary lists. The thesaurus offers six languages.
- Wordsmyth also provides free resources. Both sites limit use without a paid subscription but offer enhanced features for a small fee.
- Word Hippo, available as a website or an app, is a free online thesaurus offering synonyms, antonyms, rhymes, definitions, pronunciations, sentences and translations.

Figure 11.3 Signing Life Dictionary

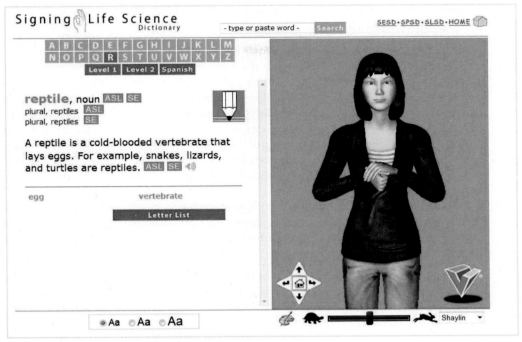

SOURCE: Image courtesy of Signing Math & Science: TERC, Inc., 2012.

The accuracy of digital translations has improved dramatically. The newest version of Google Translate has achieved high levels of accuracy for some languages. Still, understanding words and their meanings is often dependent on the social context of their use—settings and situations that no smart machine can reproduce. To generate clear understandings between teachers and students and families and schools, it is important to have human speakers facilitating educational communications.

TERC, a Massachusetts-based technology research company, has developed animated, illustrated, and interactive 3-D signing dictionary websites and signing apps for deaf and hard of hearing students (see Figure 11.3). Math and science dictionaries and pictionaries in American Sign Language (ASL) or Signed English (SE) help students learn through printed text and the signing of an on-screen avatar. There are earth science, life science, and physical science versions for upper-grade students.

Spell checking is a resource for everyone; no one knows the standard spelling of every word we speak and write. Writers who find spelling a difficult or frustrating experience can stop feeling inadequate as learners. If words are spelled incorrectly, online interactive dictionaries offer a list of possible standard spellings and, with a voice capacity, read them aloud for easy identification. Instead of stopping to change spelling while composing drafts, writers can concentrate on expressing ideas and then checking spelling afterward with the machine. Writing proceeds as a process—students put ideas on paper in a flow of written self-expression, then revise the ideas to improve reader understanding, and finally edit the piece by spelling words conventionally and adding appropriate punctuation.

> **MyLab Education Application Exercise 11.2:**
> Locating Vocabulary Words Using Online Dictionaries
>
> **MyLab Education Self-Check 11.2**

Uses of Assistive Technologies

11.3 Explain how assistive technologies increase opportunities for successful student learning.

Assistive technologies (AT) enable teachers to differentiate instruction and pursue universal design for learning. Whether it's a classroom timer, a simple pencil grip, a pair of non-prescription reading glasses, or a digital screen reader, an assistive technology is any physical item, piece of equipment, software program, or learning system that is used to maintain or improve the functional capabilities of persons with disabilities. These tools make it possible for individuals to do things they might otherwise not be able to do—large keys on a computer keyboard assist individuals with reduced hand functions, while software that reads text aloud assists individuals with reduced vision. The goal of assistive technologies is to maximize learning while minimizing barriers to success.

Matching assistive technologies with student needs is often done by a team of special education teachers, doctors, speech-language pathologists and occupational therapists, and special education coordinators. Assistive technologies are important learning resources for the following reasons:

- Assistive technologies translate text and communicate words and data to individuals with hearing, sight, mobility, or cognitive challenges. An interactive e-book can help develop a child's reading skills and reinforce the learning of key concepts. There are tools to support a wide range of learning needs, including hardware, software, and adaptive devices like screen magnification or specialized keyboards.
- Widely viewed as tools to support students with disabilities, assistive technologies create enhanced learning opportunities for all students. A single tool can produce multiple results; it is not a stand-alone device that a teacher uses specifically with one or two students. Text-to-speech software allows webpages to be read aloud, calculators speak numbers as well as perform calculations, and apps convert cursive writing or spoken words into printed text. These and many other assistive technologies facilitate learning activities for all students at all grade levels.

Matching Learners and Technologies

How do teachers decide which assistive technologies will optimally assist individual learners? The question recognizes that students learn at different rates as members of a classroom group. Teachers are constantly adjusting the pace of instruction to help individuals learn while advancing the curriculum for the classroom group. If too much time is spent on individual needs, progress for a larger group of students may be slowed. If the larger group moves on to the next academic topic, some individuals may lag behind, missing what they need to understand.

One framework for pairing students with technology devices is the **SETT** framework created by teacher and special educator Dr. Joy Smiley Zabala. SETT is an acronym for Students, Environments, Tasks, and Tools. The SETT framework focuses on "a shared understanding of the student, the customary environments in which the student spends time, and the tasks that are required for the student to be able to do or learn to do to be an active participant in the teaching/learning processes that lead to educational success" (Smiley Zabala, 2015). Find out more about this framework at Reading Rockets, a national public media initiative offering resources and information about reading, readingrockets.org.

You can learn how school districts can assess assistive technologies for students from the Quality Indicators for Assistive Technology (QIAT) Community, a national group of educators who study how to put AT tools into action. Their work has resulted in a popular list of applicable QIAT services that may be helpful in selecting AT tools for your classroom.

Speech-to-Text Software and Apps

Speech-to-text software and apps (also known as *speech recognition* or *voice to text*) display a person's spoken words as written text on a screen. Initially designed for use by sight-impaired individuals, students with fine motor disabilities that impede writing by hand or typing on a keyboard, and individuals with dyslexia who do not want to be stopped in their creative process by seeing misspellings that need changing, speech-to-text tools are now used by anyone who would rather speak than write or type their ideas.

Mobile technology includes a growing number of speech-to-text options, some free and others available for a fee. Dragon Dictation is a popular smartphone or tablet app. Siri, a voice recognition program available on iPhones and iPads, includes a dictation function that converts spoken words into text; Google Assistant provides similar functions for Android, BlackBerry, and Windows mobile devices. Google Docs has dictation capabilities. You can learn about these and other free assistive technologies from the website of the National Center for Learning Disabilities.

More advanced speech recognition programs like Dragon Naturally Speaking require users to "train the system" by speaking into a computer's microphone to make it recognize one or more primary voices. The process for training the software is accomplished in a few minutes as the speaker reads a single paragraph. The software "learns" to recognize an individual's speech patterns and tonal nuances. Once the training is completed, the software will transcribe spoken words into documents to be edited using the editorial features and options found in word processing software programs.

For students who are unwilling to write or who feel unsuccessful as writers, speech recognition software offers a new way to record their thoughts, allowing them to get their stories and conversations on paper without the anxiety of writing with a handheld implement or typing on a keyboard. For writers of all ages, conversations can become stories and poems, and the software demonstrates this in real time. Imagine the surprise of a student wearing a headset who speaks into a microphone the first time and sees a screen fill with the spoken words. The experience can be astonishing and inspiring for a reluctant writer.

The process of transferring spoken words to written text always requires revising and editing by a student and teacher, even with speech-to-text tools. After the dictation is complete, the teacher will read the student's text aloud with the student or listen to the student read it. Rereading and discussing together the software-captured version produces a revised, more conventional version of the story.

With speech recognition programs, an author's misuse of a word or the software's misinterpretation of what a speaker has said may confuse the meaning of the text. One young boy who continually says "yeah" when he means "yes" saw the software printing "yeah" on the page; the speech pattern was visible to him, prompting an edit to the text. He said "yes," and the machine transcribed the word he really wanted on the page. The software is a nonjudgmental proofreader, showing in print exactly what was said, giving instant feedback as a prompt for revising the text so it reads the way the writer wants it to read.

Word prediction tools are another type of speech-to-text technology. They act as a spelling and writing coach for young writers. The software predicts what the writer may be intending to write next and offers multiple options as the writer types. For example, type the letter *s,* and the program displays words from a list of frequently typed words beginning with *s.* Like speech recognition software, word prediction programs learn individual word usage habits. After someone types *good,* the word *morning* may automatically appear because so many writers type *good morning* in their e-mails. Or following the word *happy,* the word *birthday* may pop up as the first choice to enter to the text.

Text-to-Speech Software and Apps

Text-to-speech software and apps (also known as *text reading*) let students hear written text read aloud. These software programs are available in many versions, from simple text speech readers with few options to customized reading packages that offer selections of voices by gender or with different cadences. Software lets users choose the pace of words read aloud per minute and highlights the text as the computerized voice reads it aloud. For some learners, this highlighting feature simulates an adult physically pointing to the individual words and letters in the text. There are three basic types of text-to-speech tools. The web browser Firefox includes text-to-speech and dictionary add-ons, while users with e-mail accounts from Gmail can access a text-to-speech reader.

- **Screen readers** act as a translator of the visual page, supporting those who have "low vision" or "vision loss" in the reading of computer screens. The software reads the text and notifies the user of the frames and boundaries that are located on the screen. JAWS, a screen reader for Windows machines, is available in multiple languages, including English, Spanish, French, German, Portuguese, and Italian. VoiceOver from Apple, a standard accessibility feature on iPads and iPhones, supports learning for blind and sight-impaired students. Google Chrome's accessibility features include screen reading. TalkBack is an open-source screen reader for Android machines. NaturalReader text-to-speech reader can translate almost any printed or digital document into spoken word. All audio files are adjustable (spoken word rate and vocal tone) and are portable and translatable to multiple digital devices. Kurzweil 3000 software will read any text on a computer screen in 31 different voices; 18 languages and dialects, reading rate modification, and text magnification are also part of this ever-expanding software package. Screen magnification readers can change the size of the words and pictures on a computer screen and or graphics on the screen. SuperNova Magnifier by Dolphin Computer Access enlarges text on the computer screen, along with zoom in and zoom out features. You can learn more about screen readers from the American Foundation for the Blind website.

- **Optical character recognition and reading (OCR) tools** enable text to be read and translated into multiple modes on computers, phones, and tablets. Kurzweil 3000 for Windows and Mac is the leading commercial program; Prizmo is a powerful app that combines character recognition, text to speech, and translation in one program, with 35 voices and 10 languages. Scanning text into software that displays it on-screen supports learning English as a new language as well as learners' special needs. Pages from a favorite book or from a reading assigned for a class can be scanned and transferred into a readable document. OCR technology converts conventional text into a "living book" by adding new dimensions of flexible use. Readers can parse a text into multiple interactive versions that can be selected and highlighted, creating a personally customized version of the original document.

Interactive Whiteboards for Classroom Learning

An **interactive whiteboard** can serve as a powerful UDL technology when teachers use it to differentiate the way students experience learning in a classroom. When connected to a computer or tablet, a whiteboard becomes a large, interactive screen that can be manipulated by a finger, pen, or other touch device. Students and teachers alike become actively involved as viewers and/or presenters of on-screen material.

The whiteboard's interactivity attracts learners of all ages and generates multiple grouping formats: whole class, pairs, trios, or students working by themselves with the technology. For any size learning group, showing a slide or video presentation, using an educational website, accessing a web-based learning game, or letting students design with 2-D or 3-D opportunities, whoever is involved has a heightened learning experience with this tool.

While in use for curriculum learning, a teacher or a student can write on or add notes or symbols directly to the screen while learning happens in real time. Ideas and comments of students can be noted to include individual and group contributions in class content. These annotated pages can be saved to a teacher's computer or tablet and distributed via a website or Twitter account.

MyLab Education
Video Example 11.3
In this video, a teacher describes how she differentiates teaching and learning in the classroom. What are more ways you can invite students to participate with a smartboard for learning?

Interactive whiteboards provide flexible formats for activating multiple intelligences of learners, identified by psychologist Howard Gardner (2011b). Viewing large-size material on a whiteboard focuses on visual/spatial intelligence, hearing material read aloud supports linguistic intelligence, and being able to manipulate images and solve problems with one's own fingers and hands engages students' bodily kinesthetic and logical-mathematical intelligences. Adding music, rhythm, and sound stimulates musical intelligence, while letting students work in groups at the whiteboard uses interpersonal intelligence and intrapersonal skills.

Here are two examples of whiteboard use to enliven learning. While a high school history class does a read-aloud of the text of the Declaration of Independence, the teacher asks for modern-day language translations of unfamiliar words, phrases, and concepts. Students write these above the original words displayed on the whiteboard screen to save for future reference and for enhancing students' understanding of the importance of this nation's founding documents.

In an elementary classroom, a teacher invites students to color on the interactive whiteboard as they discover number patterns using a hundreds grid. Individual students go to the whiteboard to have a turn with the interactive grid, using it to see different number operation patterns for addition, subtraction, multiplication, and division. The patterns are then photographed with a smartphone to print and display. While every student is waiting for a turn, the teacher has achieved anticipation, focus, practice, and the opportunity to compare/contrast what students do differently from each other.

Apps such as Doceri and AirServer let you move around the classroom with your tablet connected wirelessly to a whiteboard, projector, or HDTV. One high school teacher candidate described to us how with this app she has changed the learning dynamics in the room: "I can navigate through slides and display them from anywhere in the room, and students can add to my presentation by writing and drawing on the tablet as well." You will find more information about using interactive whiteboards at the Whiteboard Blog organized by British science teacher, certified technology trainer, and writer, Danny Nicholson.

MyLab Education Self-Check 11.3

Young Writers and Technology

11.4 Analyze the roles for technology in a writing process for young writers.

Nearly two decades ago, the National Writing Project declared that writing was education's "neglected R," an essential part of the school curriculum that was being given less attention by teachers and administrators while schools emphasized improving reading and math skills across grade levels (National Commission on Writing in America's Schools and Colleges, 2003). Still today, students spend relatively little time on writing throughout the early grades, and many high school students are rarely asked to write a paper longer than three or four pages. Yet, as a group of researchers noted: "Writing has never been more important in the digital age," especially in multimedia and digital environments where "words are regularly joined with images and voices" (National Writing Project, DeVoss, et al., 2010).

Though writing is and will always be a creative intellectual process, it is far too often taught as memorizing, editing, and manipulating words with an emphasis on using standard spelling and correct conventions (National Writing Project & Nagin, 2006). At every grade level, students say they do not enjoy writing in school, for one or more of the following reasons.

- *Pressure.* For children in kindergarten through sixth grade, the physical demands of forming letters correctly in print or cursive can make writing intensely laborious. Students of all ages may also feel pressure to spell words correctly and use punctuation, grammar, and other conventions of written language appropriately, further diminishing any sense of enjoyment from writing creatively and confidently.

- *Lack of confidence.* There are writers, young and old, who are stymied by the terror of the blank page—a feeling of not knowing what to write—that begins in the early grades and continues on through middle and high school. It is very difficult for anyone to write when they do not feel confident in their ability.

- *Lack of joy.* Many students fail to discover enjoyment of and satisfaction from expressing ideas through written language. Instead, they associate writing with worksheets devoted to practicing grammar and punctuation or with research reports for teacher-assigned topics.

- *Misdirected self-evaluation.* Some students measure their proficiency as writers on mechanics alone, in how they form letters, how much they know about writing conventions, and how well they spell, not by their ideas or the value of what they might say. "You will not like my writing," one first-grader told us at an after-school writing workshop. "It is too messy." This child equated writing with neatness, and his fine motor control skills prevented him from producing neatly arranged text on a page. His own creativity in expressing ideas was not his definition of what writing is all about because that was not the definition conveyed to him by adults.

- *Lack of patience and interest.* Other students lack the patience, interest, or calmness to quietly sit and write about assigned topics. They want to be up and moving around, engaged in conversation with other students, sometimes to the distraction of the teacher and the students around them.

- *Ideas about being smart.* Still others equate ease and enjoyment of writing with being smart in school. Because they do not find writing pleasant or easy to do, they conclude they are not smart, setting in motion a downward cycle of negative feelings about being a writer and a learner that blocks confidence and creativity.

To address these concerns, many teachers seek to "fit" the process of writing and the needs of individual students—that is, to generate the most flexible possible combination of adult and technological supports to promote a sense of confidence and engagement with written language for each writer, youngest to oldest.

We call this flexible match between writing and the needs of individual writers in K–12 schools a **writing process for young writers**, a term derived from a teaching approach known as *process writing*. A writing process for young writers is the effort to inspire students to express their ideas creatively while learning how and when to use the conventions of written language (Edwards, Maloy, & Trust, 2019; Edwards, et al., 2003). In this approach, the Internet, word processing and presentation software, handheld devices, and writing-related apps provide ongoing and engaging support to children, from initial brainstorming of ideas to final publishing of written work. These technologies offer ways for teachers and students to find the combination of tools that best supports each individual student's growth and development as a writer.

Process Approaches to Writing

Process writing has been at the center of writing instruction in schools for more than 30 years. Practiced by professional and student writers of all ages, a **writing process** involves the following stages:

- *Prewriting/brainstorming.* The writer begins by free-writing, conversing with others, listening to read-alouds, webbing ideas to connect or categorize information, or engaging in other activities that serve as catalysts for generating ideas and for structuring the text.

- *Drafting.* The writer focuses on creating a draft of writing, allowing ideas to flow forth without stopping or making large changes to the text. The goal is to write whatever comes to mind and see where the ideas take the writer. While writers often talk in terms of "first draft," the process of drafting ideas may go on through many brainstorming sessions and several written copies.

- *Revising.* The writer revisits, reviews, and changes the writing to create clarity, increase interest, and support the smooth flow of ideas. Writers do not work alone in this pursuit; through questions and suggestions, a teacher or other writers become participants in the process of making writing clearer and more interesting to readers. Feedback from readers and listeners is used to guide changes that produce a final draft with improved communication between the writer and the intended audience.

- *Editing.* The writer makes additions and deletions or changes that clarify the meaning of the text. Standard punctuation and spelling are added to make reading the writing easier, which is why these conventions exist. To ensure that editing happens, a teacher knowledgeable in the rules of printed text needs to be an editor-in-chief, providing the expertise and support to assist young writers to add conventions without endless labor or confusion.

- *Publishing.* The writer shares a complete, but not necessarily completed, text using many different formats, from a read-aloud to a performance to a display of the writing in a public place, with the goal of making the writing available for audiences to read and to hear.

Brainstorming, drafting, revising, editing, and publishing interconnect to produce a process of writing. Writers generate ideas, compose initial versions, read and change their material, and share what they have done with readers and listeners. Throughout, the writer is not alone, but in conversation with other people (teachers and other students) who offer new perspectives, thoughtful comments, and appreciative support. The essence of the process is the flow of ideas that dynamically connect each element to the others.

If any of the elements of the writing process are missing, shortchanged, or hurried, then the writer and the writing does not realize its full potential. Pushing writers to write before they are have talked about, thought about, and found an idea; making the editing process precede the revising of a text; and rushing from first draft to publication create a sense of writing as a race to the finish line with the goal of getting something done as quickly as possible rather than a process of communicating something meaningful the writer wants to say.

Neglecting the audience for the writing is similarly counterproductive. Writers need readers to comment on their drafts in order to revise them, and they need to receive new responses from readers as the work evolves. In this way everyone becomes a writer, always working through part of the process. Otherwise writing is viewed as a singular activity that only a special few have the talent and mental resolve to do well, instead of a process of communicating ideas that everyone can enjoy doing.

MyLab Education
Video Example 11.4
In this video, you will see how a teacher supports young writers as they begin brainstorming personal biography poems. What elements of the writing process do you see in action?

Technology Throughout the Writing Process

Using technology, teachers can support students by differentiating responses as writers move from initial brainstorming to completed publication. Technology gives teachers multiple ways to "fit" the writing process to young writers (see Table 11.3). Additional technology resources for supporting writing by students can be found in two companion websites for the book *Kids Have All the Write Stuff: Revised and Updated for a Digital Age* (Edwards, Maloy, & Trust, 2019). Both are free online. https://sites.google.com/view/writestuff/home

Teachers have many options to engage and sustain writing without technology, but with technology, teachers can differentiate instruction to better address the needs of individual writers. This chapter's In Practice shows how a teacher uses apps as part of the writing process.

The key to unlocking a writing process for young writers is convincing students that they are writers right now. When students believe that their ideas matter—to themselves and to others—they will become ready written communicators, willing to take risks and use time to put words on paper, fingers on keyboards, or voices on podcasts. They will know that they have something to say, revise, reflect on, and claim as their own.

Inspiring and energizing young writers involves supporting the stages of the writing process so students proceed at their own pace to accomplish learning goals. Technology shifts the focus of learning from individualization to instant/immediate feedback or computer-generated teaching (e.g., the computer is teaching a student how to write and offering suggestions like a classroom teacher would do).

Artificial Intelligence (AI) is an example of a technology that is transforming the way teachers and students write in online environments. Google Smart Autofill inserts text into written documents that the computer has "learned" based on how a writer uses words. When Robert sent a draft of this paragraph to co-authors Torrey and Sharon, the autofill function inserted the phrase *"What changes would you recommend?"* directly into the e-mail. After setting up Google Smart Autofill on a personal Gmail account, a writer can just hit the tab, and text will be pasted into the document.

Table 11.3 Technology in a Writing Process for Young Writers

Writing Process	Teacher Role	Without Technology	With Technology
Prewriting/brainstorming	Teachers use openers to show children the creative possibilities of different genres and forms of writing.	Teacher openers consist of: Read-alouds of children's literature Showing examples of children's writing on overhead projectors Playing story-writing and storytelling games Discussing genres and forms	Technology openers include: Interactive storybooks, storybook apps, web materials, or audio and videotapes Microphones or sound systems for read-alouds by individuals or groups Digital projectors to make web materials, as well as children's own writing, visible to an entire class in a large-group setting Author websites with stories, interviews, and writing games **Apps** Bamboo Paper Voice Recorder Chapters—Notebooks for Writing
Drafting	Teachers provide individualized assistance for students as they write, helping create a draft in which ideas flow forth without editing of the text and from which students produce multiple drafts of their writing.	Teachers support children's writing by: Acting as scribes Sharing the pencil as co-writers and co-illustrators Finding pleasant places for children to write Responding in supportive, engaging ways to questions about spelling, punctuation, and other conventions of written language	Technology supports include: Word processing and drawing programs for generating drafts that include written words, pictures, and illustrations that can be created by students or students and teachers together Text-to-speech software, digital pens, tape recorders, and camcorders to generate drafts of ideas Brainstorming and visual thinking software **Apps** WritePad My Writing Spot iA Writer Toontastic Animation Creator HD
Revising/editing	Teachers provide feedback about the form and substance so young writers can make additions or deletions that will improve the meaning (revising) and the clarity (editing) of written text.	Teachers and young writers engage in revising or editing by using: Paper and pencils (or pens) as well as oral conversations Reading and discussing written drafts in paper copy Making annotations and suggestions in writing directly to the text or on sticky notes	Technology for revising and editing includes: Social commenting feature on Google Docs E-mail communications so teachers and young writers can respond to writing Editing software such as grammar and spell-checking programs and apps "Track changes" editing feature on word processing programs to keep a record of changes as they are made Handheld talking spellers and dictionaries **Apps** Advanced English Dictionary and Thesaurus Grammarly Rhyme Time Rhyming Dictionary
Publishing	Teachers assist young writers in sharing their writing, making what they have written available for different audiences to read and hear.	Teachers publish and celebrate students' work by: Reading children's writing aloud Displaying stories, poetry, and other genres Assembling handmade books	Technology for publishing includes a range of venues beyond paper displays: Classroom websites Google Slides Digital portfolios Voice recorders Movie-making software Desktop publishing software for choices of page layouts, as well as print fonts and styles, to emphasize visual learning and student choice and control over how information is communicated **Apps and Websites** WordPress Book Creator iMovie Printing Press from NCTE Buncee Picture Book Maker

This makes it much faster to type, and the tool's suggestions can change the way you use language by offering suggestions for word use you might not normally include. A different AI-based tool, Grammarly, serves as grammar and spelling checker for social media posts in Gmail, Facebook, Twitter, and LinkedIn. The tool offers instant suggestions and corrections for word usage.

Another example of technology supporting student writing can be found in the following learning activity using Brian Selznick's 2007 graphic novel *The Invention of Hugo Cabret* as an illustration of creative storytelling. To start, a teacher and a small group of students read the initial 30 pages, choosing words to create an oral text for the black and white no-word illustrations depicting the characters and the setting.

At the same time, another group of students watches a video selection from the Martin Scorsese movie *Hugo* to see how the novel's beginning emerges on film. A third group accesses Brian Selznick's website to experience parts of the book interactively. Before students begin writing and illustrating their own stories, they can rotate through each of the experiences to observe the different ways these storytellers express creative ideas. A teacher cannot be in three places simultaneously, but with technology it is possible for three different introductions of fiction writing to occur.

Technology also makes it possible to individualize learning in the publishing stage of the writing process. Besides the much-used word-processed book format for publishing writing, students and teachers can create movies or video slideshows with iMovie software, graphic novels or animated stories with a comic strip program, photo stories with a program that combines text and pictures, a virtual flipbook or magazine using the Flipsnack program. Or you can try Everlapse, a stop motion flipbook software program. These different formats give writers choices about how they want their work to be presented to others, and choice of ideas and methods piques creative thinking.

Apps for Poetry Writing

Utilizing apps throughout a writing process fit for young writers generates technology-based ways for students to compose poetry from their ideas, imagination, and sense of play. Apps attract students' attention, enable them to express thoughts imaginatively without worrying about spelling errors or punctuation rules, and increase their enjoyment as they hear their poems read aloud or see them displayed online. Many poetry forms can be especially appealing for young writers, including:

- *Acrostic poems.* A poet hides a word by writing it top to bottom, vertically on the left side, right side, or middle of the paper, and uses those letters in the words in the poem.
- *Concrete or picture poems.* Images and pictures are made from filling shapes or outlining images with words rather than drawing a picture.
- *Two-voice poems.* Two narrators compose a poem by transcribing the conversations they have, delineating the voice of each speaker in a different color.

At the brainstorming phase of a writing process fit for young writers, apps let students experience poetry multimodally, and in so doing inspire their creativity. Here are three examples:

- *Instant Poetry HD.* This magnetic poetry-style app lets young poets create poems from words chosen by the program. Poets can put their newly written poem onto a photo of their choosing.
- *Poetry Mobile App from the Poetry Foundation.* This app, from the publishers of *Poetry Magazine,* features poems in text and read-aloud formats (it is also online as an interactive website). Pressing the spin button, students get selections from multiple color-coded categories—"joy" is brightly displayed in orange; "worry" is a subdued blue/green. They can read the poems that appear after each spin, spin again to see what new choices appear, and search the database by moods, subjects, poets, and audio presentations.
- *Shakespeare.* There are a number of apps that collect all of Shakespeare's plays, sonnets, and poems in one location. Works by many other poets are available on

these apps as well. Combining words, audio, and video with touch-screen technology creates engagement while inspiring students to write their own poems.

Apps can propel the drafting stage of the writing process for young poets. Before digital technology, students would write on their own or a teacher might act as a scribe—a human typewriter—recording a student's oral dictation to produce a draft on paper. Apps like QuickVoice Recorder greatly expand the composing of first drafts. A teacher might record a conversation with a young writer or a draft of a poem that can be listened to multiple times. Students record themselves reading a poem and consider whether they want to re-record and change words. Final drafts of poems can then be recorded once again for uploading to a publishing venue for others to hear the poets' voices.

There are additional apps for young poets to utilize in drafting, revising, editing, and publishing their poems. Students can compose notes in the MaxJournal app and then export them to their laptop or tablet device. Using Notability, they can type or hand-write drafts and then draw and add pictures and audio to poems. Dragon, a dictation app, converts students' spoken words into typed text. Once a draft is completed, PrintCentral lets students print their work from any Wi-Fi–connected printer; Edublogs lets students publish their creative work online; a class can watch published poets performing their poems on Poetry Everywhere from PBS to see how poetry is first and foremost a performance art.

To help students find the words they want to convey their ideas, Instant Poetry lets writers drop and drag words to create poems on a tablet or computer screen. Writers can use the free online word-rhyming site, Rhyme Zone to find rhyming words, synonyms, adjectives, descriptive words, check spelling and much more. This site also offers a Spanish version of all of these resources. Word Hippo, mentioned in the dictionary list, offers many of these options as well. All the while, the teacher continues in the role as a writing coach, collaborating with students as a writer through conversations and demonstrations.

For the students, using apps throughout the writing process boosts their interest and supports the belief that individuals have important ideas to express using written language. For teachers, apps offer more ways to explore the creativity present in every student. The combination of high-tech tools and the teacher's personal involvement as a coach creates a confidence-building creative writing experience.

MyLab Education Self-Check 11.4

Technology Transformation Learning Plan

Measuring Shadows: Differentiating Science Learning Using Technology

Grade(s)	Elementary and middle school
Subject(s)	Science
Key Goal/Enduring Understanding	Shadows are a commonly seen phenomenon on a sunny day or a moonlit night when light strikes light-blocking objects. Shadows shift and change as the turning earth produces variations in the angle of sunlight or moonlight striking the earth's surface throughout the 24 hours of day and night. Throughout the year the tilt of the earth circling the sun causes seasonal differences that change shadows' lengths, widths, and shapes.
Essential Question	Why do shadow lengths vary throughout the day and during different seasons of the year?
Academic Discipline Learning Standards	**National Science Teachers Association:** *National Science Education Standards* Earth and Space Science Content Standard D **National Council for the Social Studies**: *Curriculum Standards for the Social Studies* Theme III: People, Places, and Environment
Learning Objectives	Students will know and be able to: • Explain what creates shadows and why they change in length, width, and shape • Design and conduct a shadow measurement investigation, including recording and presenting data • Create online poster displays that explain why shadows move and change continuously and why they are different lengths throughout the seasons

Technology Uses

This activity utilizes digital measuring devices, digital cameras, movie-making software, and a classroom website or blog.

Minimal Technology	Infusion of Technology
Students measure shadows using rulers and yardsticks.	Students measure shadows using digital measuring devices, such as the iPhone or iPad Measure app.
Students record measurements in a paper notebook.	Students record measurements using a spreadsheet or graphing program.
Students record observations using words and drawings in a personal notebook.	Students record observations using digital cameras to add to their writing and drawing.
Students post observations of shadows on classroom bulletin boards.	Students post observations of shadows on a class website or blog.

Evaluation

Students will be evaluated on the knowledge gained from shadow investigations based on displays of collected data, the creative format of information presentation, and the description of how shadows would appear throughout a day if the earth were revolving on a straight axis with no tilt.

Learning Plan Description

Learning Focus

"Measuring Shadows" integrates digital measuring devices, digital cameras, movie-making software, Internet resources, and a classroom website or blog into the study of shadows and seasonal change. It shows ways to use technology to achieve universal design for learning (UDL) and differentiated instruction (DI)—both necessary to create learning success for all students.

Shadow measurements are an engaging and challenging way for elementary and middle school students to learn about seasonal change. Seasons are a part of everyone's daily life—for most students, school years begin as summer becomes fall and end as spring becomes summer. Weather patterns, animal migrations, plant growth, agricultural activities, and many other parts of daily life change seasonally. The changes become routine and go unnoticed unless teachers and students closely observe and investigate them.

Massachusetts—like other states in the northern part of the country—receives almost six and a quarter more hours of daylight at the summer solstice in June than it receives at the winter solstice in December. This difference is nearly equal to the length of an entire school day.

"Measuring Shadows" consists of inquiry-based science investigations that students can do throughout the school year on sunny days. These investigations include "Changing Shadow Lengths during the Day" and "Changing Shadow Lengths during Different Seasons of the Year." It is intended for grades 2 to 9 or mixed-age science clubs.

Learning Design—Minimal Technology

Shadows are fascinating phenomena to investigate as students learn about seasonal change. To create a shadow, two ingredients must be present: light and a solid object that does not let the light pass through it. Trees, buildings, rocks, boxes, cars, and people are easy-to-understand examples of light-blocking solid objects.

Sunlight shining on the constantly rotating earth creates dramatic shadows. Because the earth is endlessly turning, sunlight strikes objects at different angles depending on the time of day. All day long, shadows are moving and changing shapes as the angle of the light shifts. Shadows are longest in the morning or the afternoon when the sun appears lower in the sky and shortest at midday when the sun's position is directly overhead.

With colored chalk, the class goes outdoors to a space where there is enough room to trace shadows on cement or pavement. Pairs of students find spots away from other pairs. To begin, one student traces around the shoes of the other student to identify the exact spot they will return to for each of the shadow tracings that day. Either on the hour or three or four times a day, the partners return to their original spots to trace the new shadow using a different color of chalk each time. As the tracings multiply, it is apparent that all the shadows are undergoing similar changes. They all point in the same direction, grow or shrink similarly in length and width, and have remarkably different shapes from the first to the final tracing.

Inside each of the tracings, the time of the day is recorded to show how shadows are like the hands on a clock face. The following day, the shadow tracing experience is repeated. Partners switch roles, and the class observes the results of the tracings from day one and day two. This experience, repeated on sunny days in different seasons, offers students the opportunity to compare and contrast shadow sizes, shapes, and lengths while acting like scientists who construct theories from their repeated observations.

For classes that cannot go outdoors, if the sun streams into a room at the same time each day, paper can be hung on the wall or affixed to the door. Lines drawn on it every 10 minutes will show the movement of the light. Seasonal change modifies this light, making it appear earlier or later in the day, higher or lower on the wall, and at a different angle from the floor.

Learning Activities Using Technology

Multiple technologies differentiate and transform how students learn about shadows, day length, and the changing of the seasons. Here are the steps to follow:

1. *Measure shadows digitally.* Using digital measuring devices, students measure the shadows created by some light-blocking object (a tree, sign, building, or box, or one of the students in the class) at the same location at different times of the day. The position and shape of the object's shadow will move from morning to noon to afternoon. Digital photographs of the same location at different times plot the movement of the shadows throughout a day. Students' shadow measurements are posted on a classroom website or blog.

2. *Collect data from different seasons.* A class can keep track of shadows in the same location throughout the school year. As the seasons change, students will notice changes in the length of the shadow of the same object in any given location. The shadow of a sign or tree is not as long in the spring and autumn as in the summer and winter. This is because of the sun's height in the sky early and late in the day relative to the earth's tilt toward or away from the sun in the summer and in the winter. Using measuring devices and digital photographs, the students determine how much the shadow lengths vary throughout the year. If students capture the same photo spot over and over, they can turn it into a stop-motion animation and watch the shadow come to life!

3. *Provide different and similar roles to all students.* From a universal design for learning perspective, students can play different roles while pursuing common learning goals. Differentiating the roles offers students the choice of recording shadow observations; writing news reports, comics, or poems; creating videos; illustrating reports by painting and sculpting; and making models. For example, one group of classmates can trace shadows and take photographs. In partners, one student stands while the other traces the shadow, and one photographs while the other suggests angles and directions of photos. On other days, partners switch roles in this activity, and then that group switches activities with other groups who are engaged in writing reports, illustrating shadows, or making models.

4. *Integrate multiple technologies to differentiate instruction.* Technology offers differentiated ways for students to learn science content. Unlike whole-group approaches with limited opportunities for students to be active participants, technology-infused activities allow for hands-on experimentation by individuals, small-group activities, and opportunities for students to teach each other what they have learned. Teachers can differentiate instruction by assigning roles and activities based on student learning needs, including:

   - A measurement and data collection team to record length and width of shadows and objects in feet and inches. Students with hands-on tools can be actively involved in measurements while other students take digital photographs of shadow movements. They switch roles the next time they go out.
   - A data entry and presentation team that produces photo slideshows and graphs that illustrate shadow differences throughout the day and year.
   - A writing team recording and drawing to show how students are learning the science concepts at the center of the lesson. Word processing and drawing programs let students document what they are learning using different genres: poetry, prose, headlines and news columns, tweets, and posters.

5. *Publish the findings of the class.* Publishing the results of the shadow experiments on a class website or blog further differentiates instruction by "providing teachers with a user-friendly online format to reinforce strategies, introduce new topics and concepts, review important class points, and provide enrichment" (Colombo & Colombo, 2007). Publishing can be the responsibility of teams of student designers and editors.

Analysis and Extensions

1. Describe two features you find useful about this lesson.
2. How widely has technology been integrated into the lesson?
3. Name two areas for extension or revision of this lesson.
4. How might students become involved in designing, using, and evaluating their technology use in the lesson?

Chapter Summary

Learning Outcome 11.1

Demonstrate how teachers use technology to differentiate instruction (DI) and implement universal design for learning (UDL).

- All students benefit from wide and varied educational experiences that activate their talents and potential as learners.

- Differentiated instruction (DI) and universal design for learning (UDL) involve changing institutional practices and classroom structures to promote learning success for every student.

- Using technology in a universally designed classroom involves changing the learning environment and/or changing the ways curriculum is delivered, and it can be organized around low-tech, mid-tech, and high-tech accommodations and adaptations.

Learning Outcome 11.2

Discuss how technology differentiates learning of culturally and linguistically diverse students.

- Multicultural education and culturally responsive teaching affirms the diversities present in school classrooms.

- Technology promotes learning for diverse students by revealing untold stories and hidden histories, expanding teaching methods and approaches, and integrating multiple languages and cultures into the curriculum.

- Technology supports the teaching of linguistically diverse students through the use of handheld spellers, dictionaries, translators, multilingual online reading materials, word clouds, and other resources.

Learning Outcome 11.3

Explain how assistive technologies increase opportunities for successful student learning.

- Assistive technologies are tools that make academic material more accessible to students by minimizing barriers while maximizing opportunities for learning.

- Speech recognition software and text reading software are examples of technologies that can promote learning success for many different students.

Learning Outcome 11.4

Analyze the roles for technology in a writing process for young writers.

- A flexible match between school-assigned writing activities and the needs of individual writers is called a writing process for young writers.

- Technology offers multiple opportunities for teachers to "fit" the writing process to the needs and interests of student writers.

- Different technologies support the prewriting, drafting, revising, editing, and publishing stages of the writing process.

Key Terms

Accessibility, p. 274
Accommodations, p. 270
Assistive technologies (AT), p. 284
Culturally responsive teaching, p. 276
Differentiated instruction (DI), p. 270
Digital translators, p. 281
Drafting, p. 288
Editing, p. 289
Handheld speller and dictionary, p. 278
High-tech accommodations, p. 273
Interactive whiteboard, p. 286

Low-tech accommodations, p. 273
Mid-tech accommodations, p. 273
Modification, p. 270
Multicultural education, p. 276
Optical character recognition and reading (OCR) tools, p. 286
Prewriting/brainstorming, p. 288
Publishing, p. 289
Revising, p. 288
Screen readers, p. 286
SETT (Students, Environments, Tasks, and Tools), p. 284

Speech-to-text software and apps, p. 285
Superdiverse, p. 278
Text-to-speech software and apps, p. 285
Universal design, p. 272
Universal design for learning (UDL), p. 272
Word clouds, p. 281
Word prediction tools, p. 285
Writing process, p. 288
Writing process for young writers, p. 288

> MyLab Education **Application Exercise 11.3:**
> Shannon's "This I Believe" Learning Activity

For Reflection and Discussion

Handheld Calculators and Student Learning

Handheld calculators in smartphones, tablets, and computers or as stand-alone tools cause some teachers and parents to think these devices prevent students from learning essential mathematical literacy skills. Other educators view calculators as invaluable learning technologies for students.

- Do you utilize handheld calculators in your own learning? Would you learn as easily without them?

- How might handheld calculators support students with different learning challenges? How might teachers differentiate instruction using these tools?

- Would you invite students to use handheld calculators when taking tests or quizzes? Why or why not?

Assistive Technologies for Differentiated Learning

John Goodlad's classic study of American education, *A Place Called School* (1984), revealed that at every grade level, from first to 12th, students spent the overwhelming majority of classroom time passively listening to teacher lectures and explanations. Many educational reformers today conclude that little has changed in the three decades since then. Assistive technologies make possible educational experiences and instructional practices that were not possible when Goodlad conducted his research. Given these revolutionary developments, respond to the following questions:

- How can teachers design classes that rely less on lecturing and more on differentiated learning by students?

- What teaching methods and assistive technologies do you think will foster increased student engagement and why?

Chapter 12

Empowering Learners Through Performance Assessments and Reflection

SOURCE: belefront/Shutterstock

Chapter Overview

Chapter 12 examines how new teachers can use technology to design and utilize performance assessments of themselves as educators and students as learners. Beginning with early field experiences and student teaching and continuing throughout their career in education, teachers continually assess the performance of students while reflecting on their work as educators. We discuss technology-supported assessment in schools by examining student-centered assessment practices (including democratic teaching practices and student feedback surveys), digital tools and apps (including online quiz games and how they can facilitate students' self-reflection about learning), and digital portfolios for teachers and students. The chapter concludes with a Technology Transformation Learning Plan, "Constructing an Encyclo-ME-dia: Recording Student Learning in a Digital Portfolio," which describes a technology-based assessment approach with elementary students.

Chapter 12 connects to the ISTE Standard for Students: Empowered Learner. The purpose for students is to learn how to proactively establish, monitor, and assess their personal educational goals. Digital portfolios, polls, student feedback surveys, democratic classroom practices, and other performance evaluation practices and technologies help students focus on what and how they are learning. Reflecting is a necessary aspect to helping them apply that learning to their lives as members of multiple communities of friends, families and schools.

Learning Outcomes

After reading this chapter, you will be able to:

12.1   Discuss different types of learning assessments.

12.2   Explore student-centered assessment practices in schools and classrooms.

12.3   Identify digital tools and instructional practices that actively involve students in assessing learning.

12.4   Learn the features of digital portfolios for teachers and students.

Chapter Learning Goal

Use digital portfolios, polls and quiz games, student feedback surveys, democratic classrooms, and other assessment strategies to involve students in self-evaluation and reflection of their learning.

Featured Technologies

Digital teaching portfolios	Student feedback surveys
Standards-based digital portfolios	Online surveys, polls, and quiz games
Digital portfolios for students	Student response systems and apps

A Teacher and Students Make Digital Portfolios

Two months into a yearlong student teaching of 10th-grade U.S. history, Tracy learned that her cooperating teacher planned to retire in December, almost midway through the school year. "Tracy, I think you should apply for my position," her mentor said. "Your creative energy, differentiated teaching methods, and use of technology are stand-out abilities. I'll write a letter of recommendation for you."

"I'm glad to hear this, and I'd like to apply," Tracy replied. "But my chances are slim really. I am a student teacher, not truly experienced, and I have not finished gaining certification. On top of that, the principal hardly knows me."

"Don't think about those things. Start from what you do skillfully. Showcase your knowledge by adding examples of student projects and information about classroom teaching techniques into a digital teacher portfolio," the teacher advised. "Everyone involved in the interviews and hiring process will notice your ideas and accomplishments. Displaying learning plans, student work, and teaching resources is how to show what you do instructionally."

While posting her resources, artifacts, and lesson plans online, Tracy began to think of how a digital portfolio might be a valuable tool for students as a performance-based measure of academic knowledge. Throughout the semester she had been puzzled by the unwillingness of some students to study for multiple-choice exams. These students seemed disconnected from learning, disengaged from educational goals, going through the motions of attending class but not putting any effort into daily participation or studying for tests. These attitudes were Tracy's impetus for launching a digital portfolio project with students.

Arriving in class the following day, Tracy announced some news: "There will be no exam to finish our next unit. Instead of a test, everyone will assemble portfolios showing what you have learned using class notes, research assignments, and homework papers. I'd like you to take pictures that illustrate what you did. You may write captions telling what you learned. You can film short videos or create animations about books we read instead of writing book reports. You are a designer of a documentary record of your learning."

Surprised by the assignment and intrigued by the options she offered, the students responded as Tracy had hoped. A new spirit of involvement in learning emerged. Everyone, even those students she thought might complain about the amount of time and effort necessary, welcomed the opportunity to assemble a personal portfolio, and the portfolio-building process prompted lively and thoughtful discussions about the importance and meaning of the academic material the class was studying. The digital portfolios were the glue that kept students involved with the learning process.

Tracy's two-way use of digital portfolios—for assessing her learning and students assessing their learning—introduces this chapter's focus on multiple ways technology can support performance-based assessments of learning *and* individuals' self-reflections about their educational accomplishments and achievements.

Performance assessments, unlike traditional tests and exams, are based on materials created by students (class and homework samples, reflective essays, and audio and video materials) as a framework for assessing academic skills and accomplishments. Teachers can create performance assessments of their professional work (learning plans, results of student feedback surveys, written reflections). Technology tools, as shown in this chapter, offer ways to make performance assessments parts of regular learning evaluations.

Performance assessments encompass a wide range of activities, all of which are ways to involve students directly in learning through reflection. **Reflection** is a process of personal self-assessment in which a learner examines past actions to identify what to maintain or change during future interactions. Reflection is tied to all the key topics in this chapter. Democratic teaching practices and student feedback surveys invite students to be active shapers of their classroom learning experiences when creating rules and codes of conduct, presenting information to peers, and evaluating their successes as learners. Question-centered instructional methods and student participation systems with online survey software and apps shift students' learning focus from memorizing information to engaging in creative and critical thinking. Finally, digital portfolios, like those Tracy used in the classroom, propel in two key ways everyone's efforts to be reflective learners:

1. As they consider the merits of materials to include in their online eportfolios, teachers and students are evaluating what they have learned as well as the process they used to achieve those results. Performance assessment and self-reflection about learning are the ways that people understand what they did to achieve new learning and enhance their skills. This is a necessary self-assessment behavior at every grade level. Being able to explain or demonstrate learning and state how it was achieved indicate enduring understandings of topics, ideas, behaviors, and attitudes.

2. As they create digital rather than paper portfolios, teachers and students are learning how to integrate technology into assessment and reflection. Digital formats enable easy updating and changes to materials based on new experiences and new insights, making online eportfolios a constantly evolving portrait of personal learning and knowledge.

As you start to think about ways in which technology might aid your and students' learning through assessment evaluations and reflection, the following questions can serve as a guide:

1. What are the multiple dimensions of educational assessment for teachers and students?

2. How can you actively involve students in assessment and evaluation using technology?

3. How can you use student feedback surveys and participation systems to enhance student engagement in schools and classrooms?

4. How can you use digital portfolios as tools for learning?

Assessment in Teaching and Learning

12.1   Discuss different types of learning assessments.

Assessment is central to the work of teachers. Even as they plan learning activities and deliver instruction, every teacher must be thinking about how to evaluate student learning. Viewing assessment as a multifaceted and collaborative process, not a singular action of assigning grades after a test or quiz, enables students and teachers to view assessment as ongoing and ever changing, and a means for students to understand what they will learn next.

Dimensions of Educational Assessment

Teachers are concerned with three interrelated dimensions of educational assessment:

1. *New teacher assessment (how supervisors are assessing your work).* As you are preparing to become a teacher, professors and supervisors are evaluating your academic and classroom performance continually. Before being hired for your first full-time teaching job, you will likely have to pass a state teacher license test, be observed teaching by mentor teachers and college supervisors, and complete written summaries of what you have learned about academic subjects, teaching methods, classroom management strategies, and professional relationships with students, families, colleagues, and administrators.

2. *Student learning assessment (how are you assessing students' learning).* As a teacher, you will be expected to provide ongoing, data-driven evaluations about the learning progress of every student in a class throughout the school year. In most schools, you will be expected to assign grades, complete report cards, conduct meetings with families, and provide oral and written feedback to individual students and their families in the form of comments and suggestions about their academic work. Evaluating students as a teacher also includes personal self-assessments in which you ask, "Are students learning?" and, if they are not, "What can I do to change this?"

3. *Student and teacher self-assessment (how are students participating in the assessment process and how are you assessing yourself as an educator).* As a teacher, you will benefit from making students active partners rather than passive participants in the process of evaluating their own learning. Involving students in assessment means that students play meaningful roles in evaluating what they know and are able to do. As they self-assess their performance, students may change how they think about themselves as learners while building an increased commitment to academic learning. The same is true for you as an educator. You benefit from continually examining your own practices, identifying strengths and areas for improvement and then acting on that information to improve your performance in the classroom.

Technology supports teacher assessment in two main ways: 1) as part of lessons, methods, and classroom experiences that show evaluators your skills as an educator; and 2) through tools that evaluate what students learn and are able to do with that knowledge. In this way, technology connects teaching with learning in a full circle, supporting teachers as they plan lessons, deliver instruction, and evaluate performance, and supporting students as they participate in activities and evaluate their own efforts and outcomes in learning. Table 12.1 shows teachers using technology tools to evaluate students while also being evaluated professionally by teaching supervisors.

The ability to engage in self-reflection creates personal assessment—both for you as a teacher and for students as learners. As part of being evaluated on an ongoing basis as a college student, you must be able to continually evaluate yourself as a teacher, improving your practice using those assessments. Classroom teachers make hundreds of decisions every day based on interactions with students. Each class and each student bring complex dynamics, and you, the teacher, are central to those dynamics. The ability to look from different perspectives—through the eyes of learners, of families, of other professionals who are teaching also—aids you in adopting behaviors that change what you do to assist the learning potential of each student.

MyLab Education
Video Example 12.1
In this video, a teacher describes the multiple ways she assesses student learning. How can you use different forms of assessment to try to meet the learning needs of students?

Table 12.1 Roles for Technology in Student and Teacher Assessment

Technology Tools	Assessments of Students by Teachers	Assessments of Teachers by Supervisors
Word processing software, PowerPoint, Google Slides, and other digital tools for preparing papers and presentations	Papers and presentations by students in classes	Papers and presentations by new teacher candidates in teacher education classes
Digital portfolios or other digital collections of materials	Examples of learning completed by students	New teacher-designed learning plans and related curriculum materials
Video and audio presentations or podcasts	Performances by students	Field observations of teaching
Websites or digital portfolios showcasing examples of best practices	College admissions letters or job applications	Interviews with future employers

The constantly shifting nature of a classroom requires that a teacher continually assess: What strategies worked to facilitate learning? What strategies did not? Why did an approach succeed with one student or one class and not with another? What activities introduce a learning activity with focusing power or bring it to a memorable end? Successful teachers reflect on their practice and thoughtfully decide about their teaching methods, what to revise, delete, or try again.

With self-reflection essential to successful teaching, how do teachers guide students to be self-reflective about their own efforts and performance with learning? Reflective learning involves changing student mind-sets from thinking that evaluations consist of something adult-controlled to experiencing school as a place where they, students, confidently participate in how learning happens and how it is assessed. A self-reflective mind-set evolves through many experiences in which students gradually are given ways to take active responsibility in their own learning.

Digital Dialog 12.1

To begin thinking about including students in the process of evaluation, recall the different types of assessments you experienced as a student. Comment and connect online about the following questions:

- Which assessment formats were most helpful to your learning as a student? Which formats were least helpful?
- As a teacher, when might you use test-based assessments (exams, quizzes, worksheets)?
- As a teacher, when might you use performance assessments (portfolios, writing, projects)?

Different Types of Assessments for Learning

The assessment of students occurs across a spectrum of approaches. At one end of the spectrum are standardized test assessments; at the other are student-centered performance assessments. In between are combinations of both types of assessments, all designed to measure successful learning and effective teaching and determine where further effort, practice and conversation are needed.

Table 12.2 shows types of student performance evaluations that you might use as a teacher side by side with ones that college and school system supervisors are likely to be using to assess your performance as a student teacher or new teacher. Of course, classroom teachers still use tests, and college students are tested in their teacher education classes as well. The lists in Table 12.2 emphasize the performance evaluation of projects and assignments done rather than test results.

Responding to the widespread use of high-stakes standardized tests, many educational researchers have endorsed efforts to rethink how assessment happens in schools. Diane Ravitch (2014a), a former supporter of curriculum standards, standardized testing, increased teacher accountability, and the No Child Left Behind law, has unreservedly declared that the goals of education reform have been distorted through moves toward privatization, increasing numbers of charter schools, and an over-reliance on

Table 12.2 Types of Performance Evaluations of Students and Teachers

Performance Evaluation of Students by Classroom Teachers	Performance Evaluation of Teachers in Teacher Preparation Programs
• Student writing or design assignments (creative, analytical, persuasive, multimodal) • Student participation • Individual and group projects • Homework assignments • Individual presentations and performances • Open-book/open-note quizzes and tests • Student self-assessments • Teacher observations of student attitudes and behaviors	• New teacher writing or design assignments (creative, analytical, persuasive, multimodal) • Teacher education course participation • Individual and group projects • Homework assignments • Individual presentations and performances • Open-book/open-note quizzes and tests • New teacher self-assessments • College supervisor or cooperating teacher observations of new teacher attitudes and behaviors

test scores to measure educational progress. The current educational standards movement, she believes, promised to establish a common knowledge base for student learning. However, "what once was an effort to improve the quality of education turned into an accounting strategy: Measure, then punish or reward" where tests are driving the curriculum instead of the curriculum driving the tests (Ravitch, 2011, p. 16).

UCLA professor W. James Popham (2014, 2011) is a leading proponent of what he calls **transformative assessment**, in which teachers use day-to-day evidence of what students know and are able to do academically to make immediate, short-term, and long-term adjustments in curriculum and instruction. In Popham's view, an "avalanche" of standardized assessments have caused teachers to focus mainly on the information and skills assessed on tests while abandoning a more wide-ranging curriculum. For students, the joy and purpose of learning are taken away by fewer and fewer opportunities to explore topics that are not on the tests.

The National Council of Teachers of English (NCTE) issued a statement about assessment in the learning process, straightforwardly rejecting a "sole reliance on standardized tests" to measure student performance in favor of a broad view of student knowledge and performance that includes the following tenets:

- Assessment must include multiple types of information.
- Teachers and families should be knowledgeable about the things the test data can and cannot demonstrate about learning.
- Teachers and schools should be permitted to select site-specific assessment tools from a bank of alternatives and/or to create their own.
- Assessment should include how students use new technology tools to analyze and communicate information.
- Students should be encouraged to take greater responsibility for assessing their own learning. (National Council of Teachers of English, 2014a, 2013a).

In NCTE's view, effective assessment requires that teachers integrate multiple assessment resources to produce a complete picture of student performance. To do so means making comparisons among multiple forms of data.

> **MyLab Education Self-Check 12.1**

Student-Centered Assessment Practices

12.2 **Explore student-centered assessment practices in schools and classrooms.**

The development of student performance rubrics, the movement for **democratic schools and classrooms**, and the implementation of student feedback surveys are all different and impactful ways to enhance the participation of students in educational decision-making, academic learning, and personal reflection. These activities depend on teachers fostering student engagement with a balance of teacher-chosen and student-chosen activities. In organizing classroom instruction, while the teacher sets the overall theme and focus for daily learning experiences, students actively contribute to the learning process in ways such as those described by Steven Zemelman, Harvey Daniels, and Arthur Hyde from National-Louis University (2012, p. 213):

- Students select themes for study, reading materials, topics for discussion, and formats for publishing their own writing.
- Students set personal learning goals and document their progress online or on paper (see Figure 12.1 for an example of student self-assessments in a kindergarten classroom).
- Students' own questions and interests are included in classroom discussion and study.
- Students take responsibility for making decisions about classroom rules and procedures.

Student Performance Rubrics

Student performance **rubrics** are a tool for evaluating student effort and accomplishments on assigned activities. These establish known-in-advance criteria, describing in precise terms what students must do to meet those criteria. They assist students and teachers to mutually understand and evaluate whether effort and creative outcomes occurred, or if change and improved outcomes are needed to meet the academic expectations.

Rubrics can assess and grade different parts of a single assignment or learning activity. For example, students of all ages using a problem-solving model might be assessed on the following four separate performances:

1. How accurately or completely they describe the problem
2. How successfully or imaginatively they design a strategy for solving the problem
3. How they implement the plan
4. How clearly or expansively they explain their findings, outcomes, and conclusions in written, filmed, audio or oral presentations

As a performance assessment approach to educational evaluation, rubrics are adjustable for use with younger or older students; they present what needs to be done for basic or more advanced work and understanding; and they may include qualities of creative design.

Rubrics can also guide students' actions and decisions during in-class learning activities. Figure 12.2 shows a presentation rubric developed by a middle school social studies teacher for a "World Forum" activity where students work in a United Nations–like format to envision solutions to global social problems: infectious diseases, water shortages, refugees, and ethnic conflicts. The rubric assesses students' performance of presentation (addressing the class), topic understanding (speaking

Figure 12.1 Students' Self-Assessments in a Kindergarten Classroom

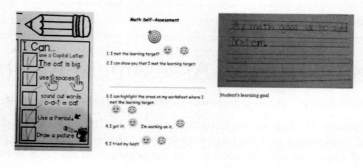

Figure 12.2 Presentation Rubric for a World Forum Activity

World Forum
Presentation Rubric

Presentation Skills: (25 points)

Makes eye contact with the audience

Speaks clearly and loudly enough for all to hear

Demonstration awareness of public speaking (not fidgetting, proper posture, etc.) _____ / 25

Demonstrating Understanding of Topic: (50 points)

Uses evidence from history and/or current events to prove this issue affects your country

Uses statistics to demonstrate impacts of this issue

Accurately represents role by acting in the best interest of your country (be able to explain your arguments and decisions) _____ / 50

Participation: (25 points)

Participates in discussion (quality)

Participates in decision-making/voting for a solution

Actively listens

Follows rules of the forum

_____ / 25

TOTAL _____ / 100

about issues during discussion), and participation/preparation (focusing on engaging with and completing work in class).

Teachers, collaborating with students, formulate rubrics to: 1) establish specific activities or accomplishments that need to be completed to achieve a learning level, score, or grade, and 2) provide an exact description of how projects, presentations, and assignments will be evaluated in the grading process. As a new teacher or student teacher, you may be asked to design rubric-based assignments, giving you an opportunity to try this form of assessment and to involve students' input in the process. MetaRubric is a game designed by Massachusetts Institute of Technology (MIT) researchers to help educators and students gain rubric design skills.

The key to constructing rubrics is unambiguously identifying what students will do as part of a class activity or assignment or as designers and creators of a project. Saying that you want students to write a high-quality persuasive essay is not a performance goal; it is the beginning of creating specific statements that will guide students in constructing essays to meet the standards of high-quality writing. These might be:

- Compose an engaging introductory paragraph to capture readers' attention.
- State a thesis sentence that clearly advocates a position.
- Include interesting details and convincing examples in each paragraph to support your argument.
- Draft a conclusion summarizing the main idea in a memorable or surprising way.

Stating the items to be evaluated—introduction, thesis sentence, examples, and conclusion—is the first step in using rubrics. You must then talk with and teach students about what makes an introduction engaging, a thesis sentence clear, examples convincing, and the conclusion punchy or memorable. If an engaging introduction is one that uses lively language, compelling facts, or a provocative claim to focus the reader's attention, then students must practice writing sentences displaying these strategies. That is how a rubric directly corresponds to what students are learning and doing in class.

Rubrics require criteria to be relentlessly concrete. For example, a teacher might expect that to earn a grade of A, a writer needs to demonstrate critical thinking, apply concepts and ideas at an advanced level, and use the conventions of written language appropriately by revising, paragraphing, and checking spelling and grammar. Each of those performance expectations can be explained in specific, measurable terms on a rubric, as follows:

- "Critical thinking" does not mean quoting what other writers have said but comprehending and comparing what other writers have said to formulate one's own view of a subject.
- "Applying concepts and ideas at an advanced level" means that the writer understands the complexities of a subject and communicates in writing about the subject from more than one point of view.
- "Using conventions of written language appropriately" means the essay displays standard conventions of grammar, sentence variety, paragraphing, spelling, and punctuation.

Students can then refer to the rubric to self-assess their knowledge about their writing on a topic.

Describing an assignment concretely, in your mind and the minds of the students, includes trying out or drafting the language and revising the directions. The advantage of a rubric lies in its level of explicit examples and how the criteria are understood by students. In our persuasive essay example, the teacher and students might choose to expand the evaluation even further—for example, by specifying how many new vocabulary words or how many pages the paper must contain to earn an A, B, or C grade. Students must know before receiving a grade, the criteria differentiating superior, good, needs improvement, and unacceptable performance.

Partnering Pedagogies and Democratic Classrooms

Meaningfully involving students in learning and assessment requires what Marc Prensky (2012, 2010) has called a **partnering pedagogy**. In today's technological age, the longstanding approach of teachers presenting information using lectures and slides is less and less relevant to the lives of students. Students need learning partnerships in which they have primary responsibility to ask questions, research information, practice skills, create presentations, and use technology in all facets of learning, while teachers have primary responsibility for guiding student investigations, explaining the meaning and relevance of academic material, and supporting individual learners by differentiating instruction (Prensky, 2010, p. 13). In assessment, a partnering pedagogy focuses on students answering questions about their own learning and progress, including "Am I improving? Am I learning? Are my skills getting better? What should I be working on?" (Prensky, 2010, p. 176). A partnering pedagogy also allows students to choose how to showcase their understanding of academic topics. Multimodal options of video and audio presentations, game design, building or drawing, writing, composing music or poetry, or creating visual descriptors on paper or digitally are available choices.

Democratic classrooms are places where students and teachers together make substantive decisions about important aspects of educational operations, from the academic curriculum to school climate and rules (Maloy & LaRoche, 2015; Hess & McAvoy, 2014; Apple, 2012; Apple & Beane, 2007). In theory, making classrooms more participatory benefits students and teachers in multiple ways. When students recognize that they have a voice in deciding how education happens, they express a greater commitment to school expectations and show increased involvement in learning. For teachers, everything about the work is easier when students show enthusiasm and interest in curriculum and instruction.

Critics of democratic classrooms suggest that, if given the opportunity to do so, students will make ill-informed or self-centered choices—doing minimal homework, spending time socializing, selecting easy problems to solve, or writing the shortest possible responses on essays or in journals, and not putting interest or effort into creating projects or portfolios. In this view, teachers cannot lead a classroom in which students make decisions because students will behave immaturely, leaving academic standards unmet.

Advocates of democratic schools and classrooms respond by noting that student engagement in decision-making is not about students controlling every decision; it is about teachers and students planning how classrooms will operate. Adults are responsible for core elements of school organizations—that reality is not negotiable. Teachers must instruct according to a curriculum and assess whether students have learned what they need to know. How learning occurs, how evaluation is conducted, and how students demonstrate what they know can be formulated through collaborative dialogue, debate, and decision-making between students and teachers.

Formally proclaimed democratic schools represent only a tiny number of the total schools in the United States, but many teachers see themselves as deliberately choosing to teach democratically, and they find multiple ways to do this within the framework of more traditionally structured organizations. They create participatory learning environments in which students are active partners in the organization of all aspects of classroom learning, from broad goals and mission statements to everyday practices in the classroom.

Robert Maloy and Irene LaRoche (2015) summarized the scope of democratic practices using seven concepts, each beginning with the letter C: 1) contrasting (integrating

MyLab Education
Video Example 12.2
In this video, a fifth-grade teacher and the students in class discuss possible roles and responsibilities of class president and vice president. How do you see the teacher promoting a democratic classroom with students?

In Practice

Assessing Student Learning with Smartphones and Tablets

Grade Level	Featured Technologies
Middle and high school	Smartphones and tablets

Learning Plan Outline

As part of a senior year honors project, Kate developed a "Smartphones and Tablets for Assessment" learning experience to explore integrating mobile devices in history and social studies classes. Before identifying this as her project, she had attended a lecture by Brian Lukoff (2013), a postdoctoral fellow at Harvard University, who discussed how students respond to teacher questions in class using personal digital devices—laptops, tablets, or phones. Lukoff believes students are more mentally and intellectually engaged if they are responding to academic subject matter in self-chosen and interactive ways. Kate then found research from higher education and high school science classrooms about the value of students taking mini-quizzes regularly to answer questions in class, with results showing improved scores on exams and higher engagement in class activities. She wondered how high school students might respond to using technology for quizzes to self-assess learning history content.

Teaching with Technology

In partnership with an interested history teacher in a local school, Kate chose a cloud-based response system for students to self-assess their understanding of assigned readings in preparation for a unit test. Then, based on the content of the class readings, Kate wrote a set of multiple-choice questions and posted them online. In class the following day, she described replacing the homework review usually done in small group conversations or by a written quiz with an approach where students would choose either their smartphones or a classroom tablet to answer questions with an online response system. None of the students had used smartphones or tablets in this way during class. This was a new method for everyone.

As Kate showed the homework review questions one by one on a screen at the front of the room, she instructed small groups to first discuss the question and answer choices before submitting their individual responses. When 100% of the class responded, the system displayed in a graph or a table the number of students making each choice. If more than 20% of students did not choose the correct answer, Kate and the class reviewed the question's answer choices and conversed about each one's content to assess its likelihood of being correct.

When the class finished the review, Kate asked for their individual evaluations of using smartphones and tablets to answer questions and assess learning and understanding of the material. In written feedback, students said they liked having the choice of devices, with most preferring the phone option. One student described seeing responses displayed in a bar graph this way: "It was exciting to see the number of people who guessed different answers. It also helped show where the class was confused." Another student appreciated the anonymity of the online responses: "What I liked the most was that no one was being called on specifically." All students agreed that the activity was interesting, helpful as a review, and they were eager to do it again.

Kate and the classroom teacher concluded that technology-based quizzes and small group discussions were an effective review of learning progress in class. The online responses show students what they know and understand about a topic; the technology provides an interesting way to focus students' attention on self-assessing personal learning; and brief discussions about answer choices help each student acquire knowledge and strategies for considering choices of answers to test questions.

multicultural content throughout the curriculum); 2) conducting (using active learning methods); 3) collaborating (managing the classroom together); 4) conversing (holding student-centered discussions); 5) conferring (getting feedback from students about teaching methods); 6) co-constructing (integrating technology); and 7) connecting (linking classroom learning with community people and concerns). Individually and collectively, each of the seven Cs of democratic practice builds a learning environment in which students feel empowered to express their ideas and take responsibility for their learning.

Importantly, democratically inclined teachers emphasize how language conveys democratic values. One second-grade teacher uses the terms *teacher* and *student* to identify everyone in the classroom, explaining to students, visitors, and families that there are 20 teachers under the age of 8 and one teacher over the age of 50 and that all members of this learning community are students. In daily routines and classroom activities, the adult teacher creates regular opportunities for children to teach each other by explaining their reading projects, writing, science, math, block building, and artwork in front of the whole class or in small groups. Words and actions together infuse democratic practices into every aspect of the classroom culture.

Student Feedback Surveys

Online **student feedback surveys** (also called student perception surveys) are opportunities for teachers and students to confer together to build positive learning communities. A student feedback survey is a series of questions given to students by teachers to gather information about how students perceive classroom learning and the larger school environment. Feedback surveys can be developed by teachers locally or implemented school- or district-wide using questionnaires developed by national educational assessment companies. Figure 12.3 shows the results from one student teacher's feedback survey.

Figure 12.3 A Teacher's Student Feedback Survey Results

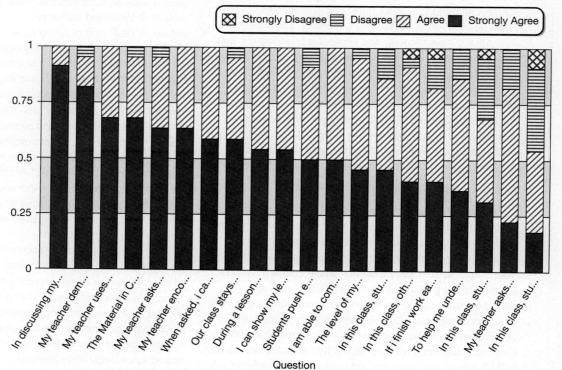

Student feedback surveys have become a widely used approach to education reform and teacher performance evaluation. More than a million students in 2014 completed formal feedback questionnaires about their teachers. Thirty-three states permit student feedback surveys as parts of the annual evaluation of K–12 teachers and Connecticut, Georgia, Hawaii, Iowa, Kentucky, Massachusetts, and Utah mandate student feedback be collected for teacher evaluation purposes. In 2016, Massachusetts began requiring student feedback surveys as part of how new teacher license candidates are evaluated by college and university teacher certification programs.

The term "confer" is at the heart of student feedback surveys. Confer comes from Latin, where "con" means together and "ferre" means bring. Bringing students and teachers together, surveys offer unique ways to improve teaching and learning based on what students say they are experiencing in classrooms and corridors. As Harvard University researcher Carly Robinson noted, when they collect *and* respond to feedback from their classes, teachers "send a strong signal to students that they care about their point of view" (quoted in Shafer, 2017).

Conferring with students shifts the focus of feedback surveys from teacher evaluation to engaging learners and improving instruction in school classrooms. By conferring, teachers learn how students think about what is happening to them educationally. The results can help teachers make changes to instructional practices that will improve student engagement and learning. In a culture of feedback, students recognize that they have a vote and power and that their opinions matter to adults; teachers gain perspectives about what works instructionally and interpersonally.

Student feedback surveys and conferring conversations can happen throughout the year—at the beginning, in the middle, or at the end of instructional units as well as in daily or weekly activities. Middle school teacher and education blogger Mari Venturino (2018, 2017) uses feedback surveys on Google forms to begin the school day by asking students how they are and how things are outside of school and again as an exit ticket at the day's end so students can reflect on their learning. She gets real-time feedback about student attitudes, which allows her to offer individualized supports to every youngster. Other teachers regularly ask students if they feel interested in what they are learning; feel challenged academically; and feel supported as a learner by adults and peers.

The specificity of written feedback questions are the key to getting meaningful, substantive student feedback. In our studies, regardless of grade level, course being taught, or students' regard for a teacher's personality, the way questions are worded impacts how students answer them (Maloy & LaRoche, 2018). Direct, content-specific questions focusing on academic content or instructional practices are more likely to receive detailed, actionable responses than are broadly stated, closed-ended questions.

Effective feedback questions ask about student learning rather than student satisfaction. While students' feelings are important and cannot be dismissed, academic learning often means hard work and sustained concentration, behaviors that some students may not like doing but are necessary to success. In Table 12.3, questions in

Table 12.3 Examples of Student Feedback Questions

Focus on Student Satisfaction	Focus on Student Learning
What did you like about working in groups while doing class work?	What changes could the teacher make to improve your learning in groups?
Did you enjoy the simulation activity and was it engaging for you as a learner?	What did you learn from the simulation that you would not have learned from reading the textbook?
Do you have any suggestions for this activity if it were taught again?	What changes could the instructor make to improve your learning if this activity were taught again?

the left-hand column ask students how they feel about an academic experience, often using value-laden verbs, "like" or "enjoy." Alternate versions in the right-hand column ask students to comment directly on what they are learning from an instructional experience.

Basic guidelines to follow when collecting student feedback include:

- Before teaching or beginning an activity, talk with students about why you feel it is important to have their feedback and how you intend to use feedback to improve your own teaching.
- Model the level of specificity you want for feedback, and give students enough time to complete the questionnaire. When students understand the importance of the feedback, and that they are the experts you are consulting, they will provide sincere ideas and suggestions. Figure 12.4 shows a sample student feedback form to use or modify for your own situation.
- Collect students' feedback forms and identify themes as you read them. Write your own reflection about the process of seeking student feedback to inform your teaching. Include comments from the student feedback surveys as well as your own ideas about how you plan to use student feedback again in your teaching.
- Share with the students what you learned from the feedback because they will want to know how their ideas and comments helped you gain insights and develop plans for teaching.
- Avoid composing "value-laden" questions ("What did you *like* about …?" or "What was your *favorite*…?").
- Limit "forced-choice" questions ("Yes/No") where students simply respond one way or the other without explaining their thinking.
- Create learning improvement questions that invite students to give specific reactions to instructional methods and classroom routines.

Used regularly throughout a school year, feedback surveys enable students to communicate with teachers and enable teachers to communicate with students about issues and topics that matter to all of them. Conferring conversations based on survey results give teachers ideas for improving instruction while building a culture of student voice and democratic participation in classroom learning communities. As Sarah Brown Wessling, the 2010 national teacher of the year and advocate of teacher- and student-developed feedback surveys, stated, "What

Figure 12.4 Teacher Online Survey

Grade: _____

Subject: _____

Feedback for _____ (teacher name) on using

_____ as a teaching method for a lesson on

_____ (topic).

Insights: How did this technology help you learn? What did you find helpful about how the teacher used this technology?

Issues: What did you find difficult in using this technology? How would you suggest the teacher improve the way he or she teaches with this technology?

Ideas: What other ways would you like to see this technology used? What other topics would you like to see this technology used to teach?

really drives my reflection is the comments they [students] offer. It is the comments that in the end—nine times out of 10—will change my instruction, or solidify my instruction" (2012, p. 1).

MyLab Education Application Exercise 12.1:
Developing a Student Feedback Survey

MyLab Education Self-Check 12.2

Digital Tools and Apps for Assessment

12.3 Identify digital tools and instructional practices that actively involve students in assessing learning.

If learning is to be lifelong and successful, assessment and reflection must be practiced by students, not only by teachers. K–12 school organizations, whose mission is to prepare young people to be active and productive members of a democratic society, often minimize or negate student voice and agency—particularly in making decisions about what students want to learn and how they want to learn it. Teachers who recognize the irony in this practice see that students learn to be passive and disconnected. To help students become reflective and feel part of decision-making, these teachers promote student engagement through collaboration about different aspects of classroom procedures and operations.

In many educational settings, students have little or no influence on curriculum topics, instructional methods, or evaluation procedures. Failure to offer students a voice in educational decision-making is an opportunity lost. From a well-established psychological perspective, individuals are more likely to become and remain invested in activities and procedures that they themselves have a role in creating and maintaining. This is true for adults at work and family members in the home, and it is true for students in schools.

Psychologists have found that students who are given a choice of homework options reported feeling more motivated to complete assignments and then performed better on tests compared with those who did not have a choice (Patall, Cooper, & Wynn, 2010). Similarly, students are more likely to follow school rules when they have been involved in creating those codes of conduct (Schimmel, 2003). So if the goal is for students to care about and engage with the curriculum, they need input in deciding what topics to study. And if the goal is for students to care about and engage with learning evaluation, they need substantive roles in the assessment process.

MyLab Education
Video Example 12.3
In this video, students become more invested in educational success as they engage in self-assessment of their learning. How will you promote student self-assessment as a teacher?

Pre-Assessment Surveys

Pre-assessments occur before introducing a new learning topic or unit for teachers to determine what students know or can already do and to inform subsequent plans for teaching. Pretests, writing prompts, graphic organizers, observations, questions, and surveys are widely used pre-assessment strategies. Pre-assessments are part of **prior knowledge–based learning**, the idea that when teaching concepts, teachers need to connect new content to what students already know or have been taught. Prior knowledge may not be immediately obvious to students; they often do not realize that they know important information about a topic. Prior knowledge needs to be activated—brought to students' attention—through readings, discussions, and pre-assessment activities.

Online surveys offer one effective way to activate prior knowledge and involve students in the pre-assessment process. An online survey is a form that collects data that can be easily accessed and analyzed online. Such surveys identify the skills and knowledge students have, as well as the information and knowledge they would like to learn. See Figure 12.4 for sample questions from a teacher's online survey.

Students have an incentive to participate in online surveys when the information gathered leads to a choice of topics to study and different ways of presenting knowledge. The surveys are not tests; they are launchers of learning. Furthermore, pre-assessment surveys demonstrate that teachers want to learn what students know about a topic before a lesson begins. Finally, because students appreciate being asked about their knowledge and skills, pre-assessment surveys create a sense of collaborative learning between students and teachers. For example, to generate discussion about books being read in an English class, teachers provide survey questions for students to answer either during or before coming to class. In class, students compare and contrast their survey responses with classmates. This digital pre-assessment survey serves to "increase opportunities for students to voice their opinions and take ownership of their learning" (Ponzio & Matthusen, 2018, p. 125).

In preparation for a community history research project, one high school teacher sent the pre-assessment survey shown in Figure 12.5 to students using an online survey-building tool with real-time mapping feedback. She had five goals for the survey:

1. To encourage students' use of technology from the beginning of the project
2. To learn about students' prior knowledge and interests
3. To generate a high level of engagement with the project
4. To show students that she appreciated and valued their ideas
5. To teach students how to use survey software and apps as data collection tools

The results of the community history survey showed that almost everyone in the class was interested in researching local history. The survey also revealed that many of the students did not have knowledge of digital media or editing and that almost half had no prior experience making PowerPoint or other online presentations.

Teachers can use the results of pre-assessment surveys to tailor instruction to emphasize learning technology skills and to ensure that everyone's research would explore different aspects of academic topics. For example, a teacher might use pre-assessment surveys to design teams of diverse learners so all the content experts or most fluent writers or most technology-savvy students are not placed in the same group. Instead, students are distributed to groups where they can share their different areas of expertise and interest to benefit a collective effort.

Student Participation Technologies

Student participation technologies, including online polls and digital quiz games, have multiple uses in K–12 classrooms. As tools for assessing student learning, polls, interactive videos, and quizzes are effective ways to: 1) assess what students know

Figure 12.5 Pre-Assessment Survey for a Community History Research Project

1. For this project you will be required to use several different technology skills. Please check the skills you feel comfortable with/have experience with:
   —PowerPoint or Other Presentation Software
   —Digital Camera
   —Scanners/Scanning Pictures
   —Camcorder
   —Web Design
   —Video Editing
   —Digital Photo Editing
   —Online Research Techniques
   —Other
2. List software programs you know how to use.
3. What technologies, software, and/or skills would you like to learn or practice with the help of this research project?
4. What level of confidence do you have in writing an interview for historical research?
5. What level of confidence do you have in conducting an interview for historical research?
6. What level of confidence do you have when calling to set up face-to-face meetings for interviews with local residents?
7. What time period in our community's history would you be interested in researching?
   —Colonial
   —Early 19th Century (Antebellum)
   —Industrial Age
   —Early 20th Century
   —Late 20th Century to Present Day
8. Do you have ideas or interests about a topic for your historical research project?

before beginning a learning experience; 2) monitor student progress while learning activities are in progress; and 3) evaluate what students have learned or are able to do after an experience or project is completed. Participation technologies also offer the following instructional advantages:

- *Active learning.* Rather than passively listening to the teacher explain, lecture, or demonstrate something, students express their opinions electronically. Student engagement is necessary because everyone's contributions matter, and interactivity is part of the lesson.

- *Student engagement.* A game-like activity with whole-group participation encourages student thinking. Because students can respond to questions anonymously, individuals worry less about the embarrassment of giving a wrong answer. Students who might otherwise not participate for fear of being wrong or appearing foolish when they answer orally can express their ideas silently.

- *Real-time feedback.* Teachers and students receive immediate feedback about students' content knowledge and test performance without doing or correcting paper-and-pencil quizzes and entering the grades.

- *Question-centered instruction.* In **question-centered instruction**, students respond to a challenging question posed by a teacher or students themselves (Rothstein & Santana, 2011). Individually, in pairs, or in small groups, students consider possible answers, then enter their choices using smartphones, computers, or tablets. A whole-class discussion of student replies and the reasoning behind those replies follows. Following this process, students have multiple opportunities to think conceptually, reason critically, and practice problem-solving skills without becoming bored by just answering questions from a teacher.

- *Student-designed quizzes.* Students, on their own or in teams, can create quizzes, interactive videos, and polls for their classmates to try out. This gives them ownership in producing the assessment process. Students can also analyze the results from their quizzes to discuss ways to improve teaching and learning.

Assessment is only one way to utilize student participation technologies instructionally. Teachers and students can design polls and surveys to explore questions that students want to answer. Teachers can ask students for their perceptions of what is happening academically in the classroom to make changes to instructional practices based on what students tell them. Students can design their own surveys for test practice or individual or group research projects for class review. Helping students analyze survey results teaches them how to draw conclusions from numerical and written data.

Digital Dialog 12.2

Quiz games using tablets or smartphones are regarded as an effective way for teachers to rapidly assess what students know and still need to learn. As you think about using quiz games in a classroom, comment and connect online about the following questions:

- What procedures could you and students utilize to make quiz games a cooperative rather than a competitive learning tool?
- What types of questions lend themselves to thoughtful responses by students—factual recall, conceptual learning, personal opinion, open-ended discussion, or a combination of these?
- How might incorrect responses become a strategy for teaching and reviewing academic material without embarrassment for students choosing a wrong answer to a question?

Revealing and correcting student misconceptions about academic material is another way for teachers to utilize online polls and quiz games. In elementary school mathematics, students find word problems asking the question "how many more" to be confusing. What do those words mean? Reviewing these types of problems in an online poll or quiz with discussion and manipulatives to move and compare, helps students to think about and learn new information. As soon as a few understand, they can help teach others. The poll or quiz becomes the doorway to further learning and students' ideas of how to teach each other. The "how many more" is only one of thousands of examples of misconceptions resulting from not understanding the academic language used to describe the concept.

Organizing Online Quiz Games

There are several key points to keep in mind when organizing online quiz games. First, depending on how they are structured, quiz games can introduce elements of competition based on scoring points to determine winners and losers (Grinias, 2017). Competing to win can be very engaging for many students, but not for all. Noncompetitively inclined youngsters or students who are struggling in a subject or learning English as a new language can resent playing for a score and mentally drop out of a quiz activity, thereby diluting its academic assistance for them as learners. Teachers need to carefully manage the intensity of competitive play while providing additional ways for everyone to succeed, such as by having students create and conduct quiz games; playing for team or class totals rather than individual scores; and creating bonus questions to help raise the scores of teams who are behind on the leaderboard.

Second, again depending on how they are organized, quiz games can emphasize lower order thinking skills of memorization and factual recall over higher order skills of application and analysis of concepts. Fact-based questions easily fit the quiz game format, and students who know the answer earn points by responding quickly, leaving other slower members of the class disengaged from the learning and bored by the game format. To ask more complex, situation- and scenario-based questions, teachers must adjust both student roles and how the game is played. For example, a scenario-based question might put students in the role of a scientist investigating the contamination of drinking water or a doctor tracking the spread of an infectious disease. Students can be given time to discuss the question and potential answers in small groups before the answer is revealed. That way, rather than quickly getting one right answer, analysis of the problem becomes the focal point of the activity. Furthermore, quiz game formats like Poll Everywhere allow teachers to embed links to video, audio, and other online resources so students can access expanded information about a question before committing to an answer.

Third, a successful quiz game requires procedures to engage students while managing the intensity of individual and/or group competition. Teachers want students to be excited to play, but not to be dismissive of or disrespectful to classmates when trying to earn a high score. We suggest the following quiz game building strategies for you to consider using:

- Compose questions for the game using a subject textbook, sample student achievement tests posted on state or district websites, and your own personal knowledge.
- Create a known-in-advance structure for the game to ensure that everyone is focused on learning the academic material addressed in the questions. Game structure determines:
  - How students will play the game—three-person teams are an optimal size so that each student feels directly involved in the game
  - Whether everyone in a group gets to submit an answer—letting each team member discuss and submit answers is important to maximizing the learning impact of the game
  - How many questions will be asked—between 5 and 10 questions is a manageable number for a single game session
  - How long will players have to answer each question—60 to 90 seconds may be a starting point; students need time to think so they do not rush through the questions, but taking too much time to respond can make the game drag
- Discuss individual questions while the game is in progress and review the entire game after it is over. Reviewing questions and answers can be an effective way to reinforce learning for students, especially questions that students did not answer correctly. Discussions give everyone the opportunity to recall the questions and what factors make one of the answers correct.

Figure 12.6 Sample Rules for the Quiz Game

---

1. Create teams of three students made by procedures students decide or by counting off. Each team creates a unique name and gets a buzzer. The team can decide who they want to operate the buzzer.
2. Quiz leaders read the question—teams must wait until the whole question is read; early buzzing disqualifies the group from answering that question.
3. The team that buzzes first has 15 seconds to respond. If they answer correctly, the team earns one point; if they answer incorrectly, a point is taken away.

*WARNING: Points CAN go negative, so think before buzzing!

BONUS QUESTION: The last question of each round is Final Jeopardy style, meaning you can wager points!

- Set rules for quiz gameplay with students (see Figure 12.6 for a variation of game rules):

  a) Teams will consist of three students. You and students choose how teams form. Each team decides on a unique name. Team members rotate answering each question, submitting answers on their smartphones or computers.
  b) Student quiz leaders will read the questions. Teams must wait until the entire question is read before answering. Early answers will disqualify the team from scoring any points for that question.
  c) Teams have a decided upon number of seconds to submit an answer. If they answer correctly, they will receive one point. If they answer incorrectly, one point is subtracted. To maintain interest, vary styles of the round's last question Final Jeopardy's format does this.

Tech Tool 12.1 discusses online polling tools, apps and quiz games that teachers can use for pre- and post-assessments of student learning.

Here are examples of poll and quiz game digital tools and apps for use in the classroom.

- *Google Forms.* This online survey tool lets you collect responses to a variety of question types (e.g., multiple choice, checkbox, grid, video/image prompt, open-ended).
- *Socrative.* This online quiz tool lets you generate exit tickets, facilitate competitive group quizzes, ask a quick question of the class, or run single-person quizzes.
- *Formative and Classkick.* These real-time assessment tools let you ask a question or show a prompt and watch students type in their results live.
- *TED-Ed, Ed Puzzle, and PlayPosit.* These interactive video tools let you embed questions and discussion prompts into videos.

Tech Tool 12.1

Interactive Participation Tools

Interactive participation tools and apps are easy-to-use technologies. Teachers can show questions to a class, and students can respond using any device with a web browser—computer, tablet, or smartphone. These tools are universally applicable to any curriculum area. Online polls, surveys, and quizzes grab students' attention almost immediately if the structure enables equal access to winning. Students enjoy the elements of game play, and there is the added appeal of being asked different kinds of questions—one answer quickly recognized, a group choice after consulting resources, or choosing two answers where both might be correct. Varied formats invite participation and level the playing field for winning.

Before choosing and using a poll or quiz game tool, it is important to know that many polling software companies keep records of respondent data on file. Be sure to examine how each company protects the privacy rights of all respondents/students because end-user agreements vary from program to program. Review privacy guarantees before using a poll or survey.

- *Survey Mapper.* This polling software invites you to generate questions, launch your polls, and collect answers with real-time mapping feedback.
- *SurveyMonkey.* This easy-to-use survey tool offers multiple ways to formulate questions and collect information, and it has a free basic subscription for up to 10 questions and 100 responses per survey.
- *MicroPoll.* This customizable poll for websites and blogs offers real-time voting and results instantly viewable by everyone in the class.
- *Quizlet.* This popular quiz builder with multiple functions for classroom use has 2.5 million study sets of already assembled quiz questions in almost every subject area and grade level. You may also create your quizzes as well as interactive diagrams.
- *Poll Everywhere.* This texting app enables students to use their phones to submit responses to questions or to submit responses on Twitter. Poll Everywhere's basic service is free; additional services must be purchased. Its MAC Presenter App lets you conduct live polls using Keynote or PowerPoint, and you can embed live links in answer choices so students can explore topics together.
- *Show of Hands.* This app lets users participate in local and national polls on topics from politics to culture to health and sports.
- *Kahoot!* This survey-style polling resource has the option for competitive quizzes called "kahoots," where scoring is based on the accuracy and speed of student responses.

MyLab Education Application Exercise 12.2:

Reviewing an Online Quiz Game

Grading Software and Apps

Many teachers use **grading software and apps** to quickly calculate and record student grades. These resources may be for a teacher's own use—such as Gradekeeper, GradeBook Pro, or Easy Grade Pro—or a part of the online record-keeping system purchased by a school district for all teachers. Schoolwide systems record grades, track attendance, support lesson planning, manage teacher correspondence, and perform other administrative and management functions.

The advantages of grading software and apps include their capacity to efficiently calculate and store multiple forms of student performance data from tests and quizzes, assignments, homework, class participation, and other activities. Teachers can assign percentage values to different types of work (for example, 50% of the student's grade is based on test scores, 25% on writing assignments, 15% on homework, and 10% on class participation), and the software instantly calculates the overall grade. Electronic calculation allows teachers to quickly report the performance of individuals and the entire class. Students have immediate access to their grades, and families are continually informed about a child's progress in class.

However, digital grading systems raise questions about how to best assess what students know and are able to do with that knowledge. Not all school learning activities, particularly in elementary and middle school classrooms, translate into a numerical score equaling a grade of A, B, C, or D. The academic performance of young learners is more nuanced than test assessments fully measure. For example, wrong answers on a test question may reveal learning misconceptions that teachers can address with further instruction. Using test assessments to record only the right answers and enter a summary score into the virtual record-keeping system may make teachers less inclined to look at the wrong answers and help students to see how and why these are wrong. Important data for teaching may be lost when the opportunity to build knowledge is overlooked.

The National Council of Teachers of English (NCTE) has expressed strong opposition to using computers to read and evaluate student writing, declaring that software programs overemphasize the surface features (spelling, punctuation, grammar) of a text while failing to honor the qualities of word use and style that make writing creative and expressive (2013b). Machine scoring disadvantages students who are learning English as a new language and those with less familiarity using technology. Students would be better served, in NCTE's view, developing portfolios of written work that can be evaluated and responded to thoughtfully by teachers.

As a teacher, you will likely be in a school that uses some form of virtual record keeping, and you may want to have your own digital gradebook as well. Although such tools simplify the work of teachers, the success of virtual grading depends on how you use the information to monitor and improve student progress.

MyLab Education Self-Check 12.3

Digital Portfolios for Teachers and Students

12.4 Learn the features of digital portfolios for teachers and students.

Being evaluated throughout your career as a teacher sets the context for developing a digital teaching portfolio. A **digital teaching portfolio**, also called a *multimedia portfolio* or *eportfolio*, is a collection of educational and professional materials stored in a digital format. Serving as an organized collection of materials that shows growth and development as a teacher over time, it contains learning plans, student work, and related curriculum materials with video, audio, presentation slides, photographs, and other multimedia artifacts that you choose to include. It can be a place to collect and share resources with members of your professional learning network (PLN) and a reflection about what you are doing as a teacher.

A digital technology portfolio lets you showcase your knowledge and skills as a technology-using educator. It has been called a "21st century digital business card" (Simon, 2014). This eportfolio illustrates your commitment to using technology as part of teaching and learning in schools and classrooms while demonstrating what you know and can do technologically as a teacher. Everyone viewing your eportfolio, from teachers and administrators to families and students themselves, will be interested in the examples you provide of technology-based learning activities and media-rich teaching.

Common elements found in most new teacher digital portfolios include:

- Resume of professional accomplishments
- Biographical sketch
- Philosophy of teaching and learning
- Letters of reference
- Learning plans, unit plans, and teaching reflections
- Academic courses and research experiences
- Teaching, tutoring, and other educational experiences
- Technology-based examples of teaching and learning (including any multimedia you've designed for your graduate classes or for teaching)
- Curated resources from your PLN (e.g., articles, images, learning ideas)

Making a digital teaching portfolio when you start taking courses toward a teaching license provides a place to store ideas, information, and activities from classes, field experiences, summer work, and community volunteering as sources of material. When you are finishing a teacher license program as an intern or student teacher, or beginning as a full-time classroom teacher, documenting professional learning accomplishments in a digital teaching portfolio provides career-related information to school administrators and teaching colleagues and offers a place for publishing personal reflections about your developing knowledge as an educator.

Elements of Digital Portfolios for Teachers

Digital portfolios by teachers follow patterns established in other fields and professions. Writers, artists, engineers, architects, musicians, graphic designers, and web developers share collections of their work to demonstrate talents and skills to employers or customers. Teachers design their portfolios in different and creative ways, but most collections include certain elements that document academic courses, teaching experiences, personal talents, and professional accomplishments. Figure 12.7 shows the homepages of two first-year teachers' online portfolios—categories on the page show pull-down menus linking to curriculum materials and assignments.

Choices for building your digital teacher portfolio range from premade sites to do-it-yourself program designs. You can decide among products that are free with limited design options that charge a fee and offer more ways to present material, or specialized versions that are more expensive and expansive in style and scope. Google Sites, Adobe Spark, and Wix are examples of easy-to-use free portfolio building sites.

Figure 12.7 Two New Teachers' Digital Portfolios

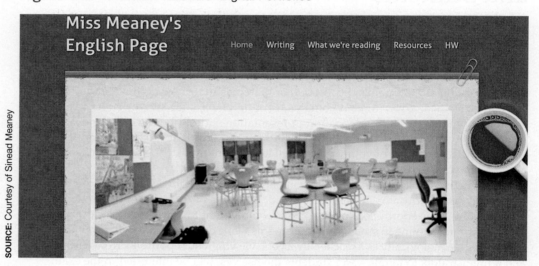

SOURCE: Courtesy of Sinead Meaney

SOURCE: Courtesy of Lauren Morton

When designing a digital teaching portfolio, it's important to showcase your technology literacy, which means ensuring your website is accessible to everyone. To make your digital portfolio accessible, use headers in order (heading 1, heading 2, heading 3), describe the visuals on your page using alternative text fields (for screen readers), make sure all videos have accurate closed captions, place periods at the end of bullet points (so the screen readers know where the sentence ends), and describe links (rather than saying "click here"). Use the Web Aim accessibility checker (http://wave.webaim.org/) to test the accessibility of your website. You can also use Grackle Suite (https://www.grackledocs.com/) to assess the accessibility of any Google Docs, Spreadsheets, or Slides you include on your digital teaching portfolio.

Another aspect of your technology knowledge is ensuring that your digital teaching portfolio is free of copyrighted materials (e.g., images pulled directly from a Google Image search). Use only media you have taken (with permission from students for any student work) or Creative Commons/public domain media on your site. You do not want anyone, employer or students, to think that you stole an image from Google and put it on your site. Also, note that adding an "image from this URL..." caption under an image does not make it legal to put a copyrighted image on your site.

Portfolios and Reflection

Learning through personal reflection is a paramount feature of portfolios. When employed as a tool for reflective practice, a digital teaching portfolio can enable both novice and accomplished teachers to showcase professional experiences. It is an eye appealing, interesting, and always accessible way to summarize the knowledge, skills, and dispositions one is gaining in the process of being a teacher.

The use of **standards-based digital portfolios** in teacher education has grown in recent years. The purpose of such portfolios is to connect teaching skills and competencies with teaching and/or curriculum standards. Standards can be a helpful way to organize portfolio material, viewing them as an opportunity to record competencies while reflecting on your personal growth as an educator instead of viewing them as a checklist of requirements that have to be fulfilled.

Using an eportfolio to explore your own teaching enables you to acquire a distinguishing quality of master teachers: the capacity to think critically and creatively about how to teach students and meet your professional goals. Assembling an eportfolio provides a structure for examining teaching practices, identifying strengths and weaknesses, and making plans to improve or change certain aspects in the future. Constructing an eportfolio without personal reflection produces an opposite outcome. Rather than documenting thinking about change, the eportfolio becomes a celebratory scrapbook of long-past activities that deters rather than promotes growth and change in a teacher's practice and knowledge.

You, too, may have wondered when building your own eportfolio about a tendency to post examples of your best efforts only (perhaps to satisfy outside evaluators of your teaching practices) and then rarely changing these entries. The intrinsic value of a digital portfolio is that its contents can be constantly changed to reflect your growth as a teacher and the growth of students as learners. Indeed, you may find yourself eagerly creating lesson plans using new strategies and technologies and then adding them to your eportfolio as evidence of changed thinking and different practices in the classroom.

Artifacts in a teacher's digital portfolio typically include lesson plans, illustrations, presentations, videos, and reflective summaries.

SOURCE: Robert W. Maloy.

Self-Tutoring for New Teachers

Learning new skills and talents is a necessary way to develop one's skills and talents as a teacher—and those skills can then be documented in a digital teaching portfolio. **Self-tutoring** (also called *self-chosen learning*) involves setting and achieving important personal or professional learning goals outside the

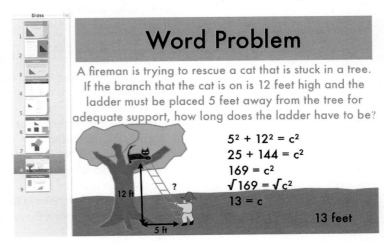

Word Problem

A fireman is trying to rescue a cat that is stuck in a tree. If the branch that the cat is on is 12 feet high and the ladder must be placed 5 feet away from the tree for adequate support, how long does the ladder have to be?

$$5^2 + 12^2 = c^2$$
$$25 + 144 = c^2$$
$$169 = c^2$$
$$\sqrt{169} = \sqrt{c^2}$$
$$13 = c$$

13 feet

requirements of college teacher license courses or school system professional development mandates. For future educators, self-tutoring learning flips the experience of becoming a teacher. Instead of focusing on what you are going to teach to students, the focus is placed on what you are choosing to learn. We have found that such self-tutoring experiences show future teachers firsthand the importance of active engagement and supportive coaching in any educational endeavor.

We have provided self-tutoring as an option for undergraduates in our course, "Tutoring in Schools." Students chose a personal or professional learning goal and then use human partners or digital resources (like YouTube videos) to help them achieve it. We were amazed by the range of activities chosen by the undergraduates who devoted many hours to their self-learning.

Three main types of self-learning projects emerged: 1) self-learning with a personal coach or tutor; 2) self-learning with a group of peers; and 3) self-learning using digital technologies. Self-tutoring with technology was the most often chosen approach. One semester, individual students used the app Duolingo to learn either French, Spanish, Italian, Turkish, or Chinese. Others found YouTube videos to gain new skills—one student started playing the guitar and another practiced playing the piano using chords. A student watched videos to learn American Sign Language; another watched jump-rope videos to get in shape so he could join the school's boxing club. A three-student group learned podcasting skills from online videos and then began a podcast at the college radio station writing, recording, and posting their own movie reviews.

Asked to reflect on these experiences, students—many of whom plan to become teachers—found self-learning surprisingly valuable. "I wouldn't have even thought that I had time to learn something new on my own," said one. Another remarked, "I learned about myself as a learner. It takes patience and practice to learn and I had forgotten how much of these students need." Many commented on how technology supports self-learning, for as one undergraduate noted: "The main thing that I learned from the app [Duolingo] was not necessarily the information in it, but rather the ways that it can be applied to help someone learn in a classroom or home environment."

Self-tutoring activities are substantive additions to a new teacher's digital portfolio. They show individual initiative and accomplishment, qualities that school systems are seeking in the educators they hire. Moreover, as individuals reflect on their self-chosen learning, they get to reconsider and think about the kind of teacher they plan to become when entering the classroom. Learning new skills and talents requires a growth mind-set, a capacity for risk-taking, a knowledge of how technology can support learning, and a willingness to work, practice, and learn from one's mistakes. Those qualities too are important for new teachers as they enter the job market as a technology-using educator. Teachers can also set up self-tutoring situations in K–12 classrooms through programs like Genius Hour, discussed in Chapter 3.

Take a moment to consider: What is something you've always wanted to learn how to do or never had time to learn how to do? Set aside time in your schedule daily or weekly to achieve your learning goal. As you engage in the learning process and reflect upon your experiences with it, reread your learning philosophy statement in your digital teaching portfolio. After self-tutoring, you may want to make revisions.

Digital Portfolios for Students

Changing from paper to digital portfolios represents a significant shift in how students communicate information about themselves and their learning. A digital portfolio may contain all the material found in a paper portfolio, but multimedia technologies are used to present the material (Reynolds & Davis, 2013; Jones & Shelton, 2011).

For students, a digital or eportfolio is both a personal and a public piece of writing. Prior to eportfolios, students stored materials in a three-ring binder and shared it only with a small number of readers. Those readers then mainly evaluated the material in a linear, page-by-page manner, viewing the early pages before the later ones. By contrast, digital portfolios make material available to many readers who can access the material electronically, navigating through the portfolio in multiple ways, moving within the linked material as they choose. This chapter's Technology Transformation Learning Plan, "Constructing an Encyclo-ME-dia," shows a digital portfolio approach for elementary students.

Teacher and blogger Matt Renwick (2014) distinguishes between two types of student digital learning collections: performance portfolios and progress portfolios. A performance portfolio displays self-chosen examples of a student's most highly developed work achieved through persistence, reflection, and reconstruction. A progress portfolio, by contrast, is an ongoing record of a student's growth in knowledge and skills over time; it may show both what a student knows and what the student is still working on learning. Viewing both gives students, teachers, families, and schools a wide-angle view of each student, allowing them to celebrate real accomplishments while setting tangible goals for what is to be learned next.

There are four important advantages of digital portfolios for K–12 students (see Table 12.4):

1. Digital portfolios are accessible and portable. Information that would fill dozens of paper pages is easily maintained and transported electronically.
2. Digital publication encourages new, creative expressions of one's ideas and accomplishments.
3. Working with technology increases portfolio builders' technological skills and confidence.
4. Digital portfolios offer connections to wider educational communities through online communications.

At the same time, there are skills necessary for digital portfolios:

1. Digital portfolios require students to know or learn how to use cameras, scanners, apps, photo and illustration software, and other tools. Though mastering these tools is a positive learning experience, it requires some class time on a regular basis with students teaching each other and you.
2. Students will also need teacher ideas and suggestions when building a portfolio template, determining what to include in it, and deciding how to describe it.
3. Not everyone in the hoped-for audiences of parents, families, other teachers, and peers will have the time to view each student's digital portfolio.
4. Some portfolio builders will spend more time fashioning the "look" of their portfolios than highlighting the substance of their academic learning.

MyLab Education Self-Check 12.4

Table 12.4 Advantages and Disadvantages of Digital Portfolios

Advantages	Disadvantages
Accessibility	Knowledge and skill requirements
Portability	Professional support
Creativity	Equipment
Technological self-confidence	Time and energy
Community	Need for increased viewer skills and equipment
	Presentation distracts from content

SOURCE: Based on *Creating Digital Teaching Portfolios* (Kilbane & Milman, 2008).

Technology Transformation Learning Plan

Constructing an Encyclo-ME-dia: Recording Student Learning in a Digital Portfolio

Grade(s)	Elementary and middle school
Subject(s)	Language arts/social studies
Key Goal/Enduring Understanding	An **Encyclo-ME-dia** collects and shares the personal milestones, memorable activities, and creative work of individual students in ways that allow everyone in a class to learn about each other's accomplishments and achievements.
Essential Question	What personal activities and accomplishments in school could become part of an Encyclo-ME-dia, and why?

Academic Discipline Learning Standards	National Council for the Social Studies: *Curriculum Standards for the Social Studies*
	        Theme III: People, Places, and Environment
	        Theme IV: Individual Development and Identity
	        Theme X: Civic Ideals and Practices

Learning Objectives	Students will know and be able to: • Describe and write in different genres, including autobiography, memoirs, letters, diary entries, poems, and stories • Choose portfolio selections to show examples of writing in class and personal interests
Technology Uses	The lesson uses tablets, smartphones, digital cameras, scanners, and editing software for collecting and publishing students' digital portfolios. A separate digital folder is made, and students add items into the Encyclo-ME-dia regularly throughout the school year.

Minimal Technology	Infusion of Technology
Students use markers, colored pencils, crayons, watercolor paint, glue sticks, tape, staplers, and paper of different sizes and colors to create items for a paper portfolio.	Students use word processors, image design or drawing programs, cameras, microphones, and editing software, tablets, and apps to create and post items for a digital portfolio.
Students collect their materials in file folders, notebooks, or other paper storage units.	Students upload photos and video to their digital portfolios.
Students publish their portfolios in a notebook or paper folder.	Students use a classroom website to publish their digital portfolios.

Evaluation	Students will be evaluated on the diversity of items showcased (video, slideshows, illustrations, and artifacts) and the range of writing genres (reports, poems, memoirs, books, essays, interviews, posters, plays, and skits) as well as their written, filmed, or recorded summaries of what they have learned and can do independently.
Learning Plan Description	An Encyclo-ME-dia is a digital collection of student-created materials that previously were stored in paper scrapbooks, journals, or diaries. An Encyclo-ME-dia shows elementary and middle school students how to assemble and develop a portfolio of personal writings, drawings, illustrations, and artwork, and audio, photographs and videos.

Although regularly used by older students to showcase their learning, digital portfolios constructed by younger students produce personally chosen creative collections of learning accomplishments.

A digital Encyclo-ME-dia serves as a technology-based learning portfolio in these ways:

- *Easy documentation and assessment of student learning.* Paper materials are sometimes misplaced and bulky to store, whereas digital materials are readily available for viewing by teachers, families, and students themselves. Classroom projects for history, science, writing, math, and creative arts are conveniently accessed digitally.
- *New forms of creative self-expression.* An Encyclo-ME-dia inspires students' choice of new forms of writing and illustrating. A student who does not enjoy writing may find digital tools for changing drafts much easier to use than rewriting by hand. Another student may discover talents as a graphic designer who captures ideas in a unique visual style to accompany poems, essays, letters, and stories, making writing more inviting. Conversely, a student who does not enjoy drawing or illustrating may be attracted to the design possibilities of desktop publishing and photo editing or the use of a tablet with drawing apps.
- *Learning about technology by using technology.* The International Society for Technology in Education (ISTE) emphasizes that all students, from first- and second-graders through high school and college students, should access technology tools in project-based learning activities. Collecting and publishing personal work digitally teaches about technology's uses and creative potentials. Using these tools demonstrates how extraordinarily fresh and new students' thinking can be in digital environments.

- *Learning about writing by writing.* An Encyclo-ME-dia showcases different writing genres. Through personal self-expression, students see themselves within the larger communities of classroom, school, neighborhood, and nation. Using tablets, cameras, and apps, students become full-fledged authors, editors, and self-publishers of their portfolios, choosing what to feature and how to showcase their writing.
- *Student engagement.* Archiving one's ideas digitally creates a powerful incentive for students to invest time and effort in their creations. When students are personally interested in the outcomes of a learning activity, they readily practice the literacy skills of reading, writing, and revising. Creating an Encyclo-ME-dia connects student engagement to the main themes of this chapter: digital portfolio development and student involvement in performance evaluation. Teachers evaluate student materials in an Encyclo-ME-dia as authentic evidence of learning; students display those same materials for self-assessment and reflection of what they have accomplished.

Learning Design—Minimal Technology
Paper portfolios, books, and posters titled "All about Me" have long been popular autobiographical writing assignments for elementary and middle school students. These formats enable students to creatively save and display personal writing and drawing. "All about Me" portfolios use minimal technology, although they often contain photocopies and photographs. "All about Me" books and paper portfolios might start at the beginning of the school year and be added to throughout the year as the curriculum evolves. Students include photos, drawings, paintings, maps, sketches, or timelines to illustrate their learning, and teachers might assign entries at any time as part of class activities and investigations.

Learning Activities Using Technology
Digital portfolios assist students in documenting and reflecting about their learning in school. You could begin the process in this way:

1. *Start your Encyclo-ME-dias.* If an Encyclo-ME-dia seems time consuming and complex, ask students what they already know about photography, uploading photos and videos from the web, and editing and downloading materials. Make a list of the skills and competencies that students possess. Students can then help teach each other about platforms and other digital tools.
2. *Choose the scale and time frame.* You can record a single science project or writing genre, an entire year of academic artifacts, or any ideas in between. In February, in connection with Black History Month and Presidents' Day, students might construct Encyclo-ME-dia entries that examine their lives and the influences that contribute to who they are in society. Usually students do not view the present as extraordinary or their own decisions as history making. By focusing attention on the importance of personal decisions as history-making activities, students act as historians of their own lives. This is a connection to learning about the lives of individuals, known and anonymous, from the past.
3. *Learn technologies collaboratively.* Together with students, learn about new apps for photo taking and video making, uploading and downloading, and inserting items into Encyclo-ME-dia folders. Slideshows, videos, greeting cards, postcards, comics, animations, stop action animations and almost anything else students design might be included in student portfolios. Supervising students' efforts requires less and less time from an adult as students become skilled in portfolio production processes and teaching each other. Students will also want to collaborate on ideas and designs for their Encyclo-ME-dias.
4. *Incorporate visual elements and video segments.* Photos and videos of students participating in learning activities are easily recorded with a digital video camera or smartphone, enabling students to 1) describe what they are doing or building; 2) ask questions of the audience as they demonstrate an experiment or explain a creative idea; and 3) perform in a play, skit, student-written commercial, public service announcement, puppet show, dance, read-aloud, news report, or other presentation.
5. *Focus on school activities.* When outside-of-school lives are included in an Encyclo-ME-dia, remember that not everyone has the same access to learning experiences and technology resources. Some students have experiences to include in their portfolio that others might not—family vacations, holiday celebrations, and trips to new places. By keeping the portfolio's contents on in-school activities and accomplishments, differences in students' lives outside of school are not important.

Analysis and Extensions
1. Describe two features you find useful about this lesson.
2. How widely has technology been integrated into the lesson?
3. Name two areas for extension or revision of this lesson.
4. How might students become more involved in designing, using, and evaluating their technology use in the lesson?

Chapter Summary

Learning Outcome 12.1

Discuss different types of learning assessments.

- Assessing student learning is an essential component of the work of teachers.
- Performance evaluations include assessments of student writing, individual and group projects, homework assignments, individual presentations and performances, as well as open-book exams, student self-assessments, and teacher observations.
- Technology is a tool for assessing performance-based learning because it allows students to display their knowledge and accomplishments using words, pictures, images, videos, and other materials.
- Student performance rubrics provide known-in-advance performance criteria for completing school assignments and offer teachers and students frameworks for fairly evaluating learning.

Learning Outcome 12.2

Explore student-centered assessment practices in schools and classrooms.

- A teacher's digital portfolio is an individually prepared collection of assets that communicates what a teacher knows and is able to do with academic subjects and classroom teaching.
- A standards-based digital portfolio serves as a way for new teacher candidates to connect experiences from classrooms to the professional teaching standards they are required to meet to earn a teaching license.
- Advantages of digital portfolios include easy online access, creative information displays, development of technology skills, and information sharing with families, friends, and other students.
- Disadvantages include consistent technology access, time to do the reflective and creative work, and the

possibility that style will override substance in the presentation of information.

Learning Outcome 12.3

Identify digital tools and instructional practices that actively involve students in assessing learning.

- Actively involving students in the process of performance evaluation builds partnerships for learning, a concept supported by advocates for democratic schools and classrooms.
- Digital portfolios allow students to participate in assessment processes, showing what they know and/or are able to do in a subject area.
- Online polls and quiz games activate students' prior knowledge about academic topics.

Learning Outcome 12.4

Learn the features of digital portfolios for teachers and students.

- Democratic practices, learning portfolios, online surveys, and rubrics promote student involvement in their education.
- Student feedback surveys provide teachers with ideas and information for developing learning activities that support students' beliefs about how they learn best.
- Student response systems enable students to anonymously respond to questions posed in a whole-group setting.
- Participation systems engage students with academic material while enabling teachers to conduct quick assessments of what students know or need or want to learn about a topic.
- Designing interesting, discussion-provoking questions is paramount to effective student participation.

Key Terms

MyLab Education Application Exercise 12.3

For Reflection and Discussion

Alfie Kohn's Critique of Standardized Tests

Education reformer Alfie Kohn (2011) believes that standardized tests are not "objective" or neutral measures of performance because adults inevitably insert biases of culture, language, and community into the test questions. In addition, students, who must take these tests, feel the stress of performance, and their "test anxiety" distorts the results. For both these reasons, Kohn believes that "the more a test is made to 'count,' the less valid the scores become" (Kohn, 1999, p. 76).

- Based on your analysis and experiences as a taker of tests, would you mostly agree with or disagree with Kohn's analysis? Explain your reasons.
- What other types of assessments can teachers utilize to assess student performance?

Test Assessments for New Teachers

In almost every state, prospective teachers must pass one or more standardized tests to receive a teaching license. As you consider this educational policy, respond to the following questions:

- Do you agree that all teacher candidates should pass a state or national competency exam before receiving a license to teach? Why or why not?
- In what ways does passing a test measure and not measure the skills and talents you display as a teacher?
- How might classroom-based performance assessments more widely measure or document your skills and talents as a teacher?

Glossary

Academic content   Ideas, information, concepts, and skills taught to students by teachers

Acceptable use policies (AUPs)   Rules for technology use by teachers and students in schools

Accessibility   Ensuring that every student can access and utilize the learning resources they need to succeed academically

Accommodation   Changes to teaching and learning practices designed to individualize and support learning for students with special educational needs

Achievement gap   Differences in academic outcomes resulting in lower test scores and graduation rates for low-income and culturally diverse youngsters, English language learners, and students with special educational needs, as well as girls or boys

Active learning   Students engaged intellectually and physically in activities that promote understanding and evaluation of academic content

Active screen time   Students being physically or cognitively involved when using screen media

Adaptive and intelligent tutoring systems (ITS)   Online or machine-based coaching or teaching for students in which a computer seeks to simulate the responses of a human tutor or teacher

Adaptation/appropriation stage   Teachers integrate technology fully into classroom learning activities as well as professional work

Administrative/professional activities   Planning, organizing, assessing, and record keeping by teachers done to support the direct instruction of students

Adoption stage   Teachers use technology without changing existing classroom instruction and practices

Alphabets and alphabet books   Student-made or student-and-teacher-made materials for teaching spelling patterns, letter sounds, vocabulary words, conventions of print, and reading strategies

Animations   Making still pictures or drawings appear to be moving images

App   An abbreviation of the word *application* that refers to software used on tablets, smartphones, and other mobile devices to perform specific functions; *see also* educational apps

Archival and primary source websites and apps   Educational materials providing original historical resources for students to access and analyze

Assessment   Evaluating a student or a teacher's learning on an activity or assignment

Assistive technologies (AT)   Tools to minimize barriers to learning and make academic material more accessible to students

Asynchronous communications   Information exchanges with time delays between responses (for example, e-mail messages or readers' responses to blog postings); *See also* synchronous communications

Augmented reality (AR)   Adding information, images, and objects to real-world scenes to create a new, computer-based environment

Augmentation stage   *See* adoption stage

Automate   Technological improvements that maintain rather than change existing practices

Avatar   Online identity adopted by students and teachers when playing games or participating in virtual reality simulations

Badware   Unscrupulous or deceitful software that allows spam or other unwanted programs to enter a device or system

Behaviorism   Theory of learning based on the idea that students learn from the repeating or reinforcing responses given by teachers; those who endorse this learning theory are called behaviorists

Blended learning   Academic experiences achieved through a combination of face-to-face and online learning experiences

Blogs   Abbreviation of *weblogs*; regularly updated online journals or websites where writers post information that can be read and responded to by readers

Bloom's taxonomy   Hierarchical system for classifying thinking skills first proposed by psychologist Benjamin Bloom

Bookmarking   Identifying and saving frequently visited web addresses on a computer; *see also* social bookmarking

Brain-based education   Educators providing different cognitive and instructional approaches as students' brains develop over time

Bring your own device/technology (BYOD/T)   Students bringing technology from home to use at school

Building and inventing tools   Programs that promote open-ended ways for students to express themselves artistically, mathematically, and/or spatially

Bullying   Unwanted threats or aggressions by one person toward another

Censorship   Approach used to block unwanted Internet content

Cheating   Accessing information without permission before or during a test or sending information about a test to other students before, during, or after an exam

Civic engagement   Efforts by students and teachers to improve communities through active involvement in social and political life; *see also* service learning

Cloud computing   Storing and managing information using web-based servers

Coding   Sequence of written commands that tell a computer what a programmer wants the machine to do

Cognitive load   Presentation of information on a webpage that either supports or restricts understanding and learning

Cognitivism   Theory of learning that focuses on the activities of the human mind and its interactions with the environment

Common Core State Standards   National curriculum standards in English/language arts/literacy and mathematics intended to help students develop conceptual and procedural knowledge needed for college and careers

Common Craft–style videos   Videos made by teachers and students using simple illustrations and paper cut-outs in the visual presentation of information

Computational thinking   Knowing how to use data, models, simulations, and algorithmic thinking to formulate and solve problems

Computer   A powerful information-processing machine that manipulates data by following instructions given by human programmers

Computer- and web-based games   Learning or entertainment activities, often featuring virtual worlds, avatars, and competition for points and a winning score

Computer literacy Learning the names, functions, and procedures of computer hardware and software

Concept/skills practice websites and apps Educational materials providing subject-specific review and practice activities for students at all grade levels

Concept and information books Student-made or student-and-teacher-made books designed to teach a single concept or idea such as shapes, sizes, fractions, opposites, or patterns

Connectivity gap A lack of available bandwidth to provide high-speed wireless connections resulting in greatly reduced access to online resources and information

Constructionism Theory of learning associated with Seymour Papert that holds the meanings individuals construct through their actions become more deeply understood when they are explained or taught to others

Constructivism Theory of learning based on the idea that individuals construct meaning through their actions and reflections on those actions

Content curation Collecting teaching and learning materials from online and print sources

Cooperative learning Group activities in which students have designated roles to perform as they work together on learning projects; *see also* groupwork

COPPA (Children's Online Privacy Protection Act) Federal law designed to protect the online privacy and security of children under age 13

Copyright Legal protection of literary, dramatic, artistic, musical, and analytical work from infringement by others

Creative Commons Licenses that allow authors to retain copyright but allow other people to copy and distribute the materials

Creativity Statements, projects, or actions by students or teachers that express new or out-of-the-ordinary ideas or approaches

Creativity apps Applications designed to support creative self-expressions by teachers and students

Criterion-referenced tests Exams that compare a test taker's performance to a set of specific objectives or standards

Critical thinking Analyzing situations, problems, or written and visual materials to determine their reliability and usefulness

Crowdfunding Using the Internet to do fundraising, generally by collecting small amounts of money from a large group of donors

Culturally responsive teaching *See* multicultural education

Cyberbullying Using computers, smartphones, or other communication technologies to threaten or harm others

Database Information organized around specific topics and easily searchable by users

Democratic schools and classrooms Educational settings that feature ongoing participation and collaborative decision-making by students and teachers

Desktop-based games Games that are downloaded to a personal device; *see also* Internet-based games

Differentiated instruction (DI) Teachers adapting instructional approaches so students with different learning styles can understand ideas and concepts

Digital art Art constructed using online tools, software, or apps

Digital badges Online credentials showing someone's accomplishments, skills, or competencies

Digital cameras Cameras that take still photographs and record video

Digital childhood Experiences of children growing up using computers, tablets, smartphones, television, video games, and other media

Digital citizenship Roles and responsibilities for acting ethically and safely in digital environments

Digital communication Digital communication is the process of devices communicating information digitally.

Digital content Academic resources and materials accessed from the Internet

Digital continuum A technology access scale ranging from older technologies at one end to the latest tools and devices at the other end

Digital disconnect Differences in technological knowledge and interest between students and teachers

Digital inequality Lack of access to interactive digital technologies by low-income students, diverse learners, and older Americans; *see also* connectivity gap, participation gap, homework gap

Digital literacy Understanding how information is produced and presented in online formats

Digital projectors Machines that project computer-based images onto a screen for classroom viewing

Digital reputation How a person is perceived online based on the digital content that they post about themselves

Digital storytelling Recording stories using digital video, pictures, and words

Digital teaching portfolio Instructional and professional materials stored in an online format, also called eportfolio; *see also* professional learning network (PLN)

Digital textbooks Online educational materials used by teachers and students; *see also* e-books

Digital translators Mobile devices that translate written or spoken words from one language to another

Digital video-editing software Application for editing and manipulating digital video material

Digital writing Written communications done on desktops, laptops, tablets, or smartphones and posted online as blog entries, tweets, e-mails, Facebook posts, or other web publication formats

Discipline-based professional organization National, regional, or state organization of educators devoted to the teaching and learning of an academic subject; e.g., National Council of Teachers of English (NCTE) or National Council of Teachers of Mathematics (NCTM)

Disruptive innovations Ways in which technology redesigns and redefines existing patterns and structures in schools and other organizations

Distance learning *See* online learning

Diversity explosion Demographic changes in schools and society marked by growing numbers of Hispanic, African American, Asian/Pacific Islander, and Native American students

Document camera Device that projects images from books and other materials onto a screen for classroom viewing

Drafting Stage of the writing process in which a writer creates a first or working document that is subsequently revised and edited

e-books Abbreviation of *electronic books*; material that is delivered digitally to teachers and students using laptops, tablets, smartphones, or other mobile devices; *see also* digital textbooks

e-book apps Applications for tablets and smartphones that enable users to access e-books; e.g., Kindle, Scribd, or Google Play Books

Editing Stage of the writing process in which a writer includes conventions of print, standard spelling, punctuation, varied sentence structure, and paragraphing to make the text clearer for readers

Educational change Innovations in school organizational structures, academic curriculum, instructional practices, and/or student learning activities

Educational digital content   Academic resources and materials accessed from the Internet; *see also* educational websites and apps

Educational websites and apps   Online digital content designed for K–12 learning

E-mail   Electronic communications sent over the Internet

Enduring understandings   Overarching ideas and essential concepts for students to learn within an Understanding by Design lesson development model; *see also* Understanding by Design (UbD)

e-newsletter   A newsletter sent via e-mail

Entertainment apps   Applications designed to provide recreation and learning for teachers and students

Entry stage   Teachers just beginning to use technology for teaching and learning

e-readers   Devices for reading e-books and digital textbooks

Essential questions   *See* enduring understandings

Exploration and discovery websites and apps   Educational materials that engage students in interactive explorations of academic subjects and topics

Exploratory learning   *See* inquiry learning

Fair use   Limited use of copyrighted materials in educational settings that do not need permission from the copyright owner

Fake and false news   Information that is deliberately misleading or not true but presented as though it were objectively and factually correct

Feedback   Responses by teachers to students about their academic work; also student responses to teachers about their instructional practices

Filtering software   Programs that block unwanted or objectionable websites from appearing on school computers

Flipped learning   Technology-based instructional approach using in-class time for group learning and one-on-one teacher instruction and outside-of-class time for independent learning and multimedia use by students

Folksonomy   Teacher- or student-created system for categorizing social bookmarking tags; derived from the words *folk* and *taxonomy*; *see also* social bookmarking

Formative assessment   Ongoing assessments done by teachers throughout a lesson or unit to monitor and evaluate student performance and progress

Game-based learning   Using games to teach academic content to students

Gamification   Using game playing to motivate people to use technology for specific purposes, such as buying a product or learning a skill

Generation Alpha   Name given to youngsters born since 2010; the children of parents from Generation Z

Generation Z   Name given to youngsters born since 2000 who have grown up using computers, the Internet, smartphones, social media, and interactive digital technologies

Genius hour   Giving students regular time during the school week to work on creative projects of personal interest

Google geographic tools   Geography learning technologies widely used in science and social studies at all grade levels; e.g., Google Earth and Google Maps

Grading software and apps   Computer-based and online student learning assessment tools

Graphic design   Process of visually arranging words, symbols, and images to communicate information on pages or screens

Groupwork   Instructional format in which small groups of students collaborate to do academic tasks; *see also* cooperative learning

Hardware   Basic machinery and circuitry of a computer

Hashtags   Symbols marking keywords in Twitter postings

Higher order thinking   Solving problems by applying, analyzing, creating, and evaluating information to promote new meanings and understandings; *see also* Bloom's taxonomy

Highly interactive, inquiry-based teaching and learning   Using technology to promote curiosity, active engagement, critical and creative thinking, and academic learning by students

High-stakes tests   Exams with significant consequences for passing or failing scores, such as graduating or not graduating from high school or gaining or not gaining a teaching license

High-tech accommodations   Changes to learning environments or curriculum delivery strategies involving extensive use of digital technologies; *see also* accommodations

Homework gap   Disadvantage experienced by students who lack the necessary digital resources at home to complete school assignments

Ill-structured problems   Issues that do not have easy or simple solutions

Immersive games   Games that fully involve players in the setting and structure of the game; *see also* non-immersive games

Inclusion   Placing students with special educational needs in the least restrictive educational environment, often in the same classroom with their regular education peers

Informate   Using technology to create new approaches to teaching and learning in schools

Information alert   Notice received by e-mail when new information about a topic becomes available online

Information apps   Applications designed to provide facts, materials, and resources; e.g. a weather app or a news app

Information and communication technologies (ICTs)   Tools, applications, and systems that make the digital publishing and sharing of information possible

Information literacy   Learning to use digital information, online communication tools, and social networks to share ideas and solve problems

Information management   System for collecting, organizing, and using information for teaching and learning

Information presentation design   Process of arranging digital content on websites or blogs to convey information clearly and interestingly; *see also* graphic design

Information research and retrieval   Locating, evaluating, and using information derived from paper or digital sources

IT (information technology) fluency   Learning to use computers, the Internet, and digital tools confidently and appropriately in and outside of school to solve problems, communicate ideas, and achieve goals

Infusion   Integration of technology into existing teaching and learning practices in K–12 schools

Inquiry-based learning   Activities in which students investigate questions, issues, and problems and propose answers or solutions based on research

Instant messaging   Real-time online exchanges between two communicators; also called *IMing*

Instructional design   Decisions and choices made by teachers in creating, teaching, and evaluating learning activities with students

Instructional practices   Methods used by teachers to convey academic ideas and content to students

Interactive participation tools and apps Real-time interactions between students and teachers using smartphones and computers

Interactive video Embedding questions, quizzes, or dialogues in a video for students to answer

Interactive videoconferencing Real-time face-to-face online meetings using video technology

Interactive whiteboard Large-screen, touch-sensitive device that interacts with a computer to enhance teaching and learning experiences in a classroom

Internet literacy Learning how to find, use, and evaluate online content

Invention stage Teachers using technology to create new instructional practices

ISTE Standards for Educators Standards for teacher learning and instructional practice with technology developed by the International Society for Technology in Education

ISTE Standards for Students Standards for student learning with technology developed by the International Society for Technology in Education

Ken Burns effect Use of zooming and panning in the editing of digital videos to give still photographs a sense of dramatic movement; pioneered by filmmaker Ken Burns

Keywords Words or phrases used by search engines to locate relevant webpages

Laptops Lightweight, portable computers, also known as *notebooks*, powered by batteries or AC current when plugged into an electrical outlet

Learning assessments Methods used to evaluate student knowledge and performance before, during, and after a lesson is taught

Learning management system (LMS) Software used by educational organizations to support the delivery of courses and online learning experiences

Lesson planning Activities performed by teachers when developing, teaching, and evaluating learning experiences for students

Lesson plan websites Online materials featuring lesson plans and related instructional materials

Lower order thinking Remembering and understanding information; also known as *recall; see also* Bloom's taxonomy

Low-tech accommodations Changes to learning environments or curriculum delivery strategies involving minimal use of technology; *see also* accommodations

Maker-based learning Approach to instruction in classrooms emphasizing learning by making

Makerspaces Areas in schools and libraries devoted to enabling students to design, tinker, invent, and construct based on their ideas and interests

Maker Movement A do-it-yourself community where people create and build objects of all kinds with electronics, robotics, smart materials, and 3-D printers

Malinformation Harmful or damaging online information

Massive open online courses (MOOCs) Online courses open to hundreds of participants

Media literacy Being able to analyze the impacts of various media platforms, e.g., television, movies, the Internet, videos, social media, and online games

Media multitasking Students using more than one media at a time

Media synergy Video, digital, and print materials combined with face-to-face instruction

Messed-up information Confusing or difficult-to-understand online information

Metacognitive thinking Process of actively reflecting on one's thinking and learning; referred to as "thinking about thinking"

Microblogging Sending short text messages, photos, or audio to friends; tweeting on Twitter is one example

Mid-tech accommodations Changes to learning environments or curriculum delivery strategies involving moderate use of technology; *see also* accommodations

Millennials Members of a population cohort born between 1981 and 1996

Mindtools Technologies that promote problem solving and critical thinking by students and teachers; term first used by David Jonassen

Misinformation False, out-of-date, or misleading online information

Modification Changes to teaching and learning situations where students with special educational needs receive less substantive experiences than regular education students

Modification stage *See* adaptation/appropriation stage

Montessori method Educational approaches developed by Maria Montessori featuring multisensory materials that engage students while providing immediate self-correcting feedback for learning

Mostly useless information Trivial and irrelevant online information

Multicultural education Learning experiences that integrate and affirm the interests, needs, talents, lives, and histories of students and families from diverse cultural, ethnic, and linguistic backgrounds

Multimedia Presentation of information using multiple media, including words, pictures, sound, and data

Multimodal learning Using information and images from multiple sources, such as words, video, graphics, and pictures, to produce learning for students

Multiuser virtual environments (MVUs) An online space where multiple people can interact with one another and the environment simultaneously

New teacher assessment Process of evaluating the readiness of teachers to enter the classroom, often through a combination of state-mandated teacher tests, school system evaluations, and college program assignments and observations

Next-generation presentation tools and apps Newer software and apps designed to create dynamic, nonlinear presentations to expand how students explore academic topics

Non-immersive games Games that do not fully involve game players in the setting and structure of a game; *see also* immersive games

Norm-referenced tests Exams that compare a test taker's performance against other test takers of the same age or grade level

Note-taking tools and apps Programs for taking and sharing digital notes using laptops, tablets, or smartphones

Object-oriented programming Software that allows teachers and students to create an object and make it do things in response to programmed instructions

One-on-one tutoring Supporting student learning through in-person or online instruction and assistance

One-to-one (or 1:1) computing Settings in which every student in a grade, school, or district has a computer, tablet, or mobile device for use in school and/or at home

One/two/three time Instructional approach in which students rotate through three different activities or centers, including meeting with a teacher, doing independent work, and using technology

Online discussions Digital forums in which teachers and students exchange information about topics of educational interest

Online learning Academic experiences delivered to students by the Internet; *see also* virtual schools

Online surveys Form that collects data, which can be easily accessed and analyzed online

Open access textbooks Textbooks published with licenses that let teachers and students freely use, adapt, and distribute the material for educational purposes

Open education Movement in education to reduce costs and eliminate barriers to learning for students

Open educational practices (OEPs) Activities that promote direct student involvement in the teaching and learning process; also known as *open pedagogy*

Open educational resources (OERs) Online teaching and learning materials freely available for use by teachers and students

Optical character recognition and reading (OCR) tools An assistive technology for teachers and students with vision impairments that converts printed text to multiple formats

Participation gap Disadvantage experienced by students who lack regular access to the latest technologies and lag behind their peers technologically and educationally

Partitions Blocking online material from school networks by identifying objectionable keywords or phrases

Partnering pedagogy Teachers actively collaborating with students in all aspects of daily instruction and school activities

Performance assessments Assessment of student learning accomplishments using presentations, projects, or class participation

Personalized learning Adapting learning activities to the needs of individual students, often using digital tools and interactive technologies

Photo sharing Posting and storing photos online

Planning and assessment websites and apps Educational materials designed to support teachers as they plan and evaluate learning activities with students

Plagiarism Copying someone else's work or ideas without attribution or misrepresenting either of these as one's own

Podcast Digital audio files delivered to computers by the Internet; *see also* vodcast

Podcatcher Software application that allows teachers or students to subscribe to podcasts

PowerPoint Multimedia presentation software used to display information visually and dynamically; *see also* presentation software

Preassessments Activities to determine what students already know or are able to do before beginning a new lesson or curriculum topic

Presentation software Multimedia tools that combine text, audio, video, images, and moving graphics for informative and engaging presentations; *see also* next-generation presentation tools and apps

Prewriting/brainstorming Initial stage of the writing process in which a writer generates ideas to write about

Prior knowledge–based learning Teaching strategies that use what students already know or are able to do to facilitate learning new concepts and knowledge

Problem-based learning (PBL) Approach to curriculum and instruction organized around problems or issues for students to solve

Problem solving Applying prior knowledge and critical thinking strategies to develop answers or solutions to a problem

Productivity and communication apps Applications designed to support presentations, communications, and teacher and student learning activities in classrooms and other educational settings

Professional learning network (PLN) Technology-based system for continual learning and professional growth through connections with people, educational spaces, and digital tools

Project-based learning (PBL) *See* team-based learning (TBL)

Projection apps Applications that enable teachers to display online content to students using tablets and smartphones

Public domain Material that can be freely used without copyright restrictions

Publishing Stage of the writing process in which a writer's work is displayed for others to read, view, and/or hear

Pull Teachers and students retrieving information from online sources

Push Information sent to teachers and students by online content providers

Question-centered instruction Teachers asking students open-ended, thought-provoking questions to generate discussion and analysis of academic topics

Real-time and recorded data websites and apps Educational materials that present scientific or mathematical data for students to access and analyze

Reciprocal teaching Students and teachers collaboratively exploring the meaning of written or visual texts

Redefinition stage *See* invention stage

Reflection Teachers and students evaluating learning goals and outcomes and making new plans as needed

Revising Stage of the writing process in which a writer reworks initial drafts by adding or deleting material, changing sentence structure or paragraphing, or restructuring how information is presented

Robotics Students and teachers designing, constructing, and using robots as part of a school curriculum

Rogers innovation curve Model depicting how people in organizations respond to innovation and change

RSS feeds Abbreviation of *Really Simple Syndication*; continually updated material sent to digital devices by news organizations, blogs, and other media

Rubrics Known-in-advance criteria explaining to students the process for grading and knowing if an assignment is completed

SAMR Model of Technology Integration Framework describing how teachers go about integrating technology into teaching and learning in schools

Screencasting The process of video recording a computer screen's output and adding voice narration as explanation

Screen readers Assistive technologies that enable computers to read aloud printed text on a computer screen

Search engine Program that locates webpages linked to its database

Self-organized learning environments (SOLEs) Online setting where students invent or create their own learning activities with technology

Self-tutoring Self-chosen learning activities intended to add to a teacher's or student's knowledge, skills, and competencies

Serious games Academic learning included within the structures of online or software and app-based game formats

Service learning Instructional activities through which students connect with local people and community organizations as part of the academic work of a class; *see also* civic engagement

SETT (Students, Environments, Tasks, Tools) Framework for connecting students and technology devices to create conditions of successful learning

Simulation game Recreations of real-world situations and settings in a game-like format

Small group learning *See* groupwork

Smart classroom A technology-enhanced learning environment featuring laptops or tablets, audio/visual capabilities, wireless microphones, a document camera, and other digital tools

Smartphones Mobile phones that allow users to access the Internet, text and talk, take and send pictures and video, and perform other communication functions

Social bookmarking Information management process in which teachers and students store and share weblinks digitally in an open public web space; *see also* bookmarking

Social informatics Social science approach in which technology's impacts are considered within the context of larger social, economic, and political realities

Social media Online forms of communication and interaction between people, including blogs, wikis, social networks, microblogs, video chats, and other tools

Social networking Using digital devices and social media to share information and connect online

Software Instructions that tell computers what functions to perform

Speech-to-text software and apps Tools that transform spoken words into printed text; also known as *speech recognition software and apps*

Standardized testing *See* high-stakes tests

Standards-based assessments Assessing the performance of students in terms of national, statewide, or local district curriculum standards

Standards-based digital portfolios Digital portfolios that link lesson plans and other educational activities done by teachers to specific professional teaching standards

Standards wiki Wikispace featuring links to local, state, or national curriculum frameworks or educational standards

Stealth learning Students learning academic information without realizing they are doing so; often embedded in game play

Storyboarding Process used by writers and videographers to first outline the action and then the sequence of video stories and presentations scene by scene or slide by slide

Streaming video Simultaneous transfer of video, voice, and data from one device to another

Student learning assessment Process of evaluating the academic performance of K–12 students, often using a combination of tests, student writing, and other measurement tools

Student-centered teaching Instructional methods that organize academic instruction around student interests and learning progress; also known as *student-centered approaches*

Student disengagement A strong lack of interest and involvement in academic learning or the overall going-to-school experience

Student feedback surveys Paper or digital formats through which students provide teachers with ideas and suggestions for improving teaching and learning in classrooms and schools

Student-initiated technology use Students voluntarily choosing how to use technology to promote personal and academic learning; *see also* teacher-facilitated technology use

Student learning objectives Goals stating what students will know or will be able to do after instruction

Student performance rubrics Known-in-advance criteria explaining to students the process for grading and knowing if an assignment is completed

Student and teacher self-assessment Process in which students and teachers evaluate personal learning goals and outcomes

Student-to-expert communication websites and apps Online materials that support exchanges of information between students and adult experts in outside-of-school organizations

Substitution stage *See* entry stage

Summative assessment Assessments by teachers to evaluate student performance after completing a learning experience, activity, or unit

Superdiverse classrooms Educational settings in which five or more languages are spoken

Synchronous communications Information exchanges that happen in real time, as in a back-and-forth telephone conversation; *see also* asynchronous communications

Tablets Wireless computing devices with touch-screen capacity and virtual keyboards

Tag cloud Visual display of keywords in which the frequently accessed terms appear in larger font sizes and in bolded or brighter colors; *see also* tags

Tags Keywords used to designate digital resources collected in social bookmarking sites

Teacher-centered teaching Instructional methods that organize instruction around teacher-decided goals and objectives

Teacher or classroom-made blogs Online materials developed by educators and devoted to educational learning activities in schools and classrooms

Teacher-facilitated technology use Teachers making decisions about what technologies to use for teaching and learning in schools; *see also* student-initiated technology use

Teaching goals, methods, and procedures Instructional strategies, interpersonal behaviors, and curriculum materials used by teachers when conducting learning activities with students

Teaching philosophy Ideas and assumptions about how to organize and conduct educational learning activities with students

Team-based learning (TBL) Instructional approach in which teachers and students use technology while working together to investigate topics, solve problems, and share information

Technological pedagogical content knowledge (TPACK) Integration of academic content, instructional practices, and technology in designing, delivering, and assessing lessons

Technology Tools and materials used by humans to solve problems and change the environment; also computers, the Internet, and digital devices used by teachers and students

Technology integration Processes of making technology a central feature of teaching and learning in schools

Test assessments Exam-based educational evaluation practices; *see also* high-stakes tests

Text messaging Typed text interactions using smartphones or other mobile devices

Textspeak Abbreviated language of letters and symbols used for quick communication in text messaging

Text-to-speech software and apps Tools that transform printed text into spoken words; also known as *text-reading software*

3-D printing A technology process in which machines produce three-dimensional solid objects based on coded instructions

Third-party apps Software applications developed by someone other than the maker of a technology device

Top-level domain name (TLD) URL ending that identifies the purpose and goal of an online site

Transformative assessment Using multiple sources of data to measure students' performance

Tweets Online posts on Twitter

Twitter Twitter is a free social networking microblogging service that allows registered members to broadcast short posts called *tweets*.

20% time *See* genius hour

21st century literacies   Knowing how to use technology to create, share, and analyze information and to solve problems collaboratively

21st century skills   Knowledge and understandings needed by students to succeed in a highly technological, information-based society

21st Century Student Outcomes for Learning   Standards for student learning with technology developed by the Partnership for 21st Century Skills

21st century technologies   Digital tools, devices, and online resources capable of providing highly interactive and inquiry-based learning

Understanding by Design (UbD)   Approach to lesson development in which teachers formulate enduring understandings and essential questions as the basis for teaching, learning, and assessment activities with students; also known as *backward design*

Uniform resource locator (URL)   Unique address that identifies a resource on the Internet

Universal design   Adapting physical environments to provide the greatest access possible for all users

Universal design for learning (UDL)   Application of universal design principles to education through methods and assessments that provide access to academic success for students

Virtual field trips   Online learning activities in which students visit museums, historic sites, scientific locations, and other places using technology

Virtual reality (VR)   Computer-based three-dimensional environments for students and teachers to explore interactively

Virtual schools   Educational organizations that deliver curriculum and instruction to students primarily over the Internet

Virtual worlds   Online learning environments where students interact as game players, often through the use of avatars

Visual dictionaries   Dictionaries that define words using pictures as well as written text

Visual learning   Learning from pictures, videos, charts, graphs, and other images from digital and print materials

Visual thinking and concept mapping tools   Software that records and extends thinking and brainstorming with pictures and webs

Vodcast   Podcast that contains video images, delivered via the Internet; *see also* podcast

Wearable technologies   Clothing and accessories containing devices and sensors that track personal health and fitness activities

WebQuests   Instructional approach in which students visit teacher-selected websites to gather academic information and engage in inquiry-based learning activities

Web 2.0 knowledge   Ideas and information created and maintained by communities of online technology users

Web 2.0/Web 3.0   Highly interactive uses of the Internet, notably blogs, wikis, social networks, and other collaborative systems of information creation and exchange

Wikipedia   Online encyclopedia edited by a worldwide community of users

WikiQuest   Instructional approach in which students visit wikis to read and view online resources

Wikis   Webpages created and maintained by multiple contributors; from the Hawaiian word for "rapid"

Wikitext   Collection of educational materials created by a group of wiki users

Word cloud   Software that presents written text in visually engaging formats with most often used terms appearing in larger font sizes and colors

Word prediction tools   Assistive technology that predicts words for a writer to use in a typed document

Writing process   Approach to writing in which teachers and students use the interconnected processes of brainstorming, drafting, revising, editing, and publishing

Writing process for young writers   Approach to writing in which teachers use technology to adapt the writing process to the needs and interests of young writers

YouTube   Popular video-hosting and -sharing website

References

Aglio, J. & Gusky, N. (2017, June 19). Here's what the ISTE Standards for Students look like in 5 #Remake Learning projects. ISTE. Retrieved from https://www.iste.org/explore/articleDetail?articleid=1004&category=Set-the-standard&article=

Alliance for Excellent Education. (2013, August). *Expanding education and workforce opportunities through digital badges*. Washington, DC: Author. Retrieved from http://all4ed.org/reports-factsheets/expanding-education-and-workforce-opportunities-through-digital-badges/

American Civil Liberties Union of Washington. (2016, September). Free speech rights of public school teachers in Washington state. Retrieved from https://www.aclu-wa.org/docs/free-speech-rights-public-school-teachers-washington-state

Anderson, M. & Jiang, J. (2018, May 31). Teens, social media & technology. *Pew Research Center*. Retrieved from http://www.pewinternet.org/2018/05/31/teens-social-media-technology-2018/

Anderson, J. (2012, February 29). Millennials will benefit and suffer due to their hyperconnected lives. *Pew Internet & American Life Project*. Retrieved from http://pewinternet.org/Reports/2012/-Hyperconnected-lives.aspx

Anderson, J., & Rainie, L. (2012, May). The future of gamification. *Pew Internet & American Life Project*. Retrieved from http://www.pewinternet.org/2012/05/18/the-future-of-gamification/

Anderson, J., & Rainie, L. (2014a, March 11). Digital life in 2025. *Pew Research Internet Project*. Retrieved from http://www.pewinternet.org/2014/03/11/digital-life-in-2025/

Anderson, J., & Rainie, L. (2014b, May 14). The Internet of Things will thrive by 2025. *Pew Research Internet Project*. Retrieved from http://www.pewinternet.org/2014/05/14/internet-of-things/

Apple, M. W. (2012). *Can education change society?* New York, NY: Routledge.

Apple, M. W., & Beane, J. A. (2007). *Democratic schools: Lessons in powerful education* (2nd ed.). Portsmouth, NH: Heinemann.

Association of College & Research Libraries. (2014). *Introduction to information literacy*. Retrieved from http://www.ala.org/acrl/issues/infolit/overview/intro

Baildon, M. & Damico, J. (2011, October). Judging the credibility of Internet sources: Developing critical and reflexive readers of complex digital texts. *Social Education, 75*(5), 269–273.

Bain, L. Z. (2015). How students use technology to cheat and what faculty can do about it. *Information Systems Education Journal, 13*(5), 92–99.

Baker, M., & Paez, M. (2018, March). *The language of the classroom: Dual language learners in Head Start, public pre-K, and private preschool programs*. Migration Policy Institute. Retrieved from https://www.migrationpolicy.org/research/language-classroom-dual-language-learners-head-start-public-pre-k-and-private-preschool

Balfanz, R., Bridgeland, J. M., Bruce, M., & Fox, J. H. (2012). *Building a grad nation: Progress and challenge in ending the high school dropout epidemic—Annual update*. Baltimore, MD: Civic Enterprises Everyone Graduates Center at Johns Hopkins University.

Balfanz, R., Bridgeland, J. M., Bruce, M., & Fox, J. H. (2013). *Building a grad nation: Progress and challenge in ending the high school dropout epidemic—2013 annual update*. Washington, DC: America's Promise Alliance, Alliance for Excellent Education, Civic Enterprises, & Everyone Graduates Center at Johns Hopkins University. Retrieved from http://www.civicenterprises.net/MediaLibrary/Docs/Building-A-Grad-Nation-Report-2013_Full_v1.pdf

Banks, J. A., & McGee Banks, C. A. (2015). *Multicultural education: Issues and perspectives* (9th ed.). San Francisco, CA: Wiley.

Barab, S. A., Gresalfi, M, & Arici, A. (2009, September). Why educators should care about games. *Educational Leadership, 67*(1), 76–80.

Barron, B., Gomez, K., Pinkard, N., & Martin, C. K. (2014). *The digital youth network: Cultivating digital media citizenship in urban communities*. Cambridge, MA: MIT Press.

Beal, C. R., Arroyo, I., Cohen, P. R., & Woolf, B. P. (2010, Spring). Evaluation of AnimalWatch: An intelligent tutoring system for arithmetic and fractions. *Journal of Interactive Online Learning, 9*(1), 64–77. Retrieved from http://www.ncolr.org/jiol/issues/pdf/9.1.4.pdf

Bennett, K. R. (2012, Winter). What can you do with just one iPad? *On Cue, 22*(1), 1, 6, 15.

Berenstain, J., & Berenstain, S. (1997). *Inside outside upside down*. New York: Random House Books for Young Readers.

Bergmann, J., & Sams, A. (2014). *Flipped learning: Gateway to student engagement*. Eugene, OR: International Society for Technology in Education.

Blair, A. M. (2011). *Too much to know: Managing information before the modern age*. New Haven: Yale University Press.

Bloom, B. S. (Ed.). Engelhart, M. D., Furst, E. J., Hill, W. H., & Krathwohl, D. R. (1956). *Taxonomy of educational objectives: The classification of educational goals. Handbook 1: Cognitive domain*. New York: David McKay.

Bogost, I. (2011). *How to do things with videogames*. Minneapolis, MN: University of Minnesota Press.

Boyd, D. (2014). *It's complicated: The social lives of networked teens*. New Haven, CT: Yale University Press.

Bronski, M. (2011). *A queer history of the United States*. Boston: Beacon Press.

Brown, A. (2017, September 11). Younger men play video games, but so do a diverse group of other Americans. *Pew Research Center FactTank*. Retrieved from http://www.pewresearch.org/fact-tank/2017/09/11/younger-men-play-video-games-but-so-do-a-diverse-group-of-other-americans/

Brown, A. D. (2011, September 14). Google Translate review: A global language translator on your phone. Retrieved from http://www.brighthand.com/default.asp?newsID=18160&news=Google+Translate+Review

Bruce, B., & Hogan, M. P. (1998). The disappearance of technology: Toward an ecological model of literacy. In D. Reinking, et al. (Eds.), *Handbook of literacy and technology: Transformations in a post-typographic world* (pp. 269–281). Mahwah, NJ: Lawrence Erlbaum.

Burbules, N. C., & Callister, T. A., Jr. (2000). *Watch IT: The risks and promises of information technologies for education*. Boulder, CO: Westview Press.

Busteed, B. (2013, January 7). The school cliff: Student engagement drops with each school year. *The Gallup Blog*. Retrieved from http://www.gallup.com/opinion/gallup/170525/school-cliff-student-engagement-drops-school-year.aspx

Campaign for a Commercial-Free Childhood, Alliance for Childhood & Teachers Resisting Unhealthy Children's Entertainment (2012, October). *Facing the screen dilemma: Young children, technology and early education*. Boston, MA: Campaign for a Commercial-Free Childhood; New York: Alliance for Childhood.

Canadian Paediatric Society. (2017, November 27). Screen time and young children: Promoting health and development in a digital world. *Paediatrics & Child Health, 22*(8), 461–468.

Campbell-Kelly, M., Aspray, W., Ensmeyer, N., & Yost, J. R. (2014). *Computer: A history of the information machine* (3rd ed.). Boulder, CO: Westview Press.

Carr, N. (2015). *The glass cage: How our computers are changing us*. New York: W. W. Norton & Company.

Carr, N. (2011). *The shallows: What the Internet is doing to our brains*. New York: W. W. Norton & Company.

Caulfield, M. A. (2017). *Web literacy for student fact-checkers*. Montreal: PressBooks.

Caumont, A. (2014, March). What would you name today's youngest generation of Americans? *Pew Research Center*. Retrieved from http://www.pewresearch.org/fact-tank/2014/03/12/what-would-you-name-todays-youngest-generation-of-americans/

CDW Government LCC (CDW-G) & Discovery Education. (2011, September). Put down your pencils: The 21st century classroom arrives for three lucky schools. *Education Letter*, 195.

Center for American Progress. (2014, October 16). *Testing overload in America's schools*. Retrieved from http://www.americanprogress.org/press/release/2014/10/16/99165/release-new-cap-report-students-tested-up-to-twice-per-month-common-core-assessments-help-shift-to-better-fairer-and-fewer-tests-2/

Center for Applied Special Technology. (2006). *What is universal design for learning?* Wakefield, MA: Author. Retrieved from http://www.cast.org/research/udl/index.html

Center for Computational Thinking. (2012). *What is computational thinking?* Carnegie Mellon University. Retrieved from http://www.cs.cmu.edu/~CompThink/

Center for Improved Engineering and Science Education (CIESE). (2002). *Exemplary collaborative projects: Higher education and K–12*. Hoboken, NJ: Stevens Institute of Technology.

Center for the Digital Future. (2013). *The Digital Future Project 2013: Surveying the digital future year eleven*. Los Angeles: University of Southern California School of Communication and Journalism. Retrieved from http://www.digitalcenter.org/wp-content/uploads/2013/06/2013-Report.pdf

Centre for Digital Media. (2019). *What is digital media?* Vancouver, BC: Author. Retrieved from https://thecdm.ca/program/digital-media

Ceruzzi, P. E. (2012). *Computing: A concise history*. Cambridge, MA: MIT Press.

Chen, J. & Moenius, J. (2017, August 5). Opinion: Two-thirds of jobs in this city could be automated by 2034. *MarketWatch*. Retrieved from https://www.marketwatch.com/story/two-thirds-of-jobs-in-this-city-could-be-automated-by-2035-2017-07-05

Churches, A. (2008, April 1). Bloom's Taxonomy blooms digitally. *Tech&Learning*. Retrieved from https://teaching.temple.edu/sites/tlc/files/resource/pdf/1%20Bloom%27s%20Taxonomy%20Blooms%20Digitally%20_%20Tech%20Learning.pdf

Clare, J. (2013, November 17). 197 educational YouTube channels you should know about. *teacherswithapps.com*. Retrieved from http://teacherswithapps.com/197-educational-youtube-channels-know/

Cleary, M. N. (2017). Top 10 reasons students plagiarized & what teachers can do about it (with apologies to David Letterman). *Phi Delta Kappan 99*(4), 66–71.

Cohen, E. G., & Lotan, R. A. (2014). *Designing groupwork: Strategies for the heterogeneous classroom* (3rd ed.). New York: Teachers College Press.

Coiro, J., Coscarelli, C., Maykel, C., & Forzani, E. (2015). Investigating criteria that seventh graders use to evaluate the quality of online information. *Journal of Adolescent & Adult Literacy, 59*(3), 287–297. doi: 10.1002/jaal.448

Collins, A., & Halverson, R. (2009). *Rethinking education in the age of technology: The digital revolution and schooling in America*. New York: Teachers College Press.

Colombo, M. W., & Colombo, P. D. (2007, September). Blogging to improve instruction in differentiated science classrooms. *Phi Delta Kappan, 89*(1), 60–63.

Colvard, N. B., Watson, C. E., & Park, H. (2018). The impact of open educational resources on various student success metrics. *International Journal of Teaching and Learning in Higher Education, 30*(2), 262–276.

Computer Science Teachers Association. (2011). Operational definition of computational thinking for K–12 education. Retrieved from https://csta.acm.org/Curriculum/sub/CurrFiles/CompThinkingFlyer.pdf

Computing Community Consortium. (2010). *A roadmap for education technology*. Washington, DC: Computing Research Association.

Common Sense Education. (2015). Our K-12 digital citizenship curriculum. Retrieved from https://www.commonsense.org/education/scope-and-sequence

Common Sense Media. (2017). The common sense census: Media use by kids age zero to eight. Retrieved from http://cdn.cnn.com/cnn/2017/images/11/07/csm_zerotoeight_full.report.final.2017.pdf

Common Sense Media. (2013, October 28). *Zero to eight: Children's media use in America 2013*. San Francisco, CA: Author. Retrieved from http://www.commonsensemedia.org/research/zero-to-eight-childrens-media-use-in-america-2013

Congressional Management Foundation. (2014). *113th Congress gold mouse awards: Best practices in online communication on Capitol Hill*. Washington, DC: Author.

Cooke, N. A. (2018). *Fake news and alternative facts: Information literacy in a post-truth era*. Chicago: American Library Association.

Coppola, E. M. (2004). *Powering up: Learning to teach well with technology*. New York: Teachers College Press.

Cortesi, S., Haduong, P., Gasser, U., Aricak, O. T., Saldana, M., & Lerner, Z. (2014, January 15). *Youth perspectives on tech in schools: From mobile devices to restrictions and monitoring*. Cambridge, MA: Berkman Center for Internet & Society at Harvard University.

Costa, A. L., & Kallick, B. (2014). *Dispositions: Reframing teaching and learning*. Thousand Oaks, CA: Corwin Press.

Cremin, L. (1988). *American education: The metropolitan experience, 1876-1980*. New York: Harper Collins.

Crimaldi, L. (2018, June 30). Writing's on the wall for state's court reporters. *The Boston Globe*, 1, 12.

Croft, M., & Moore, R. (2019, February). *Rural students: Technology, coursework and extracurricular activities*. Iowa City, IA: ACT Center for Equity in Learning. Retrieved from https://equityinlearning.act.org/wp-content/themes/voltron/img/tech-briefs/rural-students.pdf

Csikszentmihalyi, M. (2008). *Creativity: Flow and the psychology of discovery and invention*. New York: Harper Perennial.

Csikszentmihalyi, M. (2013). *Creativity: The psychology of discovery and invention*. New York: Harper Perennial.

Cuban, L. (2003). *Oversold and underused: Computers in the classroom* (New ed.). Cambridge, MA: Harvard University Press.

Cuban, L. (2009). *Hugging the middle: How teachers teach in an era of testing and accountability*. New York: Teachers College Press.

Cuban, L. (2012, February 13). "I saw the future and it works": A visit to a hybrid school. *Larry Cuban on School Reform and Classroom Practice*. Retrieved from http://larrycuban.wordpress.com/2012/02/13/i-saw-the-future-and-it-works-a-visit-to-a-hybrid-school

Cuban, L. (2013). *Inside the black box of classroom practice: Change without reform in American education*. Cambridge, MA: Harvard University Press.

Cuban, L. (2018). *The flight of a butterfly or the path of a bullet? Using technology to transform teaching and learning*. Cambridge, MA: Harvard University Press.

Dalton, B. (2014, November). e-Text and e-books are changing the literacy landscape. *Phi Delta Kappan, 96*(3), 38–43.

Darling-Hammond, L., Zielezinski, M. B., & Goldman, S. (2014, September 10). *Using technology to support at-risk students' learning*. Stanford, CA: Alliance for Excellent Education and Stanford Center for Opportunity Policy in Education.

Dean, C. B., Hubbell, E. R., Pitler, H., & Stone, B. J. (2012). *Classroom instruction that works: Research-based strategies for increasing student achievement* (2nd ed.). Alexandria, VA: Association for Supervision and Curriculum Development.

Dee, T. S., & Jacob, B. A. (2012). Rational ignorance in education: A field experiment in student plagiarism. *Journal of Human Resources, 47*(2), 397–434.

DeNisco, A. (2014). More states make computer science count. *District Administration*. Retrieved from http://www.districtadministration.com/article/more-states-make-computer-science-count

Dewey, C. (2015, May 18). If you could print out the whole Internet, how many pages would it be? *The Washington Post*. Retrieved from https://www.washingtonpost.com/news/the-intersect/wp/2015/05/18/if-you-could-print-out-the-whole-internet-how-many-pages-would-it-be/?utm_term=.1d54b5de2d15

Dewey, J. (1943). *The child and the curriculum and the school and society*. Chicago: University of Chicago Press.

Dick, R. N., McCauley, H. L., Jones, K. A., et al. (2014, November 14). Cyberdating abuse among teens using school-based health centers.

Pediatrics. Retrieved from http://pediatrics.aappublications.org/content/early/2014/11/12/peds.2014-0537

Domoff, S. E., Harrison, K., Gearhardt, A. N., Gentile, D. A., Lumeng, J. C., & Miller, A. L. (2017, November 16). Development and validation of the problematic media use measure: A parent report measure of screen media "addiction" in children. *Psychology of Popular Media Culture*, Advance online publication. http://dx.doi.org/10.1037/ppm0000163 Retrieved from: https://www.researchgate.net/publication/321115155_Development_and_Validation_of_the_Problematic_Media_Use_Measure_A_Parent_Report_Measure_of_Screen_Media_Addiction_in_Children

Donahue, C. (Ed.). (2015). *Technology and digital media in the early years: Tools for teaching and learning*. New York: Routledge.

Donovan, M. S., & Bransford, J. D. (Eds.). (2000). *How people learn: Brain, mind, experience, and school* (Expanded ed.). Washington, DC: National Academies Press.

Donovan, M. S., & Bransford, J. D. (Eds.). (2004a). *How students learn: History in the classroom*. Washington, DC: National Academies Press.

Donovan, M. S., & Bransford, J. D. (Eds.). (2004b). *How students learn: Mathematics in the classroom*. Washington, DC: National Academies Press.

Donovan, M. S., & Bransford, J. D. (Eds.). (2004c). *How students learn: Science in the classroom*. Washington, DC: National Academies Press.

Dreambox Learning. (2018). Educators believe educational technology can personalize learning—and want additional support in training and professional development. Retrieved from https://fs24.formsite.com/edweek/images/WP-Dreambox-National_Survey_How_Educators_Really_Feel_About_Educational_Technology.pdf

Dunbar-Ortiz, R. (2014). *An indigenous people's history of the United States*. Boston: Beacon Press.

Durkin, Philip P. (2014). *Borrowed words: A history of loanwords in English*. New York: Oxford University Press.

Dynarski, S. M. (2017, August 10). For better learning in college lectures, lay down the laptop and pick up the pen. *Brookings*. Retrieved from https://www.brookings.edu/research/for-better-learning-in-college-lectures-lay-down-the-laptop-and-pick-up-a-pen/

Edison Research. (2017, March 9). The infinite dial 2017. Retrieved from http://www.edisonresearch.com/infinite-dial-2017/

Education Week. (2017, June 12). State data: How do students actually use classroom computers? Retrieved from https://www.edweek.org/ew/tc/2017/state-data-how-do-students-actually-use-computers.html?intc=EW-TC17-TOC

Education Week. (2014). Diplomas count 2014—Motivation matters: Engaging students, creating learners. Retrieved from http://www.edweek.org/ew/dc/

Education Week Research Center. (2016). *Teachers and technology use in the classroom*. Bethesda, MD: Author. Retrieved from https://www.edweek.org/media/teachers-and-technology-use-in-the-classroom.pdf

EDUCAUSE Learning Initiative. (2007, August). *7 things you should know about Twitter*. Retrieved from http://www.educause.edu/ELI/7ThingsYouShouldKnowAboutTwitt/161801

EDUCAUSE Learning Initiative. (2010a, January). 7 things you should know about next-generation presentation tools. Retrieved from http://net.educause.edu/ir/library/pdf/ELI7056.pdf

EDUCAUSE Learning Initiative. (2011b, August). 7 things you should know about gamification. Retrieved from http://net.educause.edu/ir/library/pdf/ELI7075.pdf

EDUCAUSE Learning Initiative. (2012, July). 7 things you should know about ...3D printing. Retrieved from https://library.educause.edu/resources/2012/7/7-things-you-should-know-about-3d-printing

EDUCAUSE Learning Initiative. (2012, June). 7 things you should know about badges. Retrieved from http://www.educause.edu/library/resources/7-things-you-should-know-about-badges

EDUCAUSE Learning Initiative. (2013a, June). 7 things you should know about MOOCS II. Retrieved from http://www.educause.edu/library/resources/7-things-you-should-know-about-moocs-ii

EDUCAUSE Learning Initiative. (2013b, July). 7 things you should know about intelligent tutoring systems. Retrieved from http://www.educause.edu/library/resources/7-things-you-should-know-about-intelligent-tutoring-systems

Edutopia. (2013, October 30). Should coding be the "new foreign language" requirement? Retrieved from http://www.edutopia.org/blog/7-apps-teaching-children-coding-anna-adam

Edwards, S. A., Maloy, R. W., & Trust, T. (2019). *Kids have all the write stuff: Revised and updated for a digital age*. Amherst: University of Massachusetts Press.

Edwards, S. A., Maloy, R. W., & Verock-O'Loughlin, R. (2003). *Ways of writing with young kids: Teaching creativity and conventions unconventionally*. Boston: Allyn & Bacon.

Envedy, N. (2014). *Personalized instruction: New interest, old rhetoric, limited results, and the need for a new direction for computer-mediated learning*. Boulder, CO: National Education Policy Center. Retrieved from http://nepc.colorado.edu/publication/personalized-instruction

Ericson, B. (2014, June 3). Detailed data on pass rates, race and gender for 2013. *AniAniWeb for the Institute for Computing Education*. Georgia Tech University. Retrieved from http://home.cc.gatech.edu/ice-gt/556

Ertmer, P. A., Ottenbreit-Leftwich, A. T., Sadik, O., Sendurur, E., & Sendurur, P. (2012). Teacher beliefs and technology integration practices: A critical relationship. *Computers & Education*, 59, 423–435.

Evans, J. A. (2018). *Beyond engagement: Using technology to enable new learning experiences and empower educational effectiveness*. Irvine, CA: Project Tomorrow.

Eyman, B. (2009, September). Building upstander behavior in your school: Developing a peer helping network. *School Climate Matters*, 3(3), 1.

FairTest. (2018, August). Graduation test update: States that recently eliminated or scaled back high school exit exams. Retrieved from https://www.fairtest.org/graduation-test-update-states-recently-eliminated

Fay, L. (2017, September 19). 39 million students get high-speed Internet, but some schools still struggle to close the digital divide. *The 74*. Retrieved from https://www.the74million.org/article/39-million-students-get-high-speed-internet-but-some-schools-still-struggle-to-close-the-digital-divide/

Federation of American Scientists. (2006). *Summit on educational games: Harnessing the power of video games for learning*. Washington, DC: Author.

Fleming, L. (October 30, 2018). How I define a #makerspace. [Twitter Post]. Retrieved from https://twitter.com/LFlemingEDU

Foreman, S. D. (2017). *The LMS guidebook: Learning management systems demystified*. Alexandria, VA: Association for Talent Development Press.

Fox, S., & Rainie, L. (2014). The Web at 25 in the U.S. *Pew Research Center*. Retrieved from http://www.pewinternet.org/2014/02/27/the-web-at-25-in-the-u-s/

Fry, R. (2014, October 2). *U.S. high school dropout rate reaches record low, driven by improvements among Hispanics, Blacks*. Pew Research Center. Retrieved from http://www.pewresearch.org/fact-tank/2014/10/02/u-s-high-school-dropout-rate-reaches-record-low-driven-by-improvements-among-hispanics-blacks/

Frey, W. H. (2018a). *Diversity explosion: How new racial demographics are remaking America* (Revised and updated ed.). Washington, DC: Brookings Institution Press.

Frey, W. H. (2018b, June 22). US White population declines and Generation 'Z-Plus' is minority White, census shows. *Brookings*. Retrieved from https://www.brookings.edu/blog/the-avenue/2018/06/21/us-white-population-declines-and-generation-z-plus-is-minority-white-census-shows/?utm_campaign=brookings-comm&utm_source=hs_email&utm_medium=email&utm_content=63979370

Gardner, H. (2011a). *Creating minds: An anatomy of creativity seen through the lives of Freud, Einstein, Picasso, Stravinsky, Eliot, Graham, and Gandhi*. New York: Basic Books.

Gardner, H. (2011b). *Frames of mind: The theory of multiple intelligences* (3rd ed.). New York: Basic Books.

Gardner, H., & Davis, K. (2014). *The app generation: How today's youth navigate identity, intimacy and imagination in a digital world*. New Haven, CT: Yale University Press.

Gee, J. P. (2007). *What video games have to teach us about learning and literacy* (Revised and updated ed.). New York: Palgrave Macmillan.

Gee, J. P., & Hayes, E. R. (2010). *Women and gaming: The SIMS and 21st century learning*. New York: Palgrave Macmillan.

Gleeson, M. (2012, February 18). iPads can't improve learning without good teaching Pt 2—Writing. Retrieved from http://mgleeson.edublogs.com/2012/02/18/ipads-cant-improve-learning-without-good-teaching-pt-2/

GLSEN. (2013). *Out online: The experiences of lesbian, gay, bisexual and transgender youth on the Internet*. Washington, DC: Gay, Lesbian and Straight Education Network.

Gonzalez, J. (2016, September 4). Using playlists to differentiate instruction [Web log post]. Retrieved from https://www.cultofpedagogy.com/student-playlists-differentiation/

Goodlad, J. (1984). *A place called school*. New York: McGraw-Hill.

Granic, I., Lobel, A., & Engels, R. C. M. E. (2014, January). The benefits of playing video games. *American Psychologist, 69*(1), 66–78.

Greytak, E. A., Kosciw, J. G., Villenas, C. & Giga, N. M. (2016). *From teasing to torment: School climate revisited, a survey of U.S. secondary school students and teachers*. New York: GLSEN.

Greytak, E. A., Kosciw, J. G., & Diaz, E. M. (2009). *Harsh realities: The experiences of transgender youth in our nation's schools*. New York: GLSEN.

Grinberg, N., Joseph, K., Friedland, L., Swire-Thompson, B., & Lazer, D. (2019, January). Fake news on Twitter during the 2016 U.S. presidential election. *Science, 363*(6425), 374–378.

Grinias, J. P. (2017). Making a game of it: Using web-based competitive quizzes for quantitative analysis content review. *Journal of Chemical Education, 94*(9), 1363–1366.

Grunwald Associates LLC. (2013). *Living and learning with mobile devices: What parents think about mobile devices for early childhood and K–12 learning*. San Francisco, CA: Author.

Guernsey, L. (2014). *Envisioning a digital age architecture for early education*. Washington, DC: New America Education Policy Program.

Ha, T. (2014). MOOCs by the numbers: Where are we now? *Ideas. TED.com*. Retrieved from http://ideas.ted.com/2014/01/29/moocs-by-the-numbers-where-are-we-now/

Hall, T. E., Meyer, A., & Rose, D. H. (2012). *Universal design for learning in the classroom: Practical applications—What works for special-needs learners*. New York: Guilford Press.

Hamilton, E. R., Rosenberg, J. M., & Akcaoglu, M. (2016). The substitution augmentation modification redefinition (SAMR) model: A critical review and suggestions for its use. *TechTrends, 60*(5), 433–441.

Hansen, M., Levesque, E., Valant, J., & Quintero, D. (2018, June). *The 2018 Brown Center report on American education: How well are American students learning?* Washington, DC: Brown Center on Education Policy at Brookings.

Haran, M. (2015, May 25). A history of educational technology [Web log message]. Retrieved from http://institute-of-progressive-education-and-learning.org/a-history-of-education-technology/

Harel, I., & Papert, S. (Eds.). (1991). *Constructionism: Research reports and essays, 1985-1990*. Norwood, NJ: Ablex.

Harvell, E. (2018, October 24). Can you show Netflix in class? Copyright for teachers made simple. *EdSurge*. Retrieved from https://www.edsurge.com/news/2018-10-24-can-you-show-netflix-in-class-copyright-for-teachers-made-simple

Harris Poll. (2014, May 9). *Pearson Student Mobile Device Survey 2014: National report: Students in grades 4–12*. Retrieved from http://www.pearsoned.com/wp-content/uploads/Pearson-K12-Student-Mobile-Device-Survey-050914-PUBLIC-Report.pdf

Hatch, M. (2013). *The Maker Movement manifesto: Rules for innovation in the new world of crafters, hackers, and tinkerers*. New York: McGraw-Hill.

Hattie, J. (2013). *Visible learning for teachers: Maximizing impact on learning*. New York: Routledge.

Hattie, J., & Yates, G. C. R. (2014). *Visible learning and the science of how we learn*. New York: Routledge.

Hehir, T., & Katzman, L. I. (2012). *Effective inclusive schools: Designing successful schoolwide programs*. San Francisco, CA: Jossey-Bass.

Herrick, K. A., Fakhouri, T. H. I., Carlson, S. A., & Fulton, J. E. (2014, July). *TV watching and computer use in U.S. youth aged 12–15, 2012*.

NCHS Data Brief, No. 157. Retrieved from http://www.cdc.gov/nchs/data/databriefs/db157.pdf

Hess, D. E., & McAvoy, P. (2014). *The political classroom: Evidence and ethics in democratic education*, New York: Routledge.

Hicks, T. (2013). *Crafting digital writing: Composing texts across media and genres*. Portsmouth, NH: Heinemann.

Hicks, T., & Turner, K. H. (2013). No longer a luxury: Digital literacy can't wait. *English Journal, 102*(6), 58–65.

Highfill, L., Hilton, K., & Landis, S. (2016). *The hyperdoc handbook: Digital lesson design using Google apps*. Irvine, CA: EdTechTeam.

Holt, N. (2016). *The rise of the rocket girls: The women who propelled us, from missiles to the moon and Mars*. New York: Little, Brown and Company.

Honey, M. A., & Hilton, M. (Eds.) (2011). *Learning science through computer games and simulations*. Washington, DC: National Academies Press.

Horn, M. B., & Staker, H. (2015). *Blended: Using disruptive innovation to improve schools*. San Francisco, CA: Jossey-Bass.

Hostetler, A. (2012, March/April). Democratic use of blogs and online discussion boards in social studies education. *Social Education, 76*(2), 100–104.

Houston, K. (2016). *The book: A cover-to-cover exploration of the most powerful object of our time*. New York: W. W. Norton & Company.

Houssart, J., & Sams, C. (2008). Developing mathematical reasoning through games of strategy played against the computer. *The International Journal for Technology in Mathematics Education, 15*(2), 59–71.

Hrynchak, P. & Batty, H. (2012). The educational theory basis of team-based learning. *Medical Teacher, 34,* 796–801.

Hsu, Y-C., Baldwin, S., & Ching, Y-H. (2017). Learning through making and maker education. *Tech Trends, 61*: 589–594.

Hybrid Learning Institute. (2014, December 5). *Hybrid learning program results: Summary report for academic year 2013–2014*. Kutztown, PA: Dellicker Strategies, LLC.

Iding, M., & Klemm, E. B. (2005). Pre-service teachers critically evaluate scientific information on the World Wide Web: What makes information believable? *Computers in the Schools, 22*(1/2), 7–17.

Institute for the Future for Dell Technologies. (2017). *The next era in human-machine partnerships: Emerging technologies impact on society & work in 2030*. Palo Alto, CA: Author. Retrieved from https://www.delltechnologies.com/content/dam/delltechnologies/assets/perspectives/2030/pdf/SR1940_IFTFforDellTechnologies_Human-Machine_070517_readerhigh-res.pdf

International Reading Association. (2014). *Leisure reading: A joint position statement of the International Reading Association, the Canadian Children's Book Centre, and the National Council of Teachers of English*. Newark, NJ: Author. Retrieved from http://www.reading.org/Libraries/position-statements-and-resolutions/ps1082_leisure_reading.pdf

International Society for Technology in Education. (2019). *ISTE Policy Principles*. Eugene, OR: Author. Retrieved from https://www.iste.org/advocacy/advocacy-platform

International Society for Technology in Education. (2017). *ISTE Standards for Educators*. Eugene, OR: Author. Retrieved from https://www.iste.org/standards/for-educators

International Society for Technology in Education. (2016). *ISTE Standards for Students*. Eugene, OR: Author. Retrieved from https://www.iste.org/standards/for-students

International Society for Technology in Education. (2007). *ISTE Standards for Students*. Eugene, OR: Author.

International Society for Technology in Education. (2008b). *Technology and student achievement—The indelible link*. Retrieved from http://www.k12hsn.org/files/research/Technology/ISTE_policy_brief_student_achievement.pdf

ISTE Team (2017, February 6). Educators' feedback key to developing ISTE Standards for Teachers. Retrieved from https://www.iste.org/explore/articleDetail?articleid=901&category=Press-Releases&article=

Jackson, P. (1968). *Life in classrooms*. New York: Holt, Rinehart & Winston.

Jemielniak, D. (2014). *Common knowledge? An ethnography of Wikipedia.* Stanford, CA: Stanford University Press.

Jenkins, H. (2006). *Convergence culture: Where old and new media collide.* New York: New York University Press.

Jenkins, H., Ford, S., & Green, J. (2013). *Spreadable media: Creating value and meaning in a networked culture.* New York: New York University Press.

Johnson, C. Y. (2007, May 15). With simplified code, programming becomes child's play. *The Boston Globe*, pp. A1, C5.

Jonassen, D. H. (2000). *Computers as mindtools for schools: Engaging critical thinking* (2nd ed.). Upper Saddle River, NJ: Merrill.

Jonassen, D. H. (2005). *Modeling with technology: Mindtools for conceptual change* (3rd ed.). Upper Saddle River, NJ: Prentice-Hall.

Jonassen, D. H. (2010). *Learning to solve problems: A handbook for designing problem-solving learning environments.* New York: Routledge.

Jones, M., & Shelton, M. (2011). *Developing your portfolio—Enhancing your learning and showing your stuff.* New York: Routledge.

Joseph, R. (2006, March/April). The excluded stakeholder: In search of student voice in the systemic change process. *Educational Technology, 46*(2), 34–38.

Kafai, Y. B., Peppler, K. A., & Chapman, R. N. (2009). *The computer clubhouse: Constructionism and creativity in youth communities.* New York: Teachers College Press.

Kahne, J. & Bowyer, B. (2017). Educating for democracy in a partisan age: Confronting the challenges of motivated reasoning and misinformation. *American Educational Research Journal, 54*(1): 3–34.

Karchmer-Klein, R., Mouza, C., Shinas, V. H., & Park, S. (2017). Patterns in teachers' instructional design when integrating apps in middle school content-area teaching. *Journal of Digital Learning in Teacher Education, 33*, 91–102. doi: 10.1080/21532974.2017.1305305

Katz, V. S., Gonzalez, C., & Clark, K. (2017, November). Digital inequality and developmental trajectories of low-income, immigrant and minority children. *Pediatrics, 140*(s2). Retrieved from http://pediatrics.aappublications.org/content/pediatrics/140/Supplement_2/S132.full.pdf

Kilbane, C. R., & Milman, N. B. (2008). *Creating digital teaching portfolios.* New York: Pearson.

Kohn, A. (1999). *The schools our children deserve: Moving beyond traditional classrooms and "tougher standards."* Boston, MA: Houghton Mifflin.

Kohn, A. (2011). *Feel-bad education: And other contrarian essays on children and schooling.* Boston, MA: Beacon Press.

Kormos, E. (2019). An examination of social studies educators to facilitate preservice teacher development of technology integration. *Contemporary Issues in Technology and Teacher Education, 19*(1). Retrieved from https://www.citejournal.org/volume-19/issue-1-19/social-studies/an-examination-of-social-studies-educators-to-facilitate-preservice-teacher-development-of-technology-integration

Kosciw, J. G., Greytak, E. A., Zongrone, A. D., Clark, C. M., & Truong, N. L. (2018). *The 2017 national school climate survey: The experiences of lesbian, gay, bisexual, transgender, and queer youth in our nation's schools.* New York: GLSEN.

Krathwohl, D. R. (2002). A revision of Bloom's Taxonomy: An overview. *Theory into Practice, 41*(4).

Krokos, E., Plaisant, C., & Varshney, A. (2018, May). Virtual memory palaces: Immersion aids recall. *Virtual Reality.* Retrieved from https://doi.org/10.1007/s10055-018-0346-3

Ladson-Billings, G. (2009). *The dream-keepers: Successful teachers of African American children.* (2nd ed.). San Francisco: Jossey-Bass.

Lambert, J., & Hessler, B. (2018). *Digital storytelling: Capturing lives, creating community* (5th ed.). New York: Routledge.

Langville, A. N., & Meyer, C. D. (2012). *Google's pagerank and beyond: The science of search engine rankings.* Princeton, NJ: Princeton University Press.

Larson, B. E., & Keiper, T. A. (2012). *Instructional strategies for middle and high school.* New York: Routledge.

Lee, L. (2012, Winter). "A learning journey for all": American elementary teachers' use of classroom wikis. *Journal of Interactive Online Learning, 11*(3), 90–102.

Lenhart, A. (2012a, March). *Teens, smartphones & texting.* Washington, DC: Pew Internet & American Life Project. Retrieved from http://www.pewinternet.org/Reports/2012/Teens-and-smartphones/Summary-of-findings.aspx

Lenhart, A. (2012b, May). *Teens and online media.* Washington, DC: Pew Internet & American Life Project.

Lenhart, A. (2015, April 9). *Teens, social media & technology 2015 overview.* Washington, DC: Pew Internet & American Life Project. Retrieved from http://www.pewinternet.org/2015/04/09/teens-social-media-technology-2015/

Leu, D. L. (2008). "The C's of change": An extended interview with the members of the New Literacies Research Lab. Retrieved from http://www.ncte.org/magazine/extended

Leu, D. J., Forzani, E., Rhoads, C., Maykel, C., Kennedy, C., & Timbrell, N. (2015, January/February/March). The new literacies of online research and comprehension: Rethinking the reading achievement gap. *Reading Research Quarterly, 50*(1), 37–59.

Locker, M. (2018, April 25). Apple's podcasts just topped 50 billion all-time downloads and streams. *Fast Company.* Retrieved from https://www.fastcompany.com/40563318/apples-podcasts-just-topped-50-billion-all-time-downloads-and-streams

Loewen, J. W. (2018). *Lies my teacher told me: Everything your American history textbook got wrong.* New York: The New Press.

Loewen, J. W. (2009). *Teaching what really happened: How to avoid the tyranny of textbooks and get students excited about doing history.* New York: Teachers College Press.

Long, C. (2008, March). Mind the gap. *NEA Today, 26*(6), 24–31.

Lowenthal, P. R., Dunlap, J. C., & Stitson, P. (2016, April). Creating an intentional web presence: Strategies for every educational technology professional. *Tech Trends (60)*, 320–329.

Lukoff, B. (2013, February 5). *Using learning catalytics to create an interactive classroom.* STEM Tuesday Talk at the University of Massachusetts Amherst, Amherst, Massachusetts.

Lynch, M. (2017, April 8). Five reasons to teach robotics in schools. *The Edvocate.* Retrieved from https://www.theedadvocate.org/five-reasons-to-teach-robotics-in-schools/

Madden, M., Lenhart, A., Cortesi, S., Gasser, U., Duggan, M., Smith, A., & Beaton, M. (2013, May 21). *Teens, social media, and privacy.* Washington, DC: Pew Research Center. Retrieved from http://www.pewinternet.org/2013/05/21/teens-social-media-and-privacy/

Magana, S. (2017). *Disruptive classroom technologies: A framework for innovation in education.* Thousand Oaks, CA: Corwin.

Maloy, R. W. & LaRoche, I. S. (2018). "What do you think we could change to make this lesson better?" Using feedback surveys to engage students and improve instruction (pp. 53–67). In S. P. Jones & E. Sheffield (Eds.), *Why kids love (and hate) school: Reflections on practice.* Gorham, ME: Myers Education Press.

Maloy, R. W., & Malinowski, A. (2017). *Wiki works: Teaching web research and digital literacy in history and humanities classrooms.* Lanham, MD: Rowman & Littlefield.

Maloy, R. W., Trust, T., Kommers, S., Malinowski, A., & LaRoche, I. (2017). 3D modeling and printing in history/social studies classrooms: Initial lessons and insights. *Contemporary Issues in Technology and Teacher Education: Social Studies, 17*(2), 229–249. Retrieved from http://www.citejournal.org/volume-17/issue-2-17/social-studies/3d-modeling-and-printing-in-historysocial-studies-classrooms-initial-lessons-and-insights/

Maloy, R. W., & LaRoche, I. S. (2015). *We, the students and teachers: Teaching democratically in the history/social studies classroom.* Albany: State University of New York Press.

Maloy, R. W., Razzaq, L., & Edwards, S. A. (2014). Learning by choosing: Fourth-graders' use of an online multimedia tutoring system for math problem solving. *Journal of Interactive Learning Research, 25*(1), 51–64.

Markowitz, D. M., Laha, R., Perone, B. P., Pea, R. D., Bailenson, J. N. (2018). Immersive virtual reality field trips facilitate learning about climate change. *Frontiers in Psychology.* doi: 10.3389/fpsyg.2018.02364

Martinez, S. L., & Stager, G. S. (2014, May). The Maker Movement: A learning revolution. *Learning & Leading with Technology, 41*(7), 12–17.

Mayalahn, P. (2017). *COSN's 2008-2019 annual infrastructure report.* Washington, DC: Consortium for School Networking.

Mayer, R. E. (2014). *The Cambridge handbook of multimedia learning*. New York: Cambridge University Press.

McCall, J. (2011). *Gaming the past: Using video games to teach secondary history*. New York: Routledge.

McCullough, B. (2018). *How the Internet happened: From Netscape to the iPhone*. New York: Liveright.

McGrew, S., Breakstone, J., Ortega, T., Smith, M. D., & Wineburg, S. (2018, January). Can students evaluate online sources? Learning from assessments of civic reasoning. *Theory and Research in Social Education, 46*(2), 1–29.

McKenzie, J. (1998, May). The new plagiarism. Seven antidotes to prevent highway robbery in an electronic age. *The Educational Technology Journal, 7*(8).

McIntyre, L. (2018). *Post-truth*. Cambridge, MA: MIT Press.

Merrill, J., & Solbert, R. (Eds.). (1969). *A few flies and I: Haiku by Issa*. New York: Pantheon Books.

Merrow, J. (2012, March 4). Teaching kids to be "digital citizens" (not just "digital natives"). *The Washington Post: PostLocal*. Retrieved from http://www.washingtonpost.com/blogs/answer-sheet/post/teaching-kids-to-be-digital-citizens-not-just-digital-natives/2012/03/04/gIQALdFiqR_blog.htm

Metiri Group. (2008). *Multimodal learning through media: What the research says*. San Jose, CA: Cisco Systems. Retrieved from http://www.cisco.com/web/strategy/docs/education/Multimodal-Learning-Through-Media.pdf

Meyer, E. L., & Sansfacon, A. P. (Eds.). (2014). *Supporting transgender and gender creative youth: Schools, families and communities*. New York: Peter Lang.

Michels, S. (2002, November 29). The search engine that could. *Online NewsHour*. Retrieved from http://www.pbs.org/newshour/bb/business-july-dec02-google_11-29/

Millstone, J. (2012, May). *Teacher attitudes about digital games in the classroom*. New York: The Joan Ganz Cooney Center at Sesame Workshop.

Molnar, A., Miron, G., Gulosino, C., Shank, C., Davidson, C., Barbour, M.K., Huerta, L., Shafter, S.R., Rice, J.K., & Nitkin, D. (2017). *Virtual Schools Report 2017*. Boulder, CO: National Education Policy Center. Retrieved [date] from http://nepc.colorado.edu/publication/virtual-schools- annual-2017

Montessori, M. (1964). *Dr. Montessori's own handbook*. Cambridge, MA: R. Bentley.

Moore, R., Vitale, D., & Stawinoga, N. (2018, August). The digital divide and educational equity: A look at students with very limited access to electronic devices at home. *ACT Center for Equity in Learning*. Retrieved from https://equityinlearning.act.org/wp-content/themes/voltron/img/tech-briefs/the-digital-divide.pdf

Morris, S. M., & Stommel, J. (2017, June 15). A guide for resisting EdTech: The case against Turnitin. *Hybrid Pedagogy*. Retrieved from https://hybridpedagogy.org/resisting-edtech/

Moses, R. P., & Cobb, C. E., Jr. (2002). *Radical equations: Civil rights from Mississippi to the Algebra Project*. Boston, MA: Beacon Press.

Mueller, P. A., & Oppenheimer, D. M. (2014). The pen is mightier than the keyboard. *Psychological Science, 25*(6), 1159–1168.

Mundy, L. (2017). *Code girls: The untold story of the American women code breakers of World War II*. New York: Hachette Books.

Nair, P. (2014). *Blueprint for tomorrow: Redesigning schools for student-centered learning*. Cambridge, MA: Harvard Education Press.

National Academies of Science, Engineering, and Medicine. (2018). *How people learn II: Learners, contexts, and cultures*. Washington, DC: The National Academies Press.

National Center on Addiction and Substance Abuse at Columbia University. (2011, June). *Adolescent substance use: America's #1 public health problem*. New York: Columbia University.

National Center for Education Statistics. (2018a, April). *Children and youth with disabilities*. Washington, DC: Department of Education. Retrieved from https://nces.ed.gov/programs/coe/indicator_cgg.asp

National Center for Education Statistics. (2018b, April). *Student access to digital learning resources outside the classroom*. Washington, DC: Department of Education. Retrieved from https://nces.ed.gov/pubs2017/2017098/section1.asp

National Center for Education Statistics. (2019, February). *Status and trends in the education of racial and ethnic groups*. Washington, DC: Department of Education. Retrieved from https://nces.ed.gov/programs/raceindicators/indicator_rbb.asp

National Commission on Writing in America's Schools and Colleges. (2003, April). *The neglected "R": The need for a writing revolution*. Princeton, NJ: College Entrance Examination Board.

National Council of Teachers of English. (2007). *21st century literacies: A policy research brief*. Urbana, IL: Author.

National Council of Teachers of English. (2008a). *Code of best practices in fair use for media literacy education*. Urbana, IL: Author.

National Council of Teachers of English. (2008b). *The NCTE definition of 21st-century literacies*. Urbana, IL: Author.

National Council of Teachers of English. (2013a). *NCTE framework for 21st century curriculum and assessment*. Urbana, IL: Author. Retrieved from http://www.ncte.org/positions/statements/21stcentframework

National Council of Teachers of English. (2013b, April). *NCTE position statement on machine scoring*. Urbana, IL: Author. Retrieved from http://www.ncte.org/positions/statements/machine_scoring

National Council of Teachers of English. (2014a). *Formative assessment that* truly *informs instruction*. Urbana, IL: Author. Retrieved from http://www.ncte.org/positions/statements/formative-assessment

National Council of Teachers of English. (2014b). *How standardized tests shape—and limit—student learning*. Urbana, IL: Author. Retrieved from http://www.ncte.org/library/NCTEFiles/Resources/Journals/CC/0242-nov2014/CC0242PolicyStandardized.pdf

National Council of Teachers of English. (2018, October). Beliefs for integrating technology into the English Language Arts classroom. Urbana, IL: Author. Retrieved from https://www2.ncte.org/statement/beliefs-technology-preparation-english-teachers/

National Council of Teachers of Mathematics. (2011, October). Strategic Use of of Technology in Teaching and Learning Mathematics. Retrieved from https://www.nctm.org/Standards-and-Positions/Position-Statements/Strategic-Use-of-Technology-in-Teaching-and-Learning-Mathematics/

National Science Teachers Association. (2003). *National science education standards*. Arlington, VA: Author.

National Task Force on Civic Learning and Democratic Engagement. (2012). *A crucible moment: College learning and democracy's future*. Washington, DC: Association of American Colleges and Universities.

National Writing Project, & Nagin, C. (2006). *Because writing matters: Improving writing in our schools*. San Francisco, CA: Jossey-Bass.

National Writing Project with DeVoss, D. N., Eidman-Aadahl, E., & Hicks, T. (2010). *Because digital writing matters: Improving student writing in online and multimedia environments*. San Francisco, CA: Jossey-Bass.

Nelson, H. (2013). *Testing more, teaching less: What America's obsession with student testing costs in money and lost instructional time*. New York: American Federation of Teachers.

New York State School Boards Association. (2010, September). *Hey, you, get onto my cloud! How cloud computing & Web-based technologies can benefit school districts*. Latham, NY: Author.

New York Times Learning Network. (2018). The New York Times Learning Network Student Podcast Contest Rubric. Retrieved from https://static01.nyt.com/files/2018/learning/NYTLNStudentPodcastContestRubric.pdf

Newsela. (2017, December 4). Meet the 11-year-old girl who invented water-testing device. Retrieved from https://newsela.com/read/young-scientist-lead-water-testing/id/38247/

Nielsen, K. E. (2012). *A disability history of the United States*. Boston: Beacon Press.

Nieto, S. (2013). *Finding joy in teaching students of diverse backgrounds: Culturally responsive and socially just practices in U.S. classrooms*. Portsmouth, NH: Heinemann.

Nieto, S., & Bode, P. (2018). *Affirming diversity: The sociopolitical context of multicultural education* (7th ed.). New York: Pearson.

Noble, S. U. (2018). *Algorithms of oppression: How search engines reinforce racism*. New York: New York University Press.

November, A. (2009). *Empowering students with technology* (2nd ed.). Thousand Oaks, CA: Corwin Press.

November, A. (2012). *Who owns the learning? Preparing students for success in the digital age.* Bloomington, IN: Solution Tree.

NPR Hidden Brain. (2018, June 25). Fake news: An origin story. [Web log post]. Retrieved from https://www.npr.org/2018/06/25/623231337/fake-news-an-origin-story?utm_campaign=storyshare&utm_source=twitter.com&utm_medium=social&utm_source=twitter.com&utm_medium=social&utm_campaign=hiddenbrain&utm_term=artsculture&utm_content=20180626

OER Commons. (2015). *What are Open Educational Resources (OER)?* Retrieved from https://www.oercommons.org/about

Olneck, M. (2012). *Insurgent credentials: A challenge to established institutions of higher education.* Paper presented to "Education in a New Society: The Growing Interpenetration of Education in Modern Life at Radcliffe Institute for Advanced Study, Harvard University, Cambridge, Massachusetts, April 26–27.

Ormrod, J. E., Anderman, E. M., & Anderman, L. H. (2017). *Educational psychology: Developing learners.* Boston: Pearson.

Oreo, S. (2019, March 1). The surprising, research-backed benefits of active screen time. *EdSurge.* Retrieved from https://www.edsurge.com/news/2019-03-01-the-surprising-research-backed-benefits-of-active-screen-time

Ortiz, P. (2018). *An African American and Latinx history of the United States.* Boston: Beacon Press.

Papert, S. (1980). *Mindstorms: Children, computers, and powerful ideas* (2nd ed.). Cambridge, MA: Perseus.

Papert, S. (1993). *The children's machine: Rethinking school in the age of the computer.* New York: Basic Books.

Papert, S. (1996). *The connected family: Bridging the digital generation gap.* Atlanta, GA: Longstreet Press.

Pariser, E. (2011). *The filter bubble: What the Internet is hiding from you.* New York: Penguin.

Patall, E. A., Cooper, H., & Wynn, S. R. (2010, September). The effectiveness and relative importance of choice in the classroom. *Journal of Educational Psychology, 102*(4), 896–915.

Patchin, J. W., & Hinduja, S. (Eds.). (2012). *Cyberbullying prevention and response: Expert perspectives.* New York: Taylor & Francis.

Patchin, J. W., & Hinduja, S. (2016). *Bullying today: Bullet points and best practices.* Thousand Oaks, CA: Corwin.

Pearson. (2018, August). Beyond millennials: The next generation of learners. Retrieved from https://www.pearson.com/content/dam/one-dot-com/one-dot-com/global/Files/news/news-annoucements/2018/The-Next-Generation-of-Learners_final.pdf

Peelle, H. A. (2001, Spring). Alternative modes for teaching mathematical problem solving: An overview. *The Journal of Mathematics and Science, 4*(1), 119–142.

PennState University Libraries. (2018, October 30). What is fake news? Retrieved from https://guides.libraries.psu.edu/fakenews

Perez, S. (2017, May 4). Report: Smartphone owners are using 9 apps per day, 30 per month. *TechCrunch.* Retrieved from https://techcrunch.com/2017/05/04/report-smartphone-owners-are-using-9-apps-per-day-30-per-month

Pew Research Center. (2018, February 5). Mobile fact sheet. Retrieved from http://www.pewinternet.org/fact-sheet/mobile/

Piaget, J. (1968). *Six psychological studies.* Anita Tenzer (Trans.). New York: Vintage Books.

Pink, D. H. (2011). *Drive: The surprising truth about what motivates us.* New York: Riverhead Books.

Polya, G. (2009). *How to solve it: A new aspect of mathematical method.* Mountain View, CA: Ishi Press.

Ponzio, C. M. & Matthusen, A. (2018). Promoting student-centered discussion with digital tools and infographics. *English Journal, 107*(3), 123–126.

Popham, W. J. (2011). *Transformative assessment in action: An inside look at applying the process.* Alexandria, VA: Association for Supervision and Curriculum Development.

Popham, W. J. (2014). *Classroom assessment: What teachers need to know* (7th ed.). Boston, MA: Pearson.

Potter, W. J. (2010). *Media literacy* (5th ed.). Thousand Oaks, CA: Sage Publications.

Pratt, H. (2012). *The NSTA reader's guide to a framework for K–12 science education, expanded edition: Practices, crosscutting concepts, and core ideas.* Arlington, VA: National Science Teachers Association.

Prensky, M. (2001, October). Digital natives, digital immigrants. *On the Horizon, 9*(5).

Prensky, M. (2005, December 2). Shaping tech for the classroom: 21st century schools need 21st century technology. *Edutopia.* Retrieved from http://www.edutopia.org/adopt-and-adapt-shaping-tech-for-classroom

Prensky, M. (2006). *"Don't bother me Mom—I'm learning!" How computers and video games are preparing your kids for 21st century success—and how you can help!* St. Paul, MN: Paragon House.

Prensky, M. (2010). *Teaching digital natives: Partnering for real learning.* Thousand Oaks, CA: Corwin Press.

Prensky, M. (2012). *From digital natives to digital wisdom: Hopeful essays for the 21st century.* Thousand Oaks, CA: Corwin Press.

President's Committee on the Arts and the Humanities. (2011, May). *Reinvesting in arts education: Winning America's future through creative schools.* Washington, DC: Author.

Pressey, B. (2013). *Comparative analysis of national teacher surveys.* New York: Joan Ganz Cooney Center at Sesame Workshop.

Project Tomorrow. (2011b, May). *The new 3 E's of education: Enabled, engaged and empowered—How today's educators are advancing a new vision for teaching and learning.* Washington, DC: Blackboard K–12.

Project Tomorrow. (2012a, April). *Mapping a personalized learning journey—K–12 students and parents connect the dots with digital learning.* Retrieved from http://www.tomorrow.org/speakup/pdfs/SU11_PersonalizedLearning_Students.pdf

Project Tomorrow. (2012b, May). *Personalizing the classroom experience: Teachers, librarians and administrators connect the dots with digital learning.* Retrieved from http://www.tomorrow.org/speakup/pdfs/SU11_PersonalizedLearning_Educators.pdf

Project Tomorrow. (2014a, April). *The new digital learning playbook: Understanding the spectrum of students' activities and aspirations.* Retrieved from http://www.tomorrow.org/speakup/SU13DigitalLearningPlaybook_StudentReport.html

Project Tomorrow. (2014b, December). *Trends in digital learning: Students' views on innovative classroom materials.* Washington, DC: Blackboard.

Provenzano, N. (2016). *Your starter guide to makerspaces.* CreateSpace.

Puentedura, R. (2014). *SAMR and curriculum redesign.* Retrieved from http://www.hippasus.com/rrpweblog/archives/2014/08/30/SAMRAndCurriculumRedesign.pdf

Purcell, K., Heaps, A., Buchanan, J., & Friedrich, L. (2013, February 28). *How teachers are using technology at home and in their classrooms.* Washington, DC: Pew Research Center.

Purcell, K., & Rainie, L. (2014, December 8). *Americans feel better informed thanks to the Internet.* Washington, DC: Pew Research Center.

Purcell, K., Rainie, L., Heaps, A., Buchanan, J., Friedrich, L., Jacklin, L., Chen, C., & Zickuhr, K. (2012, November 1). *How teens do research in the digital world.* Washington, DC: Pew Research Center.

Qualman, E. (2014, November 13). We don't have a choice on social media [Twitter post]. Retrieved from https://twitter.com/equalman/status/533090727081689088?lang=en

Quitney, J., & Rainie, L. (2012, May 18). *Gamification: Experts expect "game layers" to expand in the future, with positive and negative results.* Washington, DC: Pew Internet & American Life Project.

Ragnedda, M., & Muschert, G. W. (Eds.). (2013). *The digital divide: The Internet and social inequality in international perspective.* New York: Routledge.

Rainie, L. (2013, November 5). The state of digital divides. *Pew Research Center: Internet, Science & Tech.* Retrieved from http://www.pewinternet.org/topics/digital-divide/pages/2/

Rainie, L., Anderson, J., & Connolly, J. (2014, October 9). Killer apps in the gigabit age. *Pew Research Center.* Retrieved from http://www.pewinternet.org/2014/10/09/killer-apps-in-the-gigabit-age/

Rainie, L., & Wellman, B. (2012). *Networked: The new social operating system.* Cambridge, MA: MIT Press.

Ramirez, A. (2016, February 29). Start that podcast! *Edutopia*. Retrieved from https://www.edutopia.org/blog/start-that-podcast-ainissa-ramirez

Ranker, J. (2010, March). The interactive potential of multiple media: A new look at inquiry projects. *Voices in the Middle*, 17(3), 36–43.

Ravitch, D. (2000). *Left back: A century of battles over school reform*. New York: Simon & Schuster.

Ravitch, D. (2011). *The death and life of the great American school system: How testing and choice are undermining education*. New York: Basic Books.

Ravitch, D. (2014a). *Reign of error: The hoax of the privatization movement and the danger to America's schools*. New York: Vintage.

Ravtich, D. (2014b, April 22). NCAA will no longer accept credits awarded by 24 K–12 virtual charter schools. *Diane Ravitch's Blog*. Retrieved from http://dianeravitch.net/2014/04/22/ncaa-will-no-longer-accept-credits-awarded-by-24-k12-virtual-charter-schools/

Ray, B., Jackson, S., & Cupaiuolo, C. (Eds.). (2014a). *Digital divide*. Chicago, IL: MacArthur Foundation Digital Media and Learning Initiative.

Ray, B., Jackson, S., & Cupaiuolo, C. (Eds.). (2014b). *Leading thinkers: Digital media & learning*. Chicago: MacArthur Foundation Digital Media and Learning Initiative.

Reardon, S. F., Fahle, E. M., Kalogrides, D., Podolsky, A., & Zárate, R. C. (2018). Gender achievement gaps in U.S. school districts: CEPA working paper No. 18–13. Stanford Center for Education Policy Analysis. Retrieved from https://cepa.stanford.edu/sites/default/files/wp18-13-v201806_0.pdf

Reich, J. & Ito, M. (2017). *From good intentions to real outcomes: Equity by design in learning technologies*. Irvine, CA: Digital Media and Learning Research Hub.

Reich, J., Murnane, R., & Willett, J. (2012). The state of wiki usage in U.S. K-12 schools. Leveraging Web 2.0 data warehouses to assess quality and equity in online learning environments. *Educational Researcher*, 41(1), 7–15.

Research Alliance for New York City Schools. (2016). Culturally relevant education: A guide for educators. Retrieved from https://steinhardt.nyu.edu/scmsAdmin/media/users/sg158/PDFs/esi_practice_guides/CRE_Practice_Guide.pdf

Resnick, M. (2017). *Lifelong kindergarten. Cultivating creating through projects, passion, peers and play*. Cambridge, MA: MIT Press.

Renwick, M. (2014). *Digital student portfolios: A whole school approach to connected learning*. Virginia Beach, VA: Powerful Learning Press.

Reyes, I., et al. (2018). "Won't somebody think of the children?" Examining COPPA compliance at scale. *Proceedings on Privacy Enhancing Technologies 3*, 63–83.

Reynolds, J. C. Jr. (1976, January). American textbooks: The first 200 years. *Educational Leadership*, 274–276. Retrieved from http://www.ascd.org/ASCD/pdf/journals/ed_lead/el_197601_reynolds.pdf

Reynolds, N., & Davis, E. (2013). *Portfolio keeping: A guide for students*. New York: Bedford/St. Martin's.

Ribble, M., & Bailey, G. (2011). *Digital citizenship in schools* (2nd ed.). Washington, DC: International Society for Technology in Education.

Ribble, M. (2015). *Digital citizenship in schools: Nine elements all students should know* (3rd ed.). Washington, DC: International Society for Technology in Education.

Richardson, W. (2010). *Blogs, wikis, podcasts, and other powerful web tools for classrooms* (3rd ed.). Thousand Oaks, CA: Corwin Press.

Richardson, W. (2011). Foreword. In N. Walser (Ed.), *Spotlight on technology in education* (pp. ix–xii). Cambridge, MA: Harvard University Press.

Richardson, W., & Mancabelli, R. (2011). *Personal learning networks: Using the power of connections to transform education*. Bloomington, IN: Solution Tree Press.

Rideout, V., Foehr, U. G., & Roberts, D. F. (2010, January). *Generation M2: Media in the lives of 8–18 year-olds*. Menlo Park, CA: Henry J. Kaiser Family Foundation.

Robers, S., Kemp, J., Rathbun, A., & Morgan, R. E. (2014). *Indicators of school crime and safety: 2013* (NCES 2014-042/NCJ 243299). Washington, DC: National Center for Education Statistics, U.S. Department of Education, and Bureau of Justice Statistics, Office of Justice Programs, U.S. Department of Justice.

Robinson, K., & Aronica, L. (2015). *Creative schools: The grassroots revolution that's transforming education*. New York: Penguin Books.

Rogers, E. M. (2003). *Diffusion of innovations* (5th ed.). New York: Free Press.

Rohrer, D. & Pashler, H. (2012). Learning styles: Where's the evidence? *Medical Education, 46*, 630–635.

Rose, T. (2013). The myth of average [YouTube video]. Retrieved from https://www.youtube.com/watch?v=4eBmyttcfU4

Rosen, L. D. (2010). *Rewired: Understanding the iGeneration and the way they learn*. New York: Palgrave Macmillan.

Rosen, L. D. (2012). *iDisorder: Understanding our obsession with technology and overcoming its hold on us*. New York: Palgrave Macmillan.

Rothstein, D., & Santana, L. (2011). *Make just one change: Teach students to ask their own questions*. Cambridge, MA: Harvard Education Press.

Russell, N. C., Reidenberg, J. R., Martin, E., & Norton, T. (2018, June 6). Transparency and the marketplace for student data. *Virginia Journal of Law and Technology*. Retrieved from http://dx.doi.org/10.2139/ssrn.3191436

Sarason, S. B. (1982). *The culture of the school and the problem of change* (2nd ed.). Boston: Allyn & Bacon.

Shafer, L. (2017, November 2). Making student feedback work. *Usable Knowledge*. Harvard Graduate School of Education. Retrieved from https://www.gse.harvard.edu/news/uk/17/11/making-student-feedback-work

Schaffhauser, D. (2014, March 27). Report: Most schools delivering BYOD programs, training teachers in mobile device usage. *THE Journal*. Retrieved from http://thejournal.com/articles/2014/03/27/report-most-schools-delivering-byod-programs-training-teachers-in-mobile-devices-usage.aspx

Schimmel, D. (2003, Summer). Collaborative rule-making and citizenship education: An antidote to the undemocratic hidden curriculum. *American Secondary Education, 31*(3), 16–35.

Schimmel, D., & Stellman, L. R. (2014). *Teachers and the law* (9th ed.). Boston, MA: Allyn & Bacon.

Schmidt, E., & Rosenberg, J. (2014). *How Google works*. New York: Grand Central.

Scholastic. (2015). *Kids & family reading report* (5th ed.). New York: Author. Retrieved from http://www.scholastic.com/readingreport/

Schwartz, S. (2019, March 14). School districts are banning teachers from using DonorsChoose. *Education Week Teacher*. Retrieved from http://blogs.edweek.org/teachers/teaching_now/2019/03/donors_choose_district_ban.html?cmp=eml-enl-eu-news1-rm&M=58776465&U=2832233&UUID=01a7816c3cddeb93bb02ef4dfef8f80b

Selingo, J. J. (2014). *MOOC U: Who is getting the most out of online education and why*. New York: Simon & Schuster.

Serafino, J. (2018, March 1). New guidelines redefine birth years for millennials, Gen-X, and post-millennials. *Mental Floss*. Retrieved from http://mentalfloss.com/article/533632/new-guidelines-redefine-birth-years-millennials-gen-x-and-post-millennials

Serico, C. (2014, December 2). Beyond giving Tuesday: Social media fuels school's "85 acts of kindness" program. *Today News*. Retrieved from http://www.today.com/news/beyond-giving-tuesday-social-media-fuels-schools-85-acts-kindness-1D80332292

Shank, J. D. (2014). *Interactive open educational resources: A guide to finding, choosing, and using what's out there to transform college teaching*. San Francisco, CA: Jossey-Bass/ACRL.

Shao, C., Ciampaglia, G. L., Varol, O, Yang, K., Flammini, A, & Menczer, F. (2018, November). The spread of low-credibility content by social bots. *Nature Communication, 9* (4787). Retrieved from https://www.nature.com/articles/s41467-018-06930–7

Shetterly, M. L. (2016). *Hidden figures: The American dream and the untold story of the Black women mathematicians who helped win the space race*. New York: HarperCollins.

Shifflet, R. & Weilbacher, G. (2015). Teacher beliefs and their influence on technology use: A case study. *Contemporary Issues in Technology and Teacher Education, 15*(3). Retrieved from https://www.citejournal.org/volume-15/issue-3-15/social-studies/teacher-beliefs-and-their-influence-on-technology-use-a-case-study

Simon, E. (2014, July 17). Do I need a digital teaching portfolio? *Edutopia*. Retrieved from http://www.edutopia.org/blog/digital-teaching-portfolio-edwige-simon

Simon, H. A. (1973, Winter). The structure of ill structured problems. *Artificial Intelligence, 4*(3–4), 181–201.

Singleton, C., Shear, L., Iwatani, E., Nielsen, N., House, A., Vasquez, S., …, Gerard, S. (2018, August). *The Apple and ConnectED initiative: Baseline and year 2 findings from principal, teacher, and student surveys.* Menlo Park, CA: SRI Education.

Skinner, B. F. (1965). *Science and human behavior.* New York: The Free Press.

Skinner, B. F. (1976). *About behaviorism.* New York: Vintage Books.

Smiley Zabala, J. (2015). Using the SETT framework to level the learning field for students with disabilities. Retrieved from http://www.joyzabala.com/uploads/Zabala_SETT_Leveling_the_Learning_Field.pdf

Smith, C. (2014, March 23). By the numbers: 150+ amazing Twitter statistics. *Digital Marketing Ramblings*. Retrieved from http://expandedramblings.com/index.php/march-2013-by-the-numbers-a-few-amazing-twitter-stats/

Smith, F. (1998). *The book of learning and forgetting.* New York: Teachers College Press.

Smith, K. (2013). *Digital outcasts: Moving technology forward without leaving people behind.* Waltham, MA: Morgan Kaufman.

Smith, R. (2017, June 25). ISTE releases new standards for educators to maximize learning for all students using technology. ISTE. Retrieved from https://www.iste.org/explore/articleDetail?articleid=1014

Smith, S. J. & Stahl, W. M. (2016, September). Determining the accessibility of K-12 materials: Tools for educators. *Journal of Special Education Leadership, 29*(2), 89–100.

Solnit, R. (2004). *River of shadows: Eadweard Muybridge and the technological wild west.* New York: Penguin.

Sophia Learning. (2014). *Growth in flipped learning.* Retrieved from http://www.sophia.org/flipped-classroom-survey

SpeakUp. (2017). Infographic: California Speaks Up! Results from SpeakUp 2016 at CUE 2017. Retrieved from https://tomorrow.org/speakup/speakup-2016-california-speaks-up-march-2017.html

Steeves, V. (2014.) *Young Canadians in a wired world, phase III: Life online.* Ottawa, ON: MediaSmarts.

Stoeckl, S. (2016, July 13). Five reasons why the 2016 ISTE Standards for Students matter. Retrieved from https://www.iste.org/explore/articleDetail?articleid=685

StopBullying.gov. (2014). *What is bullying?* Washington, DC: U.S. Department of Health & Human Services.

Strebe, J. D. (2018). *Engaging students using cooperative learning.* Second Edition. New York: Routledge.

Takaki, R. (2012). *A different mirror for young people: A history of multicultural America* (Adapted by Rebecca Stefoff). New York: Triangle Square.

Takeuchi, L. M., & Vaala, S. (2014). *Level up learning: A national survey on teaching with digital games.* New York: The Joan Ganz Cooney Center at Sesame Workshop.

Tatum, B. D. (2003). *"Why are all the black kids sitting together in the cafeteria?" and other conversations about race.* New York: Basic Books.

Tomlinson, C. A. (2017). *How to differentiate instruction in academically diverse classrooms.* (3rd ed.). Alexandria, VA: Association for Supervision and Curriculum Development.

Tomlinson, C. A. (2014). *The differentiated classroom: Responding to the needs of all learners* (2nd ed.). Alexandria, VA: Association for Supervision and Curriculum Development.

TPACK & Koehler, M. (2014). *What is TPACK?* Retrieved from http://www.tpack.org

Trust, T. (2017). Using cultural historical activity theory to examine how teachers seek and share knowledge in a peer-to-peer professional development network. *Australasian Journal of Educational Technology, 33*(1), 98–113. https://doi.org/10.14742/ajet.2593

Trust, T., Carpenter, J., & Krutka, D. G. (2018, July). Leading by learning: Exploring the professional learning networks of instructional leaders. *Educational Media International, 55*(2), 137–152.

Trust, T., Krutka, D. G., & Carpenter, J. P. (2016, November). "Together we are better": Professional learning networks for teachers. *Computers & Education, 102:* 15–34.

Trust, T., Maloy, R. W., & Edwards, S. (2018, January). Learning through making: Emerging and expanding designs for college classes. *TechTrends, 62*(1): 19–28.

Trust, T., & Maloy, R. W. (2018, Spring). Curating content for history classes: Digital tools for teachers and students. *The New England Journal of History, 74*(2), 177–201.

Trust, T., & Maloy, R.W. (2017, October). "Why 3D print? The 21st century skills students develop while engaging in 3D printing projects." *Computers in the Schools, 34*(4), 253–266.

Trust, T. (2012, September). Professional learning networks designed for teacher learning. *Journal of Digital Learning in Teacher Education, 28*(4), 133–138.

Tucher, A. (1994). *Froth and scum: Truth, beauty, goodness and the ax murder in America's first medium.* Chapel Hill: The University of North Carolina Press.

Tufte, E. R. (1990). *Envisioning information.* Cheshire, CT: Graphics Press.

Tufte, E. R. (2006). *The cognitive style of PowerPoint: Pitching out corrupts within* (2nd ed.). Cheshire, CT: Graphics Press.

Twitter. (2018). World leaders on twitter. Retrieved from https://blog.twitter.com/official/en_us/topics/company/2018/world-leaders-and-twitter.html

Tyack, D. B. (1974). *The one best system: A history of American urban education.* Cambridge, MA: Harvard University Press.

United Nations Educational, Scientific and Cultural Organization. (2017). What are open educational resources (OERs)? Retrieved from http://www.unesco.org/new/en/communication-and-information/access-to-knowledge/open-educational-resources/what-are-open-educational-resources-oers/

U.S. Census Bureau. (2015, November 3). Census Bureau reports at least 350 languages spoken in U.S. homes. Retrieved from https://www.census.gov/newsroom/press-releases/2015/cb15-185.html

U.S. Copyright Office. (2011). *Copyright basics.* Washington, DC: Library of Congress. Retrieved from http://copyright.gov/circs/circ01.pdf

U.S. Department of Commerce. (2013). *Exploring the digital nation: Americans' emerging online experience.* Washington, DC: National Telecommunications & Information Administration & Economics and Statistics Administration. Retrieved from http://www.ntia.doc.gov/files/ntia/publications/exploring_the_digital_nation_-_americas_emerging_online_experience.pdf

University of California. (2003). *UCCopyright.* Oakland, CA: The Regents of the University of California. Retrieved from http://www.universityofcalifornia.edu/copyright

University of Idaho. (2012). What is information literacy? Retrieved from http://www.webs.uidaho.edu/info_literacy

Value Based Management.net. (2011). Rogers model for the adoption and diffusion of innovations. Retrieved from http://www.value-basedmanagement.net/methods_rogers_innovation_adoption_curve.html

Valkenberg, P. M. & Piotrowski, J. T. (2017). *Plugged in: How media attract and affect youth.* New Haven, CT: Yale University Press.

Vandewater, E. A., Rideout, V. J., Wartella, E. A., Huang, X., Lee, J. H., & Shim, M. (2007, May). Digital childhood: Electronic media and technology use among infants, toddlers, and preschoolers. *Pediatrics, 119*(5), 1006–1015.

Venturino, M. (2018). Daily exit tickets with Google forms [Web log message]. Retrieved from https://mariventurino.com/2018/08/18/exitticket/

Venturino, M. (2017). Daily check-in with Google forms [Web log message]. Retrieved from https://mariventurino.com/2017/10/13/daily-check-in-with-google-forms/

Verheijen, L. (2013). The effects of text messaging and instant messaging on literacy. *English Studies, 94*(5), 582–602.

Virtual Reality Society (2017). *What is virtual reality?* Retrieved from https://www.vrs.org.uk/virtual-reality/what-is-virtual-reality.html

Visser, M. (2012, September 14). Digital literacy definition. *ALA Connect*. Retrieved from http://connect.ala.org/node/181197

Vosoughi, S., Roy, D., & Aral, S. (2018, March). The spread of true and false news online. *Science, 359*(6380), 1146–1151.

Vygotsky, L. S. (1978). *Mind in society.* London: Harvard University Press.

Wang, S. K., Hsu, H. Y., Campbell, T., Coster, D. C., & Longhurst, M. (2014, October). An investigation of middle school science teachers and students' use of technology inside and outside of classrooms. *Educational Technology Research and Development, 62*(6), 637–662. Retrieved from http://link.springer.com/article/10.1007/s11423-014-9355-4/fulltext.html

Warschauer, M. (2003). *Technology and social inclusion: Rethinking the digital divide.* Cambridge, MA: MIT Press.

Warschauer, M. (2011). *Learning in the cloud: How (and why) to transform schools with digital media.* New York: Teachers College Press.

Watanabe, M. (2012). *"Heterogenius" classrooms: Detracking math and science—A look at groupwork in action.* New York: Teachers College Press.

Wessling, S. B. (2012). "They are the experts": A national teacher of the year talks about student surveys. *Measures of Effective Teaching Project.* Retrieved from http://education.ky.gov/teachers/hieffteach/documents/met%20studentsurveys%20q%20and%20a.pdf

Wheeler, T. (2019). *From Gutenberg to Google: The history of our future.* Washington, DC: Brookings Institution Press.

Wiggins, G., & McTighe, J. (2005). *Understanding by design.* Alexandria, VA: Association for Supervision and Curriculum Development.

Wiggins, G., & McTighe, J. (2013). *Essential questions: Opening doors to student understanding.* Alexandria, VA: Association for Supervision and Curriculum Development.

Wikimedia Foundation. (2018a, July). Wikipedians. Retrieved from https://en.wikipedia.org/wiki/Wikipedia:Wikipedians

Wikimedia Foundation. (2018b, August). Wikipedia: Size comparisons. Retrieved from http://en.wikipedia.org/wiki/Wikipedia:Size_comparisons

Wikimedia Foundation. (2018c, August). Wikipedia: Core content policies. Retrieved from https://en.wikipedia.org/wiki/Wikipedia:Core_content_policies

Wiley, D. (n.d.). Defining the "open" in open content and open educational resources. Retrieved from http://opencontent.org/definition/

Wilhelm, J. (2013, November). *Massive open online courses in K–12 education.* The Florida Legislature's Office of Program Policy Analysis & Government Accountability. Retrieved from http://www.oppaga.state.fl.us/monitordocs/Presentations/P13-14.pdf

Williams, T. (2018). *Power in numbers: The rebel women of mathematics.* New York: Race Point Publishing.

Williams, L. A., & Peguero, A. A. (2011, August 23). *The impact of school bullying on racial/ethnic achievement.* Paper presented at the American Sociological Association 106th Annual Meeting. Las Vegas, Nevada.

Wineburg, S., Breakstone, J., McGrew, S., & Ortega, T. (2016, November). Executive summary: *Evaluating information—The cornerstone of civic online reasoning.* Stanford, CA: Stanford History Education Group, 1–27. Retrieved from https://stacks.stanford.edu/file/druid:fv751yt5934/SHEG%20Evaluating%20Information%20Online.pdf

Wineburg, S. (2018). *Why learn history (when it's already on your phone).* Chicago: University of Chicago Press.

Winter, J. (2014, October 12). Everything that's fit to print. *Parade,* 6–10.

Wolfe, L. (2018, May 31). Twitter user statistics 2008 through 2017. Retrieved from https://www.thebalancecareers.com/twitter-statistics-2008-2009-2010-2011–3515899

Wolk, S. (2008, October). School as inquiry. *Phi Delta Kappan, 90*(2), 115–122.

Wojcik, S., Messing, S., Smith, A., Rainie, L., & Hitlin, P. (2018, April 9). Bots in the twittersphere. Pew Research Center. Retrieved from http://www.pewinternet.org/2018/04/09/bots-in-the-twittersphere/

Yazzie-Mintz, E. (2010). *Charting the path from engagement to achievement. A report on the 2009 high school survey of student engagement.* Bloomington, IN: Center for Evaluation & Education Policy, Indiana University.

Zemelman, S., Daniels, H., & Hyde, A. (2012). *Best practice: Bringing standards to life in American classrooms* (4th ed.). Portsmouth, NH: Heinemann.

Zheng, B., Warschauer, M., Lin, C. H., & Chang, C. (2016, December). Learning in one-to-one laptop environments: A meta-analysis and research synthesis. *Review of Educational Research, 86*(4), 1052–1084.

Zickuhr, K., & Rainie, L. (2014, January 16). *A snapshot of reading in America in 2013. Pew Research Center.* Retrieved from http://www.pewinternet.org/2014/01/16/a-snapshot-of-reading-in-america-in-2013/

Zuboff, S. (1989). *In the age of the smart machine: The future of work and power.* New York: Basic Books.

Index